Lecture Notes in Computer Sc

Commenced Publication in 1973
Founding and Former Series Editors:
Gerhard Goos, Juris Hartmanis, and Jan van Leeuwen

Advanced Research in Computing and Software Science

Subline of Lectures Notes in Computer Science

Francesco Logozzo   Manuel Fähndrich (Eds.)

Static Analysis

20th International Symposium, SAS 2013
Seattle, WA, USA, June 20-22, 2013
Proceedings

 Springer

Volume Editors

Francesco Logozzo
Manuel Fähndrich
Microsoft Research
One Microsoft Way, 98052 Redmond, WA, USA
E-mail: {logozzo, maf}@microsoft.com

ISSN 0302-9743   e-ISSN 1611-3349
ISBN 978-3-642-38855-2   e-ISBN 978-3-642-38856-9
DOI 10.1007/978-3-642-38856-9
Springer Heidelberg Dordrecht London New York

Library of Congress Control Number: 2013939600

CR Subject Classification (1998): D.2.4-5, D.2.7, D.3.1-2, D.3.4, F.3.1-3, F.4.1

LNCS Sublibrary: SL 2 – Programming and Software Engineering

Typesetting: Camera-ready by author, data conversion by Scientific Publishing Services, Chennai, India

Printed on acid-free paper

Springer is part of Springer Science+Business Media (www.springer.com)

Preface

Static analysis is increasingly recognized as a fundamental tool for program verification, bug detection, compiler optimization, program understanding, and software maintenance. The series of Static Analysis Symposia has served as the primary venue for the presentation of theoretical, practical, and application advances in the area.

This year's symposium, the 20th International Static Analysis Symposium (SAS 2013), was held during June 20–22, 2013, in Seattle and co-located with ACM's PLDI Conference. Three workshops were affiliated with SAS 2013: NSAD 2013 (The 5th Workshop on Numerical and Symbolic Abstract Domains) on June 19, SASB 2013 (The 4th Workshop on Static Analysis and Systems Biology) on June 19, and TAPAS 2013 (The 4th Workshop on Tools for Automatic Program Analysis) on June 19.

We received 78 abstract and in the end 56 complete paper submissions. Each submission was reviewed on average by 3.2 Program Committee members. The committee decided to accept 23 papers. This year, for the first time, SAS invited the submission of virtual machine artifacts in support of submitted papers. We received 22 such VMs. Out of the 23 accepted papers, 11 have associated VMs. During the review process we used the VMs only in order to lend additional support to papers, not to detract from their acceptance. The VMs are archived on http://staticanalysis.org/ as a scientific record of the state of the art at this point in time and they will hopefully serve as a comparison base for future research.

We were able to secure three invited talks by Eric Lippert (Coverity) on the "Psychology of C# Analysis," Eric Goubault (CEA) on "Static Analysis by Abstract Interpretation of Numerical Programs and Systems," and FLUCTUAT, and Sriram Sankaranarayanan (University of Colorado) on "Static Analysis in the Continuously Changing World."

We would like to thank the Program Committee and all the external reviewers for their participation in the reviewing process.

We are grateful for the generous sponsorship by Microsoft Research. Our thanks go out to David Schmidt and Hans Boehm for organizing the co-location with PLDI, to Manuel Hermenegildo for help with hosting the VMs, and to the EasyChair team for the use of their very handy system.

June 2013

Manuel Fähndrich
Francesco Logozzo

Organization

Program Committee

Elvira Albert	Complutense University of Madrid, Spain
Anindya Banerjee	IMDEA Software Institute, Spain
John Boyland	University of Wisconsin-Milwaukee, USA
Wei-Ngan Chin	National University of Singapore
Mila Dalla Preda	University of Bologna, Italy
Werner Dietl	University of Washington, USA
Isil Dillig	College of William and Mary, USA
Manuel Fähndrich	Microsoft Research, USA
Arie Gurfinkel	Software Engineering Institute, Carnegie Mellon University, USA
Nicolas Halbwachs	CNRS/VERIMAG, France
Atsushi Igarashi	Graduate School of Informatics, Kyoto University, Japan
Franjo Ivancic	NEC Laboratories America, Inc., USA
Ranjit Jhala	UC San Diego, USA
Francesco Logozzo	Microsoft Research, USA
Ana Milanova	Rensselaer Polytechnic Institute, USA
Antoine Miné	CNRS and Ecole Normale Supérieure, France
Mooly Sagiv	Tel Aviv University, Israel
Helmut Seidl	TU München, Germany
Hongseok Yang	University of Oxford, UK
Enea Zaffanella	University of Parma, Italy

Additional Reviewers

Amato, Gianluca	Di Giusto, Cinzia
Apinis, Kalmer	Dillig, Thomas
Arenas, Puri	Dor, Nurit
Balakrishnan, Gogul	Flores Montoya, Antonio E.
Berdine, Josh	Gabbrielli, Maurizio
Bjorner, Nikolaj	Garoche, Pierre-Loic
Bouaziz, Mehdi	Genaim, Samir
Correas Fernández, Jesús	Gherghina, Cristian
Costea, Andreea	Gori, Roberta
Dal Lago, Ugo	Habermehl, Peter
Deutch, Daniel	Herz, Alexander

Hill, Patricia
Huch, Frank
Jeannet, Bertrand
Jin, Wesley
Joshi, Pallavi
Kahlon, Vineet
Karbyshev, Aleksandr
Kincaid, Zachary
Kinder, Johannes
Kong, Soonho
Kovács, Máté
Le, Duy Khanh
Le, Quang Loc
Lin, Anthony
Mador-Haim, Sela
Manevich, Roman
Mastroeni, Isabella
Mauborgne, Laurent
Mauro, Jacopo

Monniaux, David
Naumann, David
Petter, Michael
Ranzato, Francesco
Rinetzky, Noam
Rodríguez Carbonell, Enric
Román-Díez, Guillermo
Schwoon, Stefan
Sharma, Asankhaya
Simon, Axel
Singh, Rishabh
Soffia, Stefano
Suenaga, Kohei
Sun, Chao
Tasiran, Serdar
Thai, Trinh Minh
Trung, Ta Quang
Zanardini, Damiano

Table of Contents

Static Analysis by Abstract Interpretation of Numerical Programs and Systems, and FLUCTUAT

Eric Goubault

CEA LIST
CEA Saclay, Nanoinnov, 91191 Gif-sur-Yvette CEDEX, France
eric.goubault@cea.fr

This invited lecture is a survey of our work over the last 12 years or so[1], dealing with the precise analysis of numerical programs, essentially control programs such as the ones found in the aerospace, nuclear and automotive industry.

Our approach is now based on a rather generic abstract domain, based on "zonotopes" or "affine forms" [7], but with some specificities. For instance, our zonotopic domain provides a functional abstraction [16,13], i.e. an abstraction of the input-output relationships between values of variables, allowing for test generation and modular verification [21]. Also, our domain deals with the real number and the finite precision (for instance, floating-point or fixed-point) semantics [14,17]. It is used in practice in FLUCTUAT [20,9,4] to prove some functional properties of programs, generate (counter-) examples, identify the discrepancy between the real number and the finite precision semantics and its origin etc.

Our work is building over methods from abstract interpretation of course [8], but also over methods from applied mathematics, most notably from the "guaranteed computations" or "interval" community (affine arithmetic [7] and more general Taylor models for instance), from optimization and game theory, and from control theory (with policy iteration for instance [11] or quadratic invariants, as in [2]). In some ways, this interplay between numerical mathematics and abstract interpretation makes the calculations in the abstract much like a perturbed numerical scheme, which has its own stability and convergence properties, related to the stability and convergence of the concrete numerical scheme we are trying to prove. Similarly, we can think of our finite-precision abstract semantics as some form of a deformation of the semantics in the real numbers, i.e. the proofs we are providing are deformations of proofs in the real numbers.

Many extensions of this zonotopic abstract domain have been designed over the years: constrained affine forms [12], under-approximations [15] and more recently, "imprecise probabilistic" analyzes [5,1], where we consider that inputs of the program under analysis can be given by (non-deterministic) ranges as well as probability or sets of probability distributions.

---

[1] With a first publication at a previous SAS [18]. Acknowledgments are due to all my colleagues in the MeASI team over these last years and in particular for this talk, Olivier Bouissou, Tristan Legall, Matthieu Martel, Sylvie Putot, Franck Védrine and Sarah Zennou.

F. Logozzo and M. Fähndrich (Eds.): SAS 2013, LNCS 7935, pp. 1–3, 2013.

On the application side, we have become interested not only in certifying control software [20], potentially as part of an hybrid system [6] but also in characterizing the algorithmic error [9] (or "method" error) very early on in the software development phase, and not only the implementation error, due to finite-precision arithmetics. Recent applications of our static analyzes include "sensitivity" analysis, uncertainty propagation (in parametric models such as the ones found in robust control, or due to uncertain errors on inputs) and generating correct "optimal" fixed-point formats for programs [22].

Among the future directions of our work are the links with proof theory and program provers and the analysis of scientific computing codes, such as finite element methods for solving partial differential equations. As a matter of fact, proof-theoretic approaches, similar in spirit, have been introduced slightly later (such as [3]) and make it possible, combining it with our work, to make precise the notion of "perturbation of a proof" from real numbers to finite-precision implementations. This latter notion has actually been, implicitely at least, introduced long ago [25,24] for the study of important numerical schemes such as conjugate gradient or Lanczos methods, see [23] for a modern account. This might explain that our interest in embedded systems codes has gradually moved towards more general "cyber-physical systems" and, in parallel, towards scientific computing, which presents a real challenge to static analyzers, both on the numerical, and on the alias analysis part. One of the consequences is that we would then have to integrate our numerical domains in static analyzers dealing with concurrent programs, using our own methods [19,10]. In the realm of parallel computing, the issues concerning floating-point computations are of big concern, since in general, programs do compute a lot more numerical expressions, with even lower control on their order of evaluation, and run on hardware architectures with complicated semantics (GPUs, weak-memory models on multicore systems etc.).

References

1. Adjé, A., Bouissou, O., Goubault-Larrecq, J., Goubault, E., Putot, S.: Analyzing probabilistic programs with partially known distributions. In: VSTTE (2013)
2. Adjé, A., Gaubert, S., Goubault, E.: Coupling policy iteration with semi-definite relaxation to compute accurate numerical invariants in static analysis. Logical Methods in Computer Science 8(1) (2012)
3. Boldo, S., Filliâtre, J.C.: Formal Verification of Floating-Point Programs. In: 18th IEEE International Symposium on Computer Arithmetic (June 2007)
4. Bouissou, O., Conquet, E., Cousot, P., Cousot, R., Ghorbal, K., Lesens, D., Putot, S., Turin, M.: Space software validation using abstract interpretation. In: DASIA (2009)
5. Bouissou, O., Goubault, E., Goubault-Larrecq, J., Putot, S.: A generalization of p-boxes to affine arithmetic. Computing 94(2-4), 189–201 (2012)
6. Bouissou, O., Goubault, E., Putot, S., Tekkal, K., Vedrine, F.: HybridFluctuat: A static analyzer of numerical programs within a continuous environment. In: Bouajjani, A., Maler, O. (eds.) CAV 2009. LNCS, vol. 5643, pp. 620–626. Springer, Heidelberg (2009)

7. Comba, J.L.D., Stolfi, J.: Affine arithmetic and its applications to computer graphics. In: Proceedings of SIBGRAPI (1993)
8. Cousot, P., Cousot, R.: Abstract interpretation: A unified lattice model for static analysis of programs by construction or approximation of fixpoints. In: POPL, pp. 238–252 (1977)
9. Delmas, D., Goubault, E., Putot, S., Souyris, J., Tekkal, K., Védrine, F.: Towards an industrial use of FLUCTUAT on safety-critical avionics software. In: Alpuente, M., Cook, B., Joubert, C. (eds.) FMICS 2009. LNCS, vol. 5825, pp. 53–69. Springer, Heidelberg (2009)
10. Fajstrup, L., Goubault, É., Haucourt, E., Mimram, S., Raussen, M.: Trace spaces: An efficient new technique for state-space reduction. In: Seidl, H. (ed.) ESOP 2012. LNCS, vol. 7211, pp. 274–294. Springer, Heidelberg (2012)
11. Gawlitza, T.M., Seidl, H., Adjé, A., Gaubert, S., Goubault, E.: Abstract interpretation meets convex optimization. J. Symb. Comput. 47(12), 1416–1446 (2012)
12. Ghorbal, K., Goubault, E., Putot, S.: A logical product approach to zonotope intersection. In: Touili, T., Cook, B., Jackson, P. (eds.) CAV 2010. LNCS, vol. 6174, pp. 212–226. Springer, Heidelberg (2010)
13. Goubault, E., Gall, T.L., Putot, S.: An accurate join for zonotopes, preserving affine input/output relations. In: Proceedings of NSAD 2012, 4th Workshop on Numerical and Symbolic Abstract Domains. ENTCS, vol. 287, pp. 65–76 (2012)
14. Goubault, É., Putot, S.: Static analysis of numerical algorithms. In: Yi, K. (ed.) SAS 2006. LNCS, vol. 4134, pp. 18–34. Springer, Heidelberg (2006)
15. Goubault, E., Putot, S.: Under-approximations of computations in real numbers based on generalized affine arithmetic. In: Riis Nielson, H., Filé, G. (eds.) SAS 2007. LNCS, vol. 4634, pp. 137–152. Springer, Heidelberg (2007)
16. Goubault, E., Putot, S.: A zonotopic framework for functional abstractions. CoRR abs/0910.1763 (2009), http://arxiv.org/abs/0910.1763
17. Goubault, E., Putot, S.: Static analysis of finite precision computations. In: Jhala, R., Schmidt, D. (eds.) VMCAI 2011. LNCS, vol. 6538, pp. 232–247. Springer, Heidelberg (2011)
18. Goubault, É.: Static analyses of the precision of floating-point operations. In: Cousot, P. (ed.) SAS 2001. LNCS, vol. 2126, pp. 234–259. Springer, Heidelberg (2001)
19. Goubault, E., Haucourt, E.: A practical application of geometric semantics to static analysis of concurrent programs. In: Abadi, M., de Alfaro, L. (eds.) CONCUR 2005. LNCS, vol. 3653, pp. 503–517. Springer, Heidelberg (2005)
20. Goubault, E., Putot, S., Baufreton, P., Gassino, J.: Static analysis of the accuracy in control systems: Principles and experiments. In: Leue, S., Merino, P. (eds.) FMICS 2007. LNCS, vol. 4916, pp. 3–20. Springer, Heidelberg (2008)
21. Goubault, E., Putot, S., Védrine, F.: Modular static analysis with zonotopes. In: Miné, A., Schmidt, D. (eds.) SAS 2012. LNCS, vol. 7460, pp. 24–40. Springer, Heidelberg (2012)
22. Menard, D., Rocher, R., Sentieys, O., Simon, N., Didier, L.S., Hilaire, T., Lopez, B., Goubault, E., Putot, S., Védrine, F., Najahi, A., Revy, G., Fangain, L., Samoyeau, C., Lemonnier, F., Clienti, C.: Design of fixed-point embedded systems (defis) french anr project. In: DASIP, pp. 1–2 (2012)
23. Meurant, G.: The Lanczos and Conjugate Gradient Algorithms: From Theory to Finite Precision Computations (Software, Environments, and Tools). SIAM (2006)
24. Paige, C.C.: The computation of eigenvalues and eigenvectors of very large sparse matrices. Ph.D. thesis (1971)
25. Wilkinson, J.H.: The algebraic eigenvalue problem. Oxford University Press (1965)

Static Analysis in the Continuously Changing World

Sriram Sankaranarayanan*

University of Colorado, Boulder, CO.
firstname.lastname@colorado.edu

Abstract. In this talk, we examine static analysis techniques for continuous-time dynamical systems. Continuous time systems arise in many domains including engineered control systems, physical and biological systems. They are increasingly of interest to the static analysis community, due to the focus on *hybrid (cyber-physical) systems* that capture discrete programs interacting with a continuous external environment. We examine two types of properties that are typically verified: reachability and stability, and explore parallels between commonly used static analysis approaches and a variety of approaches to prove/disprove reachability and stability properties.

1 Introduction

Static analysis refers to a broad class of techniques that reason about the correctness of systems in the presence of uncertainties [10]. The key defining characteristics of static analysis techniques include (a) reasoning collectively about a large, often infinite set of system behaviors using *abstract domains* to represent sets of states, and (b) soundness guarantees on the results of the analysis. Static analysis has witnessed a creative explosion of techniques that focus on reasoning about programs. Abstract interpretation has been successful in providing a convenient common framework for designing, implementing and comparing various static analysis techniques [4].

In this talk, we examine parallels between the world of discrete-time computer programs and continuous-time systems defined by Ordinary Differential Equations (ODEs). The mathematical theory of differential equations provides us a framework for reasoning about these systems [9]. Continuous-time systems arise in a wide variety of engineering disciplines (control systems), physics and biology. The study of continuous systems in the formal verification community has a long history due to the intense interest in hybrid dynamical systems that model discrete programs interacting with a continuous external environment [17,8]. We explore two classes of techniques for the static analysis of continuous time and hybrid systems: (a) *flowpipe construction* approaches that use repeated forward propagation over time, and (b) automatic synthesis of *positive invariants* and *Lyapunov functions*.

Flowpipe construction techniques characterize the behavior of continuous-time and hybrid systems in the presence of uncertainties due to the initial state and input signals. Flowpipe construction techniques compute conservative approximations of the time trajectories of ODEs using numerical domains such as intervals, octagons, convex

---

* The research presented was performed in collaboration with Ashish Tiwari, Aditya Zutshi, Erika Ábraham and Xin Chen. We gratefully acknowledge the support of the US National Science Foundation (NSF) under award numbers CNS-0953941 and CPS-1035845.

F. Logozzo and M. Fähndrich (Eds.): SAS 2013, LNCS 7935, pp. 4–5, 2013.

polyhedra and Taylor models. We examine the capabilities of flowpipe construction tools such as HyTech [7], Checkmate [3], D/Dt [1], Phaver [5], SpaceEx [6] and Flow* [2].

Another class of deductive techniques derive proofs of unreachability in the form positive invariants and stability proofs using Lyapunov functions. We examine proof rules for for invariance and stability of ODEs, and the use of these rules to synthesize invariants and Lyapunov functions [16,14,12,11]. Tools such as KeYmaera support automatic invariant synthesis [13], while the SOSTools package supports the automatic synthesis of Lyapunov functions [15]. We examine some of the successes and existing shortcomings of these approaches in our talk.

References

1. Asarin, E., Dang, T., Maler, O.: The d/dt tool for verification of hybrid systems. In: Brinksma, E., Larsen, K.G. (eds.) CAV 2002. LNCS, vol. 2404, pp. 365–370. Springer, Heidelberg (2002)
2. Chen, X., Ábrahám, E., Sankaranarayanan, S.: Taylor model flowpipe construction for nonlinear hybrid systems. In: Proc. RTSS 2012, pp. 183–192. IEEE (2012)
3. Chutinan, A., Krogh, B.: Computing polyhedral approximations to flow pipes for dynamic systems. In: Proceedings of IEEE CDC. IEEE Press (1998)
4. Cousot, P., Cousot, R.: Abstract Interpretation: A unified lattice model for static analysis of programs by construction or approximation of fixpoints. ACM Principles of Programming Languages, 238–252 (1977)
5. Frehse, G.: PHAVer: Algorithmic verification of hybrid systems past hyTech. In: Morari, M., Thiele, L. (eds.) HSCC 2005. LNCS, vol. 3414, pp. 258–273. Springer, Heidelberg (2005)
6. Frehse, G., Le Guernic, C., Donzé, A., Cotton, S., Ray, R., Lebeltel, O., Ripado, R., Girard, A., Dang, T., Maler, O.: SpaceEx: Scalable verification of hybrid systems. In: Gopalakrishnan, G., Qadeer, S. (eds.) CAV 2011. LNCS, vol. 6806, pp. 379–395. Springer, Heidelberg (2011)
7. Henzinger, T.A., Ho, P.: HYTECH: The Cornell hybrid technology tool. In: Antsaklis, P.J., Kohn, W., Nerode, A., Sastry, S.S. (eds.) HS 1994. LNCS, vol. 999, pp. 265–293. Springer, Heidelberg (1995)
8. Lunze, J., Lamnabhi-Lagarrigue, F. (eds.): Handbook of Hybrid Systems Control: Theory, Tools and Applications. Cambridge University Press (2009)
9. Meiss, J.D.: Differential Dynamical Systems. SIAM Publishers (2007)
10. Nielson, F., Nielson, H.R., Hankin, C.: Principles of Program Analysis. Springer (1999)
11. Papachristodoulou, A., Prajna, S.: On the construction of lyapunov functions using the sum of squares decomposition. In: IEEE CDC, pp. 3482–3487. IEEE Press (2002)
12. Platzer, A.: Differential dynamic logic for hybrid systems. J. Autom. Reasoning 41(2), 143–189 (2008)
13. Platzer, A., Quesel, J.-D.: KeYmaera: A hybrid theorem prover for hybrid systems (System description). In: Armando, A., Baumgartner, P., Dowek, G. (eds.) IJCAR 2008. LNCS (LNAI), vol. 5195, pp. 171–178. Springer, Heidelberg (2008)
14. Prajna, S., Jadbabaie, A.: Safety verification of hybrid systems using barrier certificates. In: Alur, R., Pappas, G.J. (eds.) HSCC 2004. LNCS, vol. 2993, pp. 477–492. Springer, Heidelberg (2004)
15. Prajna, S., Papachristodoulou, A., Seiler, P., Parrilo, P.A.: SOSTOOLS: Sum of squares optimization toolbox for MATLAB (2004)
16. Sankaranarayanan, S., Sipma, H., Manna, Z.: Constructing invariants for hybrid systems. Formal Methods in System Design 32(1), 25–55 (2008)
17. Tabuada, P.: Verification and Control of Hybrid Systems: A Symbolic Approach. Springer (2009)

Abstract Interpretation over Non-lattice Abstract Domains

Graeme Gange, Jorge A. Navas, Peter Schachte,
Harald Søndergaard, and Peter J. Stuckey

Department of Computing and Information Systems,
The University of Melbourne, Victoria 3010, Australia
{gkgange,jorge.navas,schachte,harald,pstuckey}@unimelb.edu.au

Abstract. The classical theoretical framework for static analysis of programs is abstract interpretation. Much of the power and elegance of that framework rests on the assumption that an abstract domain is a lattice. Nonetheless, and for good reason, the literature on program analysis provides many examples of non-lattice domains, including non-convex numeric domains. The lack of domain structure, however, has negative consequences, both for the precision of program analysis and for the termination of standard Kleene iteration. In this paper we explore these consequences and present general remedies.

1 Introduction

The goal of static analysis is to automatically infer useful information about the possible runtime states of a given program. Because different information is pertinent in different contexts, each analysis specifies the abstraction of the computation state to use: the *abstract domain* of the analysis.

Where the abstract domain has certain desirable properties, the abstract interpretation framework of Cousot and Cousot [1,2] provides an elegant generic analysis algorithm. Under certain reasonable assumptions, the method is guaranteed to terminate with a sound abstraction of all possible program states. In particular, the abstract interpretation framework requires that the abstract domain be a lattice, and that the functions that specify how program operations affect the abstract program state be monotone.

In this paper, we focus on a class of abstract domains that do not form lattices; in particular they may not provide least upper bound and greatest lower bound operations. Such abstract domains are commonly proposed in the literature because they strike a balance, providing more detail than is offered by simpler lattice domains, while being computationally more tractable than more complex lattice domains. The reader will find several examples in Section 4.

The common response to the lack of meets and joins is to arbitrarily choose suitable but *ad hoc* lower and upper bound operators to use instead (we call them "quasi-meets" and "quasi-joins"). However, as we show, this begets other problems, such as lack of associativity of upper and lower bound operators, and

F. Logozzo and M. Fähndrich (Eds.): SAS 2013, LNCS 7935, pp. 6–24, 2013.

a lack of monotonicity, with repercussions for termination. We pinpoint some inevitable consequences of straying from the classical abstract interpretation framework and exemplify these, together with example-specific solutions.

The reader is expected to be familiar with basic concepts in order theory and abstract interpretation. In Section 2 we refresh some of these concepts, to fix our terminology and to define a notion of quasi-lattice. In Sections 3.2 and 3.3 we prove that non-lattice domains fail to preserve many principles of reasoning that we have come to depend upon in the implementation of abstract interpretation, and we discuss the ensuing problems. In Section 4 we briefly present some of the non-lattice domains found in the literature on program analysis, and show how the problems manifest themselves. In Section 5 we catalogue various remedies. Section 6 concludes.

Contributions: In this paper we

- study the impact of using quasi-lattice abstract domains, in particular the effect on precision and termination;
- identify quasi-lattice domains in the literature on program analysis and use these to exemplify the issues that the general study lays bare; and
- outline modifications to classical abstract interpretation that are sufficient to guarantee soundness and termination, while maintaining reasonable precision of analysis.

2   Lattices and Quasi-lattices

An important aim of this paper is to facilitate a discussion of "non-lattice-ness" and its consequences. The program analyses discussed in the paper are not new; they only serve to exemplify the phenomena we want to discuss. In this section we first recapitulate well-known concepts from order theory, then introduce a kind of "almost-but-not-lattice" with properties that are found in several recently proposed abstract domains.

Definition 1 (Ultimately cyclic and stationary sequences). Let $\mathbb{N} = \{0, 1, 2 \ldots\}$ and X be a set. An ω-sequence (or just *sequence*) of X-elements $[x_0, x_1, \ldots] = [x_i \mid i \in \mathbb{N}]$ is a total mapping s from $\mathbb{N}$ to X with $s(i) = x_i$. The sequence is *ultimately cyclic* iff $\exists k, m \in \mathbb{N} \ \forall n \in \mathbb{N} : n \geq k \rightarrow x_n = x_{m+n}$. In this case we refer to $[x_k, \ldots, x_{k+m-1}]$ as the sequence's *ultimate cycle*. The sequence is *ultimately stationary* iff it has an ultimate cycle of size 1. In this case we refer to the cycle's single element as the sequence's *final element*.   □

Definition 2 (Bounded poset). Consider a binary relation $\sqsubseteq$, defined on a set D. The relation is a *partial order* iff it is

1. reflexive: $\forall d \in D : d \sqsubseteq d$
2. transitive: $\forall d_1, d_2, d_3 \in D : d_1 \sqsubseteq d_2 \wedge d_2 \sqsubseteq d_3 \rightarrow d_1 \sqsubseteq d_3$
3. antisymmetric: $\forall d_1, d_2 \in D : d_1 \sqsubseteq d_2 \wedge d_2 \sqsubseteq d_1 \rightarrow d_1 = d_2$

A set equipped with a partial order is a *poset*. If the poset $\langle D, \sqsubseteq \rangle$ has a *least element* $\bot$ and a greatest element $\top$ (that is, elements $\bot, \top \in D$ such that for all $d \in D$, $\bot \sqsubseteq d \sqsubseteq \top$) then D is *bounded*. Two elements $x, y \in D$ are *comparable* iff $x \sqsubseteq y$ or $y \sqsubseteq x$; otherwise they are *incomparable*.   □

Definition 3 (Chain). A sequence $[x_i \in X \mid i \in \mathbb{N}]$ is a *chain* iff $\forall j, k \in \mathbb{N}$: $x_j \sqsubseteq x_k \vee x_k \sqsubseteq x_j$, that is, all elements are comparable.   □

Definition 4 (Monotonicity). Let $\langle D, \sqsubseteq \rangle$ be a poset. A function $f : D \to D$ is *monotone* iff $\forall x, y \in D : x \sqsubseteq y \Rightarrow f(x) \sqsubseteq f(y)$.   □

Note that the composition of monotone functions is monotone.

Definition 5 (Upper and lower bounds). Let $\langle D, \sqsubseteq \rangle$ be a bounded poset. For any $X \subseteq D$ we say that $y \in D$ is an *upper bound* (*lower bound*) of X, written $X \sqsubseteq y$ ($y \sqsubseteq X$) iff $\forall x \in X : x \sqsubseteq y$ ($\forall x \in X : y \sqsubseteq x$). An *upper-bound operator* $U : \mathscr{P}(D) \to D$ is a function which assigns to each set X some upper bound $U(X)$. A *lower-bound operator* is defined analogously. Given a set $X \subseteq D$, a *least upper bound* of X is an element $z \in D$ which satisfies two conditions:

(a) z is an upper bound of X, and
(b) for each upper bound y of X, $z \sqsubseteq y$.

Dually, a *greatest lower bound* z of X satisfies

(a) z is a lower bound of X, and
(b) for each lower bound y of X, $y \sqsubseteq z$.

A *minimal* upper bound of X is an element z satisfying

(a) z is an upper bound of X, and
(b) for each upper bound y of X, $y \sqsubseteq z \Rightarrow y = z$.

A *maximal* lower bound is defined dually. We let $lower(X)$ denote the set of lower bounds of X.   □

We follow Nielson *et al.* [12] in putting no further requirements on an upper bound operator U. It is well-known that, in general, a least upper bound of X may not exist, but when it does, it is unique. We write the least upper bound as $\bigsqcup X$. Similarly, when it exists, the greatest lower bound of X is denoted $\bigsqcap X$. As usual, we define $x \sqcup y = \bigsqcup \{x, y\}$ and $x \sqcap y = \bigsqcap \{x, y\}$, and we refer to these operations as "join" and "meet", respectively.

Infinite chains do not, in general, have least upper bounds.[1]

Definition 6 (Chain-complete poset). The poset $\langle D, \sqsubseteq \rangle$ is *chain-complete* iff every chain $C \subseteq D$ has a least upper bound $\bigsqcup C$.   □

---

[1] An infinite chain in D may not even have a *minimal* bound in D [5], witness the chain $\{x \in \mathbb{Q} \mid x^2 < 2\}$.

Definition 7 (Continuity). A function $f : D \to D$ is *continuous* iff $\bigsqcup\{f(x) \mid x \in C\} = f(\bigsqcup C)$ for all non-empty chains $C \subseteq D$. □

Definition 8 (Complete lattice). A complete *lattice* $L = \langle D, \sqsubseteq \rangle$ is a poset $\langle D, \sqsubseteq \rangle$ such that each $X \subseteq D$ has a least upper bound $\bigsqcup X$ and a greatest lower bound $\bigsqcap X$. □

Note that a complete lattice is bounded, by definition.

Definition 9 (Lattice). A *lattice* $L = \langle D, \sqsubseteq \rangle$ is a poset $\langle D, \sqsubseteq \rangle$ such that, for all $x, y \in D$, $\bigsqcup\{x, y\}$ and $\bigsqcap\{x, y\}$ exist. A lattice which is a bounded poset is a *bounded* lattice. □

Given a lattice $\langle D, \sqsubseteq \rangle$, the meet $\sqcup$ and the join $\sqcap$ have many desirable algebraic properties. In particular, they are monotone, idempotent, commutative and associative. It follows that, since a least upper bound exists for each 2-element set, a least upper bound exists for each finite set $X \subseteq D$.

Definition 10 (Quasi-lattice). A *quasi-lattice* $\langle Q, \sqsubseteq, \tilde{\bigsqcup}, \tilde{\bigsqcap} \rangle$ is a bounded poset $\langle Q, \sqsubseteq \rangle$ satisfying the following conditions:

1. $\tilde{\bigsqcup}$ is an upper-bound, and $\tilde{\bigsqcap}$ a lower-bound, operator on Q.
2. For all $x, y \in Q$, $\tilde{\bigsqcup}\{x, y\}$ is a minimal upper bound of $\{x, y\}$.
3. For all $x, y \in Q$, $\tilde{\bigsqcap}\{x, y\}$ is a maximal lower bound of $\{x, y\}$.
4. $\langle Q, \sqsubseteq \rangle$ has a "butterfly", that is, for some $a, b \in Q$, the set $\{a, b\}$ has a minimal, but no least, upper bound in Q. □

We refer to the $\tilde{\bigsqcup}$ and $\tilde{\bigsqcap}$ operations as "quasi-join" and "quasi-meet", respectively. Again, we define $x \mathbin{\tilde{\sqcup}} y = \tilde{\bigsqcup}\{x, y\}$ and $x \mathbin{\tilde{\sqcap}} y = \tilde{\bigsqcap}\{x, y\}$. Note that $\tilde{\sqcup}$ and $\tilde{\sqcap}$ are idempotent and commutative, by definition. Requirements 2 and 3 guarantee that, given two comparable elements, $\tilde{\sqcup}$ returns the larger, and $\tilde{\sqcap}$ the smaller. It also ensures that various absorption laws hold, such as $x \mathbin{\tilde{\sqcup}} x = x$, $(x \mathbin{\tilde{\sqcap}} y) \mathbin{\tilde{\sqcup}} y = y$, and $x \mathbin{\tilde{\sqcap}} (x \mathbin{\tilde{\sqcup}} y) = x$. Note that $\tilde{\sqcup}$ over-approximates each of its elements, that is, $\tilde{\sqcup}$ is conservative in the sense of abstract interpretation. It is therefore a sound replacement for the missing join. In contrast, $\tilde{\sqcap}$ is not a conservative replacement for meet. Hence it will not play a significant role in the rest of the paper. Abstract domains usually capture conjunction (or intersection of sets of runtime states) without precision loss; but not so disjunction.

Consider the bounded poset whose Hasse diagram is shown in Figure 1. It is not a lattice since it has a "butterfly"; namely, there is no least upper bound of $\{a, b\}$ (in fact, for some a, b, c, d, this structure is embedded in any bounded poset which is not a lattice). It is, however, a quasi-lattice, for several different choices of upper-bound operator. Nevertheless, each choice has shortcomings, as we now show.

Fig. 1. A "butterfly"

Theorem 1. *In a quasi-lattice $\langle Q, \sqsubseteq, \widetilde{\sqcup}, \widetilde{\sqcap} \rangle$, $\widetilde{\sqcup}$ and $\widetilde{\sqcap}$ are neither monotone nor associative.*

Proof. We show this for $\widetilde{\sqcup}$ only; the case of $\widetilde{\sqcap}$ is similar. Let $\{x, y\} \subseteq Q$ be a set for which no least upper bound exists, and let m and m' be distinct minimal upper bounds for the set. Let $u = x \mathbin{\widetilde{\sqcup}} y$. We have either (1) $m \sqsubseteq u$ or $m' \sqsubseteq u$ (or both), or we have (2) m, m', u are pairwise incomparable. In case (1) we can assume, without loss of generality, that $m \sqsubseteq u$. Note that in this case, $u \not\sqsubseteq m'$. Hence, whether we are in case (1) or (2), $u \not\sqsubseteq m'$.

Now, to see that $\widetilde{\sqcup}$ is not monotone, note that while $y \sqsubseteq m'$ (Rule 2), we also have

$$(x \mathbin{\widetilde{\sqcup}} y) = u \not\sqsubseteq m' = (x \mathbin{\widetilde{\sqcup}} m').$$

To see that $\widetilde{\sqcup}$ is not associative, note that

$$(x \mathbin{\widetilde{\sqcup}} (y \mathbin{\widetilde{\sqcup}} m')) = m' \neq (u \mathbin{\widetilde{\sqcup}} m') = ((x \mathbin{\widetilde{\sqcup}} y) \mathbin{\widetilde{\sqcup}} m'). \qquad \square$$

Definition 11 (Fixed point). A *fixed point* of a function $f : D \to D$ is an element $x \in D$ such that $f(x) = x$. The set $fp(f)$ of fixed points of f is $\{x \in D \mid f(x) = x\}$. $\qquad \square$

Theorem 2 (From the Knaster-Tarski fixed point theorem). *Let L be a complete lattice and let $f : L \to L$ be monotone. Then $fp(f)$ is a non-empty complete lattice, and $\bigsqcap fp(f)$ is the least fixed point of f.*

We denote the least fixed point of f by $lfp(f)$.

Kleene iteration is a procedure which, given $x \in D$ and function $f : D \to D$, computes the sequence $iter_f(x) = [f^j(x) \mid j \in \mathbb{N}]$ but stops as soon as a final element (a fixed point of f) is reached; if $iter_f(x)$ is not ultimately stationary, the process does not terminate. If f is monotone and there is no infinite ascending chain in D then $iter_f(\bot)$, where $\bot$ is the least element of D, is an ultimately stationary chain whose final element is $lfp(f)$.

Abstract interpretation is concerned with the approximation of program semantics, expressed as fixed points of "semantic" functions. There are essentially two fixed point approximation approaches, one based on Galois connections, and one based on "widening" [3].

Definition 12 (Galois connection). Let $\langle D, \sqsubseteq_D \rangle$ and $\langle X, \sqsubseteq_X \rangle$ be posets, and let $\alpha : D \to X$ and $\gamma : X \to D$ be monotone functions. Then $\langle D, \alpha, \gamma, X \rangle$ is a *Galois connection* between D and X iff:

$$d \sqsubseteq_D \gamma(x) \Leftrightarrow \alpha(d) \sqsubseteq_X x \quad \text{for all } d \in D \text{ and } x \in X \qquad \square$$

The intuition is that $\gamma(x)$ expresses an abstract property x in concrete terms (that is, γ provides the "meaning" of x) whereas $\alpha(d)$ expresses the concrete property d as best as it can, given X's more limited expressiveness. We can naturally express the fact that x approximates (or is an abstraction of) d by $d \sqsubseteq_D \gamma(x)$, or alternatively by $\alpha(d) \sqsubseteq_X x$, and when these two characterisations coincide, we have a Galois connection.

We can also express the fact that a function $g : X \to X$ approximates $f : D \to D$ point by point: For all $x \in X$, we have

$$f(\gamma(x)) \sqsubseteq \gamma(g(x))$$

An important result [2] states that for a chain-complete poset D (as well as for a complete lattice D) and Galois connection $\langle D, \alpha, \gamma, X \rangle$, if the monotone $g : X \to X$ approximates the monotone $f : D \to D$ then $lfp(f) \sqsubseteq_D \gamma(lfp(g))$, that is, g's least fixed point is a sound approximation of f's.

Widening-based approaches to fixed point approximation are based on the following concept.

Definition 13 (Widening). Let $\langle D, \sqsubseteq \rangle$ be a bounded poset, a widening operator $\nabla : D \times D \to D$ satisfies the following two conditions:

1. $\forall\, x, y \in D : x \sqsubseteq (x \nabla y) \wedge y \sqsubseteq (x \nabla y)$.
2. For any increasing chain $x_0 \sqsubseteq x_1 \sqsubseteq x_2 \sqsubseteq \ldots$ the alternative chain defined as $y_0 = x_0$ and $y_{k+1} = (y_k \nabla x_{k+1})$ stabilizes after a finite number of steps.

In general, a widening operator is not commutative and it is not necessarily monotone. In practice it is common to combine the Galois connection approach with the widening approach, by resorting to the use of a widening operator only after a while, to enforce or accelerate convergence. We discuss this point further, in the context of non-lattice domains, in Section 5.2.

3   The Use of Quasi-joins

There are important consequences of the absence of lattice properties. Here we discuss three important ramifications.

3.1   Impact on Predictability of Analysis

A "join node" in a control flow graph may be at the confluence of edges that come from many different nodes. In lattice-based analysis this is where a least upper bound operation is used to combine the incoming pieces of information. Commonly, this is computed through repeated use of a binary join operation $\sqcup$. In the lattice context, the order in which these binary join operations are applied is irrelevant—any order will produce the least upper bound.

In non-lattice-based analysis, the absence of a $\sqcup$ forces us to define a proxy, $\tilde{\sqcup}$, which produces an upper bound, and ideally, a minimal one. However, as shown by Theorem 1, a minimal upper bound operation is not associative. In other words, different orders of application of $\tilde{\sqcup}$ may lead to different results, and in fact, some may be less precise than others.

The order in which the elements are combined depends on quirks of the analysis implementation, details that rightly should have no bearing on the result. One consequence is unpredictable analyses: insignificant changes to a program (or to the analyzer itself) may have significant consequences for analysis results.

3.2 Impact on Precision

A brute-force approach to attacking the order-dependency problem is to exhaustively consider all possible orders of $\tilde{\sqcup}$ applications, choosing the best one. In this way we may hope to synthesize $\bigsqcup$ from $\tilde{\sqcup}$.

Alas, this is not possible. Perhaps surprisingly, it turns out that in a quasi-lattice, one may not calculate a minimal upper bound of a finite set X by performing a sequence of binary quasi-joins, in spite of the fact that each quasi-join produces a minimal upper bound. The next theorem expresses this precisely.

Theorem 3. *There exists some finite bounded poset* $\langle D, \sqsubseteq \rangle$ *for which a minimal-upper-bound operator* $U : \mathcal{P}(D) \to D$ *cannot be obtained through repeated application of a (any) binary minimal upper bound* $\tilde{\sqcup} : D^2 \to D$.

Proof. The proof is by construction. Consider a bounded poset representing containment of elements within triples. The Hasse diagram for the case that has four atoms is shown in Figure 2. Note that, for each 3-element set $\{x, y, z\}$, there is a least upper bound xyz. Hence, for this least upper bound to be produced via repeated use of a quasi-join $\tilde{\sqcup}$, it would have to be the case that, for any triple xyz, one of $(x \tilde{\sqcup} y)$, $(x \tilde{\sqcup} z)$, and $(y \tilde{\sqcup} z)$ is xyz. Consider, however, the triple-containment poset over six elements a–f. In this case, there are $\binom{6}{3} = 20$ distinct triples. However, there are only $\binom{6}{2} = 15$ pairs of elements. So there must be some triple $x'y'z'$ such that, for all pairs of elements a, b, $a \tilde{\sqcup} b \neq x'y'z'$. Then computing $x' \tilde{\sqcup} y' \tilde{\sqcup} z'$ must yield $\top$, rather than the minimal upper bound $x'y'z'$. □

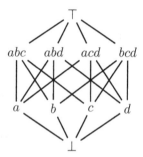

Fig. 2. A quasi-lattice with 10 elements

It follows that it is impossible to automatically synthesize a generalized minimal upper bound operator from primitive quasi-joins.

The lesson from this section and the previous one is that, in the non-lattice based case, a $\tilde{\sqcup}$ is not a suitable substitute for a minimal upper bound operator. Such an operator needs to be carefully crafted for the non-lattice domain at hand.

3.3 Impact on Termination

With quasi-lattices, including the concrete examples we turn to in Section 4, we have structures which are *almost* lattices, but lack a monotone upper-bound operation $\tilde{\sqcup}$. We now show that this lack of monotonicity has ramifications for the usual approach of solving recursive dataflow equations via Kleene iteration, even when the quasi-lattice is finite.

Theorem 4. *For any quasi-lattice Q with binary upper-bound operation $\tilde{\sqcup}$, there are elements $x \in Q$ and monotone functions $f : Q \to Q$ for which Kleene iteration of $g = \lambda y \,.\, x \,\tilde{\sqcup}\, f(y)$ fails to terminate.*

Proof. From Theorem 1 we know that $\tilde{\sqcup}$ is not monotone. Hence there are $x, y, y' \in Q$ such that

$$y \sqsubseteq y', \quad x \,\tilde{\sqcup}\, y \not\sqsubseteq x \,\tilde{\sqcup}\, y'$$

Either $(x \,\tilde{\sqcup}\, y') \sqsubset (x \,\tilde{\sqcup}\, y)$, or else $x \,\tilde{\sqcup}\, y$ and $x \,\tilde{\sqcup}\, y'$ are incomparable. Define the function $f : Q \to Q$ as follows:

$$f(v) = \begin{cases} y & \text{if } v \sqsubseteq x \,\tilde{\sqcup}\, y' \\ y' & \text{otherwise} \end{cases}$$

f is monotone, since:

$$f(v) \not\sqsubseteq f(v') \Rightarrow f(v) = y' \wedge f(v') = y \Rightarrow v \not\sqsubseteq x \,\tilde{\sqcup}\, y' \wedge v' \sqsubseteq x \,\tilde{\sqcup}\, y' \Rightarrow v \not\sqsubseteq v'$$

Note that $f(x \,\tilde{\sqcup}\, y') = y$, and $f(x \,\tilde{\sqcup}\, y) = y'$. Now consider Kleene iteration of g. Assuming $f(x \,\tilde{\sqcup}\, \bot) = y$, we observe the sequence of values:

$$[\bot, x \,\tilde{\sqcup}\, y, x \,\tilde{\sqcup}\, y', x \,\tilde{\sqcup}\, y, x \,\tilde{\sqcup}\, y', \dots]$$

This sequence will alternate between the two values indefinitely. The same oscillation occurs if we instead assume $f(x \,\tilde{\sqcup}\, \bot) = y'$.   □

At first the construction in the proof of Theorem 4 may seem artificial. However, Kleene iteration of functions of the form $\lambda y \,.\, x \sqcup f(y)$ captures exactly how one usually solves dataflow equations for simple loops, of the form shown in Figure 3. The proof of the theorem therefore gives us a recipe for constructing programs whose non-lattice-based analysis will fail to terminate, unless some remedial action is taken. Section 4 illustrates this for three concrete examples of non-lattice domains.

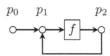

Fig. 3. A loop involving repeated use of monotone function f

4   Examples of Non-lattice Abstract Domains

In this section, we review some recent abstract domains from the literature which do not form a lattice. In each case we sketch the abstract domain and the resulting analysis. (We necessarily skip many details—the reader is referred to the cited papers for detail.) In each case we show how the phenomena identified in Sections 3.2 and 3.3 play out for the domain.

4.1   Wrapped Intervals (W-intervals)

Navas *et al.* [11] describe an abstract domain for reasoning about arithmetic operations over fixed-width machine integers. Where unbounded integers can be seen to sit on an infinite number line, fixed-width integers exist on a fixed-size number circle. One approach to handling machine arithmetic is to select a fixed wrapping point on the number circle, and represent values as intervals in the range $[v_{min}, v_{max}]$. For example, Regehr and Duongsaa [13] perform bounds analysis in a sound, wrapping-aware manner (dealing also with bit-wise operations) but as their analysis uses conventional intervals, precision is lost when sets of values cross the selected wrapping point.

Example 1 (Traditional intervals lose precision over machine arithmetic). Consider the interval $x = [0, 2]$ over 4-bit unsigned integers. The feasible values for $x - 1$ are $\{15, 0, 1\}$; however, as both 0 and 15 are contained in this set, the resulting interval is $\top$.   □

A natural alternative is to let intervals "wrap" [8,11,15]. The *wrapped intervals* (or w-intervals) of Navas *et al.* [11] still approximate a set of values as a single interval. However, there is no fixed wrapping point; a wrapped interval can begin or end at any point on the number circle.

More formally, a *w-interval* is either an empty interval, denoted $\bot$, a full interval, denoted $\top$, or a delimited interval $(\!|x, y|\!)$, where x, y are w-width bit-vectors. Let $\mathcal{B}$ be the set of all *bit-vectors* of size w, and let b^k denote k copies of bit $b \in \{0, 1\}$ in a row. Then, the concretization function is defined as:

$$\gamma(\bot) = \varnothing$$
$$\gamma(\!|x, y|\!) = \begin{cases} \{x, \ldots, y\} & \text{if } x \leqslant y \\ \{0^w, \ldots, y\} \cup \{x, \ldots, 1^w\} & \text{otherwise} \end{cases}$$
$$\gamma(\top) = \mathcal{B}$$

In the case of Example 1, the corresponding wrapped interval is $(\!|15, 1|\!)$, which succinctly represents the set of feasible values $\{15, 0, 1\}$. Unfortunately, while there is a partial ordering $\sqsubseteq$ over the set of wrapped intervals, there is no longer a unique upper bound for any pair of intervals; accordingly, the domain clearly is not a lattice. In fact, using the upper bound $\widetilde{\sqcup}$ given in [11], this domain is a quasi-lattice. Therefore, by Theorem 1, $\widetilde{\sqcup}$ is neither associative nor monotone.

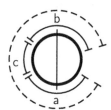

Fig. 4. The dashed interval is the minimal upper bound of $\{a, b, c\}$

Example 2 (Quasi-join over the wrapped intervals is not associative). In the context of 4-bit unsigned arithmetic, consider the three w-intervals $a = (\!|13, 2|\!)$, $b = (\!|6, 10|\!)$, and $c = (\!|3, 5|\!)$. These are shown in Figure 4. Consider that we apply the binary quasi-join $\widetilde{\sqcup}$ as follows: $(a \mathbin{\widetilde{\sqcup}} b) \mathbin{\widetilde{\sqcup}} c = (\!|6, 2|\!) \mathbin{\widetilde{\sqcup}} (\!|3, 5|\!) = (\!|6, 5|\!) = \top$.

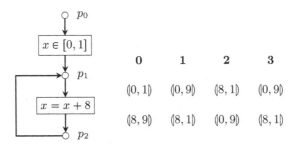

	0	**1**	**2**	**3**
	$(\!|0,1|\!)$	$(\!|0,9|\!)$	$(\!|8,1|\!)$	$(\!|0,9|\!)$
	$(\!|8,9|\!)$	$(\!|8,1|\!)$	$(\!|0,9|\!)$	$(\!|8,1|\!)$

Fig. 5. Non-terminating analysis of wrapped intervals over 4-bit integers; column i shows the interval for x in round i

However, the minimal upper bound can be obtained as $a \mathbin{\tilde{\sqcup}} (b \mathbin{\tilde{\sqcup}} c) = (\!|13,2|\!) \mathbin{\tilde{\sqcup}} (\!|3,10|\!) = (\!|13,10|\!)$. ☐

Example 3 (Any minimal quasi-join over wrapped intervals is non-monotone). Consider again the domain of intervals over 4-bit integers, with $x = (\!|0,1|\!)$, $y = (\!|8,9|\!)$, $x' = (\!|0,9|\!)$ and $y' = (\!|8,1|\!)$. Clearly, $x \sqsubseteq x'$ and $y \sqsubseteq y'$. Assume we have a quasi-join $\tilde{\sqcup}$ which selects a minimal upper bound. The two candidates for $x \mathbin{\tilde{\sqcup}} y$ are $(\!|0,9|\!)$ and $(\!|8,1|\!)$. Assume we let $x \mathbin{\tilde{\sqcup}} y = (\!|0,9|\!)$. Then we have $x \mathbin{\tilde{\sqcup}} y = (\!|0,9|\!) \not\sqsubseteq (\!|8,1|\!) = y' = x \mathbin{\tilde{\sqcup}} y'$. Similarly, if $x \mathbin{\tilde{\sqcup}} y = (\!|8,1|\!)$, we have $x \mathbin{\tilde{\sqcup}} y = (\!|8,1|\!) \not\sqsubseteq (\!|0,9|\!) = x' = x' \mathbin{\tilde{\sqcup}} y$. ☐

Given that $\tilde{\sqcup}$ is non-monotone, we can construct an instance where the analysis in the form of Kleene iteration does not terminate.

Example 4 (Analysis with w-intervals does not terminate when $\tilde{\sqcup}$ is used as the join operator). Figure 5 shows an example for bit-width $w = 4$. Recall from Example 3 that there are two equally good representations of the interval $(\!|0,1|\!) \mathbin{\tilde{\sqcup}} (\!|8,9|\!)$; namely $(\!|0,9|\!)$ and $(\!|8,1|\!)$. Assume we pick $(\!|0,9|\!)$; the other case is symmetric. In round 1, we compute $p_2 = (\!|0,9|\!) + 8 = (\!|8,1|\!)$. At the beginning of round 2, we compute $p_1 = (\!|0,1|\!) \mathbin{\tilde{\sqcup}} (\!|8,1|\!) = (\!|8,1|\!)$ (since $(\!|0,1|\!) \sqsubseteq (\!|8,1|\!)$), and p_2 then becomes $(\!|0,9|\!)$. Since $(\!|0,1|\!)$ is also contained in $(\!|0,9|\!)$, p_1 becomes $(\!|0,9|\!)$ in round 3, and we return to the state observed in round 1. The analysis will forever oscillate between the states shown in columns 1 and 2. ☐

4.2   Donut Domains

Most numerical domains are restricted to convex relations between variables; however, it is often useful to allow limited forms of non-convex reasoning. *Donut domains* [6] are constructed as the set difference of two convex domains $\langle A_1, \leqslant_1 \rangle$ and $\langle A_2, \leqslant_2 \rangle$ (relative to a given concrete powerset domain). We first consider an idealized form of donut domains. An abstract value $(x_1, x_2) \in A_1 \backslash A_2$ is interpreted according to the concretization function:

$$\gamma(x_1, x_2) = \gamma_1(x_1) \backslash \gamma_2(x_2)$$

Fig. 6. The pair of intervals $(x, y \in [-2, -1])$ and $(x, y \in [1, 2])$ has four minimal upper bounds (with respect to the inclusion ordering). In each case, the convex hull remains the same, but the *hole* component can exclude either of the rectangular regions between the two squares, or one of the two corner rectangles.

x_1 is an over-approximation of the set of reachable states, and x_2 is an under-approximation of the set of unreachable states. Assuming a suitable normalization operation, this induces a partial order over the abstract values:

$$(x_1, x_2) \sqsubseteq (y_1, y_2) \text{ iff } \gamma(x_1, x_2) \sqsubseteq \gamma(y_1, y_2)$$

This partial order clearly does not form a lattice, as there may be many minimal upper bounds of a given pair of elements.

Example 5 (The donut domain of intervals does not have a least upper bound). Consider computing the least upper bound of $a = (x, y \in [1, 2])$ and $b = (x, y \in [-2, -1])$. Four minimal upper bounds are illustrated in Figure 6. All the minimal upper bounds are of the form $(x, y \in [-2, 2]) \wedge \neg p(x, y)$ for some "hole" constraint p. For example, $p(x, y)$ may be $(x \in [-2, 2]) \wedge (y \in [-1, 1])$, or we could have $(x \in [-2, 1]) \wedge (y \in [-1, 2])$. Even though all four choices are minimal with respect to $\sqsubseteq$, the concretization of the rectangular bounds shown in the centre is larger than that of the square bounds shown to the right.   □

Given that this ordering lacks a least upper bound, any precise quasi-join will necessarily suffer the same precision and non-termination problems present in other non-lattice domains.

Example 6 (Any minimal quasi-join for the donut domain over intervals is non-associative). Consider again the intervals discussed in Example 5. Assume the quasi-join chooses the upper-left square $p = (x \in [-2, 1]) \wedge (y \in [-1, 2])$ as the hole. Then $(a \mathbin{\tilde{\sqcup}} b) \mathbin{\tilde{\sqcup}} p$ has no hole, where the minimal upper bounds have the non-empty holes $(x \in [1, 2]) \wedge (y \in [-2, 1])$ and $(x \in [-1, 2]) \wedge (y \in [-2, -1])$. For any other minimal choice made by $\tilde{\sqcup}$, we can select p similarly such that $(a \mathbin{\tilde{\sqcup}} b) \mathbin{\tilde{\sqcup}} p$ is strictly larger than $a \mathbin{\tilde{\sqcup}} (b \mathbin{\tilde{\sqcup}} p)$.   □

We now turn our attention to the formulation of donut domains presented in [6]. Given the difficulty, in general, of computing a minimal convex under-approximation of the complement of a pair of donuts, it is unsurprising that a simplified join is presented instead. The authors first define a slightly different ordering over abstract values. They define

$$(x_1, x_2) \leqslant_{1 \backslash 2} (y_1, y_2) = x_1 \leqslant_1 y_1 \wedge \left(\overline{\gamma_1(x_1) \cup \gamma_2(x_2)} \sqsupseteq \overline{\gamma_1(y_1) \cup \gamma_2(y_2)} \right)$$

Fig. 7. The two donut objects $\langle A_1, A_0 \rangle$ and $\langle A_2, A_0 \rangle$ have identical concretizations, but are incomparable under the ordering $\leqslant_{1\backslash 2}$

The bracketed component of this definition is precisely the partial order used above; $\leqslant_{1\backslash 2}$ is then a subset of $\sqsubseteq$. We suspect a misprint has crept in here, since otherwise, for some donut domains, there are values with identical concretization which are incomparable under $\leqslant_{1\backslash 2}$. An example of this is given in Figure 7. The donut objects $\langle A_1, A_0 \rangle$ and $\langle A_2, A_0 \rangle$ are built from octagons; A_0 can be expressed as $x \geqslant 0$, A_1 as $-4 \leqslant y \leqslant 4 \wedge x \leqslant y + 4$, and A_2 as $-4 \leqslant y \leqslant 4 \wedge x \leqslant -y + 4$.

The join is defined as $(x_1, x_2) \; \widetilde{\sqcup}_{1\backslash 2} \; (y_1, y_2) = (x_1 \sqcup_1 y_1, (x_1, x_2) \widetilde{\sqcap} (y_1, y_2))$, where

$$(x_1, x_2) \widetilde{\sqcap} (y_1, y_2)) = \widetilde{\alpha}((\gamma_2(x_2) \cap \gamma_2(y_2)) \cup (\gamma_2(x_2) \cap \overline{\gamma_1(y_1)}) \cup (\gamma_2(y_2) \cap \overline{\gamma_1(x_1)}))$$

The first component of the quasi-join is simply the join over A_1. $\widetilde{\sqcap}$ computes the complement by taking the intersection of each hole with the complement of the other value. Note that this only reasons about existing holes, and does not synthesize additional holes from gaps between the convex hulls; in the case of Example 6, $\widetilde{\sqcup}_{1\backslash 2}$ simply takes the convex hull of the pair. Once the complement is computed, it is mapped back to A_2 by $\widetilde{\alpha}$; this differs from α_2 in that $\widetilde{\alpha}$ under-approximates the set of concrete states, rather than over-approximates. The definition of $\widetilde{\alpha}$ is left unspecified; it is assumed to select one of the possibly many convex under-approximations of the complement.

As the previous paragraph illustrates, the donut domain, with the operations provided in [6], is not a quasi-lattice. The domain could, however, be turned into a quasi-lattice, by providing precise (minimal) upper bound operations, as these do exist. In any case, we can construct a non-terminating instance for donut domains in a similar manner as for wrapped intervals.

Example 7 (Analysis with the donut domain over intervals does not terminate).
Figure 8 shows a non-terminating example for donut domains. We start with the constraint $x, y \in [-2, 5] \wedge \neg(x, y \in (2, 4))$. At the beginning of round 1, given this definition of $\sqcup_{1\backslash 2}$, there are two minimal choices of hole. Assume we pick the hole in the top-right. This gives us the value $(x, y \in [-5, 5], x, y \in (2, 4))$. Applying f, we get $p_2 = (x, y \in [-5, 5], x, y \in (-4, -2))$. Notice that this contains p_0. In round 2, we then get $p_1 = (x, y \in [-5, 5], x, y \in (-4, -2))$. Then $p_2 = (x, y \in [-5, 5], x, y \in (2, 4))$. This again contains p_0, so round 3 returns to the state observed in round 1. As for the case of wrapped intervals, the analysis oscillates forever between the states observed in rounds 1 and 2.   □

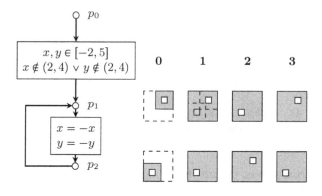

Fig. 8. Non-terminating analysis of the donut domain over intervals; column i shows the possible values for (x, y) in round i. The top entry in round 1 illustrates the two minimal upper bounds.

4.3 Segmentations for Array Content Analysis

Cousot, Cousot and Logozzo [4] propose a novel approach to the analysis of array-processing code. The idea (a further development of work by Gopan, Reps and Sagiv [7], and by Halbwachs and Péron [9]) is to summarise the content of an array by using "segmentations". These are compact descriptions that combine information about the order of indices with summary information about the content of delineated array segments. More precisely, a segmentation is of the form

$$\{e_1^1 \ldots e_{m_1}^1\} \, P_1 \, \{e_1^2 \ldots e_{m_2}^2\} \, P_2 \, \cdots P_{n-1} \, \{e_1^n \ldots e_{m_n}^n\}$$

where each e is an index expression and P_j is a description that applies to every array element between index e^{j-1} and index e^j. The lumping together (between a pair of curly brackets) of several index expressions indicates that these expressions are aliases, that is, $e_1^j = e_2^j = \cdots = e_{m_j}^j$. In our examples, index expressions will be constants or program variables, but they could be more complex. Unless otherwise indicated, the interval from e^j to e^{j+1} is assumed to be definitely non-empty. To indicate that it may be empty, the curly brackets surrounding e^{j+1} are followed by a '?'. As examples of what segmentations tell us about index relations, a segmentation of form $\{0\}..\{s\}?..\{t\}?..\{N\}$ tells us that $0 \leqslant s \leqslant t < N$, whereas one of form $\{0 \ s\}..\{u\}?..\{t \ N\}$ tells us that $0 = s \leqslant u < t = N$.

Segmentation unification is the process of, given two segmentations with "compatible" extremal segment bounds (in general for the same array), modifying both segmentations so that they coincide. By "compatible" we mean that the first and last segment bounds have a non-empty intersection.

Segmentation unification is a key operation since it is the core of the join. Sec 11.4 of [4] states the problem of segmentation unification admits a partially ordered set of solutions, but in general, not forming a lattice.

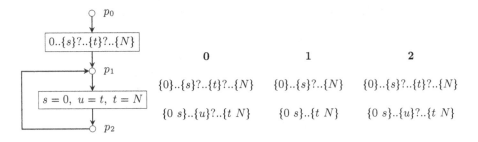

	0	**1**	**2**
	$\{0\}..\{s\}?..\{t\}?..\{N\}$	$\{0\}..\{s\}?..\{N\}$	$\{0\}..\{s\}?..\{t\}?..\{N\}$
	$\{0\ s\}..\{u\}?..\{t\ N\}$	$\{0\ s\}..\{t\ N\}$	$\{0\ s\}..\{u\}?..\{t\ N\}$

Fig. 9. Non-terminating analysis with array segmentations; column i shows the segmentation in round i

For instance, unifying $\{0\}..\{a\}..\{b\}..\{c\}$ with $\{0\}..\{b\}..\{a\}..\{c\}$ results in two incomparable minimal solutions: $\{0\}..\{a\}..\{c\}$ and $\{0\}..\{b\}..\{c\}$.

The authors describe a greedy pseudo-algorithm that scans left-to-right, keeping a point-wise consistent subset of the ordering. They also describe a *2 look-ahead* approach (in contrast with the greedy 1 look-ahead algorithm) which takes the next segment into account when unifying. As we should expect, both of these quasi-joins are non-monotone.

Example 8 (1 look-ahead segment unification is non-monotone). Let segment $A = \{0\}..\{s\}..\{t\}..\{N\}$, $B = \{0\}..\{u\}..\{s\}..\{N\}$, and $B' = \{0\}..\{s\}..\{N\}$. Clearly, $B \sqsubseteq B'$. However, we have $A \,\tilde{\sqcup}\, B = \{0\}..\{N\}$, and $A \,\tilde{\sqcup}\, B' = \{0\}..\{s\}..\{N\}$.   □

The 2 look-ahead algorithm is also clearly non-monotone, such as in the case where $A = \{0\}..\{a\}..\{b\}..\{N\}$ and $B = \{0\}..\{b\}..\{c\}..\{N\}$. (In this case, the 1 look-ahead algorithm would see that $\{a\}$ and $\{b\}$ do not match, discarding both, then again for $\{b\}$ and $\{c\}$, returning the segmentation $\{0\}..\{N\}$).

In both cases, we can construct a non-terminating instance following the structure of Theorem 4. We present only an example for the 1 look-ahead algorithm; the 2 look-ahead case can be constructed in a very similar fashion.

Example 9 (Analysis with the array segmentation domain does not terminate using the 1 look-ahead unification algorithm). Figure 9 shows an example over variables $\{s, t, u\}$. Initially, we have $0 \leqslant s \leqslant t < N$. Reaching p_2, we have the segmentation $\{0\ s\} \ldots \{u\}? \ldots \{t\ N\}$. Unifying at p_1, the $\{t\}$ and $\{u\}$ partitions are discarded, yielding $\{0\} \ldots \{s\}? \ldots \{N\}$. Since t is not in the current segmentation, u is omitted in the next round, and we reconstruct the original segmentation. It is interesting to note that this oscillates between two *comparable* values.   □

This domain does not satisfy the quasi-lattice conditions using either of the described $\tilde{\sqcup}$ definitions. For example, using the 1 look-ahead algorithm, we have $x = \{0\}..\{s\}..\{t\}..\{N\} \sqsubseteq y = \{0\}..\{t\}..\{N\}$, but $x \,\tilde{\sqcup}\, y = \{0\}..\{N\} \neq y$. However, a related quasi-lattice could be constructed by using a more precise $\tilde{\sqcup}$ which selects amongst the set of minimal upper bounds.

5 Abstract Interpretation over Bounded Posets

We have seen that, even for a domain satisfying the relatively strict quasi-lattice requirements, being a non-lattice has negative consequences for predictability, precision and termination of Kleene iteration. We now consider abstract interpretation over abstract domains that are only required to be bounded posets.

5.1 Non-associative Quasi-joins

The lack of associativity of a quasi-join cannot of itself compromise the total correctness of the abstract interpretation algorithm. However, we have seen that it can cause a loss of precision. It also means that different fixed point algorithms may lead to different results, further complicating the design of an abstract interpretation framework.

Usually analysis frameworks will define a generalized quasi-join operation in terms of a binary quasi-join:

$$\widetilde{\bigsqcup}\{x_1, \ldots, x_n\} = (\cdots(x_1 \mathbin{\widetilde{\sqcup}} x_2) \mathbin{\widetilde{\sqcup}} x_3 \cdots) \mathbin{\widetilde{\sqcup}} x_n$$

and similarly for $\widetilde{\sqcap}$ (if this operation is needed). Because quasi-joins are not associative, clearly the ordering of the x_i is important. Theorem 3 shows us that in some cases no ordering will produce a minimal upper bound, so it is preferable to specify a generalized quasi-join operation directly. For example, in the case of the wrapped interval domain, Navas *et al.* [11] present a generalized quasi-join operation defined in terms of a binary quasi-join that produces the minimal upper bound with a complexity of $O(n \log(n))$, where n is the number of w-intervals. The generalized quasi-join can compute the minimal solution by first ordering the w-intervals lexicographically. Then, it repeatedly applies the binary quasi-join to the ordered sequence while keeping track of the largest gap which is not covered by the application of the binary quasi-joins. We refer to [11] for details about the algorithm.

5.2 Non-monotone Quasi-joins

As discussed in Section 3.3, in abstract interpretation, we often wish to find the least fixed point of a function defined in terms of abstract operations (transfer functions) and joins. When using quasi-lattices, and hence quasi-joins, we may find ourselves seeking the least fixed point of a non-monotone function. In that setting, Theorem 2 does not apply, so we do not know whether a least fixed point exists, or, if it does, how to compute it. As we have seen, standard Kleene iteration may not terminate. We now show, however, that a generalized Kleene iteration algorithm will produce a sound result, under reasonable assumptions.

Theorem 5. *Let C be a complete lattice and $f : C \to C$ be continuous. Let A be a bounded poset with least element $\bot$, and let $\gamma : A \to C$ be given. If the (not necessarily monotone) $g : A \to A$ approximates f, that is,*

$$\forall y \in A : f(\gamma(y)) \sqsubseteq \gamma(g(y)) \tag{1}$$

and the sequence $g* = [\bot, g(\bot), g^2(\bot), \ldots]$ *is ultimately cyclic, then for every* y *in the ultimate cycle of* $g*$, $lfp(f) \sqsubseteq \gamma(y)$.

Proof. Let $Y = [y_0, \ldots, y_{m-1}]$ be the ultimate cycle of $g*$ and let $x_0 = \bigsqcap_{0 \leqslant i < m} \gamma(y_i)$, We then have:

$$
\begin{aligned}
f(x_0) &\sqsubseteq f(\gamma(y_i)) && \text{for all } 0 \leqslant i < m, \text{ by monotonicity of } f \\
&\sqsubseteq \gamma(g(y_i)) && \text{for all } 0 \leqslant i < m, \text{ by (1)} \\
&= \gamma(y_{i+1 \bmod m}) && \text{for all } 0 \leqslant i < m
\end{aligned}
$$

Hence $f(x_0) \sqsubseteq \bigsqcap_{0 \leqslant i < m} \gamma(y_i) = x_0$. Clearly $\bot_C \sqsubseteq x_0$, so by monotonicity of f, and the transitivity of $\sqsubseteq$, $f^k(\bot_C) \sqsubseteq x_0$ for all $k \in \mathbb{N}$. As f is continuous, $lfp(f) \sqsubseteq x_0$, so for each $y \in Y$, $lfp(f) \sqsubseteq \gamma(y)$.   □

This has two important ramifications for use in abstract interpretation:

1. Kleene iteration will not cycle (repeat) before finding a sound approximation of the true set of concrete states; and
2. In a finite abstract domain, it will reach this result in finite time.

Thus Kleene iteration can safely be used for abstract interpretation over bounded poset abstract domains, as long as we generalize the loop detection algorithm to detect cycles of cardinality greater than one. We can use the fact that any ultimately cyclic sequence must include a subsequence x_i, x_{i+1} such that $x_i \not\sqsubseteq x_{i+1}$ to reduce the overhead of the loop check. Also, since every element of the ultimate cycle is a sound approximation, we are free to return a cycle element e for which $\gamma(e)$ has minimal cardinality. We assume we are supplied with a function **better**(x_1, x_2) that returns the x_i for which $\gamma(x_i)$ has the smaller cardinality.

Algorithm 6 (Generalised Kleene Iteration)

> *procedure* ULT_CYCLE(g)
> > $result \leftarrow \bot$
> > **repeat**
> > > $prev \leftarrow result$
> > > $result \leftarrow g(result)$
> >
> > **until** $prev \not\sqsubseteq result$
> > **while** $prev \neq result$ **do**
> > > $result \leftarrow g(g(result))$
> > > $prev \leftarrow g(prev)$
> >
> > **end while**
> > $next \leftarrow g(result)$
> > **while** $prev \neq next$ **do**
> > > $result \leftarrow \textbf{better}(result, next)$
> > > $next \leftarrow g(next)$
> >
> > **end while**
> > **return** $result$
>
> *end procedure*

The **repeat** loop searches for the beginning of an ultimate cycle while repeatedly applying g. Note that the **until** condition is a strict inequality and hence, if there is a fixed point (that is, $prev = result$) the loop will also terminate. The first **while** loop iterates until it completes the ultimate cycle.[2] By Theorem 5, any solution obtained from any element in this cycle is a sound approximation of the least fixed point. The second **while** loop then chooses the most precise member of the cycle using the **better** function.

This algorithm performs very similarly to Kleene iteration in cases where the Kleene sequence is an ascending chain. In other cases it is costlier. Where performance is preferred to precision, the final **while** loop can safely be omitted.

A more efficient, but even less precise, algorithm can be had by forcibly ensuring that the Kleene sequence is increasing by defining

$$g'(x) = x \mathbin{\tilde{\sqcup}} g(x).$$

Then the standard Kleene iteration algorithm can be used on g'. Note that where the Kleene sequence for g is an ascending chain, all of these approaches yield the same result at approximately the same cost.

Example 10 (Forced climbing on wrapped intervals). Consider the program given in Example 1. After round 1, we have $p_1 = (\!(0, 9)\!)$, $p_2 = (\!(8, 1)\!)$. Where previously we compute the updated value of p_1 as $(\!(0, 1)\!) \mathbin{\tilde{\sqcup}} (\!(8, 1)\!)$, we now compute $p_1 = (\!(0, 9)\!) \mathbin{\tilde{\sqcup}} (\!(0, 1)\!) \mathbin{\tilde{\sqcup}} (\!(8, 1)\!) = \top$. The updated value of p_2 also becomes $\top$, and we have reached a fixed point.   □

Where the abstract domain is infinite, or just intractably large, another mechanism must be used to hasten termination, at the cost of some loss of precision. As has been previously observed [14], widening may be used to ensure termination:

> *The widening technique can be useful even outside abstract interpretation. For example, in a normal dataflow analysis, we can use it to make sure that the series of abstract values computed for a given program point by the analysis iterations is an ascending chain, even if the transfer functions are not monotone.*

However, care must be taken. In many cases, widening is used periodically during Kleene iteration, giving up precision only when convergence appears too slow. If this is done for Kleene iteration over a non-monotone function, it is possible that the progress that is ensured by the occasional widening step is lost in successive non-widening steps, leading to an infinite loop. That is, if the underlying function is not monotone, applying widening occasionally will not make it monotone. For example, if $g(x) = y$, $g(y) = z$, $g(z) = x$, and $x \nabla y = z$,

---

[2] This part exploits Floyd's "tortoise and hare" principle [10], and requires only two values at a time to be remembered. However, it requires more applications of g than are strictly needed. If computation of g is expensive, it may be preferable to use a hash table to store values returned by g, and to simplify the loop body so that g is called just once per iteration.

and the widening operation is applied on odd steps, then the Kleene sequence $[x, x\nabla g(x) = z, g(z) = x, \ldots]$ is not ultimately stationary. Thus to ensure termination, perhaps after a finite number of non-widening steps, widening must be performed at each step. Alternatively some other measure must be taken between widening steps (such as taking the quasi-join with the previous result) to ensure the function is monotone.

6   Conclusion

In the pursuit of increased precision, it is tempting to step outside the lattice-based framework of abstract interpretation. In the absence of a join operation, the obvious response is to seek a "quasi-join" which provides minimal upper bounds. We have shown, however, that such a quasi-join cannot always be generalized to a "minimal-upper-bound operation". This means that the precision of analysis results depends on arbitrary and insignificant design decisions that should be immaterial to the analysis. Equally, even a small semantics-preserving change to the surface structure of a subject program may have great impact on precision. Finally, the quasi-join's inevitable lack of monotonicity easily leads to non-termination of Kleene iteration.

We have exemplified these phenomena with three recently proposed non-lattice abstract domains. Usually when such domains are proposed, their proponents provide remedial tricks that overcome the problems we discuss, including non-termination of analysis. In particular, widening may be used to ensure termination. We have argued that, even so, care must be exercised if widening is interleaved with non-widening steps. Finally we have provided strategies for adapting standard Kleene iteration to the context of non-monotone functions defined on bounded posets, including forced climbing, widening, and the use of a generalised, loop-checking variant of Kleene iteration.

Acknowledgments. We wish to thank the anonymous reviewers for many insightful suggestions. This work was supported through ARC grant DP110102579.

References

1. Cousot, P., Cousot, R.: Abstract interpretation: A unified lattice model for static analysis of programs by construction or approximation of fixpoints. In: Proceedings of the Fourth Annual Symposium on Principles of Programming Languages, pp. 238–252. ACM (1977)
2. Cousot, P., Cousot, R.: Systematic design of program analysis frameworks. In: Proceedings of the Sixth Annual Symposium on Principles of Programming Languages, pp. 269–282. ACM (1979)
3. Cousot, P., Cousot, R.: Comparing the Galois connection and widening/narrowing approaches to abstract interpretation. In: Bruynooghe, M., Wirsing, M. (eds.) PLILP 1992. LNCS, vol. 631, pp. 269–295. Springer, Heidelberg (1992)

4. Cousot, P., Cousot, R., Logozzo, F.: A parametric segmentation functor for fully automatic and scalable array content analysis. In: Proceedings of the 38th Annual Symposium on Principles of Programming Languages, pp. 105–118. ACM (2011)
5. Davey, B.A., Priestley, H.A.: Introduction to Lattices and Order. Cambridge University (1990)
6. Ghorbal, K., Ivančić, F., Balakrishnan, G., Maeda, N., Gupta, A.: Donut domains: Efficient non-convex domains for abstract interpretation. In: Kuncak, V., Rybalchenko, A. (eds.) VMCAI 2012. LNCS, vol. 7148, pp. 235–250. Springer, Heidelberg (2012)
7. Gopan, D., Reps, T., Sagiv, M.: A framework for numeric analysis of array operations. In: Proceedings of the 32nd ACM SIGPLAN-SIGACT Symposium on Principles of Programming Languages, pp. 338–350. ACM (2005)
8. Gotlieb, A., Leconte, M., Marre, B.: Constraint solving on modular integers. In: Proceedings of the Ninth International Workshop on Constraint Modelling and Reformulation (September 2010)
9. Halbwachs, N., Péron, M.: Discovering properties about arrays in simple programs. SIGPLAN Notices 43, 339–348 (2008)
10. Knuth, D.E.: The Art of Computer Programming, 2nd edn., vol. 2. Addison-Wesley (1981)
11. Navas, J.A., Schachte, P., Søndergaard, H., Stuckey, P.J.: Signedness-agnostic program analysis: Precise integer bounds for low-level code. In: Jhala, R., Igarashi, A. (eds.) APLAS 2012. LNCS, vol. 7705, pp. 115–130. Springer, Heidelberg (2012)
12. Nielson, F., Nielson, H.R., Hankin, C.: Principles of Program Analysis. Springer (1999)
13. Regehr, J., Duongsaa, U.: Deriving abstract transfer functions for analyzing embedded software. In: LCTES 2006: Proceedings of the 2006 ACM SIGPLAN/SIGBED Conference on Language, Compilers, and Tool Support for Embedded Systems, pp. 34–43. ACM (2006)
14. Sălcianu, A.: Notes on abstract interpretation (2001), http://www.mit.edu/~salcianu (Unpublished Manuscript)
15. Sen, R., Srikant, Y.N.: Executable analysis using abstract interpretation with circular linear progressions. In: Proceedings of the Fifth IEEE/ACM International Conference on Formal Methods and Models for Codesign, pp. 39–48. IEEE (2007)

Localizing Widening and Narrowing

Gianluca Amato and Francesca Scozzari

Dipartimento di Economia
Università "G. d'Annunzio" di Chieti-Pescara
{gamato,fscozzari}@unich.it

Abstract. We show two strategies which may be easily applied to standard abstract interpretation-based static analyzers. They consist in 1) restricting the scope of widening, and 2) intertwining the computation of ascending and descending chains. Using these optimizations it is possible to improve the precision of the analysis, without any change to the abstract domains.

1   Introduction

In abstract interpretation-based static analysis, the program to analyze is typically translated into a set of equations describing the abstract program behavior, such as:

$$\begin{cases} x_1 = \Phi_1(x_1, \ldots, x_n) \\ \quad \vdots \\ x_n = \Phi_n(x_1, \ldots, x_n) \end{cases} \tag{1}$$

Each index $i \in \{1, \ldots, n\}$ represents a control point of the program and each Φ_i is a monotone operator. The variables in the equations range over an *abstract domain* A, which is a poset whose elements encode the properties we want to track. The analysis aims at computing the least solution of this system of equations.

In theory, it is possible to find the (exact) least solution of the system with a Kleene iteration, starting from the least element in A^n. However, in practice, many abstract domains have infinite ascending chains, therefore this procedure may not terminate. In other cases, domains may have very long finite ascending chains that would make this procedure impractical. The standard solution to these problems is to use *widening*, which ensures the termination of the analysis in exchange of a certain loss in precision.

Widening has been extensively studied, and we can find in the literature many different widenings for the most common abstract domains. Furthermore, many domain-independent techniques have been developed to improve widening precision, such as delayed widening, widening with threshold [9] and lookahead widening [17]. There are alternatives to the use of widening, such as acceleration operators [16] and strategy/policy iteration [11,15]. However, acceleration only works for programs with restricted linear assignments, while strategy/policy iteration is restricted to template domains [26]. Therefore, widening is the only general applicable mechanism.

F. Logozzo and M. Fähndrich (Eds.): SAS 2013, LNCS 7935, pp. 25–42, 2013.

Using widening in the Kleene iteration, we still get an ascending chain which stabilizes on a post-fixpoint of Φ. It is common practice to improve the precision of the analysis continuing the iteration, taking this post-fixpoint as a starting point for a descending chain. Every element of the latter is an over approximation of the least fixpoint, therefore it is possible to stop the sequence at any moment without losing correctness. Sometimes a narrowing operator may be used, with the same purpose.

While widening and ascending chains have been extensively studied, little attention has been devoted to descending chains. One of the few papers, if not the only one, which tackles the subject is [20]. Nonetheless, descending chains (with or without narrowing) are often needed to get a decent precision.

In this paper we propose two strategies for improving the way standard abstract interpretation-based static analyzers are engineered. The first improvement regards widening and ascending chains. The second improvements regards descending chains, in particular the way ascending and descending chains may be intertwined.

1.1 Improving Widening

Widening is defined by Cousot and Cousot [12] as a binary operation $\nabla : A \times A \to A$ over an abstract domain A, with the property that, given a sequence $x_0, \ldots, x_i, \ldots$ of abstract elements, the sequence $y_0 = x_0$, $y_{i+1} = y_i \nabla x_i$ is eventually constant.

It is possible to select a set of widening points $W \subseteq \{1, \ldots, n\}$ among all the control points of the program and replace, for each $i \in W$, the i-th equation in the system (1) with

$$x_i = x_i \nabla \Phi_i(x_1, \ldots, x_n) \ .$$

When W is admissible, i.e., every loop in the *dependency graph* of the system of equations contains at least one element in W, then any chaotic iteration sequence terminates. The choice of the set W of widening points may influence both termination and precision, thus should be chosen wisely.

Bourdoncle's algorithm [10] returns an admissible set of widening points. When the equations are generated by a control-flow graph, this set contains all the loop junction nodes. For structured programs, these widening points are exactly the loop heads of the program. This means that, if $i \in W$, the corresponding equation is

$$x_i = x_{in} \vee x_{back} \ ,$$

where the control points i, *in* and *back* are, respectively, the head of the loop, the input to the loop and the tail of the loop. The standard application of widening yields the equation

$$x_i = x_i \nabla (x_{in} \vee x_{back}) \ .$$

We believe that this is a source of imprecision, and show that, under certain conditions, it is possible (and generally better) to replace this equation with

$$x_i = x_{in} \vee (x_i \nabla x_{back}) \ . \tag{2}$$

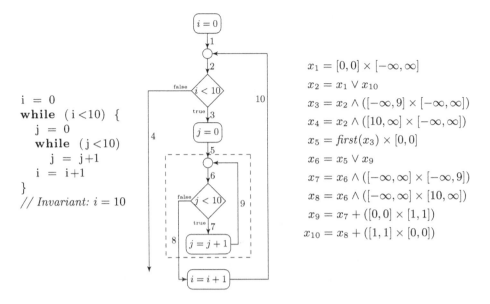

```
i = 0
while (i <10) {
   j = 0
   while (j <10)
      j = j+1
      i = i+1
}
// Invariant: i = 10
```

$$x_1 = [0,0] \times [-\infty, \infty]$$
$$x_2 = x_1 \vee x_{10}$$
$$x_3 = x_2 \wedge ([-\infty, 9] \times [-\infty, \infty])$$
$$x_4 = x_2 \wedge ([10, \infty] \times [-\infty, \infty])$$
$$x_5 = \mathit{first}(x_3) \times [0,0]$$
$$x_6 = x_5 \vee x_9$$
$$x_7 = x_6 \wedge ([-\infty, \infty] \times [-\infty, 9])$$
$$x_8 = x_6 \wedge ([-\infty, \infty] \times [10, \infty])$$
$$x_9 = x_7 + ([0,0] \times [1,1])$$
$$x_{10} = x_8 + ([1,1] \times [0,0])$$

Fig. 1. The example program **nested**

The last equation suggests that, when a junction node is entered from outside the loop, widening is replaced by least upper bound, and when a junction node is entered from inside the loop, widening is performed only on values generated inside the loop. We call *localized widening* the use of widening according to Eq. 2. Localized widening is mostly useful in the case of nested loops, where x_{in} does not change while analyzing the inner loop.

Consider the program in Figure 1 and the corresponding system of equations. Bourdouncle's algorithm outputs the set of widening points $W = \{2, 6\}$. Consider the trace of the analysis given in Figure 2, which is limited to the ascending chain and uses a recursive iteration strategy with the standard widening on the interval domain.

In the result, both x_2 and x_6 have infinite upper bounds for i. The problem is that, the second time we enter the inner loop, the new value of x_6 is computed as

$$x_6 \nabla (x_5 \vee x_9) = \{i = 0, j \geq 0\} \nabla (\{i \in [0, 9], j = 0\} \vee \{i = 0, j \in [1, 10]\})$$
$$= \{i = 0, j \geq 0\} \nabla \{i \in [0, 9], j \in [0, 10]\}$$
$$= \{i \geq 0, j \geq 0\} \ .$$

If we compute the descending sequence starting from here, we get $x_2 = \{i \geq 0\}$ and $x_6 = \{i \geq 0, j \in [0, 10]\}$. Note that, while for j we got optimal bounds, the analysis cannot determine that $i = 10$ at the end of the loops. The problem is that the descending iteration cannot improve the upper bound for i for the variable x_5, since i is not used in the inner loop. This is a well known problem, and [20] gives a detailed presentation of the issue.

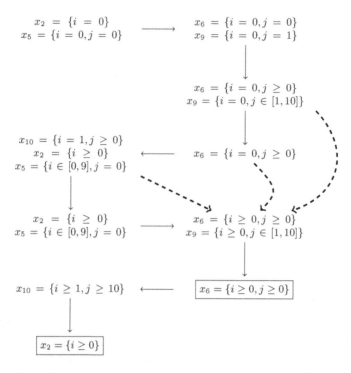

Fig. 2. Trace of the analysis (only the ascending chain) for the program in Figure 1 using standard widening. Boxed values are final values. Solid arrows depict the order of execution, while dashed arrows show which input values are used to compute a new value.

If we use localized widening as described in Eq. 2, the second time we enter the inner loop the new value of x_6 is computed as:

$$x_5 \vee (x_6 \triangledown x_9) = \{i \in [0,9], j = 0\} \vee (\{i = 0, j \geq 0\} \triangledown \{i = 0, j \geq 1\})$$
$$= \{i \in [0,9], j = 0\} \vee \{i = 0, j \geq 0\}$$
$$= \{i \in [0,9], j \geq 0\} \ .$$

At the end of the ascending chain we get $x_2 = \{i \geq 0\}$, $x_6 = \{i \in [0,9], j \geq 0\}$ and $x_{10} = \{i \in [1,10], j \geq 10\}$. This is enough to obtain, after the descending chain, the required result $x_2 = \{i \in [0,10]\}$ and $x_6 = \{i \in [0,9], j \in [0,10]\}$.

1.2   Improving Descending Sequences

The way ascending and descending sequences interact has never been fully clarified. The standard technique is to first compute an over approximation of the least solution of the equations with an ascending chain, and later refine the solution with a descending sequence. However, in the presence of nested loops, other choices are possible. In particular, when using a recursive strategy for the ascending sequence [10], it seems natural to intertwine ascending and descending sequences.

Consider again the program in Figure 1. Using either a recursive or an iterative strategy with the standard widening, the ascending chain determines the following invariants for the loops:

$$x_2 = \{i \geq 0\} \qquad x_6 = \{i \geq 0, j \geq 0\}$$

As shown in the previous section, precision may be partially recovered using a descending iteration, obtaining:

$$x_2 = \{i \geq 0\} \qquad x_6 = \{i \geq 0, j \in [0, 10]\}$$

However, it is possible to view the nodes inside the dashed rectangle in Figure 1 as if they were a single node, with input edge 5 and output edge 8. The abstract transformer for the new node is obtained performing a standard analysis of the inner loop, comprised of both ascending and descending chain. In this case, we have the following results:

$$
\begin{array}{lll}
x_2^0 = \bot & x_2^1 = \{i = 0\} & x_2^2 = \{i \in [0, \infty]\} \\
x_5^0 = \bot & x_5^1 = \{i = 0, j = 0\} & x_5^2 = \{i \in [0, 9], j = 0\} \\
x_8^0 = \bot & x_8^1 = \{i = 0, j = 10\} & x_8^2 = \{i \in [0, 9], j = 10\}
\end{array}
$$

where the values for x_8 are computed by considering the dashed rectangle as a whole. Every time it is considered, the analysis of the inner loop starts from the beginning, independently from the results of previous iterations. The last row is the fixpoint of the ascending chain (of the outer loop). Then, the descending chain (of the outer loop) begins:

$$
\begin{array}{ll}
x_2^{\downarrow 0} = \{i \in [0, \infty]\} & x_2^{\downarrow 1} = \{i \in [0, 10]\} \\
x_5^{\downarrow 0} = \{i \in [0, 9], j = 0\} & x_5^{\downarrow 1} = \{i \in [0, 9], j = 0\} \\
x_8^{\downarrow 0} = \{i \in [0, 9], j = 10\} & x_8^{\downarrow 1} = \{i \in [0, 9], j = 10\}
\end{array}
$$

In this case, we are able to prove that in the head of the outer loop $i \in [0, 10]$, since in the ascending chain we do not lose the information that $i \in [0, 9]$ holds in the inner loop.

If we look at the entire procedure without considering the abstraction given by the dashed rectangle, it happens that ascending and descending sequences are intertwined. While an ascending sequence is going on in the outer loop, either an ascending or descending sequence is going on in the inner loop. We call *localized narrowing* this strategy of intertwining ascending and descending chains. Here we use the term narrowing broadly, to mean not only the standard narrowing operator [13] but any procedure producing a descending chain.

1.3   Plan of the Paper

Localized widening and narrowing may improve precision, but it is not completely clear whether they may be applied without compromising correctness and termination.

In Section 2, we show that localized widening is correct and terminates for any iteration strategy. In Section 3, we show that localized narrowing is correct and guarantees termination. Section 4 shows that localized widening and narrowing may improve precision not only w.r.t. standard abstract interpretation, but even when compared to other optimizations.

2   Localized Widening

We now formalize the treatment of widening presented in Section 1.1. We show the conditions that allow to replace the standard widening with the localized one and prove the correctness of the resulting analysis.

In the following, we denote with Φ a system of equations as in (1), where each variable x_i ranges over a poset A, and each $\Phi_i : A^n \to A$ is a monotone function. With an abuse of notation, we denote with $\Phi = (\Phi_1, \ldots, \Phi_n)$ the function $\Phi : A^n \to A^n$ obtained as the product of the Φ_i's.

2.1   Preliminaries

We use the standard definition of widening, as appeared for the first time in [12].

Definition 1 (Widening [12]). *A* widening *for the poset A is a binary operator $\nabla : A \times A \to A$ such that:*

1. $x \leq x \nabla y$,
2. $y \leq x \nabla y$,
3. *for every sequence $(x_i)_{i \in \omega}$, the sequence $y_0 = x_0$, $y_{i+1} = y_i \nabla x_i$ is eventually constant.*

In [14] a different definition of widening is introduced, where the convergence of the sequence (y_i) is ensured only if the sequence (x_i) is ascending. Note that, every widening $\tilde{\nabla}$ satisfying [14] may be transformed in a widening ∇ satisfying [12] by defining

$$x \nabla y = x \tilde{\nabla}(x \vee y) \ . \tag{3}$$

Definition 2 (Dependency graph). *The dependency graph of the system of equations Φ is a directed graph with nodes $\{1, \ldots, n\}$ and an edge $i \to j$ iff x_i occurs in Φ_j.*

Example 1. The dependency graph for the system in Figure 1 is:

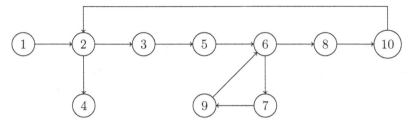

The nodes in the dependency graph correspond to the edges in the control-flow graph.

We recall from [10] the definitions of hierarchical ordering and weak topological ordering.

Definition 3 (Hierarchical ordering [10]). *A hierarchical ordering of a set S is a well-parenthesized permutation of this set without two consecutive "(".*

In other words, a hierarchical ordering is a string over the alphabet S augmented with left and right parenthesis. The elements between two matching parentheses are called a *component* and the first element of a component is called the *head*. The innermost component containing an element l is denoted by comp(l), and its head is denoted by head(l), when they exist. The set of heads of the components containing the element l is denoted by $\omega(l)$.

Example 2. For the dependency graph in Example 1, two hierarchical orderings are 1 2 3 4 5 6 7 8 9 10 and 1 (2 3 5 (6 7 9) 8 10) 4. In the second ordering, the heads are 2 and 6 and we have head(7) = 6 and head(3) = 2.

A hierarchical ordering induces a total ordering, that we denote by $\preceq$, corresponding to the permutation of the elements.

Definition 4 (Weak topological ordering [10]). *A weak topological ordering of a directed graph (w.t.o. for short) is a hierarchical ordering of its nodes such that for every edge $u \rightarrow v$, either $u \prec v$ or $v \preceq u$ and $v \in \omega(u)$.*[1]

Example 3. For the graph given in Example 1, a possible weak topological ordering is 1 (2 3 5 (6 7 9) 8 10) 4.

Every weak topological ordering of the dependency graph of Φ determines a set of admissible widening points (the set of all the heads) and two iteration strategies for solving the equations in Φ: an *iterative* and a *recursive* strategy.

   In the recursive strategy, we apply the equations in the order given by the w.t.o., but every time we enter a new component, we loop within that component until all its values are stabilized. The iterative strategy is similar, but with the ordering obtained by removing all parentheses except the ones for the outermost component.

---

[1] In [10], the first condition was $u \prec v \wedge v \notin \omega(u)$. However, the second conjunct is implied by the first one.

2.2   Localizing Widening

In the following, assume given a system Φ, its dependency graph and an associated weak topological ordering. An admissible set of widening points is implicitly defined as the set of all the heads in the weak topological ordering.

Definition 5 (Loop join node). *A loop join node is a node $l \in [1, n]$ in the dependency graph of Φ such that l is the head of a component and $\Phi_l(x_1, \ldots, x_n) = x_{v_1} \vee \cdots \vee x_{v_m}$ for some $\{v_1, \ldots, v_m\} \subseteq [1, n]$.*

Given a loop join node l, let $\{v_1^i, \ldots, v_r^i\}$ and $\{v_1^b, \ldots, v_s^b\}$ be the partition of $\{v_1, \ldots, v_m\}$ such that $v_j^i \notin \mathsf{comp}(l)$ and $v_j^b \in \mathsf{comp}(l)$. Elements of the two sets are called *input nodes* and *back nodes* respectively. We define $x_i^{in} = x_{v_1^i} \vee \cdots \vee x_{v_r^i}$ and $x_i^{back} = x_{v_1^b} \vee \cdots \vee x_{v_s^b}$.

Example 4. Nodes 2 and 6 in the system in Figure 1 are loop join nodes.

Intuitively, the above definition allows us to distinguish between join nodes generated by while loops and join nodes generated by if statements. In the first case, we separate the edges coming from inside the loop, denoted by x_i^{in}, and the edges coming from outside the loop, denoted by x_i^{back}. Note that the conditions on input and back nodes, i.e., $v_j^i \notin \mathsf{comp}(l)$ and $v_j^b \in \mathsf{comp}(l)$, are equivalent to $v_j^i \prec l$ and $l \preceq v_j^b$.

Definition 6. *We denote by $\Phi^\vee$ a new system of equations derived from Φ and such that, for each head node i, the i-th equation is replaced as follows:*

- *if i is a loop join node, by $x_i = x_i^{in} \vee (x_i \nabla x_i^{back})$;*
- *if i is not a loop join node, by $x_i = x_i \nabla \Phi_i(x_1, \ldots, x_n)$.*

The idea is that any input coming from outside of a component does not need to be guarded by the widening. In fact, either the input does not belong to any loop (and therefore it has a constant value after the first iteration) or it belongs to a loop, and therefore it is already guarded by another outer widening which ensures that it will not increase forever. This reasoning works, however, only assuming that all the head nodes are widening nodes.

Example 5. If Φ is the system in Figure 1 whose heads are 2 and 6, we have that $\Phi^\vee$ is the same as Φ but for the following equations: $x_2 = x_1 \vee (x_2 \nabla x_{10})$, $x_6 = x_5 \vee (x_6 \nabla x_9)$.

We can now prove that localized widening guarantees termination, using any fair iteration sequence. First of all, we clarify what we mean with fair iteration sequence.

An *iteration sequence* starting from $D \in A^n$ is a possibly infinite sequence (X^j) with elements $X^j \in A^n$ such that:

- $X^0 = D$.
- X^j for $j > 0$ is obtained from X^{j-1} by applying one of the equations in $\Phi^\vee$.

In the following we denote with $\delta(j)$ the equation chosen to compute X^j.

Definition 7 (Enabled equation). *Given an iteration sequence* (X^j), *we say that equation* i *is enabled* in step k *when*

- *either* i *has never been chosen before, i.e.,* $\{l \in [1, k-1] \mid \delta(l) = i\} = \emptyset$;
- *or let* $m = \max\{l \in [1, k-1] \mid \delta(l) = i\}$ *the last choice of* i: *there is* $l \in [m, k-1]$ *with* $\delta(l) = u$, $u \to i$ *is an edge in the dependency graph,* $X^l > X^{l-1}$.

An equation is enabled when its execution may produce a new value. An equation is not enabled when its execution cannot produce a new value, that is $X_i^j = \Phi_i^\vee(X^j)$. A fair iteration sequence is an iteration sequence where some enabled equations are eventually executed.

Definition 8 (Fair iteration sequence). *A fair iteration sequence starting from* $D \in A^n$ *is an iteration sequence* (X^j) *starting from* D *such that, for any step* j, *there exists* $j' \geq j$ *such that the equation* $\delta(j')$ *is enabled.*

The sequence terminates when it is not possible to choose any equation. It is immediate to see that both the iterative and recursive strategies compute fair iteration sequences. Moreover, any work-list based iteration sequence is fair.

Theorem 1. *Given a system of equations* Φ *and* $D \in A^n$ *a pre-fixpoint of* Φ, *any fair iteration sequence starting from* D *over* $\Phi^\vee$ *terminates on a post-fixpoint of* Φ *greater than* D.

There is one peculiarity when we use localized widening we should be aware of. While not specified in the definition, in the standard application of widening in the form $x_i = x_i \triangledown \Phi_i(x_1, \ldots, x_n)$, it is always the case that $\Phi_i(x_1, \ldots, x_n) \geq x_i$. This does not hold anymore with localized widening. Some libraries of abstract domains, such as PPL [8] or APRON [23], implement widening under the assumption that the second argument is bigger then the first one. In this case, the same trick of Eq. 3 may be used: it is enough to replace $x \triangledown y$ with $x \triangledown (x \vee y)$.

3   Localized Narrowing

Looking from a different perspective, what localized widening does is to decouple the analysis of the inner components from the analysis of the outer components. Each component is analyzed almost as if it were a black box. We say "almost" because every time the black box is entered, we remember the last value of the variables and continue the analysis from that point: we are still computing a fixpoint using a chaotic iteration strategy.

However, we can push further the idea of the black box, as we have shown in Section 1.2. This allows to intertwine ascending and descending sequences in order to reach better precision and generally pursuing different strategies which do not follow in the umbrella of chaotic iteration. In this section, we are going to formalize and generalize the example given in Section 1.2.

3.1 More on w.t.o. and Dependency Graphs

First of all, we make an assumption to simplify notation: we consider only systems of equations with a join regular w.t.o., according to the following definition.

Definition 9 (Join regular w.t.o.). *A w.t.o. for the dependency graph of the system of equations Φ is* join regular *iff all the heads of the components are loop join nodes.*

The reason why we use join regular w.t.o. is that, as shown for localized widening, it is possible to separate the information coming from outer components from the information coming from inner components, giving better chance of optimizations. If in the head node i we have the equation $x_i = \Phi_i(x_a, x_b)$ and Φ_i is not a join, it is not clear whether it is possible to separate the contribution of x_a and x_b.

We could easily extend the algorithm to work on non join regular graphs, along the lines of Definition 6, which chooses the right widening to be applied. However, we think it is not a particularly heavy restriction, since systems of equations used in static analysis generally come out from flow graphs or labelled transition systems, and may be rewritten in such a way that the only equations with more than one variable in right-hand side are of the form $x_i = x_{v_1} \vee \cdots \vee x_{v_n}$, therefore allowing a join regular w.t.o.

The recursive algorithm we are going to present works on the components of the w.t.o. In order to iterate over components and nodes, it uses the concepts of segments and top-level elements.

Definition 10 (Segment). *A* segment *is a set $S \subseteq [1, n]$ such that there exists a well-parenthesized substring of the w.t.o. which contains exactly the elements in S.*

Example 6. Consider the w.t.o. 1 (2 3 5 (6 7 9) 8 10) 4 from Example 3. Some of the possible segments are $\{6, 7\}$ and $\{3, 5, 6, 7, 9, 8\}$, while $\{5, 6, 7\}$ and $\{3, 6, 7, 9\}$ are not segments, because the substring 5 (6 7 is not well-parenthesized and $\{3, 6, 7, 9\}$ does not come from a substring.

Intuitively, a segment corresponds to a piece of a program which is syntactically correct, where loops are not broken apart. It is immediate to see that every component C is a segment. Moreover, if C is a component with head h, then $C \setminus \{h\}$ is a segment. Finally, the entire $[1, n]$ is a segment.

Definition 11 (Top-level elements). *A* top-level element *of a segment S is an element $t \in S$ such that $\omega(t) \cap S \subseteq \{t\}$.*

Example 7. Consider the w.t.o. 1 (2 3 5 (6 7 9) 8 10) 4 from Example 3. The top-level elements of the segment $\{3, 5, 6, 7, 9, 8\}$ are 3, 5, 6 and 8.

Algorithm 1. Analysis based on localized narrowing

The algorithm requires a system of equations Φ with a join regular w.t.o. and a global map $x : [1, n] \to A$ to keep track of the current value of the variables.

Require: S is a segment in the w.t.o. of Φ
```
 1: procedure ANALYZE(S)
 2:     for all j ← tl(S) do                                    ▷ extracted in w.t.o.
 3:         if j is head of a component then
 4:             ANALYZECOMPONENT(comp(j))
 5:         else
 6:             x_j ← Φ_j(x_1, ..., x_n)
 7:         end if
 8:     end for
 9: end procedure
```

Require: C is a component in the w.t.o. of Φ
```
10: procedure ANALYZECOMPONENT(C)
11:     i ← head of the component C
12:     input ← ⋁{x_l | l → i, l ∉ C}                           ▷ Input from outer components
13:     ⟨ initialize candidateInv ≥ input ⟩
14:     repeat                                                  ▷ Start of ascending phase
15:         x_i ← candidateInv
16:         ANALYZE(C \ {i})
17:         candidateInv ← x_i ▽ ⋁{x_l | l → i, l ∈ C}          ▷ Widening with back edges
18:     until candidateInv ≤ x_i                                ▷ End of ascending phase
19:     while ⟨ eventually false condition ⟩ do                 ▷ Start of descending phase
20:         x_i ← Φ_i(x_1, ..., x_n)
21:         y ← x
22:         ANALYZE(C \ {i})
23:         x ← x ∧ y
24:     end while                                               ▷ End of descending phase
25: end procedure
```

3.2   The Algorithm

Algorithm 1 is the formalization and generalization of the procedure illustrated in Section 1.2. It depends on a system of equations Φ with a join regular w.t.o. and on a global map $x : [1, n] \to A$ which contains the initial value and keeps track of the current value of variables. There are two procedures mutually recursive. The procedure ANALYZECOMPONENT has a parameter which is a component of the w.t.o., and calls ANALYZE to analyze the equations which are part of the component, with the exception of the head. The head is analyzed directly within ANALYZECOMPONENT, using widening to ensure convergence. The procedure ANALYZE takes as input a segment of the w.t.o., and iterates over the top-level elements, either executing equations directly, or calling ANALYZECOMPONENT for nested components. The entry point of the algorithm is the procedure ANALYZE. To analyze the entire system of equations, we call ANALYZE($[1, n]$) with x initialized to $\bot$.

The procedure ANALYZECOMPONENT depends on a policy, which initializes *candidateInv*: the value for *candidateInv* may be chosen freely, subject to the condition *candidateInv* $\geq$ *input*, where *input* is the join of all edges coming into the join node from the outer components. It starts with an ascending phase, where all the nodes on the component are dealt with, either directly, or with a recursive call for nodes which are part of a nested component. Then it follows a descending phase where the $\wedge$ operator is used to refine the result. The lines 21 and 23 are used to enforce that x is descending. Termination of the descending phase is ensured by the condition in line 19 which should be eventually false. A typical check is obtained by performing a given number of descending steps before giving up. A narrowing operating could be used instead to enforce termination.

3.3   Initialization Policies

Let us consider some of the possible initialization policies. The simplest one is the RESTART policy, given by

$$candidateInv \leftarrow input \qquad\qquad \triangleright \text{ RESTART policy} \qquad (4)$$

With this policy, every time ANALYZE is called on a component, all the results of the previous analyses are discharged and the analysis starts from the beginning. This is exactly the behavior we have shown in Section 1.2.

When the outer component is in the ascending phase, this is mostly a waste, since each time ANALYZECOMPONENT is called with an input value which is bigger than the previous one. Hence, even the resulting invariant should be bigger than the one previously computed. We use "should" since non-monotonicity of widening makes this statement potentially false. Nonetheless, it is probably better for efficiency reasons not to start the analysis from the beginning. To this purpose, we can use the CONTINUE policy, which joins the new input with the previous invariant.

$$candidateInv \leftarrow x_i \vee input \qquad\qquad \triangleright \text{ CONTINUE policy} \qquad (5)$$

Were not for the intertwining of ascending and descending sequences, this would correspond to the use of localized widening. The CONTINUE policy has a different drawback. When the outer component is in the descending phase, successive inputs generally form a descending chain. Starting from the last invariant may preclude a more precise result to be found. The HYBRID policy tries to balance efficiency and precision.

$$
\begin{aligned}
&\textbf{if } input = oldinput_i \textbf{ then} \qquad\qquad \triangleright \text{ HYBRID policy}\\
&\quad \textbf{return}\\
&\textbf{else if } input < oldinput_i \textbf{ then}\\
&\quad candidateInv \leftarrow input\\
&\textbf{else}\\
&\quad candidateInv \leftarrow x_i \vee input\\
&\textbf{end if}\\
&oldinput_i \leftarrow input
\end{aligned}
\qquad (6)
$$

```
i = 0                    i = 0                    i = 0
while (TRUE) {           while (i<4)  {           while (TRUE) {
   i = i+1                  j = 0                    // Inv: i ≥ 0
   j = 0                   while (j<4)  {            j = 0
   while (j<10) {             // Inv: i ≤ j + 3      while (j<10) {
      // Inv: 0 ≤ i ≤ 10       i = i+1                  j = j+1
      j = j+1                  j = j+1               }
   }                       }                         i = i+11−j
   if (i>9) i = 0          i = i−j+1              }
}                       }
```

Fig. 3. From left to right: programs **hybrid**, **hh** from [20] and **nested2**

This policy needs a global map *oldinput* : $H \to A$, where H is the set of loop heads, to keep track of old input values.

The HYBRID policy behaves either as the RESTART or CONTINUE policy, according to the relation between the new input and the old one. The program **hybrid** in Figure 3 is an example where the HYBRID strategy is more precise then the CONTINUE strategy. At the end of the ascending phase of the outer loop, the inner invariant is $1 \leq i, 0 \leq j < 10$. At the second iteration of the outer descending phase, the inner loop is called with input $1 \leq i \leq 10, j = 0$. However, this is joined with the previous invariant, and since i is not used in the inner loop, the improvement in precision is lost. With the HYBRID strategy, when the inner loop is called with input $1 \leq i \leq 10, j = 0$, since it is smaller then the previous input $1 \leq i, j = 0$, the analysis starts from the beginning, and the invariant of the inner loop is updated.

Since the combination of ascending and descending sequences is not something commonly considered, Algorithm 1 requires a correctness proof.

Theorem 2. *Algorithm 1 terminates and the global map x resulting from the call to* ANALYZE($[1, n]$) *is a post-fixpoint of the set of equations* Φ.

Note that, differently from the case of standard iteration strategies, we are not sure that the post-fixpoint resulting from ANALYZE($[1, n]$) is greater than the original value of x. If we want to find a solution bigger than a given $D \in A^n$, we may modify the algorithm accordingly, or insert the lower bound in the equations.

4   Related Works

In the abstract interpretation literature, many efforts have been devoted to improve the precision of the analysis by modifying the standard procedure of an ascending chain with widening followed by a descending chain.

Some frameworks propose a complete departure from the model of iterative sequences, such as the acceleration operators [16] and the strategy/policy iteration [11,15]. These are not compatible with localized widening and narrowing.

Other proposals refine the model of iterative sequences, and can be applied together with our optimizations. We recall the main ones, comparing them with our results.

Gopan and Reps' guided static analysis [18] is a technique were standard program analysis is applied to a sequence of program restrictions, which are essentially obtained by removing some edges from the control-flow graph of the program. Each restriction is analyzed starting from the result of the previous restrictions, until the original program is analyzed. Due to non-monotonicity of widening, this procedure may improve precision, especially in the case where loops contain different phases. In guided static analysis, the analyzer is treated as a black box, and therefore it may be immediately replaced with an analyzer implementing localized widening and narrowing. Henry at al. [21] enhance guide static analysis by combining it with path-focusing [24], in order to avoid merging infeasible paths. This optimization helps in finding precise disjunctive invariants, avoiding the use of disjunctive completion. The basic idea is to exploit an SMT-solver to find feasible paths, which are gradually discovered and analysed.

Guided static analysis and the strategies we propose try to fix complementary defects of standard iterative sequences. Guided static analysis focuses on improving analysis of loops whose behavior evolves along time, while localization improves results of nested loops.

Similar arguments hold for Monniaux and Le Guen's stratified static analysis by variable dependency [25]. The idea is similar to guided static analysis in that restrictions of the program are considered, but in this case the restriction is not on the edges of the control-flow graph, but on the variables. Successive approximations of the program are considered, where later approximations consider more variables than former ones. The result of an approximation is used within the successive approximations to restrict the results. If in a program node it turns out that $i \geq 0$, then the same should hold for all the successive approximations. This approach requires to modify the standard abstract interpretation procedure to use results from the previous restrictions, but the modifications may also be applied immediately to our localized strategies.

Halbwachs and Henry [20] propose a procedure to improve the result of static analysis which consists in successive static analysis phases. After each phase, the result of some special nodes are chosen, and another analysis is restarted from that point. As for guided static analysis, the standard analysis procedure is considered as a black box, and therefore can be combined with localization.

While localized narrowing seems to be more precise, we believe that combining localized widening with the optimizations in [20] is not worth, and we would obtain essentially the same results of localized widening, since both proposals essentially improve the result of nested loops. For an experimental comparison, see Section 4. We think, however, that localized widening is simpler to implement and may be easily integrated with other techniques.

Finally, localization may directly exploit any improvement to the design and implementation of widening operators (such as delayed widening, widening with threshold [9], lookahead widening [17], etc...), since we use standard definitions for widening, although applied in a different way.

4.1   Examples and Experiments

We have performed three different experiments to validate our techniques, and we plan to make more in the future. In these experiments we have used three tools: INTERPROC, PAGAI and our prototype JANDOM[2].

JANDOM implements both localized widening and narrowing, and is the successor of our previous analyzer RANDOM [7,3]. RANDOM implements many numerical abstract domains, included the recent parallelotopes [6] and template parallelotopes [4,2,5,1].

INTERPROC [22] performs inter-procedural analysis of a simple imperative language. It support standard abstract interpretation analysis, policy iteration for intervals and guided static analysis. PAGAI [21] is a path-sensitive static analyzer. It implements several different techniques, such as lookahead widening, guided static analysis, path focusing, and the optimizations to narrowing in [20].

As a first experiment, we tried to understand whether localized widening or narrowing was in use in other analyzers (apart from RANDOM and our prototype). Therefore, we tried the program **nested** in Figure 1, and the programs in Figure 3 in INTERPROC and PAGAI, using standard abstract interpretation over the domain of closed polyhedra. In INTERPROC we used delayed widening with 4 delays and a two step descending sequence. None of the two analyzers, with this standard settings, were able to prove the optimal invariant. After this experiment, and given the current literature, we are confident that localized narrowing and widening have never been implemented before.

Later, we used PAGAI on the same programs, but selecting different known optimization techniques, and comparing the results with that of localized widening and narrowing. The aim was not to provide a full evaluation, but to give an idea of the kind of programs that may benefit from localization or other techniques. Table 1 reports the result of the comparison, using the domains of strict convex polyhedra. The results show that localized narrowing with the hybrid policy proves the required invariant for all the programs, but this is hardly surprising since programs were chosen ad-hoc. Lookahead widening and guided static analysis do not work very well with this examples, but this was expected since the aim of these optimizations is different than ours. The optimized narrowing in [20] behaves better, since it was developed to improve precision on nested loops too.

As a rough evaluation of the overhead of our strategies, we count the number of times that the widening and narrowing operators are executed. It happens that, for all the programs in Table 1, using the localized widening only, we execute 8 widenings and 4 narrowings, using the localized narrowing with the continue policy we execute 8 widenings and 8 narrowings, and using the localized narrowing with the hybrid policy, we execute 11 widenings and 8 narrowings.

---

[2] https://github.com/jandom-devel/Jandom

Table 1. Results of the comparison (loc_widening=localized widening, continue=localized narrowing with continue policy, hybrid=localized narrowing with hybrid policy, guided=guided static analysis, lookahead=lookahead widening, narrowing=optimized narrowing in [20])

program	loc_widening	continue	hybrid	guided	lookahead	narrowing
nested	yes	yes	yes	no	no	yes
nested2	no	yes	yes	no	yes	no
hybrid	no	no	yes	no	no	yes
hh	yes	no	yes	no	no	yes

Finally, we implemented localized widening in PAGAI. As a testament of the simplicity of the idea, the core of the implementation, which is everything but user-interface, only required to modify one line of code. This was possible since PAGAI puts a widening on each head node, as required in Theorem 1. Using PAGAI we executed the benchmarks of the Mälardalen WCET research group [19], which contains programs such as sorts, matrix transformations, fft, simple loops, etc... We compare the result of standard abstract interpretation with and without localized widening.

We analyzed a total of 114 functions. In 29 of these we improved the results of the analysis. In particular, there are a total of 379 head nodes, and for 164 of them we improved the result. In no case we got worse results than standard widening. This improvement was obtained by reducing at the same time the number of iterations. With the standard widening the analysis took a total of 19522 ascending steps and 23415 descending steps, while with localized widening we had 19363 ascending steps and 22528 descending steps. Nonetheless, the analysis with localized widening took 5.25 seconds, against 4.49 seconds of the classic analysis. We argue that it took more time despite a reduction in the number of steps since the join operator is more costly than widening.

We also compared the results of localized widening and the refined narrowing in [20]. For the 379 heads nodes, we got more precise results in 91 cases, worse results in 2 cases, while we had incomparable results in other 2 cases.

Overall, the results of localized widening are excellent, because it can improve precision even considerably without incurring in performance penalties.

More evaluations should be performed on localized narrowing. Potentially it can improve precision much more than localized widening alone. However, the performance penalty it may incur is bigger. Also, its implementation is more difficult, and that is why we have not performed a similar comparison in PAGAI as for localized widening.

5   Conclusions

We have shown two strategies for improving precision of abstract interpretation. Localized widening is simple, effective and has negligible computational cost. Therefore, can be easily implemented in already existent abstract analyzers. Localized narrowing is more complex, potentially slower but generally more precise than localized widening. More experiments should be conducted to check the power and applicability of the latter.

References

1. Amato, G., Lipton, J., McGrail, R.: On the algebraic structure of declarative programming languages. Theoretical Computer Science 410(46), 4626–4671 (2009)
2. Amato, G., Parton, M., Scozzari, F.: Deriving numerical abstract domains via principal component analysis. In: Cousot, R., Martel, M. (eds.) SAS 2010. LNCS, vol. 6337, pp. 134–150. Springer, Heidelberg (2010)
3. Amato, G., Parton, M., Scozzari, F.: A tool which mines partial execution traces to improve static analysis. In: Barringer, H., Falcone, Y., Finkbeiner, B., Havelund, K., Lee, I., Pace, G., Roşu, G., Sokolsky, O., Tillmann, N. (eds.) RV 2010. LNCS, vol. 6418, pp. 475–479. Springer, Heidelberg (2010)
4. Amato, G., Parton, M., Scozzari, F.: Discovering invariants via simple component analysis. Journal of Symbolic Computation 47(12) (2012)
5. Amato, G., Scozzari, F.: Observational completeness on abstract interpretation. Fundamenta Informaticae 106(2-4), 149–173 (2011)
6. Amato, G., Scozzari, F.: The abstract domain of parallelotopes. In: Midtgaardand, J., Might, M. (eds.) The Fourth International Workshop on Numerical and Symbolic Abstract Domains (NSAD 2012). ENTCS, vol. 287, pp. 17–28. Elsevier (November 2012)
7. Amato, G., Scozzari, F.: Random: R-based Analyzer for Numerical Domains. In: Bjørner, N., Voronkov, A. (eds.) LPAR-18 2012. LNCS, vol. 7180, pp. 375–382. Springer, Heidelberg (2012)
8. Bagnara, R., Hill, P.M., Zaffanella, E.: The Parma Polyhedra Library: Toward a complete set of numerical abstractions for the analysis and verification of hardware and software systems. Science of Computer Programming 72(1-2), 3–21 (2008)
9. Blanchet, B., Cousot, P., Cousot, R., Feret, J., Mauborgne, L., Miné, A., Monniaux, D., Rival, X.: A static analyzer for large safety-critical software. In: Proceedings of the ACM SIGPLAN 2003 Conference on Programming Language Design and Implementation (PLDI 2003), San Diego, California, USA, 2003, June 7–14, pp. 196–207. ACM Press (2003)
10. Bourdoncle, F.: Efficient chaotic iteration strategies with widenings. In: Pottosin, I.V., Bjorner, D., Broy, M. (eds.) FMP&TA 1993. LNCS, vol. 735, pp. 128–141. Springer, Heidelberg (1993)
11. Costan, A., Gaubert, S., Goubault, É., Martel, M., Putot, S.: A policy iteration algorithm for computing fixed points in static analysis of programs. In: Etessami, K., Rajamani, S.K. (eds.) CAV 2005. LNCS, vol. 3576, pp. 462–475. Springer, Heidelberg (2005)
12. Cousot, P., Cousot, R.: Static determination of dynamic properties of programs. In: Proceedings of the Second International Symposium on Programming, Paris, France, pp. 106–130. Dunod (1976)
13. Cousot, P., Cousot, R.: Abstract interpretation: A unified lattice model for static analysis of programs by construction or approximation of fixpoints. In: POPL 1977: Proceedings of the 4th ACM SIGACT-SIGPLAN Symposium on Principles of Programming Languages, pp. 238–252. ACM Press, New York (1977)
14. Cousot, P., Cousot, R.: Comparing the Galois connection and widening/narrowing approaches to abstract interpretation. In: Bruynooghe, M., Wirsing, M. (eds.) PLILP 1992. LNCS, vol. 631, pp. 269–295. Springer, Heidelberg (1992)

15. Gawlitza, T.M., Seidl, H.: Solving systems of rational equations through strategy iteration. ACM Transactions on Programming Languages and Systems 33(3), 1–48 (2011)
16. Gonnord, L., Halbwachs, N.: Combining widening and acceleration in linear relation analysis. In: Yi, K. (ed.) SAS 2006. LNCS, vol. 4134, pp. 144–160. Springer, Heidelberg (2006)
17. Gopan, D., Reps, T.: Lookahead widening. In: Ball, T., Jones, R.B. (eds.) CAV 2006. LNCS, vol. 4144, pp. 452–466. Springer, Heidelberg (2006)
18. Gopan, D., Reps, T.: Guided static analysis. In: Riis Nielson, H., Filé, G. (eds.) SAS 2007. LNCS, vol. 4634, pp. 349–365. Springer, Heidelberg (2007)
19. Gustafsson, J., Betts, A., Ermedahl, A., Lisper, B.: The Mälardalen WCET benchmarks – past, present and future. In: Lisper, B. (ed.) Proc. 10th International Workshop on Worst-Case Execution Time Analysis (WCET 2010), Brussels, Belgium, pp. 137–147. OCG (July 2010)
20. Halbwachs, N., Henry, J.: When the decreasing sequence fails. In: Miné, A., Schmidt, D. (eds.) SAS 2012. LNCS, vol. 7460, pp. 198–213. Springer, Heidelberg (2012)
21. Henry, J., Monniaux, D., Moy, M.: PAGAI: A path sensitive static analyser. Electronic Notes in Theoretical Computer Science 289, 15–25 (2012)
22. Jeannet, B.: Interproc Analyzer for Recursive Programs with Numerical Variables. In: INRIA (2004), Software and documentation are available at the following URL: `http://pop-art.inrialpes.fr/interproc/interprocweb.cgi` (accessed: April 3, 2013)
23. Jeannet, B., Miné, A.: APRON: A library of numerical abstract domains for static analysis. In: Bouajjani, A., Maler, O. (eds.) CAV 2009. LNCS, vol. 5643, pp. 661–667. Springer, Heidelberg (2009)
24. Monniaux, D., Gonnord, L.: Using bounded model checking to focus fixpoint iterations. In: Yahav, E. (ed.) SAS 2012. LNCS, vol. 6887, pp. 369–385. Springer, Heidelberg (2011)
25. Monniaux, D., Le Guen, J.: Stratified static analysis based on variable dependencies. In: Massé, D., Mauborgne, L. (eds.) Proceedings of the Third International Workshop on Numerical and Symbolic Abstract Domains, NSAD 2011. ENTCS, vol. 288, pp. 61–74. Elsevier (December 2012)
26. Sankaranarayanan, S., Sipma, H.B., Manna, Z.: Scalable analysis of linear systems using mathematical programming. In: Cousot, R. (ed.) VMCAI 2005. LNCS, vol. 3385, pp. 25–41. Springer, Heidelberg (2005)

The Abstract Domain of Segmented Ranking Functions

Caterina Urban

École Normale Supérieure - CNRS - INRIA, Paris, France
`urban@di.ens.fr`

Abstract. We present a parameterized abstract domain for proving program termination by abstract interpretation. The domain automatically synthesizes piecewise-defined ranking functions and infers sufficient conditions for program termination. The analysis uses over-approximations but we prove its soundness, meaning that all program executions respecting these sufficient conditions are indeed terminating.

The abstract domain is parameterized by a numerical abstract domain for environments and a numerical abstract domain for functions. This parameterization allows to easily tune the trade-off between precision and cost of the analysis. We describe an instantiation of this generic domain with intervals and affine functions. We define all abstract operators, including widening to ensure convergence.

To illustrate the potential of the proposed framework, we have implemented a research prototype static analyzer, for a small imperative language, that yielded interesting preliminary results.

1 Introduction

Static analysis has made great progress since the introduction of Abstract Interpretation [10,12]. Most results in this area are concerned with the verification of safety properties. The verification of liveness properties (and, in particular, termination) has received considerable attention recently.

The traditional method for proving program termination is based on the synthesis of ranking functions, which map program states to elements of a well-founded domain. Termination is guaranteed if a ranking function that decreases during computation is found. In [14], Patrick Cousot and Radhia Cousot proposed a unifying point of view on the existing approaches to termination, and introduced the idea of the computation of a ranking function by abstract interpretation. We build our work on their proposed general framework, and we design and implement a suitable parameterized abstract domain for proving termination of imperative programs by abstract interpretation.

The domain automatically synthesizes piecewise-defined ranking functions through backward invariance analysis. The analysis does not rely on assumptions about the structure of the analyzed program: for example, is not limited to simple loops, as in [22]. The ranking functions can be used to give upper bounds on the computational complexity of the program in terms of execution steps.

F. Logozzo and M. Fähndrich (Eds.): SAS 2013, LNCS 7935, pp. 43–62, 2013.

Moreover, the domain infers sufficient conditions for program termination. The analysis uses over-approximations but we prove its soundness, meaning that all program executions respecting these sufficient conditions are indeed terminating, while a program execution that does not respect these conditions might not terminate.

We employ segmentations to handle disjunctions arising in static program analysis, as proposed in [15] for array content analysis. The analysis automatically partitions the space of values for the program variables by means of abstract environments. A segment is a pair of an abstract environment and an abstract function. During the analysis (similarly to other partitioning approaches in static analysis [19,24]), segments are split by tests, modified by assignment and joined when merging control flows. Widening limits the number of segments of a ranking function to a maximum given as a parameter of the analysis.

The segmented ranking functions abstract domain is parameterized by the choice of the abstract environments (e.g. intervals, as in Section 3.1) and the choice of the abstract functions (e.g. affine functions, as in Section 3.2). This parameterization allows a wide range of instantiations of the domain making it possible to easily tune the trade-off between analysis precision and cost.

Motivating Example. To illustrate the potential of segmentations, let us consider the following program annotated with numbered labels to denote control points:

$$\text{while } {}^1(x \geq 0) \text{ do}$$
$$\qquad {}^2x := -2x + 10$$
$$\text{od}^3$$

The program terminates if we consider variables with integer values (if we admit non-integer values, for $x = \frac{10}{3}$ the program is not terminating). However, it does not have a linear ranking function. As a result, well-known methods to synthesize ranking functions like [22,5], would not be capable to guarantee its termination.

Figure 1 illustrates the details of our backward invariance analysis. We will map each program control point to a function $f \in \mathbb{Z} \mapsto \mathbb{N}$ of the (integer-valued) variable x, representing an upper bound on the number of execution steps before termination. We denote by $2[x \geq 0]$ the function obtained from the test $x \geq 0$ applied to the function at program point 2. Similarly, $3[x < 0]$ denotes the function obtained from the test $x < 0$ applied to the function at program point 3.

The analysis is performed backwards starting with the totally undefined function $\perp$ at each program point. The first iteration begins from the total function $f(x) = 0$ at program point 3. The test $x < 0$ enforces loop exit: it splits the domain of the function and enforces termination in 1 step. At program point 1, the function $3[x < 0]$ is unmodified by the join with the yet totally undefined function $2[x \geq 0]$. At program point 2, the assignment $x := -2x + 10$ propagates the function increasing its value to 2. Then, the test $x \geq 0$, since it does not need to split further the function domain, just propagates the function increasing again its value to 3. Finally, a second iteration starts joining once more the functions $3[x < 0]$ and $2[x \geq 0]$ at program point 1.

		1st iteration	2nd iteration	...	5th/6th iteration
3	⊥	$f(x) = 0$	$f(x) = 0$	...	$f(x) = 0$
$3[x < 0]$	⊥	$f(x) = \begin{cases} 1 & x < 0 \\ \perp & x \geq 0 \end{cases}$	$f(x) = \begin{cases} 1 & x < 0 \\ \perp & x \geq 0 \end{cases}$	...	$f(x) = \begin{cases} 1 & x < 0 \\ \perp & x \geq 0 \end{cases}$
1	⊥	$f(x) = \begin{cases} 1 & x < 0 \\ \perp & x \geq 0 \end{cases}$	$f(x) = \begin{cases} 1 & x < 0 \\ \perp & 0 \leq x \leq 5 \\ 3 & x > 5 \end{cases}$	...	$f(x) = \begin{cases} 1 & x < 0 \\ 5 & 0 \leq x \leq 2 \\ 9 & x = 3 \\ 7 & 4 \leq x \leq 5 \\ 3 & x > 5 \end{cases}$
2	⊥	$f(x) = \begin{cases} \perp & x \leq 5 \\ 2 & x > 5 \end{cases}$	$f(x) = \begin{cases} 4 & x \leq 2 \\ \perp & 3 \leq x \leq 5 \\ 2 & x > 5 \end{cases}$	...	$f(x) = \begin{cases} 4 & x \leq 2 \\ 8 & x = 3 \\ 6 & 4 \leq x \leq 5 \\ 2 & x > 5 \end{cases}$
$2[x \geq 0]$	⊥	$f(x) = \begin{cases} \perp & x \leq 5 \\ 3 & x > 5 \end{cases}$	$f(x) = \begin{cases} \perp & x < 0 \\ 5 & 0 \leq x \leq 2 \\ \perp & 3 \leq x \leq 5 \\ 3 & x > 5 \end{cases}$	...	$f(x) = \begin{cases} \perp & x < 0 \\ 5 & 0 \leq x \leq 2 \\ 9 & x = 3 \\ 7 & 4 \leq x \leq 5 \\ 3 & x > 5 \end{cases}$

Fig. 1. Motivating Example Analysis. The analysis starts from $f(x) = 0$ at program point 3. At program point 1, the functions $3[x < 0]$ (obtained from the test $x < 0$) and $2[x \geq 0]$ (obtained from the test $x \geq 0$) are joined.

In this particular case, there is no need for convergence acceleration and the analysis is rather precise: at the sixth iteration, a fix-point is reached providing the following ranking function $f \in \mathbb{Z} \mapsto \mathbb{N}$ as loop invariant at program point 1:

$$f(x) = \begin{cases} 1 & x < 0 \\ 5 & 0 \leq x \leq 2 \\ 9 & x = 3 \\ 7 & 4 \leq x \leq 5 \\ 3 & x > 5 \end{cases}$$

Unlike [22,5], our method is not impaired from the fact that the program does not have a linear ranking function.

Our Contribution. In summary, this paper proposes a new abstract domain for proving termination of imperative programs. We introduce the family of parameterized abstract domains of segmented ranking functions (Section 3). We also describe the design (Section 3.3) and implementation (Section 4) of a particular instance of these generic domains based on affine functions.

Outline of the Paper. Section 2 introduces the syntax and concrete semantics of our language. In Section 3 we define the segmented ranking functions abstract domain. We describe the implementation of our prototype static analyzer, in Section 4. Finally, Section 5 discusses related work and Section 6 concludes and envisions future work.

2 Concrete Termination Semantics

In the following, we briefly recall some results presented in a language independent way in [14]. Then, we tailor these results for a small imperative language.

2.1 Termination Semantics

We consider a programming language with non-deterministic programs. We describe the small-step operational semantics of a program by means of a transition system $\langle \Sigma, \tau \rangle$. Σ is the set of all program states, and $\tau \subseteq \Sigma \times \Sigma$ is the transition relation: a binary relation describing the transitions between a state and its possible successors during program execution. Let β_τ denote the set of final states: $\beta_\tau \triangleq \{ s \in \Sigma \mid \forall s' \in \Sigma : \langle s, s' \rangle \notin \tau \}$. The program trace semantics generated by a transition system $\langle \Sigma, \tau \rangle$ is the set of all infinite traces over the states in Σ and all finite traces that end with a final state in β_τ.

The traditional method for proving program termination is based on ranking functions, mapping program states to elements of a well-founded domain (e.g., ordinals in $\mathbb{O}$). Termination is guaranteed if a ranking function that decreases during computation is found.

In [14], Patrick Cousot and Radhia Cousot prove the existence of a most precise ranking function that can be expressed in fix-point form by abstract interpretation of the program trace semantics. This function[1] $v_\tau \in \Sigma \nrightarrow \mathbb{O}$ associates to each program state definitely leading to a final state in β_τ (i.e. a program state such that all traces to which it belongs end up at a final state in β_τ), an ordinal in $\mathbb{O}$ representing an upper bound on the number of remaining program execution steps to termination. Otherwise stated, v_τ is a partial function which domain $\mathsf{dom}(v_\tau)$ is the set of states leading to program termination: any trace starting in a state $s \in \mathsf{dom}(v_\tau)$ must terminate in at most $v_\tau(s)$ execution steps, while a trace starting in a state $s \notin \mathsf{dom}(v_\tau)$ might not terminate.

Let us define a computational partial order $\preccurlyeq$:

$$v_1 \preccurlyeq v_2 \triangleq \mathsf{dom}(v_1) \subseteq \mathsf{dom}(v_2) \wedge \forall x \in \mathsf{dom}(v_1) : v_1(x) \leq v_2(x).$$

Its related join operator is:

$$v_1 \curlyvee v_2 \triangleq \lambda \rho. \begin{cases} v_1(\rho) & \text{if } \rho \in \mathsf{dom}(v_1) \setminus \mathsf{dom}(v_2) \\ \sup\{v_1(\rho), v_2(\rho)\} & \text{if } \rho \in \mathsf{dom}(v_1) \cap \mathsf{dom}(v_2) \\ v_2(\rho) & \text{if } \rho \in \mathsf{dom}(v_2) \setminus \mathsf{dom}(v_1) \end{cases}$$

---

[1] $A \nrightarrow B$ is the set of partial maps from a set A to a set B.

Then, the ranking function v_τ is computed by fix-point iteration[2] starting from the totally undefined function $\dot{\emptyset}$:

$$v_\tau \triangleq \mathsf{lfp}_{\dot{\emptyset}}^{\preccurlyeq} \phi_\tau$$

$$\phi_\tau(v) \triangleq \lambda s. \begin{cases} 0 & \text{if } s \in \beta_\tau \\ \sup\{v(s')+1 \mid \langle s, s' \rangle \in \tau\} & \text{if } s \in \widetilde{\mathsf{pre}}(\mathrm{dom}(v)) \end{cases}$$

The idea is to extract the well-founded part of the transition relation τ: starting from the states in β_τ and, through a backward computation based on the inverse of the transition relation τ, mapping all the states definitely leading to a final state to their ordinal rank. In case of a non-deterministic transition system $\langle \Sigma, \tau \rangle$, using $\widetilde{\mathsf{pre}}$ ensures that we take into account all the possibly infinite choices made at each execution step, eliminating all traces potentially branching (through local non-determinism) to non-termination.

The next example is taken from [14].

Example 1. Let us consider the following trace semantics:

The fix-point iterates for the corresponding ranking function are:

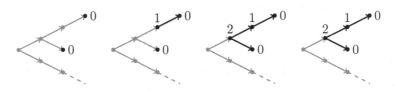

$\square$

Note that the computational order $\preccurlyeq$ does not coincide (see [12,13] for further discussion) with the approximation order $\sqsubseteq$. The order $\sqsubseteq$ is defined as follows:

$$v_1 \sqsubseteq v_2 \triangleq \mathrm{dom}(v_1) \supseteq \mathrm{dom}(v_2) \wedge \forall x \in \mathrm{dom}(v_2) : v_1(x) \leq v_2(x).$$

Its corresponding join operator is:

$$v_1 \sqcup v_2 \triangleq \lambda \rho \in \mathrm{dom}(v_1) \cap \mathrm{dom}(v_2). \ \sup\{v_1(\rho), v_2(\rho)\}.$$

The partial orders coincide only when the functions have the same domain:

Lemma 1. $\mathrm{dom}(v_1) = \mathrm{dom}(v_2) \Rightarrow (v_1 \sqsubseteq v_2 \Leftrightarrow v_1 \preccurlyeq v_2).$

---

[2] $\widetilde{\mathsf{pre}}(X) \triangleq \{s \in \Sigma \mid \forall s' \in \Sigma : \langle s, s' \rangle \in \tau \Rightarrow s' \in X\}.$

$X \in \mathcal{X}, \; n, n_1, n_2 \in \mathbb{I}$

$A ::= \; X \mid n \mid [n_1, n_2] \mid ? \mid \; - A \mid A_1 \diamond A_2 \qquad\qquad\qquad\qquad \diamond \in \{+, -, *, /\}$

$B ::= \; \mathsf{true} \mid \mathsf{false} \mid ? \mid !B \mid B_1 \vee B_2 \mid B_1 \wedge B_2 \mid A_1 \bowtie A_2 \quad \bowtie \in \{<, \leq, =, \neq, >, \geq\}$

$S ::= \; X := A \mid \mathsf{if} \; B \; \mathsf{then} \; S_1 \; \mathsf{else} \; S_2 \; \mathsf{fi} \mid \mathsf{while} \; B \; \mathsf{do} \; S \; \mathsf{od} \mid S_1; S_2$

Fig. 2. Syntax

The termination semantics v_τ is sound and complete to prove termination of a program P with initial states in I:

Theorem 1. *A program P, with trace semantics generated by a transition system $\langle \Sigma, \tau \rangle$, terminates for all traces starting from initial states in $I \in \wp(\Sigma)$ if and only if there exists $v \in \Sigma \not\mapsto \mathbb{O}$ such that $v_\tau \sqsubseteq v \wedge I \subseteq \mathsf{dom}(v)$.*

Proof. See [14]. □

2.2 A Small Imperative Language

In the following, we give a denotational definition of $v_\tau \in \Sigma \not\mapsto \mathbb{O}$ for a simple imperative language. We consider a small sequential non-deterministic programming language with no procedures, no pointers and no recursion. Let $\mathcal{X}$ be a finite set of variables and let $\mathbb{I}$ be a set of values, where $\mathbb{I} \in \{\mathbb{Z}, \mathbb{Q}, \mathbb{R}\}$. In Figure 2, we define inductively the syntax of programs.

An environment $\rho \in \mathcal{X} \mapsto \mathbb{I}$ maps each variable in $\mathcal{X}$ to a value in $\mathbb{I}$. Let $\mathcal{E}$ denote the set of all environments. The semantics of an arithmetic expression A is a function $\mathcal{A}[\![A]\!] \in \mathcal{E} \mapsto \wp(\mathbb{I})$ mapping an environment to the set of all possible values for the expression in the given environment. Similarly, the semantics of a boolean expression B is a function $\mathcal{B}[\![B]\!] \in \mathcal{E} \mapsto \wp(\{\mathsf{T}, \mathsf{F}\})$ mapping an environment to the set of all possible truth values for the expression in the environment. We need power-sets because we also consider non-deterministic arithmetic and boolean expressions (cf. Figure 2). Non-determinism comes in handy to model program input and to approximate non-linear expressions.

Let $\mathcal{L}$ be a finite set of labels. The initial and final labels of a program are denoted by i and e, respectively. A state $s \in \mathcal{L} \times \mathcal{E}$ is a pair consisting of a program control point $l \in \mathcal{L}$ and an environment $\rho \in \mathcal{E}$. Let Σ denote the set of all program states. The program initial states belong to $\Sigma_i \triangleq \{s \in \Sigma \mid \exists \rho \in \mathcal{E} : s = \langle i, \rho \rangle\}$ while $\Sigma_e \triangleq \{s \in \Sigma \mid \exists \rho \in \mathcal{E} : s = \langle e, \rho \rangle\}$ is the set of program final states. The semantics of a statement S is a function $\mathcal{S}[\![S]\!] \in (\Sigma \not\mapsto \mathbb{O}) \mapsto (\Sigma \not\mapsto \mathbb{O})$ mapping a partial function from states to ordinals into a partial function from states to ordinals with greater value. The program semantics $v_\tau \in \Sigma \not\mapsto \mathbb{O}$ is computed backwards, starting from the partial function $\lambda s(s \in \Sigma_e). 0$ and propagating it towards the initial states by means of $\mathcal{S}[\![S]\!]$.

Note that we can redefine $v_\tau \in \Sigma \not\mapsto \mathbb{O} = (\mathcal{L} \times \mathcal{E}) \not\mapsto \mathbb{O}$ in an isomorphic way by point-wise lifting to $\mathcal{L}$ of the partial function from environments to ordinals: $v_\tau \in \mathcal{L} \mapsto (\mathcal{E} \not\mapsto \mathbb{O})$. In a similar way, we can redefine the statement semantics:

$$\mathcal{S}[\![X := A]\!]v \triangleq \lambda\rho.\ \sup\{v(\rho[X \mapsto n]) + 1 \mid \forall n \in \mathcal{A}[\![A]\!]\rho : \rho[X \mapsto n] \in \mathrm{dom}(v)\}$$

$$\mathcal{S}[\![\text{if } B \text{ then } S_1 \text{ else } S_2 \text{ fi}]\!]v \triangleq (\lambda\rho(\rho \in \mathrm{dom}(v_1) \wedge \mathsf{F} \notin \mathcal{B}[\![B]\!]\rho).\ v_1(\rho))$$

$$\curlyvee (\lambda\rho(\rho \in \mathrm{dom}(v_2) \wedge \mathsf{T} \notin \mathcal{B}[\![B]\!]\rho).\ v_2(\rho))\ \curlyvee\ (v_1 \sqcup v_2)$$

$$\text{where } v_1 \triangleq \lambda\rho(\rho \in \mathrm{dom}(\mathcal{S}[\![S_1]\!]v) \wedge \mathsf{T} \in \mathcal{B}[\![B]\!]\rho).\ (\mathcal{S}[\![S_1]\!]v)(\rho) + 1$$

$$v_2 \triangleq \lambda\rho(\rho \in \mathrm{dom}(\mathcal{S}[\![S_2]\!]v) \wedge \mathsf{F} \in \mathcal{B}[\![B]\!]\rho).\ (\mathcal{S}[\![S_2]\!]v)(\rho) + 1$$

$$\mathcal{S}[\![\text{while } B \text{ do } S \text{ od}]\!]v \triangleq \mathrm{lfp}_{\emptyset}^{\preccurlyeq}\ \phi$$

$$\text{where } \phi \triangleq \lambda x.\ (\lambda\rho(\rho \in \mathrm{dom}(v_1) \wedge \mathsf{F} \notin \mathcal{B}[\![B]\!]\rho).\ v_1(\rho))$$

$$\curlyvee (\lambda\rho(\rho \in \mathrm{dom}(v_2) \wedge \mathsf{T} \notin \mathcal{B}[\![B]\!]\rho).\ v_2(\rho))\ \curlyvee\ (v_1 \sqcup v_2))$$

$$v_1 \triangleq \lambda\rho(\rho \in \mathrm{dom}(\mathcal{S}[\![S_1]\!]x) \wedge \mathsf{T} \in \mathcal{B}[\![B]\!]\rho).\ (\mathcal{S}[\![S_1]\!]x)(\rho) + 1$$

$$v_2 \triangleq \lambda\rho(\rho \in \mathrm{dom}(v) \wedge \mathsf{F} \in \mathcal{B}[\![B]\!]\rho).\ v(\rho) + 1$$

$$\mathcal{S}[\![S_1; S_2]\!]v \triangleq \mathcal{S}[\![S_1]\!](\mathcal{S}[\![S_2]\!]v)$$

Fig. 3. Concrete Semantics

$\mathcal{S}[\![S]\!] \in (\mathcal{E} \nrightarrow \mathbb{O}) \mapsto (\mathcal{E} \nrightarrow \mathbb{O})$ is defined by induction on the syntax of programs in Figure 3. In this form, we can consider $v_\tau \in \mathcal{L} \mapsto (\mathcal{E} \nrightarrow \mathbb{O})$ as an invariance semantics: to each program control point $l \in \mathcal{L}$, it associates a partial function in $\mathcal{E} \nrightarrow \mathbb{O}$ representing the program ranking function in that particular program point. Loop semantics requires the computation of a loop invariant as the least fix-point of a monotonic function $\phi \in (\mathcal{E} \nrightarrow \mathbb{O}) \mapsto (\mathcal{E} \nrightarrow \mathbb{O})$. However, such a fix-point is usually not computable.

In the next section, we will present a decidable abstraction of v_τ by means of piecewise-defined functions computed through backward invariance analysis.

3   An Abstract Domain Functor for Termination

We derive an approximate program semantics by abstract interpretation [10,12]. We look for $v_\tau^\# \in \mathcal{L} \mapsto \mathcal{V}^\#$ mapping each program point $l \in \mathcal{L}$ to an abstraction of the program ranking function in that specific program point.

In particular, we abstract the ranking functions in $\mathcal{E} \nrightarrow \mathbb{O}$ by piecewise-defined ranking functions in $\mathcal{V}^\#$. To this end, we introduce the family of segmented ranking functions abstract domains $\mathsf{V}(\mathsf{E}, \mathsf{P})$, parameterized by the environments abstract domains E and the functions abstract domains P. Adopting an OCaml terminology, each V is an abstract domain functor: a function mapping the parameter abstract domains E and P into a new abstract domain $\mathsf{V}(\mathsf{E}, \mathsf{P})$. V can be applied to various implementations of E and P yielding the corresponding implementations of $\mathsf{V}(\mathsf{E}, \mathsf{P})$, with no need for further programming effort.

In the following, in order we present the family of environments abstract domains E, the family of functions abstract domains P, and the family of parameterized abstract domains of segmented ranking function $\mathsf{V}(\mathsf{E}, \mathsf{P})$. We also describe the design of particular instances, based on intervals and affine functions, of each one of these abstract domains.

To ensure the soundness of our abstraction, throughout the rest of the paper we will continue to maintain a strict separation between approximation and computational orders (as we already did in Section 2).

3.1   Environments Abstract Domain

The environments abstract domain E abstracts sets of concrete environments in $\wp(\mathcal{E})$. The abstract properties $\rho^{\#} \in \mathcal{E}^{\#}$ are called abstract environments. The concretization function $\gamma_{\mathsf{E}} \in \mathcal{E}^{\#} \mapsto \wp(\mathcal{E})$ maps an abstract property to the set of concrete environments having that abstract property.

In case E is a non-relational domain, $\wp(\mathcal{E}) = \wp(\mathcal{X} \mapsto \mathbb{I})$ is abstracted to $\mathcal{X} \mapsto \wp(\mathbb{I})$, and we have $\mathcal{E}^{\#} \triangleq \mathcal{X} \mapsto \mathcal{B}^{\#}$, where the abstract domain B abstracts properties of values in $\mathbb{I}$ with concretization function $\gamma_{\mathsf{B}} \in \mathcal{B}^{\#} \mapsto \wp(\mathbb{I})$.

Intervals Abstract Domain. In the literature, numerous environments abstract domains have already been proposed (e.g., the numerical abstract domains of intervals [9], octagons [21], and convex polyhedra [16]).

In the following, as a simple example of non-relational environments abstract domain, we will consider the intervals abstract domain [9]. The abstract properties in $\mathcal{B}^{\#}$ are empty ($\bot_{\mathsf{B}}$) or non-empty ($[a, b]$) intervals with bounds in $\mathbb{I} \cup \{-\infty, +\infty\}$. We denote the abstract partial order by $\sqsubseteq_{\mathsf{B}}$, the join operator by $\sqcup_{\mathsf{B}}$, the meet operator by $\sqcap_{\mathsf{B}}$ and the widening operator by $\triangledown_{\mathsf{B}}$.

As for the abstract transformers for assignments and tests, we recall that our program concrete semantics is *defined* backwards (cf. Section 2), and we will see (in Section 3.4) that the program abstract semantics is *computed* backwards as well. Consequently, we consider backward assignment and test transfer functions, denoted by $\mathrm{ASSIGN}_{\mathsf{B}}$ and $\mathrm{FILTER}_{\mathsf{B}}$, respectively. The primitive $\mathrm{ASSIGN}_{\mathsf{B}}$ returns an abstraction of a set of environments that can lead to another given abstraction of a set of environments by an assignment $X := A$. The primitive $\mathrm{FILTER}_{\mathsf{B}}$ filters out environments that do not verify a boolean expression B.

Example 2. Let us consider the ranking function at program point 2 in the second iteration column of Figure 1. The test $x \geq 0$ is applied to each segment of the function, yielding the function $2[x \geq 0]$. In particular, we consider one of the segments on which such function is defined: the segment represented by the environment $\rho^{\#} \equiv x \mapsto [-\infty, 2]$. The result of $\mathrm{FILTER}_{\mathsf{B}}$ for $x \geq 0$ on $\rho^{\#}$ is $x \mapsto [0, 2]$.

Let us consider now the assignment $x := -2x + 10$ applied segment-wise to the ranking function at program point 1 in the last column of the table. In particular, the result of $\mathrm{ASSIGN}_{\mathsf{B}}$ on the segment represented by the environment $x \mapsto [4, 5]$ is the segment represented by $x \mapsto [3, 3]$ (recall that we consider the space of values for the variable x to be the set of integers $\mathbb{Z}$).   □

3.2   Functions Abstract Domain

The functions abstract domain P is itself a functor $\mathsf{P}(\mathsf{E})$, parameterized by the environment abstract domain E. It abstracts partial functions $\mathcal{E} \not\mapsto \mathbb{O}$ from environments to ordinals by natural-valued partial functions of the $\mathbb{I}$-valued variables in $\mathcal{X}$. Let n denote $|\mathcal{X}|$. The abstract properties of P belong to $\mathcal{E}^{\#} \times \mathcal{F}^{\#}$, where $\mathcal{F}^{\#} \triangleq \{\perp_{\mathsf{F}}\} \cup \{f^{\#} \mid f^{\#} \in \mathbb{I}^{n} \mapsto \mathbb{N}\} \cup \{\top_{\mathsf{F}}\}$. The bottom function $\perp_{\mathsf{F}}$ denotes the totally undefined function, and the top function $\top_{\mathsf{F}}$, abstracts all functions mapping environments to infinite ordinals.

The concretization function $\gamma_{\mathsf{P}} \in (\mathcal{E}^{\#} \times \mathcal{F}^{\#}) \mapsto (\mathcal{E} \not\mapsto \mathbb{O})$ depends on the value of the variables in $\mathcal{X}$ according to an abstract environment $\rho^{\#} \in \mathcal{E}^{\#}$:

$$\gamma_{\mathsf{P}}(\langle \rho^{\#}, \perp_{\mathsf{F}} \rangle) = \dot{\emptyset}$$
$$\gamma_{\mathsf{P}}(\langle \rho^{\#}, f^{\#} \rangle) = \lambda \rho \in \gamma_{\mathsf{E}}(\rho^{\#}). \; f^{\#}(\rho(x_1), \ldots, \rho(x_n))$$
$$\gamma_{\mathsf{P}}(\langle \rho^{\#}, \top_{\mathsf{F}} \rangle) = \dot{\emptyset}$$

We define the abstract approximation preorder $\sqsubseteq_{\mathsf{P}}$, in such a way that $\langle \rho_1^{\#}, f_1^{\#} \rangle \sqsubseteq_{\mathsf{P}} \langle \rho_2^{\#}, f_2^{\#} \rangle \Leftrightarrow \gamma_{\mathsf{P}}(\langle \rho_1^{\#}, f_1^{\#} \rangle) \sqsubseteq \gamma_{\mathsf{P}}(\langle \rho_2^{\#}, f_2^{\#} \rangle)$, as follows:

$$\langle \rho_1^{\#}, f_1^{\#} \rangle \sqsubseteq_{\mathsf{P}} \langle \rho_2^{\#}, f_2^{\#} \rangle \triangleq \rho_2^{\#} \sqsubseteq_{\mathsf{E}} \rho_1^{\#} \wedge f_1^{\#} \sqsubseteq_{\mathsf{F}} f_2^{\#}$$

where

$$f_1^{\#} \sqsubseteq_{\mathsf{F}} f_2^{\#} \triangleq \forall \rho \in \gamma_{\mathsf{E}}(\rho_1^{\#} \sqcap_{\mathsf{E}} \rho_2^{\#}) : f_1^{\#}(\rho(x_1), \ldots, \rho(x_n)) \leq f_2^{\#}(\rho(x_1), \ldots, \rho(x_n)).$$

Theorem 2. $\langle \rho_1^{\#}, f_1^{\#} \rangle \sqsubseteq_{\mathsf{P}} \langle \rho_2^{\#}, f_2^{\#} \rangle \Leftrightarrow \gamma_{\mathsf{P}}(\langle \rho_1^{\#}, f_1^{\#} \rangle) \sqsubseteq \gamma_{\mathsf{P}}(\langle \rho_2^{\#}, f_2^{\#} \rangle).$

The result proves that γ_{P} is monotonic.

We also define a computational partial order $\preccurlyeq_{\mathsf{P}}$:

$$\langle \rho_1^{\#}, f_1^{\#} \rangle \preccurlyeq_{\mathsf{P}} \langle \rho_2^{\#}, f_2^{\#} \rangle \triangleq \rho_1^{\#} \sqsubseteq_{\mathsf{E}} \rho_2^{\#} \wedge f_1^{\#} \sqsubseteq_{\mathsf{F}} f_2^{\#}.$$

Lemma 2.

$$(\rho_1^{\#} \sqsubseteq_{\mathsf{E}} \rho_2^{\#} \wedge \rho_2^{\#} \sqsubseteq_{\mathsf{E}} \rho_1^{\#}) \Rightarrow (\langle \rho_1^{\#}, f_1^{\#} \rangle \sqsubseteq \langle \rho_2^{\#}, f_2^{\#} \rangle \Leftrightarrow \langle \rho_1^{\#}, f_1^{\#} \rangle \preccurlyeq \langle \rho_2^{\#}, f_2^{\#} \rangle).$$

Finally, in addition to a join operator $\sqcup_{\mathsf{P}}$, P is equipped with backward assignment and test abstract transformers $\mathrm{ASSIGN}_{\mathsf{P}}$ and $\mathrm{FILTER}_{\mathsf{P}}$. In the following, we will define these operators for the affine functions abstract domain.

Affine Functions Abstract Domain. As an example of functions abstract domain, we instantiate the functor P with the intervals environment abstract domain E described above, and as abstract properties $f^{\#} \in \mathcal{F}^{\#}$ we choose affine functions of the form:

$$y = f(x_1, \ldots, x_n) = m_1 x_1 + \cdots + m_n x_n + q$$

where $x_1, \ldots, x_n$ are variables in $\mathcal{X}$, $y \notin \mathcal{X}$ is a special variable not included in $\mathcal{X}$, and $m_1, \ldots, m_n, q$ are constants.

The operators of the affine functions abstract domain include the join operator $\sqcup_{\mathsf{P}}$, and the abstract property transformers $\mathrm{ASSIGN}_{\mathsf{P}}$ for backward assignments and $\mathrm{FILTER}_{\mathsf{P}}$ for backward tests.

Join. The join operator $\sqcup_P$, given two partial functions $\langle \rho_1^{\#}, f_1^{\#} \rangle$ and $\langle \rho_2^{\#}, f_2^{\#} \rangle$, determines $\rho^{\#} \equiv \rho_1^{\#} \sqcap_E \rho_2^{\#}$ and then computes $f^{\#} \equiv f_1^{\#} \sqcup_F f_2^{\#}$ within $\rho^{\#}$.

Let $\rho^{\#} \equiv \{x_1 \mapsto [a_1, b_1], \ldots, x_n \mapsto [a_n, b_n]\}$, $f_1^{\#} \equiv y = f_1(x_1, \ldots, x_n)$ and $f_2^{\#} \equiv y = f_2(x_1, \ldots, x_n)$. The operator $\sqcup_F$ basically reuses the join of polyhedra [16]; it transforms $f_1^{\#}$ and $f_2^{\#}$ into two set of constraints of the form:

$$\{a_1 \leq x_1 \leq b_1, \ldots, a_n \leq x_n \leq b_n, 0 \leq y \leq f_i(x_1, \ldots, x_n)\}$$

for $i = 1, 2$. Then, it computes their convex hull:

$$\{a_1 \leq x_1 \leq b_1, \ldots, a_n \leq x_n \leq b_n, 0 \leq y \leq f(x_1, \ldots, x_n)\}$$

and transforms it back to $\langle \rho^{\#}, f^{\#} \rangle$, where $f^{\#} \equiv y = f(x_1, \ldots, x_n)$. In case the convex hull contains more than one constraint on y (except for the constraint $0 \leq y$), we are in presence of several not comparable choices for $f^{\#}$. In such situation, we prefer a deterministic behavior for $\sqcup_F$, and we choose $f^{\#} = \top_F$.

Example 3. Let us consider the abstract functions

$$f_1^{\#} \equiv y = f_1(x_1, x_2) = -\frac{1}{2}x_2 + 2$$

$$f_2^{\#} \equiv y = f_2(x_1, x_2) = -\frac{1}{2}x_1 + 2$$

within the environment $\rho^{\#} \equiv \{x_1 \mapsto (-\infty, 4], x_2 \mapsto (-\infty, 4]\}$. Their join is the convex hull of the sets of constraints $\{x_1 \leq 4, x_2 \leq 4, 0 \leq y \leq -\frac{1}{2}x_2 + 2\}$ and $\{x_1 \leq 4, x_2 \leq 4, 0 \leq y \leq -\frac{1}{2}x_1 + 2\}$. Thus $f_1^{\#} \sqcup_F f_2^{\#} = f^{\#}$ where $f^{\#} \equiv y = f(x_1, x_2) = -\frac{1}{2}x_1 - \frac{1}{2}x_2 + 4$ (see Figure 4).   □

In the particular case where $f_1^{\#} \equiv \bot_F$ or $f_2^{\#} \equiv \bot_F$, their join $f_1^{\#} \sqcup_F f_2^{\#}$ is $f^{\#} \equiv \bot_F$. In all the other cases, $f_1^{\#} \sqcup_F f_2^{\#}$ is $f^{\#} \equiv \top_F$.

The following result proves the soundness of the join operator $\sqcup_P$.

Theorem 3. $\gamma_P(\langle \rho_1^{\#}, f_1^{\#} \rangle) \sqcup \gamma_P(\langle \rho_2^{\#}, f_2^{\#} \rangle) \sqsubseteq \gamma_P(\langle \rho_1^{\#}, f_1^{\#} \rangle \sqcup_P \langle \rho_2^{\#}, f_2^{\#} \rangle)$.

Assignments. In order to handle assignments $X := A$, the abstract domain P is equipped with an operation to substitute an arithmetic expression A for a variable X within an abstract function $f^{\#}$. Given $\langle \rho^{\#}, f^{\#} \rangle \in \mathcal{E}^{\#} \times \mathcal{F}^{\#}$, the backward abstract transformer ASSIGN$_P$, applies the assignment independently to $\rho^{\#}$, by means of ASSIGN$_E$, and to $f^{\#}$. Let $f^{\#} \equiv f(x_1, \ldots, X, \ldots, x_n)$. The transformer ASSIGN$_F$ has to take into account the assignment $X := A$ and increase the value of $f^{\#}$: the result is the function $f(x_1, \ldots, A, \ldots, x_n) + 1$.

Example 4. Let consider again the ranking function at program point 1 in the last column of Figure 1. The result of the assignment $x := -2x + 10$, on the segment represented by the environment $x \mapsto [4, 5]$ and the function $f(x) = 7$, is represented by $\rho^{\#} \equiv x \mapsto [3, 3]$ and $f^{\#} \equiv f(-2x + 10) = 7 + 1 = 8$.   □

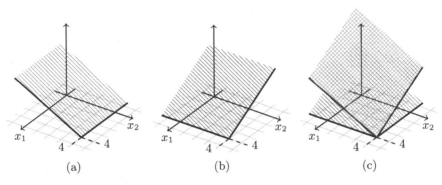

Fig. 4. Example of join of two abstract functions of two variables. The function $f_1(x_1, x_2) = -\frac{1}{2}x_2 + 2$ (shown in (a)) is joined with $f_2(x_1, x_2) = -\frac{1}{2}x_1 + 2$ (shown in (b)), within the environment $\{x_1 \mapsto (-\infty, 4], x_2 \mapsto (-\infty, 4]\}$. The result is the function $f(x_1, x_2) = -\frac{1}{2}x_1 - \frac{1}{2}x_2 + 4$ (shown in (c)).

Example 5. Let us consider $f(x) = 2x + 1$ within the environment $x \mapsto [4, 6]$, and the assignment $x := x + 1$. The result of the assignment is $\langle \rho^\#, f^\# \rangle$, where $\rho^\# \equiv x \mapsto [3, 5]$ and $f^\# \equiv f(x + 1) + 1 = 2(x + 1) + 1 + 1 = 2x + 4$.   □

In case of a non-linear expression A, the limited expressiveness of the domain forces the assignment to be approximated using non-determinism and taking into account all possible outcomes of the resulting non-deterministic assignment.

Note that the assignment abstract transformer ASSIGN$_P$ is *not sound* due to the over-approximation introduced by the environments transformer ASSIGN$_E$.

Example 6. Let us consider $\rho^\# \equiv x \mapsto [2, 3]$ and $f^\# \equiv f(x) = x + 1$, and the assignment $x := x + [1, 2]$. The result of the assignment is $\langle \bar{\rho}^\#, \bar{f}^\# \rangle$, where $\bar{\rho}^\# \equiv x \mapsto [0, 2]$ and $\bar{f}^\# \equiv f(x + [1, 2]) \equiv \bar{f}(x) = x + 4$. It is not sound because $\mathcal{S}[\![x := x + [1, 2]]\!] \gamma_P(\langle \rho^\#, f^\# \rangle) \not\sqsubseteq \gamma_P(\langle \bar{\rho}^\#, \bar{f}^\# \rangle)$: in fact, the domain of $\gamma_P(\langle \bar{\rho}^\#, \bar{f}^\# \rangle)$, that is $\{x \mapsto 0, x \mapsto 1, x \mapsto 2\}$, is not included in the domain of $\mathcal{S}[\![x := x + [1, 2]]\!] \gamma_P(\langle \rho^\#, f^\# \rangle)$, that is $\{x \mapsto 1\}$.   □

However, in the next section, we will exploit ASSIGN$_P$ to define ASSIGN$_V$, for the abstract domain $V(E, P)$, and we will prove the soundness of such transformer, despite the fact that it uses an unsound ASSIGN$_P$.

Tests. The test abstract transformer FILTER$_P$, given $\langle \rho^\#, f^\# \rangle \in \mathcal{E}^\# \times \mathcal{F}^\#$, simply narrows the domain of $f^\#$, represented by the environment $\rho^\#$, by means of the environments transformer FILTER$_E$.

3.3   Segmented Ranking Functions Abstract Domain

The segmented ranking functions abstract domain $V(E, P)$ introduces segmentations into P: it abstracts ranking functions in $\mathcal{E} \nrightarrow \mathbb{O}$ by piecewise-defined abstract ranking functions belonging to:

$$\mathcal{V}^\# \triangleq \{(\mathcal{E}^\# \times \mathcal{F}^\#)^k \mid k \geq 0\}.$$

An abstract property $v^\# \in \mathcal{V}^\#$ has the form $v^\# \equiv \langle \rho_1^\#, f_1^\# \rangle \dots \langle \rho_k^\#, f_k^\# \rangle$, where $\rho_1^\#, \dots, \rho_k^\#$ are non-overlapping abstract environments forming a partition of the space of values for the program variables in $\mathcal{X}$.

Let $\perp_\mathsf{V}$ denote the totally undefined function.

The concretization function $\gamma_\mathsf{V} \in \mathcal{V}^\# \mapsto (\mathcal{E} \nrightarrow \mathbb{O})$ is defined as follows[3]:

$$\gamma_\mathsf{V}(v^\#) = \gamma_\mathsf{V}(\langle \rho_1^\#, f_1^\# \rangle \dots \langle \rho_k^\#, f_k^\# \rangle) = \dot{\bigcup_i} \gamma_\mathsf{P}(\langle \rho_i^\#, f_i^\# \rangle)$$

As in [15], the abstract domain $\mathsf{V}(\mathsf{E}, \mathsf{P})$ relies on a segmentation unification algorithm: given two functions $v_1^\#$ and $v_2^\#$, it modifies their segments so that they form a common refined partition of the space of values for each program variable. The abstract order $\sqsubseteq_\mathsf{V}$ applies such segmentation unification and then compares the abstract ranking functions. First, their domains are compared considering the number of segments $\langle \rho^\#, f^\# \rangle$ in which each of the functions is defined (i.e. in which $f^\# \neq \perp_\mathsf{F}$ and $f^\# \neq \top_\mathsf{F}$). Then, if $v_1^\#$ is defined on less segments than $v_2^\#$, the functions are compared piecewise using the functions order $\sqsubseteq_\mathsf{P}$.

Theorem 4. $v_1^\# \sqsubseteq_\mathsf{V} v_2^\# \Leftrightarrow \gamma_\mathsf{V}(v_1^\#) \sqsubseteq \gamma_\mathsf{V}(v_2^\#)$

The result shows that γ_V is monotonic.

We define as well a computational partial order $\preccurlyeq_\mathsf{V}$ that also exploits the segmentation unification algorithm. Then, it compares the domains of the functions $v_1^\#$ and $v_2^\#$ (as $\sqsubseteq_\mathsf{V}$ does) and, if $v_1^\#$ is defined on less segments than $v_2^\#$, it compares the functions piecewise using the partial order $\preccurlyeq_\mathsf{P}$.

Note that, *the approximation order $\sqsubseteq_\mathsf{V}$ and the computational order $\preccurlyeq_\mathsf{V}$ coincide when the functions are defined on the same segments.*

Let $\sqcup_\mathsf{V}$ denote the join operator, $\triangledown_\mathsf{V}$ the widening operator, and let $\mathsf{ASSIGN}_\mathsf{V}$ and $\mathsf{FILTER}_\mathsf{V}$ denote the backward assignment and test transfer functions, respectively. In the following, we will define these operators and prove their soundness for an instance of $\mathsf{V}(\mathsf{E}, \mathsf{P})$ with intervals and affine functions.

Segmented Affine Ranking Functions Abstract Domain As an example of segmented ranking functions abstract domain, we apply the functor V to the interval environments abstract domain E (described in Section 3.1) and to the affine functions abstract domain $\mathsf{P}(\mathsf{E})$ (described in Section 3.2). The abstract properties $v^\# \in \mathcal{V}^\#$ are piecewise-defined affine ranking functions.

In this case, since the segments are determined by abstract intervals with constant bounds, the segmentation unification algorithm is rather simple: the unification simply introduces new bounds consequently splitting intervals in both segmentations. An example of segmentation unification is illustrated in Figure 5.

---

[3] $\dot{\cup}$ joins partial functions with disjoint domains: $(f_1 \dot{\cup} f_2)(x) \triangleq f_1(x)$, if $x \in \mathsf{dom}(f_1)$, and $(f_1 \dot{\cup} f_2)(x) \triangleq f_2(x)$, if $x \in \mathsf{dom}(f_2)$, where $\mathsf{dom}(f_1) \cap \mathsf{dom}(f_2) = \emptyset$.

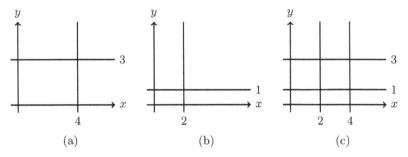

Fig. 5. Example of segmentation unification. The segmentation shown in (a) is joined with the one shown in (b). The resulting segmentation is depicted in (c).

Join. As the order $\sqsubseteq_V$, also the join operator $\sqcup_V$ depends on the segmentation unification algorithm. After the unification, the abstract ranking functions are joined piecewise by means of the abstract functions join operator $\sqcup_P$.

The next result proves the soundness of $\sqcup_V$.

Theorem 5. $\gamma_V(v_1^{\#}) \sqcup \gamma_V(v_2^{\#}) \sqsubseteq \gamma_V(v_1^{\#} \sqcup_V v_2^{\#})$

We now define another join operator $\curlyvee_V$ that we will use in the following to join two functions $v_1^{\#}$ and $v_2^{\#}$, the segmentations of which have different lower and upper bounds. Where both segmentation are defined, $\curlyvee_V$ applies the segmentation unification algorithm and then joins the ranking functions piecewise using the join operator $\sqcup_P$. To the resulting segmented function, segments are added, where only one of the functions is defined.

Example 7. Let us consider the abstract piecewise-defined ranking functions $v_1^{\#} \equiv \langle x \mapsto [2,4], y = 2 \rangle$ and $v_2^{\#} \equiv \langle x \mapsto (-\infty, 4], y = -x + 4 \rangle$ represented in Figure 6a and Figure 6b, respectively. Their join is the piecewise-defined ranking function $v^{\#} \equiv \langle x \mapsto (-\infty, 2), y = -x + 4 \rangle \langle x \mapsto [2,4], y = 2 \rangle$ of Figure 6c.   □

Assignments. The backward assignment abstract transformer ASSIGN$_V$, given a segmented function $v^{\#}$, applies piecewise the transformer ASSIGN$_P$ and then joins the resulting segments using the join operator $\curlyvee_V$. In this way, it refines the segmentation of the function so as to avoid overlapping segments.

Example 8. Let us consider $v^{\#} \equiv \langle x \mapsto [-\infty, 9], \bot_F \rangle \langle x \mapsto [10, +\infty], y = 0 \rangle$ and the assignment $x := x + [0, 2]$. The result of the assignment on $v^{\#}$ is $\langle x \mapsto [-\infty, 9], \bot_F \rangle \curlyvee_V \langle x \mapsto [8, +\infty], y = 1 \rangle$. That is the segmented function $\langle x \mapsto [-\infty, 7], \bot_F \rangle \langle x \mapsto [8, 9], \bot_F \rangle \langle x \mapsto [10, +\infty], y = 1 \rangle$.

The following result proves the soundness of ASSIGN$_V$.

Theorem 6. $\mathcal{S}[\![X := A]\!] \gamma_V(v^{\#}) \sqsubseteq \gamma_V(\text{ASSIGN}_V(X := A, v^{\#}))$.

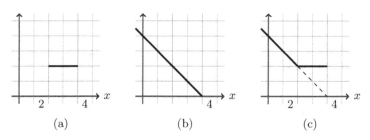

Fig. 6. Example of join of partial piecewise-defined ranking functions. $v_1^\#$ (shown in (a)) is joined with $v_2^\#$ (shown in (b)). The result $v^\#$ is shown in (c).

We omit the proof due to space limits. Intuitively, as we have seen in the previous section, the transformer ASSIGN$_P$ is unsound because it introduces over-approximations. In particular, over-approximations are more likely to appear because of non-determinism (cf. Example 8). However, since the resulting segments are joined by means of Υ_V, we recover from the unsoundness of ASSIGN$_P$. In fact, by definition of Υ_V, the possible overlaps are handled with the sound join operator $\sqcup_P$ and this yields a sound backward assignment transformer ASSIGN$_V$.

Tests. The transformer FILTER$_V$ for backward tests simply applies piecewise the transformer FILTER$_P$.

In the following (cf. Figure 8), we will exploit FILTER$_V$ and the operator Υ_V to define the abstract counterpart of the concrete semantics for the if statement, and the abstract counterpart $\phi^\# \in \mathcal{V}^\# \mapsto \mathcal{V}^\#$ of $\phi \in (\mathcal{E} \not\mapsto \mathbb{O}) \mapsto (\mathcal{E} \not\mapsto \mathbb{O})$, as defined in Figure 3 for the while statement. The soundness of these operators relies on an argument similar to the one we used to justify ASSIGN$_V$.

Widening. The widening operator ∇_V prevents the number of pieces of an abstract ranking function from growing indefinitely. First, to avoid infinite chains, it performs a segmentation unification that keeps only the bounds occurring in the first segmentation. Then, it widens the functions piecewise (basically reusing[4] the widening on polyhedra) and toward the adjacent segments (cf. Example 9).

Example 9. Let us consider the widening between the segmented functions $v_1^\#$ and $v_2^\#$ represented in Figure 7a and Figure 7b, respectively. The operator ∇_V keeps only the segmentation of $v_1^\#$. Thus, the segments $\langle x \mapsto (-\infty, 3), \perp_F \rangle$ and $\langle x \mapsto [3, 5), y = 5 \rangle$ of $v_2^\#$, are joined into a single segment $\langle x \mapsto (-\infty, 5), y = 5 \rangle$. Then, $\langle x \mapsto (-\infty, 5), y = 5 \rangle$ is widened toward $\langle x \mapsto [5, 10), y = 3 \rangle$: both segments are considered as sets of constraints (as we have seen for the definition of the operator $\sqcup_F$ of Section 3.2) and their convex-hull

$$\{x \leq 10, 0 \leq y, y \leq 3, y \leq -\frac{2}{5}x + 7\}$$

---

[4] In a similar way as the join of polyhedra was reused to define $\sqcup_F$ in Section 3.2.

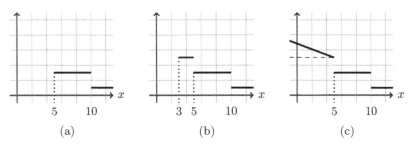

Fig. 7. Example of widening of abstract piecewise-defined ranking functions. The result of widening $v_1^{\#}$ (shown in (a)) with $v_2^{\#}$ (shown in (b)) is shown in (c).

is shrunk by the constraint $x < 5$ originating from the first segment:

$$\{x < 5, 0 \le y \le -\frac{2}{5}x + 7\}.$$

The resulting widened segmented function is

$$v^{\#} \equiv \langle x \mapsto (-\infty, 5), y = -\frac{2}{5}x + 7\rangle\langle x \mapsto [5, 10), y = 3\rangle\langle x \mapsto [10, +\infty), y = 1\rangle$$

represented in Figure 7c.   □

Note that this widening does not respect the traditional definition [10], since the property $\gamma_V(v_1^{\#}) \sqcup \gamma_V(v_2^{\#}) \sqsubseteq \gamma_V(v_1^{\#} \triangledown_V v_2^{\#})$ does not always hold.

However, we are able to prove the following weaker result (that will be decisive for the soundness of the iterations with widening):

Lemma 3. $(X \triangledown_V Y = X) \Rightarrow Y \sqsubseteq_V X$

Proof. When $X \triangledown_V Y = X$, we have $Y \preccurlyeq_V X$. Moreover, since the widening force the segmentation of X on Y, having $X \triangledown_V Y = X$ means that X and Y are defined on the same segments. In this case, as we have already observed, the orders $\sqsubseteq_V$ and $\preccurlyeq_V$ coincide, and we have $Y \sqsubseteq_V X$.   □

3.4   Abstract Termination Semantics

We now use the operators of $V(E, P)$ to define the statement abstract semantics $S^{\#}[\![S]\!] \in V^{\#} \mapsto V^{\#}$ by induction on the syntax of programs in Figure 8.

The program abstract semantics $r_\tau^{\#} \in \mathcal{L} \mapsto V^{\#}$ is computed through backward invariance analysis, starting from the program final control point $e \in \mathcal{L}$ with the constant function equals to 0. The ranking function is then propagated towards the program initial control point $i \in \mathcal{L}$ taking assignments and tests into account with widening around loops [4]. The upward iteration sequence with widening

$$\mathcal{S}^\#[\![X := A]\!]v \triangleq \mathrm{ASSIGN}_\mathsf{V}(X := A, v)$$

$$\mathcal{S}^\#[\![\text{if } B \text{ then } S_1 \text{ else } S_2 \text{ fi}]\!]v \triangleq \mathrm{FILTER}_\mathsf{S}(B, \mathcal{S}^\#[\![S_1]\!]v) \curlyvee_\mathsf{V} \mathrm{FILTER}_\mathsf{S}(\neg B, \mathcal{S}^\#[\![S_2]\!]v)$$

$$\mathcal{S}^\#[\![\text{while } B \text{ do } S \text{ od}]\!]v \triangleq \mathsf{lfp}^{\#\preccurlyeq_\mathsf{V}}_{\perp_\mathsf{V}} \phi^\#$$

$$\text{where } \phi^\# \triangleq \lambda x.\ \mathrm{FILTER}_\mathsf{S}(\neg B, v) \curlyvee_\mathsf{V} \mathrm{FILTER}_\mathsf{S}(B, \mathcal{S}^\#[\![S]\!]x)$$

$$\mathcal{S}^\#[\![S_1; S_2]\!]v \triangleq \mathcal{S}^\#[\![S_1]\!](\mathcal{S}^\#[\![S_2]\!]v)$$

Fig. 8. Abstract Semantics

$$X_0 = \perp_\mathsf{V}$$
$$X_{i+1} = X_i \ \triangledown_\mathsf{V} \ \phi^\#(X_i)$$

is ultimately stationary and we prove that its limit $\mathsf{lfp}^{\#\preccurlyeq_\mathsf{V}}_{\perp_\mathsf{V}} \phi^\#$ is a sound over-approximation of $\mathsf{lfp}^{\preccurlyeq}_{\dot{\emptyset}} \phi$:

Lemma 4. $\mathsf{lfp}^{\preccurlyeq}_{\dot{\emptyset}} \phi \sqsubseteq \gamma_\mathsf{V}(\mathsf{lfp}^{\#\preccurlyeq_\mathsf{V}}_{\perp_\mathsf{V}} \phi^\#)$

Proof. Follows from the soundness of the function $\phi^\#$ and Lemma 3.   □

Finally, thanks to the soundness of all abstract operators, with the following result we establish the soundness of the program semantics $r^\#_\tau$ for proving program termination for initial states in I.

Theorem 7. *Let $v^\#$ be such that $r^\#_\tau \sqsubseteq_\mathsf{V} v^\# \wedge I \subseteq \mathsf{dom}(\gamma_\mathsf{V}(v^\#))$. Then, a program P, with trace semantics described by a transition system $\langle \Sigma, \tau \rangle$, terminates for all traces starting from initial states in $I \in \wp(\Sigma)$.*

4   Implementation

We have implemented a research prototype static analyzer, based on our abstract domain of segmented ranking functions. It is written in OCaml on top of the Apron library [20], and we have used it to analyze programs written in the small non-deterministic imperative language presented in Section 2.2.

To improve precision, we avoid trying to compute a ranking function for the non-reachable states: our tool runs an iterated forward and backward invariance analysis to over-approximate the reachable states definitely leading to final states [11]. Then, it runs the backward analysis to infer the ranking function, intersecting its domain at each step with the states identified by the previous analysis.

The analysis proceeds by structural induction on the program syntax, iterating loops until an abstract fix-point is reached. In case of nested loops, a fix-point on the inner loop is computed for each iteration of the outer loop, following [4].

To illustrate the expressiveness of our domain, we consider more examples, besides the one shown in Section 1.

Example 10. Let us consider the following program:

$$\text{while } {}^1(x_1 \geq 0 \wedge x_2 \geq 0) \text{ do}$$
$$\quad \text{if } {}^2(?) \text{ then}$$
$$\qquad {}^3x_1 := x_1 - 1$$
$$\quad \text{else}$$
$$\qquad {}^4x_2 := x_2 - 1$$
$$\quad \text{fi}$$
$$\text{od}^5$$

The presence of the test within the loop does not impair our method.

We run our analysis delaying widening of 2 iterations, and we obtained the following loop invariant at program point 1:

$$f(x_1, x_2) = \begin{cases} 1 & x_1 < 0 \\ 1 & x_2 < 0 \\ 3 & 0 \leq x_1 < 1 \wedge 0 \leq x_2 < 1 \\ 5 & 0 \leq x_1 < 1 \wedge 1 \leq x_2 < 2 \\ 5 & 1 \leq x_1 < 2 \wedge 0 \leq x_2 < 1 \\ 2x_1 + 3 & 2 \leq x_1 \wedge 0 \leq x_2 < 1 \\ 2x_2 + 3 & 0 \leq x_1 < 1 \wedge 2 \leq x_2 \\ 2x_1 + 2x_2 + 3 & 1 \leq x_1 \wedge 1 \leq x_2 \end{cases}$$

Note how the ranking function, since its value represents an upper bound on the number of steps to termination, also provides information on the program computational complexity.   □

Example 11. Let us consider the following program:

$$\text{while } {}^1(x < 10) \text{ do}$$
$$\quad {}^2x := 2x$$
$$\text{od}^3$$

Such program always terminates if and only if $x > 0$.

Our tool, with delayed widening of 2 iterations, is able to provide the following loop invariant:

$$f(x) = \begin{cases} 3 & 5 \leq x < 10 \\ 1 & 10 \leq x \end{cases}$$

We can see that even when the analysis fails to prove whole program termination, it can still infer useful sufficient conditions for termination.

Besides, in this case, if we assume that the variable x takes values in $\mathbb{Z}$, it is sufficient to further delay the widening, to obtain the most precise ranking function:

$$
f(x) = \begin{cases}
9 & x = 1 \\
7 & x = 2 \\
5 & 3 \leq x \leq 4 \\
3 & 5 \leq x \leq 9 \\
1 & 10 \leq x
\end{cases}
$$

□

5 Related Work

Termination analysis has attracted increased interest over the years (cf. [8]). Proving termination of programs is necessary for ensuring the correct behavior of systems, especially those for which unexpected behavior can be catastrophic.

The first results in this field date back to [26] and [18]. In the recent past, despite the undecidability of termination, termination analysis has benefited from many research advances and powerful termination provers have emerged.

Many results are developed on the basis of the transition invariants method introduced in [23]. In particular, the Terminator prover [7] is based on an algorithm for the iterative construction of transition invariants. This algorithm search for counterexamples (i.e. single paths of a program) to termination, computes a ranking function for each one of them individually (as in [22]), and combines them into a single termination argument. Our approach differs in that it aims to prove termination for all program paths at the same time, without resorting to counterexample-guided analysis. Moreover, it avoids the cost of explicit checking for the well-foundedness of the termination argument. The approach presented in [25] shares similar motivations, but prefers loop summarization to iterative fix-point computation with widening, as considered in this paper.

Among the methods based on transition invariants, we also recall the strategy, proposed in [3], based on the *indirect* use of invariants to prove program termination (and liveness properties). On the other hand, our approach infers ranking functions *directly* as invariants.

In [2], the invariants are pre-computed as in [3], but each program point is assigned with a ranking function (that also provides information on the program computational complexity), as in our technique.

Finally, in the literature, we found only few works that have addressed the problem of automatically finding preconditions to program termination. In [6], the authors proposed a method based on preconditions generating valid ranking functions. Our approach somehow goes the other way around, using the computation of ranking functions to infer sufficient condition for termination.

6   Conclusions and Future Work

In this paper, we presented a family of parameterized abstract domains for proving termination of imperative programs. These domains automatically synthesize piecewise-defined ranking functions through backward invariance analysis.

We also described the design and implementation of a particular instance of these generic abstract domains based on intervals and affine functions. We have seen that the piecewise-definition of the functions allows us to overcome the non-existence of a linear ranking function for a program (cf. Section 1). Our invariance analysis is not limited to simple loop (cf. Example 10) and, even when it fails to prove whole program termination, it can still infer useful information as sufficient conditions for termination (cf. Example 11).

As might be expected, the implemented domain has a limited expressiveness that translates into an imprecision of the analysis especially in the case of nested loops (and, in general, of programs with non-linear complexity). For this reason, we would like to consider the possibility of structuring computations as suggested by [14]. It also remains for future work to design more abstract domains, based on non-linear functions as exponentials [17] or polynomials. In addition, we plan to extend our research to proving other liveness properties.

We are interested as well in exploring further the possible potential of our approach in the termination-related field of automatic cost analysis [1].

Finally, another line of research would be proving definite non-termination by abstraction of the potential termination semantics proposed in [14].

Acknowledgments. We are deeply grateful to Patrick Cousot, Radhia Cousot, Antoine Miné, Xavier Rival, Jérôme Feret, Damien Massé and the anonymous referees for all their useful comments and helpful suggestions.

References

1. Albert, E., Arenas, P., Genaim, S., Puebla, G.: Closed-Form Upper Bounds in Static Cost Analysis. J. Autom. Reasoning 46(2), 161–203 (2011)
2. Alias, C., Darte, A., Feautrier, P., Gonnord, L.: Multi-dimensional Rankings, Program Termination, and Complexity Bounds of Flowchart Programs. In: Cousot, R., Martel, M. (eds.) SAS 2010. LNCS, vol. 6337, pp. 117–133. Springer, Heidelberg (2010)
3. Berdine, J., Chawdhary, A., Cook, B., Distefano, D., O'Hearn, P.W.: Variance Analyses from Invariance Analyses. In: POPL, pp. 211–224 (2007)
4. Bourdoncle, F.: Efficient Chaotic Iteration Strategies with Widenings. In: FMPA, pp. 128–141 (1993)
5. Bradley, A.R., Manna, Z., Sipma, H.B.: The Polyranking Principle. In: Caires, L., Italiano, G.F., Monteiro, L., Palamidessi, C., Yung, M. (eds.) ICALP 2005. LNCS, vol. 3580, pp. 1349–1361. Springer, Heidelberg (2005)
6. Cook, B., Gulwani, S., Lev-Ami, T., Rybalchenko, A., Sagiv, M.: Proving Conditional Termination. In: Gupta, A., Malik, S. (eds.) CAV 2008. LNCS, vol. 5123, pp. 328–340. Springer, Heidelberg (2008)

7. Cook, B., Podelski, A., Rybalchenko, A.: TERMINATOR: Beyond Safety. In: Ball, T., Jones, R.B. (eds.) CAV 2006. LNCS, vol. 4144, pp. 415–418. Springer, Heidelberg (2006)

8. Cook, B., Podelski, A., Rybalchenko, A.: Proving Program Termination. Commun. ACM 54(5), 88–98 (2011)

9. Cousot, P., Cousot, R.: Static Determination of Dynamic Properties of Programs. In: Proceedings of the Second International Symposium on Programming, pp. 106–130 (1976)

10. Cousot, P., Cousot, R.: Abstract Interpretation: a Unified Lattice Model for Static Analysis of Programs by Construction or Approximation of Fixpoints. In: POPL, pp. 238–252 (1977)

11. Cousot, P., Cousot, R.: Abstract Interpretation and Application to Logic Programs. J. Log. Program. 13(2&3), 103–179 (1992)

12. Cousot, P., Cousot, R.: Abstract Interpretation Frameworks. J. Log. Comput. 2(4), 511–547 (1992)

13. Cousot, P., Cousot, R.: Higher Order Abstract Interpretation (and Application to Comportment Analysis Generalizing Strictness, Termination, Projection, and PER Analysis. In: ICCL, pp. 95–112 (1994)

14. Cousot, P., Cousot, R.: An Abstract Interpretation Framework for Termination. In: POPL, pp. 245–258 (2012)

15. Cousot, P., Cousot, R., Logozzo, F.: A Parametric Segmentation Functor for Fully Automatic and Scalable Array Content Analysis. In: POPL, pp. 105–118 (2011)

16. Cousot, P., Halbwachs, N.: Automatic Discovery of Linear Restraints Among Variables of a Program. In: POPL, pp. 84–96 (1978)

17. Feret, J.: The Arithmetic-Geometric Progression Abstract Domain. In: Cousot, R. (ed.) VMCAI 2005. LNCS, vol. 3385, pp. 42–58. Springer, Heidelberg (2005)

18. Floyd, R.W.: Assigning Meanings to Programs. In: Proceedings of Symposium on Applied Mathematics, vol. 19, pp. 19–32 (1967)

19. Jeannet, B.: Dynamic Partitioning in Linear Relation Analysis: Application to the Verification of Reactive Systems. Formal Methods in System Design 23(1), 5–37 (2003)

20. Jeannet, B., Miné, A.: APRON: A Library of Numerical Abstract Domains for Static Analysis. In: Bouajjani, A., Maler, O. (eds.) CAV 2009. LNCS, vol. 5643, pp. 661–667. Springer, Heidelberg (2009)

21. Miné, A.: The Octagon Abstract Domain. HOSC 19(1), 31–100 (2006)

22. Podelski, A., Rybalchenko, A.: A Complete Method for the Synthesis of Linear Ranking Functions. In: Steffen, B., Levi, G. (eds.) VMCAI 2004. LNCS, vol. 2937, pp. 239–251. Springer, Heidelberg (2004)

23. Podelski, A., Rybalchenko, A.: Transition Invariants. In: LICS, pp. 32–41 (2004)

24. Rival, X., Mauborgne, L.: The Trace Partitioning Abstract Domain. ACM Transactions on Programming Languages and Systems 29(5) (2007)

25. Tsitovich, A., Sharygina, N., Wintersteiger, C.M., Kroening, D.: Loop Summarization and Termination Analysis. In: Abdulla, P.A., Leino, K.R.M. (eds.) TACAS 2011. LNCS, vol. 6605, pp. 81–95. Springer, Heidelberg (2011)

26. Turing, A.: Checking a Large Routine. In: Report of a Conference on High Speed Automatic Calculating Machines, pp. 67–69 (1948)

Symbolic Automata for Static Specification Mining

Hila Peleg[1], Sharon Shoham[2], Eran Yahav[3], and Hongseok Yang[4]

[1] Tel Aviv University, Israel
[2] Tel Aviv-Yaffo Academic College, Israel
[3] Technion, Israel
[4] University of Oxford, UK

Abstract. We present a formal framework for static specification mining. The main idea is to represent partial temporal specifications as symbolic automata – automata where transitions may be labeled by variables, and a variable can be substituted by a letter, a word, or a regular language. Using symbolic automata, we construct an abstract domain for static specification mining, capturing both the partialness of a specification and the precision of a specification. We show interesting relationships between lattice operations of this domain and common operators for manipulating partial temporal specifications, such as building a more informative specification by consolidating two partial specifications.

1 Introduction

Programmers make extensive use of frameworks and libraries. To perform standard tasks such as parsing an XML file or communicating with a database, programmers use standard frameworks rather than writing code from scratch. Unfortunately, a typical framework API can involve hundreds of classes with dozens of methods each, and often requires sequences of operations to be invoked on specific objects to perform a single task (e.g., [14,6,12,3,13]). Even experienced programmers might spend hours trying to understand how to use a seemingly simple API [6].

Static specification mining techniques (e.g., [10,7,2,15]) have emerged as a way to obtain a succinct description of usage scenarios when working with a library. However, although they demostrated great practical value, these techniques do not address many interesting and challenging technical questions.

In this paper, we present a formal framework for static specification mining. The main idea is to represent *partial temporal specifications* as symbolic automata, where transitions may be labeled by variables representing unknown information. Using symbolic automata, we present an abstract domain for static specification mining, and show interesting relationships between the *partialness* and the *precision* of a specification.

Representing Partial Specifications Using Symbolic Automata. We focus on generalized typestate specifications [11,7]. Such specifications capture legal sequences of method invocations on a given API, and are usually expressed as finite-state automata where a state represents an internal state of the underlying API, and transitions correspond to API method invocations.

To make specification mining more widely applicable, it is critical to allow mining from *code snippets*, i.e., code fragments with unknown parts. A natural approach for

F. Logozzo and M. Fähndrich (Eds.): SAS 2013, LNCS 7935, pp. 63–83, 2013.

mining from code snippets is to capture gaps in the snippets using gaps in the specification. For example, when the code contains an invocation of an unknown method, this approach reflects this fact in the mined specification as well (we elaborate on this point later). Our *symbolic automaton* is conceived in order to represent such partial information in specifications. It is a finite-state machine where transitions may be labeled by variables and a variable can be substituted by a letter, a word, or a regular languages in a context sensitive manner — when a variable appears in multiple strings accepted by the state machine, it can be replaced by different words in all these strings.

An Abstract Domain for Mining Partial Specifications. One challenge for forming an abstract domain with symbolic automata is to find appropriate operations that capture the subtle interplay between the partialness and the precision of a specification. Let us explain this challenge using a preorder over symbolic automata.

When considering non-symbolic automata, we typically use the notion of language inclusion to model "precision" — we can say that an automaton A_1 overapproximates an automaton A_2 when its language includes that of A_2. However, this standard approach is not sufficient for symbolic automata, because the use of variables introduces *partialness* as another dimension for relating the (symbolic) automata. Intuitively, in a preorder over symbolic automata, we would like to capture the notion of a symbolic automaton A_1 being *more complete* than a symbolic automaton A_2 when A_1 has fewer variables that represent unknown information. In Section 4, we describe an interesting interplay between *precision* and *partialness*, and define a preorder between symbolic automata, that we later use as a basis for an abstract domain of symbolic automata.

Consolidating Partial Specifications. After mining a large number of partial specifications from code snippets, it is desirable to combine consistent partial information to yield consolidated temporal specifications. This leads to the question of *combining consistent symbolic automata*. In Section 7, we show how the join operation of our abstract domain leads to an operator for consolidating partial specifications.

Completion of Partial Specifications. Having constructed consolidated specifications, we can use symbolic automata as queries for code completion. Treating one symbolic automaton as a query being matched against a database of consolidated specifications, we show how to use simulation over symbolic automata to find automata that match the query (Section 5), and how to use *unknown elimination* to find completions of the query automaton (Section 6).

Main Contributions. The contributions of this paper are as follows:

- We formally define the notion of *partial typestate specification* based on a new notion of *symbolic automata*.
- We explore relationships between partial specifications along two dimensions: (i) *precision* of symbolic automata, a notion that roughly corresponds to containment of non-symbolic automata; and (ii) *partialness* of symbolic automata, a notion that roughly corresponds to an automata having fewer variables, which represent unknown information.

- We present an abstract domain of symbolic automata where operations of the domain correspond to key operators for manipulating partial temporal specifications.
- We define the operations required for algorithms for consolidating two partial specifications expressed in terms of our symbolic automata, and for completing certain partial parts of such specifications.

Related Work. Mishne et. al [7] present a practical framework for static specification mining and query matching based on automata. Their framework imposes restrictions on the structure of automata and they could be viewed as a restricted special case of the formal framework introduced in this paper. In contrast to their informal treatment, this paper presents the notion of symbolic automata with an appropriate abstract domain.

Weimer and Necula [14] use a lightweight static analysis to infer simple specifications from a given codebase. Their insight is to use exceptional program paths as negative examples for correct API usage. They learn specifications consisting of pairs of events $\langle a, b \rangle$, where a and b are method calls, and do not consider larger automata.

Monperrus et. al [8] attempt to identify missing method calls when using an API by mining a codebase. They only compare objects with identical type and same containing method signature, which only works for inheritance-based APIs. Their approach deals with identical histories minus k method calls. Unlike our approach, it cannot handle incomplete programs, non-linear method call sequences, and general code queries.

Wasylkowski et. al [13] use an intraprocedural static analysis to automatically mine object usage patterns and identify usage anomalies. Their approach is based on identifying usage patterns, in the restricted form of pairs of events, reflecting the order in which events should be used.

Gruska et. al [5] considers limited specifications that are only pairs of events. [1] also mines pairs of events in an attempt to mine partial order between events. [12] mine specifications (operational preconditions) of method parameters to detect problems in code. The mined specifications are CTL formulas that fit into several pre-defined templates of formulas. Thus, the user has to know what kind of specifications she is looking for.

Shoham et. al [10] use a whole-program analysis to statically analyze clients using a library. Their approach is not applicable in the setting of partial programs and partial specification since they rely on the ability to analyze the complete program for complete alias analysis and for type information.

Plandowski [9] uses the field of word equations to identify assignments to variables within conditions on strings with variable portions and regular expression. Ganesh et. al [4] expand this work with quantifiers and limits on the assignment size. In both cases, the regular language that the assignments consist of does not allow variables, disallowing the concept of symbolic assignments of variables within the branching of the automata for the regular language. In addition, while word equations allow all predicate arguments to have symbolic components, the equation is solved by a completely concrete assignment, disallowing the concept of assigning a symbolic language.

2 Overview

We start with an informal overview of our approach by using a simple `File` example.

```
1   void process(File f) {
2       f.open();
3       doSomething(f);
4       f.close();
5   }
```

(a)   (b)

Fig. 1. (a) Simple code snippet using `File`. The methods `open` and `close` are API methods, and the method `doSomething` is unknown. (b) Symbolic automaton mined from this snippet. The transition corresponding to `doSomething` is represented using the variable X. Transitions corresponding to API methods are labeled with method name.

(a)   (b)

Fig. 2. Automata mined from programs using `File` to (a) read after canRead check; (b) write

2.1   Illustrative Example

Consider the example snippet of Fig. 1(a). We would like to extract a temporal specification that describes how this snippet uses the `File` component. The snippet invokes `open` and then an unknown method `doSomething(f)` the code of which is not available as part of the snippet. Finally, it calls `close` on the component. Analyzing this snippet using our approach yields the partial specification of Fig. 1(b). Technically, this is a symbolic automaton, where transitions corresponding to API methods are labeled with method name, and the transition corresponding to the unknown method `doSomething` is labeled with a variable X. The use of a variable indicates that some operations may have been invoked on the `File` component between `open` and `close`, but that this operation or sequence of operations is unknown.

Now consider the specifications of Fig. 2, obtained as the result of analyzing similar fragments using the `File` API. Both of these specifications are *more complete* than the specification of Fig. 1(b). In fact, both of these automata do not contain variables, and they represent non-partial temporal specifications. These three separate specifications come from three pieces of code, but all contribute to our knowledge of how the `File` API is used. As such, we would like to be able to compare them to each other and to combine them, and in the process to eliminate as many of the unknowns as possible using other, more complete examples.

Our first step is to *consolidate* the specifications into a more comprehensive specification, describing as much of the API as possible, while losing no behavior represented by the original specifications.

Next, we would like to *eliminate unknown operations* based on the extra information that the new temporal specification now contains with regard to the full API. For instance, where in Fig. 1 we had no knowledge of what might happen between `open` and `close`, the specification in Fig. 3(a) suggests it might be either `canRead` and `read`, or `write`. Thus, the symbolic placeholder for the unknown operation is now no longer needed, and the path leading through X becomes redundant (as shown in Fig. 3(b)).

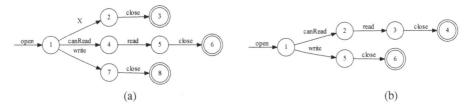

Fig. 3. (a) Automaton resulting from combining all known specifications of the `File` API, and (b) the `File` API specifications after partial paths have been subsumed by more concrete ones

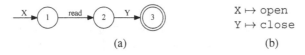

Fig. 4. (a) Symbolic automaton representing the query for the behavior around the method `read` and (b) the assignment to its symbolic transitions which answers the query

We may now note that all three original specifications are still *included* in the specification in Fig. 3(b), even after the unknown operation was removed; the concrete paths are fully there, whereas the path with the unknown operation is represented by both the remaining paths.

The ability to find the inclusion of one specification with unknowns within another is useful for performing queries. A user may wish to use the `File` object in order to read, but be unfamiliar with it. He can query the specification, marking any portion he does not know as an unknown operation, as in Fig. 4(a).

As this very partial specification is included in the API's specification, there will be a match. Furthermore, we can deduce what should replace the symbolic portions of the query. This means the user can get the reply to his query that x should be replaced by open and y by close.

Fig. 5 shows a more complex query and its assignment. The assignment to the variable x is made up of two different assignments for the different contexts surrounding x: when followed by `write`, x is assigned `open`, and when followed by `read`, x is assigned the word `open,canRead`. Even though the branching point in Fig. 3(b) is not identical to the one in the query, the query can still return a correct result using contexts.

2.2   An Abstract Domain of Symbolic Automata

To provide a formal background for the operations we demonstrated here informally, we define an abstract domain based on symbolic automata. Operations in the domain correspond to natural operators required for effective specification mining and answering code search queries. Our abstract domain serves a dual goal: (i) it is used to represent partial temporal specification during the analysis of each individual code snippet; (ii) it is used for consolidation and answering code search queries across multiple snippets

In its first role — used in the analysis of a single snippet — the abstract domain can further employ a quotient abstraction to guarantee that symbolic automata do not grow

(*,X,read) ↦ open,canRead
(*,X,write) ↦ open
Y ↦ close
Z ↦ close

(a)   (b)

Fig. 5. (a) Symbolic automaton representing the query for the behavior around `read` and `write` methods and (b) the assignment with contexts to its symbolic transitions which answers the query

without a bound due to loops or recursion [10]. In Section 4.2, we show how to obtain a lattice based on symbolic automata.

In second role — used for consolidation and answering code-search queries — query matching can be understood in terms of *unknown elimination* in a symbolic automata (explained in Section 6), and consolidation can be understood in terms of *join* in the abstract domain, followed by "minimization" (explained in Section 7).

3   Symbolic Automata

We represent partial typestate specifications using symbolic automata:

Definition 1. *A deterministic symbolic automaton (DSA) is a tuple $\langle \Sigma, Q, \delta, \iota, F, Vars \rangle$ where:*

- *Σ is a finite alphabet $a, b, c, \ldots$;*
- *Q is a finite set of states $q, q', \ldots$;*
- *δ is a partial function from $Q \times (\Sigma \cup Vars)$ to Q, representing a transition relation;*
- *$\iota \in Q$ is an initial state;*
- *$F \subseteq Q$ is a set of final states;*
- *Vars is a finite set of variables $x, y, z, \ldots$.*

Our definition mostly follows the standard notion of deterministic finite automata. Two differences are that transitions can be labeled not just by alphabets but by variables, and that they are partial functions, instead of total ones. Hence, an automaton might get stuck at a letter in a state, because the transition for the letter at the state is not defined.

We write $(q, l, q') \in \delta$ for a transition $\delta(q, l) = q'$ where $q, q' \in Q$ and $l \in \Sigma \cup Vars$. If $l \in Vars$, the transition is called *symbolic*. We extend δ to words over $\Sigma \cup Vars$ in the usual way. Note that this extension of δ over words is a partial function, because of the partiality of the original δ. When we write $\delta(q, sw) \in Q_0$ for such words sw and a state set Q_0 in the rest of the paper, we mean that $\delta(q, sw)$ is defined and belongs to Q_0.

From now on, we fix Σ and *Vars* and omit them from the notation of a DSA.

3.1   Semantics

For a DSA A, we define its *symbolic language*, denoted $SL(A)$, to be the set of all words over $\Sigma \cup Vars$ accepted by A, i.e.,

$$SL(A) = \{ sw \in (\Sigma \cup Vars)^* \mid \delta(\iota, sw) \in F \}.$$

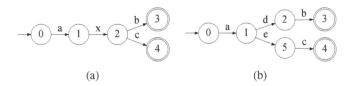

Fig. 6. DSAs (a) and (b)

Words over $\Sigma \cup$ *Vars* are called *symbolic words*, whereas words over Σ are called *concrete words*. Similarly, languages over $\Sigma \cup$ *Vars* are *symbolic*, whereas languages over Σ are *concrete*.

The symbolic language of a DSA can be interpreted in different ways, depending on the semantics of variables: (i) a variable represents a sequence of letters from Σ; (ii) a variable represents a regular language over Σ; (iii) a variable represents *different* sequences of letters from Σ under different contexts.

All above interpretations of variables, except for the last, assign some value to a variable while ignoring the context in which the variable lies. This is not always desirable. For example, consider the DSA in Fig. 6(a). We want to be able to interpret x as d when it is followed by b, and to interpret it as e when it is followed by c (Fig. 6(b)). Motivated by this example, we focus here on the last possibility of interpreting variables, which also considers their context. Formally, we consider the following definitions.

Definition 2. *A* context-sensitive assignment, *or in short assignment,* σ *is a function from* $(\Sigma \cup Vars)^* \times Vars \times (\Sigma \cup Vars)^*$ *to* $NonEmptyRegLangOn(\Sigma \cup Vars)$.

When σ maps (sw_1, x, sw_2) to SL, we refer to (sw_1, sw_2) as the *context* of x. The meaning is that an occurrence of x in the context (sw_1, sw_2) is to be replaced by SL (i.e., by any word from SL). Thus, it is possible to assign multiple words to the same variable in different contexts. The context used in an assignment is the *full* context preceding and following x. In particular, it is not restricted in length and it can be symbolic, i.e., it can contain variables. Note that these assignments consider a *linear* context of a variable. A more general definition would consider the branching context of a variable (or a symbolic transition).

Formally, applying σ to a symbolic word behaves as follows. For a symbolic word $sw = l_1 l_2 \ldots l_n$, where $l_i \in \Sigma \cup$ *Vars* for every $1 \leq i \leq n$,

$$\sigma(sw) = SL_1 SL_2 \ldots SL_n$$

where (i) $SL_i = \{l_i\}$ if $l_i \in \Sigma$; and (ii) $SL_i = SL$ if $l_i \in$ *Vars* is a variable x and $\sigma(l_1 \ldots l_{i-1}, x, l_{i+1} \ldots l_n) = SL$.

Accordingly, for a symbolic language SL, $\sigma(SL) = \bigcup \{\sigma(sw) \mid sw \in SL\}$.

Definition 3. *An assignment* σ *is* concrete *if its image consists of concrete languages only. Otherwise, it is* symbolic.

If σ is concrete then $\sigma(SL)$ is a concrete language, whereas if σ is symbolic then $\sigma(SL)$ can still be symbolic.

Fig. 7. DSA before and after assignment

In the sequel, when σ maps some x to the same language in several contexts, we sometimes write $\sigma(C_1, x, C_2) = SL$ as an abbreviation for $\sigma(sw_1, x, sw_2) = SL$ for every $(sw_1, sw_2) \in C_1 \times C_2$. We also write $*$ as an abbreviation for $(\Sigma \cup Vars)^*$.

Example 1. Consider the DSA A from Fig. 6(a). Its symbolic language is $\{axb, axc\}$. Now consider the concrete assignment $\sigma : (*, x, b*) \mapsto d, (*, x, c*) \mapsto e$. Then $\sigma(axb) = \{adb\}$ and $\sigma(axc) = \{aec\}$, which means that $\sigma(SL(A)) = \{adb, aec\}$. If we consider $\sigma : (*, x, b*) \mapsto d^*, (*, x, c*) \mapsto (e|b)^*$, then $\sigma(axb) = ad^*b$ and $\sigma(axc) = a(e|b)^*c$, which means that $\sigma(SL(A)) = (ad^*b)|(a(e|b)^*c)$.

Example 2. Consider the DSA A depicted in Fig. 7(a) and consider the symbolic assignment σ which maps $(*ab, x, *)$ to g, and maps x in any other context to x. The assignment is symbolic since in any incoming context other than $*ab$, x is assigned x. Then Fig. 7(b) presents a DSA for $\sigma(SL(A))$.

Completions of a DSA. Each concrete assignment σ to a DSA A results in some "completion" of $SL(A)$ into a language over Σ (c.f. Example 1). We define the semantics of a DSA A, denoted $[\![A]\!]$, as the set of all languages over Σ obtained by concrete assignments:

$$[\![A]\!] = \{\sigma(SL(A)) \mid \sigma \text{ is a concrete assignment}\}.$$

We call $[\![A]\!]$ the set of *completions* of A.

For example, for the DSA from Fig. 6(a), $\{adb, aec\} \in [\![A]\!]$ (see Example 1). Note that if a DSA A has no symbolic transition, i.e. $SL(A) \subseteq \Sigma^*$, then $[\![A]\!] = \{SL(A)\}$.

4   An Abstract Domain for Specification Mining

In this section we lay the ground for defining common operations on DSAs by defining a preorder on DSAs. In later sections, we use this preorder to define an algorithm for query matching (Section 5), completion of partial specification (Section 6), and consolidation of multiple partial specification (Section 7).

The definition of a preorder over DSAs is motivated by two concepts. The first is *precision*. We are interested in capturing that one DSA is an overapproximation of another, in the sense of describing more behaviors (sequences) of an API. When DFAs are considered, language inclusion is suitable for capturing a precision (abstraction) relation between automata. The second is *partialness*. We would like to capture that a DSA is "more complete" than another in the sense of having less variables that stand for unknown information.

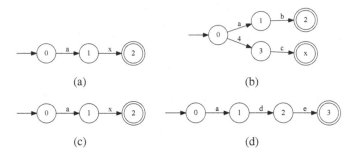

Fig. 8. Dimensions of the preorder on DSAs

4.1 Preorder on DSAs

Our preorder combines precision and partialness. Since the notion of partialness is less standard, we first explain how it is captured for symbolic words. The consideration of symbolic words rather than DSAs allows us to ignore the dimension of precision and focus on partialness, before we combine the two.

Preorder on Symbolic Words

Definition 4. *Let sw_1, sw_2 be symbolic words. $sw_1 \leq sw_2$ if for every concrete assignment σ_2 to sw_2, there is a concrete assignment σ_1 to sw_1 such that $\sigma_1(sw_1) = \sigma_2(sw_2)$.*

This definition captures the notion of a symbolic word being "more concrete" or "more complete" than another: Intuitively, the property that no matter how we fill in the unknown information in sw_2 (using a concrete assignment), the same completion can also be obtained by filling in the unknowns of sw_1, ensures that every unknown of sw_2 is also unknown in sw_1 (which can be filled in the same way), but sw_1 can have additional unknowns. Thus, sw_2 has "no more" unknowns than sw_1. In particular, $\{\sigma(sw_1) \mid \sigma$ is a concrete assignment$\} \supseteq \{\sigma(sw_2) \mid \sigma$ is a concrete assignment$\}$. Note that when considering two concrete words $w_1, w_2 \in \Sigma^*$ (i.e., without any variable), $w_1 \leq w_2$ iff $w_1 = w_2$. In this sense, the definition of $\leq$ over symbolic words is a relaxation of equality over words.

For example, $abxcd \geq ayd$ according to our definition. Intuitively, this replationship holds because $abxcd$ is more complete (carries more information) than ayd.

Symbolic Inclusion of DSAs.
We now define the preorder over DSAs that combines precision with partialness. On the one hand, we say that a DSA A_2 is "bigger" than A_1, if A_2 describes more possible behaviors of the API, as captured by standard automata inclusion. For example, see the DSAs (a) and (b) in Fig. 8. On the other hand, we say that a DSA A_2 is "bigger" than A_1, if A_2 describes "more complete" behaviors, in terms of having less unknowns. For example, see the DSAs (c) and (d) in Fig. 8.

However, these examples are simple in the sense of "separating" the precision and the partialness dimensions. Each of these examples demonstrates one dimension only.

We are also interested in handling cases that combine the two, such as cases where A_1 and A_2 represent more than one word, thus the notion of completeness of symbolic words alone is not applicable, and in addition the language of A_1 is not included in the language of A_2 per se, e.g., since some of the words in A_1 are less complete than those of A_2. This leads us to the following definition.

Definition 5 (symbolic-inclusion). *A DSA A_1 is symbolically-included in a DSA A_2, denoted by $A_1 \preceq A_2$, if for every concrete assignment σ_2 of A_2 there exists a concrete assignment σ_1 of A_1, such that $\sigma_1(SL(A_1)) \subseteq \sigma_2(SL(A_2))$.*

The above definition ensures that for each concrete language L_2 that is a completion of A_2, A_1 can be assigned in a way that will result in its language being included in L_2. This means that the "concrete" parts of A_1 and A_2 admit the inclusion relation, and A_2 is "more concrete" than A_1. Equivalently: A_1 is symbolically-included in A_2 iff for every $L_2 \in [\![A_2]\!]$ there exists $L_1 \in [\![A_1]\!]$ such that $L_1 \subseteq L_2$.

Example 3. The DSA depicted in Fig. 6(a) is symbolically-included in the one depicted in Fig. 6(b), since for any assignment σ_2 to (b), the assignment σ_1 to (a) that will yield a language that is included in the language of (b) is $\sigma : (*, x, b*) \mapsto d, (*, x, c*) \mapsto e$. Note that if we had considered assignments to a variable without a context, the same would not hold: If we assign to x the sequence d, the word adc from the assigned (a) will remain unmatched. If we assign e to x, the word aeb will remain unmatched. If we assign to x the language $d|e$, then both of the above words will remain unmatched. Therefore, when considering context-free assignments, there is no suitable assignment σ_1.

Theorem 1. $\preceq$ *is reflexive and transitive.*

Structural Inclusion. As a basis for an algorithm for checking if symbolic-inclusion holds between two DSAs, we note that provided that any alphabet Σ' can be used in assignments, the following definition is equivalent to Definition 5.

Definition 6. *A_1 is structurally-included in A_2 if there exists a symbolic assignment σ to A_1 such that $\sigma(SL(A_1)) \subseteq SL(A_2)$. We say that σ witnesses the structural inclusion of A_1 in A_2.*

Theorem 2. *Let A_1, A_2 be DSAs. Then $A_1 \preceq A_2$ iff A_1 is structurally-included in A_2.*

The following corollary provides another sufficient condition for symbolic-inclusion:

Corollary 1. *If $SL(A_1) \subseteq SL(A_2)$, then $A_1 \preceq A_2$.*

Example 4. The DSA depicted in Fig. 9(a) is not symbolically-included in the one depicted in Fig. 9(b) since no symbolic assignment to (a) will substitute the symbolic word $axbg$ by a (symbolic) word (or set of words) in (b). This is because assignments cannot "drop" any of the contexts of a variable (e.g., the outgoing bg context of x). Such assignments are undesirable since removal of contexts amounts to removal of observed behaviors.

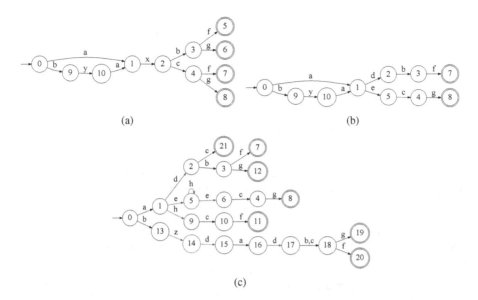

Fig. 9. Example for a case where there is no assignment to either (a) or (b) to show (a) $\preceq$ (b) or (b) $\preceq$ (a), and where there is such an assignment for (a) so that (a) $\preceq$ (c)

On the other hand, the DSA depicted in Fig. 9(a) is symbolically-included in the one depicted in Fig. 9(c), since there is a witnessing assignment that maintains all the contexts of x: $\sigma : (a, x, b*) \mapsto d, (a, x, cf*) \mapsto h, (a, x, cg*) \mapsto eh^*e, (bya, x, *) \mapsto d, (*, y, *) \mapsto zd$. Assigning σ to (a) results in a DSA whose symbolic language is strictly included in the symbolic language of (c). Note that symbolic-inclusion holds despite of the fact that in (c) there is no longer a state with an incoming c event and both an outgoing f and an outgoing g events while being reachable from the state 1. This example demonstrates our interest in linear behaviors, rather than in branching behavior. Note that in this example, symbolic-inclusion would not hold if we did not allow to refer to contexts of any length (and in particular length > 1).

4.2 A Lattice for Specification Mining

As stated in Theorem 1, $\preceq$ is reflexive and transitive, and therefore a preorder. However, it is not antisymmetric. This is not surprising, since for DFAs $\preceq$ collapses into standard automata inclusion, which is also not antisymmetric (due to the existence of different DFAs with the same language). In the case of DSAs, symbolic transitions are an additional source of problem, as demonstrated by the following example.

Example 5. The DSAs in Fig. 10 satisfy $\preceq$ in both directions even though their symbolic languages are different. DSA (a) is trivially symbolically-included in (b) since the symbolic language of (a) is a subset of the symbolic language of (b) (see Corollary 1). Examining the example closely shows that the reason that symbolic-inclusion also holds in the other direction is the fact that the symbolic language of DSA

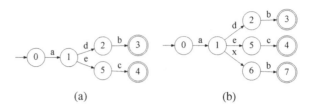

Fig. 10. Equivalent DSAs w.r.t. symbolic-inclusion

(b) contains the symbolic word axb, as well as the concrete word adb, which is a completion of axb. In this sense, axb is subsumed by the rest of the DSA, which amounts to DSA (a).

In order to obtain a partial order we follow a standard construction of turning a preordered set to a partially ordered set. We first define the following equivalence relation based on $\preceq$:

Definition 7. *DSAs A_1 and A_2 are symbolically-equivalent, denoted by $A_1 \equiv A_2$, iff $A_1 \preceq A_2$ and $A_2 \preceq A_1$.*

Theorem 3. $\equiv$ *is an equivalence relation over the set* **DSA** *of all DSAs.*

We now lift the discussion to the quotient set **DSA**/$\equiv$, which consists of the equivalence classes of **DSA** w.r.t. the $\equiv$ equivalence relation.

Definition 8. *Let $[A_1], [A_2] \in$ **DSA**/$\equiv$. Then $[A_1] \sqsubseteq [A_2]$ if $A_1 \preceq A_2$.*

Theorem 4. $\sqsubseteq$ *is a partial order over* **DSA**/$\equiv$.

Definition 9. *For DSAs A_1 and A_2, we use $union(A_1, A_2)$ to denote a union DSA for A_1 and A_2, defined similarly to the definition of union of DFAs. That is, $union(A_1, A_2)$ is a DSA such that $SL(union(A_1, A_2)) = SL(A_1) \cup SL(A_2)$.*

Theorem 5. *Let $[A_1], [A_2] \in$ **DSA**/$\equiv$ and let $union(A_1, A_2)$ be a union DSA for A_1 and A_2. Then $[union(A_1, A_2)]$ is the least upper bound of $[A_1]$ and $[A_2]$ w.r.t. $\sqsubseteq$.*

Corollary 2. $(\mathbf{DSA}/\equiv, \sqsubseteq)$ *is a join semi-lattice.*

The $\bot$ element in the lattice is the equivalence class of a DSA for $\emptyset$. The $\top$ element is the equivalence class of a DSA for Σ^*.

5   Query Matching Using Symbolic Simulation

Given a query in the form of a DSA, and a database of other DSAs, query matching attempts to find DSAs in the database that symbolically include the query DSA. In this section, we describe a notion of simulation for DSAs, which precisely captures the preorder on DSAs and serves a basis of core algorithms for manipulating symbolic automata. In particular, in Section 5.2, we provide an algorithm for computing symbolic simulation that can be directly used to determine when symbolic inclusion holds.

5.1 Symbolic Simulation

Let A_1 and A_2 be DSAs $\langle Q_1, \delta_1, \iota_1, F_1 \rangle$ and $\langle Q_2, \delta_2, \iota_2, F_2 \rangle$, respectively.

Definition 10. *A relation* $H \subseteq Q_1 \times (2^{Q_2} \setminus \{\emptyset\})$ *is a symbolic simulation from* A_1 *to* A_2 *if it satisfies the following conditions:*

(a) $(\iota_1, \{\iota_2\}) \in H$;
(b) for every $(q, B) \in H$, *if* q *is a final state, some state in* B *is final;*
(c) for every $(q, B) \in H$ *and* $q' \in Q_1$, *if* $q' = \delta_1(q, a)$ *for some* $a \in \Sigma$,

$$\exists B' \text{ s.t. } (q', B') \in H \wedge B' \subseteq \{q_2' \mid \exists q_2 \in B \text{ s.t. } q_2' = \delta_2(q_2, a)\};$$

(d) for every $(q, B) \in H$ *and* $q' \in Q_1$, *if* $q' = \delta_1(q, x)$ *for* $x \in$ Vars,

$$\exists B' \text{ s.t. } (q', B') \in H \wedge B' \subseteq \{q_2' \mid \exists q_2 \in B \text{ s.t. } q_2' \text{ is reachable from } q_2\}.$$

We say that (q', B') *in the third or fourth item above is a* witness *for* $((q, B), l)$, *or an* l-witness *for* (q, B) *for* $l \in \Sigma \cup$ Vars. *Finally,* A_1 *is symbolically simulated by* A_2 *if there exists a symbolic simulation* H *from* A_1 *to* A_2.

In this definition, a state q of A_1 is simulated by a nonempty set B of states from A_2, with the meaning that their union overapproximates all of its outgoing behaviors. In other words, the role of q in A_1 is "split" among the states of B in A_2. A "split" arises from symbolic transitions, but the "split" of the target of a symbolic transition can be propagated forward for any number of steps, thus allowing states to be simulated by sets of states even if they are not the target of a symbolic transition. This accounts for splitting that is performed by an assignment with a context longer than one. Note that since we consider *deterministic* symbolic automata, the sizes of the sets used in the simulation are monotonically decreasing, except for when a target of a symbolic transition is considered, in which case the set increases in size.

Note that a state q_1 of A_1 can participate in more than one simulation pair in the computed simulation, as demonstrated by the following example.

Example 6. Consider the DSAs in Fig. 9(a) and (c). In this case, the simulation will be

$$H = \{ (0, \{0\}), (1, \{1\}), (2, \{2, 6, 9\}), (3, \{3\}), (4, \{4, 10\}), (5, \{7\}), (6, \{12\})$$
$$(7, \{11\}), (8, \{8\}), (9, \{13\}), (10, \{15\}), (1, \{16\}), (2, \{17\}), (4, \{18\}),$$
$$(7, \{20\}), (8, \{19\}), (3, \{18\}), (5, \{20\}), (6, \{19\}) \}.$$

One can see that state 2 in (a), which is the target of the transition labeled x, is "split" between states 2, 6 and 9 of (c). In the next step, after seeing b from state 2 in (a), the target state reached (state 3) is simulated by a singleton set. On the other hand, after seeing c from state 2 in (a), the target state reached (state 4), is still "split", however this time to only two states: 4 and 10 in (c). In the next step, no more splitting occurs.

Note that the state 1 in (a) is simulated both by $\{1\}$ and by $\{16\}$. Intuitively, each of these sets simulates the state 1 in another incoming context (a and b respectively).

Theorem 6 (Soundness). *For all DSAs* A_1 *and* A_2, *if there is a symbolic simulation* H *from* A_1 *to* A_2, *then* $A_1 \preceq A_2$.

Our proof of this theorem uses Theorem 2 and constructs a desired symbolic assignment σ that witnesses structural inclusion of A_1 in A_2 explicitly from H. This construction shows, for any symbolic word in $SL(A_1)$, the assignment (completion) to all variables in it (in the corresponding context). Taken together with our next completeness theorem (Theorem 7), this construction supports a view that a symbolic simulation serves as a finite representation of symbolic assignment in the preorder. We develop this further in Section 6.

Theorem 7 (Completeness). *For al DSAs A_1 and A_2, if $A_1 \preceq A_2$, then there is a symbolic simulation H from A_1 to A_2.*

5.2   Algorithm for Checking Simulation

A maximal symbolic simulation relation can be computed using a greatest fixpoint algorithm (similarly to the standard simulation). A naive implementation would consider all sets in 2^{Q_2}, making it exponential.

More efficiently, we obtain a symbolic simulation relation H by an algorithm that traverses both DSAs simultaneously, starting from $(\iota_1, \{\iota_2\})$, similarly to a computation of a product automaton. For each pair (q_1, B_2) that we explore, we make sure that if $q_1 \in F_1$, then $B_2 \cap F_2 \neq \emptyset$. If this is not the case, the pair is removed. Otherwise, we traverse all the outgoing transitions of q_1, and for each one, we look for a *witness* in the form of another simulation pair, as required by Definition 10 (see below). If a witness is found, it is added to the list of simulation pairs that need to be explored. If no witness is found, the pair (q_1, B_2) is removed. When a simulation pair is removed, any simulation pair for which it is a witness and no other witness exists is also removed (for efficiency, we also remove all its witnesses that are not witnesses for any other pairs). If at some point $(\iota^1, \{\iota^2\})$ is removed, then the algorithm concludes that A_1 is not symbolically simulated by A_2. If no more pairs are to be explored, the algorithm concludes that there is a symbolic simulation, and it is returned.

Consider a candidate simulation pair (q_1, B_2). When looking for a witness for some transition of q_1, a crucial observation is that if some set $B_2' \subseteq Q_2$ simulates a state $q_1' \in Q_1$, then any superset of B_2' also simulates q_1'. Therefore, as a witness we add the *maximal* set that fulfills the requirement: if we fail to prove that q_1' is simulated by the maximal candidate for B_2', then we will also fail with any other candidate, making it unnecessary to check.

Specifically, for an a-transition, where $a \in \Sigma$, from q_1 to q_1', the witness is (q_1', B_2') where $B_2' = \{q_2' \mid \exists q_2 \in B_2 \text{ s.t. } q_2' = \delta_2(q_2, a)\}$. If $B_2' = \emptyset$ then no witness exists. For a symbolic transition from q_1 to some q_1', the witness is (q_1', B_2') where B_2' is the set of all states reachable from the states in B_2 (note that $B_2' \neq \emptyset$ as it contains at least the states of B_2). In both cases, if q_1' is a final state, we make sure that B_2' contains at least one final state as well. Otherwise, no witness exists.

In order to prevent checking the same simulation pair, or related pairs, over and over again, we keep all removed pairs. When a witness (q_1', B_2') is to be added as a simulation pair, we make sure that no simulation pair (q_1', B_2'') where $B_2' \subseteq B_2''$ was already removed. If such a pair was removed, then clearly, (q_1', B_2') will also be removed. Moreover, since B_2' was chosen as the maximal set that fulfills the requirement, any other possible witness will comprise of its subset and will therefore also be removed. Thus, in this case, no witness is obtained.

As an optimization, when for some simulation pair (q_1, B_2) we identify that all the witnesses reachable from it have been verified and remained as simulation pairs, we mark (q_1, B_2) as verified. If a simulation pair (q_1, B_2') is to be added as a witness for some pair where $B_2' \supseteq B_2$, we can automatically conclude that (q_1, B_2') will also be verified. We therefore mark it immediately as verified, and consider the witnesses of (q_1, B_2) as its witnesses as well. Note that in this case, the obtained witnesses are not maximal. Alternatively, it is possible to simply use (q_1, B_2) instead of (q_1, B_2'). Since this optimization damages the maximality of the witnesses, it is not used when maximal witnesses are desired (e.g., when looking for all possible unknown elimination results).

Example 7. Consider the DSAs depicted in Fig. 9(a) and (c). A simulation between these DSAs was presented in Example 6. We now present the simulation computed by the above algorithm, where "maximal" sets are used as the sets simulating a given state.

$$H = \{(0, \{0\}), (1, \{1\}), (2, \{1, ..., 12, 21\}), (3, \{3\}), (4, \{4, 10, 21\}), (5, \{7\}),$$
$$(6, \{12\}), (7, \{11\}), (8, \{8\}), (9, \{13\}), (10, \{13, ..., 20\}), (1, \{16\}),$$
$$(2, \{16, ..., 20\}), (3, \{18\}), (4, \{18\}), (5, \{20\}), (6, \{19\}), (7, \{20\}), (8, \{19\})\}.$$

For example, the pair $(2, \{1, ..., 12, 21\})$ is computed as an x-witness for $(1, \{1\})$, even though the subset $\{2, 6, 9\}$ of $\{1, ..., 12, 21\}$ suffices to simulate state 2.

6   Completion Using Unknown Elimination

Let A_1 be a DSA that is symbolically-included in A_2. This means that the "concrete parts" of A_1 exist in A_2 as well, and the "partial" parts of A_1 have some completion in A_2. Our goal is to be able to eliminate (some of) the unknowns in A_1 based on A_2. This amounts to finding a (possibly symbolic) assignment to A_1 such that $\sigma(SL(A_1)) \subseteq SL(A_2)$ (whose existence is guaranteed by Theorem 2).

We are interested in providing some *finite* representation of an assignment σ derived from a simulation H. Namely, for each variable $x \in$ *Vars*, we would like to represent in some finite way the assignments to x in *every* possible context in A_1. When the set of contexts in A_1 is finite, this can be performed for every symbolic word (context) separately as described in the proof of Theorem 6. However, in this section we also wish to handle cases where the set of possible contexts in A_1 is infinite.

We choose a unique witness for every simulation pair (q_1, B_2) in H and every transition $l \in \Sigma \cup$ *Vars* from q_1. Whenever we refer to an l-witness of (q_1, B_2) in the rest of this section, we mean this chosen witness. The reason for making this choice will become clear later on.

Let $x \in$ *Vars* be a variable. To identify the possible completions of x, we identify all the symbolic transitions labeled by x in A_1, and for each such transition we identify all the states of A_2 that participate in simulating its source and target states, q_1 and q_1' respectively. The states simulating q_1 and q_1' are given by states in simulation pairs $(q_1, B_2) \in H$ and $(q_1', B_2') \in H$ respectively. The paths in A_2 between states in B_2 and B_2' will provide the completions (assignments) of x, where the corresponding contexts will be obtained by tracking the paths in A_1 that lead to (and from) the corresponding simulation pairs, where we make sure that the sets of contexts are pairwise disjoint.

Formally, for all q_1, q_1', x with $\delta(q_1, x) = q_1'$, we do the following:

(a) For every simulation pair $(q_1, B_2) \in H$ we compute a set of incoming contexts, denoted $in(q_1, B_2)$ (see *computation of incoming contexts* in the next page). These contexts represent the incoming contexts of q_1 under which it is simulated by B_2. The sets $in(q_1, B_2)$ are computed such that the sets of different B_2 sets are pairwise-disjoint, and form a partition of the set of incoming contexts of q_1 in A_1.

(b) For every $(q_1', B_2') \in H$ which is an x-witness of some $(q_1, B_2) \in H$, and for every $q_2' \in B_2'$, we compute a set of outgoing contexts, denoted $out(q_1', B_2', q_2')$ (see *computation of outgoing contexts*). These contexts represent the outgoing contexts of q_1' under which it is simulated by the state q_2' of B_2'. The sets $out(q_1', B_2', q_2')$ are computed such that the sets of different states $q_2' \in B_2'$ are pairwise-disjoint and form a partition of the set of outgoing contexts of q_1' in A_1.

(c) For every pair of simulation pairs $(q_1, B_2), (q_1', B_2') \in H$ where (q_1', B_2') is an x-witness, and for every pair of states $q_2 \in B_2$ and $q_2' \in B_2'$, such that q_2 "contributes" q_2' to the witness (see *computation of outgoing contexts*), we compute the set of words leading from q_2 to q_2' in A_2. We denote this set by $lang(q_2, q_2')$. The "contribution" relation ensures that for every state $q_2 \in B_2$ there is at most one state $q_2' \in B_2'$ such that $lang(q_2, q_2') \neq \emptyset$.

(d) Finally, for every pair of simulation pairs $(q_1, B_2), (q_1', B_2') \in H$ where (q_1', B_2') is an x-witness of (q_1, B_2), and for every pair of states $q_2 \in B_2$ and $q_2' \in B_2'$, if $in(q_1, B_2) \neq \emptyset$ and $out(q_1', B_2', q_2') \neq \emptyset$ and $lang(q_2, q_2') \neq \emptyset$, then we define $\sigma(in(q_1, B_2), x, out(q_1', B_2', q_2')) = lang(q_2, q_2')$. For all other contexts, σ is defined arbitrarily.

Note that in step (d), for all the states $q_2 \in B_2$ the same set of incoming contexts is used $(in(q_1, B_2))$, whereas for every $q_2' \in B_2'$, a separate set of outgoing contexts is used $(out(q_1, B_2', q_2'))$. This means that assignments to x that result from states in the same B_2 do not differ in their incoming context, but they differ by their outgoing contexts, as ensured by the property that the sets $out(q_1', B_2', q_2')$ of different states $q_2' \in B_2'$ are pairwise-disjoint. Assignments to x that result from states in different B_2 sets differ in their incoming context, as ensured by the property that the sets $in(q_1, B_2)$ of different B_2 sets are pairwise-disjoint. Assignments to x that result from different transitions labeled by x also differ in their incoming contexts, as ensured by the property that A_1 is deterministic, and hence the set of incoming contexts of each state in A_1 are pairwise disjoint. Altogether, there is a unique combination of incoming and outgoing contexts for each assignment of x.

Computation of Incoming Contexts: To compute the set $in(q_1, B_2)$ of incoming contexts of q_1 under which it is simulated by B_2, we define the *witness graph* $G_W = (Q_W, \delta_W)$. This is a labeled graph whose states Q_W are all simulation pairs, and whose transitions δ_W are given by the witness relation: $((q_1', B_2'), l, (q_1'', B_2'')) \in \delta_W$ iff (q_1'', B_2'') is a l-witness of (q_1', B_2').

To compute $in(q_1, B_2)$, we derive from G_W a DSA, denoted $A_W(q_1, B_2)$, by setting the initial state to $(\iota^1, \{\iota^2\})$ and the final state to (q_1, B_2). We then define $in(q_1, B_2)$

to be $SL(A_W(q_1, B_2))$, describing all the symbolic words leading from $(\iota^1, \{\iota^2\})$ to (q_1, B_2) along the witness relation. These are the contexts in A_1 for which this witness is relevant.

By our particular choice of witnesses for H, the witness graph is deterministic and hence each incoming context in it will lead to at most one simulation pair. Thus, the sets $in(q_1, B_2)$ partition the incoming contexts of q_1, making the incoming contexts $in(q_1, B_2)$ of different sets B_2 pairwise-disjoint.

Computation of Outgoing Contexts: To compute the set $out(q'_1, B'_2, q'_2)$ of outgoing contexts of q'_1 under which it is simulated by the state q'_2 of B'_2, we define a *contribution relation* based on the witness relation, and accordingly a *contribution graph* G_C. Namely, for $(q_1, B_2), (q''_1, B''_2) \in H$ such that (q''_1, B''_2) is an l-witness of (q_1, B_2), we say that $q_2 \in B_2$ "contributes" $q''_2 \in B''_2$ to the witness if q_2 has a corresponding l-transition (if $l \in \Sigma$) or a corresponding path (if $l \in Vars$) to q''_2. If two states $q_2 \neq q'_2$ in B_2 contribute the same state $q''_2 \in B''_2$ to the witness, then we keep only one of them in the contribution relation.

The *contribution graph* is a labeled graph $G_C = (Q_C, \delta_C)$ whose states Q_C are triples (q_1, B_2, q_2) where $(q_1, B_2) \in H$ and $q_2 \in B_2$. In this graph, a transition $((q_1, B_2, q_2), l, (q''_1, B''_2, q''_2)) \in \delta_C$ exists iff (q''_1, B''_2) is an l-witness of (q_1, B_2) and q_2 contributes q''_2 to the witness. Note that G_C refines G_W in the sense that its states are substates of G_W and so are its transitions. However, unlike W_C, G_C is nondeterministic since multiple states $q_2 \in B_2$ can have outgoing l-transitions.

To compute $out(q'_1, B'_2, q'_2)$ we derive from G_C a nondeterministic version of our symbolic automaton, denoted $A_C(q'_1, B'_2, q'_2)$, by setting the initial state to (q'_1, B'_2, q'_2) and the final states to triples (q_1, B_2, q_2) where q_1 is a final state of A_1 and q_2 is a final state in A_2. Then $out(q'_1, B'_2, q'_2) = SL(A_C(q'_1, B'_2, q'_2))$. This is the set of outgoing contexts of q'_1 in A_1 for which the state q'_2 of the simulation pair (q'_1, B'_2) is relevant. That is, it is used to simulate some outgoing path of q'_1 leading to a final state.

However, the sets $SL(A_C(q'_1, B'_2, q'_2))$ of different $q'_2 \in B'_2$ are not necessarily disjoint. In order to ensure disjoint sets of outgoing contexts $out(q'_1, B'_2, q'_2)$ for different states q'_2 within the same B'_2, we need to associate contexts in the intersection of the outgoing contexts of several triples with one of them. Importantly, in order to ensure "consistency" in the outgoing contexts associated with different, but related triples, we require the following *consistency property*: If $\delta_W((q_1, B_2), sw) = (q'_1, B'_2)$ then for every $q'_2 \in B'_2$, $\{sw\} \cdot out(q'_1, B'_2, q'_2) \subseteq \bigcup \{out(q_1, B_2, q_2) \mid q_2 \in B_2 \wedge (q'_1, B'_2, q'_2) \in \delta_C((q_1, B_2, q_2), sw)\}$.

This means that the outgoing contexts associated with some triple (q'_1, B'_2, q'_2) are a subset of the outgoing contexts of triples that lead to it in G_C, truncated by the corresponding word that leads to (q'_1, B'_2, q'_2).

Note that this property holds trivially if $out(q'_1, B'_2, q'_2) = SL(A_C(q'_1, B'_2, q'_2))$, as is the case if these sets are already pairwise-disjoint and no additional manipulation is needed. The following lemma ensures that if the intersections of the *out* sets of different q'_2 states in the same set B'_2 are eliminated in a way that satisfies the consistency property, then correctness is guaranteed. In many cases (including the case where A_1 contains no loops, and the case where no two symbolic transitions are reachable from each other) this can be achieved by simple heuristics. In addition, in many cases the simulation H can be manipulated such that the sets $SL(A_C(q_1', B_2', q_2'))$ themselves will become pairwise disjoint.

Lemma 1. *If for every $(q_1', B_2', q_2') \in Q_C$, $out(q_1', B_2', q_2') \subseteq SL(A_C(q_1', B_2', q_2'))$,* · *and for every $(q_1', B_2') \in Q_W$, $\bigcup_{q_2' \in B_2'} out(q_1', B_2', q_2') = \bigcup_{q_2' \in B_2'} SL(A_C(q_1', B_2', q_2'))$, and the consistency property holds then the assignment σ defined as above satisfies $\sigma(SL(A_1)) \subseteq SL(A_2)$.*

Example 8. Consider the simulation H from Example 6, computed for the DSAs from Fig. 9(a) and (c). Unknown elimination based on H will yield the following assignment: $\sigma(a, x, b(f|g)) = d, \sigma(a, x, cg) = eh^*e, \sigma(a, x, cf) = h, \sigma(bya, x, (b|c)(f|g)) = d, \sigma(b, y, ax(b|c)(f|g)) = zd$. All other contexts are irrelevant and assigned arbitrarily. The assignments to x are based on the symbolic transition $(1, x, 2)$ in (a) and on the simulation pairs $(1, \{1\}), (1, \{16\})$ and their x-witnesses $(2, \{2, 6, 9\}), (2, \{17\})$ respectively. Namely, consider the simulation pair $(q_1, B_2) = (1, \{1\})$ and its witness $(q_1', B_2') = (2, \{2, 6, 9\})$. Then $B_2 = \{1\}$ contributed the incoming context $in(1, \{1\}) = a$, and each of the states $2, 6, 9 \in B_2' = \{2, 6, 9\}$, contributed the outgoing contexts $out(2, \{2, 6, 9\}, 2) = b(f|g), out(2, \{2, 6, 9\}, 6) = cg, out(2, \{2, 6, 9\}, 9) = cf$ respectively. In this example the *out* sets are pairwise-disjoint, thus no further manipulation is needed. Note that had we considered the simulation computed in Example 7, where the x-witness for $(1, \{1\})$ is $(2, \{2, \ldots 12, 20\})$, we would still get the same assignment since for any $q \neq 2, 6, 9$, $out(2, \{2, \ldots 12, 20\}, q) = \emptyset$. Similarly, $(1, \{16\})$ contributed $in(1, \{16\}) = bya$ and the (only) state $17 \in \{17\}$ contributed $out(2, \{17\}, 17) = (b|c)(f|g)$. The assignment to y is based on the symbolic transition $(9, x, 10)$ and the corresponding simulation pair $(9, \{13\})$ and its y-witness $(10, \{15\})$.

7   Consolidation Using Join and Minimization

Consolidation consists of (1) union, which corresponds to join in the lattice over equivalence classes, and (2) choosing a "most complete" representative from an equivalence class, where "most complete" is captured by having a minimal set of completions.

Note that DSAs A, A' in the same equivalence class do not necessarily have the same set of completions. Therefore, it is possible that $[\![A]\!] \neq [\![A']\!]$ (as is the case in Example 5). A DSA A is "most complete" in its equivalence class if there is no equivalent DSA A' such that $[\![A']\!] \subset [\![A]\!]$. Thus, A is most complete if its set of completions is minimal.

Let A be a DSA for which we look for an equivalent DSA A' that is most complete. If $[\![A]\!]$ itself is not minimal, there exists A' such that A' is equivalent to A but $[\![A']\!] \subset [\![A]\!]$. Equivalence means that (1) for every $L' \in [\![A']\!]$ there exists $L \in [\![A]\!]$ such that $L \subseteq L'$, and (2) conversely, for every $L \in [\![A]\!]$ there exists $L' \in [\![A']\!]$ such that $L' \subseteq L$. Requirement (1) holds trivially since $[\![A']\!] \subset [\![A]\!]$. Requirement (2) is satisfied iff for every $L \in [\![A]\!] \setminus [\![A']\!]$ (a completion that does not exist in the minimal DSA), there exists $L' \in [\![A']\!]$ such that $L' \subseteq L$ (since for $L \in [\![A]\!] \cap [\![A']\!]$ this holds trivially).

Namely, our goal is to find a DSA A' such that $[\![A']\!] \subset [\![A]\!]$ and for every $L \in [\![A]\!] \setminus [\![A']\!]$ there exists $L' \in [\![A']\!]$ such that $L' \subseteq L$. Clearly, if there is no $L' \in [\![A]\!]$ such that $L' \subseteq L$, then the requirement will not be satisfied. This means that the only completions L that can be removed from $[\![A]\!]$ are themselves non-minimal, i.e., are supersets of other completions in $[\![A]\!]$.

Note that it is in general impossible to remove from $[\![A]\!]$ all non-minimal languages: as long as $SL(A)$ contains at least one symbolic word $sw \in (\Sigma \cup \mathit{Vars})^* \setminus \Sigma^*$, there are always comparable completions in $[\![A]\!]$. Namely, if assignments σ and σ' differ only on their assignment to some variable x in sw (with the corresponding context), where σ assigns to it L_x and σ' assigns to it L'_x where $L_x \supset L'_x$, then $L = \sigma(SL(A)) = \sigma(SL(A) \setminus \{sw\}) \cup \sigma(sw) \supset \sigma'(SL(A) \setminus \{sw\}) \cup \sigma'(sw) = \sigma'(SL(A')) = L'$. Therefore $L \supset L'$ where both $L, L' \in [\![A]\!]$. On the other hand, not every DSA has an equivalent concrete DSA, whose language contains no symbolic word. For example, consider a DSA A_x such that $SL(A_x) = \{x\}$, i.e. $[\![A_x]\!] = 2^{\Sigma^*} \setminus \{\emptyset\}$. Then for every concrete DSA A_c with $[\![A_c]\!] = \{SL(A_c)\}$, there is $L_x \in [\![A_x]\!]$ such that either $L_x \supset SL(A_c)$, in which case $A_x \not\preceq A_c$, or $SL(A_c) \supset L_x$, in which case $A_c \not\preceq A_x$. Therefore, symbolic words are a possible source of non-minimlaity, but they cannot always be avoided.

Below we provide a condition which ensures that we remove from $[\![A]\!]$ only non-minimal completions. The intuition is that non-minimality of a completion can arise from a variable in A whose context matches the context of some known behavior. In this case, the minimal completion will be obtained by assigning to the variable the matching known behavior, whereas other assignments will result in supersets of the minimal completion. Or in other words, to keep only the minimal completion, one needs to remove the variable in this particular context.

Example 9. This intuition is demonstrated by Example 5, where the set of completions of the DSA from Fig. 10(b) contains non-minimal completions due to the symbolic word axb that co-exists with the word adb in the symbolic language of the DSA. Completions resulting by assigning d to x are strict subsets of completions assigning to x a different language, making the latter non-minimal. The DSA from Fig. 10(a) omits the symbolic word axb, keeping it equivalent to (b), while making its set of completions smaller (due to removal of non-minimal completions resulting from assignments that assign to x a language other than d).

Definition 11. *Let A be a DSA. An accepting path π in A is* redundant *if there exists another accepting path π' in A such that $\pi \preceq \pi'$. A symbolic word $sw \in SL(A)$ is* redundant *if its (unique) accepting path is redundant.*

This means that a symbolic word is redundant if it is "less complete" than another symbolic word in $SL(A)$. In particular, symbolic words where one can be obtained from the other via renaming are redundant. Such symbolic words are called *equivalent* since their corresponding accepting paths π and π' are symbolically-equivalent.

In Example 9, the path $\langle 0, 1, 6, 7 \rangle$ of the DSA in Fig. 10(b) is redundant due to $\langle 0, 1, 2, 3 \rangle$. Accordingly, the symbolic word axb labeling this path is also redundant.

An equivalent characterization of redundant paths is the following:

Definition 12. *For a DSA A and a path π in A we use $A \setminus \pi$ to denote a DSA such that $SL(A \setminus \pi) = SL(A) \setminus SL(\pi)$.*

Lemma 2. *Let A be a DSA. An accepting path π in A is redundant iff $\pi \preceq A \setminus \pi$.*

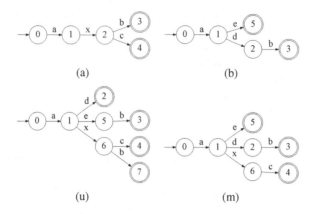

Fig. 11. Inputs (a) and (b), union (u) and minimized DSA (m)

Theorem 8. *If π is a redundant path, then $(A \setminus \pi) \equiv A$, and $[\![A \setminus \pi]\!] \subseteq [\![A]\!]$, i.e. $A \setminus \pi$ is at least as complete as A.*

Theorem 8 leads to a natural semi-algorithm for minimization by iteratively identifying and removing redundant paths. Several heuristics can be employed to identify such redundant paths.

In fact, when considering minimization of A into some A' such that $SL(A') \subseteq SL(A)$, it turns out that a DSA without redundant paths cannot be minimized further:

Theorem 9. *If $A \equiv (A \setminus \pi)$ for some accepting path π in A then π is redundant in A.*

The theorem implies that for a DSA A without redundant paths there exists no DSA A' such that $SL(A') \subset SL(A)$ and $A' \equiv A$, thus it cannot be minimized further by removal of paths (or words).

Fig. 11 provides an example for consolidation via union (which corresponds to join in the lattice), followed by minimization.

8   Putting It all Together

Now that we have completed the description of symbolic automata, we describe how they can be used in a static analysis for specification mining. We return to the example in Section 2, and emulate an analysis using the new abstract domain. This analysis would combine a set of program snippets into a typestate for a given API or class, which can then be used for verification or for answering queries about API usage.

Firstly, the DSAs in Fig. 1 and Fig. 2 would be mined from user code using the analysis defined by Mishne et. al [7]. In this process, code that may modify the object but is not available to the analysis becomes a variable transition.

Secondly, we generate a typestate specification from these individual DSAs. As shown in Section 2, this is done using the join operation, which consolidates the DSAs and generates the one in Fig. 3(b). This new typestate specification is now stored in our specification database. If we are uncertain that all the examples which we are using to create the typestate are correct, we can add weights to DSA transitions, and later prune low-weight paths, as suggested by Mishne et. al.

Finally, a user can query against the specification database, asking for the correct sequence of operations between `open` and `close`, which translates to querying the symbolic word $open \cdot x \cdot close$. Unknown elimination will find an assignment such that $\sigma(x) = canRead \cdot read$, as well as the second possible assignment, $\sigma(x) = write$.

The precision/partialness ordering of the lattice captures the essence of query matching. A query will always have a $\preceq$ relationship with its results: the query will always be *more partial* than its result, allowing the result to contain the query's assignments, as well as *more precise*, which means a DSA describing a great number of behaviors can contain the completions for a very narrow query.

Acknowledgements. The research was partially supported by The Israeli Science Foundation (grant no. 965/10). Yang was partially supported by EPSRC. Peleg was partially supported by EU's FP7 Program / ERC agreement no. [321174-VSSC].

References

1. Acharya, M., Xie, T., Pei, J., Xu, J.: Mining API patterns as partial orders from source code: from usage scenarios to specifications. In: ESEC-FSE 2007, pp. 25–34 (2007)
2. Alur, R., Cerny, P., Madhusudan, P., Nam, W.: Synthesis of interface specifications for Java classes. In: POPL (2005)
3. Beckman, N.E., Kim, D., Aldrich, J.: An empirical study of object protocols in the wild. In: Mezini, M. (ed.) ECOOP 2011. LNCS, vol. 6813, pp. 2–26. Springer, Heidelberg (2011)
4. Ganesh, V., Minnes, M., Solar-Lezama, A., Rinard, M.: Word equations with length constraints: what decidable? In: Haifa Verification Conference (2012)
5. Gruska, N., Wasylkowski, A., Zeller, A.: Learning from 6,000 projects: Lightweight cross-project anomaly detection. In: ISSTA 2010 (2010)
6. Mandelin, D., Xu, L., Bodik, R., Kimelman, D.: Jungloid mining: helping to navigate the API jungle. In: PLDI 2005, pp. 48–61 (2005)
7. Mishne, A., Shoham, S., Yahav, E.: Typestate-based semantic code search over partial programs. In: OOPSLA 2012: Proceedings of the 27th ACM SIGPLAN Conference on Object-Oriented Programming, Systems, Languages and Applications (2012)
8. Monperrus, M., Bruch, M., Mezini, M.: Detecting missing method calls in object-oriented software. In: D'Hondt, T. (ed.) ECOOP 2010. LNCS, vol. 6183, pp. 2–25. Springer, Heidelberg (2010)
9. Plandowski, W.: An efficient algorithm for solving word equations. In: Proceedings of the Thirty-Eighth Annual ACM Symposium on Theory of Computing, STOC 2006 (2006)
10. Shoham, S., Yahav, E., Fink, S., Pistoia, M.: Static specification mining using automata-based abstractions. In: ISSTA 2007 (2007)
11. Strom, R.E., Yemini, S.: Typestate: A programming language concept for enhancing software reliability. IEEE Trans. Software Eng. 12(1), 157–171 (1986)
12. Wasylkowski, A., Zeller, A.: Mining temporal specifications from object usage. In: Autom. Softw. Eng., vol. 18 (2011)
13. Wasylkowski, A., Zeller, A., Lindig, C.: Detecting object usage anomalies. In: FSE 2007, pp. 35–44 (2007)
14. Weimer, W., Necula, G.C.: Mining temporal specifications for error detection. In: Halbwachs, N., Zuck, L.D. (eds.) TACAS 2005. LNCS, vol. TACAS, pp. 461–476. Springer, Heidelberg (2005)
15. Whaley, J., Martin, M.C., Lam, M.S.: Automatic extraction of object-oriented component interfaces. In: ISSTA 2002 (2002)

Predicate Abstraction for Relaxed Memory Models

Andrei Marian Dan[1], Yuri Meshman[2], Martin Vechev[1], and Eran Yahav[2]

[1] ETH Zurich
{andrei.dan,martin.vechev}@inf.ethz.ch
[2] Technion
{yurime,yahave}@cs.technion.ac.il

Abstract. We present a novel approach for predicate abstraction of programs running on relaxed memory models. Our approach consists of two steps.

First, we reduce the problem of verifying a program P running on a memory model M to the problem of verifying a program P_M that captures an abstraction of M as part of the program.

Second, we present a new technique for discovering predicates that enable verification of P_M. The core idea is to extrapolate from the predicates used to verify P under sequential consistency. A key new concept is that of cube extrapolation: it successfully avoids exponential state explosion when abstracting P_M.

We implemented our approach for the x86 TSO and PSO memory models and showed that predicates discovered via extrapolation are powerful enough to verify several challenging concurrent programs. This is the first time some of these programs have been verified for a model as relaxed as PSO.

1   Introduction

One approach for efficiently utilizing multi-core architectures, used by major CPU designs (e.g., [27,28,20]), is to define architectural *relaxed (weak) memory models (RMMs)* [14]. Some of those relaxations can be modeled using one or more per-processor FIFO buffers, where a store operation adds values to the buffer and a flush operation propagates the stored value to main memory. Programs running under those models exhibit unique caveats and verifying their correctness is challenging.

The Problem. Given a program P, a specification S and a memory model M, we would like to answer whether P satisfies S under M, denoted as $P \models_M S$.

Unfortunately, even for finite-state programs, automatic verification under relaxed memory models is a hard problem. The problem is either undecidable or has a non-primitive recursive complexity for stronger models such as x86 TSO and PSO (see [4] for details). It is therefore natural to explore the use of abstraction for verification of such programs.

Predicate abstraction [16] is a widely used approach for abstract interpretation [9]. Since predicate abstraction has been successfully applied to verify a wide range of sequential and concurrent programs (e.g., [6,13,15]), we are interested in the question:

how to apply predicate abstraction to programs running on relaxed models?

F. Logozzo and M. Fähndrich (Eds.): SAS 2013, LNCS 7935, pp. 84–104, 2013.
© Springer-Verlag Berlin Heidelberg 2013

Given a program P and a vocabulary (set of predicates) $V = \{p_1, \ldots, p_n\}$ with corresponding boolean variables $\hat{V} = \{b_1, \ldots, b_n\}$, standard predicate abstraction (e.g. [16,6]) constructs a boolean program $\mathcal{BP}(P, V)$ that conservatively represents the behaviors of P using only boolean variables from $\hat{V}$. When considering predicate abstraction in the context of relaxed memory models, two key challenges need to be addressed: (i) *soundness*: the boolean program must faithfully abstract the behaviors of P running on model M; (ii) *predicate discovery*: there should be a mechanism for automatically discovering predicates that enable successful verification of P running on memory model M.

Soundness. Under sequential consistency (SC), predicate abstraction is sound and we know that $\mathcal{BP}(P, V) \models_{SC} S$ implies $P \models_{SC} S$. Unfortunately, we observed this does not hold for relaxed memory models (see Section 2.2).

Intuitively, the problem is as follows: under sequential consistency, a shared variable has only one value — the value stored in main memory. Predicates used for predicate abstraction can therefore refer to that shared value and relate it to the values of other shared variables or thread-local variables. In contrast, for a program running on a relaxed model, threads may observe *different values for the same shared variable* as they have their own local buffered copies. This means that in a relaxed model, one cannot directly apply classic predicate abstraction, as the variables used in predicates are assumed to refer to a single value at a time.

Predicate Discovery. A key challenge with predicate abstraction is to discover a set of predicates that enable verification. Following classic abstraction refinement, one would start with a program that is to be verified on a particular relaxed model together with an initial set of predicates. Then, proceed to iteratively apply refinement until we find a set of predicates under which the program verifies (or the process times out).

We take a different approach to predicate discovery for programs running on RMMs. In our approach, we first obtain the predicates that enable verification of the program on sequential consistency (SC). Then, we automatically *extrapolate* from these SC predicates to produce a new set of predicates that can be used as a basis for verification on the relaxed model.

Our Approach. Given a program P, a specification S and a memory model M, our approach consists of the following steps:

1. *verify under SC*: find a set of predicates V, sufficient to verify P under sequential consistency, i.e., a set V such that $\mathcal{BP}(P, V) \models_{SC} S$.
2. *reduce to SC*: automatically construct a new program P_M such that if $P_M \models_{SC} S$ then $P \models_M S$. The program P_M contains an abstraction of the store buffers used in M.
3. *discover new predicates*: automatically compute a new set of predicates V_M that are used for predicate abstraction of P_M. This is a challenging step and the key idea is to leverage the verification of P under SC. We present two approaches: predicate extrapolation which discovers new predicates based on the predicates in V and cube extrapolation which discovers new predicates based on both V and $\mathcal{BP}(P, V)$.

4. *construct a new boolean program*: given the new program P_M and the new predicates V_M, automatically construct a boolean program $\mathcal{BP}(P_M, V_M)$ such that $\mathcal{BP}(P_M, V_M) \models_{SC} S$ ensures that $P_M \models_{SC} S$, which in turn guarantees that $P \models_M S$. Here, cube extrapolation enables us to build $\mathcal{BP}(P_M, V_M)$ *without* suffering from the usual problem of exponential search.

5. *check*: whether $\mathcal{BP}(P_M, V_M) \models_{SC} S$.

Main Contributions

– We provide a novel approach for predicate abstraction of programs running on relaxed memory models, extrapolating from the predicate abstraction proof of the same program for sequential consistency.

– One of our insights is that the predicates used to verify P under SC can be automatically *extrapolated* to discover new predicates for verification of the program with M encoded in it, P_M. We present two approaches for discovering new predicates called predicate extrapolation and cube extrapolation.

– We instantiated our approach for the x86 TSO and PSO memory models. We implemented our approach and applied it to verify several challenging concurrent algorithms (both finite and infinite-state) under these models. We show that extrapolation is powerful enough to verify these algorithms and in particular, cube extrapolation enables verification of Lamport's Bakery algorithm, which otherwise (without cube extrapolation) times out when building the boolean program.

2 Overview

In this section, we give an informal overview of our approach using simple examples.

2.1 Motivating Example

Fig. 1 shows an implementation of an infinite state alternating bit protocol (ABP) with two concurrent threads. We use capitalized variable names to denote global shared variables, and variable names in lowercase to denote local variables. In this program, global shared variables Msg and Ack have an initial value 0. We use this algorithm as our illustrative example, additional examples are discussed in Section 6.

Specification. When executing on a sequentially consistent memory model, this program satisfies the invariant:

$$((lRCnt = lSCnt) \vee ((lRCnt + 1) = lSCnt))$$

Here, the local variable $lRCnt$ is the local counter for the receiver thread containing the number of received messages. Similarly, local variable $lSCnt$ is the local counter for the sender thread containing the number of sent messages.

Predicate Abstraction under Sequential Consistency. A traditional approach to predicate abstraction is shown in Fig. 2(a). To verify that ABP satisfies its specification under SC, we instantiate predicate abstraction with the following predicates:

$$(Msg = 0), (Ack = 0), (lSSt = 0), (lAck = 0)$$
$$(lMsg = 0), (lRSt = 0), (lRCnt = lSCnt), ((lRCnt + 1) = lSCnt)$$

initially: Msg = Ack = 0

Sender (thread 0):   Receiver (thread 1):

```
1   lAck = Ack;                                       1   lMsg = Msg;
2   if ((lAck = 0 & lSSt = 0)                         2   if ((lMsg = 0 & lRSt != 0)
    | (lAck != 0 & lSSt != 0))                            | (lMsg = 0 & lRSt != 0))
3                                                     3
4            if (lSSt != 0) lSSt = 0;                 4            lRSt = lMsg;
5            else lSSt = 1;                           5            lRCnt++;
6            lSCnt++;                                 6            Ack = lRSt;
7            Msg = lSSt;                              7
8   goto 1;                                           8   goto 1;
```

Fig. 1. An alternating bit protocol example with two threads

The result of predicate abstraction using these predicates is a concurrent boolean program that conservatively represents all behaviors of the original ABP program. In Fig. 2(a), this boolean program is denoted as the oval named Boolean Program B.

In the worst case, the construction of the concurrent boolean program, following standard predicate abstraction techniques (e.g., [16,6,15]) involves an exponential number of calls to an underlying theorem prover. A critical part of the construction of the boolean program is searching the "cubes" — conjunctions of predicates — that imply a certain condition. This search is exponential in the number of predicates.

An Informal Overview of PSO. In the partial-store-order (PSO) memory model, each thread maintains a private buffer (a sequence) for each global variable. When the thread writes to a global variable, the value is enqueued into the buffer for that variable. Non-deterministically, the values can be dequeued from the buffer and written to main memory. When the thread reads from a global variable, it first checks if the buffer is empty and if so, it reads as usual from main memory. Otherwise, it reads the last value written in the buffer. The model is further equipped with a special *fence* instruction which can be executed by a thread to empty all buffers for that thread and write the most recent value in each buffer to the corresponding shared location. In our example, thread 0 maintains one buffer, the buffer for global variable Msg and thread 1 also maintains one buffer, the buffer for global variable Ack. For instance, the store Msg = lSST leads to the value of lSST being enqueued into the private buffer for thread 0. This value can be flushed to main memory at any point in the execution, non-deterministically.

An Informal Overview of TSO. In the total-store-order (TSO) memory model, each thread maintains a single private buffer for all global variables. Similarly to PSO, values stored to global variables are first written to the buffer, and then are non-deterministically flushed to main memory. A *fence* instruction empties the thread's private buffer.

The challenges we address are: (i) how to verify programs such as ABP under relaxed memory models such as x86 TSO and PSO, and (ii) how to deal with the exponential complexity of standard predicate abstraction in our setting of RMM.

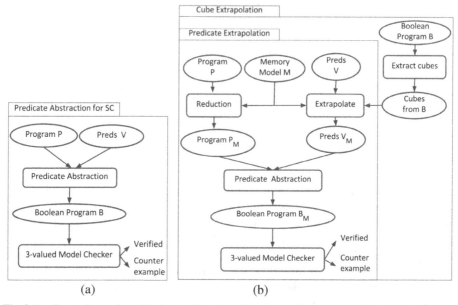

Fig. 2. Predicate abstraction: (a) classic algorithm, (b) with predicate extrapolation and cube extrapolation. Here, a rectangle shape represents an algorithm, while an oval shape represents input-output information (data).

2.2 Standard (Naive) Predicate Abstraction under RMM Is Unsound

We now consider the following scheme for predicate abstraction: (i) construct a boolean program directly from the program of Fig. 3 using standard predicate abstraction; (ii) execute the boolean program using PSO semantics. This scheme is simple, but unfortunately, it is unsound. We now show that following this scheme, we can produce a boolean program that successfully verifies our assertion. This is unsound because we know the existence of an assertion violation, namely the one shown in Fig. 4(a).

```
                    initial: X=Y=0
Thread 0:                        Thread 1:

1   X = Y+1              1   Y = X+1
2   fence(X)            2   fence(Y)

        assert(X≠Y)
```

Fig. 3. Unsoundness example

To capture the assertion breach, we need to keep track of the relationship between X and Y. Consider the predicates:

$$P_1 : X = Y, P_2 : X = 1, P_3 : Y = 1, P_4 : X = 0, P_5 : Y = 0$$

Each P_i has been assigned a boolean variable B_i (with a buffer for each thread) where the effect of a thread writing to X or Y will write to a local buffer of $X = Y$ of that thread, and the effect of flushing X or Y will also flush the buffer associated with $X = Y$. Unfortunately this approach is insufficient. The problem is shown in Fig. 4(b). When thread 0 updates X to 1, and thread 1 updates Y to 1, the predicate $X = Y$ will be updated to *false* in both (denoted as F) and stored in the store buffer of each thread

	Thread 0 (X,Y)	Thread 1 (X,Y)	Global (X,Y)	Thread 0 (X=Y,X=1,Y=1,X=0,Y=0)	Thread 1 (X=Y,X=1,Y=1,X=0,Y=0)	Global (X=Y,X=1,Y=1,X=0,Y=0)
	(0,0)	(0,0)	(0,0)	(T, F, F, T, T)	(T, F, F, T, T)	(T, F, F, T, T)
T0: $X = Y+1$	(1,0)	(0,0)	(0,0)	(F, T, F, F, T)	(T, F, F, T, T)	(T, F, F, T, T)
T1: $Y = X+1$	(1,0)	(0,1)	(0,0)	(F, T, F, F, T)	(F, F, T, T, F)	(T, F, F, T, T)
T0: flush(X)	(1,0)	(1,1)	(1,0)	**(F, T, F, F, T)**	(F, T, T, F, F)	**(F, T, F, F, T)**
T1: flush(Y)	(1,1)	(1,1)	(1,1)	(F, T, F, F, T)	**(F, T, T, F, F)**	**(F, T, T, F,F)**

Fig. 4. (a) an error trace for Fig. 3 under PSO. Thread i are values observed by thread i, Global are the values in global memory. (b) Values of predicates in a boolean program corresponding to the program of Fig. 3 under PSO semantics.

(since neither of the two threads can see the update of the other). When the value of X is flushed from the buffer of thread 0, our setting flushes the value of the predicate $X = Y$ (F) to main memory. Similarly, when Y is flushed in thread 1, the value of $X = Y$ (F) is flushed. The main memory state after these two flushes is inconsistent, as it has $X = 1$ set to T, $Y = 1$ set to T and $X = Y$ set to F.

2.3 Predicate Abstraction for Relaxed Memory Models

In Fig. 2(b), we illustrate the ingredients and flow of our approach for solving the verification problem under relaxed memory models. The figure contains two approaches for adapting predicate abstraction to our setting called Predicate Extrapolation and Cube Extrapolation (which includes Predicate Extrapolation). Next, we discuss the steps of our approach.

Step 1: Verify P under SC. The first step is to verify the program P under sequential consistency using standard predicate abstraction as outlined earlier in Fig. 2(a). Once the program is verified, we can leverage its set of predicates as well as its boolean program in the following steps.

Step 2: Construct the reduced program P_M. This step is named "Reduction" in Fig. 2(b). To enable sound predicate abstraction of a program P under a relaxed memory model M, we first reduce the problem into predicate abstraction of a sequentially consistent program. We do so, by constructing a program P_M that conservatively represents the memory model M effects as part of the program.

The key idea in constructing P_M is to represent an abstraction of the store buffers of M as additional variables in P_M. Since the constructed program P_M represents (an abstraction of) the details of the underlying memory model, we can soundly apply predicate abstraction to P_M. The formal details of the reduction for x86 TSO and PSO are discussed later in the paper. Here, we give an informal description.

For PSO, it is sufficient to consider a program P_{PSO} where every global variable X in P is also associated with: (i) additional k *local* variables for each thread t: $x_{1\_t}, \ldots, x_{k\_t}$, representing the content of a local store buffer for this variable in each thread t, (ii) a buffer counter variable x_{cnt_t} that records the current position in the store buffer of X in thread t.

The x86 TSO model maintains a single local buffer per process. This buffer is updated with stores to *any* of the global variables. However, we need additional variables to capture information about which global variable is stored in the buffer. The lhs variables contain the index of which global variable is addressed for each buffer element. The other variables are similar to PSO: (i) k *local* variables for each thread t: $lhs_{1\_t}, \ldots, lhs_{k\_t}$, representing the index of the global variable stored at a local store buffer in each thread t, (ii) k *local* variables for each thread t: $rhs_{1\_t}, \ldots, rhs_{k\_t}$, representing the value content of a local store buffer in each thread t, (iii) a buffer counter variable cnt_t that records the current position in the store buffer of thread t.

Step 3: Discover new predicates for P_M After verifying P under SC and constructing P_M, the remaining challenge is to discover a sufficient set of predicates for verifying that P_M satisfies a given specification. One of our main insights is that for buffered memory models such as x86 TSO and PSO, the predicates (and boolean program) used for verifying P under SC can be automatically leveraged to enable verification of P_M. This step corresponds to the "Extrapolate" box. This step takes as input the set of predicates V that were successful for verifying P under SC and outputs a new set V_M.

Predicates for the motivating example. Next, we illustrate via our running example how to generate new predicates under PSO (the process under x86 TSO is similar).

Consider again the ABP algorithm of Fig. 1 and the 8 predicates listed earlier in Section 2.1. Following the structure of the additional variables in P_M, we can introduce additional predicates by cloning each predicate over a global variable X into new predicates over store-buffer variables $x_{1\_t}, \ldots, x_{k\_t}$. For example, assuming $k = 1$, in addition to $Msg = 0$, we introduce $Msg\_1\_t0 = 0$.

To keep track of the buffer size for each buffered variable, we introduce additional predicates. For instance, for a global variable Msg, to register possible values for Msg_cnt_t0, assuming $k = 1$, we introduce $Msg\_cnt\_t0 = 0$ and $Msg\_cnt\_t0 = 1$. Note that we do not introduce predicates such as $Msg\_cnt\_t1 = 0$ and $Msg\_1\_t1 = 0$ as thread 1 always accesses Msg via main memory. Another predicate we could have added is $Msg\_1\_t0 = Msg$. This predicate is not needed for the verification of ABP, however, we observe that such predicates can greatly reduce the state space of the model checker. In Section 5, we discuss rules and optimizations for generating new predicates for the PSO memory model and in [10] we present the details for the x86 TSO model (which are similar).

Finally, to ensure soundness, we add a designated flag $overflow$ to track when the buffer size grows beyond our predetermined bound k. Overall, with a bound of $k = 1$, from 8 predicates used for sequential consistency we generate 15 predicates for PSO:

$(Msg = 0), (Ack = 0), (lSSt = 0), (lAck = 0), (lMsg = 0), (lRSt = 0), (lRCnt = lSCnt),$
$((lRCnt + 1) = lSCnt), (Msg\_cnt\_t0 = 0), (Msg\_cnt\_t0 = 1), (Ack\_cnt\_t1 = 0),$
$(Ack\_cnt\_t1 = 1), (Msg\_1\_t0 = 0), (Ack\_1\_t1 = 0), (overflow = 0)$

Cube Search Space. A critical part of the predicate abstraction algorithm is finding the weakest disjunction of cubes that implies a given formula (see [13,6] for details). This is done by exploring the cube search space, typically ordered by cube size. Because the search is exponential in the number of predicates, most previous work on predicate abstraction has bounded the cube space by limiting the maximal cube size to 3.

The translation of SC predicates to PSO predicates implies a polynomial (in the buffer limit k, number of threads and number of shared variables) growth in the number of predicates. Unfortunately, since cube search space is exponential in the number of predicates, exploration of the PSO cube space can sometimes be prohibitively expensive in practice.

For example, for ABP running on sequential consistency, the total number of cubes is $3^8 = 6561$. Here, 8 is the maximal sized cube which is the same as the number of predicates. And 3 means that we can use the predicate directly, its negation or the predicate can be absent. However, for PSO, the total number of cubes is 3^{15} exceeding 14 million cubes! If we limit cube size to 4, the SC cube search space becomes bounded by $\Sigma_{i=1}^4 2^i \binom{8}{i} = 288$, and the PSO cube space to be explored becomes bounded by $\Sigma_{i=1}^4 2^i \binom{15}{i} = 25630$.

The situation is worsened as the cube space is explored for every abstract transformer computation. Further, while in previous work, which mostly targets sequential programs, limiting the cube size to 3 seemed to work, with concurrency, where one needs to capture correlations between different threads, it is possible that we need a cube size of 4 or greater. As the number of predicates increases, directly exploring cubes of size 4 or more, even with standard optimizations, becomes infeasible (our experiments confirm that).

Reducing the PSO Cube Space using SC Cubes. One of our main insights is that we can leverage the boolean program (the proof) under sequential consistency to simplify reasoning under relaxed memory models. Technically, we realize this insight by using the cubes from the boolean program under SC in order to guide the search in the cube space under the weak memory model.

In Fig. 2(b), this step is denoted under Cube Extrapolation where in addition to the steps in Predicate Extrapolation, we also extract the cubes that appear in the boolean program of P under SC.

For example, for ABP, we examine the boolean program $\mathcal{BP}(ABP, V)$ where V are the eight predicates listed earlier in Section 2.1, and observe the following cubes:

$$c_1 = (lSSt = 0) \wedge (lAck = 0)$$
$$c_2 = (lSSt = 0) \wedge \neg(lAck = 0)$$
$$c_3 = (lMsg = 0) \wedge \neg(lRSt = 0)$$
$$c_4 = \neg(lSSt = 0) \wedge \neg(lAck = 0)$$
$$c_5 = \neg(lSSt = 0) \wedge (lAck = 0)$$

Since these cubes do not use the two global variables Msg and Ack, it stands to reason that the same cubes would be obtained from the PSO cube space exploration, which is indeed the case.

In this simple example, the above cubes from the predicate abstraction under SC could be used directly for the predicate abstraction under PSO, *without* needing to search for these cubes. Of course, there are cases where SC cubes do contain buffered variables (such as Msg or Ack) and in that case we need to extrapolate from these cubes in order to obtain useful cubes under PSO (see Section 5).

Building the Boolean Program. An enabling factor with cube extrapolation is that it changes the way we build the boolean program. We no longer require exponential search over the cube search space. In Section 4, we show how to use the cubes under SC as constraints over the cube space to reduce the size of the cube space to be explored under

$[X = r]_k^t$	$[r = X]_k^t$	$[\text{fence}]_k^t$	$[\text{flush}]_k^t$

if $x_{cnt\_t} = k$ **then**
 abort("overflow")
 	
 $x_{cnt\_t} = x_{cnt\_t} + 1$
 	
 if $x_{cnt\_t} = 1$ **then**
 $x_{1\_t} = r$
 ...
 if $x_{cnt\_t} = k$ **then**
 $x_{k\_t} = r$
	if $x_{cnt\_t} = 0$ **then**
	 $r = X$
	 if $x_{cnt\_t} = 1$ **then**
	 $r = x_{1\_t}$
	 ...
	 if $x_{cnt\_t} = k$ **then**
	 $r = x_{k\_t}$
		▷ for each
		 $X \in Gvar$
		 generate:
		
		 assume $(x_{cnt\_t} = 0)$
		
		 ▷ end of generation
			while * **do**
			 ▷ for each $X \in Gvar$ generate:
			 if $x_{cnt\_t} > 0$ **then**
			 if * **then**
			 $X = x_{1\_t}$
			 if $x_{cnt\_t} > 1$ **then**
			 $x_{1\_t} = x_{2\_t}$
			 ...
			 if $x_{cnt\_t} = k$ **then**
			 $x_{(k-1)\_t} = x_{k\_t}$
			
			 $x_{cnt\_t} = x_{cnt\_t} - 1$
			 ▷ end of generation

Fig. 5. PSO Translation Rules: each sequence of statements is atomic

the weak memory model. Technically, the idea is to lift the cubes under SC to buffered counterparts by a translation similar to the way in which we extrapolated predicates under SC (described above).

We can then pack the extrapolated cubes as new predicates provided to the predicate abstraction procedure for the weak memory model, and limit cube size to 1. Limiting the maximal cube size to 1 turns the process of cube search from exponential to linear (in the number of predicates and cubes obtained from extrapolation). This is key to making predicate abstraction tractable for relaxed memory models.

In Fig. 2(b), to reduce clutter, both Predicate Extrapolation and Cube Extrapolation lead to the same Predicate Abstraction box. However, it is important to note that the process of predicate abstraction for Cube Extrapolation *does not* perform exponential search while the process for predicate extrapolation does. As we will see in the experimental results, Predicate Extrapolation is sufficient for simpler programs, while Cube Extrapolation is necessary for more complex programs.

Step 4: Model checking. Once the boolean program is built (either via Predicate or Cube Extrapolation), the final step is to model check the program. This step is exactly the same as in the standard case of traditional predicate abstraction shown in Fig. 2(a).

3 Reduction

In this section, we describe a translation that transforms a program running on a relaxed memory model into a program with no weak memory model effects. The basic idea is to translate the store buffers in the semantics into variables that are part of the program. This translation enables us to leverage classic program analysis techniques such as predicate abstraction. Further, because the translation is parametric on the size of the buffer, it allows us to tailor the abstraction to the buffer size required by the particular concurrent algorithm. We show the process for the PSO memory model, the process for x86 TSO is similar and is shown in [10].

Reduction: PSO to SC. The reduction takes as input a thread identifier (whose statements are to be handled), as well as a bound on the maximum buffer size k for the per-variable buffer. Here, k denotes the maximum number of writes to global variables without a fence in-between the writes. While the translation presented here uses a fixed k for all global variables, we can easily use different k's for different variables.

The translation considers in turn every statement that involves global variables. We introduce a translation function, which takes as input a statement, a thread identifier, and a bound on the maximum buffer size and produces a new statement as output:

$$[\![\ ]\!] \in Stmt \times Thread \times \mathbb{N} \to Stmt$$

As a shorthand we write $[\![S]\!]_k^t$ for $[\![S, t, k]\!]$. $[\![S]\!]_k^t$ denotes the statement obtained from translating statement S in thread t with buffer bound k.

To perform the translation, the entries of the per-variable buffer are translated into thread-local variables and a local counter is introduced to maintain its depth. That is, for each global variable X and thread t, we introduce the following local variables:

- buffer content variables: $x_{1\_t}, \dots, x_{k\_t}$, where k is the maximum size of the buffer.
- a buffer counter variable: x_{cnt_t}.

Fig. 5 presents the translation of the three program code statements and the memory subsystem statement (flush). In the translation, the newly generated sequence of statements is atomic.

Store to a global variable $[\![X = r]\!]_k^t$***:*** The store to a global variable X first checks if we are about to exceed the buffer bound k and if so, the program aborts. Otherwise, the counter is increased. The rest of the logic checks the value of the counter and updates the corresponding local variable. The global variable X is not updated and only local variables are involved.

Load from a global variable $[\![r = X]\!]_k^t$***:*** The load from a global variable X checks the current depth of the buffer and then loads from the corresponding local variable. When the buffer is empty (i.e., $x_{cnt\_t} = 0$), the load is performed directly from the global store. We do not need to check whether the buffer limit k is exceeded as that is ensured by the global store.

Fence statement $[\![fence]\!]_k^t$***:*** For *each* shared variable X, the fence statement waits for the buffer of X to be empty (flush instructions to be executed). The fence has no effect on X.

Flush action $[\![flush]\!]_k^t$***:*** The flush action is translated into a loop with a non-deterministic exit condition (we use $*$). New statements are introduced for each global variable X. If the buffer counter for the variable is positive, then it non-deterministically decides whether to update the global variable X or to continue the iteration. If it has decided to update X, the earliest write (i.e. x_{1_t}) is stored in X. The contents of the local variables are then updated by shifting: the content of each x_{i_t} is taken from the content of the successor $x_{(i+1)\_t}$ where $1 \leq i < k$. Finally, the buffer count is decremented. The composite statement inside the while loop is generated for each global variable. To ensure a faithful translation of the flush action, the whole newly generated statement is placed after *each* statement of the resulting program. The atomic statements are translated directly, without change (not shown in the figure).

The translation extends naturally to a sequence of statements and to programs with n concurrent threads: $[\![P]\!]_k = [\![S]\!]_k^1 \parallel \cdots \parallel [\![S]\!]_k^n$, leading to the following theorem:

Theorem 1 (Soundness of Translation). *For a given program, P and a safety specification S, if $P \not\models_{pso} S$ then there exists a $k \in \mathbb{N}$ such that $[\![P]\!]_k \not\models_{sc} S$.*

From the theorem it follows that if $[\![P]\!]_k \models_{sc} S$ then $P \models_{pso} S$. When we successfully verify the program with a given k, it is guaranteed that no execution of the program ever requires a buffer of size larger than k. If the program does have an execution which exceeds k, then during verification we will encounter overflow and can attempt a higher value of k. That is, if we verify the program for a certain bound k, then the algorithm is correct for any size of the buffer greater or equal to k. In our experience, most concurrent algorithms exhibit low values for k as typically they use fences after a small number of global stores.

4 Predicate Abstraction for Relaxed Memory Models

In this section we describe how predicate abstraction is used to verify concurrent programs running on relaxed memory models. The central point we address is how to discover the predicates necessary for verification under the relaxed model from the predicates and the proof that was successful for verification of the program under sequential consistency (SC).

4.1 Predicate Abstraction

Predicate abstraction [16] is a special form of abstract interpretation that employs cartesian abstraction over a given set of predicates. Given a program P, and vocabulary (set of predicates) $V = \{p_1, \ldots, p_n\}$ with corresponding boolean variables $\hat{V} = \{b_1, \ldots, b_n\}$, predicate abstraction constructs a boolean program $\mathcal{BP}(P, V)$ that conservatively represents behaviors of P using only boolean variables from $\hat{V}$ (corresponding to predicates in V). We use $[b_i]$ to denote the predicate p_i corresponding to the boolean variable b_i. We similarly extend $[b]$ to any boolean function b.

Next we explain how to construct $\mathcal{BP}(P, V)$. A literal is a boolean variable or its negation. A *cube* is a conjunction of literals, the size of a cube is the number of literals it contains. The concrete (symbolic) domain is defined as formulae over the predicates $p_1, \ldots, p_n$. The abstract domain is a disjunctions of cubes over the variables $b_1, \ldots, b_n$. The abstraction function α maps a formula φ over predicates from V to the weakest disjunction of cubes d such that $[d] \Rightarrow \varphi$.

The abstract transformer of a statement st w.r.t. a given vocabulary V can be computed using weakest-precondition computation and performing implication checks using a theorem prover:

$$b_i = choose(\alpha(wp(st, p_i)), \alpha(wp(st, \neg p_i,)))$$

where

$$choose(\varphi_t, \varphi_f) = \begin{cases} 1, & \varphi_t \text{ evaluates to true;} \\ 0, & \text{only } \varphi_f \text{ evaluates to true;} \\ \star, & \text{otherwise.} \end{cases}$$

Different predicate abstraction techniques use different heuristics for reducing the number of calls to the prover.

Input: Vocabulary V, Statement st, Maximum cube size k
Output: Abstract transformer for st over predicates from V

function COMPUTETRANSFORMER(V, st, k)
  for each $p \in V$ **do**
    $\psi_p^+ = \psi_p^- = false$
    $\varphi^+ = wp(st, p)$
    $\varphi^- = wp(st, \neg p)$
    for each $i = 1 \ldots k$ **do**
      $cubes^+ = $ BUILDBOUNDEDCUBES(V, i, ψ_p^+)
      if $cubes^+ = \emptyset$ **then break**
      $\psi_p^+ = $ COMPUTEAPPROX$(cubes^+, \varphi^+, \psi_p^+)$
    for each $i = 1 \ldots k$ **do**
      $cubes^- = $ BUILDBOUNDEDCUBES(V, i, ψ_p^-)
      if $cubes^- = \emptyset$ **then break**
      $\psi_p^- = $ COMPUTEAPPROX$(cubes^-, \varphi^-, \psi_p^-)$
    $\psi(p) = choose(\psi_p^+, \psi_p^-)$
(a)

Input: RMM predicates V_{rmm}, RMM cubes C_{rmm}, Statement st,
Output: Abstract transformer for st over predicates from $V_{rmm} \cup C_{rmm}$

function COMPUTETRANSFORMER(V_{rmm}, C_{rmm}, st)
  for each $p \in V_{rmm}$ **do**
    $\psi_p^+ = \psi_p^- = false$

    $\varphi^+ = wp(st, p)$
    $\psi_p^+ = $ COMPUTEAPPROX$(V_{rmm} \cup C_{rmm}, \varphi^+, \psi_p^+)$

    $\varphi^- = wp(st, \neg p)$
    $\psi_p^- = $ COMPUTEAPPROX$(V_{rmm} \cup C_{rmm}, \varphi^-, \psi_p^-)$

    $\psi(p) = choose(\psi_p^+, \psi_p^-)$
(b)

Fig. 6. Computing abstract transformers: (a) classical predicate abstraction; (b) using extrapolation. COMPUTEAPPROX is shown in Fig. 7.

function COMPUTEAPPROX($cubes, \varphi, \psi$)
  for each $c \in cubes$ **do**
    if $c \Rightarrow \varphi$ **then**
      $\psi = \psi \vee c$
  return ψ

Fig. 7. Predicate abstraction - helper function

Fig. 6 (a) shows a standard predicate abstraction algorithm in the spirit of [6]. The algorithm takes as input a statement st and a set of predicates (vocabulary) V. It then computes an abstract transformer for st using combinations of predicates from V. The algorithm works by computing an update formula $\psi(p)$ for every predicate p. The update formula is constructed as a choice between two sub-formulae, ψ_p^+ which holds when p should be set to $true$, and ψ_p^- which holds when p should be set to $false$.

The function BUILDBOUNDEDCUBES builds cubes of size i over predicates from V, checking that cubes of size i are not subsumed by previously generated cubes in ψ_p^+ or ψ_p^-. This function is standard, and we do not list it here due to space restrictions.

There are other algorithms that can be used here, such as the Flanagan&Qadeer's [15], or the one of Das et al. [11]. However, our focus is not on these optimizations, but on leveraging information from the verification of the SC program to discover the new predicates for verification under the relaxed memory model.

4.2   Predicate Extrapolation: From Predicates under SC to Predicates under Relaxed Model

Given a program which successfully verified under SC, our first approach to verifying the program under x86 TSO or PSO is to:

- Reduce the program as described in Section 3. That is, given a statement st of the original program, obtain a new statement st_{pso} or st_{tso} from the translation.
- Compute $V_{pso} = $ EXTRAPOLATEPSO(V) for PSO as discussed in Section 5, or for TSO: $V_{tso} = $ EXTRAPOLATETSO(V) (the TSO extrapolation is discussed in [10] and is similar to PSO). This extrapolates from the set of input predicates under SC and derives new predicates under x86 TSO or PSO.
- Invoke COMPUTETRANSFORMER(V_{pso}, st_{pso}, k) to build the abstract transformer under PSO. Similarly, invoke COMPUTETRANSFORMER(V_{tso}, st_{tso}, k) for x86 TSO. Here, k is the appropriate buffer bound. The function COMPUTETRANSFORMER is shown in Fig. 6 (a).

That is, with this approach, the entire predicate abstraction tool chain remains the same except we change the input to the function for computing abstract transformers to be the new predicates V_{pso} and the new statement st_{pso}.

4.3   Cube Extrapolation: From SC Proof to PSO Predicates

As we will see in our experimental results, predicate extrapolation is effective only in some cases. The problem is that on more complex programs, the cube search space increases significantly meaning the function COMPUTETRANSFORMER as described in Fig. 6 (a) times out. Next, we discuss another approach for computing abstract transformers under the relaxed memory model.

Core Idea. The core idea is that cubes generated during SC predicate abstraction capture invariants that are important for correctness under SC, but the same relationships between variables can be extrapolated to relationships between variables in the relaxed setting. Based on this observation, we extrapolate from these cubes similarly to the way we extrapolated from the predicates under SC. We use the function $C_{pso} = $ EXTRAPOLATEPSO(C) where C denotes the cubes under SC. The newly generated extrapolated cubes C_{pso} are then used as predicates for the verification.

The key point is that the cube search over C_{pso} is now limited to cubes of size 1! The steps are as follows:

- Compute $V_{pso} = $ EXTRAPOLATEPSO(V)
- Compute $C_{pso} = $ EXTRAPOLATEPSO(C)
- Invoke COMPUTETRANSFORMER(V_{pso}, C_{pso}, st) as shown in Fig. 6 (b) and taking as input extrapolated predicates and extrapolated cubes together with the statement.

The process for the x86 TSO model is identical.

Search vs. Extrapolation. In contrast to the standard COMPUTETRANSFORMER of Fig. 6 (a), the algorithm of Fig. 6 (b) *does not* perform exhaustive search of the cube space. In particular, it does not take as input the parameter k. That is, our new way of building transformers is based on extrapolating from a previous (SC) proof.

5   Extrapolating Predicates: SC to PSO

In this section, we elaborate on how the function $preds_{pso} = \text{EXTRAPOLATEPSO}$ $(preds_{sc})$ operates. The operation $\text{EXTRAPOLATETSO}(preds_{sc})$ for TSO is similar and is discussed in [10]. The function EXTRAPOLATEPSO computes the ingredients, that is, the new predicates $preds_{pso}$, using which the final abstraction is built. We discuss the core reasons for introducing the new predicates. This reasoning is independent of predicate abstraction and can be used with other verification approaches.

Any abstraction for store buffer based RMMs such as PSO must be precise enough to preserve the following properties: (i) Intra-thread coherence: If a thread stores several values to shared variable X, and then performs a load from X, it should not see any value it has itself stored except the most recent one. (ii) Inter-thread coherence: A thread T_i should not observe values written to shared variable X by thread T_j in an order different from the order in which they were written. (iii) Fence semantics: If a thread T_i executes a fence when its buffer for variable X is non-empty, the value of X visible to other threads immediately after the fence should be the most recent value T_i wrote.

Fig. 8 shows a simple example in which a single thread stores two values into a shared variable X and then loads the value of X into $l1$. To successfully verify this program, the abstraction we use must be precise enough to capture intra-thread coherence.

Thread 1:

```
1    X=0;
2    X=1;
3    l1=X;
4    fence;
5    assert (X = l1);
```

Fig. 8. Intra-thread coherence example

5.1   Generic Predicates

For a shared variable X, if we use a buffer with a max size of 1, our translation adds the predicates: $X\_cnt\_t1 = 0, X\_cnt\_t1 = 1$ indicating the last location of the buffer for X which has been written to by thread 1, but not yet flushed. These predicates serve multiple purposes: (i) track the store buffers size; (ii) provide knowledge during store and load operations on where to write/read the value of X. (iii) preserve *Intra-thread coherence* in the abstraction.

Another predicate we generate is: $overflow = 0$. This predicate supplements the previously described predicates, giving indication of when the number of subsequent stores to a shared variable X, without a fence or a flush in between these stores, exceeds the limit k of our abstraction. This is crucial to ensure soundness of the abstraction.

The general extrapolation rule, which is independent of the verified program and of the input SC predicates $preds_{sc}$, is:

Rule 1. *For a buffer size bound k, add the following predicates to $preds_{pso}$:*

- $\{\mathbf{V}\_cnt\_\mathbf{T} = i \mid 1 \leq i \leq k, \mathbf{V} \in Gvar, \mathbf{T} \in Thread\}$
- $overflow = 0$

5.2   Extrapolating from $preds_{sc}$

We now describe how to extrapolate from the predicates in the set $preds_{sc}$ in order to compute new predicates that become part of $preds_{pso}$. The rule below ensures that the SC executions of the new program can be verified.

Rule 2. *Update the set $preds_{pso}$ to contain the set $preds_{sc}$*

Next, we would like properties on the values of a shared variable X captured by predicates in $preds_{sc}$ to also be captured for the buffered values of X. For example if $preds_{sc}$ contains $X = 0$, we add the predicate $X\_1\_t1 = 0$ for a buffer of X for thread T_1. This can be seen in the example of Fig. 8 where we need to track that the buffered value of X is 0 at line 1. We summarize these observations in the following rule:

Rule 3. *Update $preds_{pso}$ to contain the set $\bigcup_{p_{sc} \in preds_{sc}} lift(p_{sc})$*

Here, $lift(p_{sc})$ generates from each SC predicate a set of PSO predicates where the original variables are replaced with buffered versions of the variables (for each buffered version of a variable and their combination).

In addition to the above rules, adding a predicate $X\_1\_t1 = X$ ensures that the shared value of X and the buffered value of X are in agreement (when the predicate is set to *true*). This reduces the time and space of model checking. Following similar reasoning, the predicate $X\_1\_t1 = X\_2\_t1$ is also added.

Rule 4. *For $\mathbf{V} \in Gvar$, $\mathbf{T} \in Thread$ and k the buffer bound, update $preds_{pso}$ to contain the sets:*

- $\{\mathbf{V}\_(i-1)\_\mathbf{T} = \mathbf{V}\_i\_\mathbf{T} \mid 2 \leq i \leq k\}$
- $\{\mathbf{V}\_i\_\mathbf{T} = \mathbf{V} \mid 1 \leq i \leq k\}$

The above rules add both: generic predicates that are independent of $preds_{sc}$ as well as predicates that are extrapolated from $preds_{sc}$. But these rules may sometimes generate a larger set of predicates than necessary for successful verification. We now describe several optimizations that substantially reduce that number.

Rule 5 *Read-only shared variables.* *If a thread t never writes to a shared variable X do not extrapolate the SC predicates referencing X to their PSO counterparts for t.*

Rule 6 *Predicates referencing a shared variable more than once.* *Replace all occurrences of the shared variable with the same buffered location.*

For example, for $X \leq Y \wedge 0 \leq X$, where X is referred to more than once, we generate the new predicate $X\_1\_t1 \leq Y \wedge 0 \leq X\_1\_t1$, but we do not generate the predicate $X\_1\_t1 \leq Y \wedge 0 \leq X\_1\_t2$. The intuition is that the SC predicate captures information regarding the value of X at some point in the execution and when extrapolating the predicate to PSO, we need to capture that information regarding the shared value of X or its buffered value, yet the mixture of the two is redundant. Similarly for $Y2 \leq Y1$, we do not necessarily need to generate the predicate $Y2\_1\_t2 \leq Y1\_1\_t1$.

Rule 7 *Predicates referencing different shared variables.* *For a predicate referencing more than one shared variable, if it can be guaranteed that a fence will be executed between every two shared location writes , restrict to generating predicates that relate to one buffered location at most.*

In summary, EXTRAPOLATEPSO is computed by applying the above seven rules for the predicates in V and C (both obtained from the verification under SC).

6   Experimental Evaluation

We implemented predicate abstraction based on predicate extrapolation (PE) and cube extrapolation (CE) as outlined earlier in our tool called CUPEX. Then, we thoroughly evaluated the tool on a number of challenging concurrent algorithms. All experiments were conducted on an Intel(R) Xeon(R) 2.13GHz with 250GB RAM. The key question we seek to answer is whether predicate extrapolation and cube extrapolation are precise and scalable enough to verify all of our (relaxed) programs.

6.1   Prototype Implementation

CUPEX works in two phases. In the first phase, given an input program, it applies abstraction and produces a boolean program. In the second phase, the boolean program is verified using a three-valued model checker for boolean programs. To reduce the cube search space, CUPEX uses optimizations such as bounded cube size search and cone of influence. For every assignment statement in the original program, it updates only the boolean variables corresponding to predicates which contain the assigned variable from the statement (subject to aliasing). The search in the cube space is performed in increasing cube size order, thus we find the weaker (smaller) cubes first. CUPEX uses Yices 1.0.34 as the underlying SMT solver.

The second phase relies on a three-valued model checker to verify the boolean program. Our model checker uses 3-valued logic for compact representation, and handles assume statements in a number of clever ways, performs partial concretization of assume conditions and merges states after updates.

6.2   Results

We evaluated CUPEX on the following concurrent algorithms: Dekker's mutual exclusion algorithm [12], Peterson's mutual exclusion algorithm [26], Szymanski mutual exclusion algorithm [29], Alternating Bit protocol (already discussed in Section 2), an Array-based Lock-Free Queue (here, we verified its memory safety), Lamport's Bakery algorithm [24] and the Ticket locking algorithm [3]. The first three algorithms are finite-state, while the last four are infinite-state. For each algorithm, we evaluated our tool for x86 TSO and PSO models. We ran tests with buffer bounds ranging from $k \in 1 \dots 3$. For each k, we tested various fence configurations. We present in the result tables values for $k = 1$, obtained for the minimal fence configurations which successfully verified.

Meaning of table columns. Our results are summarized in Table 1 and Table 2. The meaning of most table columns is self explanatory, but we elaborate on the following columns of Table 1:

- Build Boolean Program (i) # input preds: number of initial input predicates. For x86 TSO and PSO, these are obtained by extrapolating from the predicates in the # input preds column of the corresponding SC program. (ii) # SMT calls: total number of calls (in thousands) to the SMT solver required to build the boolean program (BP). (iii) time: time in seconds that it took to build the boolean program. We use T/O for timed out (keeps running after 10 hours). (iv) # cubes used: total

Table 1. Results for Predicate Extrapolation

algorithm	memory model	Build Boolean Program					Model check		
		# input preds	# SMT calls (K)	time (sec)	# cubes used	cube size	# states (K)	memory (MB)	time (sec)
Dekker	SC	7	0.7	0.1	0		14	6	1
	PSO	20	26	6	0	1	80	31	5
	TSO	18	22	5	0		45	20	3
Peterson	SC	7	0.6	0.1	2		7	3	1
	PSO	20	15	3	2	2	31	13	3
	TSO	18	13	3	2		25	11	2
ABP	SC	8	2	0.5	5		0.6	1	0.6
	PSO	15	20	4	5	2	2	3	1
	TSO	17	23	5	5		2	3	1
Szymanski	SC	20	16	3.3	1		12	6	2
	PSO	35	152	33	1	2	61	30	4
	TSO	37	165	35	1		61	31	5

number of cubes in the boolean program whose size is greater than 1, that is, these are cubes composed of 2 or more input predicates. (v) cube size: maximum cube size found in the boolean program. For instance, cube size 4 means that there exist cubes which combine 4 input predicates.

- Model check (i) # states: total number of states (thousands) explored by the underlying three-valued model checker.

Table 2 contains two additional columns in the Build Boolean Program column: (i) method used to build the boolean program: PE , CE or, for SC programs where no new predicates are generated, Trad (Traditional). (ii) # input cubes: These are obtained by extrapolating from the cubes in the # cubes used column of the corresponding SC program. These cubes are then added to the initial # input preds and CE is performed.

6.3   Observations

Sequential Consistency. We assume that the predicates for the original SC program are provided by the programmer or inferred using existing SC verification tools such as [17]. For our benchmarks we manually provided the SC predicates, since we focus on the relaxed memory verification.

Predicate Extrapolation. We first focus on the results of Table 1. Here, PE was quick enough to verify all programs under x86 TSO and PSO. For example for Dekker's algorithm, even though there was a significant increase in the number of predicates (7 input predicates required to verify the program under SC yet under PSO, 20 predicates were needed), the newly generated predicates were precise enough to prove the program. A similar pattern can be observed for Peterson, ABP and Szymanski. For all four algorithms, a small cube size (at most 2) was sufficient for verification. Furthermore, the number of cubes of size 2 that are used in the boolean program is fairly small. Overall, these four programs require a small cube size to verify, at most 2, leading to quick building of the boolean program. For these programs, CE was unnecessary.

Table 2. Results for Predicate Extrapolation and Cube Extrapolation

algorithm	memory model	method	# input preds	# input cubes	# SMT calls (K)	time (sec)	# cubes used	cube size	# states (K)	memory (MB)	time (sec)
Queue	SC	Trad	7	-	20	5	50		1	2	1
	PSO	PE	15	-	5,747	1,475	412		1	4	1
		CE		99	98	17	99	4	11	6	2
	TSO	PE	16	-	11,133	2,778	412		12	4	1
		CE		99	163	31	99		12	7	2
Bakery	SC	Trad	15	-	1,552	355	161		20	8	2
	PSO	PE	38	-	-	T/O	-		-	-	-
		CE		422	9,018	1,773	381	4	979	375	104
	TSO	PE	36	-	-	T/O	-		-	-	-
		CE		422	7,048	1,386	383		730	285	121
Ticket	SC	Trad	11	-	218	51	134		2	2	1
	PSO	PE	56	-	-	T/O	-		-	-	-
		CE		622	15,644	2,163	380	4	193	123	40
	TSO	PE	48	-	-	T/O	-		-	-	-
		CE		622	6,941	1,518	582		71	67	545

Cube Extrapolation. Next, we discuss the results of Table 2. We first observe that for Queue, under PSO, PE required around 6 million calls to the SMT solver and took a little over 24 minutes to complete in building the boolean program. Indeed, the combination of increased cube size (4) together with 15 initial input predicates significantly affected the running time for building the boolean program. Interestingly, we observe that CE, was able to reduce the number of calls to the SMT solver by a factor of 60 and reduce the running time by a factor of 80. Importantly, CE was precise enough to verify the program. Here we see that CE generated 99 new cubes which were extrapolated from the 50 SC cubes. The final program used exactly these 99 cubes, meaning that CE did not generate redundant cubes.

For both Bakery and Ticket, the benefits of CE are even more startling. With PE, building the boolean program fails under both x86 TSO and PSO due to a time out. However, CE massively reduced the number of SMT calls enabling successful generation of the boolean program. The set of cubes CE returned was fairly close to the set of cubes used during the boolean program verification. For instance, in Bakery under PSO, 422 input cubes were generated out of which 381 were used in the boolean program (fairly close to ideal).

It is worth noting that in all benchmarks we experimented on, the minimal fence placement required was different for x86 TSO and PSO.

Discussion. Next we note two observations from our approach which we encountered experimentally and which we believe are interesting items for future work.

First, when we directly applied CE to the Ticket algorithm, it took hours to verify for PSO. To solve this problem, we hypothesized that given a safety property, which does not reference buffered values, we may allow inconsistent values at buffered locations, and that inconsistency would be resolved when those values are flushed and before an error state is reached. Therefore, to enable quicker verification, we first applied CE as usual, and then automatically removed all predicates referencing buffered values from the resulting cubes found in the boolean program after CE. Such a reduction preserves soundness while abstracting the proof. We note that although this approach worked for Ticket under PSO, when we tried it under x86 TSO this additional pass introduced too much imprecision and the program failed to verify (the table reports results for Ticket on PSO using this additional pass and on x86 TSO without this pass).

Second, for the Queue algorithm our initial successful SC proof was insufficient to extrapolate from. Portions of the program where the boolean program under SC lost precision due to abstraction were amplified by the extrapolation. For instance, where the SC proof used a predicate $Tail < Head$ which was unknown through parts of the SC proof with no adverse effects, the extrapolated proof propagated this uncertainty causing an error state to be reached. Adding $Tail \leq Head$ strengthened the SC proof and enabled successful extrapolation (this is the result we report in the Table).

Summary. For cubes of small size, 2 or less, with PE, CUPEX builds the boolean program quickly and is precise enough to verify the program. For larger cube sizes, PE takes too long to build the boolean program or times out. However, CUPEX with CE enables us to build the boolean program in reasonable time and critically, is precise enough to verify the program both for x86 TSO and PSO.

7   Related Work

There has been almost no work on automatically verifying *infinite-state* concurrent programs running on relaxed memory models. We briefly survey some of the more closely related work.

Model Checking for Relaxed Memory Models. The works of [25,21,22,19] describe explicit-state model checking under several memory models. In [7], instead of working with operational memory models and explicit model-checking, they convert programs into a form that can be checked against an axiomatic model specification. These approaches do not handle infinite-state programs. The work in [23] focuses on programs that are finite-state under SC but infinite-state under x86 TSO and PSO and suggests an abstraction to deal with the issue. Unfortunately, it also cannot handle general infinite-state programs (i.e., the program must be finite-state under SC).

The works of [2,5] present a code-to-code transformation which encodes the relaxed memory semantics into the program. Our approach goes beyond this transformation and tackles the difficulty of verifying the newly obtained relaxed program. These new programs are more difficult to verify because of the complexity added by the encoded semantics. Our approach solves this problem by learning from the proof under sequential consistency.

The work of [1] builds on [23] and handles infinite state programs (on x86 TSO) by applying both predicate abstraction and store buffers abstraction. Their approach discovers predicates via traditional abstraction refinement and does not reuse information from the proof under SC, while in our approach we present a technique which leverages an existing proof under SC in order to derive a new proof for a more relaxed program.

Further, we also handle a memory model (PSO) that allows for more behaviors and complexity than x86 TSO.

Lazy abstraction. The work of [18] introduces the concept of adjusting the level of abstraction for different sections of the verified program's state space. This is achieved by applying on-the-fly refinement for search-tree sub-graphs. Their approach does not construct a boolean program during verification. However, encoding the weak memory semantics in the code and extrapolating from the SC proof are concepts applicable for extending lazy abstraction to relaxed memory models. The backwards counter-example analysis phase, which requires costly calls to the theorem prover, may in part be avoided by anticipating in each branch of the search tree which predicates are required.

8   Conclusion and Future Work

We introduced a novel approach for predicate abstraction of concurrent programs running on relaxed memory models such as x86 TSO and PSO. The essence of our approach is extrapolation: learning from an existing proof of the program under sequential consistency in order to obtain a proof for a more relaxed version of the program.

We implemented our extrapolation approach and successfully applied it to automatically verify several challenging concurrent algorithms for both x86 TSO and PSO. This is the first time some of these programs have been verified for a model as relaxed as PSO.

As future work, we plan to investigate how these techniques apply to other relaxed models, both hardware models such as Power, as well as software programming models such as [8].

References

1. Abdulla, P.A., Atig, M.F., Chen, Y.-F., Leonardsson, C., Rezine, A.: Automatic fence insertion in integer programs via predicate abstraction. In: Miné, A., Schmidt, D. (eds.) SAS 2012. LNCS, vol. 7460, pp. 164–180. Springer, Heidelberg (2012)
2. Alglave, J., Kroening, D., Nimal, V., Tautschnig, M.: Software verification for weak memory via program transformation. In: Felleisen, M., Gardner, P. (eds.) ESOP 2013. LNCS, vol. 7792, pp. 512–532. Springer, Heidelberg (2013)
3. Andrews, G.R.: Concurrent programming - principles and practice. Benjamin/Cummings (1991)
4. Atig, M.F., Bouajjani, A., Burckhardt, S., Musuvathi, M.: On the verification problem for weak memory models. In: POPL (2010)
5. Atig, M.F., Bouajjani, A., Parlato, G.: Getting rid of store-buffers in tso analysis. In: Gopalakrishnan, G., Qadeer, S. (eds.) CAV 2011. LNCS, vol. 6806, pp. 99–115. Springer, Heidelberg (2011)
6. Ball, T., Majumdar, R., Millstein, T., Rajamani, S.K.: Automatic predicate abstraction of C programs. In: PLDI (2001)
7. Burckhardt, S., Alur, R., Martin, M.M.K.: CheckFence: checking consistency of concurrent data types on relaxed memory models. In: PLDI (2007)
8. Burckhardt, S., Baldassin, A., Leijen, D.: Concurrent programming with revisions and isolation types. In: OOPSLA (2010)

 9. Cousot, P., Cousot, R.: Abstract interpretation: A unified lattice model for static analysis of programs by construction of approximation of fixed points. In: POPL (1977)
10. Dan, A., Meshman, Y., Vechev, M., Yahav, E.: Predicate abstraction for relaxed memory models. Tech. rep
11. Das, S., Dill, D.L., Park, S.: Experience with Predicate Abstraction. In: Halbwachs, N., Peled, D.A. (eds.) CAV 1999. LNCS, vol. 1633, pp. 160–171. Springer, Heidelberg (1999)
12. Dijkstra, E.: Cooperating sequential processes, TR EWD-123. Tech. rep., Technological University, Eindhoven (1965)
13. Donaldson, A., Kaiser, A., Kroening, D., Wahl, T.: Symmetry-aware predicate abstraction for shared-variable concurrent programs. In: Gopalakrishnan, G., Qadeer, S. (eds.) CAV 2011. LNCS, vol. 6806, pp. 356–371. Springer, Heidelberg (2011)
14. Dubois, M., Scheurich, C., Briggs, F.A.: Memory access buffering in multiprocessors. In: ISCA (1986)
15. Flanagan, C., Qadeer, S.: Predicate abstraction for software verification. In: POPL (2002)
16. Graf, S., Saïdi, H.: Construction of abstract state graphs with PVS. In: Grumberg, O. (ed.) CAV 1997, vol. 1254, pp. 72–83. Springer, Heidelberg (1997)
17. Gupta, A., Popeea, C., Rybalchenko, A.: Threader: A constraint-based verifier for multithreaded programs. In: Gopalakrishnan, G., Qadeer, S. (eds.) CAV 2011. LNCS, vol. 6806, pp. 412–417. Springer, Heidelberg (2011)
18. Henzinger, T.A., Jhala, R., Majumdar, R., Sutre, G.: Lazy abstraction. In: POPL (2002)
19. Huynh, T.Q., Roychoudhury, A.: Memory model sensitive bytecode verification. Form. Methods Syst. Des. (2007)
20. IBM. Power ISA v.2.05. (2007)
21. Jonsson, B.: State-space exploration for concurrent algorithms under weak memory orderings. SIGARCH Comput. Archit. News (2008)
22. Kuperstein, M., Vechev, M., Yahav, E.: Automatic inference of memory fences. In: FMCAD (2010)
23. Kuperstein, M., Vechev, M., Yahav, E.: Partial-coherence abstractions for relaxed memory models. In: PLDI (2011)
24. Lamport, L.: A new solution of Dijkstra's concurrent programming problem. Commun. ACM (1974)
25. Park, S., Dill, D.L.: An executable specification and verifier for relaxed memory order. IEEE Trans. on Computers 48 (1999)
26. Peterson, G.L.: Myths about the mutual exclusion problem. Inf. Process. Lett. 12(3) (1981)
27. Sarkar, S., Sewell, P., Nardelli, F.Z., Owens, S., Ridge, T., Braibant, T., Myreen, M.O., Alglave, J.: The semantics of x86-cc multiprocessor machine code. In: POPL (2009)
28. SPARC International, Inc. The SPARC architecture manual (version 9). Prentice-Hall, Inc., Upper Saddle River, NJ, USA (1994)
29. Szymanski, B.K.: A simple solution to Lamport's concurrent programming problem with linear wait. In: ICS (1988)

On Solving Universally Quantified Horn Clauses

Nikolaj Bjørner[1], Ken McMillan[1], and Andrey Rybalchenko[1,2]

[1] Microsoft Research
[2] Technische Universität München

Abstract. Program proving can be viewed as solving for unknown relations (such as loop invariants, procedure summaries and so on) that occur in the logical verification conditions of a program, such that the verification conditions are valid. Generic logical tools exist that can solve such problems modulo certain background theories, and therefore can be used for program analysis. Here, we extend these techniques to solve for *quantified* relations. This makes it possible to guide the solver by constraining the form of the proof, allowing it to converge when it otherwise would not. We show how to simulate existing abstract domains in this way, without having to directly implement program analyses or make certain heuristic choices, such as the terms and predicates that form the parameters of the abstract domain. Moreover, the approach gives the flexibility to go beyond these domains and experiment quickly with various invariant forms.

1 Introduction

Many problems of inference in program verification can be reduced to relational post-fixed point solving [13,4]. That is, to prove correctness of a program, we apply the rules of a program proof system to obtain purely logical proof subgoals. These subgoals are called the *verification conditions* or VC's. Proving validity of the VC's implies correctness of the program. The VC's generally contain auxiliary predicates such as inductive invariants, that must be *inferred*. Leaving these auxiliary predicates undefined (that is, as symbolic constants) the problem of inference becomes a problem of *solving* for unknown relations satisfying a set of logical constraints. In the simplest case, this is an SMT (satisfiability modulo theories) problem.

procedure $\pi(\text{ref } a : \text{int array}, N : \text{int})$:
   var i : int := 0;
   while $i < N$ **invariant** $P(a, i, N)$ **do**
     $a[i] := 0$;
     $i := i + 1$;
   done
   assert $\forall 0 \leq j < N.\ a[j] = 0$;

Consider, for example, the simple procedure on the left. The procedure sets elements $0 \ldots N - 1$ of array a to zero in a loop. We want to prove that on return, these array elements are in fact zero (leaving aside the question of array over-run). The loop is annotated with an invariant $P(a, i, N)$, an unknown predicate which we wish to discover in order to prove correctness.

F. Logozzo and M. Fähndrich (Eds.): SAS 2013, LNCS 7935, pp. 105–125, 2013.
© Springer-Verlag Berlin Heidelberg 2013

The *verification conditions* of this program are the following three logical formulas:

$$i = 0 \implies P(a, i, N) \tag{1}$$

$$P(a, i, N) \wedge i < N \implies P(a[i \leftarrow 0], i + 1, N) \tag{2}$$

$$P(a, i, N) \wedge \neg(i < N) \implies \forall 0 \leq j < N.\ a[i] = 0 \tag{3}$$

These are just the three proof obligations of the Hoare logic rule for while loops translated into logic. They say, respectively, that invariant $P(a, i, N)$ is initially true, that it is preserved by an iteration of the loop, and that it implies the post-condition of the loop on exit. Note in particular that $P(a[i \leftarrow 0], i + 1, N)$ is just the weakest precondition of $P(a, i, N)$ with respect to the loop body. The notation $a[i \leftarrow 0]$ means "array a with index i updated to 0".

The problem of proving the program thus reduces to finding an interpretation of the unknown predicate (or relation) P that makes the VC's valid. In the simplest case (technically, when the background theory is complete) a program proof is a satisfying assignment for the VC's. In our example, one solution is:

$$P(a, i, N) \equiv \forall 0 \leq j < i.\ a[j] = 0.$$

Of course this does not mean that we can in practice solve the VC's using existing SMT solvers. The VC's are valid when they are true with the free variables a, i, N universally quantified. SMT solvers generally cannot produce models for arbitrary quantified formulas.

There are specialized solvers, however, that can take advantage of the fact that the VC's fit a particular pattern. We will use the notation $\phi[X]$ to stand for a formula or term with free variables X. Our VC's have the form $\forall X.B[X] \implies H[X]$. We will call $B[X]$ the *body* of the VC and $H[X]$ the head. Our unknown relations such as P occur only in a limited way in these formulas: as the head, or as a conjunct of the body. Thus, supposing P, Q are our unknown relations, we could have $\forall x.\ x < 0 \wedge P(x) \implies Q(x)$ or $\forall x, y.\ P(x) \wedge Q(x, y) \implies x < y$ as VC's, but not $\forall x, y.\ x < y \implies P(x) \vee Q(x)$. Another way to say this is that our VC's are *constrained Horn clauses*.

Alternatively, we can view the VC's as a Constraint Logic Program (CLP) [20]. In our example, (1) and (2) are the clauses of the program. The VC (3) can be viewed as a safety property to be proved of the program, or its negation can be considered a *goal*, an *answer* to which would be a counterexample to program correctness. In fact, numerous schemes for capturing program semantics in CLP have been proposed [7,10,22].

A number of tools exist for solving constrained Horn clauses modulo different theories, or equivalently proving CLP programs. For example, QARMC can solve such problems modulo rational linear arithmetic. It uses a technique based on predicate abstraction [12] and Craig interpolation [26] that was generalized to trees [15]. Bjørner and Hoder describe a technique for the same theory that is an extension of property-driven reachability analysis [17]. A system called Duality [30] uses an extension of the IMPACT algorithm [27] to solve

$$i = 0 \implies \forall j. \ P(a[j], i) \tag{4}$$

$$\forall j. \ P(a[j], i) \wedge i < N \implies \forall j. \ P(a[i \leftarrow 0][j], i + 1) \tag{5}$$

$$\forall j. \ P(a[j], i) \wedge \neg(i < N) \implies \forall 0 \leq j < N. \ a[j] = 0 \tag{6}$$

Fig. 1. VC's generated for array initialization, with quantified invariant

problems in the combined theory of integer linear arithmetic and arrays, using an interpolating decision procedure for these theories [29]. Likewise, the Eldarica tool [32,19] takes as input constrained Horn clauses over Presburger arithmetic. The SPACER tool [24] combines CEGAR (counter example guided abstraction refinement) with 2BMC (bounded model checking based model checking) for solving Horn clauses.

Tools based on CLP include CiaoPP [16] which takes an abstract interpretation approach and TRACER [21] that uses a hybrid of symbolic execution, interpolation and abstract interpretation.

The advantage of such solvers is that they abstract away from particular programming languages and program proof systems. We can apply these solvers so long as we have a VC generator that produces VC's as (generalized) Horn formulas. Moreover, as we will see, they give us considerable flexibility to generate VC's in a way that guides or constrains the solution.

In this paper, we will consider such techniques, and show that by writing the VC's in an appropriate form, we can convey domain knowledge about the problem in a way that can simulate the effect of various abstract domains, without having to design and implement a custom program analysis, and without having to specify many of the parameters of these domains, as they can be inferred automatically by the solver. This makes it possible to experiment rapidly with various analyses. Based on this experience, one could then implement a custom analysis (say, using parameters of the abstract domain discovered by the solver for a class of programs) or simply apply the Horn solvers directly if their performance is adequate.

In particular, in this paper we will show that the process of solving for program proofs can be guided by choosing the logical form of the unknown assertions. To obtain universally quantified invariants in this way, we extend Horn solvers to handle *quantified predicates*. That is, we allow an unknown predicate P to appear in a VC as $\forall X. P(t[X])$, where $t[X]$ is a vector of terms with free variables X. This allows us to replace the invariant $P(a, i)$ in our example with, say, $\forall j. P(j, a[j], i, N)$. This tells us, in effect, that we have to write the invariant as a formula universally quantified over j, using just the terms j, $a[j]$, i and N. This new invariant assertion gives us the VC's shown in Figure 1, with quantified predicates.

One solution for these VC's is:

$$P(j, x, i, N) \equiv 0 \leq j < i \implies x = 0$$

Notice that substituting this definition into $\forall j.\ P(j, a[j], i, N)$ gives us $\forall j.\ 0 \leq j < i \implies a[j] = 0$, exactly the invariant we obtained previously.

The advantage of using this formulation of the problem is that it constrains the space of solutions in a way that causes the solver to converge, whereas with the more general formulation it may not converge. Another way to say this is that we have provided a restricted language for the inductive invariant. This restriction thus takes the heuristic role of an abstract domain, even though the solver itself may not be based on abstract interpretation. Note, though, that it is a rich abstract domain, since it does not restrict the Boolean structure of P or the set of arithmetic terms or relations that may occur in P.

We will show experimentally that, solving for quantified invariants in this form, we can simulate the effect of different abstract domains, such as the array segmentation domain of [6] and the Fluid Updates array abstraction of [9]. That is, we can induce a Horn clause solver to produce inductive proofs in a language at least as rich as these abstract domains, without implementing a custom program analysis, and without providing abstract domain parameters such as the segment boundary terms or data abstractions. Rather, we simply write the invariants to be solved for in an appropriate form. Moreover, quantified predicates provide us flexibility to solve problems that cannot be solved in these domains.

Related Work. Quite a variety of approaches have been taken to generation of quantified inductive invariants. Here, we will survey some of these methods and compare them to the present one. One line of work is based on interpolants. Quantification is used for interpolants describing unbounded ranges of arrays [23]; and in more recent work [2] by leveraging Model Checking Modulo Theories. Super-position theorem provers work directly with clauses corresponding to quantified formulas and this has been leveraged for extracting quantified invariants [28], [18]. Common to these approaches, and different from the current work, is that they aim to produce quantified invariants directly. The shape of quantification is left mostly unrestricted. In contrast, the current work takes as starting point a template space of quantified invariants and reduces the problem to quantifier-free invariant generation. A number of abstract interpretation methods have domains that represent universally quantified facts [14,11,5,31]. Here, we aim to avoid the explicit construction of abstract post operators, widenings and refinement procedures needed in these approaches. The constraint-based approach of [25] synthesizes a class of universally quantified linear invariants of array programs. We synthesize a broader class of invariants, without hints as to the index terms occurring in the invariants. In principle, however, a constraint-based linear invariant generator can be a back-end solver in our procedure.

There also exist solving techniques that support existential quantification in Horn clauses, i.e., a quantifier alternation in the form of forall/exists [3]. This approach computes witnesses to existential quantification in form of Skolem relations. The method also relies on a back-end Horn clause solver, however, an abstraction refinement loop is used to iteratively discover required witnesses.

That is, in contrast to the method presented here, [3] calls the back-end solver repeatedly.

2   Preliminaries

We use standard first-order logic over a signature Σ of function and predicate symbols of defined arities. Generally, we use a, b, c for constants (nullary function symbols), f, g for functions, P, Q, R for predicates, x, y, z for individual variables, t, u for terms. When we say a formula is *valid* or *satisfiable*, this is relative to a fixed background theory $\mathcal{T}$. A subset of the signature $\Sigma_I \subseteq \Sigma$ is considered to be *interpreted* by the theory. The *vocabulary* of a formula ϕ (the subset of Σ occurring in it) is denoted $L(\phi)$. The variables occurring free in ϕ are denoted $V(\phi)$. We will write $\phi[X]$ and $t[X]$ for a formula or term with free variables X. If P is a predicate symbol, we will say that a P-formula is a formula of the form $P(t_1, \ldots, t_n)$. If R is a set of symbols, we say ϕ is R-free when $L(\phi) \cap R = \emptyset$.

3   The Quantified Relational Post-fixed Point Problem

We now give a precise definition of the problem to be solved.

Definition 1. *A* constrained Horn clause *(in the sequel* CHC*) over a vocabulary of predicate symbols* $\mathcal{R}$ *is a formula of the form* $\forall X.B[X] \Rightarrow H[X]$ *where*

- *The* head $H[X]$ *is either a* P-formula, *or is* $\mathcal{R}$-free, *and*
- *The* body $B[X]$ *is a formula of the form* $\exists Y. \phi \wedge \psi_1 \wedge \cdots \psi_k$ *where* ϕ *is* $\mathcal{R}$-free *and* ψ_i *is a* P-formula for some $P \in \mathcal{R}$.

The clause is called a query *if the head is* $\mathcal{R}$-free, *else a* rule. *A rule with body* TRUE *is a* fact.

Definition 2. *A* relational post-fixed point problem *(RPFP) is a pair* $(\mathcal{R}, \mathcal{C})$, *where* $\mathcal{R}$ *is a set of predicate symbols (called the* nodes*) and* $\mathcal{C}$ *is a set of CHC's over* $\mathcal{R}$.

An RPFP is satisfiable if there is an interpretation of the predicate symbols $\mathcal{R}$, such that each constraint in $\mathcal{C}$ is true under the interpretation. Thus, an interpretation provides a *solution* to an RPFP. We are here interested in effective ways to establish satisfiability of RPFPs and will search for interpretations that can be expressed as formulas using the existing vocabulary. We call the resulting solutions *symbolic solutions*, explained next.

We will refer to $\Sigma \setminus \mathcal{R}$ as the *background vocabulary*. A *symbolic relation* is a term of the form $\lambda.\bar{x}. \phi[\bar{x}]$ where $\bar{x}$ is a vector of distinct variables, such that $L(\phi) \subseteq \Sigma \setminus \mathcal{R}$ (that is, ϕ is over only the background vocabulary). A symbolic relational interpretation σ over $\mathcal{R}$ is a map from symbols in $\mathcal{R}$ to symbolic relations of the appropriate arity. If ψ is a formula, we write $\psi\sigma$ to denote ψ with $\sigma(R)$ substituted for each $R \in \mathcal{R}$ and β-reduction applied. For example, if ψ is $R(a, b)$ and $\sigma(R)$ is $\lambda x, y. \ x < y$, then $\psi\sigma$ is $a < b$.

Definition 3. *A symbolic solution of RPFP $(\mathcal{R}, \mathcal{C})$ is a symbolic relational interpretation over $\mathcal{R}$ such that, for all $C \in \mathcal{C}$, $C\sigma$ is valid (relative to theory $\mathcal{T}$).*

A subtle point worth noting here is that a solution of an RPFP depends on the interpretation of the background symbols. If the background theory is complete (meaning it has a unique model up to isomorphism) then this gives a unique interpretation of $\mathcal{R}$. We can therefore think of an RPFP as a special case of an SMT problem. If $\mathcal{T}$ is incomplete, however (say it includes uninterpreted function symbols) then the symbolic solution effectively gives an interpretation of $\mathcal{R}$ for each theory model. This allows us to leave aspects of the program semantics (say, the heap model) incompletely defined, yet still prove the program correct.

3.1 Refutations and Derivation Trees

If a solution of the VC's corresponds to a proof of the program, one might ask what corresponds to a counterexample (that is, a proof the program is incorrect). One way to view this is that a set of rules has a minimal model, that is, a least interpretation of the predicate symbols by set containment that satisfies the rules. An RPFP is satisfiable exactly when the minimal model of its rules satisfies all of its queries. The minimal model of the rules is the set of ground facts that can be derived from ground instances of the rules by unit resolution. An RPFP can thus be refuted (proved unsatisfiable) by a ground derivation of FALSE.

As an example, consider the following RPFP:

$$x = y \implies P(x, y) \tag{7}$$
$$P(x, y) \wedge z = y + 1 \implies P(x, z) \tag{8}$$
$$P(x, y) \wedge P(y, z) \implies Q(x, z) \tag{9}$$
$$Q(x, z) \implies x + 2 \leq z \tag{10}$$

We can think of these formulas as the VC's of a program with two procedures, P and Q. Procedure P is recursive and either returns its input (7) or calls itself and returns the result plus one (8). Procedure Q calls P twice (9). The query represents a specification that Q increments its argument by at least two (10). The program does not satisfy this specification, which we can prove by the following ground derivation. First, from (7), setting $x = y = 0$, we derive the ground fact $P(0, 0)$. Then from (9), setting $x = y = z = 0$, we obtain $P(0, 0) \wedge P(0, 0) \implies Q(0, 0)$. Resolving with $P(0, 0)$, we derive $Q(0, 0)$. Then from (10), setting $x = z = 0$, we obtain $Q(0, 0) \implies$ FALSE. Resolving with $Q(0, 0)$, we obtain FALSE. This refutation can also be thought of as an execution of the program that does not satisfy the specification.

We can discover a refutation by constructing a *derivation tree*, by a process that is essentially logic program execution. A derivation tree is obtained by starting with a query and successively unifying $\mathcal{R}$-predicates in bodies with heads of rules until we reach facts. In our example, we might obtain the derivation tree

$\neg x + 2 \leq z \wedge Q(x,z) \Rightarrow false$ $\neg(x + 2 \leq z)$ $Q(0,1) \Rightarrow false$

$P(x,y) \wedge P(y,z) \Rightarrow Q(x,z)$ $true$ $P(0,0) \wedge P(0,1) \Rightarrow Q(0,1)$

$x = y \Rightarrow P(x,y)$ $x = y$ $P(0,0)$

$P(y,y') \wedge z = y' + 1 \Rightarrow P(y,z)$ $z = y' + 1$ $P(0,0) \Rightarrow P(0,1)$

$y = y' \Rightarrow P(y,y')$ $y = y'$ $P(0,0)$

(a)   (b)   (c)

Fig. 2. Deriving a refutation (a) Derivation tree. Arrows represent unification steps. (b) Constraint tree. (c) Resulting ground refutation.

of Figure 2(a). Extracting the constraints from these clauses, we obtain the constraint tree shown in Figure 2(b). If these constraints are satisfiable, substituting the satisfying assignment into the derivation tree gives us a ground derivation of FALSE, as shown in Figure 2(c). On the other hand, showing satisfiability of the RPFP is equivalent to proving unsatisfiability of all possible derivation trees. This view will be useful later when we discuss quantifier instantiation.

3.2 Solving RPFP's

A variety of techniques can be applied to solve RPFP's symbolically or produce refutations. For example, ARMC [13] applies predicate abstraction [12]. Given a set $\mathcal{P}$ of atomic predicates, it synthesizes the strongest map from $\mathcal{R}$ to Boolean combinations (alternatively cubes) over $\mathcal{P}$ that solves the problem. The predicates are derived from interpolants for unsatisfiable derivation trees. Various other methods are available [30,17] but all synthesize the solution in some manner from solutions of finite unwindings of the clause set.

All these methods may diverge by producing an infinite sequence of approximations to a solution. For example, in our array initialization example above, we may first consider just one iteration of the loop, deriving an approximation of the loop invariant $P(i, a, N)$ that involves the predicate $a[0] = 0$. Then we consider two iterations of the loop, obtaining $a[1] = 0$ and so on *ad infinitum*. In short, we need some way to tell the tool that the invariant must involve a quantifier.

3.3 Quantified Predicates

To do this, we will allow our symbolic program assertions to contain quantifiers. We say that a $\forall P$-formula is a formula of the form $\forall Y.P(t)$. We extend constrained Horn clauses to *quantified* Horn clauses as follows:

Definition 4. *A* quantified Horn clause *(in the sequel* QHC*) over a vocabulary of predicate symbols $\mathcal{R}$ is a formula of the form $\forall X.B[X] \Rightarrow H[X]$ where*

- *The* head $H[X]$ *is either a $\forall P$-formula, or is $\mathcal{R}$-free, and*

– *The body $B[X]$ is a formula of the form $\exists Y.\ \phi \wedge \psi_1 \wedge \cdots \psi_k$ where ϕ is $\mathcal{R}$-free and ψ_i is a $\forall P$-formula for some $P \in \mathcal{R}$.*

The only difference from the previous definition is that we use $\forall P$-formulas in place of P-formulas. This allows us to express VC's such as those in our second version of the array initialization problem (4–6).

We first observe that a universal quantifier in the head of a rule poses no difficulty, as it can simply be shifted to prenex position. That is, the formula

$$\forall X.\ B[X] \implies \forall Y.P(t)$$

is equi-valid to

$$\forall X, S.\ B[X] \implies P(t)\langle S/Y \rangle$$

where S is a set of fresh variables. The difficulty lies, rather, in the $\forall P$-formulas that occur as conjuncts in the body $B[X]$. We can think of these formulas as representing an infinity of groundings.

As a result, derivation trees are now infinitely branching. Consider, for example, this rule:

$$(\forall y.\ P(x, y)) \implies Q(x)$$

The rule requires an infinite set of tuples $P(x, y)$ to derive a single tuple $Q(x)$. One can also easily construct cases where the only feasible derivation tree has infinite height. For example, in the theory of arithmetic:

$$x = 0 \implies P(x)$$
$$P(x) \implies P(x + 1)$$
$$(\forall 0 \le y.\ P(y)) \implies Q$$

A derivation of Q requires an infinite set of subtrees corresponding to $P(0), P(1),$ $P(2), \ldots,$ where the derivation of $P(k)$ is of height $k + 1$. Thus, the height of the derivation of Q is ω.

A similar example illustrates that finite quantifier instantiation is incomplete for establishing satisfiability of RPFP's. Consider the system below.

$$P(0, 1)$$
$$P(x, y) \implies P(x, y + 1)$$
$$P(x, y) \implies P(x + 1, y + 1)$$
$$(\forall x.\ P(x, y)) \implies Q(y) \tag{11}$$
$$Q(x) \implies \text{FALSE}$$

It exploits that compactness does not hold for the theory of natural numbers. It is satisfiable with symbolic solution $P(x, y) \equiv x < y$, $Q(y) \equiv \text{FALSE}$; yet every finite instantiation $P(a_1, y) \wedge \ldots P(a_n, y) \implies Q(y)$ of the quantified clause (11) produces a stronger system that is unsatisfiable. We have yet to encounter applications from program analysis where this source of incompleteness is significant.

The approach we will take to quantifiers is the same as is typically taken in SMT solvers: we will replace a universally quantified formula by a finite set of its instances. Say that an *instantiation* of a formula $\forall Y. P(t)$ is $P(t)\langle S/Y \rangle$ for some vector of terms S. We can show:

Theorem 1. *Let Π be a quantified RPFP and let Π' be an unquantified RPFP obtained by shifting quantifiers in the heads of the rules to prenex position and replacing each $\forall P$ formula in a body by a finite conjunction of its instantiations. Then a solution of Π' is also a solution of Π.*

Proof. A conjunction of instantiations of a universal formula ϕ is implied by ϕ. Thus, the body of a QHC in the instantiated Π' is implied by the corresponding body in Π. Since the bodies are on the left-hand side of the implications, it follows that the constraints in Π' imply the corresponding constraints in Π. A solution of Π' is thus a solution of Π.   □.

This means that if we replace any $\forall P$-formula with a finite instantiation, any proof of the program we obtain is valid. However, a counterexample may not be valid. By adding one more instance, we may find the counterexample ruled out. Thus, finite instantiation is a conservative abstraction.

In this paper we will consider a simple syntactic approach to generate finite instantiations, relying on Theorem 1. It uses pattern-matching heuristics to instantiate the universals in the QHC bodies. The resulting problem Π' can then be solved by any of the available RPFP solvers. Any solution of Π' is also a solution of Π and thus implies correctness of the program. This approach has the advantage that it leaves the solver itself unchanged. Thus, we can apply any available solver for unquantified Horn clauses.

4 Trigger-Based Quantifier Instantiation

The syntactic approach can be applied as a pre-processing step on the RPFP. It operates in a matter that is inspired by quantifier instantiation in SMT solvers [8]. We begin with the theory of equality and uninterpreted functions, and then extend to cover the theory of arrays. For the programs we have analyzed here, it was sufficient to treat arithmetical symbols $+, \times$ as uninterpreted.

4.1 Theory of Equality

Trigger-based instantiation [8] is a method for instantiating universal quantifiers. The *current goal* of the prover is a set of literals whose satisfiability is to be determined. Quantifiers in the current goal are annotated by triggers, that is, terms containing all the quantified variables. A *match* is any variable substitution that takes a trigger to an existing ground term from the current goal, modulo the set of asserted equalities in the current goal.

$$i_0 = 0 \implies P(a_0[k_0], i_0) \tag{12}$$

$$\forall j_1.\ P(a_1[j_1], i_1) \wedge i_1 < N_1 \implies P(a_1[i_1 \leftarrow 0][k_1], i_1 + 1) \tag{13}$$

$$\forall j_2.\ P(a_2[j_2], i_2) \wedge \neg(i_2 < N_2) \implies 0 \leq k_2 < N_2 \implies a_2[k_2] = 0 \tag{14}$$

Fig. 3. VC's generated for array initialization, after shifting head quantifiers to prenex

The intuition behind trigger-based instantiation as stated in [8] is that an instance of a universal is likely to be relevant if it contains many terms that can be proved equal to existing terms. Here, unlike in [8], we wish to find such instances in advance of doing any actual deduction. Thus we will produce an *over-approximation* of the equality relation, considering terms equal if they *may* be proved equal in some propositional case. Moreover, we wish to produce enough instantiations to make all of the derivation trees unsatisfiable. Thus the proofs we are considering are proofs of unsatisfiability of the constraints in these trees. For this reason, we will consider two terms possibly equal if two instances of these terms may be inferred to be equal in some derivation tree.

To discover instantiations of $\forall P$-formulas in quantified clauses we build a structure called an E-graph [8]. The E-graph is a term DAG with an equivalence relation over the nodes. It provides a compact representation of a collection of terms that might be generated by instantiating axioms of the theory of equality. We produce instantiations by matching terms containing bound variables against terms represented in the E-graph.

Consider, for example, our array initialization problem of Figure 1. For now, we consider the array operators $\cdot[\cdot]$ and $\cdot[\cdot \leftarrow \cdot]$ to be uninterpreted functions. We begin by shifting head quantifiers to prenex (introducing fresh variables k_i) to obtain the QHC's of Figure 3. We also rename the bound variables so they are distinct.

The E-graph we obtain from these formulas is shown in Figure 4. It contains all of the terms occurring outside of $\forall P$-formulas. It merges the terms i_0, 0 and $a_2[k_2]$ into an equality class, due to the presence of equalities in the formulas. Then we try to match certain terms within $\forall P$-formulas called *triggers* with terms represented in the E-graph, to produce instantiations of the variables. We never match bare variables, hence the matched terms must always agree on at least the top-level function symbol. In practice, we use array select terms as triggers. The process of matching triggers against the E-graph to produce instantiations is called E-matching. The exact set of matching terms we produce from the E-graph is a heuristic choice.

In the example, we can match $a_2[j_2]$ with the E-graph term $a_2[k_2]$, using the unifier $j_2 = k_2$. We use this assignment to instantiate the quantifier in (14). This gives us the instance $P(a_2[k_2], i_2)$. We now merge the arguments of P in this term with corresponding arguments in the heads of the rules. Thus, we merge $a_2[k_2]$ with $a_1[i_1 \leftarrow 0][k_1]$ and with $a_0[k_0]$, and we merge i_2 with $i_1 + 1$ and i_0 in the E-graph. We do this because these terms might be unified in the construction

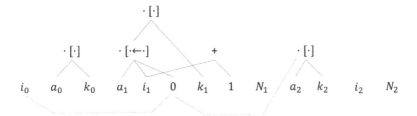

Fig. 4. Starting E-graph for formulas of Figure 3. Dashed lines represent equality classes.

of a derivation tree. In principle this merge might give us new matches, but in this case no new matches result. In particular, there is no match for $a_1[\cdot]$, so we still have no instances of P in the body of rule (13), leaving the instantiated system unsolvable.

4.2 Theory of Arrays

To solve this problem, we need to attach semantics to the array operations select and store. In particular, we need to take into account that $a[x \leftarrow y][z]$ may equal $a[z]$ (in the case when $x \neq z$). We do this by adding the axioms of the array theory to the mix. These are:

$$\forall a, i, d.\ a[i \leftarrow d][i] = d$$
$$\forall a, i, j, d.\ (i = j) \vee a[i \leftarrow d][j] = a[j]$$

The trigger associated with the first axiom is $a[i \leftarrow d][i]$. The second axiom contains the sub-term $a[i \leftarrow d][j]$ that contains all the bound variables and we use it as a trigger. In our example, this trigger matches the term $a_1[i_1 \leftarrow 0][k_1]$ in the E-graph, producing the instance $(i_1 = k_1) \vee a_1[i_1 \leftarrow 0][k_1] = a_1[k_1]$. This contributes the term $a_1[k_1]$ to the E-graph, which then matches $a_1[j_0]$ to give the instance $P(a_1[k_1], i_1)$. Adding this instance, we merge $a_1[k_1]$ with $a_1[i_1 \leftarrow 0][a_0]$ and i_1 with $i_1 + 1$ in the E-graph. This results in no further matches, so instantiation terminates. Note that matching with the first axiom never produces new terms, so we need not consider it. The final E-graph after quantifier instantiation is shown in Figure 5.

Now, replacing the $\forall P$-formulas with the obtained instantiations, we have the instantiated problem Π' shown in Figure 6. This problem has a solution, for example, the same solution we obtained for the original quantified problem:

$$P(j, x, i, N) \equiv 0 \leq j < i \implies x = 0$$

One can verify this solution by plugging in the definition of P and checking validity of the resulting quantifier free formulas with an SMT solver.

As a side-remark we note that trigger-based quantifier instantiation becomes a complete decision procedure for the existential theory of non-extensional arrays

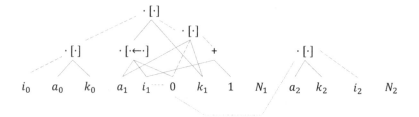

Fig. 5. Final E-graph for formulas of Figure 1

$$i_0 = 0 \implies P(a_0[k_0], i_0) \tag{15}$$
$$P(a_1[k_1], i_1) \wedge i_1 < N_1 \implies P(a_1[i_1 \leftarrow 0][k_1], i_1 + 1) \tag{16}$$
$$P(a_2[k_2], i_2) \wedge \neg(i_2 < N_2) \implies 0 \leq k_2 < N_2 \implies a_2[k_2] = 0 \tag{17}$$

Fig. 6. VC's generated for array initialization example, after instantiation

if we also add the two terms $a[i \leftarrow d], a[j]$ as a joint trigger (called multi-pattern) to the second array axiom. But it is well recognized that this axiom is irrelevant for verification conditions from programs (where the same array does not get updated in two different ways), so we disregard this trigger in our experiments.

4.3   Algorithm

Figure 7 shows a high-level algorithm for trigger-based instantiation, based on standard techniques for E-matching [8]. We start by shifting quantifiers, then collect the $\forall P$-formulas from the bodies, adding axioms of the theory. These are the universal formulas to be instantiated. Then we build an E-graph, merging terms based on equalities in the formulas. We then enter a loop, instantiating the quantified formulas using the E-graph. Each time an instance matches the head of a rule, we merge the corresponding arguments in the E-graph. Finally, for each $\forall P$-formula in a rule C, we gather the instances that are expressed using the variables of C (thus if the instance contains a variable from another constraint, we reject it as irrelevant). The conjunction of these instances replaces the $\forall P$-formula.

In principle, we may have a matching loop. For example, suppose we have the quantified formula $\forall y.\ P(g(y), g(f(y)))$ in $\mathcal{P}$ and associated trigger $g(y)$ and a term $g(a)$ in the E-graph. We can then obtain an infinite sequence of instantiations: First y is instantiated with a producing the grounding $P(g(a), g(f(a)))$. The E-graph is updated with the term $g(f(a))$ terms $g(a), g(f(a)), g(f(f(a))), \ldots$ Though we have not seen this in practice, it would be possible to terminate such loops by putting a bound on term size.

As in SMT solvers, the trigger-based instantiation approach is heuristic. It may or may not generate the instances needed to obtain a proof. Moreover, we

Algorithm *Trigger-instantiate*
Input: a set of QHC's C
Output: instantiations of C

Shift head quantifiers in C to prenex position.
Let $\mathcal{P}$ be the set of $\forall P$-formulas in C.
Let $\mathcal{Q}$ be $\mathcal{P}$ with the array theory axioms added.
Let E be an empty E-graph.
Add the ground terms of C to E.
For every ground equality $x = y$ in C, merge x and y in E.
Let $\mathcal{I}$ be the empty set of formulas.
Repeat:
    Let $\mathcal{G}$ be the instances of $\mathcal{Q}$ obtained by E-matching with E.
    Add $\mathcal{G}$ to $\mathcal{I}$.
    Add the ground terms of $\mathcal{G}$ to E.
    For every instance $G \in \mathcal{G}$ of some formula $\forall Y.\ P(t)$ in $\mathcal{P}$, do
        For every head $P(u)$ of a rule in C, do
            Merge t with u in E. (*)
Until no change in $\mathcal{I}$.
For each formula ϕ in $\mathcal{P}$, where ϕ occurs in QHC $C \in \mathcal{C}$ do
    Let $\mathcal{I}_\phi$ be the set of instances ψ of ϕ in $\mathcal{I}$ s.t. $V(\psi) \subseteq V(C)$
        Substitute $\wedge \mathcal{I}_\phi$ for ϕ in C
Return C.

Fig. 7. Trigger-based instantiation algorithm

must view the counterexamples (*i.e.*, derivation trees) generated by the solver as
suspect, since they contain only a finite subset of the instances of the universals.
We will observe in Section 5, however, that a reasonably precise analysis can be
obtained with these fairly simple heuristics.

In fact, in our experiments, we have found a more restrictive instantiation
policy to be adequate. That is, we only instantiate variables with *existing* terms
(not all terms represented in the E-graph) and we instantiate each QHC in isolation. Reducing the number of irrelevant instances in this way tends to improve
the solver performance.

In summary we have the following variants and restrictions of Algorithm
Trigger-instantiate:

Inter vs. intraprocedural: The algorithm takes a set C of Horn clauses as
input. In one extreme take C as the entire set of clauses to be checked for
satisfiability. In the other extreme process each clause C_i by setting C to
$\{C_i\}$ and invoke the instantiation algorithm.

Instantiation vocabulary: The E-graph represents potentially an infinite
number of terms. For example, if a and $f(a)$ are merged in E, then E
encodes that $f(f(a)) = a$. Each of the terms $f(a)$, $f(f(a))$, $f(f(f(a)))$,
etc. can be used as representatives for a. Different instances of Algorithm
Trigger-instantiate are obtained by bounding the number of representatives

admitted for each match. Since the algorithm uses *may* equality, it becomes highly incomplete if only a single match is admitted.

Instantiation depth: SMT solvers manage quantifier instantiations using a priority queue of instances. An instantiation is *heavy* if it uses terms that were constructed by a long sequence of instantiations. Lighter (younger) terms are preferred. Likewise, our pre-processing instantiation can cut off instantiations based on a maximal weight.

5   Applications

We now consider some applications of quantified RPFP solving. We will observe that by choosing our symbolic invariants appropriately, we can simulate the effect of some abstract domains from the literature. In this way, we can avoid implementing a custom analysis. As we sill see, we can also avoid the problem of tuning the parameters of the abstract domain, since the values of these parameters can be extracted automatically.

5.1   Simulating Array Segmentation Abstractions

Cousot, Cousot and Logozzo describe an *array segmentation functor* for analyzing programs that manipulate arrays [6]. This is a parametrized class of abstract domains that characterize the contents of an array. An abstract array is divided into segments, that is, consecutive subsets of the array elements that are divided by symbolic index expressions. The elements in each segment are characterized by a chosen abstract domain on data. Both the segment boundary expressions and the data domain may depend on scalar variables in the program.

As an example, the following expression represents an array that contains a segment of zeros for indices $0 \ldots i - 1$ and a segment of arbitrary values for indices $\geq i$:

{0} 0 {i}? T {A.Length}?

The symbol T stands for the top element of the data domain. The question marks indicate that the preceding segment may be empty. This abstract array can be expressed in logical form as

$$\forall x.\ 0 \leq \mathtt{i} \leq \mathtt{A.Length} \wedge (0 \leq x < i \implies \mathtt{A}[x] = 0)$$

In fact, *any* abstract array can be expressed by a predicate in integer linear arithmetic of the form $\forall x.\ P(x, A[x], \boldsymbol{v})$ where A is the array and $\boldsymbol{v}$ are the scalar variables of the program, provided the data domain is expressible in the logic. Now suppose we decorate a program with symbolic invariants of this form, for every array A in the program. It follows that if the array segmentation functor can prove the program for some value of its parameters, then the resulting RPFP has a solution, thus we can in principle prove the program using an RPFP solver.

```
public Random(int Seed) {
  Contract.Requires(Seed != Int32.MinValue);
  int num2 = 161803398 - Math.Abs(Seed);
  this.SeedArray = new int [56];
  this.SeedArray [55] = num2;
  int num3 = 1;
  // Loop 1
  for (int i = 1; i < 55; i++) {
    int index = (21 * i) % 55;
    this.SeedArray [index] = num3;  // (*)
    num3 = num2 - num3;
    if (num3 < 0) num3 += 2147483647;
    num2 = this.SeedArray [index];
  }
  Contract.Assert (Contract.Forall( // (**)
    0, this.SeedArray.Length - 1, i => a[i] >= -1));
  // Loop 2
  for (int j = 1; j < 5; j++) {
    // Loop 3
    for (int k = 1; k < 56; k++) {
      this.SeedArray [k] -= this.SeedArray [1 + (k + 30) % 55];
      if (this.SeedArray [k] < 0)
        this.SeedArray [k] += 2147483647;
  } }
  Contract.Assert (Contract.Forall (0, // (***)
    this.SeedArray.Length, i => a[i] >= -1));
}
```

Fig. 8. Motivating example for Array Segmentation Functor

As a motivating example, consider the program from [6], shown in Figure 8. When the array this.SeedArray is created, it is implicitly initialized to all zero. After the first loop, we must prove that all the elements of array but the last are ≥ -1 (this is the semantics of Contract.Forall). We decorate Loop 1 with a symbolic invariant $\forall x.\ P(x, \text{this.SeedArray}[x], v)$, where v contains the program's integer variables. We then generate the verification conditions for the loop. The VC's are encoded into integer arithmetic. Since the actual program variables are bit vectors, we must test each integer operation for overflow. This gives us an RPFP Π with one unknown predicate P. We instantiate Π using trigger-based instantiation to get the quantifier-free problem Π'. We then used Duality to solve Π' for P, obtaining the following inductive invariant for the loop:

$$\forall x.\ \begin{pmatrix} (\text{num2} \geq -2147483648 \vee \text{num2} \leq 2147483647) \\ \wedge(0 \leq \text{num3} + 1) \\ \wedge(0 \leq \text{this.SeedArray}[x] + 1 \vee 0 \leq x - 55) \end{pmatrix}$$

The first conjunct of this invariant is equivalent to TRUE. The second says that the scalar num3 is ≥ -1 while the third says that the array value is ≥ -1 for all all indices < 55. Note, this applies to negative indices as well, though it would be a run-time error to access these.

Notice that we obtained this result using a generic solver, without implementing a custom analysis. Notice also that the segment boundary 55 and the data predicate $0 \leq$ this.SeedArray$[x] + 1$ were generated in the solving process, so we did not have to provide these as a parameter of the abstraction. The run-time of the tool was 0.3 seconds. This is undoubtedly slower than the custom analysis of [6]. On the other hand, it might be fast enough for some applications. The method can similarly solve for an inductive invariant of the second loop.

A more significant advantage to this approach is the flexibility it provides to experiment with abstractions. For example, suppose we need an invariant that relates the values of corresponding elements of two arrays a and b. We could use the symbolic invariant $\forall x.\ P(x, a[x], b[x], v)$. Or suppose we need to relate distant elements of the arrays. We could then use two quantifiers, expressing the desired invariant in the form $\forall x, y,\ (x, a[x], y, b[y], v)$. This would allow us to express the fact, for example, that a is the reverse of b, as follows: $\forall x, y.\ 0 \leq x < N \wedge y = N - x \implies a[x] = b[y]$. To implement this using the array segmentation functor would be a significant manual effort, as we would have to implement a component abstract domain that names array segments with a corresponding segment unification procedure, introduce auxiliary variables to represent array segment values and introduce the appropriate terms and relations, including the relation $y = N - x$, into the scalar abstraction. Here, we simply change the form of the symbolic invariant that annotates the program. The necessary terms and predicates can be synthesized by the Horn solvers.

5.2   Simulating the Fluid Updates Abstraction

The Fluid Updates method of Aiken, Dillig and Dillig [9] provides a richer abstract domain for arrays. The abstraction can symbolically represent pair-wise points-to relations between arrays. A points-to relation is represented by a triple $a[x] \to \phi \to b[y]$, where a and b are symbolic terms representing locations and containing parameters x and y, and ϕ is a may- or must-condition for $a[x]$ to point to $b[y]$. For example, to write that all the elements of the array pointed to by a up to $i - 1$ are zero, we would write a must relation $(*a)[j] \to 0 \leq j < N \to *0$, where we think of the constant zero as a pointer to a zero object.

We can express all such relationships logically using predicates of the form $\forall x, y.\ P(x, a[x], b[y], v)$, where $a[x]$ and $b[y]$ are location terms and v contains scalar program variables. For example, the must relationship

$$a[x] \to 0 \leq x < N \wedge y = N - x \to b[y]$$

says that element x of array a must point to element $N - x$ of array b. This can be expressed as

$$\forall x, y.\ 0 \leq x < N \wedge y = N - x \implies \text{pto}(a[x], b[y])$$

where pto represents the points-to relation. The corresponding may relationship is

$$\forall x, y.\ \text{pto}(a[x], b[y]) \implies 0 \leq x < N \wedge y = N - x.$$

In the case where $b[x]$ is $*t$ for some integer-valued term t, the relation pto becomes simply equality over integers.

Using this scheme, we can capture the information available in the Fluid Updates abstraction by simply decorating the program with symbolic invariants of the form $\forall x, y.\ P(x, a[x], b[y], \boldsymbol{v})$, for any pairs of location terms $a[x]$ and $b[y]$ we wish to track. We can, if desired, narrow down the pairs tracked using any available points-to analysis.

To test this idea, we constructed the VC's manually for the set of synthetic test programs used in [9]. We used the quantifier instantiation procedure of section 4 in the intraprocedural mode, with the restrictive instantiation policy. No matching loops were observed. Table 1 shows the performance we obtained solving these instantiated VC's using the Horn solving engine of Z3 [17], ARMC [13], and Duality, compared to the results of [9]. Run times should be considered approximate as machine speeds may differ slightly. A question mark indicates the tool could not process the problem. In Duality, we used a recent interpolation technique that handles linear rational arithmetic [1]. It is slower, but has better convergence behavior than the proof-based method of [29]. Integer arithmetic and the theory of arrays are handled by eager axiom instantiation. We observe that each tool is able to solve most of the problems, though the performance is not always as good as the Fluid Updates method. All tools fail for one case (init_even). This requires a divisibility constraint in the invariant, which none of the tools supports. All the other problems can be solved by at least one tool. Thus, using generic Horn solvers, we obtain results similar to what can be obtained using a specialized abstract domain.

Again, however, we observe that using symbolic invariants gives us flexibility not available in an analysis tool implementing a particular abstract domain. Consider, for example, the following simple fragment:

```
var i : int := 0;
while i < N do
    c[i] := a[i] - b[i];
    i := i + 1;
done
assert ∀0 ≤ j < N. c[j] = a[j] − b[j];
```

To prove the assertion, we must track the values in three arrays. To extend Fluid Updates to handle this case would require modifying the tool. To handle this example using symbolic invariants, we simply decorate the loop with the predicate $\forall x.\ P(x, a[x], b[x], c[x], i, N)$ and solve for P. If we need to relate distinct indices in the arrays, we can simply add another quantifier.

Table 1. Performance on synthetic array benchmarks. Run times in seconds.

example	[9]	Z3 Horn	ARMC	Duality
init	0.01	0.06	0.15	0.72
init_non_constant	0.02	0.08	0.48	6.60
init_partial	0.01	0.03	0.14	2.60
init_partial_BUG	0.02	0.01	0.07	0.03
init_even	0.04	TO	?	TO
_2Darray_init	0.04	0.18	?	TO
copy	0.01	0.04	0.20	1.40
copy_partial	0.01	0.04	0.21	1.80
copy_odd	0.04	TO	?	4.50
reverse	0.03	0.12	2.28	8.50
reverse_BUG	0.04	0.01	0.08	0.03
check_swap	0.12	0.41	3.0	40.60
check_double_swap	0.16	1.37	4.4	TO
check_strcpy	0.07	0.05	0.15	0.62
check_strlen	0.02	0.07	0.02	0.20
check_strlen_BUG	0.01	0.07	?	0.03
check_memcpy	0.04	0.04	0.20	16.30
find	0.02	0.01	0.08	0.38
find_first_nonnull	0.02	0.01	0.08	0.39
array_append	0.02	0.04	1.76	1.50
merge_interleave	0.09	0.04	?	1.50
alloc_fixed_size	0.02	0.02	0.09	0.69
alloc_nonfixed_size	0.03	0.03	0.13	0.42

5.3   Proving Termination

Using the generic Horn solver at the back-end allows one to prove termination of array manipulating problem without constructing a specialized termination checker for programs over arrays.

For example, our approach proves termination of the following program.

```
void main () {
  int i, n, x, a[n];
  for(i = 0; i < n; i++) {
    a[i] = 1;
  }
  x = read_int();
  while (x > 0) {
    for(i = 0; i < n; i++) x = x-a[i];
  }
}
```

Here, termination of the while loop depends on the values stored in the array. We trigger termination proving by requiring that the restriction of the transition relation of the program with the quantified invariants, which needs to be inferred accordingly, is disjunctively well-founded. After the quantifier instantiation step, ARMC [13] proves termination of all loops in 1.7 sec.

6   Conclusion

Program proving can be reduced to solving a symbolic relation post-fixed point problem. We decorate the program with suitable symbolic invariants (which may be loop invariants, procedure summaries, and so on) yielding the verification conditions which can then be *solved* to produce a program proof. Generic solvers exist to solve these problems modulo various background theories.

We observed that by adjusting the form of the desired proof, we can guide the solver to produce a proof when it would otherwise fail. In particular, we extended RPFP solvers to handle *quantified* symbolic invariants. This allows us to solve for invariants within a restricted domain by choosing the form of the invariant, chiefly its quantifier structure. This allows us to simulate existing abstract domains using a generic solver, without having to directly implement these domains or make certain heuristic choices, such as the terms and predicates that form the parameters of the abstract domain. Moreover the approach gives the flexibility to go beyond these domains and experiment quickly with various invariant forms. It also allows us to guide the proof search by using alternative proof decompositions, without changing the underlying solver.

One view of this approach is as a way of rapidly prototyping program analyses. If the performance of the prototype is adequate, we may simply apply the generic logical solver. If not, we may use the results as a guide to a more efficient custom implementation.

We observed that the primary difficulty in solving for quantified symbolic invariants is in *quantifier instantiation*. We apply simple trigger-based heuristics, similar to those used in SMT solvers, but adapted to our purpose. These heuristics were found adequate in some cases, but clearly more work is needed in this area, perhaps applying model-based quantifier instantiation methods, or judiciously leveraging quantifier elimination methods when they are available, or controlling instantiation using an abstraction refinement methodology. This remains for future work, as does the question of synthesizing quantifier alternations.

Finally, we have here explored only a small part of the space of possible applications of such methods. For example, properties involving the shape of heap data structures can in principle be expressed, for example, using a reachability predicate. It remains to be seen whether relational fixed point solving techniques could be applied to generate invariants in rich domains such as this.

Acknowledgements. This research was supported in part by ERC project 308125 VeriSynth.

References

1. Albarghouthi, A., McMillan, K.L.: Beautiful interpolants. In: CAV (2013)
2. Alberti, F., Bruttomesso, R., Ghilardi, S., Ranise, S., Sharygina, N.: Lazy abstraction with interpolants for arrays. In: Bjørner, N., Voronkov, A. (eds.) LPAR-18 2012. LNCS, vol. 7180, pp. 46–61. Springer, Heidelberg (2012)
3. Beyene, T.A., Popeea, C., Rybalchenko, A.: Solving existentially quantified Horn clauses. In: CAV (2013)
4. Bjørner, N., McMillan, K.L., Rybalchenko, A.: Program verification as Satisfiability Modulo Theories. In: SMT (2012)
5. Cousot, P.: Verification by abstract interpretation. In: Dershowitz, N. (ed.) Verification (Manna Festschrift). LNCS, vol. 2772, pp. 243–268. Springer, Heidelberg (2004)
6. Cousot, P., Cousot, R., Logozzo, F.: A parametric segmentation functor for fully automatic and scalable array content analysis. In: POPL (2011)
7. Delzanno, G., Podelski, A.: Model Checking in CLP. In: Cleaveland, W.R. (ed.) TACAS 1999. LNCS, vol. 1579, pp. 223–239. Springer, Heidelberg (1999)
8. Detlefs, D., Nelson, G., Saxe, J.B.: Simplify: a theorem prover for program checking. J. ACM 52(3) (2005)
9. Dillig, I., Dillig, T., Aiken, A.: Fluid updates: Beyond strong vs. weak updates. In: Gordon, A.D. (ed.) ESOP 2010. LNCS, vol. 6012, pp. 246–266. Springer, Heidelberg (2010)
10. Flanagan, C.: Automatic software model checking using clp. In: Degano, P. (ed.) ESOP 2003. LNCS, vol. 2618, pp. 189–203. Springer, Heidelberg (2003)
11. Flanagan, C., Qadeer, S.: Predicate abstraction for software verification. In: POPL, pp. 191–202 (2002)
12. Graf, S., Saïdi, H.: Construction of abstract state graphs with PVS. In: Grumberg, O. (ed.) CAV 1997. LNCS, vol. 1254, pp. 72–83. Springer, Heidelberg (1997)
13. Grebenshchikov, S., Lopes, N.P., Popeea, C., Rybalchenko, A.: Synthesizing software verifiers from proof rules. In: PLDI (2012)
14. Gulwani, S., McCloskey, B., Tiwari, A.: Lifting abstract interpreters to quantified logical domains. In: Necula, G.C., Wadler, P. (eds.) POPL, pp. 235–246. ACM (2008)
15. Gupta, A., Popeea, C., Rybalchenko, A.: Solving recursion-free Horn clauses over LI+UIF. In: Yang, H. (ed.) APLAS 2011. LNCS, vol. 7078, pp. 188–203. Springer, Heidelberg (2011)
16. Hermenegildo, M., Puebla, G., Bueno, F., López-García, P.: Program development using abstract interpretation (and the ciao system preprocessor). In: Cousot, R. (ed.) SAS 2003. LNCS, vol. 2694, pp. 127–152. Springer, Heidelberg (2003)
17. Hoder, K., Bjørner, N.: Generalized property directed reachability. In: Cimatti, A., Sebastiani, R. (eds.) SAT 2012. LNCS, vol. 7317, pp. 157–171. Springer, Heidelberg (2012)
18. Hoder, K., Kovács, L., Voronkov, A.: Case studies on invariant generation using a saturation theorem prover. In: Batyrshin, I., Sidorov, G. (eds.) MICAI 2011, Part I. LNCS, vol. 7094, pp. 1–15. Springer, Heidelberg (2011)
19. Hojjat, H., Konečný, F., Garnier, F., Iosif, R., Kuncak, V., Rümmer, P.: A verification toolkit for numerical transition systems - tool paper. In: Giannakopoulou, D., Méry, D. (eds.) FM 2012. LNCS, vol. 7436, pp. 247–251. Springer, Heidelberg (2012)

20. Jaffar, J., Maher, M.J.: Constraint logic programming: A survey. J. Log. Program. 19(20), 503–581 (1994)
21. Jaffar, J., Murali, V., Navas, J.A., Santosa, A.E.: Tracer: A symbolic execution tool for verification. In: Madhusudan, P., Seshia, S.A. (eds.) CAV 2012. LNCS, vol. 7358, pp. 758–766. Springer, Heidelberg (2012)
22. Jaffar, J., Santosa, A.E., Voicu, R.: Modeling Systems in CLP. In: Gabbrielli, M., Gupta, G. (eds.) ICLP 2005. LNCS, vol. 3668, pp. 412–413. Springer, Heidelberg (2005)
23. Jhala, R., McMillan, K.L.: Array abstractions from proofs. In: Damm, W., Hermanns, H. (eds.) CAV 2007. LNCS, vol. 4590, pp. 193–206. Springer, Heidelberg (2007)
24. Komuravelli, A., Gurfinkel, A., Chaki, S., Clarke, E.: Automatic Abstraction in SMT-Based Unbounded Software Model Checking. In: CAV (2013)
25. Larraz, D., Rodríguez-Carbonell, E., Rubio, A.: SMT-Based Array Invariant Generation. In: Giacobazzi, R., Berdine, J., Mastroeni, I. (eds.) VMCAI 2013. LNCS, vol. 7737, pp. 169–188. Springer, Heidelberg (2013)
26. McMillan, K.L.: An interpolating theorem prover. Theor. Comput. Sci. 345(1) (2005)
27. McMillan, K.L.: Lazy abstraction with interpolants. In: Ball, T., Jones, R.B. (eds.) CAV 2006. LNCS, vol. 4144, pp. 123–136. Springer, Heidelberg (2006)
28. McMillan, K.L.: Quantified invariant generation using an interpolating saturation prover. In: Ramakrishnan, C.R., Rehof, J. (eds.) TACAS 2008. LNCS, vol. 4963, pp. 413–427. Springer, Heidelberg (2008)
29. McMillan, K.L.: Interpolants from Z3 proofs. In: FMCAD (2011)
30. McMillan, K.L., Rybalchenko, A.: Computing relational fixed points using interpolation. Technical Report MSR-TR-2013-6, Microsoft Research (2013), http://research.microsoft.com/apps/pubs/?id=180055
31. Pnueli, A., Ruah, S., Zuck, L.D.: Automatic deductive verification with invisible invariants. In: Margaria, T., Yi, W. (eds.) TACAS 2001. LNCS, vol. 2031, pp. 82–97. Springer, Heidelberg (2001)
32. Rümmer, P., Hojjat, H., Kuncak, V.: Disjunctive interpolants for horn-clause verification. In: CAV (2013)

From Concrete Examples to Heap Manipulating Programs

Subhajit Roy

Computer Science and Engineering Department,
Indian Institute of Technology Kanpur
`subhajit@cse.iitk.ac.in`

Abstract. Data-structure manipulation is not just a perplexing ordeal
for newbies, but also a tedious errand for seasoned programmers. Even after a programmer gets the "hang of things", programming complex pointer
manipulations (like reversing a linked list) still makes one reach for a note-
book to draw some *box-and-arrow* diagrams to work out the low-level
pointer jugglery. These diagrams are, not surprisingly, used as a basic tool
to introduce heap manipulations in introductory programming courses.

We propose a synthesis technology to automatically create programs
that manipulate heap data-structures from such diagrams. The programmer is needed to provide a set of concrete examples of her high-level
strategy for the low-level manipulations to be discharged automatically.
We plan the synthesis task as a sequence of "fast" stages, making it usable in an integrated development environment. We envisage that such
a tool will be useful to programmers as a *code-assist* comfortably tucked
away in their favorite integrated development environment.

1 Introduction

Conjuring data-structure manipulations is a perplexing ordeal — irrespective of
the years of professional experience tucked away in one's Curriculum Vitae. Consider the task of reversing a linked list: it is easy to guess that such a task will require constructing a loop that visits each node in the list, each iteration of the loop
flipping the "next" pointers till the last node is encountered; however, wording the
same effectively using low-level pointer manipulations still remains a challenge.

Most often, our intuition of pointer jugglery is built on visualizing heap data-
structures as *box-and-arrow* diagrams. Such diagrams, introduced in our *Programming 101* classes, remain a potent weapon in our armory while warring
complex data-structures.

Let us attempt to conjure *box-and-arrow* diagrams for the above problem of
reversing a linked list. With the initial state as a "correct" linked list (of, say, five
nodes), the desired program should produce a reversed list of the same nodes
(for the final state). As we are interested in an iterative algorithm, the desired
program should attempt to reverse these links starting from the head node. It
is also trivial to guess that the program would typically require four iterations
to get the job done; Figure 1 illustrates our expectation of the state of the list
at the end of each iteration.

F. Logozzo and M. Fähndrich (Eds.): SAS 2013, LNCS 7935, pp. 126–149, 2013.
© Springer-Verlag Berlin Heidelberg 2013

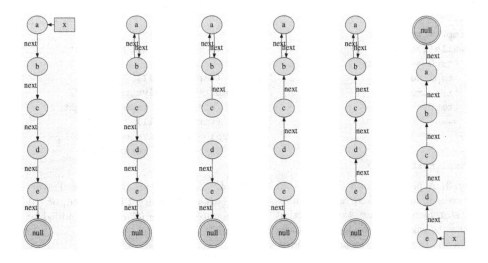

Fig. 1. State changes caused by an iterative program for reversing a linked list (Program variables are shown in boxes, heap nodes by ellipses, the labels on the arrows indicate the fields and "null" is indicated by a double circle)

Consider the similar case for the depth-first traversal of a binary search tree (Figure 2). It is very clear that the pointer x should visit the nodes of the tree in the order [a,b,c,d,e,f] (at the entry of each recursive call that is made), but writing down the exact piece of code, with the correct null-checks for the base case, needs a careful programmer.

Bottom line: data-structure manipulations are complex, but *box-and-arrow* diagrams come as a surprisingly intuitive instrument in planning any jugglery with the heap pointers. Wouldn't it be nice if the encoding of these high-level intuitions, designed using these diagrams, into the corresponding low-level pointer manipulations — that would sweat its way through a jungle of get-field and set-field operations — could be materialized automatically?

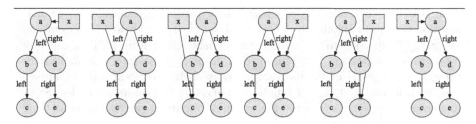

Fig. 2. State changes caused by a recursive program while performing a depth-first traversal of a binary tree (Program variables are shown in boxes, heap nodes by ellipses, the labels on the arrows indicate the fields; any field for a heap cell that is not shown must be assumed as set to "null")

```
0 tmp1 = x
1 ---
2 tmp2 = tmp1.next
  while(not (tmp2 == null)) {
3   tmp0 = tmp2.next
4   tmp2.next = x
5   x = tmp2
6   tmp2 = tmp0
7   ---
  }
8 ---
9 tmp1.next = tmp0
```

Fig. 3. A program from SYNBAD that reverses a singly linked list; the missing statements (—) are statements that SYNBAD was able to optimize away from the frame that the user provided

```
formal parameter: x
0 --
1 --
2 if (x != null) tmp0 = x.left
3 --
4 if (tmp0 != null)
     tmp1 = recursive_call(tmp0)
5 if (x != null) tmp0 = x.right
6 if (tmp0 != null)
     tmp1 = recursive_call(tmp0)
7 if (x != null) return(tmp1)
```

Fig. 4. Generated program (Tree Traversal): either (a) Figure 2 is provided, or (b) the counterexample (Figure 9) is added to Figure 7

In this paper, we propose a tool — **SYNBAD** (Program **SYN**thesizer from **B**ox and **A**rrow **D**iagrams) — that synthesizes programs from a sequence of such *box-and-arrow* diagrams. SYNBAD is able to synthesize both iterative and recursive programs for heap manipulation tasks.

Figure 3 shows the program that SYNBAD synthesizes for reversing the linked list. Note that with high-level examples — involving only the *interesting* variable x — SYNBAD automatically materializes the jugglery involving x, and three temporary variables (tmp0, tmp1 and tmp2) that is necessary to enforce the desired state changes. Similarly, for the recursive tree traversal (described by Figure 2), SYNBAD generates the procedure[1] shown in Figure 4.

We envisage that SYNBAD will be appreciated by seasoned programmers as a code-assist comfortably tucked away within their favorite IDE. This tool may also serve as a guide to students en route to mastering the art of data-structure manipulations. We have a committed goal to make this device still easier for such *Programming 101* students by augmenting the tool with additional heuristics and a knowledge-base of data-structure manipulating programs in the future.

The power of "box and arrow" diagrams for capturing a data-structure manipulation was also exploited by Singh et al. for their Storyboard Programming Tool (SPT) [1,2]. SYNBAD primarily distinguishes itself from SPT in the way the program specification is captured: SPT feeds from *abstract* box and arrow diagrams, where parts of the data structure is abstracted away with summary nodes, with formal fold/unfold functions describing the summary nodes; SYNBAD , however, attempts to serve the group of impatient programmers at their IDEs who may be ready to scratch in a set of *concrete* examples within their IDE, but would shy away from providing detailed, formal descriptions. To be

---

[1] The synthesized procedure is supposed to have a default return statement at the end of the procedure (not shown in the figure) that returns "null".

usable in an IDE environment, SYNBAD also needs to respond quickly; most of the programs we synthesized were discharged in less than 30 seconds. Section 2 provides a more detailed comparison of these two tools.

SYNBAD also attempts to materialize "optimal" programs: in our current implementation the optimal program is defined by the smallest possible program which accomplishes the desired task; however, our algorithm can be tuned to any definition of optimality that can be measured over static program properties (like size of the program, number of temporaries, number of pointer dereferences etc.). To meet the deadlines set by the patience of frantic programmers at their IDE, we break this search for the optimal program into simpler, "quick" phases rather than tackling it as one massive activity. As examples are an underspecification, we also attempt to drive refinement by drawing from ideas in the domain of automatic test case generation.

Following are the contributions of this paper:

- We propose an inductive synthesis algorithm to generate *iterative* and *recursive* programs from concrete box and arrow diagrams.
- We purport an algorithm to fragment the synthesis activity into multiple simple phases, to generate solutions within reasonable time. The phases in SYNBAD accomplish the following tasks:
  - Generate a program that satisfy the concrete examples;
  - Optimize the above program;
  - Produce runs from automatically generated test inputs to enable selection of counterexamples to drive refinement.

2   Let's Meet SYNBAD

SYNBAD essentially needs the following information to perform its task:

- Program structure
  - **program frame:** the program frame specifies program features like the number of loops, approximate number of statements within the loop and outside, and the number and approximate positions of the recursive calls. The frame restricts the search space, forcing the solver to "mould" the solution into a program having the desired form;
  - **input/output variables:** the variables that are used to specify the program state at a different points of execution;
  - **number and types of temporary variables:** the maximum number of temporary variables (of each type: pointer and integer) that the synthesized program is allowed to employ.
- A set of examples describing the user intent (SYNBAD provides a graphical frontend to enter the box-and-arrow diagrams for the examples); for each example, SYNBAD accepts the following descriptions:
  - **pre-conditions and post-conditions:** the input and final state of the heap and of the input/output variables;

Frame	(3,5,2)
variables	x: pointer
temp variables	(3:pointer, 0:integer)
fields	next: pointer
heap nodes	{a, b, c, d, e}
#examples	1
program type	iterative
hints	lp: (*, *, pointer)

Template	(4,6,0)
variables	x: pointer
temp variables	(1:pointer, 1:integer)
fields	left: pointer, right:pointer, value:integer
heap nodes	{a, b, c, d, e}
#examples	1
program type	recursive
hints	none

(a) The specifications for a program to reverse a singly linked list   (b) Specification for the tree traversal routine

Fig. 5. Specification of program templates

- **intermediate states:** intermediate program states can be specified to describe the generated program more succinctly; as it also constrains the search space, SYNBAD is able to discharge the synthesis faster;
- **print-buffer:** the programmer has an option of requesting SYNBAD to place print statements such that the generated program emits a certain output; as will be illustrated later, certain tasks can be expressed completely only if such a specification mechanism is provided.
- Additional hints
  - SYNBAD can be provided additional hints for certain program points, like what statements to use and the type of predicates to employ. These hints not only allow a finer control over the to-be-generated program, but it also speeds up the synthesis.

Once fed with the above specification, SYNBAD moves as follows:
1. SYNBAD produces a candidate program that meets the provided specification. Additionally, it produces a set of test inputs, along with the results of the test runs on the generated program.
2. The programmer either
   (a) accepts the program, or
   (b) produces a counterexample (possibly from the set of test runs presented); in this case, the specification is modified by adding the counterexample to the set of examples. SYNBAD moves to step (1) to reattempt the synthesis taking the counterexample under consideration.

This process continues till the programmer either accepts the program, or SYNBAD declares the specification unsatisfiable. Let us, now, present a couple of examples to illustrate how SYNBAD operates.

Reversing a Linked-list. Figures 1 and 5a form the specification provided for the task of reversing a singly-linked list. The program frame is summarized as (3,5,2): for iterative programs, it corresponds to the number of statements in the header, loop-body and the tail sections of the program[2] (see Figure 6a).

---

[2] At this point of time, SYNBAD can generate programs with only a single loop. However, our algorithm is general enough to generate looping structure of any depth.

```
<head> [3]
while (...) {
    <loop> [5]
}
<tail> [2]
```

(a) Frames for iterative programs: this program frame will be summarized as (3,5,2)

```
...
3 recursive_call
...
5 recursive_call
...
9 recursive_call
...
12 return
```

(b) Frames for a recursive programs: this frame will be summarized as (3,5,9,2)

Fig. 6. Specification of Program Frames

The input/output variables, fields, and number of temporaries are described next. The specification, then, declares that the examples will be described using the five heap nodes (named {a,b,c,d,e}). Next, it declares that only a single example is provided and that an iterative algorithm is desired. We defer the description of the hints to section 5.

The program generated by SYNBAD for the above specification is shown in Figure 3. All temporary variables are assumed to be initialized to null at the entry to the function. An important fact to be noted is that though the programmer had provided *loose* bounds for the sizes of the head, loop-body and the tail sections, the program generated by SYNBAD is the smallest program possible — this is due to the optimization phase built into SYNBAD (details in section *3.2*).

Note that we needed to provide very high-level descriptions of the program states involving the heap nodes and the interesting program variables — the intricate program states involving the not-very-interesting program variables and temporaries involved in the low-level pointer manipulations were completely left out! All of that was automatically planned out by SYNBAD.

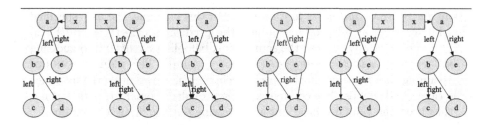

Fig. 7. State changes caused by a recursive program while performing a depth-first traversal of a binary tree (Program variables are shown in boxes, heap nodes by ellipses, the labels on the arrows indicate the fields; any field for a heap cell that is not shown must be assumed as set to "null")

```
formal parameter: x
0 --
1 --
2 if (x != null) tmp0 = x.left
3 --
4 if (tmp0 != null)
     tmp1 = recursive_call(tmp0)
5 if (tmp0 != null) tmp0 = x.right
6 if (tmp0 != null)
     tmp1 = recursive_call(tmp0)
7 if (x != null) return(tmp1)
```

Fig. 8. Generated program (Tree Traversal): when only Figure 7 is provided

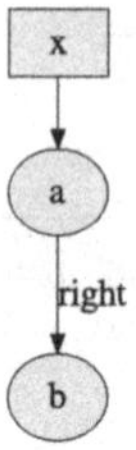

Fig. 9. Counterexample for the program in Figure 8

Traversing a Binary Tree. Figures 7 and 5b form the specification of a recursive program for depth-first traversal of a binary tree. The specification mentions that the program would require two recursive calls to do the job and the pointer variable x touches each of the nodes in the intermediate states. The specification (Figure 5b) also lays out the program frame and the participating entities (variables, temporaries, fields, heap nodes). The program frame for a recursive program is summarized (see Figure 6b) as the positions of the recursive calls followed by the number of statements in the trailing section (till the return statement is reached).

In this case, SYNBAD produces the program shown in Figure 8: once again SYNBAD is able to identify the low-level details — including the formal/actual parameters, return values and guards for the recursive calls.

After synthesizing the program, SYNBAD goes about generating test-inputs for the program: in fact, one of these test-inputs (Figure 9) generated by SYNBAD exemplifies a problem with the generated program — the program does not seem to work correctly on binary trees that are not full (see the guard at line 5 in Figure 8). Adding the counterexample (Figure 9) to the set of examples makes SYNBAD spell out the "correct" program (Figure 4).

Why did SYNBAD *fail in its first attempt?* In this example, the user specified a *full* binary tree: at all program points, the predicates $(x.left! = null)$ and $(x.right! = null)$ always shared the same value, befooling SYNBAD into guessing a *false invariant* $(x.left == null) \Leftrightarrow (x.right == null)$. This induced SYNBAD into assuming that these predicates are interchangeable, preventing the inference of the right conditionals. The counterexample provided a binary tree that is not full, thus breaking the false invariant and drawing out the desired program.

However, if the user had specified the example shown in Figure 2 at the onset, SYNBAD would have brought forth the "correct" program in its very first attempt. This points out a weakness of inductive synthesis: the produced programs are "correct" only with respect to the provided examples. Good examples from the user is essential for the synthesis to be successful — we discuss more on the adequacy of examples in section 5.

Let us, now, attempt to generate the programs for preorder and inorder traversals. The careful reader will realize that the program description essentially remains the same (as in Figure 2), the only difference being the order in which a `print` statement (or any operation that processes the visited nodes) process the nodes. This is accomplished by the description of the *print-buffer*: Figure 10 illustrates how a different specification of the order in which the nodes should be printed gives different programs.

SYNBAD Versus SPT. The Storyboard Programming Tool (SPT) [1] accepts a *storyboard*, composed of a set of scenarios (input-output pairs as box and arrows describing operations on an *abstract* data-structure), a set of fold and unfold operations (describing the structure of the summary nodes) and a skeleton of the looping structure of the desired program. While the storyboard framework attempts to synthesize programs from a more formal *abstract* box and arrow examples riding the power of abstract interpretation, SYNBAD attempts at inductive synthesis with concrete examples.

SPT and SYNBAD serve orthogonal goals: While SPT works with a specification provided as abstract scenarios, SYNBAD would appeal to frenzied programmers on an IDE who would like to provide concrete examples and refine those on demand. Though SPT advocates supplementing concrete examples along with the abstract scenarios, it does not perform well when only concrete examples are provided: the authors have remarked that when SPT was provided concrete examples alone, SPT either synthesizes undesired manipulations or times out (section 6 in [1]). Via SYNBAD we attempt to assert that, at least for the domain of data-structure manipulations, concrete examples are also a powerful mode of user-interaction. SYNBAD suits users who would like to draw out the concrete states of a manipulation rather than structuring an abstract description.

A bonus of concrete examples is the easy creation of a visual front-end. SYNBAD leverages the ease of specifying concrete examples to provide a *graphical frontend* where the programmers can simply "draw" the program specification.

An important consideration that influenced the design of SYNBAD was an objective to produce an optimal program — the current implementation attempts to produce the smallest program; however, our algorithm can be tuned to any definition of optimality that is measurable over a set of static program properties (like size of the program, number of temporaries, number of pointer dereferences). SPT, on the other hand, makes no such attempt: for example, the program produced by SPT in (Figure 7 in [1]) has a dead assignment "`head.next = head`" (the authors also mention it in section 2.3 of [1]).

The use of abstraction makes it difficult for SPT to use off-the-shelf SMT solvers (the authors resort to the sketch solver [3,4] to solve their constraints) as their constraint system requires the computation of a least fixpoint solution. SYNBAD, on the other hand, easily uses an off-the-shelf SMT solver to solve its constraints: rather than overwhelming the solver for the optimal program at the very onset, it first generates "simple" constraints and iteratively refines the constraints while cleverly exploiting previous (unoptimized) solution in its search

Specifying Heap Nodes	a.value = 101; b.value = 102; c.value = 103; d.value = 104; e.value = 105
For preorder traversal	print-buffer = **[103, 102, 104, 101, 105]** frame: (4, 6, 0)
For inorder traversal	print-buffer = **[101, 102, 103, 104, 105]** frame: (2, 6, 0)

(a) User-provided specifications

```
formal parameter: x                      formal parameter: x
0 --                                      0 --
1 if (x != null) tmp1 = x.value           1 if (x != null) tmp0 = x.left
2 if (x != null) print tmp1               2 if (tmp0 != null)
3 if (x != null) tmp0 = x.left                tmp0 = call(tmp0)
4 if (tmp0 != null)                       3 if (x != null) tmp1 = x.value
      tmp0 = call(tmp0)                   4 if (x != null) tmp0 = x.right
5 if (x != null) tmp0 = x.right           5 if (x != null) print tmp1
6 if (tmp0 != null)                       6 if (tmp0 != null)
      tmp0 = call(tmp0)                       tmp0 = call(tmp0)
7 if (x != null) return(tmp0)             7 if (x != null) return(tmp0)
```

(b) Preorder and Inorder tree traversals synthesized (left and right respectively)

Fig. 10. Describing tree traversals using the print-buffer specification

for the optimal program. This allows SYNBAD to have impressive run-times of less than 30 seconds for most of our benchmarks.

Finally, while SPT is limited to generating only iterative programs, SYNBAD is capable of generating recursive programs as well. Handling recursive programs is challenging as the execution trace of a recursive program grows exponentially with the size of the concrete example. Also, the the tool needs to handle storing (restoring) of the state of local variables at each recursive call (return). SYNBAD also provides interesting mechanisms like specification of *print-buffers* and hints about commands to be used to enable effective synthesis.

However, we must caution the reader that it is not fair to compare the run-times of these two tools as the specification provided to these tools vary significantly. While, SPT is provided abstract input-output examples with no intermediate states (in most of the cases), SYNBAD is provided concrete examples, not only of the input and output states, but also of intermediate states inside each loop iteration or recursive call invocation. Hence, SYNBAD surfs through a much smaller search space than what SPT needs to cover. For instance, for reversing a singly linked list, SPT takes **1m49sec** on "an Intel Core-i7 1.87GHz CPU with 4GB of RAM" (as reported in [1]), SYNBAD accomplishes the task in less than **7 seconds** (for the best frame), and even produces the most compact program in another 18.1 seconds. Similarly, for reversing a doubly linked list, SPT takes **3min47sec** (as reported in [1]), while SYNBAD takes only **32 seconds**. We assert that such intermediate states (shown in Figure 1, 2 and 7) are easy for the programmers to provide (SYNBAD makes it still easier via a graphical frontend).

Our results for SYNBAD (reported above) were produced on a laptop running Intel Core i7 1.73 GHz with 8 GB RAM.

We feel that SPT and SYNBAD serve orthogonal goals: while SPT would be appreciated by careful programmers who are willing to write formal abstract configurations, SYNBAD will be loved by frenzied programmers chased by close deadlines who would prefer to draw concrete examples on a visual canvas.

3 The Synthesis Algorithm

The overview of our synthesis algorithm is presented in Figure 11; we illustrate the algorithm in this section.

Program State. The entities of a program are given in terms of a set of program variables λ_V, heap nodes λ_H, and fields λ_F of these heap nodes. The program variables $\lambda_V : \lambda_{VI} \cup \lambda_{VT}$, where λ_{VI} are the set of all program identifiers and λ_{VT} are the temporaries.

The state ($\mathcal{S}_i$) of the program at a point i in an execution captures values of each program entity (variable and heap nodes):

$\mathcal{S}: \mathcal{V} \times \mathcal{H}$

The maps $\mathcal{V}$ and $\mathcal{H}$ define the values for the integer/pointer variables $v \in \lambda_V$ and the heap nodes $h \in \lambda_H$ via all their possible fields $f \in \lambda_F$.

$\mathcal{V}: \lambda_V \to \lambda_H$

$\mathcal{H}: (\lambda_H \times \lambda_F) \to \lambda_H$

The map Υ returns the type of each program entity; at present SYNBAD supports only two types: integer and pointer.

The Synthesis Problem. Each example provided by the user corresponds to an execution of the to-be-synthesized program. We view the synthesis problem as inferring this execution as a linear transition system — via a sequence of states

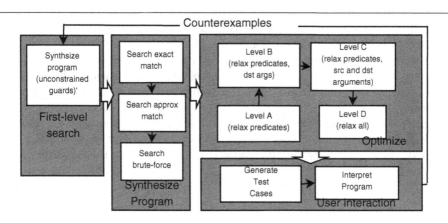

Fig. 11. An eagle's view of our synthesis algorithm

(nodes), realizable by a sequence of appropriate statements/commands (edges). All loops in the program frame are unrolled and all recursive calls inlined to produce these transition systems — one for each example provided. Some of the states are constrained (either partially or fully) via specifications of the box-and-arrow diagrams. The state transition from $\mathcal{S}_i$ to $\mathcal{S}_{i+1}$ is constrained by the semantics of commands that appear along the edge $(\mathcal{S}_i \to \mathcal{S}_{i+1})$.

Additionally, we use a set of guard variables $g_i \in \mathcal{G}$ for each transition $(\mathcal{S}_i \to \mathcal{S}_{i+1})$ that allow the command on the transition to be "switched off": if the guard variable is true, the command on the edge $(\mathcal{S}_i \to \mathcal{S}_{i+1})$ has the appropriate semantics; if false, then $\mathcal{S}_i = \mathcal{S}_{i+1}$.

These boolean guard variables for the transitions provide a lot of advantages:
- they allow us to split the complex task of synthesizing the commands and the branch predicates into simpler phases;
- by bounding the number of guard variable that are active, we speed up the SMT solver (constraining the search to a smaller number of transitions).

3.1   Generating Programs

Each example (provided by the user) is "explained" by an *execution trace* of the program; the state of a program after executing i steps (from the initial state) in the transition system is given by:

$\mathcal{S}_i : \mathcal{V}_i \times \mathcal{H}_i$

The heap node pointed to by a variable $v \in \lambda_V$ after i steps is given by $\mathcal{V}_i(v)$ and that pointed to by a field $f \in \lambda_F$ of a heap node $h \in \lambda_H$ is given by $\mathcal{H}_i(h, f)$.

The function π maps points in the execution trace to static program points in the to-be-synthesized program. In other words, it maps the dynamic instance of each instruction (and the corresponding program points) to their static counterparts.

For each example, SYNBAD encodes the primary constraint as:

$$\Phi \wedge \prod_{i=1}^{n}((g_i \implies T_{\pi(i)}) \wedge (\neg g_i \implies T_{skip})) \tag{1}$$

where Φ is the state specifications (provided as box and arrow diagrams) and there exists n steps in the execution trace. The constraint enforces the specification Φ and, then, attempts to explain it as a sequence of guarded transitions; the guard variables g_i allow the corresponding transition function $T_{\pi(i)}$ to be switched on or off. Table 1 describes the transition function for each program statement[3].

For iterative programs, at all points in the transition system where the loop entry condition is evaluated (say $1 \ldots \delta$), the loop entry condition is satisfied for all but the last instance (when the loop is exited); we encode this condition as:

$$(\prod_{i=1}^{\delta-1}(g_i = true)) \wedge (g_\delta = false) \tag{2}$$

---

[3] In Table 1, rn is the transition identifier where the corresponding call returns; cn is the transition identifier where the call corresponding to this return is made.

Table 1. Semantics of program statements for synthesis

Cmd	Precondition	$\forall v \in V : \mathcal{V}_{i+1}(v)$	$\forall (h,f) \in (H,F):$ $\mathcal{H}_{i+1}(h,f)$
$T_{asgn}(x,y)$ $[x = y]$	$\Upsilon(x) = \Upsilon(y)$	$\begin{cases} \mathcal{V}_i(y) & \text{if } v = x \\ \mathcal{V}_i(v) & \text{otherwise} \end{cases}$	$\mathcal{H}_i(h,f)$
$T_{getfld}((x,y,g)$ $[x = y.g]$	$\mathcal{V}_i(y) \neq null$ $\Upsilon(x) =$ $\Upsilon(\langle \mathcal{V}_i(y), g \rangle)$ $\Upsilon(y) =\text{pointer}$	$\begin{cases} \mathcal{H}_i(\mathcal{V}_i(y),g) & \text{if } v = x \\ \mathcal{V}_i(v) & \text{otherwise} \end{cases}$	$\mathcal{H}_i(h,f)$
$T_{setfld}(x,g,y)$ $[x.g = y]$	$\mathcal{V}_i(x) \neq null$ $\Upsilon(y) =$ $\Upsilon(\langle \mathcal{V}_i(x), g \rangle)$ $\Upsilon(x) =\text{pointer}$	$\mathcal{V}_i(v)$	$\begin{cases} \mathcal{V}_i(y) & \text{if } h = \mathcal{V}_i(x) \\ & \wedge g = f \\ \mathcal{H}_i(h,f) & \text{otherwise} \end{cases}$
T_{skip} $[skip]$	none	$\mathcal{V}_i(v)$	$\mathcal{H}_i(h,f)$
$T_{call}(x,y : z, rn)$ $[x = call(y : z, rn)]$	$\Upsilon(y) = \Upsilon(z)$	$\begin{cases} \mathcal{V}_i(y) & \text{if } v = z \\ init & \text{otherwise} \end{cases}$	$\mathcal{H}_i(h,f)$
$T_{ret}(y : x, cn)$ $[ret(y : x, cn)]$	$\Upsilon(y) = \Upsilon(x)$	$\begin{cases} \mathcal{V}_i(y) & \text{if } v = x \\ \mathcal{V}_{cn}(v) & \text{otherwise} \end{cases}$	$\mathcal{H}_i(h,f)$
$T_{prnt}(x)$ $[print\ x]$	$\Upsilon(x) =\text{integer}$	$\mathcal{V}_i(v)$	$\mathcal{H}_i(h,f)$

$$prntbuf_{i+1} = \begin{cases} prntbuf_i.append(\mathcal{V}_i(x)) & \text{if } T_{prnt}(x) \\ prntbuf_i & \text{otherwise} \end{cases}$$

For recursive programs, the guards corresponding to the body of a call invocation are determined by the state of the guard to the statement where the function call is made; for example, if the guard for a function call is `false`, none of the statements within the body of this call can execute:

$$\left(\prod_{i=1}^{n} (g_i \implies g_{call(i)}) \right) \tag{3}$$

SYNBAD generates a program as a sequence of guarded commands. Hence, to synthesize the complete program, SYNBAD needs to identify both the program statements as well as the *guard predicates* corresponding to each of these statements. To allow for an efficient search, SYNBAD tackles this task in two stages:

Search with Unconstrained Guards. In this stage, SYNBAD essentially enforces constraint (1) (along with (2) for iterative programs and (3) for recursive programs) to generate a solution φ_1 (let $\varphi_1[cmd_i]$, $\varphi_1[src_i]$, $\varphi_1[dst_i]$ and $\varphi_1[prd_i]$ refer to the command type, source arguments, destination arguments and guarded predicate for the ith guarded command within the solution φ_1).

Table 2. Semantics of predicate template for synthesis of the branch and loop conditions

predicate (t)	Precondition	$\gamma_i(t)$
$(true)$	none	$true$
$(false)$	none	$false$
$(x = null)$	$\Upsilon(x) =$ pointer	$\begin{cases} true & \text{if } \mathcal{V}_i(x) = null \\ false & \text{otherwise} \end{cases}$
$(x = y)$	$\Upsilon(x) = \Upsilon(y)$	$\begin{cases} true & \text{if } \mathcal{V}_i(x) = \mathcal{V}_i(y) \\ false & \text{otherwise} \end{cases}$
$(x > y)$	$\Upsilon(x) = \Upsilon(y)$ $\Upsilon(x) =$ Integer	$\begin{cases} true & \text{if } \mathcal{V}_i(x) > \mathcal{V}_i(y) \\ false & \text{otherwise} \end{cases}$
$(x < y)$	$\Upsilon(x) = \Upsilon(y)$ $\Upsilon(x) =$ Integer	$\begin{cases} true & \text{if } \mathcal{V}_i(x) < \mathcal{V}_i(y) \\ false & \text{otherwise} \end{cases}$

For the negated forms, the γ functions returns the negated values from that of their direct form: $\gamma_i(\neg t) = \neg(\gamma_i(t))$

Note that the guard variables are free to assume any value as long as the trace satisfies the specified examples. Often, the values assumed by the guard variables in this solution cannot be enforced by any set of guard predicates, implying that the solution does not correspond to a "realizable" program. But, at the same time, we observed that the *command types* synthesized in this solution are same, or at least "close" (spatially) to that of a realizable program. We use this solution to stiffen our search space for the second stage.

Search for the Complete Program. For the search for a complete candidate program (statements and guards), SYNBAD enforces the following constraints on the guard variables so as to generate realizable guard predicates:

- predicates corresponding to the guarded commands: each guard g_i should be explained by a predicate $(\gamma_{\pi(i)})$ at the respective program point $\pi(i)$:

$$\prod_{i=1}^{n} g_i = \gamma_{\pi(i)} \tag{4}$$

- loop-entry predicates: say for δ iterations of the loop, for each iteration $1 \ldots \delta - 1$, the loop predicate should evaluate to true; for the last iteration, the guard should evaluate to false:

$$(\prod_{i=1}^{\delta-1} g_i = \gamma_{\pi(i)} = true) \wedge (g_\delta = \gamma_{\pi(\delta)} = false) \tag{5}$$

The semantics of the predicates can be found in Table 2.

Enabled with the above solution φ_1, SYNBAD makes three attempts at synthesizing a solution φ_2 that yields a realizable program:

1. **Exact Match:** In this attempt, SYNBAD tries to synthesize guard predicates meeting the constraints (4) and (5) while assuming that the solution φ_2 has exactly the same sequence of command (types) as φ_1:

$$\prod_{i=1}^{k} (\varphi_1[cmd_i] = \varphi_2[cmd_i]) \tag{6}$$

where $\varphi_1[cmd_i]$ refers to the command type corresponding to the ith guarded command within the solution φ_1 and the program has k guarded commands (i.e. the user specified the program frame to have k statements).

2. **Approximate Match:** If the above attempt fails, SYNBAD tries to synthesize guard predicates meeting the constraints (4) and (5) while assuming that the sequence of command types in solution φ_2, though not an exact match, is *close* to the sequence of command types in φ_1; *closeness* is defined as "most of the time, the type of the command at i in φ_2 appears near i in φ_1". To establish our notion of closeness, we define the following score for each program location i:

$$closeness(i) = \begin{cases} 5 & \varphi_2[cmd_i] = \varphi_2[cmd_{i-1}] \\ 0 & \varphi_2[cmd_i] = \varphi_2[cmd_i] \\ 5 & \varphi_2[cmd_i] = \varphi_2[cmd_{i+1}] \\ 10 & \text{otherwise} \end{cases} \tag{7}$$

We set GETFLD as the missing neighbors of the first and the last statements. In our current implementation, we naively assume an uniform probability distribution among the above four outcomes: thus, we get an expected *closeness* score of 5 for each statement. We use this closeness score for all statements in φ_2 to restrict the search space, facilitating a faster search:

$$\sum_{i=1}^{k} closeness(i) \leq 5k \tag{8}$$

when the program has k guarded commands.

3. **Brute-Force Search:** If an approximate match fails as well, we resort to a brute-force search by dropping the constraint (8).

Understandably, the brute-force search is much more expensive than approximate match, which in turn is more expensive than exact match. Our experience with SYNBAD showed that mostly a solution is obtained with exact match, a few cases requiring an approximate match, while almost none permeate to brute-force search.

3.2   Optimizing the Program

The program synthesized in the above phase is most often inefficient — containing dead and faint code, and circuitous manipulations. This phase aims for the smallest program that meets the specification. For the purpose of optimization, among all programs that satisfy the specifications, SYNBAD attempts to search for the program that has the maximum number of guard predicates γ_i set to the constant predicate "(false)". Alongside, it also attempts to simplify the guard and loop-entry predicates: simplicity can be measured by the number of variables involved in a predicate: (true) is a simpler than (x == null), which is simpler than (x == y).

To achieve the same, SYNBAD defines the following cost function on predicates:

$$predicate\_cost(i) = \begin{cases} 0 & \text{if } \gamma_i = "(false)" \\ 1 & \text{if } \gamma_i = "(true)" \\ 5 & \text{if } \gamma_i = "(x = null)" \\ 10 & \text{otherwise} \end{cases}$$

SYNBAD attempts to **minimize** the following optimization score[4]:

$$opt\_score = \sum_{i=1}^{k} predicate\_cost(i) + predicate\_cost(l) \qquad (9)$$

when the program has k guarded commands; l is the predicate guarding entry to the loop.

We run optimizations at four levels, each time striving for a lower *opt_score* than the previous solution. Each level is designed to allow a *controlled* transformation of the candidate program:

Level A (Relax Predicates). In this level, SYNBAD enforces the command types and arguments from the solution φ_2 while attempting to improve *opt_score*. Given an unoptimized solution φ_u (in this case $\varphi_u = \varphi_2$), the following constraints are imposed while deriving an optimized solution φ_o:

$$\prod_{i=1}^{k} (\varphi_o[cmd_i] = \varphi_u[cmd_i]) \qquad (10)$$

$$\prod_{i=1}^{k} (\varphi_o[src_i] = \varphi_u[src_i]) \qquad (11)$$

$$\prod_{i=1}^{k} (\varphi_o[dst_i] = \varphi_u[dst_i]) \qquad (12)$$

when the program has k guarded commands.

Level B (Relax Predicates and Destination Arguments). SYNBAD, in this level, relaxes the destination arguments, i.e. it does not enforce constraint (12).

Level C (Relax Predicates, Destination Arguments and Source Arguments). Now, SYNBAD relaxes even the source arguments to the commands by dropping constraint (11), while constraining only the command types to the synthesized program.

---

[4] For an alternate measure for optimality, we simply need to define *op_score* differently.

```
0 x.next = y
1 tmp0 = x.next
2 tmp1 = tmp0.value
3 tmp1 = y.value
  while (...) {
4   x = tmp0
5   tmp0 = y
6   tmp0 = x.next
  }
7 y.next = tmp0
8 x.next = y
```

(a) Search with unre-
stricted guards

```
0 ---
1 if (!(y == null))
    tmp2 = y.value
2 if (!(y == x))
    tmp0 = x.next
3 if (!(tmp0 == null))
    tmp1 = tmp0.value
  while (tmp2 > tmp1) {
4   if (!(x == tmp0))
    x = tmp0
5   if (!(tmp1 == tmp2))
    tmp0 = tmp0.next
6   if (!(tmp1 > tmp2))
    tmp1 = tmp0.value
  }
7 y.next = tmp0
8 if (!(y == x))
    x.next = y
```

(b) Search with approximate
matching

```
0 ---
1 tmp2 = y.value
2 tmp0 = x.next
3 tmp1 = tmp0.value
  while (tmp2 > tmp1)
{
4   x = tmp0
5   tmp0 = tmp0.next
6   tmp1 = tmp0.value
  }
7 y.next = tmp0
8 x.next = y
```

(c) Final program after optimizations

Fig. 12. Inserting a node in a sorted linked list: the variable y points to the node to be inserted and the variable x points to the list head

Level D (Relax All). Finally SYNBAD drops all the above constraints — even constraint (10) — allowing the synthesis to conjure a completely new program, but having a still lower *opt_score*. However, if a command has already been identified as a skip statement, we fix it perennially.

As the amount of change allowed by an optimization level (and hence its potency) increases, the search tends to be more expensive. These optimization can be stopped at any of the levels, yielding a program that meets all the specifications. While experimenting with SYNBAD, we discovered that level D is often very expensive and almost never achieves any additional improvement over level C (see section 6). It may be a good option to discard level D if SYNBAD is employed in IDE environments.

Example 1. Figure 12 shows some of the steps in how a program gets synthesized by SYNBAD. Figure 12a shows how the search with unrestricted guards simply synthesizes the commands without the guards. In this case, search for the predicates with an exact match fails. Figure 12b shows how approximate matching generates a candidate program. Interestingly, though these programs differ significantly, the command types in the corresponding lines are *almost* the same. Note that Figure 12b is very inefficient. The optimization pass transforms this program to Figure 12c: it is able to change many of the guard predicates to the constant predicate (true).

4 Refinement Using Counterexample Generation

After producing the program, SYNBAD simulates the execution of the program on a set of test cases which are then presented to the programmer. The programmer may exhibit her discontent with the synthesized program by selecting an appropriate test case (as a counterexample) to be added to the set of examples to invoke SYNBAD with.

The test case generator in SYNBAD requires the following from the user:

- a set of pre-conditions to seed test case generation;
- a sanity_check() function to assert that a generated input is valid i.e. the input data-structure generated meets all the required assumptions (for example, that a linked list is acyclic);
- a bound on the number of heap nodes generated.

The routine starts off by priming its variable and heap maps according to the preconditions; any entity (variable or heap cell) that is unspecified is set to undefined. SYNBAD, then, starts off an interpreter on the program. At any point that an undefined entity is used, its value is initialized as follows:

- if the entity is of integer type: it is set to a random integer value
- if the entity is of pointer type: SYNBAD carries out a systematic search along all the following:

  - the entity set to null
  - the entity set to an existing node
  - if the bound on the number of nodes is not reached yet, then the entity set to a new node with all its fields set to undefined (the set of existing nodes is updated accordingly)

  The user has an option of restricting the search to a smaller subset of the above.

```
0 tmp3 = y.value
1 tmp2 = x.value
2 ---
3 ---
  while (not (tmp3 < tmp2)) {
4   x = x.next
5   tmp0 = x.next
6   tmp2 = tmp0.value
  }
7 y.next = tmp0
8 x.next = y
```

Fig. 13. Inserting an element in a sorted linked list (fails on short lists): the variable y points to the node to be inserted and the variable x points to the list head

```
0 tmp2 = x.next
1 skip
  while (tmp1 == null) {
2   x.next = tmp1
3   tmp1 = x
4   x = tmp2.next
5   x.next = tmp2
  }
6 tmp2.next = tmp1
```

Fig. 14. Reversal of a (short) linked list of 3 nodes: the variable x points to the list head

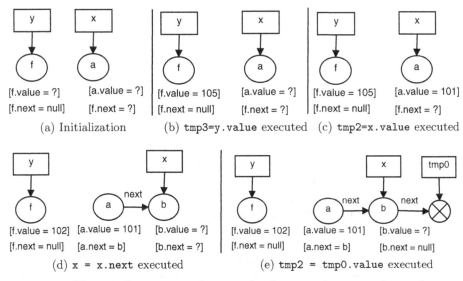

Fig. 15. Counterexample generation from test-input creation

SYNBAD also mirrors the same change on the input that was used to run this test case. A sanity check is performed on this corresponding input state (by calling `sanity_check()` on this structure); if it passes, the interpreter continues with the newly assigned value, else this newly created structure is discarded; this process continues till a sane structure is generated.

SYNBAD is bound to terminate as only a bounded number of new nodes can be generated. In the current implementation of SYNBAD, we require manual inspection of the results of these tests; in the future, we plan to allow the user to provide a `check_test()` function to automatically report for failures.

Example 2. Figure 13 shows a case where SYNBAD generated a program to insert a node in a sorted linked list from an example list of **five** nodes; note that this program would fail on short lists. Let us see how SYNBAD is able to generate a counterexample:

- Figure 15(a): The test case generation phase is primed with x and y pointing to heap nodes (named a and f respectively). Note that all fields except `f.next` were left unspecified by the user.
- Figure 15(b): As the program statement "tmp3 = y.value" is executed, y.value is found to have an undefined value (shown as ?); being an integer it is assigned a random value (105 in this case). The same is then assigned to tmp3.
- Figure 15(c): The program statement "tmp2 = x.value" is executed. A random value (101) is assigned to a.value and tmp2.
- Figure 15(d): On executing "x = x.next", x.next is found to be undefined. Hence, the interpreter makes a non-deterministic choice, in this case creating a new node b. The variable x is then updated to point to the new node.

- Figure 15(e): On executing "tmp0 = x.next", x.next is again found to be undefined. The interpreter makes a non-deterministic choice, setting x.next to null in this case. tmp0 is accordingly set to null as well.
- On executing "tmp2 = tmp0.value", the program raises a *"null pointer exception"*, thus providing a counterexample.

5   Discussion

Adequacy of Examples Examples form an under-specification; at the same time, they also turn out to be the easiest to provide. The performance of any device drawing on examples as a means of specification must care about the quality of examples provided to it. We developed a few suggestions that are useful towards providing examples for SYNBAD :

- **Size of the heap-structure:** the number of nodes in the data-structure is an important concern. One useful guideline is to ensure that *the number of nodes is greater than the number of variables* (input/output + temporary). For example, for reversing a linked list, the total number of variables is four (Figure 5a): if we select an example with just three nodes, SYNBAD synthesizes an incorrect program (Figure 14). The reason is that with the large number of variables available with respect to the number of nodes, the loop was deemed unnecessary.
- **Complexity of the heap-structure:** As discussed in section 2, if provided a full binary tree as an example, SYNBAD guesses a *false invariant* $(x.left == null) \Leftrightarrow (x.right == null)$. Hence, when providing examples, non-symmetrical graphs are generally better choices over symmetrical ones.

Programmer Hints. As synthesis is a compute intensive activity, hints provided by the programmer go a long way in helping a synthesis tool move quicker through its search space. Programmers have an option to help SYNBAD by asserting any subset of the following:

- command type (at a program point);
- type of the guarded predicate (at a program point);
- data-type for the variables within the guard predicates (at a program point).

For example, in Figure 5a, the specification asserts that for the predicate guarding the entry to the loop[5], the variables participating in the predicate are of pointer types. No other hint (for command type or type of the guarded predicate for any program point) is provided in this case.

6   Implementation and Experiments

We have implemented SYNBAD in Python using the Z3 SMT solver [5]. We have used SYNBAD to generate a variety of iterative and recursive programs on a laptop running quad-core Intel i7 1.73 GHz with 8 GB RAM. Table 3 describes each task and the time taken by SYNBAD to synthesize a program:

---

[5] Specified by 'lp'; for other statements, the statement number is provided instead.

- **Task:** describes the task
- **Entities:** these columns describe the number of entities specified by the user: input/output variables (Var), temporaries (Tmp), fields (Flds) and heap nodes (HN). For all these entities (except HN), the type of the entity is listed (p: pointer, i: integer)
- **R/I:** whether the user desires an iterative (I) or a recursive (R) implementation; for iterative programs, the loop bound and for the recursive programs the recursion depth is provided
- **Frame:** the frame of the program specified by the user is summarized in this column (see Figure 6a and 6b)
- **E:** the number of examples provided
- **Hints:** any hints provided to SYNBAD is specified
- **Timings:** the time taken by SYNBAD is detailed:
  - T_{gen}: the time taken to generate a program that satisfies the specifications
  - T_{opt}: the total time taken to optimize the generated program
  - T_{hl}: the time taken by the last level of optimization (level D)
  - O_{eff}: the highest optimization level where any improvement in the program is noticed
  - T_{eff}: the effective time taken (total time from the invocation of SYNBAD to where the last improvement was seen)

The total time taken by SYNBAD is $T_{gen} + T_{opt}$ while T_{eff} gives the time where SYNBAD is involved in activities that turn out fruitful.

Optimization Levels. Overall, SYNBAD is quick: it is able to produce a program in less than a minute for most of the tasks. Moreover, the effective time (i.e. time till when the last improvement in the program is seen) is less than 20 seconds for most of the tasks. This implies that SYNBAD is able to produce the optimal program very fast, but then loses time in a vain attempt to optimize it further. The examination of the column (O_{eff}) sheds more light into this matter: most of the times, the optimal program is produced in the very first level of optimization (level A). Also, the highest level of optimization (level D) takes a significant fraction of the time (T_{hl}) and seldom brings about any further improvement in the program. This hints at a possibility of dropping out the level D optimizer; however, the caveat is that, in doing so, we would lose the assertion that SYNBAD *always* produces the optimal program. Another possibility (when used inside an IDE) is to flash the program to the user without invoking the level D optimizer. Meanwhile, this optimizer (level D) could run in the background; in the rare cases that an improvement is actually noticed, a message can be flashed to the user to enable replacing the generated code segment by the optimal one.

A Tight Frame. The task RL (in Table 3) shows the effect of providing a loose frame. As the frame size increases, SYNBAD is made to work harder at both generating and optimizing the program. For the most loose frame, even the level C optimizer needed to kick in. For recursive programs (see task IT), the situation is still worse: the performance drops very rapidly as the frame is loosened. This is not surprising considering the fact the frame needs to be recursively inlined for synthesizing recursive programs.

Programmer Hints. The task PG illustrates the effect of programmer hints: as more hints are provided, SYNBAD is more efficient at its job.

7   Related Work

Researchers have employed examples [6,7,8,9], traces [10,11,12], to a partial program with "holes" [3,4,13,14] to capture user intent. [15,16] describe systems that efficiently synthesize loop-free programs from a given set of components. [17] allows a programmer to provide templates for the looping structure of programs, form of the loop invariants etc. as a scaffold to generate iterative programs that can satisfy the scaffold. Even functional programming has received attention: [18,19] suggest techniques for synthesis of recursive functional programs.

SYNBAD also uses this Programming-By-Example (PBE) paradigm to capture user-intent. For SYNBAD, the user has the option of controlling the operation of the synthesized programs at various granularity — from just the input-output pairs to a full (high-level) trace. However, to allow SYNBAD to respond in reasonable time, we always invoke SYNBAD with intermediary states provided, like those at the beginning (or end) of each loop iteration and at the beginning (or end) of each recursive call.

The Sketch tool [3,4,13,14] uses a counterexample guided loop to synthesize its programs. As a program sketch enjoys the luxury of formal assertions, the sketch tool employs a automatic verifier to generate a counterexample that can be used to refine the solution. In the absence of formal specifications, SYNBAD employs the user as an oracle to verify the solution (similar to [16]). To ease out the process, SYNBAD automatically generates runs over automatically generated test cases that are presented to the user; this scheme is suggested in [16], though the authors (in [16]) use test-input generation like techniques to generate distinguishing inputs (to single out a program among all programs that have different semantics but that pass on the provided examples).

The counterexample generation phase of SYNBAD shares some ideas with CUTE [20] that performs concolic execution: a concrete execution serving as a test run alongside a symbolic execution to generate new test inputs. However, unlike CUTE, SYNBAD does not perform concolic execution; SYNBAD employs random testing, with an ability to perform a lazy, non-deterministic initialization of heap cells.

The optimization problem in SYNBAD resembles the goal of superoptimization [21,22,23]: deriving the most efficient sequence of loop-free instructions for a task. Most often compilers employ a brute-force search over the available machine instructions to meet this goal. SYNBAD performs this search in a controlled, phased manner — cheaper to expensive — reducing the "cost" of the program fragment with each optimization level. It unleashes a brute-force search in the last level (level D) but with a clear goal of beating an already optimized program.

Table 3. SYNBAD at work

Task	Entities				R/I	Frame	E	Hints	Timings (sec)				
	Var	Tmp	Flds	HN					T_{gen}	T_{opt}	T_{hl}	O_{eff}	T_{eff}
(RL) Reversing a linked list	1p	3p	1p	5	I (4)	(2,4,1)	1	lp:(*, *, ptr)	6.2	18.1	16.2	A	7.1
	1p	3p	1p	5	I (4)	(2,5,1)	1	lp:(*, *, ptr)	15.5	25.7	22.3	A	17.6
	1p	3p	1p	5	I (4)	(3,5,2)	1	lp:(*, *, ptr)	32.1	24.6	18.5	C	37.5
(IS) Insert element in sorted linked list	2p	1p,2i	1p,1i	6	I(3,0)	(3,3,2)	2	lp:(*, *, int)	10.4	11.8	4.3	A	15.5
	1p,1i	1p,2i	1p,1i	5	I(5)	(1,3,0)	1	lp:(*, *, ptr), 2:(PRT, *, int)	4.1	2.9	1.0	A	5.1
(PG) Print all elements greater than 'n' in a linked list	1p,1i	1p,2i	1p,1i	5	I(5)	(1,3,0)	1	lp:(*, *, ptr)	7.5	4.6	3.3	A	7.9
(DL) Delete a node from linked list	1p,1i	1p,2i	1p,1i	5	I(5)	(1,3,0)	1	-	10.9	5.2	3.9	A	11.2
	1p,1i	2p,1i	1p,1i	5	I(3)	(3,2,2)	1	lp:(*, *, int)	3.6	4.5	1.7	A	5.1
(IT) Inorder Binary Tree Traversal	1p	1p,1i	2p,1i	5	R(2)	(2,6,1)	1	-	15.3	35.1	22.5	A	15.3
	1p	1p,1i	2p,1i	5	R(2)	(3,7,1)	1	-	20.6	48.8	30.5★	A	24.6
	1p	1p,1i	2p,1i	5	R(2)	(3,7,2)◆	1	-	146.7	80.2	54.2	A	157.4
(PT) Preorder Binary Tree Traversal	1p	1p,1i	2p,1i	5	R(2)	(4,6,0)	2	-	13.0	46.9	30.5★	A	19.6
(DD) Delete a node from a doubly-linked list	1p,1i	2p,1i	2p,1i	5	I(3)	(1,2,4)	1	lp:(*, *, int)	2.9	4.9	1.5	A	5.7
(RD) Reverse a doubly-linked list	1p,0i	4p,0i	2p,0i	5	I(4)	(2,6,2)	1	lp:(*, *, ptr)	31.7	652.7	596.0	D	380.5
(TS) Search BST (element always present)	1p,1i	0p,1i	2p,1i	9	I(3)	(1,3,0)	1	-	1.9	2.7	1.2	A	2.5
(OT) Postorder traversal of Binary Tree	1p	1p,1i	2p,1i	5	R(2)	(2,4,2)	1	-	19.8	28.0	17.3	A	21.3
(PA) Preorder binary tree traversal (asymmetric example)	1p	1p,1i	2p,1i	5	R(2)	(4,6,0)	1	-	20.3	47.5	30.5*	A	26.6

Note: for all the above task, SYNBAD was provided box and arrow diagrams at the beginning (or end) of each loop iteration and recursive call invocation

Special cases:

★ a timeout of 30s was used for the SMT solver for this case

◆ timeout of the solver was increased to 300s for this case

8   Conclusions and Future Work

Our experience with SYNBAD strengthened our belief that heap manipulations can be described with concrete examples — a form of specification that is dear to most users. We intend to integrate SYNBAD within a programming IDE. Another important direction of work is towards still reducing the amount of specification demanded from the user. We intend to investigate as to if a good program frame and number of temporaries can be guessed by SYNBAD by examining the box and arrow diagrams.

References

1. Singh, R., Solar-Lezama, A.: Synthesizing data structure manipulations from storyboards. In: ESEC/FSE 2011, pp. 289–299. ACM, New York (2011)
2. Singh, R., Solar-Lezama, A.: SPT: Storyboard programming tool. In: Madhusudan, P., Seshia, S.A. (eds.) CAV 2012. LNCS, vol. 7358, pp. 738–743. Springer, Heidelberg (2012)
3. Solar Lezama, A.: Program Synthesis By Sketching. PhD thesis, EECS Department, University of California, Berkeley (December 2008)
4. Solar-Lezama, A.: The sketching approach to program synthesis. In: Hu, Z. (ed.) APLAS 2009. LNCS, vol. 5904, pp. 4–13. Springer, Heidelberg (2009)
5. De Moura, L., Bjørner, N.: Z3: an efficient SMT solver. In: Ramakrishnan, C.R., Rehof, J. (eds.) TACAS 2008. LNCS, vol. 4963, pp. 337–340. Springer, Heidelberg (2008)
6. Gulwani, S.: Automating string processing in spreadsheets using input-output examples. In: POPL 2011, pp. 317–330. ACM, New York (2011)
7. Gulwani, S., Harris, W.R., Singh, R.: Spreadsheet data manipulation using examples. Communications of the ACM (2012)
8. Harris, W.R., Gulwani, S.: Spreadsheet table transformations from examples. In: PLDI 2011, pp. 317–328. ACM, New York (2011)
9. Singh, R., Gulwani, S.: Learning semantic string transformations from examples. Proc. VLDB Endow. 5(8), 740–751 (2012)
10. Biermann, A.W., Baum, R.I., Petry, F.E.: Speeding up the synthesis of programs from traces. IEEE Trans. Comput. 24(2), 122–136 (1975)
11. Cypher, A., Halbert, D.C., Kurlander, D., Lieberman, H., Maulsby, D., Myers, B.A., Turransky, A.: Watch what I do: programming by demonstration. MIT Press, Cambridge (1993)
12. Lau, T., Domingos, P., Weld, D.S.: Learning programs from traces using version space algebra. In: K-CAP 2003, pp. 36–43. ACM, New York (2003)
13. Solar-Lezama, A., Rabbah, R., Bodík, R., Ebcioğlu, K.: Programming by sketching for bit-streaming programs. In: PLDI 2005, pp. 281–294. ACM, New York (2005)
14. Solar-Lezama, A., Tancau, L., Bodik, R., Seshia, S., Saraswat, V.: Combinatorial sketching for finite programs. In: ASPLOS-XII, pp. 404–415. ACM, New York (2006)
15. Gulwani, S., Jha, S., Tiwari, A., Venkatesan, R.: Synthesis of loop-free programs. In: PLDI 2011, pp. 62–73. ACM, New York (2011)
16. Jha, S., Gulwani, S., Seshia, S.A., Tiwari, A.: Oracle-guided component-based program synthesis. In: ICSE 2010, pp. 215–224. ACM, New York (2010)

17. Srivastava, S., Gulwani, S., Foster, J.S.: From program verification to program synthesis. In: POPL 2010, pp. 313–326. ACM, New York (2010)
18. Armando, A., Smaill, A., Green, I.: Automatic synthesis of recursive programs: The proof-planning paradigm. Automated Software Engg. 6(4), 329–356 (1999)
19. Banerjee, D.: A methodology for synthesis of recursive functional programs. ACM Trans. Program. Lang. Syst. 9(3), 441–462 (1987)
20. Sen, K., Marinov, D., Agha, G.: CUTE: a concolic unit testing engine for C. In: ESEC/FSE-13, pp. 263–272. ACM, New York (2005)
21. Bansal, S., Aiken, A.: Automatic generation of peephole superoptimizers. In: ASPLOS-XII, pp. 394–403. ACM, New York (2006)
22. Bansal, S., Aiken, A.: Binary translation using peephole superoptimizers. In: OSDI 2008, pp. 177–192. USENIX Association, Berkeley (2008)
23. Massalin, H.: Superoptimizer: a look at the smallest program. In: ASPLOS-II, pp. 122–126. IEEE Computer Society Press, Los Alamitos (1987)

Local Shape Analysis for Overlaid Data Structures[*]

Cezara Drăgoi[1], Constantin Enea[2], and Mihaela Sighireanu[2]

[1] IST Austria
cezarad@ist.ac.at
[2] Univ Paris Diderot, Sorbonne Paris Cite, LIAFA CNRS UMR 7089, Paris
{cenea,sighirea}@liafa.univ-paris-diderot.fr

Abstract. We present a shape analysis for programs that manipulate overlaid data structures which share sets of objects. The abstract domain contains Separation Logic formulas that (1) combine a per-object separating conjunction with a per-field separating conjunction and (2) constrain a set of variables interpreted as sets of objects. The definition of the abstract domain operators is based on a notion of homomorphism between formulas, viewed as graphs, used recently to define optimal decision procedures for fragments of the Separation Logic. Based on a Frame Rule that supports the two versions of the separating conjunction, the analysis is able to reason in a modular manner about non-overlaid data structures and then, compose information only at a few program points, e.g., procedure returns. We have implemented this analysis in a prototype tool and applied it on several interesting case studies that manipulate overlaid and nested linked lists.

1 Introduction

Automatic synthesis of valid assertions about heap-manipulating programs, such as loop invariants or procedure summaries, is an important and highly challenging problem. In this paper, we address this problem for sequential programs manipulating overlaid and nested linked lists. The term overlaid refers to the fact that the lists share some set of objets. Such data structures are often used in low-level code in order to organize a set of objects with respect to different criteria. For example, the network monitoring software Nagios (www.nagios.com) groups sets of tasks in nested lists, according to the user that spawned them, but also in two lists of pending and, respectively, executed tasks. These structures are overlaid because they share the objects that represent tasks.

We propose an analysis based on abstract interpretation [10], where the elements of the abstract domain are formulas in *NOLL* [13], a fragment of Separation Logic (SL) [17]. The main features of *NOLL* are (1) two separating conjunction operators, the *per-object* separation $*$ and the *per-field* separation $*_w$, (2) recursive predicates indexed by *set variables*, which are interpreted as the set of all heap objects in the data structure described by the predicate, and (3) constraints over set variables, which relate sets of objects that form different data structures. The analysis has as parameter the set of recursive predicates used in the *NOLL* formulas. Although per-object separation can be expressed using per-field separation and constraints on set variables, we prefer to keep

---

[*] This work was supported in part by the Austrian Science Fund NFN RiSE, by the ERC Advanced Grant QUAREM, and by the French ANR Project Veridyc.

F. Logozzo and M. Fähndrich (Eds.): SAS 2013, LNCS 7935, pp. 150–171, 2013.
© Springer-Verlag Berlin Heidelberg 2013

both versions for two reasons: (i) the formulas are more concise and (ii) as a design principle, the analysis should introduce per-field separation only when it is necessary, i.e., when it detects overlaid data structures.

The main characteristics of the analysis are (1) *compositionality*: we define a frame rule for *NOLL*, which allows to reason locally, on a subset of allocated objects and considering only a subset of their fields and (2) abstract domain operators based on *graph homomorphism*, used recently in optimal decision procedures for SL fragments [9,13].

The frame rule for SL with only per-object separation [17] states that, in order to compute the effect of a program P on the input specified by a formula ϕ, one has to split ϕ into $\phi_i * \sigma$, where ϕ_i describes all the heap objects reachable from program variables read in P without being written before, compute the post-condition ϕ_o of P on ϕ_i and then, infer that the effect of P on ϕ is $\phi_o * \sigma$. Programs with overlaid data structures can be usually partitioned in blocks, e.g. procedures, that manipulate just one non-overlaid data structure at a time. Thus, for the sake of compositionality, only the description of this data structure should be considered when computing the effect of some block. Having both the per-field and the per-object separation, the frame rule we define refines the decomposition of ϕ into $(\phi_i *_w \sigma_1) * \sigma_2$, where ϕ_i describes *the list segments in the heap built with fields accessed in P*, which start in variables read in P. As before, if ϕ_o represents the effect of P on ϕ_i then the post-condition of P on ϕ is $(\phi_o *_w \sigma_1) * \sigma_2$.

The constraints on set variables are important to define a precise local analysis. They are used to relate heap regions accessed in different blocks of the program. For example, consider a program that traverses a list segment L_1 and then, another list segment L_2, these list segments being overlaid. In a local analysis that considers only one list segment at a time, the constraints on set variables are used to preserve the fact that some heap objects, materialized on the list segment L_1, belong also to L_2. This information may be used when fields of these heap objects are accessed.

The elements of the abstract domain are existentially-quantified disjunctions of *NOLL* formulas that use only (separating) conjunctions. To obtain efficient abstract domain operators, we use a graph representation for *NOLL* formulas. Each disjunction-free formula φ is represented by a graph where nodes correspond to variables of φ and edges correspond to atoms of φ that describe (nested) list segments.

The definition of the order relation $\preceq$ between the abstract domain values uses the entailment relation $\models$ between *NOLL* formulas. One can prove [9,13] that $\varphi_1 \models \varphi_2$ whenever there exists an *homomorphism* from the graph representations of φ_2 to the one of φ_1. Assuming that atoms describe only singly-linked lists, an homomorphism from a graph G_1 to a graph G_2 maps edges of G_1 to (possibly empty) paths of G_2 such that the paths of G_2 associated to two distinct edges of G_1 do not share edges. If atoms include recursive predicates that describe nested list segments, the homomorphism maps edges of G_1 to more general sub-graphs of G_2 that represent unfoldings of these predicates. Comparing to the previous approaches for proving entailments of SL formulas, which are based on inference rules, the homomorphism approach has the same precision but it is more efficient because, intuitively, it defines also a strategy for applying the inference rules. We introduce an effective procedure for checking graph homomorphism, which is based on testing membership in languages described by tree automata.

The widening operator ∇ is based on two operations: (1) a fold operator that "recognizes" data structures used in the program, if they are describable by one of the predicates parametrizing the analysis and (2) a procedure that uses graph homomorphism in order to identify the constraints which are true in both of its arguments (implicitly, it tries to preserve the predicates discovered by fold). More precisely, given two graphs G_1 and G_2, the widening operator searches for a maximal sub-graph of G_1 which is homomorphic to a sub-graph of G_2 (and thus weaker) and a maximal sub-graph of G_2 which is homomorphic to a sub-graph of G_1. All these graphs should be disjoint. If all edges of G_1 and G_2 are included in these sub-graphs then the widening returns the union of the two weaker sub-graphs. Otherwise, it returns a disjunction of two graphs or, if the number of nodes which correspond to existential variables is greater than some fixed bound, it applies the operator fold which replaces unfoldings of recursive predicates by instantiations of these predicates. Folding the same set of nodes in two different list segments introduces the per-field separation although the initial formula may use only the per-object separation.

The analysis is implemented in a prototype tool that has been successfully applied on some interesting set of benchmarks that includes fragments from Nagios.

Related Work: There are many works that develop static analyses based on SL, e.g., [2,7,6,8,11,12,14,16,19,20]. Most of them, except the work in [16], are not precise enough in order to deal with overlaid data structures. The abstract domain operators defined in [7,20] can be seen as instantiations of the operators based on graph homomorphism introduced in this paper (provided that the definition of the graph homomorphism is adapted to the respective logics). In [16], overlaid data structures are described using the classical conjunction, instead of the per-field separation as in our work. The analysis is defined as a reduced product of several sub-analyses, where each sub-analysis "observes" a different set of fields. The reduction operator, used to exchange information between the sub-analyses, is called at control points, which are determined using a preliminary data-flow analysis. The same data-flow analysis is used to anticipate the updates on the set variables. In our work, compositionality is achieved using the frame rule and thus, it avoids the overhead of duplicate domain operations and calls to the reduction operator. Moreover, the updates on the set variables are determined during the analysis and thus, they can produce more precise results. Static analyses for reasoning about the size of memory regions are introduced in [15]. They are based on combining a *set domain*, that partitions the memory into (not necessarily) disjoint regions, and a numerical domain, that is used to relate the cardinalities of the memory regions. The abstract domain defined in this paper can be seen as an instance of a set domain.

2   Overview

Our running example is extracted from the network monitoring software Nagios which uses a task manager to store pending and executed tasks, grouped or linked according to different criteria. The implementation given in Fig. 1 wraps tasks in objects of type Task composed of a field op, which stores a description of the task, a field succ, which links the tasks spawned by the same user, and fields next and prev, which link pending or executed tasks. A task manager is implemented by an object of type Manager containing

```
typedef struct Task {                     Task* add(Task* x,Task* log)
  char* op;                               { x->prev = NULL;
  struct Task* succ;                        x->next = log;
  struct Task* prev, *next;                 return x;
} Task;                                   }
                                          Task* cut(Task* x,Task* todo)
typedef struct NestedList {               {
  int user;                                 Task* tmp = x->next;
  struct NestedList* nextu;                 if (tmp != NULL)      tmp->prev = x->prev;
  Task* tasks;                              if (x->prev == NULL)  return tmp;
} NestedList;                               else
                                            { x->prev->next = tmp;
typedef struct Manager {                      return todo; }
  NestedList* tab;                        }
  Task* todo;                             void execute(int user,char* str,Manager* man)
  Task* log;                              {
} Manager;                                  Task* x = lookup(user,str,man->tab);
                                            if ( x != NULL && (x->prev != NULL || x==man->todo) )
Task* lookup(int user,char* str,            { man->todo = cut(x,man->todo);
            NestedList* tab)                  man->log = add(x,man->log); }
{ ... return ret; }                       }
```

Fig. 1. Task manager

a field tab, which stores the tasks of each user using a NestedList object, a field todo which is used to access the pending tasks, and a field log, which points to the list of executed tasks. Each element of type NestedList has an integer field encoding the user id and a field tasks pointing to the list of tasks spawned by the user. To specify the lists pointed to by the fields of an object of type Manager, we use the following SL formula:

$$\varphi \triangleq \mathtt{nll}_\alpha(\mathtt{tab},\mathrm{NULL},\mathrm{NULL}) *_w \big(\mathtt{dll}_\beta(\mathtt{todo},\mathrm{NULL}) * \mathtt{sll}_\gamma(\mathtt{log},\mathrm{NULL},\mathrm{NULL})\big) \\ \wedge\ \alpha(\mathtt{Task}) = \beta \cup \gamma, \tag{1}$$

where $\mathtt{nll}_\alpha(\mathtt{tab},\mathrm{NULL},\mathrm{NULL})$ describes a list of lists pointed to by tab and ending in NULL, where all the inner lists end also in NULL, $\mathtt{dll}_\beta(\mathtt{todo},\mathrm{NULL})$ describes[1] a doubly-linked list from todo to NULL, and $\mathtt{sll}_\gamma(\mathtt{log},\mathrm{NULL},\mathrm{NULL})$ describes a list of objects with two fields next and prev such that prev points always to NULL (this is a common way to factorize one type declaration in order to represent both doubly-linked and singly-linked lists). In general, the list segments described by these predicates can be empty. (For a formal definition of these predicates, we defer the reader to Sec. 4.) The set variables α, β, and γ are interpreted as the set of heap objects in the list segments described by the corresponding predicates. Also, $\alpha(\mathtt{Task})$ is interpreted as the set of heap objects of type Task in the interpretation of α. To simplify the notation, we represent an object of type Manager by three pointer variables tab, todo, and log. The per-field separation $*_w$ allows the list of lists to share objects with the other two lists.

Such formulas have an equivalent graph representation, which is more intuitive and easier to work with. For example, Fig. 2 shows the graph representation of φ. In $\mathtt{nll}_\alpha(\mathtt{tab},\mathrm{NULL},\mathrm{NULL})$, the first two arguments represent the start and, resp., the end of the list of NestedList objects. Therefore, this atom is represented by an edge from tab to NULL labeled by $\mathtt{nll}_\alpha$ (actually, the edge label contains also the third argument

---

[1] This predicate is actually a shorthand for the formula $\mathtt{todo} \mapsto \{(\mathrm{prev},\mathrm{NULL})\} *_w$ $\mathtt{dll}_\beta(\mathtt{todo},u') *_w u' \mapsto \{(\mathrm{next},\mathrm{NULL})\}$, where $\mathtt{dll}_\beta$ is the recursive predicate defined in Ex. 1, page 159, and u' an existential variable.

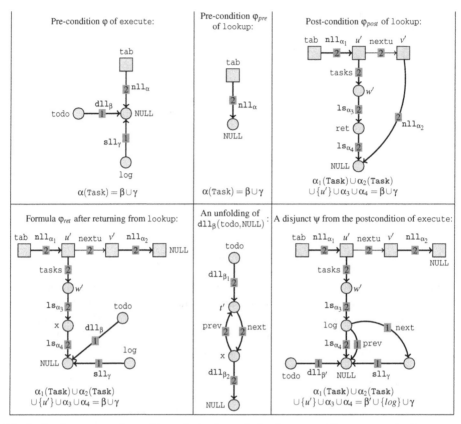

Fig. 2. Graph representations of formulas in the analysis of execute (the square nodes have type NestedList and the circle nodes have type Task)

NULL but we have omit it for simplicity). Any two edges labeled by the same integer (resp., different integers) represent per-object (resp., per-field) separated atoms.

We define an abstract domain, denoted $\mathcal{ASL}$, which is parametrized by a set of (recursive) predicates as above and contains disjunctions of formulas as in (1).

Next, we focus on the analysis of the procedure execute, which moves a task from the list of pending tasks, pointed to by todo, to the list of executed tasks, pointed to by log. To check that the task pointed to by x belongs to the todo list, it tests if x equals the head of this list or if the prev field is not NULL. Given the precondition φ in (1), the analysis proves that, at the end of the procedure, the property φ remains true, i.e., all the data structures are preserved.

The procedure starts by calling lookup in order to search for an object of type Task. The analysis we define is compositional in two ways. First, each procedure is analyzed on its "local heap", i.e., the heap region reachable from the actual parameters of the call. Second, we restrict the local heap to paths that use only fields accessed by the procedure. For example, the procedure lookup accesses only the fields nextu, tasks, and succ and consequently, it is analyzed on a sub-formula φ_{pre} of φ that contains only $nll_\alpha(\text{tab}, \text{NULL}, \text{NULL}) \wedge \alpha(\text{Task}) = \beta \cup \gamma$. The constraint on set variables is included because it constrains a set of objects in the local heap of lookup. The graph representation of φ_{pre} is given in Fig. 2.

The post-condition of lookup computed by the analysis contains several disjuncts; one of them, denoted φ_{post}, is given in Fig. 2. This graph represents an unfolding of the list segment described by $\text{nll}_\alpha(\text{tab}, \text{NULL}, \text{NULL})$, where u', v', and w' are existentially quantified variables (by convention, all the existential variables are primed). Edges labeled by fields, e.g., the edge from u' to v' labeled by nextu, represent values of fields. The term $\{u'\}$ in the constraint on set variables is interpreted as the singleton containing the object u'. The output parameter ret points to an object in some inner list of the nested list segment pointed to by tab. The inner lists are described by the predicate ls.

The abstract value reached when returning from the call to lookup, φ_{ret}, is given in Fig. 2. It is obtained from φ by replacing the sub-formula φ_{pre} with φ_{post} (we consider two copies of the node labeled by NULL for readability).

We now consider the if statement in execute. The abstract element where we assume that x!=NULL is true is obtained from φ_{post} by adding the constraint $x \neq \text{NULL} \wedge x \in \alpha_4$ (the object pointed to by x belongs to α_4 only if $x \neq \text{NULL}$; otherwise, the interpretation of α_4 is $\emptyset$). To compute the abstract element where we assume that x->prev != NULL, we need to materialize the prev field of x. For this, we use the fact that the set constraints imply that $x \in \beta \cup \gamma$ and we compute a disjunction of three graphs where we unfold either the predicate $\text{dll}_\beta(\text{todo}, \text{NULL})$ (with x as the first element or as some element different from the first one) or $\text{sll}_\gamma(\text{log}, \text{NULL}, \text{NULL})$ (with x as some arbitrary element). Only one graph satisfies x->prev != NULL and this graph contains the unfolding of $\text{dll}_\beta(\text{todo}, \text{NULL})$ given in the second row of Fig. 2. With this unfolding, the set variable β is replaced by $\beta_1 \cup \{t'\} \cup \beta_2$. Note that the node labeled by x in this unfolding is the same as the node labeled by x in the unfolding of $\text{nll}_\alpha(\text{tab}, \text{NULL}, \text{NULL})$.

If we continue on the branch of the if statement where x!=NULL and x->prev!=NULL are true then, we analyze the call to cut starting from a precondition that contains only the sub-formula describing the unfolding of $\text{dll}_\beta(\text{todo}, \text{NULL})$ and the constraint on the set variables. This is because cut accesses only the fields prev and next, and the list $\text{sll}_\gamma(\text{log}, \text{NULL}, \text{NULL})$ is per-object separated from the doubly-linked list. A similar analysis is done for the call to add. One of the disjuncts from the post-condition of execute, denoted by ψ, is given in Fig. 2 (local variables have been projected out and, for simplicity, we abstract the unfolding of $\text{dll}_{\beta'}$).

The analysis proves that the data structures are preserved by a call to execute, i.e., its postcondition implies φ in (1). This is because there exists an homomorphism from φ to every disjunct in the post-condition. Intuitively, the homomorphism maps nodes of φ to nodes of the disjunct, labeled by at least the same set of program variables, and edges e of φ to sub-graphs of the disjunct, that represent unfoldings of the predicate labeling e. For example, this is the case for the disjunct ψ in Fig. 2. Concerning the constraints on set variables, the edge mapping defines a substitution Γ for set variables of φ to terms over variables of ψ, e.g., α is substituted by the union of all set variables in the unfolding of $\text{nll}_\alpha(\text{tab}, \text{NULL}, \text{NULL})$, i.e., $\alpha_1 \cup \alpha_2 \cup \{u'\} \cup \alpha_3 \cup \alpha_4$ ($\{u'\}$ is also considered because some field of u' is explicit in this unfolding). If Λ_1 and Λ_2 are the constraints over set variables in ψ, resp., φ, then Λ_1 implies $\Lambda_2[\Gamma]$.

3 Programs

We consider strongly typed imperative programs. The types used in the program are references to record types belonging to some set $\mathcal{T}$. A record type contains a set of fields, each field being a reference to a record type. We suppose that each field has a unique name and we denote by *Flds* the set of field names. Let τ be a typing function, that maps each variable into a type in $\mathcal{T}$ and each field into a function type over $\mathcal{T}$.

Program Configurations: We use a classical storage model, where a *program configuration* is a pair $C = (S, H)$, where S represents the stack of program variables and H represents the heap of dynamically allocated objects. To give a formal definition, we consider three additional countable sets which are pairwise disjoint and disjoint from *Flds*: a set *Loc* of addresses (called also *locations*), a set *Vars* of program variables x, y, z, and a set *Vars'* of "primed" variables x', y', z' that do not appear in the program but only in assertions where they are implicitly existentially quantified. We assume that all these elements are typed by τ to records in $\mathcal{T}$. For simplicity, we also assume that NULL is an element of *Vars* mapped always to a distinguished location $\sharp \in Loc$. Then,

$$S \in \text{Stacks} = [(Vars \cup Vars') \to Loc] \qquad H \in \text{Heaps} = [Loc \times Flds \rightharpoonup Loc]$$
$$C \in \text{Configs} = \text{Stacks} \times \text{Heaps}$$

We consider that S and H are *well typed*, e.g., if $S(x) = \ell$ then $\tau(x) = \tau(\ell)$. For simplicity, the constant NULL and the location $\sharp$ are typed by τ in any record in $\mathcal{T}$.

The set of locations l for which $H(l, f)$ is defined, for some f, is called the set of locations in C, and it is denoted by $Loc(C)$. The component S (resp. H) of a heap C is denoted by S^C (resp. H^C).

Programs: Aside the definition of record types, programs are collections of procedures. The procedures are written in a classical imperative programming language that contains memory allocation/deallocation statements (new/free), field updates ($x\text{->}f :=$ ...), variable assignments ($x := y/x := y\text{->}f$), call statements (call $\text{Proc}(\vec{x})$), and composed statements like sequential composition ;, if-then-else, and while loops. The formal meanings of the *basic statements* (not containing ;, conditionals, loops, and procedure calls) are given in terms of functions from 2^{Configs} to 2^{Configs}, where Configs contains a special value $C_\perp$ that corresponds to a memory fault.

4 Assertion Language

The language we consider for writing program assertions, that describe sets of program configurations, is the logic *NOLL* [13] enriched with existential quantifiers and disjunction (to simplify the notation, we use primed variables instead of existential quantifiers).

Syntax: The logic *NOLL* is a multi-sorted fragment of Separation Logic [17]. It is defined over two sets of variables *LVars* = *Vars* $\cup$ *Vars'* and *SetVars*, called *location variables* and *set variables*, respectively. We assume that the typing function τ associates a sort, resp., a set of sorts, to every variable in *LVars*, resp., *SetVars*. A variable in *LVars* is interpreted as a location in *Loc* while a variable in *SetVars* is interpreted as a set of locations in *Loc*. The syntax of *NOLL* is given in Fig. 3.

$E, F, E_i \in LVars$ location variables
$f, f_i \in Flds$ field names
$R \in \mathcal{T}$ sort

$\vec{E} \in LVars^+$ tuple of location variables
$\alpha \in SetVars$ set variable
$P \in \mathcal{P}$ list segment predicate

$\Phi ::= \Pi \wedge \Sigma \wedge \Lambda \mid \Phi \vee \Phi$ $\qquad\qquad\qquad\qquad\qquad$ *NOLL* formulas

$\Pi ::= E = F \mid E \neq F \mid \Pi \wedge \Pi$ $\qquad\qquad\qquad\qquad\qquad$ pure formula

$\Sigma ::= true \mid emp \mid E \mapsto \{(f_1, E_1), \ldots, (f_k, E_k)\} \mid P_\alpha(\vec{E}) \mid \Sigma * \Sigma \mid \Sigma *_w \Sigma$ $\quad$ spatial formula

$\Lambda ::= E \in t \mid E \notin t \mid t = t' \mid t \cap t' = \emptyset \mid \Lambda \wedge \Lambda$ $\qquad\qquad\qquad$ sharing formula

$t ::= \{E\} \mid \alpha \mid \alpha(R) \mid t \cup t'$ $\qquad\qquad\qquad\qquad\qquad\qquad$ set terms

Fig. 3. Syntax of *NOLL* formulas

The atoms of *NOLL* are either (1) *pure*, i.e., (dis)equalities between location variables, (2) *spatial*, i.e., the predicate *emp* denoting the empty heap, points-to constraints $E \mapsto \{(f_1, E_1); \ldots; (f_k, E_k)\}$, saying that the value stored by the field f_i of E equals E_i, for any $1 \le i \le k$, or predicate applications $P_\alpha(\vec{E})$, or (3) *sharing*, i.e., membership and inclusion constraints over set terms. The predicates P in $P_\alpha(\vec{E})$ are used to describe recursive data structures starting or ending in locations denoted by variables in $\vec{E}$. The set variable α is interpreted as the set of all locations in the data structure defined by P.

NOLL includes two versions of the separating conjunction: the *per-object separating conjunction* $*$ expresses the disjointness between two sets of heap objects (of record type) while the *per-field separating conjunction* $*_w$ expresses the disjointness between two sets of heap cells, that correspond to fields of heap objects.

The values of the set variables can be constrained in a logic that uses the classical set operators $\in$, $\subseteq$, and $\cup$.

Semantics: The formal semantics of *NOLL* formulas is given by a satisfaction relation $\models$ between pairs (C, J), where $C = (S, H)$ is a program configuration and $J : SetVars \rightarrow 2^{Loc}$ interprets variables in *SetVars* to finite subsets of *Loc*, and *NOLL* formulas. Sample clauses of the definition of $\models$ appear in Fig. 4. Given Φ_1 and Φ_2, $\Phi_1 \models \Phi_2$ iff for any (C, J), if $(C, J) \models \Phi_1$ then $(C, J) \models \Phi_2$.

Two spatial atoms are *object separated*, resp. *field separated*, if their least common ancestor in the syntactic tree of the formula is $*$, resp. $*_w$.

Recursive Predicates for Describing (Nested) List Segments: In the following, we consider a set of predicates $\mathcal{P}$ that describe *nested list segments* and have recursive definitions of the following form:

$$P_\alpha(in, out, \vec{nhb}) \triangleq (in = out) \vee \qquad\qquad\qquad\qquad\qquad\qquad (2)$$
$$(\exists u', \vec{v}', \alpha', \vec{\beta}. \ \Sigma(in, u', \vec{v}', \vec{nhb}, \vec{\beta}) *_w P_{\alpha'}(u', out, \vec{nhb}) \wedge T_\Sigma \cap \alpha' = \emptyset)$$

where $in, out, u' \in LVars$, $\vec{nhb}, \vec{v}' \in LVars^*$, $\alpha' \in SetVars$, $\vec{\beta} \in SetVars^*$, Σ is a spatial formula, and T_Σ is a set term, defined as the union of (1) the location variables appearing in the left of a points-to constraint, *except* u', and (2) the set variables in $\vec{\beta}$.

A predicate $P_\alpha(in, out, \vec{nhb})$ defines possibly empty list segments starting from *in* and ending in *out*. The fields of each element in this list segment and the nested lists to which it points to are defined by Σ. The parameters $\vec{nhb}$ are used to define the "boundaries" of the nested list segment described by P, in the sense that every location described by P belongs to a path between *in* and some location in $out \cup \vec{nhb}$ (this path may be

$$
\begin{aligned}
(C,J) &\models emp && \text{iff } Loc(C) = \emptyset \\
(C,J) &\models E = F && \text{iff } S^C(E) = S^C(F) \\
(C,J) &\models E \mapsto \cup_{i \in I}\{(f_i, E_i)\} && \text{iff } \mathrm{dom}(H^C) = \{(S^C(E), f_i) \mid i \in I\}, \forall i \in I. H^C(S^C(E), f_i) = S^C(E_i) \\
(C,J) &\models P_\alpha(\vec{E}) && \text{iff } (C,J) \in \llbracket P_\alpha(\vec{E}) \rrbracket \text{ and } J(\alpha) = Loc(C). \\
(C,J) &\models E \in t && \text{iff } S^C(E) \in [t]_{S^C,J} \\
(C,J) &\models t \subseteq t' && \text{iff } [t]_{S^C,J} \subseteq [t']_{S^C,J} \\
(C,J) &\models \varphi_1 * \varphi_2 && \text{iff there exist program heaps } C_1 \text{ and } C_2 \text{ s.t. } C = C_1 * C_2, \\
& && \quad (C_1, J) \models \varphi_1, \text{ and } (C_2, J) \models \varphi_2 \\
(C,J) &\models \varphi_1 *_w \varphi_2 && \text{iff there exist program heaps } C_1 \text{ and } C_2 \text{ s.t. } C = C_1 *_w C_2, \\
& && \quad (C_1, J) \models \varphi_1, \text{ and } (C_2, J) \models \varphi_2
\end{aligned}
$$

Separation operators over program configurations:

$$
\begin{aligned}
C = C_1 * C_2 \quad &\text{iff } Loc(C) = Loc(C_1) \cup Loc(C_2) \text{ and } Loc(C_1) \cap Loc(C_2) = \emptyset, \\
& \quad H^{C_1} = H^C|_{Loc(C_1)}, H^{C_2} = H^C|_{Loc(C_2)}, \text{ and } S^C = S^{C_1} = S^{C_2} \\
C = C_1 *_w C_2 \quad &\text{iff } \mathrm{dom}(H^C) = \mathrm{dom}(H^{C_1}) \cup \mathrm{dom}(H^{C_2}) \text{ and } \mathrm{dom}(H^{C_1}) \cap \mathrm{dom}(H^{C_2}) = \emptyset, \\
& \quad H^{C_1} = H^C|_{\mathrm{dom}(H^{C_1})}, H^{C_2} = H^C|_{\mathrm{dom}(H^{C_2})}, \text{ and } S^C = S^{C_1} = S^{C_2}
\end{aligned}
$$

Interpretation of a set term t, $[t]_{S,J}$:

$$
[\{E\}]_{S,J} = \{S(E)\}, \quad [\alpha]_{S,J} = J(\alpha), \quad [\alpha(R)]_{S,J} = J(\alpha) \cap Loc_R, \quad [t \cup t']_{S,J} = [t]_{S,J} \cup [t']_{S,J}.
$$

Fig. 4. Semantics of *NOLL* formulas (the set of program configurations satisfying $P(\vec{E})$ is denoted by $\llbracket P(\vec{E}) \rrbracket$, $\mathrm{dom}(F)$ denotes the domain of the function F, and Loc_R denotes the set of elements in Loc of type R)

$$
\begin{aligned}
(C,J) &\in \llbracket P_\alpha(in, out, \vec{nhb}) \rrbracket && \text{iff there exists } k \in \mathbb{N} \text{ s.t. } (C,J) \in \llbracket P_\alpha^k(in, out, \vec{nhb}) \rrbracket \\
(C,J) &\in \llbracket P_\alpha^0(in, out, \vec{nhb}) \rrbracket && \text{iff } S(in) = S(out) \text{ and } J(\alpha) = \emptyset \\
(C,J) &\in \llbracket P_\alpha^{k+1}(in, out, \vec{nhb}) \rrbracket && \text{iff } S(in) \neq S(out) \text{ and}
\end{aligned}
$$

$$
\text{there exists } \rho : \{u'\} \cup \vec{v} \to Loc \text{ and } \nu : \{\alpha'\} \cup \vec{\beta} \to 2^{Loc} \text{ s.t.}
$$
$$
(C[S \mapsto S \cup \rho], J \cup \nu) \models \Sigma(in, u', \vec{v}, \vec{nhb}, \vec{\beta}) *_w P_{\alpha'}^k(u', out, \vec{nhb}) \wedge T_\Sigma \cap \alpha' = \emptyset
$$
$$
\text{and } J(\alpha) = \nu(\alpha') \cup [T_\Sigma]_{\rho,\nu}.
$$

Fig. 5. Semantics of list segments predicates ($S \cup \rho$ denotes a new mapping $K : \mathrm{dom}(S) \cup \mathrm{dom}(\rho) \to Loc$ s.t. $K(in) = \rho(x)$, $\forall x \in \mathrm{dom}(\rho)$ and $K(y) = S(y)$, $\forall y \in \mathrm{dom}(S)$)

defined by more than one field). The constraint $T_\Sigma \cap \alpha = \emptyset$ expresses the fact that the inner list segments are disjoint. We assume several restrictions on the definition of P_α: (1) $\tau(in) = \tau(out) = \tau(u')$, and $\tau(in) \neq \tau(v')$, for every $v' \in \vec{v}$; this is to ensure that the nesting of different predicates is bounded, and (2) the predicate P does not occur in Σ.

For any predicate P_α, $Flds_0(P_\alpha)$ is the set of all fields used in points-to constraints of Σ. Also, $Flds(P_\alpha) = Flds_0(P_\alpha) \cup \bigcup_{Q_\beta \text{ in } \Sigma} Flds(Q_\beta)$. If Σ has only points-to constraints then P_α is a 1-*level predicate*. For any $n \geq 2$, if Σ contains only m-level predicates with $m \leq n - 1$ and at least one $(n-1)$-level predicate then P_α is a n-*level predicate*.

To simplify the presentation of some constructions, we may use less expressive predicates of the form (Σ contains no points-to constraints having u' on the left side):

$$
P_\alpha(in, out, \vec{nhb}) \triangleq (in = out) \vee (\exists u', \vec{v}, \alpha', \vec{\beta}. \Sigma(in, u', \vec{v}, \vec{nhb}, \vec{\beta}) * P_{\alpha'}(u', out, \vec{nhb})) \quad (3)
$$

Example 1. The predicates used in the analysis from Sec. 2 are defined as follows:

$$\texttt{nll}_\alpha(x,y,z) \triangleq (x = y) \vee \left(\exists u', v', \alpha', \beta. x \mapsto \{(\texttt{nexth}, u'), (\texttt{tasks}, v')\} * \texttt{ls}_\beta(v', z) * \texttt{nll}_{\alpha'}(u', y, z)\right),$$
$$\text{where } \texttt{ls}_\alpha(x, y) \triangleq (x = y) \vee \left(\exists u', \alpha'. x \mapsto \{(\texttt{succ}, u')\} * \texttt{ls}_{\alpha'}(u', y)\right)$$

$$\texttt{dll}_\alpha(x,y) \quad \triangleq (x = y) \vee \left(\exists u', \alpha'. (x \mapsto \{(\texttt{next}, u')\} * u' \mapsto \{(\texttt{prev}, x)\}) *_w \texttt{dll}_{\alpha'}(u', y) \wedge x \notin \alpha'\right)$$

$$\texttt{sll}_\alpha(x,y,z) \triangleq (x = y) \vee \left(\exists u', \alpha'. x \mapsto \{(\texttt{next}, u'), (\texttt{prev}, z)\} * \texttt{sll}_{\alpha'}(u', y, z)\right)$$

5 Abstract Domain

We define an abstract domain parametrized by a set of predicates $\mathcal{P}$, denoted by $\mathcal{ASL}(\mathcal{P})$, whose elements are *NOLL* formulas over $\mathcal{P}$ represented as sets of graphs. We define the order relation $\preceq$ between two sets of graphs and a widening operator $\triangledown$. We assume that the definitions in $\mathcal{P}$ are not mutually recursive.

5.1 Abstract Domain Elements

Each disjunct φ of an $\mathcal{ASL}(\mathcal{P})$ element is represented by a labeled directed multi-graph $G[\varphi]$, called *heap graph* [13].

Given $\varphi = \Pi \wedge \Sigma \wedge \Lambda$, every node of $G[\varphi]$ represents a maximal set of equal location variables (according to Π) and it is labeled by the location variables in this set. If Π contains both $E \neq F$ and $E = F$ then $G[\varphi]$ is the bottom element $\perp$. We also assume that nodes are typed according to the variables they represent.

The set of edges in $G[\varphi]$ represent spatial or disequality atoms different from *true* and *emp*. An atom $E \neq F$ is represented by an unlabeled edge from the node labeled by E to the node labeled by F, called a *disequality edge*. An atom $E \mapsto \{(f, F)\}$ is represented by an edge labeled by f from the node of E to the node of F, called a *points-to edge*. An atom $P_\alpha(E, F, \vec{B})$, where $E, F \in LVars$ and $\vec{B} \in LVars^*$, is represented by an edge from the node of E to the node of F labeled by $(P_\alpha, \vec{N}_B)$, where $\vec{N}_B$ is the sequence of nodes labeled by $\vec{B}$; such an edge is called a *predicate edge*. A *spatial edge* is a points-to or a predicate edge. The spatial formula *true* is represented by a special node labeled by *true*. A heap graph that does not contain this node is called *precise*. The object separated spatial constraints are represented in $G[\varphi]$ by a binary relation Ω_* over edges. The sharing constraints of φ are kept unchanged in $G[\varphi]$.

Formally, $G[\varphi] = (V, E, \pi, \ell, \Omega_*, \Lambda)$, where V is the set of nodes, E is the set of edges, π is the node typing function, ℓ is the node labeling function, and Ω_* is a symmetric relation over edges in E. The set of all heap graphs is denoted by $\mathcal{HG}$.

In the following, $V(G)$, denotes the set of nodes in the heap graph G; we use a similar notation for all the other components of G. For any node $n \in V(G)$, $PVars_G(n)$ denotes the set of all *program variables* labeling the node n in G, i.e., $PVars_G(n) = \ell(n) \cap Vars$. A node n is called *anonymous* iff $PVars_G(n) = \emptyset$.

The concretization of an $\mathcal{ASL}(\mathcal{P})$ element Φ is defined as the set of models of Φ.

Remark 1. In the elements of $\mathcal{ASL}(\mathcal{P})$, the disjunction is used only at the top most level. In practice, this may be a source of redundancy and inefficiency and some specialized techniques have been proposed in order to deal with disjunctive predicates, e.g., [8] and inner-level disjunction, e.g., [1,16]. For example, [16] allows disjunctions under the level of the field separated formulas instead of the top-most level. These techniques can be embedded in our framework, by adapting the graph homomorphism approach for defining the order relation between $\mathcal{ASL}(\mathcal{P})$ elements.

5.2   Order Relation

The order relation between abstract elements, denoted by $\preceq$, over-approximates the entailment (i.e., if $\Phi_1 \preceq \Phi_2$ then $\Phi_1 \models \Phi_2$) and it is defined using the graph homomorphism approach [9,13], extended to disjunctions of existentially quantified formulas.

Given two elements $\varphi_1 = \Pi_1 \wedge \Sigma_1 \wedge \Lambda_1$ and $\varphi_2 = \Pi_2 \wedge \Sigma_2 \wedge \Lambda_2$ of $\mathcal{ASL}$, $\varphi_1 \preceq \varphi_2$ iff $G[\varphi_1] = \bot$ or there exists an homomorphism from $G[\varphi_2]$ to $G[\varphi_1]$ defined as follows.

Let G_1 and G_2 be two heap graphs such that G_1 is not precise. An *homomorphism* from G_1 to G_2 is a mapping $h : V(G_1) \rightarrow V(G_2)$ such that the following conditions hold. The constraints imposed by $*$ and $*_w$ are expressed using the function $used : E(G_1) \rightarrow 2^{E(G_2) \times 2^{Flds}}$, defined meanwhile edges of G_1 are mapped to sub-graphs of G_2.

node labeling preservation: For any $n \in V(G_1)$, $PVars_{G_1}(n) \subseteq PVars_{G_2}(h(n))$.

disequality edge mapping: For any disequality edge $(n,n') \in E(G_1)$, there exists a disequality edge $(h(n), h(n'))$ in $E(G_2)$.

points-to edge mapping: For any points-to edge $e = (n,n') \in E(G_1)$ labeled by f, there exists a points-to edge $e' = (h(n), h(n'))$ labeled by f in $E(G_2)$. We define $used(e) = (e', f)$.

predicate edge mapping: Let $e = (n,n')$ be an edge in G_1 representing a predicate $P_\alpha(in, out, \vec{nhb})$ as in (3) (the extension to predicate definitions as in (2) is straightforward). We assume that $\preceq$ is a partial order on the predicates in $\mathcal{P}$ which is an (over-approximation of) the semantic entailment $\models$ [2].

It is required that either $h(n) = h(n')$ or there exists an homomorphism h_e from the graph representation of a formula that describes an unfolding of P_α to a sub-graph $G_2(e)$ of G_2. Formulas that describe unfoldings of P are of the form:

$$\psi := \phi[E_0, E_1] * \phi[E_1, E_2] * \ldots * \phi[E_{n-1}, E_n], \qquad (4)$$

where $E_0 = E$, $E_n = F$, $n \geq 1$, and for any $0 \leq i < n$, $\phi[E_i, E_{i+1}]$ is the formula

$$\Sigma(E_i, E_{i+1}, u', \vec{v}', \vec{nhb}, \vec{\beta}) \quad \text{or} \quad P'_{\alpha_i}(E_i, E_{i+1}, \vec{nhb}) \text{ with } P'_\alpha \preceq P_\alpha.$$

If $\phi[E_i, E_{i+1}]$ is of the form $P'_{\alpha_i}(E_i, E_{i+1}, \vec{B}')$, then h_e must match the edge corresponding to $\phi[E_i, E_{i+1}]$ with exactly one edge of $G_2(e)$. That is, if m and m' are the nodes labeled by E_i, resp., E_{i+1}, then $G_2(e)$ contains an edge $(h_e(m), h_e(m'))$ labeled by $(P'_{\alpha_i}, \vec{N}_{B'})$, where $\vec{N}_{B'}$ are the nodes labeled by the variables in $\vec{B}'$.

Above, we have reduced the definition of the homomorphism for n-level predicate edges to the definition of the homomorphism for $(n-1)$-level predicate edges. For 1-level predicates, the sub-formula Σ contains only points-to constraints and the definition above reduces to matching points-to edges and checking the order relation between predicates in $\mathcal{P}$.

We define $used(e)$ as the union of $used(e')$ for any edge e' in the graph representation of ψ. If e' is a points-to edge then $used(e')$ is defined as above. If e' is the edge representing some formula $\phi[E_i, E_{i+1}]$ of the form $P'_{\alpha_i}(E_i, E_{i+1}, \vec{nhb})$ and e'' the edge associated to e' by h_e then $used(e') = \{(e'', f) \mid f \in Flds_0(P_\alpha)\}$, where $Flds_0(P_\alpha)$ denotes the set of fields used in points-to constraints of Σ.

---

[2] For the set of predicates we have used in our experiments, $\models$ can be checked syntactically.

separating conjunctions semantics: The semantics of $*_w$ requires that, for any two spatial edges e_1 and e_2 in G_1, $used(e_1) \cap used(e_2) = \emptyset$. The semantics of $*$ requires that for any two edges e_1 and e_2 s.t. $(e_1, e_2) \in \Omega_*(G_1)$, we have that $(e_1', e_2') \in \Omega_*(G_2)$, for any edge e_1' in $used(e_1)$ and any edge e_2' in $used(e_2)$.

entailment of sharing constraints: Based on the mapping of edges in $E(G_1)$ to subgraphs of G_2, we define a substitution Γ for set variables in $\Lambda(G_1)$ to terms over variables in $\Lambda(G_2)$. Let α be a variable in $\Lambda(G_1)$. If α is not bound to a spatial atom then $\Gamma(\alpha) = \alpha$. Otherwise, let α be bound to a spatial atom represented by some edge $e \in E(G_1)$. Then, $\Gamma(\alpha)$ is the union of (1) the set variables bound to spatial atoms denoted by predicate edges in $used(e)$ and (2) the terms $\{x\}$, where x labels the left-end of a points-to edge in $used(e)$. It is required that $\Lambda(G_1)[\Gamma] \Rightarrow \Lambda(G_2)$.

If both G_1 and G_2 are precise then we add the following constraints: (1) predicate ordering $\preceq$ is the equality relation, (2) every edge of G_2 belongs to the image of $used$, and (3) the paths of G_2 associated by h to predicate edges of G_1 can not be interpreted into lasso-shaped or cyclic paths in some model of G_2. Also, by convention, there exists no homomorphism from a precise heap graph to one which is not precise.

The order relation is extended to general $\mathcal{ASL}$ elements as usual: $\Phi_1 \preceq \Phi_2$ iff for each disjunct φ_1 of Φ_1 there exists a disjunct φ_2 in Φ_2 such that $\varphi_1 \preceq \varphi_2$.

The complexity of our procedure for finding a homomorphism is NP time. It extends the unique mapping induced by program variables in a non-deterministic way to the anonymous nodes.

5.3   An Effective Homomorphism Check for Predicate Edges

In order to check that some predicate edge of G_1 is homomorphic to a sub-graph of G_2, we define an effective procedure based on tree automata. For the simplicity of the presentation, we consider that predicates in $\mathcal{P}$ have the following form:

$$P(in, out, \vec{nhb}) \triangleq (in = out) \vee (\exists u', v'. \tag{5}$$
$$in \mapsto \{(f, u'), (g, b_1), (h, v')\} * R(v', b_2, \vec{b}) \ * \ P(u', out, \vec{nhb})),$$

$$\text{where } b_1, b_2, \vec{b} \subseteq \vec{nhb}, f, h, g \in Flds, \text{ and } R \in \mathcal{P}.$$

Such predicates describe nested list segments where every two consecutive elements are linked by f, the g field of every element points to some fixed location b, and the h field of every element points to a list segment described by R. Note that the results below can be extended to predicates describing doubly-linked list segments like in (2) or cyclic nested list segments.

Essentially, we model heap graphs by (unranked) labeled trees and then, for each recursive predicate P, we define a (non-deterministic) top-down tree automaton that recognizes exactly all the heap graphs that describe unfoldings of P. The fact that some predicate edge e of G_1 is homomorphic to a sub-graph of G_2 reduces to the fact that the tree-modeling of the sub-graph of G_2 is accepted by the tree automaton corresponding to the predicate labeling e.

Tree Automata: A *tree* over an alphabet Σ is a partial mapping $t : \mathbb{N}^* \to \Sigma$ such that $\mathrm{dom}(t)$ is a finite, prefix-closed subset of $\mathbb{N}^*$. Let ε denote the empty sequence. Each sequence $p \in \mathrm{dom}(t)$ is called a *vertex* and a vertex p with no children (i.e., for all $i \in \mathbb{N}$, $pi \notin \mathrm{dom}(t)$) is called a *leaf*.

A *(top-down) tree automaton* is a tuple $\mathcal{A} = (Q, \Sigma, I, \delta)$, where Q is a finite set of states, $I \subseteq Q$ is a set of initial states, Σ is a finite alphabet, and δ is a set of transition rules of the form $q \xrightarrow{f} (q_1, \ldots, q_n)$, where $n \geq 0$, $q, q_1, \ldots, q_n \in Q$, and $f \in \Sigma$.

A *run* of $\mathcal{A}$ on a tree t over Σ is a mapping $\pi : \operatorname{dom}(t) \to Q$ such that $\pi(\varepsilon) \in I$ and for each non-leaf vertex $p \in \operatorname{dom}(t)$, δ contains a rule of the form $q \xrightarrow{t(p)} (q_1, \ldots, q_n)$, where $q = \pi(p)$ and $q_i = \pi(pi)$, for all i such that $pi \in \operatorname{dom}(t)$. The *language* of $\mathcal{A}$ is the set of all trees t for which there exists a run of $\mathcal{A}$ on t.

Tree-modeling of Heap Graphs: Note that the minimal heap graphs that are homomorphic to a predicate edge have a special form: nodes with more than one incoming edge have no successors. Such heap graphs are transformed into tree-shaped graphs with labeled nodes by (1) moving edge labels to the source node and (2) introducing copies of nodes with more than one incoming edge (i.e., for every set of edges E' having the same destination n, introduce $|E'|$ copies of n and replace every edge (m, n) by (m, n_m), where n_m is a copy of n). We also replace labels of predicate edges of the form $(P_\alpha, \vec{N}_B)$ with $(P, \vec{B})$, where $\vec{B}$ is a tuple of variables labeling the nodes in N_B.

Given a finite set of variables $\mathcal{V}$, let $\Sigma_{\mathcal{V}} = 2^{Flds \cup \mathcal{V}} \cup \{(P, \vec{B}) \mid P \in \mathcal{P}, \vec{B} \in \mathcal{V}^+\}$. The *tree-modeling* of a heap graph G is the tree $t[G]$ over $\Sigma_{\mathcal{V}}$ isomorphic to the tree-shaped graph described above; $\mathcal{V}$ is the set of variables labeling nodes of the graph.

Tree Automata Recognizing Unfoldings of Recursive Predicates: The definition of the tree-automata associated to a predicate P as in (5), denoted $\mathcal{A}_P$, follows its recursive definition. $I(\mathcal{A}_P) = \{q_0^P\}$ and the transition rules in $\delta(\mathcal{A}_P)$ are defined as follows:

$$q_0^P \xrightarrow{\{in, f, g, h\}} (q_{rec}^P, q_g^P, q_h^P) \qquad q_{rec}^P \xrightarrow{\{f, g, h\}} (q_{rec}^P, q_g^P, q_h^P) \qquad q_h^P \xrightarrow{h} q_0^R$$

$$q_0^P \xrightarrow{\{in, out\}} \varepsilon \qquad q_{rec}^P \xrightarrow{(P', \vec{B})} q_{rec}^P, \text{ with } P'(E, F, \vec{B}) \preceq P(E, F, \vec{B}) \qquad q_g^P \xrightarrow{b} \varepsilon$$

$$q_{rec}^P \xrightarrow{out} \varepsilon \qquad\qquad Rules(R)[\Upsilon]$$

where q_0^R is the initial state of $\mathcal{A}_R$, the tree automaton for R, and $Rules(R)[\Upsilon]$ denotes the set $\delta(\mathcal{A}_R)$ where variables are substituted by the actual parameters v', b_2, and $\vec{b}$.

6   Widening

We describe the widening operator $\triangledown$, which satisfies the following properties: (1) it defines an upper bound for any two elements of $\mathcal{ASL}$, i.e., given $\Phi_1, \Phi_2 \in \mathcal{ASL}$, $\Phi_1 \preceq \Phi_1 \triangledown \Phi_2$ and $\Phi_2 \preceq \Phi_1 \triangledown \Phi_2$, and (2) for any infinite ascending chain $\Phi_1 \preceq \Phi_2 \preceq \ldots \preceq \Phi_n \preceq \ldots$ in $\mathcal{ASL}$, there exists a finite chain $\Phi_1^\triangledown \preceq \ldots \preceq \Phi_k^\triangledown$ in $\mathcal{ASL}$ such that $\Phi_1^\triangledown = \Phi_1$, $\Phi_i^\triangledown = \Phi_{i-1}^\triangledown \triangledown \Phi_{i+1}$, for every $2 \leq i \leq k$, and $\Phi_k^\triangledown = \Phi_k^\triangledown \triangledown \Phi_{k+1}$. The widening operator is used to ensure the termination of fixed point computations over elements of $\mathcal{ASL}$.

We define $\varphi_1 \triangledown \varphi_2$, for any φ_1 and φ_2 two disjunction-free formulas in $\mathcal{ASL}$. The extension to disjunctions is straightforward. The widening operator is parametrized by a natural number K such that $\varphi_1 \triangledown \varphi_2$ returns a set of heap graphs with at most $max(annon(\varphi_1), K)$ anonymous nodes, where $annon(\varphi_1)$ is the number of anonymous nodes in $G[\varphi_1]$. Therefore, an infinite ascending chain is over-approximated by a finite one, whose elements have at most as many anonymous nodes as either the first element of the infinite ascending chain or the parameter K, depending on which one is bigger.

Widening Operator Description: Intuitively, the result of $\varphi_1 \nabla \varphi_2$ should preserve the properties which are present in both φ_1 and φ_2. To this, each graph $G_i = G[\varphi_i]$, $i \in \{1,2\}$, is split into three sub-graphs G_i^+, G_i^-, and $G_i^\approx$ such that:

- the sets of spatial edges in these sub-graphs form a partition of the set of spatial edges in G_i;
- there exists an homomorphism $h_\rightarrow$ from the sub-graph G_1^+ to G_2^- and an homomorphism $h_\leftarrow$ from G_2^+ to G_1^-;
- G_1^+ and G_2^+ are maximal.

Here, a heap graph G' is called a *sub-graph* of a heap graph G if it contains only a subset of the nodes and edges in G, for each node n, the labeling of n in G' is a subset of the labeling of n in G such that $PVars_G(n) \neq \emptyset$ implies $PVars_{G'}(n) \neq \emptyset$, and the Ω_* and Λ components of G' are also subsets of the corresponding components of G.

The two tuples of sub-graphs are called an *homomorphism induced partition*.

Example 2. Let G_1 and G_2 be the graphs pictured in the first row of Fig. 7. The tuples of sub-graphs $(G_1^+, G_1^-, G_1^\approx)$ and $(G_2^+, G_2^-, G_2^\approx)$ given in the second row of Fig. 7 define homomorphism induced partitions for G_1 and, resp., G_2. These partitions correspond to the homomorphisms $h_{ij} : G_i^+ \rightarrow G_j^-$, which map the node labeled by y (resp., z) in G_i^+ to the node labeled by y (resp., z) in G_j^-, for all $1 \leq i \neq j \leq 2$.

If $G_1^\approx = \emptyset$ and $G_2^\approx = \emptyset$ then each spatial edge of G_1 is homomorphic to a sub-graph of G_2 or vice-versa. In this case, the result of the widening is the graph defined as the union of G_1^+ and G_2^+, i.e., the weakest among the comparable sub-graphs. The union operator $\uplus$ is parametrized by the two homomorphisms $h_\rightarrow$ and $h_\leftarrow$ in order to (1) merge nodes which are matched according to these homomorphisms, (2) identify the object separated spatial constraints in the union of the two sub-graphs, and (3) compute the union of the sharing constraints. In this case, the number of anonymous nodes in $\varphi_1 \nabla \varphi_2$ is bounded by the number of anonymous nodes in φ_1.

Otherwise, the widening operator tries to return two graphs G_1' and G_2', each of them being obtained from G_1 resp. G_2, by replacing the sub-graph G_i^- with its weaker version G_j^+, where $i, j \in \{1,2\}$ and $i \neq j$. However, to preserve the bound on the number of anonymous nodes, this operation is possible only if the number of anonymous nodes in G_1' and G_2' is smaller than $max(annon(\varphi_1), K)$.

Example 3. In Fig. 7, if $K = 3$ then $G_1 \nabla G_2$ has two disjuncts. The first one, G_1', is obtained from G_1 using the homomorphism h_{21}: (1) the graph G_1^- is replaced by G_2^+, and (2) the sharing constraints $\beta = \alpha^1 \cup \alpha^2$ become $\alpha = \beta$, where β is the set of locations in the doubly-linked list defined by dll_β. The second disjunct, G_2', is obtained similarly from G_2 using h_{12}.

Operator fold: If the above condition on the number of anonymous nodes is not satisfied then, we apply an operator called fold on each of the two graphs. Given a heap graph G and some $b \in \mathbb{N}$, fold builds a graph F with at most b anonymous nodes, obtained from G by replacing edges used by non-empty unfoldings of recursive predicates with predicate edges (labeled with fresh set variables). Moreover, nodes in F without incident edges are removed. The graph F is homomorphic to G and fold also returns the homomorphism h from F to G. The operator fold may fail to obtain a graph with at most b anonymous nodes in which case it returns $\top$.

The object/field separation between predicate edges copied from G to F is preserved. Two predicate edges in F are object separated if (1) they replace two unfoldings in G that contain disjoint sets of nodes and any two predicate edges from the two unfoldings are object separated in G or (2) one of them, denoted by e_1, replaces an unfolding in G, the other one, denoted by e_2, is copied from G, and all the edges from the unfolding are object separated from e_2 in G. Otherwise, the predicate edges are field separated.

$G_1 \triangledown G_2 \triangleq$

    let $(G_1^+, G_1^-, G_1^\approx)$ and $(G_2^+, G_2^-, G_2^\approx)$
      be an homomorphism induced partition
      of G_1 and G_2

    let $\pi = (h_\rightarrow, h_\leftarrow)$

    if $(G_1^\approx = \emptyset \wedge G_2^\approx = \emptyset)$ **then**

      return $G_1^+ \uplus^\pi G_2^+$;

    else

      $G_1' = (G_1^+ \cup G_1^\approx) \uplus^{h_\leftarrow} G_2^+$;
      $G_2' = (G_2^+ \cup G_2^\approx) \uplus^{h_\rightarrow} G_1^+$;
      $bound = max(annon(\varphi_1), K)$;
      if $(annon(G_1') \leq bound$
        $\wedge \, annon(G_2') \leq bound)$ **then**
        return $G_1' \triangledown G_2'$;
      else
        for each $1 \leq i \leq 2$ **do**
          $b_i = bound - annon(G_i^+ \cup G_i^-)$;
          $(F_i, h_i) = fold(G_i^\approx, b_i)$;
          $G_i' = (G_i^+ \cup G_i^-) \uplus^{h_i} F_i$;
        return $G_1' \triangledown G_2'$;

    Fig. 6. The definition of $\triangledown$

Another important property of fold is to maintain relations between sets of locations that correspond to unfoldings of recursive predicates, replaced by predicate edges. For any sub-graph G' of G representing the unfolding of a recursive predicate, let $T_{G'}$ be the set term defined as the union of all set variables labeling edges in G' and all location variables, which are the source of at least one points-to edge in G'. Based on the equalities between location variables in G, the sharing constraints $\Lambda(G)$, and the inference rule "if $t_1 = t_1'$ and $t_2 = t_2'$ then $t_1 \cup t_2 = t_1' \cup t_2'$", for any set terms t_1, t_1', t_2, and t_2', fold generates new equalities between (unions of) set terms $T_{G'}$ or between (unions of) set terms $T_{G'}$ and set variables labeling edges copied from G to F. Once a predicate edge e in F replaces the unfolding of a recursive predicate G', the set term $T_{G'}$ is substituted by the set variable labeling e. Similarly, fold generates constraints of the form $t \cap t' = \emptyset$ with t and t' set terms, and constraints of the form $x \in t$ or $x \notin t$.

In the definition of $\triangledown$, the argument of fold is the graph $G_i^\approx$ where anonymous nodes that are incident to edges in G_i^+ or G_i^- are labeled by ghost program variables so they are preserved in the output of fold. Then, the graph G_i' is defined by replacing the subgraph $G_i^\approx$ of G_i with the one returned by fold, i.e., F_i. This replacement is written as the union of the sub-graph $G_i^+ \cup G_i^-$ with F_i, where the homomorphism h_i is used to merge nodes which are associated by h_i and to identify the object separated constraints. Finally, the widening operator is called recursively on the new graphs. Notice that, the widening operator contains at most one recursive call. The first execution of $\triangledown$ recognizes unfoldings of recursive predicates and, if needed, eliminates enough anonymous nodes in order to make the recursive call succeed.

Example 4. In Fig. 7, if $K = 0$ then $bound = 1$ because G_1 contains one anonymous node. The computation of $\triangledown$ based only on $\uplus$ doesn't satisfy the bound on the number of anonymous nodes because $G_2^\approx$ contains two anonymous nodes labeled by v' and u'. Therefore, we apply $fold(G_2^\approx, 1)$ and the result is the graph F_2 given on the third row of Fig. 7. The graph F_2 is obtained from $G_2^\approx$ by replacing the sub-graph of $G_2^\approx$ that consists of all edges labeled by succ with a predicate edge labeled by ls_δ and the sub-graph of

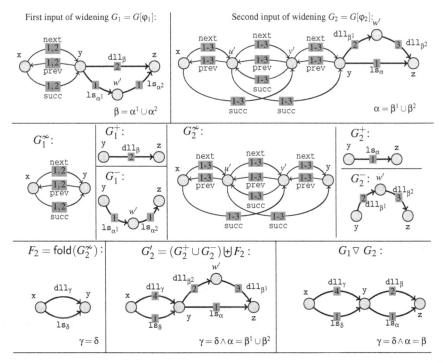

Fig. 7. Steps in the computation of $\triangledown$ (the object separated edges are defined by $\Omega_* = \{(e, e') \mid$ the integers labeling e are included in the integers labeling e' or vice-versa$\}$)

$G_2^{\approx}$ that consists of all edges labeled by next and prev with a predicate edge labeled by dll_γ. The set terms which correspond to these two unfoldings are $\{x\} \cup \{u'\} \cup \{v'\}$ and respectively, $\{x\} \cup \{u'\} \cup \{v'\}$. Since they contain exactly the same location variables the equality $\gamma = \delta$ is added to the sharing constraints of the output graph. Also, because all the edges incident to u' and v' are included in the two unfoldings, these two nodes are removed. The two edges of F_2 are field separated because the corresponding unfoldings share some node. Since $G_1^{\approx}$ has no anonymous nodes, $\text{fold}(G_1^{\approx}, 1) = G_1^{\approx}$ and $G_1' = (G_1^+ \cup G_1^-) \uplus^{h_i} F_1 = G_1$.

The second column in the last row of Fig. 7 shows the graph G_2' obtained by replacing in G_2, $G_2^{\approx}$ with F_2. Finally, $G_1 \triangledown G_2$ equals $G_1 \triangledown G_2'$, which is given in the bottom right corner of Fig 7. Notice that the computation of $G_1 \triangledown G_2'$ requires only the union.

Operator $\uplus^h$: Formally, $\uplus^h$ replaces in a given graph G, a sub-graph G' by another graph G'' s.t. h is an homomorphism from G'' to G'. For example, $(G_1^+ \cup G_1^{\approx}) \uplus^{h_\leftarrow} G_2^+$ replaces the sub-graph G_1^- of G_1 with the graph G_2^+ ($h_\leftarrow$ is an homomorphism from G_2^+ to G_1^-). The result of $\uplus^h$ on G, G', G'', and h is the heap graph $(V, E, \pi, \ell, \Omega_*, \Lambda)$, where:

- V is obtained from $V(G \setminus G') \cup V(G'')$, where $V(G \setminus G')$ is the set of nodes in G, which have at least an incident edge not included in G', by merging every $m \in V(G)$ with one of the nodes in $h^{-1}(m)$, provided that $h^{-1}(m) \neq \emptyset$;
- for any $n \in V$, the set of variables $\ell(n)$ is the union of the label of n in G, $\ell(G)(n)$, and the label of n in G'', $\ell(G'')(n)$;

- $E = (E(G) \setminus E(G')) \cup E(G'')$;
- Ω_* is defined from $\Omega_*(G)$ and $\Omega_*(G'')$ as follows: $(e, e') \in \Omega_*$ iff either (i) $(e, e') \in \Omega_*(G)$, (ii) $(e, e') \in \Omega_*(G'')$, or (iii) $e \in E(G)$, $e'' \in E(G'')$, and for any edge e' in the sub-graph of G to which e'' is mapped by the homomorphism h, $(e, e') \in \Omega_*(G)$;
- Λ is the union of (1) the constraints $\Lambda(G'')$ in G'' and (2) the constraints $\Lambda(G)$ in G where every set term t, denoting all the locations in some heap region described by a sub-graph of G' associated by the homomorphism h to an edge e'' of G'', is replaced by the set variable α in the label of e''. Note that Λ contains only set variables which appear in labels of E.

Operator $\uplus^\pi$: Given $(G_1^+, G_1^-, G_1^\sim)$ and $(G_2^+, G_2^-, G_2^\sim)$ two homomorphism induced partitions of G_1 and resp., G_2, and $\pi = (h_\to, h_\leftarrow)$, $G_1^+ \uplus^\pi G_2^+$ is defined similarly to $G_1^+ \uplus^{h_\leftarrow} G_2^+$ [3] except for the fact that the constraint on set variables is defined as the conjunction of all the constraints which appear in both $G_1^+ \uplus^{h_\leftarrow} G_2^+$ and $G_2^+ \uplus^{h_\to} G_1^+$.

Complexity: The search for homomorphism induced partitions is done in linear time in the size of the input graphs. The correspondence between anonymous nodes in $h_\leftarrow$ and $h_\to$ is chosen arbitrarily (in practice, they are chosen according to some heuristics). In order to obtain a more precise result, one should enumerate an exponential number of such mappings. Given an arbitrary but fixed order relation on the recursive predicates, the complexity of the operator fold which replaces predicate unfoldings with predicate edges according to this order is PTIME. In our implementation, the operator fold is parametrized by a set of order relations among recursive predicates (in practice, we have used a small number of such order relations) and it enumerates all of them until it succeeds to eliminate the required number of anonymous nodes.

7   Abstract Transformers

In this section, we describe the abstract transformers associated with intra-procedural statements (in Sec. 7.1) and procedure calls and returns (in Sec. 7.2).

7.1   Intra-procedural Analysis

For any basic statement C, which does not contain a procedure call, the analysis uses an abstract transformer $[\![C]\!]^\sharp : \mathcal{HG} \to 2^{\mathcal{HG}}$ that, given a heap graph $G \in \mathcal{HG}$, it returns either $\top$ meaning that a possible memory error has been encountered, or a set of heap graphs representing the effect of the statement C on G. The transformers $[\![C]\!]^\sharp$ are defined as the composition of three (families of) functions:

materialization $\to_{x,f}$: transforms a heap graph, via case analysis, into a set of heap graphs where the value of the field f stored at the address pointed to by the program variable x is concretized. It returns $\top$ if it can not prove that x is allocated in the input.

symbolic execution $\leadsto$: expresses the concrete semantics of the statements in terms of heap graphs, e.g., for an assignment $x := y$, it merges the nodes labeled by x and y.

---

[3] In $G_1^+ \uplus^{h_\leftarrow} G_2^+$, G_1^- is replaced by G_2^+.

consistency check $\to^{\#}$: takes the graphs from the output of the symbolic execution and checks if their concretization is empty or if they contain garbage. All graphs with empty concretization are removed and if garbage is detected then the result is $\top$.

Materialization $\to_{x,f}$: The relation $\to_{x,f}$ for dereferencing the field f of the object pointed to by x is defined by a set of rewriting rules over $\mathcal{ASL}$ elements. When the value of f is characterized by a predicate edge that starts or ends in a node labeled by x then the rules are straightforward. If the sharing constraints imply that x belongs to the list segment described by some predicate edge (which is not incident to a node labeled by x) and this list segment uses the field f then, we use the following rules:

$$G \quad \to_{x,f} \quad \texttt{unfoldMiddle}(G,e,x)$$

    if e is a predicate edge in G labeled by P_α such that $\Lambda(G) \Rightarrow x \in \alpha$
    and $f \in Flds_0(P_\alpha)$

$$G \quad \to_{x,f} \quad \texttt{unfoldMiddle}(G,e,\_)$$

    if e is a predicate edge in G labeled by P_α such that $\Lambda(G) \Rightarrow x \in \alpha$
    and $f \in Flds(P_\alpha) \setminus Flds_0(P_\alpha)$

The function $\texttt{unfoldMiddle}(G,e,\xi)$ concretizes the fields of an *arbitrary* object in the list segment described by e, that has the same type as the nodes incident to e. Suppose that e starts in the node n, labeled by y_1, and ends in the node n', labeled by y_2. For simplicity, suppose that e is labeled by a predicate P_α defined as in (3). Then, $\texttt{unfoldMiddle}$ replaces the edge e with the graph representation of $P_{\alpha'}(y_1,u'_1,n\vec{h}b) *_w$ $\Sigma(u'_1,u'_2,\vec{v},n\vec{h}b,\vec{\beta}) *_w P_{\alpha''}(u'_2,y_2,n\vec{h}b)$. If ξ is a program variable and the formula Σ in the definition of P_α contains a points-to constraint of the form $in \mapsto \{(f,w)\}$, for some $w \in LVars$, i.e., the direction of f is from x to y then, the node labeled by ξ is merged with the node labeled by u'_1. Otherwise, the node labeled by ξ is merged with the node labeled by u'_2. Finally, the constraints $T_\Sigma \cap \alpha' = \emptyset$, $T_\Sigma \cap \alpha'' = \emptyset$, $\alpha' \cap \alpha'' = \emptyset$ are added to $\Lambda(G)$ and all occurrences of α in $\Lambda(G)$ are substituted with $\alpha' \cup T_\Sigma \cup \alpha''$.

In general, the output of $\to_{x,f}$ depends on the (dis)equalities which are explicit in the input heap graph (e.g., an equality $x_1 = x_2$ is explicit if there exists a node labeled by both x_1 and x_2). In order to make explicit all the (dis)equalities which are implied by the input graph, (e.g., $ls(x,y) * ls(x,z) * y \mapsto \{(f,t)\}$ implies $x = z$), one can use the normalization procedure introduced in [13], based on SAT solvers.

7.2   Inter-procedural Analysis

We consider an inter-procedural analysis based on the *local heap* semantics [18]. The analysis explores the call graph of the program starting from the `main` procedure and proceeds downward, computing for each procedure `Proc`, a set of summaries of the form (φ_i, Φ_o), where φ_i and Φ_o are $\mathcal{ASL}$ elements, φ_i disjunction-free. Essentially, φ_i is an abstract element built at the entry point of the procedure `Proc` by the transformer associated to `call Proc`$(\vec{x})$, which describes the part of the heap reachable from the actual parameters $\vec{x}$. Then, Φ_o is the abstract element obtained by analyzing the effect of `Proc` on the input described by φ_i. The transformer associated to the `return` statement takes a summary (φ_i, Φ_o) of `Proc` and returns a set of heap graphs obtained from the ones associated to the control point of the caller that precedes the procedure call by replacing the graph φ_i with each of the graphs in Φ_o. The important operations for the inter-procedural analysis are the computation of the local heap at the procedure call and the substitution of the local heap with the output heap at the procedure return.

These operations are more difficult in the presence of *cutpoints*, i.e., locations in the local heap of the callee which are reachable from local variables of other procedures in the call stack without passing through the actual parameters. For simplicity, we define the `call` transformer such that it returns $\top$ whenever it detects cutpoints. This is still relevant, because in practice most of the procedure calls are cutpoint-free.

Frame Rules: We follow the approach in Gotsman et al. [14] and define these transformers based on a frame rule for procedure calls. The fragment of *NOLL* without $*_w$ and sharing constraints satisfies the following frame rule [14]:

$$\frac{\phi \models \phi_{call}\sigma * \phi_1 \quad \phi_{ret}\sigma * \phi_1 \models \phi' \quad \{\phi_{call}\}\texttt{Proc}(\vec{x})\{\phi_{ret}\}}{\{\phi\}\texttt{Proc}(\vec{x}\sigma)\{\phi'\}}$$

where σ is the substitution from formal to actual parameters. Intuitively, this means that it is possible to analyze the effect of $\texttt{Proc}(\vec{x})$ on a part of the heap, ϕ_{call}, while holding the rest of the heap ϕ_1 aside, to be added to the heap ϕ_{ret} that results from executing Proc. In general, $\phi_{call}\sigma$ and ϕ_1 can be chosen arbitrarily but, in order to be precise, $\phi_{call}\sigma$ should contain all the heap locations reachable from the actual parameters.

In the following, we extend this frame rule to work for both per-object and per-field separating conjunction. Given a disjunction-free *NOLL* formula φ, $T[\varphi]$ denotes the set term which is the union of all set variables in φ and all location variables which are on the left side of a points-to constraint. Then, the following holds:

$$\frac{\phi \models (\phi_{call}\sigma *_w \phi_1) * \phi_2 \quad (\phi_{ret}\sigma *_w \phi_1) * \phi_2 \wedge \Lambda \models \phi' \quad \{\phi_{call}\}\texttt{Proc}(\vec{x})\{\phi_{ret}\}}{\{\phi\}\texttt{Proc}(\vec{x}\sigma)\{\phi'\}}$$

where σ is the substitution from formal to actual parameters and

$\Lambda \triangleq T[\phi_{ret}] \cap T_1 = \emptyset$ with T_1 a set term over variables in ϕ_1 s.t. $\phi \models T[\phi_{call}\sigma] \cap T_1 = \emptyset$.

The formula Λ expresses the fact that if all heap locations in the interpretation of T_1 are disjoint from the ones included in the local heap of Proc then, they will remain disjoint from all the locations in the output of Proc.

Computing the Local Heap: To compute ϕ_{call}, we proceed as follows (as before, this is important only for precision). For any procedure Proc, *Flds*(Proc) denotes the set of fields accessed by Proc, which consists of (1) the fields f such that x->f appears in some expression and (2) all the fields of the type *RT* such that Proc contains a free statement over a variable of type *RT*. This set of fields can be computed easily from the syntactic tree of Proc. Given an $\mathcal{ASL}$ element ϕ, a spatial edge in ϕ is called a Proc-edge iff it is a points-to edge labeled by some $f \in \textit{Flds}(\texttt{Proc})$ or a predicate edge labeled by P_α with $\textit{Flds}(P_\alpha) \cap \textit{Flds}(\texttt{Proc}) \neq \emptyset$.

The set of spatial edges in ϕ_{call} is the union of (1) the subgraph G_r of ϕ that contains all the Proc-edges which are reachable from the actual parameters using only Proc-edges and (2) all the Proc-edges e such that the set of locations characterized by e is not disjoint from the set of locations characterized by G_r, according to ϕ (e.g., if e is a

Table 1. Experimental results on an Intel Core i3 2.4 GHz with 2GB of memory ($3 \times$ dll means 3 instances of the predicate dll over 3 disjoint sets of pointer fields)

program	size		spec NOLL	analysis − max			time (sec)
	#fun	#lines	$\mathcal{P}$	#iter	#graphs	#anon (K)	
list-dio	5	134	$2 \times$ dll	5	16	3	<3
many-keys	4	87	$3 \times$ dll	3	8	2	<1
cache	4	88	dll	3	5	2	<1
nagios-event	4	90	nll, $2 \times$ ls	3	5	2	<2
nagios-task	4	112	nll, dll, sll, ls	5	8	3	<2
nagios-queue	4	101	nll, dll, ls	3	5	2	<2

predicate edge labeled by P_α then $\phi \not\Rightarrow \alpha \cap T[G_r] = \emptyset$). The pure and sharing constraints in ϕ_{call} are all the pure and the sharing constraints in ϕ that contain variables from the spatial constraints in ϕ_{call}.

8   Experiments

We have implemented our inter-procedural analysis in the plugin CELIA [3,5] of the FRAMA-C platform [4] for C program analysis. The domain $\mathcal{ASL}$ has been implemented as a C library which takes as input a set of predicates defined in the logic ACSL of FRAMA-C. To reduce the number of disjuncts in a formula, we define an heuristic for choosing when to replace pairs of disjuncts G_1, G_2 by their widening $G_1 \triangledown G_2$.

We have considered two classes of programs. The first class contains the examples from [16] which manipulate (i.e., create, find, add, delete) doubly linked lists (DLL): (list-dio) manipulates two overlaid, circular DLL per-object separated from a third circular DLL; (many-keys) manipulates three overlaid and circular DLL; (cache) manipulates one circular DLL with a pointer to the last added cell. The second class of examples is extracted from the Nagios data structures and work on nested linked lists (NLL) combined with singly (SLL) or doubly linked lists: (nagios-event) manipulates an NLL where all the nested cells are shared with a SLL, (nagios-task) is the example considered in the overview, and (nagios-queue) manipulates an NLL where some of the nested list cells are shared with a DLL.

Table 1 presents the results of our analysis on the above benchmark. Column $\mathcal{P}$ indicates the set of predicates used by the analysis for each example. The last five columns gives collected informations about the analysis, e.g., the number of widening points, the maximal number of graphs in the abstract values and the maximal size of these graphs, and the maximal time for the analysis of included functions. For the first three examples, the comparison with the execution times reported in [16] raises the following comments. The experiments have been done on different hardware configurations and the set of recursive predicates supported in [16] does not include predicates for describing nested lists, but predicates for describing tree data structures.

The precision and the efficiency of our analysis depends on several factors. One factor is the choice of an adequate set $\mathcal{P}$ of recursive predicates. The set $\mathcal{P}$ should be expressive enough to describe all the data structures manipulated by the program and, for efficiency, it should be minimal and not contain unused predicates (such predicates may slow down the fold procedure used in the widening operator). The scalability of our analysis also depends on the modularity of the input program: if the code is structured in functions that deal with one non-overlapped list at a time then the analysis is more efficient. However, this does not have an influence on the precision of the analysis.

References

1. Ball, T., Podelski, A., Rajamani, S.K.: Boolean and cartesian abstraction for model checking c programs. In: Margaria, T., Yi, W. (eds.) TACAS 2001. LNCS, vol. 2031, pp. 268–283. Springer, Heidelberg (2001)
2. Berdine, J., Calcagno, C., Cook, B., Distefano, D., O'Hearn, P.W., Wies, T., Yang, H.: Shape analysis for composite data structures. In: Damm, W., Hermanns, H. (eds.) CAV 2007. LNCS, vol. 4590, pp. 178–192. Springer, Heidelberg (2007)
3. Bouajjani, A., Dragoi, C., Enea, C., Sighireanu, M.: On inter-procedural analysis of programs with lists and data. In: PLDI, pp. 578–589. ACM (2011)
4. CEA. Frama-C Platform, http://frama-c.com
5. Celia plugin, http://www.liafa.univ-paris-diderot.fr/celia
6. Chang, B.-Y.E., Rival, X.: Relational inductive shape analysis. In: POPL, pp. 247–260. ACM (2008)
7. Chang, B.-Y.E., Rival, X., Necula, G.C.: Shape analysis with structural invariant checkers. In: Riis Nielson, H., Filé, G. (eds.) SAS 2007. LNCS, vol. 4634, pp. 384–401. Springer, Heidelberg (2007)
8. Chin, W.-N., Gherghina, C., Voicu, R., Le, Q.L., Craciun, F., Qin, S.: A specialization calculus for pruning disjunctive predicates to support verification. In: Gopalakrishnan, G., Qadeer, S. (eds.) CAV 2011. LNCS, vol. 6806, pp. 293–309. Springer, Heidelberg (2011)
9. Cook, B., Haase, C., Ouaknine, J., Parkinson, M.J., Worrell, J.: Tractable reasoning in a fragment of separation logic. In: Katoen, J.-P., König, B. (eds.) CONCUR 2011. LNCS, vol. 6901, pp. 235–249. Springer, Heidelberg (2011)
10. Cousot, P., Cousot, R.: Abstract interpretation: A unified lattice model for static analysis of programs by construction or approximation of fixpoints. In: POPL. ACM (1977)
11. Distefano, D., O'Hearn, P.W., Yang, H.: A local shape analysis based on separation logic. In: Hermanns, H., Palsberg, J. (eds.) TACAS 2006. LNCS, vol. 3920, pp. 287–302. Springer, Heidelberg (2006)
12. Dudka, K., Müller, P., Peringer, P., Vojnar, T.: Predator: A verification tool for programs with dynamic linked data structures - (competition contribution). In: Flanagan, C., König, B. (eds.) TACAS 2012. LNCS, vol. 7214, pp. 545–548. Springer, Heidelberg (2012)
13. Enea, C., Saveluc, V., Sighireanu, M.: Compositional invariant checking for overlaid and nested linked lists. In: Felleisen, M., Gardner, P. (eds.) ESOP 2013. LNCS, vol. 7792, pp. 129–148. Springer, Heidelberg (2013)
14. Gotsman, A., Berdine, J., Cook, B.: Interprocedural shape analysis with separated heap abstractions. In: Yi, K. (ed.) SAS 2006. LNCS, vol. 4134, pp. 240–260. Springer, Heidelberg (2006)
15. Gulwani, S., Lev-Ami, T., Sagiv, M.: A combination framework for tracking partition sizes. In: POPL, pp. 239–251. ACM (2009)
16. Lee, O., Yang, H., Petersen, R.: Program analysis for overlaid data structures. In: Gopalakrishnan, G., Qadeer, S. (eds.) CAV 2011. LNCS, vol. 6806, pp. 592–608. Springer, Heidelberg (2011)

17. Reynolds, J.C.: Separation logic: A logic for shared mutable data structures. In: LICS, pp. 55–74. IEEE Computer Society (2002)
18. Rinetzky, N., Bauer, J., Reps, T.W., Sagiv, S., Wilhelm, R.: A semantics for procedure local heaps and its abstractions. In: POPL, pp. 296–309. ACM (2005)
19. Toubhans, A., Chang, B.-Y.E., Rival, X.: Reduced product combination of abstract domains for shapes. In: Giacobazzi, R., Berdine, J., Mastroeni, I. (eds.) VMCAI 2013. LNCS, vol. 7737, pp. 375–395. Springer, Heidelberg (2013)
20. Yang, H., Lee, O., Berdine, J., Calcagno, C., Cook, B., Distefano, D., O'Hearn, P.W.: Scalable shape analysis for systems code. In: Gupta, A., Malik, S. (eds.) CAV 2008. LNCS, vol. 5123, pp. 385–398. Springer, Heidelberg (2008)

Quantified Data Automata on Skinny Trees: An Abstract Domain for Lists

Pranav Garg[1], P. Madhusudan[1], and Gennaro Parlato[2]

[1] University of Illinois at Urbana-Champaign, USA
[2] University of Southampton, UK

Abstract. We propose a new approach to heap analysis through an abstract domain of automata, called *automatic shapes*. Automatic shapes are modeled after a particular version of *quantified data automata on skinny trees* (QSDAs), that allows to define universally quantified properties of programs manipulating acyclic heaps with a single pointer field, including data-structures such singly-linked lists. To ensure convergence of the abstract fixed-point computation, we introduce a subclass of QSDAs called elastic QSDAs, which forms an abstract domain. We evaluate our approach on several list manipulating programs and we show that the proposed domain is powerful enough to prove a large class of these programs correct.

1 Introduction

The abstract analysis of heap structures is an important problem in program verification as dynamically evolving heaps are ubiquitous in modern programming, either in terms of low level pointer manipulation or in object-oriented programming. Abstract analysis of the heap is hard because abstractions need to represent the heap which is of unbounded size, and must capture both the *structure* of the heap as well as the unbounded *data* stored in the heap. While several data-domains have been investigated for data stored in static variables, the analysis of unbounded structure and unbounded data that a heap contains has been less satisfactory. The primary abstraction that has been investigated is the rich work on *shape analysis* [25]. However, unlike abstractions for data-domains (like intervals, octagons, polyhedra, etc.), shape analysis requires carefully chosen *instrumentation* predicates to be given by the user, and often are particular to the program that is being verified. Shape analysis techniques typically *merge* all nodes that satisfy the same unary predicate, achieving finiteness of the abstract domain, and interpret the other predicates using a 3-valued (must, must not, may) abstraction. Moreover, these instrumentation predicates often require to be encoded in particular ways (for example, capturing binary predicates as particular kinds of unary predicates) so as to not lose precision.

For instance, consider a sorting algorithm that has an invariant of the form:

$$\forall x, y. \left(\; (x \to_{next}^* y \wedge y \to_{next}^* i) \Rightarrow d(x) \leq d(y) \; \right)$$

which says that the sub-list before pointer i is sorted. In order to achieve a shape-analysis algorithm that discovers this invariant (i.e., captures this

F. Logozzo and M. Fähndrich (Eds.): SAS 2013, LNCS 7935, pp. 172–193, 2013.

invariant precisely during the analysis), we typically need instrumentation predicates such as $p(z) = z \to_{next}^{*} i$, $s(x) = \forall y.((x \to_{next}^{*} y \wedge y \to_{next}^{*} i) \Rightarrow d(x) \leq d(y))$, etc. The predicate $s(x)$ says that the element that is at x is less than or equal to the data stored in every cell between x and i. These instrumentation predicates are clearly too dependent on the precise program and property being verified.

In this paper, we investigate an abstract domain for heaps that works *without user-defined instrumentation predicates* (except we require that the user fix an abstract domain for data, like octagons, for comparing data elements).

We propose a radically new approach to heap analysis through an abstract domain of automata, called *automatic shapes* (automatic because we use automata). Our abstract domain are modeled after a particular kind of automata, called *quantified data automata*, that define, logically, universally quantified properties of heap structures. In this paper, we restrict our attention to acyclic heap structures that have only *one pointer field*; our analysis is hence one that can be used to analyze properties of heaps containing lists, with possible aliasing (merging) of them, especially at intermediate stages in the program. One-pointer acyclic heaps can be viewed as *skinny trees* (trees where the number of branching nodes is bounded).

Automata, in general, are classical ways to capture an infinite set of objects using finite means. A class of (regular) skinny trees can hence be represented using tree automata, capturing the structure of the heap. While similar ideas have been explored before in the literature [14], our main aim is to also represent properties of the *data* stored in the heap, building automata that can express universally quantified properties on lists, in particular those of the form

$$\bigwedge_i \forall \overline{x}.\, (\mathit{Guard}_i(\overline{p}, \overline{x}) \Rightarrow \mathit{Data}_i(d(\overline{p}), d(\overline{x})))$$

where $\overline{p}$ is the set of static pointer variables in the program. The Guard_i formulas express structural constraints on the universally quantified variables and the pointer variables, while the Data_i formulas express properties about the data stored at the nodes pointed to by these pointers. In this paper, we investigate an abstract domain that can infer such quantified properties, parameterized by an abstract numerical domain $\mathcal{F}_d$ for the data formulas and by the number of quantified variables $\overline{x}$.

The salient aspect of the automatic shapes that we build is that (a) there is no requirement from the user to define instrumentation predicates for the structural *Guard* formulas; (b) since the abstraction will not be done by merging unary predicates and since the automata can define how data stored at *multiple* locations on the heap are related, there is no need for the user to define carefully crafted unary predicates that relate structure and data (e.g., the unary predicate $s(x)$ defined above that says that the location x is sorted with respect to all successive locations that come after x but before i). Despite this lack of help from the user, we show how our abstract domain can infer properties of a large number of list-manipulating programs adequately to prove interesting quantified properties.

The crux of our approach is to use a class of automata, called quantified data automata on skinny trees (QSDA), to express a class of single-pointer heap structures and the data contained in them. QSDAs read skinny trees with data along with *all* possible valuations of the quantified variables, and for each of them check whether the data stored in these locations (and the locations pointed to by pointer variables in the program) relate in particular ways defined by the abstract data-domain $\mathcal{F}_d$.

We show, for a simple heap-manipulating programming language, that we can define an abstract post operator over the abstract domain of QSDAs. This abstract post preserves the structural aspects of the heap *precisely* (as QSDAs can have an arbitrary number of states to capture the evolution of the program) and that it soundly abstracts the quantified data properties. The abstract post is nontrivial to define and show effective as it requires automata-theoretic operations that need to simultaneously preserve structure as well as data properties; this forms the hardest technical aspect of our paper. We thus obtain an effective sound transfer function for QSDAs. However, it turns out that QSDAs are not complete lattices (infinite sets may not have least upper-bounds), and hence do not form an abstract domain to interpret programs. Furthermore, typically, in each iteration, the QSDAs obtained would grow in the number of states, and it is not easy to find a fixed-point.

Traditionally, in order to handle loops and reach termination, abstract domains require some form of widening. Our notion of widening is founded on the principle that lengths of stretches of the heap that are neither pointed to by program variables nor by the quantified variables (in one particular instantiation of them) must be ignored. We would hence want the automaton to check the same properties of the instantiated heap no matter how long these stretches of locations are. This notion of abstraction is also suggested by our earlier work where we have shown that such abstractions lead to *decidability*; in other words, properties of such abstracted automata fall into decidable logical theories [10,18]. Assume that the programmer computes a QSDA as an invariant for the program at a particular point, where there is an assertion expressed as a quantified property p over lists (such as "the list pointed to by *head* is sorted"). In order to verify that the abstraction proves the assertion, we will have to check if the language of lists accepted by the QSDA is contained in the language of lists that satisfy the property p. However, this is in general *undecidable*. However, this inclusion problem is decidable if the automata abstracts the lengths of stretches as above. Our aim is hence to *over-approximate* the QSDA into a larger language accepted by a particular kind of data automata, called *elastic* QSDA (EQSDA) that ignores the stretches where variables do not point to, and where "merging" of the pointers do not occur [10,18].

This *elastification* will in fact serve as the basis for widening as well, as it turns out that there are only a *finite* number of elastic QSDAs that express structural properties, discounting the data-formulas. Consequently, we can combine the elastification procedure (which over-approximates a QSDA into an elastic QSDA) and widening over the numerical domain for the data in order to obtain widening procedures that can be used to accelerate the computation for loops. In fact, the domain of EQSDAs is an abstract domain and a complete lattice (where infinite sets also have least upper-bounds), and there is a natural abstract interpretation between sets of concrete heap configurations and EQSDAs, where the EQSDAs permit widening procedures. We show a unique elastification theorem that shows that for any QSDA, there is a unique elastic QSDA that over-approximates it. This allows us to utilize the abstract transfer function on QSDAs (which is more precise) on a linear block of statements, and then elastify them to EQSDAs at join points to have computable fixed-points.

We also show that EQSDA properties over lists can be translated to a decidable fragment of the logic STRAND [18] over lists, and hence inclusion checking an elastic QSDA with respect to any assertion that is also written using the decidable sublogic of STRAND over lists is decidable. The notion of QSDAs and elasticity are extensions of recent work in [10], where such notions were developed for *words* (as opposed to trees) and where the automata were used for *learning* invariants from examples and counter-examples.

We implement our abstract domain and transformers and show, using a suite of list-manipulating programs, that our abstract interpretation is able to prove the naturally required (universally-quantified) properties of these programs. While several earlier approaches (such as shape analysis) can tackle the correctness of these programs as well, our abstract analysis is able to do this *without* requiring program-specific help from the user (for example, in terms of instrumentation predicates in shape analysis [25], and in terms of guard patterns in the work by Bouajjani et al [5]).

Related Work. Shape analysis [25] is the one of the most well-known technique for synthesizing invariants about dynamically evolving heaps. However, shape analysis requires user-provided instrumentation predicates which are often too particular to the program being verified. Hence coming up with these instrumentation predicates is not an easy task. In recent work [5,6,12,21], several abstract domains have been explored which combine the shape and the data constraints. Though some of these domains [6,21] can handle heap structures more complex than singly-linked lists, all these domains require the user to provide a set of data predicates [12] or a set of structural guard patterns [5] or predicates over both the structure and the data constraints [6,21]. In contrast, the only assistance our technique requires from the user is specifying a numerical domain over data formulas and the number of universally quantified variables.

For singly-linked lists, [20] introduces a family of abstractions based on a set of instrumentation predicates which track uninterrupted list segments. However these abstractions only handle structural properties and not the more-complex quantified data properties. Several separation logic based shape analysis techniques have also been developed over the years [3,4,9,13]. But they too mostly handle only the shape properties (structure) of the heap.

Our automaton model for representing quantified invariants over lists is inspired by the decidable fragment of STRAND [18] and can track invariants with guard constraints of the form $y \leq t$ or $t \leq y$ for a universal variable y and some term t. These structural constraints on the guard are very similar to array partitions in [8,11,15]. However, our automata model is more general. For instance, none of these related works can handle sortedness of arrays which requires quantification over more than one variable.

Techniques based on *Craig's interpolation* have recently emerged as an orthogonal way for synthesizing quantified invariants over arrays and lists [1,17,22,26]. These methods use different heuristics like term abstraction [26] or introduction of existential ghost variables [1] or finding interpolants over a restricted language [17,22] to ensure the convergence of the interpolant from a small number of spurious counter-examples. The shape analysis proposed in [24] is also counter-example driven. [24] requires certain quantified predicates to be provided by the user. Given these predicates, it uses a CEGAR-loop for incrementally improving the precision of the abstract transformer and also discovering new predicates on the heap objects that are part of the invariant.

Automata based abstract interpretation has been explored in the past [14] for inferring shape properties about the heap. However, in this paper we are interested in strictly-richer universally quantified properties on the data stored in the heap. [2] introduces a streaming transducer model for algorithmic verification of single-pass list-processing programs. However the transducer model severely constrains the class of programs it can handle; for example, [2] disallows repeated or nested list traversals which are required in sorting routines, etc.

In this paper we introduce a class of automata called quantified skinny-tree data automata (QSDA) to capture universally quantified properties over skinny-trees. The QSDA model is an extension of recent work in [10] where a similar automata model was introduced for words (as opposed to trees). Also, the automata model in [10] was parameterized by a *finite* set of data formulas and was used for *learning* invariants from examples and counter-examples. In contrast, we extend the automata in [10] to be instantiated with a (possibly-infinite) abstract domain over data formulas and develop a theory of abstract interpretation over QSDAs.

2   Programs Manipulating Heap and Data

We consider sequential programs manipulating acyclic singly-linked data structures. A *heap structure* is composed of locations (also called nodes). Each location is endowed with a *pointer field* `next` that points to another location or it is undefined, and a *data field* called `data` that takes values from a potentially infinite domain $\mathbb{D}$ (i.e. the set of integers). For simplicity we assume a special location, called *dirty*, that models an un-allocated memory space. We assume that the `next` pointer field of *dirty* is undefined. Besides the heap structure, a program also has a finite number of *pointer variables* each pointing to a location in the heap structure, and a finite number of *data variables* over $\mathbb{D}$. In our programming language we do not have procedure calls, and we handle non-recursive procedures calls by inlining the code at call points. In the rest of the section we formally define the syntax and semantics of these programs.

Syntax. The syntax of programs is defined by the grammar of Figure 1. A program starts with the declaration of pointer variables followed by a declaration of data variables. Data variables range over a potentially infinite data

$$\langle prgm \rangle ::= \text{pointer } p_1, \ldots, p_k; \text{ data } d_1, \ldots, d_\ell; \langle pc\_stmt \rangle^+$$
$$\langle pc\_stmt \rangle ::= pc : \langle stmt \rangle;$$
$$\langle stmt \rangle ::= \langle ctrl\_stmt \rangle \mid \langle heap\_stmt \rangle$$
$$\langle ctrl\_stmt \rangle ::= d_i := \langle data\_expr \rangle \mid \text{skip} \mid \text{assume}(\langle pred \rangle)$$
$$\mid \text{ if } \langle pred \rangle \text{ then } \langle pc\_stmt \rangle^+ \text{ else } \langle pc\_stmt \rangle^+ \text{ fi}$$
$$\mid \text{ while } \langle pred \rangle \text{ do } \langle pc\_stmt \rangle^+ \text{ od}$$
$$\langle heap\_stmt \rangle ::= \text{new } p_i \mid p_i := \text{nil} \mid p_i := p_j$$
$$\mid p_i := p_j \rightarrow \text{next} \mid p_i \rightarrow \text{next} := \text{nil} \mid p_i \rightarrow \text{next} := p_j$$
$$\mid p_i \rightarrow \text{data} := \langle data\_expr \rangle$$

Fig. 1. Simple programming language

domain $\mathbb{D}$. We assume a language of data expressions built from data variables and terms of the form $p_i \rightarrow \text{data}$ using operations over $\mathbb{D}$. Predicates in our language are either data predicates built from predicates over $\mathbb{D}$ or structural predicates concerning the heap built from atoms of the form $p_i == p_j$, $p_i == \text{nil}$, $p_i \rightarrow \text{next} == p_j$ and $p_i \rightarrow \text{next} == \text{nil}$, for some $i, j \in [1, k]$. Thereafter, there is a non-empty list of labelled statements of the form $pc : \langle stmt \rangle$ where pc is the *program counter* and $\langle stmt \rangle$ defines a language of either C-like statements or statements which modify the heap. We do not have an explicit statement to *free* locations of the heap: when a location is no longer reachable from any location pointed by a pointer variable we assume that it automatically disappears from the memory. For a program P, we denote with PC the set of all program counters of P statements. Figure 2(a) shows the code for program *sorted list-insert* which is a running example in the paper. The program inserts a *key* into the sorted list pointed to by variable *head*.

Semantics. A *configuration* C of a program P with set of pointer variables PV and data variables DV is a tuple $\langle pc, H, pval, dval \rangle$ where

- $pc \in PC$ is the program counter of the next statement to be executed;
- H is a *heap configuration* represented by a tuple $(Loc, \text{next}, \text{data})$ where (1) Loc is a finite set of heap locations containing special elements called *nil* and *dirty*, (2) $\text{next} : Loc \mapsto Loc$ is a partial map defining an edge relation among locations such that the graph (Loc, next) is acyclic, and (3) $\text{data} : Loc \mapsto \mathbb{D}$ is a map that associates each *non-nil* and *non-dirty* location of Loc with a data value in $\mathbb{D}$;
- $pval : \widehat{PV} \rightarrow Loc$, where $\widehat{PV} = PV \cup \{\text{nil}, \text{dirty}\}$, associates each pointer variable of P with a location in H. If $pval(p) = v$ we say that node v is *pointed* by variable p. Furthermore, each node in Loc is reachable from a node pointed by a variable in PV. There is no outgoing (next) edge from location *dirty* and there is a next edge from the location pointed by nil to *dirty* (henceforth we use PV everywhere instead of the $\widehat{PV}$);
- $dval : DV \rightarrow \mathbb{D}$ is a valuation map for the data variables.

Figure 2(b) graphically shows a program configuration which is reachable at program counter 8 of the program in Figure 2(a) (as explained later we encode the data variable *key* as a pointer variable in the heap configuration). The *transition relation* of a program P, denoted $\xrightarrow{stmt}_P$ for each statement *stmt* of P, is defined as usual. The control-flow statements update the program counter, possibly depending on a predicate (condition). The assignment statements update the variable valuation or the heap structure other than moving to the next program counter. Let us define the concrete transformer $F^\natural = \lambda C.\{C' \mid C \xrightarrow{stmt}_P C'\}$. The concrete semantics of a program is given as the least fixed point of a set of equations of the form $\psi = F^\natural(\psi)$.

To simplify the presentation of the paper, we assume that our programs do not have data variables. This restriction, indeed, does not reduce their expressiveness: we can always transform a program P into an *equivalent* program P' by translating each data variable d into a pointer variable that will now point to a fresh node in the heap structure, in which the value d is now encoded by $d \to \mathtt{data}$. The node pointed by d is not pointed by any other pointer, further, $d \to \mathtt{next}$ points to *dirty*. Obviously, wherever d is used in P will now be replaced by $d \to \mathtt{data}$ in P'.

3   Quantified Skinny-Tree Data Automata

In this section we define *quantified skinny-tree data automata* (QSDAs, for short), an accepting mechanism of program configurations (represented as special labeled trees) on which we can express properties of the form $\bigwedge_i \forall y_1, \ldots, y_\ell.\, Guard_i \Rightarrow Data_i$, where variables y_i range over the set of locations of the heap, $Guard_i$ represent quantifier-free structural constraints among the pointer variables and the universally quantified variables y_i, and $Data_i$ (called *data formulas*) are quantifier-free formulas that refer to the data stored at the locations pointed either by the universal variables y_i or the pointer variables, and compare them using operators over the data domain. In the rest of this section, we first define *heap skinny-trees* which are a suitable labeled tree encodings for program configurations; we then define *valuation trees* which are heap skinny-trees by adding to the labels an instantiation of the universal variables. *Quantified skinny-tree data automata* is a mechanism designed to recognize valuation trees. The *language* of a QSDA is the set of all heap skinny-trees such that all valuation trees deriving from them are accepted by the QSDA. Intuitively, the heap skinny-trees in the language defined by the QSDA are all the program configurations that verify the formula $\bigwedge_i \forall y_1, \ldots, y_\ell.Guard_i \Rightarrow Data_i$.

Let T be a tree. A node u of T is *branching* whenever u has more than one child. For a given natural number k, T is *k-skinny* if it contains at most k branching nodes.

Heap Skinny-Trees. Let PV be the set of pointer variables of a program P and $\Sigma = 2^{PV}$ (let us denote the empty set with a blank symbol b). We associate with each P configuration $C = \langle pc, H, pval, dval \rangle$ with $H = (Loc, \mathtt{next}, \mathtt{data})$, the $(\Sigma \times \mathbb{D})$-labeled graph $\mathcal{H} = (T, \lambda)$ whose nodes are those of Loc, and where (u, v) is an edge of T iff $\mathtt{next}(v) = u$ (essentially we reverse all $\mathtt{next}$ edges). From the definition of program configurations, since all locations are required to be reachable from some program variable, it is easy to see that T is a k-skinny tree

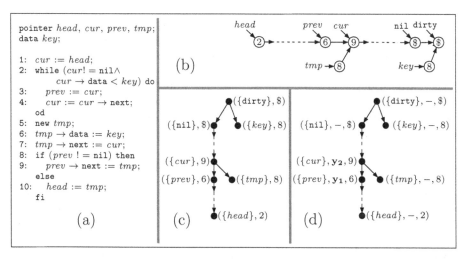

Fig. 2. **(a)** *sorted list-insert* program P; **(b)** shows a P configuration at program counter 8; **(c)** is the heap skinny-tree associated to (b); **(d)** is a valuation tree of (c)

where $k = |PV|$. The labeling function $\lambda : Loc \rightarrow (\Sigma \times \mathbb{D})$ is defined as follows: for every $u \in Loc$, $\lambda(u) = (S, d)$ where S is the set of all pointer variables p such that $pval(p) = u$, and $d = \texttt{data}(u)$. We call $\mathcal{H}$ the *heap skinny-tree* of C.

Heap skinny-trees are formally defined as follows.

Definition 1 (HEAP SKINNY-TREES). *A heap skinny-tree over a set of pointer variables PV and data domain $\mathbb{D}$, is a $(\Sigma \times \mathbb{D})$-labeled k-skinny tree (T, λ) with $\Sigma = 2^{PV}$ and $k = |PV|$, such that:*

- *for every leaf v of T, $\lambda(v) = (S, d)$ where $S \neq \emptyset$;*
- *for every $p \in PV$, there is a unique node v of T such that $\lambda(v) = (S, d)$ with $p \in S$ and some $d \in \mathbb{D}$;*
- *for a node v of T such that $\lambda(v) = (S, d)$, if $\texttt{nil} \in S$ then v is one of the children of the root of T; if v is the root of T then $S = \{\texttt{dirty}\}$.* □

Figure 2(c) shows the heap skinny-tree corresponding to the program configuration of Figure 2(b). Note that though the program handles a singly linked list, in the intermediate operations we can get trees. However they are special trees with bounded branching. This example illustrates that program configurations of list manipulating programs naturally correspond to heap skinny-trees. It also motivates why we need to extend automata over words introduced in [10] to quantified data automata over skinny-trees. We now define valuation trees.

Valuation Trees. Let us fix a finite set of *universal* variables Y. A *valuation tree* over Y of a heap skinny-tree $\mathcal{H}$ is a $(\Sigma \times (Y \cup \{-\}) \times \mathbb{D})$-labeled tree obtained from $\mathcal{H}$ by adding an element from the set $Y \cup \{-\}$ to the label, in which every element in Y occurs exactly once in the tree. We use the symbol '$-$' at a node v if there is no variable from Y labeling v. A valuation tree corresponding to the heap skinny-tree of Figure 2(c) is shown in Figure 2(d).

Quantified skinny-tree data automata are a mechanism to accept skinny-trees. To express properties on the data present in the nodes of the skinny-trees, QSDAs are parameterized by a set of data formulas F over $\mathbb{D}$ which form a complete-lattice $\mathcal{F} = (F, \sqsubseteq_{\mathcal{F}}, \sqcup_{\mathcal{F}}, \sqcap_{\mathcal{F}}, \textit{false}, \textit{true})$ where $\sqsubseteq_{\mathcal{F}}$ is the partial-order on the data-formulas, $\sqcup_{\mathcal{F}}$ and $\sqcap_{\mathcal{F}}$ are the least upper bound and the greatest lower bound and $\textit{false}$ and $\textit{true}$ are formulas required to be in F and correspond to the bottom and the top elements of the lattice, respectively. Also, we assume that whenever $\alpha \sqsubseteq_{\mathcal{F}} \beta$ then $\alpha \Rightarrow \beta$. Furthermore, we assume that any pair of formulas in F are non-equivalent. For a logical domain as ours, this can be achieved by having a canonical representative for every set of equivalent formulas. Let us now formally define QSDAs.

Definition 2 (QUANTIFIED SKINNY-TREE DATA AUTOMATA). *A quantified skinny-tree data automaton (QSDA) over a set of pointer variables PV (with $|PV| = k$), a data domain $\mathbb{D}$, a set of universal variables Y, and a formula lattice $\mathcal{F}$, is a tuple $\mathcal{A} = (Q, \Pi, \Delta, \mathcal{T}, f)$ where:*

- *Q is a finite set of states;*
- *$\Pi = \Sigma \times \widehat{Y}$ is the alphabet where $\Sigma = 2^{PV}$ and $\widehat{Y} = Y \cup \{-\}$;*
- *$\Delta = (\Delta_0, \Delta_1, \ldots, \Delta_k)$ where, for every $i \in [1, k]$, $\Delta_i : (Q^i \times \Pi) \mapsto Q$ is a partial function and defines a (deterministic) transition relation;*
- *$\mathcal{T} : Q \to 2^{PV \cup Y}$ is the type associated with every state $q \in Q$;*
- *$f : Q \to \mathcal{F}$ is a final-evaluation.* □

A valuation tree (T, λ) over Y of a program P, where N is the set of nodes of T, is *recognized* by a QSDA $\mathcal{A}$ if there exists a node-labeling map $\rho : N \mapsto Q$ that associates each node of T with a state in Q such that for each node t of T with $\lambda(t) = (S, y, d)$ the following holds (here $\lambda'(t) = (S, y)$ is obtained by projecting out the data values from $\lambda(t)$):

- if t is a leaf then $\Delta_0(\lambda'(t)) = \rho(t)$ and $\mathcal{T}(\rho(t)) = S \cup \{y\} \setminus \{-\}$.
- if t is an internal node, with sequence of children $t_1, t_2, \ldots, t_i$ then
  - $\Delta_i\left(\, (\rho(t_1), \ldots, \rho(t_i)),\ \lambda'(t)\,\right) = \rho(t)$;
  - $\mathcal{T}(\rho(t)) = S \cup \{y\} \setminus \{-\} \cup \left(\bigcup_{j \in [1,i]} \mathcal{T}(\rho(t_j)) \right)$.
- if t is the root then the formula $f(\rho(t))$, obtained by replacing all occurrences of terms $y \to \mathtt{data}$ and $p \to \mathtt{data}$ with their corresponding data values in the valuation tree, holds true.

A QSDA can be thought as a *register* automaton that reads a valuation tree in a bottom-up fashion and stores the data at the positions evaluated for Y and locations pointed by elements in PV, and checks whether the formula associated to the state at the root holds true by instantiating the data values in the formula with those stored in the registers. Furthermore, the role of map $\mathcal{T}$ is that of enforcing that each element in $PV \cup Y$ occurs exactly once in the valuation tree.

A QSDA $\mathcal{A}$ *accepts* a heap skinny-tree $\mathcal{H}$ if $\mathcal{A}$ recognizes all valuation trees of $\mathcal{H}$. The *language* accepted by $\mathcal{A}$, denoted $L(\mathcal{A})$, is the set of all heap skinny-trees $\mathcal{H}$ accepted by $\mathcal{A}$. A language $\mathcal{L}$ of heap skinny-trees is *regular* if there is a QSDA $\mathcal{A}$ such that $\mathcal{L} = L(\mathcal{A})$. Similarly, a language $\mathcal{L}$ of valuation trees is *regular* if there is a QSDA $\mathcal{A}$ such that $\mathcal{L} = L_v(\mathcal{A})$, where $L_v(\mathcal{A})$ is the set of all valuation trees recognized by $\mathcal{A}$.

QSDAs are a generalization of *quantified data automata* introduced in [10] which handle only lists, as opposed to QSDAs that handle skinny-trees. We now introduce various characterizations of QSDAs which are used later in the paper.

Unique Minimal QSDA. In [10] the authors show that it is not possible to have a unique minimal (with respect to the number of states) quantified data automaton over words which accepts a given language over linear heap configurations. The proof gives a set of heap configurations over a linear heap-structure that is accepted by two different automata having the same number of states. Since QSDAs are a generalization of quantified data automata, the same counter-example language holds for QSDAs. However, under the assumption that all data formulas in $\mathcal{F}$ are pairwise non-equivalent, there does exist a canonical automaton at the level of *valuation trees*. In [10], the authors prove the canonicity of quantified data automata, and their result extends to QSDAs in a straight forward manner.

Theorem 1. *For each* QSDA $\mathcal{A}$ *there is a unique minimal* QSDA $\mathcal{A}'$ *such that* $L_v(\mathcal{A}) = L_v(\mathcal{A}')$.

We give some intuition behind the proof of Theorem 1. First, we introduce a central concept called *symbolic trees*. A symbolic tree is a $(\Sigma \times (Y \cup \{-\}))$-labeled tree that records the positions of the universal variables and the pointer variables, but does not contain concrete data values (hence the word symbolic). A valuation tree can be viewed as a symbolic tree augmented with data values at every node in the tree. There exists a unique tree automaton over the alphabet Π that accepts a given regular language over symbolic trees. It can be shown that if the set of formulas in $\mathcal{F}$ are pairwise non-equivalent, then each state q in the tree automaton, at the root, can be decorated with a unique data formula $f(q)$ which extends the symbolic trees with data values such that the corresponding valuation trees are in the given language of valuation trees.

Hence, a language of valuation trees can be viewed as a function that maps each symbolic tree to a uniquely determined formula, and a QSDA can be viewed as a Moore machine (an automaton with output function on states) that computes this function. This helps us separate the structure of valuation trees (the height of the trees, the cells the pointer variables point to) from the data contained in the nodes of the trees. We formalize this notion by introducing *formula trees*.

Formula Trees. A *formula tree* over pointer variables PV, universal variables Y and a set of data formulas $\mathcal{F}$ is a tuple of a $\Sigma \times (Y \cup \{-\})$-labeled tree (or in other words a symbolic tree) and a data formula in $\mathcal{F}$. For a QSDA which captures a universally quantified property of the form $\bigwedge_i \forall y_1, \ldots, y_\ell . Guard_i \Rightarrow Data_i$, the symbolic tree component of the formula tree corresponds to guard formulas like $Guard_i$ which express structural constraints on the pointers pointing into the valuation tree. The data formula in the formula trees correspond to $Data_i$ which express the data values with which a symbolic tree (read $Guard_i$) can be extended so as to get a valuation tree accepted by the QSDA. In our running example, consider a QSDA with a formula tree which has the same symbolic tree as the valuation tree in Figure 2(d) (but without the data values in the nodes) and a data-formula $\varphi = y_1 \rightarrow \texttt{data} \leq y_2 \rightarrow \texttt{data} \wedge y_1 \rightarrow \texttt{data} < key \wedge y_2 \rightarrow \texttt{data} \geq key$. This formula tree represents all valuation trees (including the one shown in Figure 2(d)) which extend the symbolic tree with data values which satisfy φ.

By introducing formula trees we explicitly take the view of a QSDA as an automaton that reads symbolic trees and outputs data formulas. We say a formula tree (t, φ) is accepted by a QSDA $\mathcal{A}$ if $\mathcal{A}$ reaches the state q after reading t and $f(q) = \varphi$. Given a QSDA $\mathcal{A}$, the language of valuation trees accepted by $\mathcal{A}$ gives an equivalent language of formula trees accepted by $\mathcal{A}$ and vice-versa. We denote the set of formula trees accepted by $\mathcal{A}$ as $L_f(\mathcal{A})$. A language over formula trees is called regular if there exists a QSDA accepting the same language.

Theorem 2. *For each QSDA $\mathcal{A}$ there is a unique minimal QSDA $\mathcal{A}'$ that accepts the same set of formula trees.*

4   A Partial Order over QSDAs

In the previous section we introduced quantified skinny-tree data automata as an automaton model for expressing universally quantified properties over heap skinny-trees. In this section, we first establish a partial order over the class of QSDAs and then show that QSDAs do not form a complete lattice with respect to this partial order. This motivates us to introduce a subclass of QSDAs called elastic QSDAs which we show, in Section 6, form a complete lattice and can be to compute the semantics of programs. The partial order over EQSDAs with respect to which they form a lattice is the same as the partial order over QSDAs we introduce in this section.

Given a set of pointer variables PV and universal variables Y, let $\mathcal{Q}_{\mathcal{F}}$ be the class of all QSDAs over the lattice of data formulas $\mathcal{F}$. Clearly $\mathcal{Q}_{\mathcal{F}}$ is a partially-ordered set where the most natural partial order is the set-inclusion over the language of QSDAs. However, QSDAs are not closed under unions. Thus, a *least upper bound* for a pair of QSDAs does not exist with respect to this partial order. So we consider a new partial-order on QSDAs which allows us to define a least upper bound for every pair of QSDAs.

If we view a QSDA as a mapping from symbolic trees to formulas in $\mathcal{F}$, we can define a new partial-order relation on QSDAs as follows. We say $\mathcal{A}_1 \sqsubseteq \mathcal{A}_2$ if $L_f(\mathcal{A}_1) \subseteq L_f(\mathcal{A}_2)$, which means that for every symbolic tree t if $(t, \varphi_1) \in L_f(\mathcal{A}_1)$ and $(t, \varphi_2) \in L_f(\mathcal{A}_2)$ then $\varphi_1 \sqsubseteq_{\mathcal{F}} \varphi_2$. Note that, whenever $\mathcal{A}_1 \sqsubseteq \mathcal{A}_2$ implies that $L(\mathcal{A}_1) \subseteq L(\mathcal{A}_2)$. QSDAs, with respect to this partial order, form a lattice. Unfortunately, QSDAs do not form a complete lattice with respect to this above defined partial order (infinite sets of QSDAs may not have least upper-bounds). Consequently, we invent a subclass of QSDAs called elastic QSDAs (or EQSDAs) which we show form a complete lattice with respect to the above defined partial order. We also show that EQSDAs form an abstract domain by establishing an abstraction function and a concretization function between a set of heap skinny-trees and EQSDAs and showing that they form a Galois-connection. Even though QSDAs do not form a complete-lattice, we describe next a sound abstract transformer over QSDAs, a variant of which we use in Section 6 for abstracting the semantics of programs over EQSDAs.

5   Abstract Transformer over QSDAs

In this section we describe an abstract transformer over QSDAs which soundly over-approximates the concrete transformer over heap skinny-trees. We will later use a variant of this transformer when we compute the semantics of programs abstractly over EQSDAs.

Given a QSDA $\mathcal{A}$, the concrete transformer $F^\natural$ guesses a pre-state accepted by $\mathcal{A}$ (which involves existential quantification), and then constrains the post-state with respect to this guessed pre-state according to the semantics of the statement. For instance, consider the statement $p_i := p_j$. Given a QSDA accepting a universally quantified property $\forall y_1, \ldots, y_\ell.\psi$, its strongest post-condition with respect to this statement is the formula: $\exists p_i'.\forall y_1, \ldots, y_\ell.\psi[p_i/p_i'] \wedge p_i = p_j$. Note that, an interpretation of the existentially quantified variable p_i' in a model of this formula gives the location node pointed to by variable p_i in the pre-state, such that the formula $\forall y_1, \ldots, y_\ell.\psi$ was satisfied by the pre-state. However it is not possible to express these precise post-conditions, which are usually of the form $\exists^*\forall^*\psi$, in our automaton model. So we over-approximate these precise post-conditions by a QSDA which semantically moves the existential quantifiers inside the universally quantified prefix – $\forall y_1 \ldots y_\ell.\exists p_i'.\psi[p_i/p_i'] \wedge p_i = p_j$. The existential quantifier can now be eliminated using a combination of automata based quantifier elimination, for the structure, and the quantifier elimination procedures for the data-formula lattice $\mathcal{F}$. In the above example, intuitively, the abstract post-condition QSDA guesses a position for the pointer variable p_i for every valuation of the universal variables, such that the valuation tree augmented with this guessed position is accepted by the precondition QSDA. More generally, the abstract transformer computes the most precise post-condition over the language of valuation trees accepted by a QSDA, instead of computing the precise post-condition over the language of heap skinny-trees. In fact, we go beyond valuation trees to formula trees; the abstract transformer evolves the language of formula trees accepted by a QSDA by tracking the precise set of symbolic trees to be accepted in the post-QSDA and their corresponding data formulas.

We assume that the formula lattice $\mathcal{F}$ supports quantifier-elimination. We encourage the reader to keep in mind numerical domains over the theory of integers with constants (0, 1, etc.), addition, and the usual relations (like $<, \leq, =$)

Table 1. Abstract Transformer $F_f^\sharp$ over the language of formula trees. The abstract transformer over QSDAs $F^\sharp(\mathcal{A}) = \mathcal{A}'$ where $\mathcal{A}'$ is the unique minimal QSDA such that $L_f(\mathcal{A}') = (F_f^\sharp)\, L_f(\mathcal{A})$. The predicate *update* and the set *label* are defined below.

Statements	Abstract Transformer $F_f^\sharp$ on a regular language over formula trees
$p_i := nil$	$\lambda L_f.\ \{(t', \varphi') \mid \varphi' = \bigsqcup \{\exists d. \varphi[p_i \to \mathbf{data}/d] \mid (t, \varphi) \in L_f,$ $update(t, p_i := nil, t')\}\}$
$p_i := p_j$	$\lambda L_f.\ \{(t', \varphi') \mid \varphi' = (p_i \to \mathbf{data} = p_j \to \mathbf{data}) \sqcap$ $\bigsqcup \{\exists d.\varphi[p_i \to \mathbf{data}/d] \mid (t, \varphi) \in L_f,$ $update(t, p_i := p_j, t')\}\}$
$p_i := p_j \to \mathbf{next}$	$\lambda L_f.\ \{(t', \varphi') \mid \varphi' = \bigsqcup\{\exists d.\varphi[p_i \to \mathbf{data}/d] \mid (t, \varphi) \in L_f,$ $update(t, p_i := p_j \to \mathbf{next}, t')\}$ $\sqcap \{p_i \to \mathbf{data} = v \to \mathbf{data} \mid v \in label(t', p_i)\}\}$
$p_i \to \mathbf{next} := nil$	$\lambda L_f.\ \{(t', \varphi') \mid \varphi' = \bigsqcup\{\varphi \mid (t, \varphi) \in L_f, update(t, p_i \to \mathbf{next} := nil, t')\}\}$
$p_i \to \mathbf{next} := p_j$	$\lambda L_f.\ \{(t', \varphi') \mid \varphi' = \bigsqcup\{\varphi \mid (t, \varphi) \in L_f, update(t, p_i \to \mathbf{next} := p_j, t')\}\}$
$p_i \to \mathbf{data} :=$ $data\_expr$	$\lambda L_f.\ \{(t, \varphi') \mid \varphi' = \exists d.(\varphi[v_1 \to \mathbf{data}/d, \dots, v_\ell \to \mathbf{data}/d] \sqcap$ $\sqcap\{v \to \mathbf{data} = data\_expr[v_1 \to \mathbf{data}/d, \dots, v_\ell \to \mathbf{data}/d] \mid v \in V\}),$ $V = \{v_1, \dots, v_\ell\} = label(t, p_i), (t, \varphi) \in L_f\}$
assume ψ_{struct}	$\lambda L_f.\ \{(t', \varphi') \mid (t', \varphi') \in L_f,\ t' \models \psi_{struct}\}$
assume ψ_{data}	$\lambda L_f.\ \{(t', \varphi') \mid \varphi' = \varphi \sqcap \psi_{data}, (t', \varphi') \in L_f\}$
new p_i	$\lambda L_f.\{(t', \varphi') \mid \varphi' = (y \to \mathbf{data} = p_i \to \mathbf{data}) \sqcap$ $\bigsqcup\{\exists d_1 d_2.\varphi[p_i \to \mathbf{data}/d_1, y \to \mathbf{data}/d_2] \mid (t, \varphi) \in L_f,$ $update(t, \mathbf{new}^{\{y\}}\, p_i, t')\},\ y \in Y\}$ $\cup\ \{(t', \varphi') \mid \varphi' = \bigsqcup\{\exists d.\varphi[p_i \to \mathbf{data}/d] \mid (t, \varphi) \in L_f,$ $update(t, \mathbf{new}^{\{-\}}\, p_i, t')\}\}$

as an example of the formula lattice. Table 1[1] gives the abstract transformer $F_f^\sharp$ which takes a regular language over formula trees L_f and gives, as output, a set of formula trees. We know from Theorem 2 that for any regular set of formula trees there exists a unique minimal QSDA that accepts it. We show below (see Lemma 2) that for a QSDA $\mathcal{A}$, the language over formula trees given by $(F_f^\sharp)\, L_f(\mathcal{A})$ is regular. Hence, we can define the abstract transformer $F^\sharp$ as $F^\sharp = \lambda\mathcal{A}.\mathcal{A}'$ where $\mathcal{A}'$ is the unique minimal QSDA such that $L_f(\mathcal{A}') = (F_f^\sharp)\, L_f(\mathcal{A})$.

In Table 1, $label(t, p_i)$ is the set of pointer and universal variables which label the same node in t as variable p_i. The predicate $update(t, stmt, t')$ is true if symbolic trees t and t' are related such that the execution of statement $stmt$ updates precisely the symbolic tree t to t'. As an example, the abstract transformer for the statement $p_i := nil$ in the first row of Table 1 states that the post-QSDA maps the symbolic tree t' to the data-formula φ' where φ' is the join of all formulas of the form $\exists d.\varphi[p_i \to \mathbf{data}/d]$ where φ is the data-formula associated with symbolic tree t in the pre-QSDA such that $update(t, p_i := nil, t')$ is true.

---

[1] The abstract transformer defined in Table 1 assumes that there are no memory errors in the program. It can be extended to handle memory errors.

We now briefly describe the predicate $update(t, \mathtt{new}^{\{\hat{y}\}}\ p_i, t')$, where $\hat{y} \in Y \cup \{-\}$, which is used in the definition of the transformer for the $\mathtt{new}$ statement and is slightly more involved. The statement $\mathtt{new}\ p_i$ allocates a new memory location. After the execution of this statement, pointer p_i points to this allocated node. Besides, the universal variables also need to valuate over this new node apart from the valuations over the previously existing locations in the heap. The superscript $\{y\}$ in the predicate $update(t, \mathtt{new}^{\{y\}}\ p_i, t')$ tracks the case when variable $y \in Y$ valuates over the newly allocated node (analogously, the superscript $\{-\}$ tracks the case when no universal variable valuates over the newly allocated node). Hence, if $update(t, \mathtt{new}^{\{y\}}\ p_i, t')$ holds true then the symbolic trees t and t' agree on the locations pointed to by all variables except p_i and the universal variable y; both these variables point, in t', to a new location v which is not in t and a new edge exists in t' from the root to v.

An important point to note is that the abstract transformer for the statement $p_i \to \mathtt{next}$ (i.e., the predicate $update(t, p_i \to \mathtt{next} := p_j, t')$) assumes that the program does not introduce cycles in the heap configurations.

From the construction in Table 1 it can be observed that given a language of valuation trees obtained uniquely from a language of formula trees, $F_f^{\#}$ applies the most-precise concrete transformer on each valuation tree in the language, and then constructs the smallest regular language of valuation trees (or equivalently formula trees) which approximates this set. As we have already discussed, the abstract transformer by reasoning over valuation/formula trees (and not heap skinny-trees) leads to a loss in precision. To regain some of the lost precision, we define a function $Strengthen$ which takes a formula language L_f and finds a smaller language over formula trees, which accepts the same set of heap trees. Here $t \downarrow_y$ stands for a $\Pi \backslash \{y\}$ -labeled tree which agrees with t on the locations pointed to by all variables except y.

$$Strengthen = \lambda y.\lambda L_f.\{(t', \varphi') \mid \varphi' = \varphi'' \sqcap \phi,\ (t', \varphi'') \in L_f,$$
$$\phi = \bigsqcap\{\exists d.\varphi[y \to \mathtt{data}/d] \mid (t, \varphi) \in L_f, t \downarrow_y = t' \downarrow_y\}\}$$

We now reason about the soundness of the operator $Strengthen$. Fix a $y \in Y$. Consider a QSDA $\mathcal{A}$ with a language over formula trees L_f and consider all symbolic trees t such that $t \downarrow_y = t' \downarrow_y$. This implies that the trees t have the pointer variables pointing to the same positions as t' and have the same valuations for variables in $Y \backslash \{y\}$. Since our automaton model has a universal semantics, any heap tree accepted by $\mathcal{A}$ should satisfy the data formulas annotated at the final states reached for every valuation of the universal variables. If we look at a fixed valuation for variables in $Y \backslash \{y\}$ (which is same as that in t') and different valuations for y, any heap tree accepted should satisfy the formula $\exists d.\varphi[y \to \mathtt{data}/d]$ for all such $(t, \varphi) \in L_f$. Hence the $Strengthen$ operator can safely strengthen the formula φ'' associated with the symbolic tree t' to $\varphi'' \sqcap \phi$. It can be shown that for a given universal variable y and a regular language L_f, the language over formula trees $(Strengthen)\ y\ L_f$ is regular. In fact, the QSDA accepting the language $(Strengthen)\ y\ L_f(\mathcal{A})$ for a QSDA $\mathcal{A}$ can be easily constructed. The abstract transformer $F_f^\sharp$ can thus be soundly strengthened by an application of *Strengthen* at each step, for each variable $y \in Y$.

It is clear that the abstract transformer $F_f^\sharp$ in Table 1 as well as the function *Strengthen* are monotonic. We now show that the language over formula trees given by $(F_f^\sharp)L_f(\mathcal{A})$ is a regular language for any QSDA $\mathcal{A}$. This helps us to construct the abstract transformer $F^\sharp : \mathcal{Q}_{\mathcal{F}} \to \mathcal{Q}_{\mathcal{F}}$. Finally, we show that this abstract transformer is a sound approximation of the concrete transformer $F^\natural$.

Lemma 1. *The abstract transformer $F_f^\sharp$ is sound with respect to the concrete semantics.*

Lemma 2. *For a QSDA $\mathcal{A}$, the language $(F_f^\sharp)\ L_f(\mathcal{A})$ over formula trees is regular.*

From Lemma 2 and Theorem 2, it follows that there exists a QSDA $\mathcal{A}'$ such that $\mathcal{A}' = (F^\sharp)\mathcal{A}$. The monotonicity of $F^\sharp$, with respect to the partial order defined in Section 4 over QSDAs, follows from the monotonicity of $F_f^\sharp$. The soundness of $F^\sharp$ can be stated as the following theorem.

Theorem 3. *The abstract transformer $F^\sharp$ is sound with respect to the concrete transformer $F^\natural$.*

Hence $F^\sharp$ is both monotonic, and sound with respect to the concrete transformer $F^\natural$. In the next section we introduce elastic QSDAs, a subclass of QSDAs, which form an abstract domain and we use the above defined transformer $F^\sharp$ over QSDAs to define an abstract transformer over elastic QSDAs. Note that the abstract transformer $F^\sharp$, in general, might require a powerset construction over the input QSDA, very similar to the procedure for determinizing a tree automaton. Hence the worst-case complexity of the abstract transformer is exponential in the size of the QSDA. However our experiments show that this worst-case is not achieved for most programs in practice.

6   Elastic Quantified Skinny-Tree Data Automata

As we saw in Section 4, a least upper bound might not exist for an infinite set of QSDAs. Therefore, we identify a sub-class of QSDAs called elastic quantified skinny-tree data automata (EQSDAs) such that elastic QSDAs form a complete lattice and provide a mechanism to compute the abstract semantics of programs.

Let us denote the symbol $(b, -) \in \Pi$ indicating that a position does not contain any variable by $\underline{b}$. A QSDA $A = (Q, \Pi, \Delta, \mathcal{T}, f)$ where $\Delta = (\Delta_0, \Delta_1, \ldots, \Delta_k)$ is called elastic if each transition on $\underline{b}$ in Δ_1 is a self loop i.e. $\Delta_1(q_1, \underline{b}) = q_2$ implies $q_1 = q_2$.

We first show that the number of states in a minimal EQSDA is bounded for a fixed set PV and Y. Consider all skinny-trees where a blank symbol $\underline{b}$ occurs only at branching points. Since the number of branching points is bounded and since every variable can occur only once, there are only a bounded number of such trees. Consider any minimal EQSDA. Consider all states that are part of the run of the EQSDA on the trees of the kind above. Clearly, there are only a bounded number of states in this set. Now, we argue that on *any* tree, the run on that tree can only use these states. For any tree t, consider the tree t' obtained by removing the nodes of degree one marked by blank. The run on tree t will label common states of t and t' identically, and the nodes that are removed will be labeled by the state of its child, since blank transitions cannot cause state-change. Since in any minimal automaton, for any state, there must be some tree that uses this state, we know that the number of state is bounded.

We next show the following result that every QSDA $\mathcal{A}$ can be *most precisely over-approximated* by a language of valuation trees (or equivalently formula trees) that can be accepted by an EQSDA $\mathcal{A}_{el}$. We will refer to this construction, which we outline below, as *elastification*. This result is an extension of the unique over-approximation result for quantified data automata over words [10]. Using this result, we can show that elastic QSDAs form a complete lattice and there exists a Galois-connection $\langle \alpha, \gamma \rangle$ between a set of heap skinny trees and EQSDAs. This lets us define an abstract transformer over the abstract domain EQSDAs such that the semantics of a program can be computed over EQSDAs in a sound manner.

Let $\mathcal{A} = (Q, \Pi, \Delta, \mathcal{T}, f)$ be a QSDA such that $\Delta = (\Delta_0, \Delta_1, \ldots, \Delta_k)$ and for a state q let $R_{\underline{b}}(q) := \{q' \mid q' = q$ or $\exists q''.q'' \in R_{\underline{b}}(q)$ and $\Delta_1(q'', \underline{b}) = q'\}$ be the set of states reachable from q by a (possibly empty) sequence of $\underline{b}$-unary-transitions. For a set $S \subseteq Q$ we let $R_{\underline{b}}(S) := \bigcup_{q \in S} R_{\underline{b}}(q)$.

The set of states of $\mathcal{A}_{el}$ consists of sets of states of $\mathcal{A}$ that are reachable by the following transition function Δ^{el} (where $\Delta_i(S_1, \ldots, S_i, a)$ denotes the standard extension of the transition function of $\mathcal{A}$ to sets of states):

$$\Delta_0^{el}(a) = R_{\underline{b}}(\Delta_0(a))$$

$$\Delta_1^{el}(S, a) = \begin{cases} R_{\underline{b}}(\Delta_1(S, a)) & \text{if } a \neq \underline{b} \\ S & \text{if } a = \underline{b} \text{ and } \Delta_1(q, \underline{b}) \text{ is defined for some } q \in S \\ \text{undefined} & \text{otherwise.} \end{cases}$$

$$\Delta_i^{el}(S_1, \ldots, S_i, a) = R_{\underline{b}}(\Delta_i(S_1, \ldots, S_i, a)) \text{ for } i \in [2, k]$$

Note that this construction is similar to the usual powerset construction except that in each step we apply the transition function of $\mathcal{A}$ to the current set of states and take the $\underline{b}$-closure. However, if the input letter is $\underline{b}$ on a unary transition, $\mathcal{A}_{el}$ loops on the current set if a $\underline{b}$-transition is defined for some state in the set.

It can be argued inductively, starting from the leaf states, that the type for all states in a set is the same. Hence we define the type of a set S as the type of any state in S. The final evaluation formula for a set is the least upper bound of the formulas for the states in the set: $f^{el}(S) = \bigsqcup_{q \in S} f(q)$. We can now show that $\mathcal{A}_{el}$ is the *most precise over-approximation* of the language of valuation trees accepted by QSDA $\mathcal{A}$.

Theorem 4. *For every QSDA $\mathcal{A}$, the EQSDA $\mathcal{A}_{el}$ satisfies $L_v(\mathcal{A}) \subseteq L_v(\mathcal{A}_{el})$, and for every EQSDA $\mathcal{B}$ such that $L_v(\mathcal{A}) \subseteq L_v(\mathcal{B})$, $L_v(\mathcal{A}_{el}) \subseteq L_v(\mathcal{B})$ holds.*

The proof of Theorem 4 is similar to the proof of a similar theorem in [10] for the case of words. The above theorem can also be stated over a language of formula trees in the same way, that $\mathcal{A}_{el}$ is the most precise over-approximation of the language of formula trees accepted by QSDA $\mathcal{A}$.

We can now show that EQSDAs form a complete lattice $(\mathcal{Q}_{\mathcal{F}}{}^{el}, \sqsubseteq, \sqcup, \sqcap, \bot, \top)$. The partial order on EQSDAs is the same as the partial order on QSDAs. For EQSDAs $\mathcal{A}_1$ and $\mathcal{A}_2$, $\mathcal{A}_1 \sqsubseteq \mathcal{A}_2$ if $L_f(\mathcal{A}_1) \subseteq L_f(\mathcal{A}_2)$, meaning that for every symbolic tree t if $(t, \varphi_1) \in L_f(\mathcal{A}_1)$ and $(t, \varphi_2) \in L_f(\mathcal{A}_2)$ then $\varphi_1 \sqsubseteq_{\mathcal{F}} \varphi_2$. Given EQSDAs $\mathcal{A}_1$ and $\mathcal{A}_2$ and a symbolic tree t such that $(t, \varphi_1) \in L_f(\mathcal{A}_1)$ and $(t, \varphi_2) \in L_f(\mathcal{A}_2)$, the meet $\mathcal{A}_1 \sqcap \mathcal{A}_2$ is the EQSDA that maps t to the unique formula $\varphi_1 \sqcap_{\mathcal{F}} \varphi_2$, and can be realized using a product construction. The meet for EQSDAs, $\mathcal{A}_1 \sqcup \mathcal{A}_2$, is obtained by constructing a QSDA which maps the symbolic tree t to the formula $\varphi_1 \sqcup_{\mathcal{F}} \varphi_2$ followed by its unique elastification to obtain an EQSDA. We can also similarly compute $\sqcup$ and $\sqcap$ for an infinite number of EQSDAs— we build a product automaton, which can potentially have infinitely many states, but because of the restriction that these are EQSDAs, we can show that the number of states of this product automaton is also bounded as above.

We can now view the space of EQSDAs as an abstraction over sets of heap skinny trees. Let us define an abstraction function $\alpha : \mathcal{H} \to \mathcal{Q}_{\mathcal{F}}{}^{el}$ and a concretization function $\gamma : \mathcal{Q}_{\mathcal{F}}{}^{el} \to \mathcal{H}$ such that $(\mathcal{H}, \alpha, \gamma, \mathcal{Q}_{\mathcal{F}}{}^{el})$ form a Galois-connection. Note that, abstract interpretation [7] requires that the abstraction function α maps a concrete element (a language of heap skinny-trees) to a unique element in the abstract domain and that α be surjective; similarly γ should be an injective function. Also note that given a regular language of heap skinny-trees there might be several QSDAs (and thus EQSDAs) accepting that language. In such a case defining a surjective function α is not possible. Therefore, we first restrict ourselves to a set of EQSDAs in $\mathcal{Q}_{\mathcal{F}}{}^{el}$ where each EQSDA accepts a different language. Under this assumption, we define an α and a γ as follows: for a set of heap configurations H, $\alpha(H) = \sqcap\{\mathcal{A} \mid H \subseteq L(\mathcal{A})\}$ and $\gamma(\mathcal{A}) = L(\mathcal{A})$. Note that both α and γ are order-preserving; α is surjective and γ is an injective function. Also for a set of heap configurations H, $H \subseteq \gamma(\alpha(H))$ and for an EQSDA $\mathcal{A}$, $\mathcal{A} = \alpha(\gamma(\mathcal{A}))$. Hence $(\mathcal{H}, \alpha, \gamma, \mathcal{Q}_{\mathcal{F}}{}^{el})$ forms a Galois-connection.

Theorem 5. *Let $(\mathcal{H}, \subseteq)$ be the class of sets of heap skinny-trees and $(\mathcal{Q}_{\mathcal{F}}{}^{el}, \sqsubseteq)$ be the class of EQSDAs (accepting pairwise inequivalent languages) over data formulas $\mathcal{F}$, then $(\mathcal{H}, \alpha, \gamma, \mathcal{Q}_{\mathcal{F}}{}^{el})$ forms a Galois-connection.*

Let us define the abstract transformer over EQSDAs as $F_{el}^{\sharp} : \mathcal{Q}_{\mathcal{F}}{}^{el} \to \mathcal{Q}_{\mathcal{F}}{}^{el} = F_{el} \circ F^{\sharp}$ where F_{el} is the *elastification* operator which returns the most precise EQSDA over-approximating a language of valuation trees accepted by a QSDA. The soundness of $F_{el}^{\sharp}$ follows from the soundness of $F^{\sharp}$ (and the fact that F_{el} is extensive, i.e., $F_{el}(\mathcal{A}) \sqsupseteq \mathcal{A}$). Similarly its monotonicity follows from the monotonicity of $F^{\sharp}$ and the monotonicity of F_{el}. The semantics of a program can be thus computed over the abstract domain $\mathcal{Q}_{\mathcal{F}}{}^{el}$ as the least fix-point of a set of equations of the form $\psi = F_{el}^{\sharp}(\psi)$. Since the number of states in an EQSDA is bounded (for a given set of program variables PV and universal variables Y), this least fix-point computation terminates (modulo the convergence of the data formulas in the formula lattice $\mathcal{F}$ in which case termination can be achieved by defining a suitable widening operator on the data formula lattice).

6.1   From EQSDAs to a Decidable Fragment of STRAND

In this section we show that EQSDAs can be converted to formulas that fall in a decidable fragment of first order logic, in particular the decidable fragment of STRAND over lists. Hence, once the abstract semantics has been computed over EQSDAs, the invariants expressed by the EQSDAs can be used to validate assertions in the program that are also written using the decidable sublogic of STRAND over lists. We assume that the assertions in our programs express quantified properties over *disjoint* lists, like sortedness of lists, etc. and properties relying on mutual sharing or aliasing of list-structures are not allowed.

Given an EQSDA $\mathcal{A}$ and for every pointer variable p, we construct a QSDA over words that are projections of trees accepted by $\mathcal{A}$ and where the first node is p. A key property in the decidable fragment of STRAND is that universal quantification is not permitted to be over elements that are only a bounded distance away from each other. In other words universally quantified variables are only allowed to be related by elastic relations. As a result, we can safely elastify the constructed QSDA over words and obtain an EQSDA over words expressing quantified properties in the decidable sublogic of STRAND. [10] details the translation from an EQSDA over words to a quantified formula in the decidable fragment of STRAND over lists. The formula, thus obtained, can be used to validate assertions in the program and thus prove the program correct.

7   Experimental Evaluation

We implemented the abstract domain over EQSDAs presented in this paper, and evaluated it on several list-manipulating programs. We now first present the implementation details followed by our experimental results. Our prototype implementation along with the experimental results and programs can be found at http://web.engr.illinois.edu/~garg11/qsdas.html.

Implementation Details. Given a program P we compute the abstract semantics of the program over the abstract domain $\mathcal{Q}_{\mathcal{F}}{}^{el}$ over EQSDAs. A program is a sequence of statements as defined by the grammar in Figure 1. In addition to those statements, a program is also annotated with a pre-condition and a bunch of assertions. The pre-condition formulas belong to the decidable fragment of STRAND over lists and can express quantified properties over disjoint lists (aliasing of two list-structures is not allowed), like sortedness of lists, etc. Given a pre-condition formula φ, we construct the EQSDA which accepts all the heap skinny-trees which satisfy φ. This EQSDA precisely captures the set of initial configurations of the program. Starting from these configurations we compute the abstract semantics of the program over $\mathcal{Q}_{\mathcal{F}}{}^{el}$. The assert statements in the program are ignored during the fix-point computation. Once the convergence of the fix-point has been achieved, the EQSDAs can be converted back into

Table 2. Experimental results. Property checked — LIST: the return pointer points to a list; INIT: the list is properly initialized with some key; MAX: returned value is the maximum of all data values in the list; GEK: the list (or some parts of the list) have data values greater than or equal to a key k; SORT: the list is sorted; LAST: returned pointer is the last element of the list; EMPTY: the returned list is empty.

Programs	#PV	#Y	#DV	Property checked	#Iter	Max. size of QSDA	Time (s)
INIT	2	1	1	INIT, LIST	4	19	0.0
ADD-HEAD	2	1	1	INIT, LIST	-	11	0.1
ADD-TAIL	3	1	1	INIT, LIST	4	29	0.1
DELETE-HEAD	2	1	1	INIT, LIST	-	10	0.0
DELETE-TAIL	4	1	1	INIT, LIST	5	51	0.5
MAX	2	1	1	MAX, LIST	4	19	0.1
CLONE	4	1	1	INIT, LIST	4	44	0.7
FOLD-CLONE	5	1	1	INIT, LIST	5	57	3.2
COPY-GE5	4	1	0	GEK, LIST	9	53	2.6
FOLD-SPLIT	3	1	1	GEK, LIST	4	33	0.3
CONCAT	4	1	1	INIT, LIST	5	44	0.7
SORTED-FIND	2	2	2	SORT, LIST	5	38	0.3
SORTED-INSERT	4	2	1	SORT, LIST	6	163	5.8
BUBBLE-SORT	4	2	1	SORT, LIST	5/18	191	42.8
SORTED-REVERSE	3	2	0	SORT, LIST	5	43	1.5
EXPRESSOS-LOOKUP-PREV	3	2	1	SORT, LIST	6	73	2.2
GSLIST-APPEND	4	0	1	LIST	8	3	0.0
GSLIST-PREPEND	2	0	1	LIST	-	3	0.0
GSLIST-LAST	3	0	0	LAST, LIST	3	7	0.0
GSLIST-FREE	3	0	0	EMPTY, LIST	1	3	0.0
GSLIST-POSITION	4	0	0	LIST	3	13	0.0
GSLIST-REVERSE	3	0	0	LIST	3	5	0.0
GSLIST-CUSTOM-FIND	3	1	1	GEK, LIST	4	29	0.1
GSLIST-NTH	3	0	1	LIST	3	7	0.0
GSLIST-REMOVE	4	0	1	LIST	4	10	0.0
GSLIST-REMOVE-LINK	5	0	0	LIST	4	16	0.0
GSLIST-REMOVE-ALL	5	1	1	GEK, LIST	5	51	0.6
GSLIST-INSERT-SORTED	5	2	1	SORT, LIST	6	279	27.4

decidable STRAND formula over lists (as described in Section 6.1) and the STRAND decision procedure can be used for validating the assertions.

We recall that the abstract transformer $F_{el}^\sharp$ is a function composition of the abstract transformer $F^\sharp$ over QSDAs and the unique elastification operator F_{el}. So that we are as precise as possible, for every statement in the program we apply the more precise transformer $F^\sharp$ (and not $F_{el}^\sharp$). However, we apply the elastification operator F_{el} at the header of loops before the join to ensure convergence of the computation of the abstract semantics. The intermediate semantic facts (QSDAs) in our analysis are thus not necessarily elastic.

Our abstract domains are parameterized by a quantifier-free domain $\mathcal{F}$ over the data formulas. In our experiments, we instantiate $\mathcal{F}$ with the octagon abstract domain [23] from the Apron library [16]. It is sufficient to capture the pre/post-conditions and the invariants of all our programs.

Experimental Results. We evaluate our abstract domain on a suite of list-manipulating programs (see Table 2). For every program we report the number of pointer variables (PV), the number of universal variables (Y), the number of data variables (DV) and the property being checked for the program. We also report the number of iterations required for the fixed-point to converge, the maximum size of the intermediate QSDAs and finally the time taken, in seconds, to analyze the programs.

The names of the programs in Table 2 are self-descriptive, and we only describe some of them. The program COPY-GE5, from [5], copies all those entries from a list whose data value is greater than or equal to 5. Similarly, the program FOLD-SPLIT [5] splits a list into two lists – one which has entries whose data values are greater than or equal to a key k and the other list with entries whose data value is less than k. The program EXPRESSOS-LOOKUP-PREV is a method from the module cachePage in a verified-for-security platform for mobile applications [19]. The module cachePage maintains a cache of the recently used disc pages as a priority queue based on a sorted list. This method returns the correct position in the cache at which a disc page could be inserted. The programs in the second part of the table are various methods adapted from the Glib list library which comes with the GTK+ toolkit and the Gnome desktop environment. The program GSLIST-CUSTOM-FIND finds the first node in the list with a data value greater or equal to k and GSLIST-REMOVE-ALL removes all elements from the list whose data value is greater or equal to k. The programs GSLIST-INSERT-SORTED and SORTED-INSERT insert a key into a sorted list.

All experiments were completed on an Intel Core i5 CPU at 2.4GHz with 6Gb of RAM. The number of iterations is left blank for programs which do not have loops. BUBBLE-SORT program converges on a fix-point after 18 iterations of the inner loop and 5 iterations of the outer loop. The size of the intermediate QSDAs depends on the number of universal variables and the number of pointer variables and largely governs the time taken for the analysis of the programs. For all programs, our prototype implementation computes their abstract semantics in reasonable time. Moreover we manually verified that the final EQSDAs in all the programs were sufficient for proving them correct (this validity check for assertions can be mechanized in the future). The results show that the abstract domain we propose in this paper is reasonably efficient and powerful enough to prove a large class of programs manipulating singly-linked list structures.

Acknowledgements. This work is partially supported by NSF CAREER award #0747041.

References

1. Alberti, F., Bruttomesso, R., Ghilardi, S., Ranise, S., Sharygina, N.: Lazy abstraction with interpolants for arrays. In: Bjørner, N., Voronkov, A. (eds.) LPAR-18 2012. LNCS, vol. 7180, pp. 46–61. Springer, Heidelberg (2012)

2. Alur, R., Černý, P.: Streaming transducers for algorithmic verification of single-pass list-processing programs. In: POPL, pp. 599–610 (2011)

3. Berdine, J., Calcagno, C., Cook, B., Distefano, D., O'Hearn, P.W., Wies, T., Yang, H.: Shape analysis for composite data structures. In: Damm, W., Hermanns, H. (eds.) CAV 2007. LNCS, vol. 4590, pp. 178–192. Springer, Heidelberg (2007)

4. Berdine, J., Cook, B., Ishtiaq, S.: SLAyer: Memory safety for systems-level code. In: Gopalakrishnan, G., Qadeer, S. (eds.) CAV 2011. LNCS, vol. 6806, pp. 178–183. Springer, Heidelberg (2011)

5. Bouajjani, A., Dragoi, C., Enea, C., Sighireanu, M.: On inter-procedural analysis of programs with lists and data. In: PLDI, pp. 578–589 (2011)

6. Chang, B.-Y.E., Rival, X.: Relational inductive shape analysis. In: POPL, pp. 247–260 (2008)

7. Cousot, P., Cousot, R.: Abstract interpretation: A unified lattice model for static analysis of programs by construction or approximation of fixpoints. In: POPL, pp. 238–252 (1977)

8. Cousot, P., Cousot, R., Logozzo, F.: A parametric segmentation functor for fully automatic and scalable array content analysis. In: POPL, pp. 105–118 (2011)

9. Distefano, D., O'Hearn, P.W., Yang, H.: A local shape analysis based on separation logic. In: Hermanns, H., Palsberg, J. (eds.) TACAS 2006. LNCS, vol. 3920, pp. 287–302. Springer, Heidelberg (2006)

10. Garg, P., Löding, C., Madhusudan, P., Neider, D.: Learning Universally Quantified Invariants of Linear Data Structures. In: CAV (2013) (to appear)

11. Gopan, D., Reps, T.W., Sagiv, S.: A framework for numeric analysis of array operations. In: POPL, pp. 338–350 (2005)

12. Gulwani, S., McCloskey, B., Tiwari, A.: Lifting abstract interpreters to quantified logical domains. In: POPL, pp. 235–246 (2008)

13. Guo, B., Vachharajani, N., August, D.I.: Shape analysis with inductive recursion synthesis. In: PLDI, pp. 256–265 (2007)

14. Habermehl, P., Holík, L., Rogalewicz, A., Šimáček, J., Vojnar, T.: Forest automata for verification of heap manipulation. In: Gopalakrishnan, G., Qadeer, S. (eds.) CAV 2011. LNCS, vol. 6806, pp. 424–440. Springer, Heidelberg (2011)

15. Halbwachs, N., Péron, M.: Discovering properties about arrays in simple programs. In: PLDI, pp. 339–348 (2008)

16. Jeannet, B., Miné, A.: Apron: A library of numerical abstract domains for static analysis. In: Bouajjani, A., Maler, O. (eds.) CAV 2009. LNCS, vol. 5643, pp. 661–667. Springer, Heidelberg (2009)

17. Jhala, R., McMillan, K.L.: Array abstractions from proofs. In: Damm, W., Hermanns, H. (eds.) CAV 2007. LNCS, vol. 4590, pp. 193–206. Springer, Heidelberg (2007)

18. Madhusudan, P., Parlato, G., Qiu, X.: Decidable logics combining heap structures and data. In: POPL, pp. 611–622 (2011)

19. Mai, H., Pek, E., Xue, H., King, S.T., Madhusudan, P.: Verifying security invariants in ExpressOS. In: ASPLOS, pp. 293–304 (2013)

20. Manevich, R., Yahav, E., Ramalingam, G., Sagiv, M.: Predicate abstraction and canonical abstraction for singly-linked lists. In: Cousot, R. (ed.) VMCAI 2005. LNCS, vol. 3385, pp. 181–198. Springer, Heidelberg (2005)

21. McCloskey, B., Reps, T., Sagiv, M.: Statically inferring complex heap, array, and numeric invariants. In: Cousot, R., Martel, M. (eds.) SAS 2010. LNCS, vol. 6337, pp. 71–99. Springer, Heidelberg (2010)

22. McMillan, K.L.: Quantified invariant generation using an interpolating saturation prover. In: Ramakrishnan, C.R., Rehof, J. (eds.) TACAS 2008. LNCS, vol. 4963, pp. 413–427. Springer, Heidelberg (2008)
23. Miné, A.: The octagon abstract domain. In: WCRE, pp. 310–319 (2001)
24. Podelski, A., Wies, T.: Counterexample-guided focus. In: POPL, pp. 249–260 (2010)
25. Sagiv, S., Reps, T.W., Wilhelm, R.: Parametric shape analysis via 3-valued logic. ACM Trans. Program. Lang. Syst. 24(3), 217–298 (2002)
26. Seghir, M.N., Podelski, A., Wies, T.: Abstraction refinement for quantified array assertions. In: Palsberg, J., Su, Z. (eds.) SAS 2009. LNCS, vol. 5673, pp. 3–18. Springer, Heidelberg (2009)

Static Validation of Dynamically Generated HTML Documents Based on Abstract Parsing and Semantic Processing

Hyunha Kim[1,*], Kyung-Goo Doh[1,*], and David A. Schmidt[2,**]

[1] Hanyang University, Ansan, South Korea
hhkim@plasse.hanyang.ac.kr, doh@hanyang.ac.kr
[2] Kansas State University, Manhattan, Kansas, USA
das@ksu.edu

Abstract. Abstract parsing is a static-analysis technique for a program that, given a reference LR(k) context-free grammar, statically checks whether or not every dynamically generated string output by the program conforms to the grammar. The technique operates by applying an LR(k) parser for the reference language to data-flow equations extracted from the program, immediately parsing all the possible string outputs to validate their syntactic well-formedness.

In this paper, we extend abstract parsing to do semantic-attribute processing and apply this extension to statically verify that HTML documents generated by JSP or PHP are always valid according to the HTML DTD. This application is necessary because the HTML DTD cannot be fully described as an LR(k) grammar. We completely define the HTML 4.01 Transitional DTD in an attributed LALR(1) grammar, carry out experiments for selected real-world JSP and PHP applications, and expose numerous HTML validation errors in the applications. In the process, we experimentally show that semantic properties defined by attribute grammars can also be verified using our technique.

Keywords: static analysis, string analysis, abstract parsing, HTML validation.

1 Introduction

Most HTML documents viewed from the web are dynamically generated by scripts that mix dynamic input with static structure. As a result, many dynamically generated documents are grammatically malformed, and some even contain user-supplied attacks that exploit the malformedness [18, 19]. HTML validation tools are provided at the W3C site, but the tools are impractical or impossible

---

* This work was supported by the Engineering Research Center of Excellence Program of Korea Ministry of Education, Science and Technology(MEST) / National Research Foundation of Korea(NRF) (Grant 2012-0000469).
** Research partially supported by National Science Foundation Project, NSF CNS-1219746.

F. Logozzo and M. Fähndrich (Eds.): SAS 2013, LNCS 7935, pp. 194–214, 2013.

to use with scripts that dynamically generate HTML. Therefore, our goal is to validate, in advance of execution, the syntactic *and* semantic properties of the HTML documents generated dynamically by an application.

Since HTML-document structure is context-sensitive, we wish to employ parsing theory and semantic-analysis techniques from compiling theory to do validation. *Abstract parsing* does this [7, 8]: It extracts from a script a set of flow equations that overapproximate the documents (strings) that the script might generate, and it solves the equations in the domain of *LR-parse stacks*, which encodes the documents' context-free structure.

In this paper, we explain how we employ abstract parsing to validate JSP and PHP scripts. When our implementation is applied to a standard suite of JSP and PHP programs, we found it to be sound, precise (it yields very few false positives — false indications of errors), and reasonably efficient.

1.1   Motivating Examples

We show two HTML-generated PHP scripts, the first generating syntactically invalid HTML, the second generating semantically invalid HTML:

Validating Syntactic Structure. The following code shows a portion of a PHP program that generates one of two different HTML pages depending on the value of a conditional expression isset($_POST["mode"]) determined at run-time.

```
<body>
  <table>
    <tr><th>
    ...
<?php
  if (isset($_POST["mode"])) {
    echo "<tr>";
    $result = DB_query(...);
    while($fruit = DB_fetch_array($result) {
      echo "<td>" . $fruit . "</td>";
    }
    echo "</table>";
  }
?>
  ...
```

If the conditional evaluates to true, the program always generates a syntactically valid page. <table> is required to be paired with </table>, which is the case in the generated page. It is acceptable that <tr> has no matching </tr>, because the HTML definition allows that </tr> be omitted. However, if the conditional evaluates to false, </table> is missing in the generated page, making the page syntactically invalid.

Validating Semantic Properties. The following PHP program fetched from DiscountCategories.php in WEBERP always generates a form element if the conditional in the first line is true. In the form, a table is built using data retrieved from a database and contains a submit button.

```
if (isset($_POST['selectchoice'])) {
  echo '<form id="update" method="post" action=" ... "';
  echo '<div>'; echo '<input type="hidden" name="FormID" value="...">'';
  $sql = "SELECT DISTINCT discountcategory FROM stockmaster WHERE discountcategory <>''";
  $result = DB_query($sql, $db);
  if (DB_num_rows($result) > 0) {
    echo '<table class="selection"><tr><td>';
    echo '<select name="DiscCat" onchange="ReloadForm(update.select)">';
    while ($myrow = DB_fetch_array($result)){
        echo '... <option selected="selected" value="..."> ...';
    }
    echo '</select></td>';
    echo '<td><input type="submit" name="select" value="'._('Select').'" /></td>
        </tr></table><br />';
  }
  echo '</div></form>';
}
```

However, when nothing is retrieved from the database, the second conditional is false, no submit button is generated, and the result is a useless form that never transmits data. (When there is nothing to submit, no form should be generated.)

Our abstract-parsing technique will analyze and detect both forms of errors — both the syntax *and semantics* of the dynamically generated documents can be predicted prior to run-time.

1.2   Contributions

The contributions of this paper are

- We extend abstract-parsing with an implementation of semantic-attribute processing, which makes it amenable to a wide range of static-analysis problems on document-generating scripts.
- We define a complete LALR(1) attribute grammar for the HTML 4.01 DTD Transitional definition, a nontrivial task.
- We statically validate JSP and PHP programs that dynamically generate HTML documents, by submitting the HTML attributed grammar to the abstract parser equipped with semantic processing. The implementation statically validates all the features that W3C HTML Validator does dynamically, as well as semantic properties. Our earlier work shown in [7] was only able to validate a subset of HTML, essentially XHTML, the part definable in LALR(1) grammar.

The paper's next section summarizes abstract-parsing methodology (c.f. [7]), and Section 3 explains semantic processing, extending earlier work [8]. Section 4 explains the difficulties and our achievement of defining precisely an attributed grammar for the HTML DTD. Sections 5 and 6 present our work and our results of validating syntactic and semantic properties of scripts that dynamically generate HTML. Section 7 examines related research in the field, and Section 8 concludes.

```
      r = ']'                        R = ]
      x = '[' . r                    X0 = [ · R
      while ...                      X1 = X0 ⊔ X2
          x = '[' . x . r            X2 = [ · X1 · R
      print x                        X3 = X1 · !
```

(Read . as an infix string-append operation.)

Fig. 1. Sample program and its data-flow equations

2 Fundamentals of Abstract Parsing

This section is a summary of [7], improved to support modular definitions. We present abstract parsing with an example: Say that a script must generate an output string that conforms to this grammar,

$$S \rightarrow [] \mid [S] \mid SS$$

where S is the only nonterminal. (HTML, XML, and SQL are such bracket languages.) The grammar can be difficult to enforce even for simple programs, like the one in Figure 1, left column. Say this program must print only well-formed S-phrases.

Figure 1's right column shows the data-flow equations extracted from the program. Previous approaches have used type checking [3, 6, 17], regular expressions [4, 5, 12, 13], and language inclusion [14, 16, 15, 17], but all of these fail at some point to track precisely the context-free structure implicit in the string-valued document. For example, a standard regular-expression analysis solves the flow equations in the domain of regular expressions, determining that $X3$'s values conform to the regular expression, $[^* \cdot [\cdot] \cdot]^*$, which does not validate the demand. (It is possible to "jazz up" such an analysis [16, 15], but at some point, context-free structure is lost.)

We validate the desired property by solving the flow equations in Figure 1 in the domain of *LR-parse stacks* — $X3$'s meaning is the *set of parse stacks* of the strings that might be denoted by x. Our technique simultaneously unfolds and LR-parses the strings defined by $X3$, computing parse stacks that express structure in both the flow equations and the reference grammar. (Of course, a script might generate infinitely many different strings, and therefore the analysis might compute an infinite set of parse stacks. We finitely approximate an infinite set of parse stacks by exploiting a key feature of LR-parse theory, described in Section 2.2.)

First, let's understand the parser for the example grammar: Figure 2 gives the LALR(1)-parse-controller and parse of the string, [[] []]. The controller's transitions are coded as shift/reduce rewriting rules, which parse the string. The current state, $[s_i]$, of the parse appears at the top of the parse stack, $s_0 :: s_1 :: \cdots :: [s_i]$. Input symbols, i, are supplied to parse state s in the format, $[i \hookrightarrow s]$. The parser starts from the stack, $[s_0]$ and consumes the input string symbol by symbol, generating the parse in the Figure.

Input symbols label the transitions and ! denotes end of input:

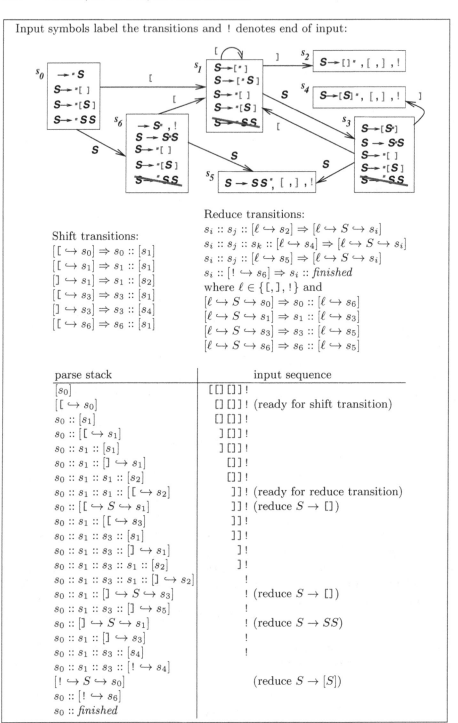

Shift transitions:

$[[\hookrightarrow s_0] \Rightarrow s_0 :: [s_1]$
$[[\hookrightarrow s_1] \Rightarrow s_1 :: [s_1]$
$] \hookrightarrow s_1] \Rightarrow s_1 :: [s_2]$
$[[\hookrightarrow s_3] \Rightarrow s_3 :: [s_1]$
$] \hookrightarrow s_3] \Rightarrow s_3 :: [s_4]$
$[[\hookrightarrow s_6] \Rightarrow s_6 :: [s_1]$

Reduce transitions:

$s_i :: s_j :: [\ell \hookrightarrow s_2] \Rightarrow [\ell \hookrightarrow S \hookrightarrow s_i]$
$s_i :: s_j :: s_k :: [\ell \hookrightarrow s_4] \Rightarrow [\ell \hookrightarrow S \hookrightarrow s_i]$
$s_i :: s_j :: [\ell \hookrightarrow s_5] \Rightarrow [\ell \hookrightarrow S \hookrightarrow s_i]$
$s_i :: [! \hookrightarrow s_6] \Rightarrow s_i :: \text{finished}$

where $\ell \in \{[,],!\}$ and

$[\ell \hookrightarrow S \hookrightarrow s_0] \Rightarrow s_0 :: [\ell \hookrightarrow s_6]$
$[\ell \hookrightarrow S \hookrightarrow s_1] \Rightarrow s_1 :: [\ell \hookrightarrow s_3]$
$[\ell \hookrightarrow S \hookrightarrow s_3] \Rightarrow s_3 :: [\ell \hookrightarrow s_5]$
$[\ell \hookrightarrow S \hookrightarrow s_6] \Rightarrow s_6 :: [\ell \hookrightarrow s_5]$

parse stack	input sequence
$[s_0]$	$[[] []] !$
$[[\hookrightarrow s_0]$	$[] []] !$ (ready for shift transition)
$s_0 :: [s_1]$	$[] []] !$
$s_0 :: [[\hookrightarrow s_1]$	$] []] !$
$s_0 :: s_1 :: [s_1]$	$] []] !$
$s_0 :: s_1 :: [] \hookrightarrow s_1]$	$[]] !$
$s_0 :: s_1 :: s_1 :: [s_2]$	$[]] !$
$s_0 :: s_1 :: s_1 :: [[\hookrightarrow s_2]$	$]] !$ (ready for reduce transition)
$s_0 :: [[\hookrightarrow S \hookrightarrow s_1]$	$]] !$ (reduce $S \to []$)
$s_0 :: s_1 :: [[\hookrightarrow s_3]$	$]] !$
$s_0 :: s_1 :: s_3 :: [s_1]$	$]] !$
$s_0 :: s_1 :: s_3 :: [] \hookrightarrow s_1]$	$] !$
$s_0 :: s_1 :: s_3 :: s_1 :: [s_2]$	$] !$
$s_0 :: s_1 :: s_3 :: s_1 :: [] \hookrightarrow s_2]$	$!$
$s_0 :: s_1 :: [] \hookrightarrow S \hookrightarrow s_3]$	$!$ (reduce $S \to []$)
$s_0 :: s_1 :: s_3 :: [] \hookrightarrow s_5]$	$!$
$s_0 :: [] \hookrightarrow S \hookrightarrow s_1]$	$!$ (reduce $S \to SS$)
$s_0 :: s_1 :: [] \hookrightarrow s_3]$	$!$
$s_0 :: s_1 :: s_3 :: [s_4]$	$!$
$s_0 :: s_1 :: s_3 :: [! \hookrightarrow s_4]$	
$[! \hookrightarrow S \hookrightarrow s_0]$	(reduce $S \to [S]$)
$s_0 :: [! \hookrightarrow s_6]$	
$s_0 :: \text{finished}$	

Fig. 2. Disambiguated LALR(1) parser for $S \to [\ ] \mid [S] \mid S\,S$, where $S\,S$ is made left associative

Our abstract parsing technique will apply the shift/reduce transition rules to the flow equations in the right column of Figure 1. To validate that the program prints only S-structured phrases at $X3$, we must evaluate the start stack, $[s_0]$, and (the string(s) denoted by) $X3$. We portray this as the function call, $X3[s_0]$ — *we treat the program-flow equations in Figure 1 as functions defined in combinator notation*, where we apply a function to the state used to parse it.

Starting from $X3[s_0]$, we use the flow equation, $X3 = X1$, to generate this calculation:

$$X3[s_0] = (X1 \cdot !)[s_0]$$
$$= X1[s_0] \oplus !$$

The first line says that the value of $X1 \cdot !$ must be parsed starting from $[s_0]$. The second line says that the string value of $X1$ is parsed first and the resulting parse stack, say, $s_0 :: s_i :: \cdots :: [s_j]$, is then used to parse $!$. (This will be $s_0 :: s_i :: \cdots :: ![s_j]$. The $\oplus$ operator is defined precisely below; for now, read $E_1(s) \oplus E_2$ as "$E_1(s)$ generates a parse stack whose top state is passed as the argument to E_2, which extends the stack.")

The call, $X1[s_0]$, generates this equation:

$$X1[s_0] = X0[s_0] \cup X2[s_0]$$

That is, the union of the parses of strings at $X0$ and $X2$ from s_0 must be computed. (*Important:* this computes a set of parse stacks, which must be finitely approximated in the implementation.) We consider first $X0[s_0]$:

$$X0[s_0] = ([\cdot R)[s_0] = [[s_0] \oplus R = [[\hookrightarrow s_0] \oplus R$$
$$= (s_0 :: [s_1]) \oplus R = s_0 :: (R[s_1])$$
$$\text{and} \quad R[s_1] =][s_1] = [] \hookrightarrow s_1] = \{s_1 :: [s_2]\}$$
$$\text{so,} \quad X0[s_0] = s_0 :: (R[s_1]) = \{s_0 :: s_1 :: [s_2]\}$$

That is, the parse of $[\cdot R$ from $[s_0]$ generates the stack, $s_0 :: s_1 :: [s_2]$, which is one transition step from reducing $S \to []$ (which occurs when the next input symbol is encountered and is verified in S's *follow set*).

The $\oplus$ is a "continuation operator": For parse stack, st, and combinator expression, E, define $st \oplus E = tail(st) :: E[head(st)]$. That is, stack st's top state feeds to E. (More generally, for a set of stacks, S, define $S \oplus E = \{tail(st) :: E[head(st)] \mid st \in S\}$.)

Next,

$$X2[s_0] = ([\cdot X1 \cdot R)[s_0] = [[\hookrightarrow s_0] \oplus (X1 \cdot R)$$
$$= (s_0 :: [s_1]) \oplus (X1 \cdot R) = s_0 :: (X1 \cdot R)[s_1]$$
$$= s_0 :: (X1[s_1] \oplus R)$$

The call to parse $X1$'s string from $[s_1]$ generates $X1[s_1] = X0[s_1] \cup X2[s_1]$ which in turn generates calls to $X0[s_1]$ and $X2[s_1]$. Here is the list of residual equations generated from the initial call, $X3[s_0]$:

$X3[s_0] = X1[s_0] \oplus !$	$X2[s_0] = s_0 :: (X1[s_1] \oplus R)$
$X1[s_0] = X0[s_0] \cup X2[s_0]$	$X1[s_1] = X0[s_1] \cup X2[s_1]$
$X0[s_0] = \{s_0 :: s_1 :: [s_2]\}$	$X0[s_1] = \{s_1 :: s_1 :: [s_2]\}$
$R[s_1] \ = \{s_1 :: [s_2]\}$	$X2[s_1] = s_1 :: (X1[s_1] \oplus R)$

These equations will be solved by a least-fixed point calculation in the domain of sets of parse stacks. (That is, the meaning of each $X_i[s_j]$ computes to a set of stacks.)

More equations can and will be generated, in demand-driven fashion, during the fixed-point calculation. To show how this proceeds, we will solve the mutually recursive equations for $X1[s_0]$, $X2[s_0]$, $X1[s_1]$, and $X2[s_2]$, in stages:

$$X1_0[s_0] = X2_0[s_0] = X1_0[s_1] = X2_0[s_1] = \emptyset$$

$$
\begin{aligned}
X1_1[s_0] &= \{s_0 :: s_1 :: [s_2]\} & X2_2[s_0] &= s_0 :: (X1_1[s_1] \oplus R) \\
X2_1[s_0] &= \emptyset & &= s_0 :: s_1 :: s_1 :: R[s_2] \\
X1_1[s_1] &= \{s_1 :: s_1 :: [s_2]\} & &= \{s_0 :: s_1 :: s_3 :: [s_4]\} \\
X2_1[s_1] &= s_1 :: (X1_1[s_1] \oplus R) & X1_2[s_1] &= \{s_1 :: s_1 :: [s_2], \ s_1 :: s_1 :: s_3 :: [s_4]\} \\
&= s_1 :: s_1 :: s_1 :: R[s_2] & X2_2[s_1] &= s_1 :: (X1_2[s_1] \oplus R) \\
&\quad \text{where } R[s_2] = [] \hookrightarrow s_2] & &= \{s_1 :: s_1 :: s_1 :: R[s_2], \\
&= s_1 :: s_1 :: s_1 :: [] \hookrightarrow s_2] & &\quad s_1 :: s_1 :: s_1 :: s_3 :: R[s_4]\} \\
&= s_1[] \hookrightarrow S \hookrightarrow s_1] & &= \{s_1 :: s_1 :: s_3 :: [s_4]\} \\
&= s_1 :: s_1 :: [] \hookrightarrow s_3] & X1_3[s_0] &= \{s_0 :: s_1 :: [s_2], \ s_0 :: s_1 :: s_3 :: [s_4]\} \\
&= \{s_1 :: s_1 :: s_3 :: [s_4]\} & X2_3[s_0] &= s_0 :: (X1_2[s_1] \oplus R) \\
& & &= \{s_0 :: s_1 :: s_3 :: [s_4]\}
\end{aligned}
$$

At this point, the equations converge. Note that

$$X1[s_0] = \{s_0 :: s_1 :: [s_2], \ s_0 :: s_1 :: s_3 :: [s_4]\}$$

signifying that the parses of the value of x in the loop body come either from $[]$ or from $[\cdot S \cdot]$, where S represents a parse of some S-structured string. For this reason, we have

$$
\begin{aligned}
X3[s_0] &= X1[s_0] \oplus \,! \\
&= \{s_0 :: s_1 :: \,![s_2], \ s_0 :: s_1 :: s_3 :: \,![s_4]\} \\
&= \{s_0 :: \textit{finished}\}
\end{aligned}
$$

This validates that the strings printed at the hot spot must be S-phrases. The algorithm that generates the residual equations and simultaneously solves them is a worklist algorithm like those used for demand-driven data-flow analysis [2, 9, 11].

2.1 Simplifying the Calculation: Higher-Order Parse States

It is disappointing that the calculation of $X0[s_0]$ yields $\{s_0 :: s_1 :: [s_2]\}$ and not the nonterminal, S, since the assignment x = ' [' . r assigns the string, ' [] ', to x. The issue, of course, is that a lookahead symbol, ℓ, is required to validate the reduction of ' [] ' to S. This is formalized in the transitions stated in Figure 2:

$$
\begin{aligned}
s_i :: s_j :: [\ell \hookrightarrow s_2] &\Rightarrow [\ell \hookrightarrow S \hookrightarrow s_i], \text{ if } \ell \in \{[,],!\} \\
[\ell \hookrightarrow S \hookrightarrow s_0] &\Rightarrow s_0 :: [\ell \hookrightarrow s_6]
\end{aligned}
$$

If we make the current parse state "higher order" by parameterizing it on the lookahead symbol, we can simplify the situation — we use this variation of the above reduction transition:

Conditional reduce transitions:

$$s_i :: s_j :: [s_2] \Rightarrow [S_F \hookrightarrow s_i]$$
$$s_i :: s_j :: s_k :: [s_4] \Rightarrow [S_F \hookrightarrow s_i]$$
$$s_i :: s_j :: [s_5] \Rightarrow [S_F \hookrightarrow s_i]$$
$$\text{where } F = \{[,], !\}$$

Lookahead application transitions:

$$[\ell \hookrightarrow S_F \hookrightarrow s_0] \Rightarrow s_0 :: [\ell \hookrightarrow s_6] \text{ if } \ell \in F$$
$$[\ell \hookrightarrow S_F \hookrightarrow s_1] \Rightarrow s_1 :: [\ell \hookrightarrow s_3] \text{ if } \ell \in F$$
$$[\ell \hookrightarrow S_F \hookrightarrow s_3] \Rightarrow s_3 :: [\ell \hookrightarrow s_5] \text{ if } \ell \in F$$
$$[\ell \hookrightarrow S_F \hookrightarrow s_6] \Rightarrow s_6 :: [\ell \hookrightarrow s_5] \text{ if } \ell \in F$$

Reworked abstract parse of example program:

$$X0[s_0] = \{s_0 :: s_1 :: [s_2]\} = \{[S_F \hookrightarrow s_0]\}$$
$$R[s_1] \quad = \{s_1 :: [s_2]\}$$
$$R[s_2] \quad = \{[] \hookrightarrow s_2]\}$$
$$R[s_4] \quad = \{[] \hookrightarrow s_4]\}$$
$$X1[s_0] = X1[s_0] \oplus \; ! \; = \{s_0 :: s_1 :: [s_2], s_0 :: s_1 :: s_3 :: [s_4]\} = \{[S_F \hookrightarrow s_0]\}$$
$$X2[s_0] = s_0 :: (X1[s_1] \oplus R) = \{s_0 :: s_1 :: s_3 :: [s_4]\} = \{[S_F \hookrightarrow s_0]\}$$
$$X1[s_1] = X0[s_1] \cup X2[s_1] = \{[S_F \hookrightarrow s_1]\}$$
$$X2[s_1] = s_1 :: (X1[s_1] \oplus R) = \{[S_F \hookrightarrow s_1]\}$$
$$X3[s_0] = X1[s_0] \oplus \; ! \; = \; ![S_F \hookrightarrow s_0] = [! \hookrightarrow S_F \hookrightarrow s_0] = \{s_0 :: [! \hookrightarrow s_6]\}$$
$$\qquad\quad = \{s_0 :: \textit{finished}\}$$

Fig. 3. Reformatted transition rules and reworked example

$$s_i :: s_j :: [s_2] \Rightarrow [S_F \hookrightarrow s_i], \text{where } F = \{[,], !\}$$

$[S_F \hookrightarrow s_i]$ is actually an abbreviation for $\lambda\ell \in F. [\ell \hookrightarrow S \hookrightarrow s_i]$.

The new rule reduces $s_0 :: s_1 :: [s_2]$ *before* the lookahead symbol arrives, conditionally on the value of the lookahead. The accompanying transition rule does application and validation:

$$[\ell \hookrightarrow S_F \hookrightarrow s_0] \Rightarrow s_0 :: [\ell \hookrightarrow s_6], \text{ if } \ell \in F$$

Using the new rules, we calculate that

$$X0[s_0] = \{[S_F \hookrightarrow s_0]\}$$

That is, $X0$ generates an "S-typed" string and supplies it to s_0, conditional on the arrival of the lookahead symbol.

Figure 3 presents the higher-order variants of the reduction rules from Figure 2 and recalculates the abstract parse of the example program, producing more intuitive answers.

2.2 Finite Convergence by Stack Folding

The previous example converged in finitely many calculation steps, but in general, an infinite set of parse stacks can be computed, e.g.,

```
x = ’[’
while ...
    x = x . ’[’
    x = x . ’]’
```

$$X0 = [$$
$$X1 = X0 \sqcup X2$$
$$X2 = X1 \cdot [$$
$$X3 = X1 \cdot] \cdot !$$

At conclusion, x holds zero or more left brackets and an S-phrase. The analysis confirms this:

$$X0[s_0] = s_0 :: [s_1]$$
$$X1[s_0] = \{s_0 :: s_1^i :: [s_1] \mid i \geq 0\}$$
$$X2[s_0] = \{s_0 :: s_1^i :: [s_1] \mid i > 0\}$$
$$X3[s_0] = \{(s_0 :: s_1^i :: [s_1]) \oplus] \oplus ! \mid i \geq 0\}$$
$$= \{s_0 :: s_1^i :: [! \hookrightarrow s_2] \mid i \geq 0\}$$
$$= \{[! \hookrightarrow S \hookrightarrow s_0]\} \cup \{s_0 :: s_1^i :: [! \hookrightarrow S \hookrightarrow s_1] \mid i \geq 0\}$$
$$= \{s_0 :: \mathit{finished}\} \cup \{s_0 :: s_1^j :: [! \hookrightarrow s_3] \mid j > 0\}$$

Since we want a finitely convergent analysis, we bound the infinite sets by "folding" their stacks so that no state repeats in a stack. Thus, the worklist algorithm calculates

$$X0[s_0] = s_0 :: [s_1]$$
$$X1[s_0] = \{s_0 :: s_1^* :: [s_1]\}$$
$$X2[s_0] = \{s_0 :: s_1^+ :: [s_1]\}$$
$$X3[s_0] = \{s_0 :: \mathit{finished}, \quad s_0 :: s_1^* :: [! \hookrightarrow s_3]\}$$

Since the set of parse-state names is finite, folding produces a finite set of finite-sized stacks (that contain cycles). This works because each parse stack is a finite path through the LR-parser's finite-state controller, and folding a parse stack generates a (smallest) subgraph of the automaton that covers the path. Indeed, the subgraph can be represented by a regular expression, because it is a *viable prefix* [10] of the LR-parse.

Stack folding lets us generalize the abstract-parsing technique to arbitrary LALR(k) grammars with good success in practice.

3   Abstract Semantic-Processing

We now build on the proposal in [8] to implement a useful form of semantic processing. Since we can parse dynamically generated strings, we can predict their *semantics* as well by incorporating syntax-directed-translation (synthesized-attribute) techniques from compiling theory. For the bracket language,

$$S \rightarrow \texttt{[]} \mid \texttt{[}S\texttt{]} \mid S\,S$$

we might wish to track the *depth* at each point in a string as well as the *height* of each completed S-phrase. For example, for $(\alpha)\,\texttt{[}\texttt{[}(\beta)\texttt{]}\,\texttt{[}\texttt{]}\texttt{]}$, the depth at α is 0, the depth at β is 2, the height of $\texttt{[]}$ is 1, and the height of the entire string is 2. The depth and height attributes typify the semantical information one must collect to validate HTML semantic properties, so we develop this example in detail.

Figure 4 gives a Madsen-Watt-style attribute grammar that defines depth and height, along with modified transition rules that compute the attributes, and also a calculation of the example string. All parse states are annotated with a depth attribute, d, since all parse points within the string possess depth. Nonterminals, S, are annotated with a height attribute, h, since a well-formed S-phrase has

Semantic attributes : depth, d (inherited), annotates all parse states;
height, h (synthesized), annotates s_3, s_5, s_6.

$$\rightarrow\ \downarrow 0\ S \uparrow d$$

attributes rules :
$$\downarrow d\ S \uparrow 1 \rightarrow [\ ]$$
$$\downarrow d\ S \uparrow h+1 \rightarrow [\ \downarrow d\ S \uparrow h\ ]$$
$$\downarrow d\ S \uparrow max(h,h') \rightarrow \downarrow d\ S \uparrow h\ \ \downarrow d\ S \uparrow h'$$

Attributed reduce transitions:

$$s_i :: s_j :: [l \hookrightarrow s_2] \Rightarrow [l \hookrightarrow S^1 \hookrightarrow s_i]$$

Attributed Shift transitions:

$$s_i :: s_j :: s_k^h :: [l \hookrightarrow s_4] \Rightarrow [l \hookrightarrow S^{h+1} \hookrightarrow s_i]$$

$$[[\hookrightarrow s_0^d] \Rightarrow s_0^d :: [s_1^{d+1}]$$

$$s_i :: s_j^h :: [l \hookrightarrow s_5^{h'}] \Rightarrow [l \hookrightarrow S^{max(h,h')} \hookrightarrow s_i]$$

$$[[\hookrightarrow s_1^d] \Rightarrow s_1^d :: [s_1^{d+1}]$$

$$s_i :: [! \hookrightarrow s_6^h] \Rightarrow s_i^h :: finished$$

$$[] \hookrightarrow s_1^d] \Rightarrow s_1^d :: [s_2^{d-1}]$$

where $l \in \{[,],!\}$ and

$$[[\hookrightarrow s_3^d] \Rightarrow s_3^d :: [s_1^{d+1}]$$

$$[l \hookrightarrow S^h \hookrightarrow s_0^d] \Rightarrow s_0^d :: [l \hookrightarrow s_6^{d,h}]$$

$$[] \hookrightarrow s_3^d] \Rightarrow s_3^d :: [s_4^{d-1}]$$

$$[l \hookrightarrow S^h \hookrightarrow s_1^d] \Rightarrow s_1^d :: [l \hookrightarrow s_3^{d,h}]$$

$$[[\hookrightarrow s_6^d] \Rightarrow s_6^d :: [s_1^{d+1}]$$

$$[l \hookrightarrow S^h \hookrightarrow s_3^d] \Rightarrow s_3^d :: [l \hookrightarrow s_5^{d,h}]$$

$$[l \hookrightarrow S^h \hookrightarrow s_6^d] \Rightarrow s_6^d :: [l \hookrightarrow s_5^{d,h}]$$

(Read ! as symbol of end of string)

parse stack (top lies at right)	input sequence (front lies at left)
$[s_0^0]$	$[[]\ []]\ !$
$[[\hookrightarrow s_0^0]$	$[]\ []]\ !$ (ready for shift transition)
$s_0^0 :: [s_1^1]$	$[]\ []]\ !$
$s_0^0 :: [[\hookrightarrow s_1^1]$	$]\ []]\ !$
$s_0^0 :: s_1^1 :: [s_1^2]$	$]\ []]\ !$
$s_0^0 :: s_1^1 :: [] \hookrightarrow s_1^2]$	$[]]\ !$
$s_0^0 :: s_1^1 :: s_1^2 :: [s_2^1]$	$[]]\ !$
$s_0^0 :: s_1^1 :: s_1^2 :: [[\hookrightarrow s_2^1]$	$]]\ !$ (ready for reduce transition)
$s_0^0 :: [[\hookrightarrow S^1 \hookrightarrow s_1^1]$	$]]\ !$ (reduce $S \rightarrow []$)
$s_0^0 :: s_1^1 :: [[\hookrightarrow s_3^{1,1}]$	$]]\ !$
$s_0^0 :: s_1^1 :: s_3^{1,1} :: [s_1^2]$	$]]\ !$
$s_0^0 :: s_1^1 :: s_3^{1,1} :: [] \hookrightarrow s_1^2]$	$]\ !$
$s_0^0 :: s_1^1 :: s_3^{1,1} :: s_1^2 :: [s_2^1]$	$]\ !$
$s_0^0 :: s_1^1 :: s_3^{1,1} :: s_1^2 :: [] \hookrightarrow s_2^1]$	$!$
$s_0^0 :: s_1^1 :: [] \hookrightarrow S^1 \hookrightarrow s_3^{1,1}]$	$!$ (reduce $S \rightarrow []$)
$s_0^0 :: s_1^1 :: s_3^{1,1} :: [] \hookrightarrow s_5^{1,1}]$	$!$
$s_0^0 :: [] \hookrightarrow S^1 \hookrightarrow s_1^1]$	$!$ (reduce $S \rightarrow SS$)
$s_0^0 :: s_1^1 :: [] \hookrightarrow s_3^{1,1}]$	$!$
$s_0^0 :: s_1^1 :: s_3^{1,1} :: [s_4^1]$	$!$
$s_0^0 :: s_1^1 :: s_3^{1,1} :: [! \hookrightarrow s_4^1]$	
$[! \hookrightarrow S^2 \hookrightarrow s_0^0]$	(reduce $S \rightarrow [S]$)
$s_0^0 :: [! \hookrightarrow s_6^{0,2}]$	
$s_0^{0,2} :: finished$	

Fig. 4. $S \rightarrow [\ ]\ |\ [S]\ |\ S\ S$, annotated with depth and height *concrete* semantic attributes

height: the height attributes are attributes of parse states, s_3, s_5, s_6, since these states are reached by transitions labelled by S.

As noted earlier, an LR(1) state has form, $[\ell_1 \hookrightarrow \ell_0 \hookrightarrow s]$, where s is the parser state, ℓ_0 the input, and ℓ_1 the lookahead. When a reduce transition occurs, the corresponding semantic rule is computed. For the example bracket language, [[] []], the computed result is $height = 2$, as expected.

Of course, precision of semantic attributes can be affected by stack folding, but as demonstrated in the following sections, loss of precision has not been a significant problem in practice.

4   Attributed LR(1) Grammar for the HTML DTD

The W3C recommends every HTML document be validated according to the DTD (Document Type Definition). But the commonly used standard, HTML 4.01 Transitional DTD [1], cannot be defined in LALR(1); indeed, some parts are not LR(k) and are even ambiguous. We now review trouble spots in the HTML DTD and explain how we handled them with a synthesized-attribute-based LALR(1)-grammar.

4.1   Unordered Occurrences of Elements

In a HEAD element, its contents, TITLE, ISINDEX and BASE, may appear in any order, with the restrictions that TITLE must appear once, and ISINDEX and BASE may appear once or none:

```
<!ELEMENT HEAD O O (%head.content;) +(%head.misc;) >
<!ENTITY % head.content "TITLE & ISINDEX? & BASE?">
<!ENTITY % head.misc  "SCRIPT|STYLE|META|LINK|OBJECT" -- repeatable head elements -->
<!ELEMENT TITLE - - (#PCDATA) -(%head.misc;) -- document title -->
<!ELEMENT ISINDEX - O EMPTY -- single line prompt -->
<!ELEMENT BASE - O EMPTY -- document base URI -->
```

The tag inclusion +(%head.misc;) indicates that elements in head.misc can appear in HEAD. However, the declarations of TITLE, ISINDEX, and BASE prevent elements in head.misc from propagating inside head.content. The TITLE element excludes head.misc, and the ISINDEX and BASE elements have their bodies empty. Due to the unorderedness of head.content, a LALR(1)-grammatical expansion would grow exponentially, so we utilized synthesized attributes instead: An attribute tag for each of three elements counts the occurrences of its element and checks if the number of occurrences falls within the boundaries. The synthesized-attribute LALR(1) grammar is defined in Figure 5.

4.2   Tag Inclusion and Exclusion

Tag inclusion, +(A), which is an SGML feature, signifies that element A may appear anywhere within its defining element. There are only two occurrences of tag inclusion in HTML DTD, one of which is the following:

production	semantic rules
$head \rightarrow head_{\circ}^{?}$	
$contents$	$\{\ (t,b,i) = contents.count;$ $\quad$ check $t == 1 \wedge 0 \leq b \leq 1 \wedge 0 \leq i \leq 1;\ \}$
$head_{\bullet}^{?}$	
$contents \rightarrow contents_1$	
$content$	$\{\ contents.count = contents_1.count +\!+\!+ content.count\ \}$
$contents \rightarrow content$	$\{\ contents.count = content.count\ \}$
$content \rightarrow title$	$\{\ content.count = (1,0,0)\ \}$
$content \rightarrow base$	$\{\ content.count = (0,1,0)\ \}$
$content \rightarrow isindex$	$\{\ content.count = (0,0,1)\ \}$
$content \rightarrow misc$	$\{\ content.count = (0,0,0)\ \}$

where the attribute $count$ is (t,b,i):
$\quad head_{\circ}$ is start tag of HEAD element $\qquad$ t is the number of TITLE elements
$\quad head_{\bullet}$ is end tag of HEAD element $\qquad$ b is the number of BASE elements
$\qquad\qquad\qquad\qquad\qquad\qquad\qquad\qquad$ i is the number of ISINDEX elements
and $(t_1,b_1,i_1)+\!+\!+(t_2,b_2,i_2) = (min(2,t_1+t_2), min(2,b_1+b_2), min(2,i_1+i_2))$

Fig. 5. Attribute grammar for head elements

```
<!ELEMENT BODY 0 0 (%flow;)* +(INS|DEL) >
<!ELEMENT (INS|DEL) - - (%flow;)* -- inserted text, deleted text -->
```

That is, INS and DEL elements may appear anywhere in BODY element. This is not directly definable in LALR(1), so we manually expanded the grammar by adding production rules for INS and DEL to every nested element.

The tag exclusion, -(A), which is another SGML feature, signifies that the element A cannot appear in the defining element. For example, consider the following declaration of anchor element A:

```
<!ELEMENT A - - (%inline;)* -(A)>
```

-(A) indicates that the element A cannot be nested. A simple-minded construction of LALR(1) grammar for tag exclusion results in an exponentially large number of productions, and thus we chose to use synthesized attributes in Figure 6.

4.3   Validation of Attributes in an HTML Element

Attributes[1] in each HTML element have to be validated according to the ATTLIST declaration, where for each attribute, defined are its name, its type, and whether it is required or implied. We employed synthesized-attribute semantic processing to validate attributes in an HTML element. A global environment for attributes are constructed from element declarations. We get the necessary information about the attributes from the global environment as follows:

- defined($n_{\circ}$) : the set of all attribute names in $n_{\circ}$

---

[1] The reader should be careful not to confuse HTML "attributes" with the synthesized attributes used by the abstract parser.

production	semantic rules
$a \rightarrow a_o$	
inlines	{ check name(a_o) $\notin$ inlines.names }
$a_\bullet$	{ $a.names = \{$ name(a_o) $\} \cup$ inlines.names }

inlines $\rightarrow$ inlines$_1$	
inline	{ inlines.names $=$ inlines$_1$.names $\cup$ inline.names }
inlines $\rightarrow$ inline	{ inlines.names $=$ inline.names }

$n \rightarrow n_o$	
some	{ $n.names = \{$ name(n_o) $\} \cup$ some.names }
$n_\bullet$?	

name(a_o) : element name of $a_o = a$

Fig. 6. Attribute grammar for Tag exclusion

- well-typed(a,n_o) : the value of attribute a in n_o is well-typed
- required(n_o) : the set of all required attribute names in n_o, where $\forall n_o$. required(n_o) $\subseteq$ defined(n_o)

For example, consider the following attribute definition of PARAM:

```
<!ELEMENT PARAM - O EMPTY>
<!ATTLIST PARAM
   id           ID               #IMPLIED
   name         CDATA            #REQUIRED
   value        CDATA            #IMPLIED
   valuetype    (DATA|REF|OBJECT) DATA
   type         %ContentType;    #IMPLIED>
```

- defined($param_o$) $= \{$id,name,value,valuetype,type$\}$
- well-typed(valuetype,$param_o$) $= true$
  if the value of valuetype in $param_o$ is among $\{$DATA,REF,OBJECT$\}$
- required($param_o$) $= \{$name$\}$

Semantic rules for validating attributes in an element are defined as follows:

production semantic rules
$n \rightarrow n_o$ { check $\forall a \in$ parsed(n_o). $a \in$ defined(n_o);
check $\forall a \in$ parsed(n_o). well-typed(a,n_o);
check $\forall a \in$ required(n_o). $a \in$ parsed(n_o) ; }
where parsed(n_o) is the set of parsed attribute names in n_o

Each semantic rule for the production $n \rightarrow n_o$ asserts the following for attributes in n_o:

- every parsed attribute name is declared
- every parsed attribute value is well-typed
- every required attribute is present

5 Experiments: Static HTML Validation

Applying abstract parsing enhanced with attribute grammars, we implemented a static validator for JSP and PHP scripts. The architecture of our platform is

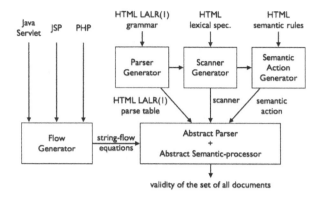

Fig. 7. Architecture of static HTML validator

shown in Figure 7. Java Servlets, JSP pages and PHP scripts are converted to sets of flow equations, and the LALR(1) grammar for HTML 4.01 Transitional DTD is given to `ocamlyacc`, generating its parsing table. A lexical specification is given to `ocamllex`, generating a scanner. Semantic rules are given to the semantic-action generator, emitting semantic actions. All of these are forwarded to the static validator, which is a generic abstract parser equipped with a semantic-attribute processor. The static validator analyzes all the documents generated by the input program. When a validation error occurs, the original position of the source that causes the error is returned. The entire implementation is written in Objective Caml.

We experimented with our static validator on a suite of JSP programs (the same one as Møller and Schwarz [15]) and PHP programs. The experiment was done with Mac OS X 10.8.2 Mountain Lion with Intel Core 2 Duo processor (2.56GHz) and 8GB memory. The results are summarized in Table 1.

The execution time measured is the total time used to validate each set of valid programs after all errors found are fixed manually. The average running time for each program is approximately one second except one case (WebChess, in PHP) averaged close to 5 seconds. Building the LALR(1) parse table takes only a few seconds and is not counted in the analysis time.

The details of detected errors are summarized in Table 2. The errors are classified into three groups: *tag matching*, *misplaced element*, and *attributes*. There are some false positives (only in PHP programs) that are all due to the lack of path-sensitive analysis. The number of false positives is shown inside parentheses.

5.1   Tag Matching

Missing matched tag errors are abundant. Examples are <strong> with no matching </strong> (unmatched start/end tag) and <h3> followed by </h2> (mismatched tags). More serious errors are "improperly nested tags" as follows:

Table 1. Summary of experimental results

	program	Files	SLOC	Errors	FP	Time
	Pebble	117	41,893	36	0	118.0s
	Bookstore1	6	919	8	0	6.2s
	Bookstore2	7	532	5	0	7.0s
	Bookstore3	11	753	5	0	11.0s
JSP	Bookstore4	6	279	3	0	6.0s
	Bookstore5	7	249	6	0	7.1s
	Bookstore6	8	1,960	1	0	7.9s
	JSP Chat	14	920	21	0	16.1s
	JPivot	7	635	0	0	7.0s
	JSTL Book	53	1,457	18	0	52.7s
	Schoolmate	65	6,470	149	0	62s
	FaqForge	19	940	68	0	10s
PHP	WebChess	24	2,906	11	2	106s
	HGB	20	645	92	0	27s
	WEBERP	572	183,511	600	54	590s

Table 2. Classification of errors in JSP and PHP programs

categories	errors	JSP						PHP					
		A	B	C	D	E	total	F	G	H	I	J	total
tag matching	unmatched start/end tag	3	16	2	2	0	23	4	57	2(2)	14	145(16)	268(18)
	mismatched tags	0	0	1	0	0	1	0	0	0	0	1	3
	improperly nested tags	0	9	6	2	0	17	0	0	0	0	4	38
misplaced element	no TITLE in HEAD	0	0	0	0	0	0	0	0	0	2	38	40
	misplaced </head>	0	0	0	0	0	0	0	0	0	1	2	3
	misplaced <body>	0	0	0	0	0	0	1	0	0	0	4	5
	misplaced </body>	0	0	0	0	0	0	1	0	0	0	2	3
	misplaced </html>	0	0	0	0	0	0	0	0	0	0	2	2
	illegal appearance of *blocks* in P	16	0	0	0	0	16	0	0	3	0	5	40
	illegal appearance of *blocks* in FONT	0	0	0	0	0	0	0	0	0	3	0	3
	illegal appearance of NOFRAMES	0	0	1	0	0	1	0	0	0	0	0	2
	illegal appearance of LINK	0	0	0	0	0	0	0	0	2	0	0	2
	illegal appearance of META	0	0	0	0	0	0	0	0	0	0	7	7
	improperly closed FORM	0	0	0	0	0	0	1	3	0	5	4	13
	illegal appearance of HTML before HTML	0	0	0	0	0	0	0	0	0	0	1	1
	illegal appearance of TABLE before BODY	0	0	0	0	0	0	0	1	0	0	0	1
	no TR in TABLE	0	1	1	0	0	2	0	0	0	0	0	4
	missing TR outside TD or TH	2	0	0	0	0	2	0	0	0	3	13(6)	20(6)
	missing TD or TH in TR	4	0	1	0	0	5	0	1	0	0	13(3)	24(3)
	missing both TR and TD(or TH)	0	0	0	0	0	0	1	1	0	6	41	49
	improperly missing <tbody>	4	1	0	0	0	5	0	0	0	0	0	10
	no OPTIONs in SELECT	0	0	0	0	0	0	31	0	1	0	282(29)	314(29)
	nonstandard element name	0	0	0	2	0	2	20	0	1	0	0	25
attributes	missing required attributes	5	1	6	9	0	21	24	3	1	6	14	90
	using undefined attributes	1	0	3	3	0	7	15	1	0	26	2	58
misc.	lexical errors	1	0	0	0	0	1	0	2	0	0	10	14
	total	36	28	21	18	0	103	98	69	10(2)	66	590(54)	1039(56)

A = Pebble, B = Bookstore, C = JSP Chat, D = JSTP Book, E = JPivot,
F = Schoolmate, G = FaqForge, H = WebChess, I = HGB, J = WEBERP.

$m(n)$ means that n of m errors are false positives
blocks = block-level elements

- `<p><strong>` ... `</p></strong>`
- `<tr><form><td>` ... `</td></form><tr>`

These should have been generated respectively as follows:

- `<p><strong>` ... `</strong></p>`
- `<tr><td><form>` ... `</form></td><tr>`

5.2   Misplaced Element

Block-level elements, such as TABLE, FORM, DIV, and UL, in P element are detected as errors, e.g., `<p><table>` ... `</table></p>`.

Errors related to TABLE elements are also found. According to TABLE DTD, a TABLE element should contain at least one TBODY or TR element and a TR element should contain at least one TD or TH element. The followings are the detected example patterns that violate the DTD:

- `<table>` text : both TR and TD are missing
- `<table><td>` text : TR is missing
- `<table><tr>` text : TD is missing

The correct pattern should have been: `<table><tr><td>` text. The requirement is: If TABLE element contains either THEAD or TFOOT, TBODY element cannot be omitted. Errors in Pebble 2.6.2 have the following common pattern:

- `<table><thead>` ... `</thead> <tr>` ... `</table>`

which should have been written as follows:

- `<table><thead>` ... `</thead> <tbody> <tr>` ... `</table>`

According to the HTML DTD, a SELECT element must contain at least one OPTION. The following program excerpted from WEBERP violates this when the loop is not executed:

```
$result = execute_query("SELECT ... ");
echo "<select>";
while($result) {
   ... echo "<option> ...";
}
echo "</select>"
```

Some programs carefully avoid this by filtering out empty data as follows:

```
if (DB_num_rows($result) == 0) then {
   ...
} else {
  echo "<select>";
  while($result) {
     ... echo "<option> ...";
  }
  echo "</select>"
}
```

Our tool falsely decides this situation is an error due to its ignorance of conditional expressions.

5.3 Attributes in HTML Elements

Our tool detected multiple misuses of attributes in HTML elements. The TD element has an undefined attribute background as follows:

– <td class='b' width=10 background='./images/left.gif'>

The TEXTAREA has no required attributes rows and cols:

– <textarea name='task'>

6 Static Validation of Semantic Properties

Additional semantic requirements, beyond those described in the DTD, are abundant in the HTML specification and listed in natural language. We carefully chose several critical semantic properties and specified them in an attributed LALR(1) grammar and then supplied the grammar to our static analyzer based on attributed-abstract parsing.

The semantic errors found are classified in Table 3. False positives here are also due to the lack of path-sensitive analysis. We examine the table in detail in the following subsections.

Table 3. Classification of semantic errors in PHP programs

errors	WebChess	HGB	WEBERP	total
non-unique id attribute	0	8	1(1)	9(1)
unmatched id and name in a single element	0	0	4	4
href or hrefs refer undefined identifier	0	0	0	0
unsubmittable FORM field	10(7)	4(4)	26	40(11)

6.1 Properties of Element Identifiers

According to the HTML 4.01 Specification, element identifiers must have the following properties:

– the value of id attribute must be unique in a document
– the values of id and name must be the same when both appear in an element's start tag
– the values of href and hrefs attributes should refer to defined identifiers in the same document

production	semantic rules

$element \rightarrow element_o$	{ if $element_o(\texttt{id})$ is given then
	     check $element_o(\texttt{id}) \notin element.idset(\texttt{id})$;
	  if $element_o(\texttt{name})$ is given then
	     check $element_o(\texttt{id}) == element_o(\texttt{name})$;
	  $element.idset = element.idset \cup \{element_o(\texttt{id})\}$;
	
	  if $element_o(\texttt{href})$ is given then
	     $element.hrefset = element.hrefset \cup \{element_o(\texttt{href})\}$;
	
	  if $element_o(\texttt{hrefs})$ is given then
	     $element.hrefset = element.hrefset \cup element_o(\texttt{hrefs})$; }

$\begin{array}{c}contents\\element_\bullet\end{array}^{?}$	
$document \rightarrow$ $html$	{ $html.idset = \emptyset$; $html.hrefset = \emptyset$; } { check $\forall \texttt{id} \in html.hrefset,\ \texttt{id} \in html.idset$ }

Fig. 8. Attribute grammar for checking properties of element indentifiers

Figure 8 shows an attribute grammar for checking the above properties.

Errors found in HGB are all from `header.php` originate from eight redundant uses of the same value, `tl`, as follows:

```
// hgb/header.php
<?php if($block === false){ ?>
<div align=center>
<a id=tl href="./admin.php">Admin HOME</a> || <a id=tl href="filter.php">Spam Filter</a> ||
<a id=tl href="ipblock.php">IP Blocker</a> || <a id=tl href="passwrd.php">Change Password</a> ||
<a id=tl href="about.php?out=signout">Sign out</a><br>
<a id=tl href="url.php">Properties</a> || <a id=tl href="about.php">About</a> ||
<a id=tl href="readme.php">Read me</a> || <a id=tl target="_blank"  ...
```

An error found in `AccountGroups.php` of WEBERP is a false positive: Two conditional branches share the same value `AccountGroups` of id, but only one branch of the two will be executed, i.e., if one is executed, the other isn't. Since our analyzer does not take into account the meaning of conditional, it announces an error.

```
// WEBERP/AccountGroups.php
 ...
} elseif (isset($_GET['delete'])) {
  ...
  if ($myrow['groups']>0) {
    echo '... <br /><form method="post" id="AccountGroups"
      action="' . htmlspecialchars($_SERVER['PHP_SELF'], ENT_QUOTES, 'UTF-8') . '"> ...';
  }
}
 ...
if (!isset($_GET['delete'])) {
  echo '<form method="post" id="AccountGroups"
      action="' . htmlspecialchars($_SERVER['PHP_SELF'], ENT_QUOTES, 'UTF-8') . '">';
```

6.2 Submission of FORM Fields

A FORM field only transfers its data when one of the following conditions is true:

- it contains at least one INPUT element whose type is submit or image,
- it contains one and only INPUT element whose type is text,
- it contains a BUTTON element whose name is submit.

Another way of transferring data is to use the submit() function of JavaScript. An attribute grammar for validating FORM data submission is defined as follows:

production	semantic rules
form $\rightarrow$ form$_o$ contents form$_\bullet$	{ *form.submittable* = false; *form.textcount* = 0; } { check *contents.submittable* $\vee$ *contents.textcount* == 1 }
input $\rightarrow$ input$_o$	{ if input$_o$(disabled) $\neq$ true $\wedge$ input$_o$(type) $\in$ { submit, image } then *input.submittable* =true; if input$_o$(disabled) $\neq$ true $\wedge$ input$_o$(type) = text then *input.textcount* = $min(2, input.textcount + 1)$; }
button $\rightarrow$ button$_o$	{ if button$_o$(disabled) $\neq$ true $\wedge$ button$_o$(type) = submit then *button.submittable* =true; }
...	

submittable is a synthesized attribute becoming true when one of the first and third conditions above is true. *textcount* is also a synthesized attribute counting the number of text elements. Note that the domain of these attribute values are finite. The value of *textcount* is one of 0, 1, and 2.

Eleven errors are classified as false positives because all use JavaScript function submit() to submit FORM field data and JavaScript code itself is not analyzed by the tool. For instance,

```
print("<script language='JavaScript'>
  function schoolInfo() {
    document.admin.page2.value=1;
    document.admin.submit();
  } ... </script>");
...
  print("...
    <form name='admin' action='./index.php' method='POST'>
      <a class='menu' href='javascript: schoolInfo();' ... >School</a>
      ...
      <input type='hidden' name='page2' value='$page2'>
      <input type='hidden' name='logout'>
      <input type='hidden' name='page' value='$page'>
    </form> ...");
```

Three hidden input fields are submitted by function schoolInfo(), the first link of A in FORM. However, if JavaScript is unsupported or disabled in a web browser, the submission would not be working, hence they might well be classified as true positives. An additional analysis of JavaScript would remedy this problem.

7   Related Research

Because of the popularity of HTML-document generators there exist a variety of approaches for static validation.

Minamide's initial efforts used data-flow equations to approximate the documents generated from PHP programs and then treats the equations as a grammar, matching it against an HTML/XHTML grammar [13]. However, since the language inclusion problem for context-free grammar is undecidable, nesting depth of elements must be bounded, making the approach miss errors.

Later, Minamide's and Møller's groups independently developed sound methods of validating dynamically generated XML documents based on balanced grammars [12, 14], but their methods are difficult to generalize to HTML features such as tag omission and inclusion/exclusion. Some improvement has been made by Nishiyama and Minamide, who translate a subclass of the SGML DTD (including HTML) into a regular hedge grammar, avoiding undecidability [16]. However, this method does not support start tag omission and tag inclusion, and the translation to support exclusion causes exponential blowup of the grammar.

Recently, Møller and Schwarz developed an HTML validation algorithm [15] that is a generalization of the core algorithm for SGML parsing to work on context-free-grammar representation of documents. The approach is stated sound, precise, and efficient, and handles tag omissions and inclusions/exclusions; it is comparable to our work, limited to the extent of JSP validation. The comparison of JSP experimental results of ours and theirs (what is in the paper) reveals that ours finds more errors in J2EE Bookstore. We also located errors (in 4 pages from Bookstore 2) that are not mentioned in their paper, as follows:

- bookcashier.jsp : unmatched `</strong>` at line 32
- bookcatalog.jsp :
  - improperly nested tag `<p><strong>` at line 62 and `</p></strong>` at line 66
  - unmatched `<strong>` at 117 line
- booldetails.jsp : improperly nested tag `<p><strong>` at line 60 and `</p></strong>` at line 73
- bookshowcart.jsp : unmatched `</td>` at line 143

Extending the SGML parsing algorithm to handle semantic-attribute processing remains to be seen. Interestingly, our tool found no errors in JPivot, whereas Møller and Schwarz's tool found errors in 2 pages out of 3. The possible explanation might be that our tool skipped one JSP page that generates documents through XSL transformation, which our JSP-to-Java translator has yet to handle.

8   Conclusion

We have demonstrated the utility of marrying parsing, semantic processing, and data-flow analysis in the form of attributed abstract parsing, which can predict, parse, and semantically process with surprising accuracy the documents dynamically generated by scripts. The application domain described here, JSP and PHP scripts that generate HTML documents that conform with the HTML 4.01 Transitional DTD, demonstrates the feasibility of the approach.

Acknowledgements. We thank anonymous referees for valuable suggestions and comments.

References

[1] HTML 4.01 Transitional DTD W3C Recommendation (December 24, 1999), http://www.w3.org/TR/html4/loose.dtd

[2] Agrawal, G.: Simultaneous demand-driven data-flow and call graph analysis. In: Proc. International Conference on Software Maintenance, Oxford (1999)

[3] Brabrand, C., Møller, A., Schwartzbach, M.I.: The <bigwig> project. ACM Transaction on Internet Technology 2 (2002)

[4] Choi, T.-H., Lee, O., Kim, H., Doh, K.-G.: A practical string analyzer by the widening approach. In: Kobayashi, N. (ed.) APLAS 2006. LNCS, vol. 4279, pp. 374–388. Springer, Heidelberg (2006)

[5] Christensen, A.S., Møller, A., Schwartzbach, M.I.: Static analysis for dynamic XML. In: Proc. PLAN-X 2002 (2002)

[6] Christensen, A.S., Møller, A., Schwartzbach, M.I.: Extending Java for high-level web service construction. ACM TOPLAS 25 (2003)

[7] Doh, K.-G., Kim, H., Schmidt, D.A.: Abstract parsing: static analysis of dynamically generated string output using LR-parsing technology. In: Palsberg, J., Su, Z. (eds.) SAS 2009. LNCS, vol. 5673, pp. 256–272. Springer, Heidelberg (2009)

[8] Doh, K.-G., Kim, H., Schmidt, D.A.: Abstract LR-parsing. In: Agha, G., Danvy, O., Meseguer, J. (eds.) Talcott Festschrift. LNCS, vol. 7000, pp. 90–109. Springer, Heidelberg (2011)

[9] Duesterwald, E., Gupta, R., Soffa, M.L.: A practical framework for demand-driven interprocedural data flow analysis. ACM TOPLAS 19, 992–1030 (1997)

[10] Hopcroft, J., Ullman, J.: Formal Languages and their Relation to Automata. Addison Wesley (1969)

[11] Horwitz, S., Reps, T., Sagiv, M.: Demand interprocedural dataflow analysis. In: Proc. 3rd ACM SIGSOFT Symposium on Foundations of Software Engineering (1995)

[12] Kirkegaard, C., Møller, A.: Static analysis for Java Servlets and JSP. In: Yi, K. (ed.) SAS 2006. LNCS, vol. 4134, pp. 336–352. Springer, Heidelberg (2006)

[13] Minamide, Y.: Static approximation of dynamically generated web pages. In: Proc. 14th International Conference on World Wide Web, pp. 432–441 (2005)

[14] Minamide, Y., Tozawa, A.: XML validation for context-free grammars. In: Kobayashi, N. (ed.) APLAS 2006. LNCS, vol. 4279, pp. 357–373. Springer, Heidelberg (2006)

[15] Møller, A., Schwarz, M.: HTML validation of context-free languages. In: Hofmann, M. (ed.) FOSSACS 2011. LNCS, vol. 6604, pp. 426–440. Springer, Heidelberg (2011)

[16] Nishiyama, T., Minamide, Y.: A translation from the HTML DTD into a regular hedge grammar. In: Ibarra, O.H., Ravikumar, B. (eds.) CIAA 2008. LNCS, vol. 5148, pp. 122–131. Springer, Heidelberg (2008)

[17] Thiemann, P.: Grammar-based analysis of string expressions. In: Proc. ACM SIGPLAN International Workshop on Types in Languages Design and Implementation, pp. 59–70 (2005)

[18] Wassermann, G., Su, Z.: The essence of command injection attacks in web applications. In: Proc. 33rd ACM Symp. POPL, pp. 372–382 (2006)

[19] Wassermann, G., Su, Z.: Sound and precise analysis of web applications for injection vulnerabilities. In: Proc. ACM PLDI, pp. 32–41 (2007)

Byte-Precise Verification of Low-Level List Manipulation*

Kamil Dudka, Petr Peringer, and Tomáš Vojnar

FIT, Brno University of Technology, IT4Innovations Centre of Excellence, Czech Republic

Abstract. We propose a new approach to shape analysis of programs with linked lists that use low-level memory operations. Such operations include pointer arithmetic, safe usage of invalid pointers, block operations with memory, reinterpretation of the memory contents, address alignment, etc. Our approach is based on a new representation of sets of heaps, which is to some degree inspired by works on separation logic with higher-order list predicates, but it is graph-based and uses a more fine-grained (byte-precise) memory model in order to support the various low-level memory operations. The approach was implemented in the Predator tool and successfully validated on multiple non-trivial case studies that are beyond the capabilities of other current fully automated shape analysis tools.

1 Introduction

Dealing with programs with pointers and dynamic linked data structures belongs among the most challenging tasks of formal analysis and verification due to a need to cope with infinite sets of reachable program configurations having the form of complex graphs. This task becomes even more complicated when considering low-level memory operations such as pointer arithmetic, safe usage of pointers with invalid targets, block operations with memory, reinterpretation of the memory contents, or address alignment. Despite the rapid progress in the area of formal program analysis and verification, fully automated approaches capable of efficiently handling sufficiently general classes of dynamic linked data structures in the form used in low-level code are still missing.

In this paper, we propose a new fully automated approach to formal verification of list manipulating programs designed to cope with all of the above mentioned low-level memory operations. Our approach is based on a new representation of sets of heaps, which is to some degree inspired by works on separation logic with higher-order list predicates [1], but it is graph-based and uses a much more fine-grained memory model. In particular, our memory model allows one to deal with *byte-precise* offsets of fields of objects, offsets of pointer targets, as well as object sizes. Together with the new heap representation, we propose original algorithms for all the operations needed for a use of the new representation in a fully automated shape analysis. As our experiments show, these algorithms allow our analysis to successfully handle many programs on which other state-of-the-art fully automated approaches fail (by not terminating or by producing false positives or even false negatives).

---

* This work was supported by the Czech Science Foundation (project P103/10/0306), the Czech Ministry of Education (project MSM 0021630528), the EU/Czech IT4Innovations Centre of Excellence project CZ.1.05/1.1.00/02.0070, and the BUT FIT project FIT-S-12-1.

F. Logozzo and M. Fähndrich (Eds.): SAS 2013, LNCS 7935, pp. 215–237, 2013.

In particular, we represent sets of heap graphs using the so-called *symbolic memory graphs* (SMGs) with two kinds of nodes: *objects* and *values*. Objects represent allocated memory and are further divided into *regions* representing individual memory areas and *list segments* encoding linked sequences of n or more regions uninterrupted by external pointers (for some $n \geq 0$). Values represent addresses and other data stored inside objects. Objects and values are linked by two kinds of edges: *has-value* edges from objects to values and *points-to* edges from value nodes representing addresses to objects. For efficiency reasons, we represent equal values by a single value node. We explicitly track sizes of objects, byte-precise offsets at which values are stored in them, and we allow pointers to point to objects with an arbitrary offset, i.e., a pointer can point *inside* as well as *outside* an object, not just at its beginning as in many current analyses.

We are capable of handling possibly cyclic, nested (with an arbitrary depth), and/or shared singly- as well as doubly-linked lists (for brevity, below, we concentrate on doubly-linked lists only). Our analysis can fully automatically recognise linking fields of the lists as well as the way they are possibly hierarchically nested. Moreover, the analysis can easily handle lists in the form common in system software (in particular, the Linux kernel), where list nodes are linked through the middle of them, pointer arithmetic is used to get to the beginning of the nodes, pointers iterating through such lists can sometimes safely point to unallocated memory, the forward links are pointers to structures while the backward ones are pointers to pointers to structures, etc.

To reduce the number of SMGs generated for each basic block of the analysed program, we propose a join operator working over SMGs. Our join operator is based on simultaneously traversing two SMGs while trying to merge the encountered pairs of objects and values according to a set of rules carefully tuned through many experiments to balance precision and efficiency (see Section 3.2 for details). Moreover, we use the join operator as the core of our abstraction, which is based on merging neighbouring objects (together with their sub-heaps) into list segments. This approach leads to a rather easy to understand and—according to our experiments—quite efficient abstraction algorithm. In the abstraction algorithm, the join is not applied to two distinct SMGs, but a single one, starting not from pairs of program variables, but the nodes to be merged. Further, we use our join operator as a basis for checking entailment on SMGs too (by observing which kind of pairs of objects and values are merged when joining two SMGs). In order to handle lists whose nodes *optionally* refer to some regions or sub-lists (which can make some program analyses diverge and/or produce false alarms [16]), our join and abstraction support the so-called 0/1 abstract objects.

Since on the low level, the same memory contents can be interpreted in different ways (e.g., via unions or type-casting), we incorporate into our analysis the so-called read, write, and join *reinterpretation*. In particular, we formulate general conditions on the reinterpretation operators that are needed for soundness of our analysis, and then instantiate these operators for the quite frequent case of dealing with blocks of nullified memory. Due to this, we can, e.g., efficiently handle initialization of structures with tens or hundreds of fields commonly allocated and nullified in practice through a single call of calloc, at the same time avoiding false alarms stemming from that some field was not explicitly nullified. Moreover, we provide a support for block operations like memmove or memcpy. Further, we extend the basic notion of SMGs to support pointers having the form of not just a single address, but an interval of addresses. This is needed, e.g., to cope with address alignment or with list nodes that are equal up to their incoming pointers arrive with different offsets (as common, e.g., in memory allocators).

We have implemented the proposed approach in a new version of our tool Predator [7]. Predator automatically proves absence of various memory safety errors, such as invalid dereferences, invalid free operations, or memory leaks. Moreover, Predator can also provide the user with the derived shape invariants. Due to SMGs provide a rather detailed memory model, Predator produces fewer false alarms compared with other tools, and on the other hand, it can discover bugs that may be undetected by other state-of-the-art tools (as illustrated by our experimental results). In particular, Predator can discover out-of-bound dereferences (including stack smashing or buffer overflows) as well as nasty bugs resulting from dealing with overlapping blocks of memory in operations like memcpy. We have successfully validated the new version of Predator on a number of case studies, including various operations on lists commonly used in the Linux kernel as well as code taken directly from selected low-level critical applications (without any changes up to adding a test environment). In particular, we considered the memory allocator from the Netscape portable runtime (NSPR), used, e.g., in Firefox, and the lvm2 logical volume manager. All of the case studies are available within the distribution of Predator. To the best of our knowledge, many of our case studies are out of what other currently existing fully automated shape analysis tools can handle.

Related Work. Many approaches to formal analysis and verification of programs with dynamic linked data structures have been proposed. They differ in their generality, level of automation, as well as the formalism on which they are based. As said already above, our approach is inspired by the fully automated approaches [1,17] based on separation logic with higher-order list predicates implemented in two well-known tools, namely, Space Invader and SLAyer [2]. Compared with them, however, we use a purely graph-based memory representation. In fact, a graph-based representation was used already in the older version of our tool Predator [7]. However, that representation was a rather straightforward graph-based encoding of separation logic formulae, which is no more the case for the representation proposed in this paper. Our new heap representation is much finer, which on one hand complicates its formalization, but on the other hand, it allows us to treat the different peculiarities of low-level memory manipulation. Moreover, somewhat surprisingly, despite our new heap representation is rather detailed, it still allowed us to propose algorithms for all the needed operations such that they are quite efficient. Indeed, the new version of Predator is much faster than the old one while at the same time producing fewer false positives. Compared with Space Invader and SLAyer, Predator based on the new memory representation and new algorithms is not only faster, but also terminates more often, avoids false positives and, in particular, is able to detect additional classes of program errors that the other tools silently ignore (as illustrated in the section on experiments).

Both Space Invader and SLAyer provide some support for pointer arithmetic, but its systematic description is (to the best of our knowledge) not available, and moreover, the support seems to be rather basic as illustrated by our experimental results. The same is the case with some other fully automated tools for verification of programs with dynamic linked data structures based on other formalisms, such as Forester [9] based on automata. A support for pointer arithmetic in combination with separation logic appears in [5], which is, however, highly specialised for a particular kind of linked lists with variable length entries used in some memory allocators.

As for the memory model, probably the closest to our work is [11], which uses the so-called separating shape graphs. They support tracking of the size of allocated memory areas, pointers with byte-precise offsets wrt. addresses of memory regions, dealing with offset ranges, as well as multiple views on the same memory contents. A major difference is that [11] and the older work [6], on which [11] is based, use the so-called summary edges annotated by *user-supplied* data structure invariants to summarize parts of heaps of an unbounded size. This approach is more general in terms of the supported shapes of data structures but less automatic because the burden of describing the shape lies on the user. We use abstract objects (list segments) instead, which are capable of encoding various forms of hierarchically nested lists (very often used in practice) and are carefully designed to allow for *fully automatic* and *efficient* learning of the concrete forms of such lists (the concrete fields used, the way the lists are hierarchically nested, their possible cyclicity, possibly shared nodes, optional nodes, etc.). Also, the level of nesting is not fixed in advance—our list segments are labelled by an integral nesting level, which allows us to represent hierarchically nested data structures as flattened graphs. Finally, although [11] points out a need to reinterpret the memory contents upon reading/writing, the corresponding operations are not formalized there. One of our contributions is thus also a definition of read/write reinterpretation operators in a way that can be used by a fully automatic shape analysis algorithm.

A graph-based abstraction of sets of heap configurations is used in [12] too. On one hand, the representation allows one to deal even with tree-like data structures, but on the other hand, the case of doubly-linked lists is not considered. Further, the representation does not consider the low-level memory features covered by our symbolic memory graphs. Finally, the abstraction and join operations used in [12] are more aggressive and hence less precise than in our case.

The work [10], which is based on an instantiation of the TVLA framework [14], focuses on analysis of Linux-style lists, but their approach relies on an implementation-dependent way of accessing list nodes, instead of supporting pointer arithmetics, unions, and type-casts in a generic way. Finally, the work [15] provides a detailed treatment of low-level C features such as alignment, byte-order, padding, type-unsafe casts, etc. in the context of theorem proving based on separation logic. Our reinterpretation operators provide a lightweight treatment of these features designed to be used in the context of a fully automated analysis based on abstraction.

2   Symbolic Memory Graphs

We encode sets of program configurations using the so-called *symbolic memory graphs* (SMGs) together with a mapping from global (static) and local (stack) variables to nodes of the SMGs. In particular, SMGs have a form of node- and edge-labelled directed graphs. Below, we start by an informal description of SMGs, followed by their formalisation. For an illustration of the notions discussed below, we refer the reader to Fig. 1, which shows how SMGs represent cyclic Linux-style DLLs (with a head node without any data part, other nodes including the head structure as well as custom data, and with the next/prev pointers pointing *inside* list nodes, not at their beginning). Some more examples illustrating the notion of SMGs, including its use for encoding various low-level Linux-style lists, can be found in [8].

2.1   The Intuition behind SMGs

An SMG consists of two kinds of nodes: *objects* and *values* (in Fig. 1, they are represented by boxes and circles, respectively). Objects are further divided to *regions* and (doubly-linked) *list segments* (DLSs)[1]. A region represents a contiguous area of memory allocated either statically, on the stack, or on the heap.

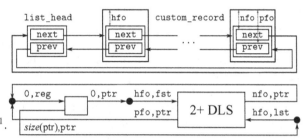

Fig. 1. A cyclic Linux-style DLL (top) and its SMG (bottom), with some SMG attributes left out for readability.

Each consistent SMG contains a special region called the *null object*, denoted #, which represents the target of NULL. DLSs arise from abstracting sequences of doubly-linked regions that are not interrupted by any external pointer. For example, in the lower part of Fig. 1, the left box is a region corresponding to the list head from the upper part of the figure whereas the right box is a DLS summarizing the sequence of custom_record objects from the upper part. Values are then used to represent *addresses* and other *data* stored in objects. All values are abstract in that we only distinguish whether they represent equal or possibly different concrete values. The only exception is the value 0 that is used to represent sequences of zero bytes of any length, which includes the zeros of all numerical types, the address of the null object, as well as nullified blocks of any size. Zero values are supported since they play a rather crucial role in C programs. In the future, a better distinction of values can be easily added.

SMGs have two kinds of *edges*: namely, *has-value edges* leading from objects to values and *points-to edges* leading from addresses to objects (cf. Fig. 1). Intuitively, the edges express that objects have values and addresses point to objects. Has-value edges are labelled by the *offset* and *type* of the *field* in which a particular value is stored within an object. Note that we allow the fields to overlap. This is used to represent different *interpretations* that a program can assign to a given memory area in order not to have to recompute them again and again. Points-to edges are labelled by an *offset* and a *target specifier*. The offset is used to express that the address from which the edge leads may, in fact, point *before, inside, or behind* an object. The target specifier is only meaningful for list segments to distinguish whether a given edge represents the address (or addresses) of the first, last, or each concrete region abstracted by the segment. The last option is

---

[1] Our tool Predator supports *singly-linked list segments* too. Such segments can be viewed as a restriction of DLSs, and we omit them from the description in order to simplify it.

used to encode links going to list nodes from the structures nested below them (e.g., in a DLL of DLLs, each node of the top-level list may be pointed from its nested list).

A key advantage of representing values (including addresses) as a separate kind of nodes is that a single value node is then used to represent values which are guaranteed to be equal in all concrete memory configurations encoded by a given SMG. Hence, distinguishing between *equal* values and *possibly different* values reduces to a simple identity check, not requiring a use of any prover. Thanks to identifying fields of objects by offsets (instead of using names of struct/union members), comparing their addresses for equality simplifies to checking identity of the address nodes. For example, (x == &x->next) holds iff next is the first member of the structure pointed by x, in which case both x and &x->next are guaranteed to be represented by a single address node in SMGs. Finally, the distinction of has-value and points-to edges saves some space since the information present on points-to edges would otherwise have to be copied multiple times for a single target.

Objects and values in SMGs are labelled by several *attributes*. First, each object is labelled by its *kind*, allowing one to distinguish regions and DLSs. Next, each object is labelled by its *size*, i.e., the amount of memory allocated for storing it. For DLSs, the size gives the size of their nodes. All objects and values have the so-called *nesting level* which is an integer specifying at which level of hierarchically nested structures the object or value appears (level 0 being the top level). All objects are further labelled by their *validity* in order to allow for safe pointer arithmetic over freed regions (which are marked invalid, but kept as long as there is some pointer to them).

Next, each DLS is labelled by the *minimum length* of the sequence of regions represented by it.[2] Further, each DLS is associated with the offsets of the *"next"* and *"prev"* *fields* through which the concrete regions represented by the segment are linked forward and backward. Each DLS is also associated with the so-called *head offset* at which a sub-structure called a *list head* is stored in each list node (cf. Fig. 1). The usage of list heads is common in system software. They are predefined structures, typically containing the next/prev fields used to link list nodes. When a new list is defined, its node structure contains the list head as a nested structure, its nodes are linked by pointers pointing not at their beginning but inside of them (in particular, to the list head), and pointer arithmetic is used to get to the beginning of the actual list nodes.

Global and stack *program variables* are represented by regions like heap objects and can thus be manipulated in a similar way (including their manipulation via pointers, checking for out-of-bounds accesses leading to stack smashing, etc.). Regions corresponding to program variables are tagged by their names and hence distinguishable whenever needed (e.g., when checking for invalid frees of stack/global memory, etc.).

2.2 Symbolic Memory Graphs

Let $\mathbb{B}$ be the set of Booleans, $\mathbb{T}$ a set of types, $size(t)$ the size of instances of a type $t \in \mathbb{T}$, $\texttt{ptr} \in \mathbb{T}$ a unique pointer type[3], $\mathbb{K} = \{\texttt{reg}, \texttt{dls}\}$ the set of kinds of objects

---

[2] Later, in Section 4, special list segments of length 0 or 1 are mentioned too.

[3] We assume $size(\texttt{ptr})$ to be a constant, which implies that separate verification runs are needed for verifying a program for target architectures using different address sizes.

(distinguishing regions and DLSs), and $\mathbb{S} = \{\texttt{fst}, \texttt{lst}, \texttt{all}, \texttt{reg}\}$ the set of points-to target specifiers. A *symbolic memory graph* is a tuple $G = (O, V, \Lambda, H, P)$ where:

- O is a finite set of objects including the special null object $\#$.
- V is a finite set of *values* such that $O \cap V = \emptyset$ and $0 \in V$.
- Λ is a tuple of the following labelling functions:
  - The kind of objects $kind : O \to \mathbb{K}$ where $kind(\#) = \texttt{reg}$, i.e., $\#$ is formally considered a region. We let $R = \{r \in O \mid kind(r) = \texttt{reg}\}$ be the set of regions and $D = \{d \in O \mid kind(d) = \texttt{dls}\}$ be the set of DLSs of G.
  - The nesting level of objects and values $level : O \cup V \to \mathbb{N}$.
  - The size of objects $size : O \to \mathbb{N}$.
  - The minimum length of DLSs $len : D \to \mathbb{N}$.
  - The validity of objects $valid : O \to \mathbb{B}$.
  - The head, next, and prev field offsets of DLSs $hfo, nfo, pfo : D \to \mathbb{N}$.
- H is a partial edge function $O \times \mathbb{N} \times \mathbb{T} \rightharpoonup V$ which defines *has-value edges* $o \xrightarrow{of, t} v$ where $o \in O$, $v \in V$, $of \in \mathbb{N}$, and $t \in \mathbb{T}$. We call (of, t) a *field* of the object o that stores the value v of the type t at the offset of.
- P is a partial injective edge function $V \rightharpoonup \mathbb{Z} \times \mathbb{S} \times O$ which defines *points-to edges* $v \xrightarrow{of, tg} o$ where $v \in V$, $o \in O$, $of \in \mathbb{Z}$, and $tg \in \mathbb{S}$ such that $tg = \texttt{reg}$ iff $o \in R$. Here, of is an offset wrt. the base address of o.[4] If o is a DLS, tg says whether the edge encodes pointers to the *first*, *last*, or *all* concrete regions represented by o.

We define the first node of a list segment such that the next field of the node points inside the list segment (and the last node such that the prev field of the node points inside the list segment). As already mentioned, the *all* target specifier is used in hierarchically nested list structures where each nested data structure points back to the node of the parent list below which it is nested. Fig. 2 illustrates how the target specifier affects the semantics of points-to edges (and the corresponding addresses): The DLS d is concretized to the two regions r_1 and r_2, and the nested abstract region r' to the two concrete regions r_1' and r_2'. Note that if r' was not nested, i.e., if it had $level(r') = 0$, it would concretise into a single region pointed by both r_1 and r_2.

Let $G = (O, V, \Lambda, H, P)$ be an SMG with a set of regions R and a set of DLSs D. We denote a DLS $d \in D$ of minimum length n, for which $len(d) = n$, as an $n+$ DLS. We use $\bot$ to denote cases where H or P is not defined. For any $v \in V$ for which $P(v) \neq \bot$, we denote by $of(P(v))$, $tg(P(v))$, and $o(P(v))$ the particular items of the triple $P(v)$. Further, for $o \in O$, we let $H(o) = \{H(o, of, t) \mid of \in \mathbb{N}, t \in$

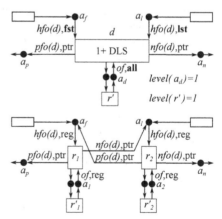

Fig. 2. An SMG and its possible concretisation for the case when the DLS d represents exactly two regions (only important attributes are shown).

---

[4] Note that the offset can even be negative, which happens, e.g., when traversing a Linux list.

$\mathbb{T}$, $H(o, of, t) \neq \perp\}$. We let $A = \{v \in V \mid P(v) \neq \perp\}$ be the set of all *addresses* used in G. Next, a *path* in G is a sequence (of length one or more) of values and objects such that there is an edge between every two neighbouring nodes of the path. An object or value $x_2 \in O \cup V$ is *reachable* from an object or value $x_1 \in O \cup V$ iff there is a path from x_1 to x_2.

We call G *consistent* iff the following holds:

- *Basic consistency of objects.* The null object is invalid, has size and level 0, and its address is 0, i.e., $valid(\#) = false$, $size(\#) = level(\#) = 0$, and $0 \xrightarrow{0, \text{reg}} \#$. All DLSs are valid, i.e., $\forall d \in D : valid(d)$. Invalid regions have no outgoing edges.

- *Field consistency.* Fields do not exceed boundaries of objects, i.e., $\forall o \in O \; \forall of \in \mathbb{N}$ $\forall t \in \mathbb{T} : H(o, of, t) \neq \perp \Rightarrow of + size(t) \leq size(o)$.

- *DLS consistency.* Each DLS $d \in D$ has a next pointer and a prev pointer, i.e., there are addresses $a_n, a_p \in A$ s.t. $H(d, nfo(d), \text{ptr}) = a_n$ and $H(d, pfo(d), \text{ptr}) = a_p$ (cf. Fig. 2). The next pointer is always stored in memory before the prev pointer, i.e., the next and prev offsets are s.t. $\forall d \in D : nfo(d) < pfo(d)$. Points-to edges encoding links to the first and last node of a DLS d are always pointing to these nodes with the appropriate head offset, i.e., $\forall a \in A : tg(P(a)) \in \{\text{fst}, \text{lst}\} \Rightarrow$ $of(P(a)) = hfo(d)$ where $d = o(P(a))$.[5] Finally, there is no cyclic path containing 0+ DLSs (and their addresses) only in a consistent SMG since its semantics would include an address not referring to any object.

- *Nesting consistency.* Each nested object $o \in O$ of level $l = level(o) > 0$ has precisely one *parent DLS*, denoted *parent*(o), that is of level $l - 1$ and there is a path from *parent*(o) to o whose inner nodes are of level l and higher only (e.g., in Fig. 2, d is the parent of r'). Addresses with fst, lst, and reg targets are always of the same level as the object they refer to (as is the case for a_f, a_l, a_1, a_2 in Fig. 2), i.e., $\forall a \in A : tg(P(a)) \in \{\text{fst}, \text{lst}, \text{reg}\} \Rightarrow level(a) = level(o(P(a)))$. On the other hand, addresses with the all target go up one level in the nesting hierarchy, i.e., $\forall a \in A : tg(P(a)) = \text{all} \Rightarrow level(a) = level(o(P(a))) + 1$ (cf. a_d in Fig. 2). Finally, edges representing back-pointers to all nodes of a list segment can only lead from objects (transitively) nested below that segment (e.g., in Fig. 2, such an edge leads from region r' back to the DLS d, but it cannot lead from any other regions). Formally, for any $o, o' \in O$, $a \in H(o)$, $o(P(a)) = o'$, and $level(o) > level(o')$, $tg(P(a)) = \text{all}$ iff $o' = parent^k(o)$ for some $k \geq 1$.

From now on, we assume working with consistent SMGs only. Let *GVar* be a finite set of global variables, *SVar* a countable set of stack variables such that *GVar* $\cap$ *SVar* $= \emptyset$, and let *Var* $=$ *GVar* $\cup$ *SVar*. A symbolic program configuration (SPC) is a pair $C = (G, \nu)$ where G is an SMG with a set of regions R, and $\nu :$ *Var* $\rightarrow R$ is a finite injective map such that $\forall x \in Var : level(\nu(x)) = 0 \wedge valid(\nu(x))$. Note that ν gives the regions in which values of variables are stored, not directly the values themselves. We call each object o such that $\nu(x) = o$ for some $x \in GVar$ a *static object*, and each object o such that $\nu(x) = o$ for some $x \in SVar$ a *stack object*. All other objects are called *heap objects*. An SPC is called *garbage-free* iff all its heap objects are reachable from static or stack objects.

---

[5] The last two requirements are not necessary, but they significantly simplify the below presented algorithms (e.g., the DLS materialisation given in Section 2.3).

We define the *empty SMG* to consist solely of the null object, its address 0, and the points-to edge between them. The *empty SPC* then consists of the empty SMG and the empty variable mapping. An SMG $G' = (O', V', \Lambda', H', P')$ is a *sub-SMG* of an SMG $G = (O, V, \Lambda, H, P)$ iff (1) $O' \subseteq O$, (2) $V' \subseteq V$, and (3) H', P', and Λ' are restrictions of H, P, and Λ to O' and V', respectively. The sub-SMG of G *rooted at* an object or value $x \in O \cup V$, denoted G_x, is the smallest sub-SMG of G that includes x and all objects and values reachable from x. Given $F \subseteq \mathbb{N}$, the *F-restricted* sub-SMG of G rooted at an object $o \in O$ is the smallest sub-SMG of G that includes o and all objects and values reachable from o apart from the addresses $A_F = \{H(o, of, \texttt{ptr}) \mid of \in F\}$ and nodes that are reachable from o through A_F only. Finally, the sub-SMG of G *nested below* $d \in D$, denoted $\widehat{G}_d$, is the smallest sub-SMG of G including d and all objects and values of level higher than *level*(d) that are reachable from d via paths that, apart from d, consist exclusively of objects and values of a level higher than *level*(d).

2.3   The Semantics of SMGs

We define the semantics of SMGs in two steps, namely, by first defining it in terms of the so-called memory graphs whose semantics is subsequently defined in terms of concrete memory images. In particular, a *memory graph* (MG) is defined exactly as an SMG up to it is not allowed to contain any list segments. An SMG then represents the class of MGs that can be obtained (up to isomorphism) by applying any number of times the following two transformations: (1) *materialisation* of fresh regions from DLSs (i.e., intuitively, "pulling out" concrete regions from the beginning or end of segments) and (2) *removal* of 0+ DLSs (which may have become 0+ due to the preceding materialisation).

Materialisation and Removal of DLSs. Let $G = (O, V, \Lambda, H, P)$ be an SMG with the sets of regions R, DLSs D, and addresses A. Let $d \in D$ be a DLS of level 0. Further, let $a_n, a_p \in A$ be the next and prev addresses of d, i.e., $H(d, pfo(d), \texttt{ptr}) = a_p$ and $H(d, nfo(d), \texttt{ptr}) = a_n$. The DLS d can be *materialised* as follows—for an illustration of the operation, see the upper part of Fig. 3:

1. G is extended by a fresh copy G'_r of the sub-SMG $\widehat{G}_d$ nested below d. In G'_r, d is replaced by a fresh region r such that $size(r) = size(d)$, $level(r) = 0$, and $valid(r) = true$. The nesting level of each object and value in G'_r (apart from r) is decreased by one.
2. Let $a_f \in A$ be the address pointing to the beginning of d, i.e., such that $P(a_f) = (hfo(d), \texttt{fst}, d)$. If a_f does not exist in G, it is added. Next, A is extended by a fresh address a_d that will point to the beginning of the remaining part of d after the concretisation (while a_f will be the address of r). Finally, H and P are changed s.t. $P(a_f) = (hfo(d), \texttt{reg}, r)$, $H(r, pfo(d), \texttt{ptr}) = a_p$, $H(r, nfo(d), \texttt{ptr}) = a_d$, $P(a_d) = (hfo(d), \texttt{fst}, d)$, and $H(d, pfo(d), \texttt{ptr}) = a_f$.
3. For any object o of $\widehat{G}_d$, let o' be the corresponding copy of o in G'_r (for $o = d$, let $o' = r$). For each field $(of, t) \in (\mathbb{N} \times \mathbb{T})$ of each object o in $\widehat{G}_d$ whose value is of level 0, i.e., $level(H(o, of, t)) = 0$, the corresponding field of o' in G'_r is set to the same value, i.e., the set of edges is extended such that $H(o', of, t) = H(o, of, t)$.
4. If $len(d) > 0$, $len(d)$ is decreased by one.

Next, let $d \in D$ be a DLS as above with the additional requirement of $len(d) = 0$ with the addresses a_n, a_p, a_f, and a_l defined as in the case of materialisation. The DLS d can be *removed* as follows—for an illustration, see the lower part of Fig. 3: (1) Each has-value edge $o \xrightarrow{of,t} a_f$ is replaced by the edge $o \xrightarrow{of,t} a_n$. (2) Each has-value edge $o \xrightarrow{of,t} a_l$ is replaced by the edge $o \xrightarrow{of,t} a_p$. (3) The subgraph $\widehat{G}_d$ is removed together with the addresses a_f, a_l, and the edges adjacent with the removed objects and values.

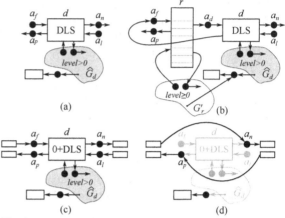

Fig. 3. Materialisation of a DLS: (a) input, (b) output (region r got materialised from DLS d). Removal of a DLS: (c) input, (d) output. Sub-SMGs $\widehat{G}_d$ and G'_r are highlighted without their roots.

Given an SMG $G = (O, V, \Lambda, H, P)$ with a set of DLSs D, we denote by $MG(G)$ the class of all MGs that can be obtained (up to isomorphism) by materializing each DLS $d \in D$ at least $len(d)$ times and by subsequently removing all DLSs.

Concrete Memory Images. The semantics of an MG $G = (R, V, \Lambda, H, P)$ is the set $MI(G)$ of *memory images* $\mu : \mathbb{N} \to \{0, \ldots, 255\}$ mapping *concrete addresses* to *bytes* such that there exists a function $\pi : R \to \mathbb{N}$, called a *region placement*, for which the following holds:

1. Only the null object is placed at address zero, i.e., $\forall r \in R : \pi(r) = 0 \Leftrightarrow r = \#$.
2. No two valid regions overlap, i.e., $\forall r_1, r_2 \in R : valid(r_1) \wedge valid(r_2) \Rightarrow \langle \pi(r_1), \pi(r_1) + size(r_1) \rangle \cap \langle \pi(r_2), \pi(r_2) + size(r_2) \rangle = \emptyset$.
3. Pointer fields are filled with the concrete addresses of the regions they refer to. Formally, for each pair of has-value and points-to edges $r_1 \xrightarrow{of_1,\mathtt{ptr}} a \xrightarrow{of_2,\mathtt{reg}} r_2$ in H and P, resp., $addr(bseq(\mu, \pi(r_1)+of_1, size(\mathtt{ptr}))) = \pi(r_2)+of_2$ where $bseq(\mu, p, size)$ is the sequence of bytes $\mu(p)\mu(p + 1)\ldots\mu(p + size - 1)$ for any $p, size > 0$, and $addr(\sigma)$ is the concrete address encoded by the byte sequence σ.
4. Fields having the same values are filled with the same concrete values (up to nullified blocks that can differ in their length), i.e., for every two has-value edges $r_1 \xrightarrow{of_1,t_1} v$ and $r_2 \xrightarrow{of_2,t_2} v$ in H, where $v \neq 0$, $bseq(\mu, \pi(r_1) + of_1, size(t_1)) = bseq(\mu, \pi(r_2) + of_2, size(t_2))$.
5. Finally, nullified fields are filled with zeros, i.e., for each has-value edge $r \xrightarrow{of,t} 0$ in H, $\mu(\pi(r) + of + i) = 0$ for all $0 \leq i < size(t)$.

For an SMG G, we let $MI(G) = \bigcup_{G' \in MG(G)} MI(G')$. Note that it may happen that it is not possible to find concrete values satisfying the needed constraints. In such a case, the semantics of an (S)MG is empty. Note also that we restrict ourselves to a flat address space, which is, however, sufficient for most practical cases.

3   Operations on SMGs

In this section, we propose algorithms for all the operations on SMGs that are needed for their application in program verification. In particular, we discuss data reinterpretation, join of SMGs (which we use for entailment checking, too), abstraction, inequality checking, and symbolic execution of C programs. Due to limited space, the description is mostly informal. More details can be found in [8].

Below, we denote by $I(of, t)$ the right-open integer interval $\langle of, of + size(t)\rangle$, and for a has-value edge $e : o \xrightarrow{of, t} v$, we write $I(e)$ as the abbreviation of $I(of, t)$.

3.1   Data Reinterpretation

SMGs allow fields of a single object to overlap and even to have the same offset and size, being distinguishable by their types only. In line with this feature of SMGs, we introduce the so-called *read reinterpretation* that can create multiple views (*interpretations*) of a single memory area without actually changing the semantics. On the other hand, if we write to a field that overlaps with other fields, we need to reflect the change of the memory image in the overlapping fields, for which the so-called *write reinterpretation* is used. These two operations form the basis of all operations reading and writing memory represented by SMGs. Apart from them, we also use *join reinterpretation* which is applied when joining two SMGs to preserve as much information shared by the SMGs as possible even when this information is not explicitly represented in the same way in both the input SMGs.

Defining reinterpretation for all possible data types (and all of their possible values) is hard (cf. [15]) and beyond the scope of this paper. Instead of that, we define minimal requirements that must be met by the reinterpretation operators so that our verification approach is sound. This allows different concrete instantiations of these operators to be used in the future. Currently, we instantiate the operators for the particular case of dealing with nullified blocks of memory, which is essential for handling low-level pointer manipulating programs that commonly use functions like `calloc()` or `memset()` to obtain large blocks of nullified memory.[6]

Read Reinterpretation. A read reinterpretation operator takes as input an SMG G with a set of objects O, an object $o \in O$, and a field (of, t) to be read from o such that $of + size(t) \leq size(o)$. The result is a couple (G', v) where G' is an SMG with a set of has-value edges H' such that (1) $H'(o, of, t) = v \neq \bot$ and (2) $MI(G) = MI(G')$. The operator thus preserves the semantics of the SMG but ensures that it contains a has-value edge for the field being read. This edge can lead to a value already present in the SMG but also to a new value derived by the operator from the edges and values existing in the SMG. In the extreme case, a fresh, completely unconstrained value node can be added, representing an unknown value, which can, however, become constrained by the further program execution. In other words, read reinterpretation installs a new view on some part of the object o, but it cannot modify the semantics of the SMG in any way.

---

[6] Apart from the nullified blocks, our implementation also supports tracking of uninitialized blocks of memory and certain manipulations of null-terminated strings.

For the particular case of dealing with nullified memory, we use the following concrete read reinterpretation (cf. [8]). If G contains an edge $o \xrightarrow{of,t} v$, (G, v) is returned. Otherwise, if each byte of the field (of, t) is nullified by some edge $o \xrightarrow{of',t'} 0$ present in G, $(G', 0)$ is returned where G' is obtained from G by adding the edge $o \xrightarrow{of,t} 0$. Otherwise, (G', v) is returned with G' obtained from G by adding an edge $o \xrightarrow{of,t} v$ leading to a fresh value v (representing an unknown value). It is easy to see that with the current support of types and values in SMGs, this is the most precise read reinterpretation that is possible from the point of view of reading nullified memory.

Write Reinterpretation. The write reinterpretation operator takes as input an SMG G with a set of objects O, an object $o \in O$, a field (of, t) within o, i.e., such that $of + size(t) \leq size(o)$, and a value v that is to be written into the field (of, t) of the object o. The result is an SMG G' with a set of has-value edges H' such that (1) $H'(o, of, t) = v$ and (2) $MI(G) \subseteq MI(G'')$ where G'' is the SMG G' without the edge $e : o \xrightarrow{of,t} v$. In other words, the operator makes sure that the resulting SMG contains the edge e that was to be written while the semantics of G' without e over-approximates the semantics of G. Indeed, one cannot require equality here since the new edge may collide with some other edges, which may have to be dropped in the worst case.

For the case of dealing with nullified memory, we propose the following write reinterpretation (cf. [8], which include an illustration too). If G contains the edge $e : o \xrightarrow{of,t} v$, G is returned. Otherwise, all has-value edges leading from o to a non-zero value whose fields overlap with (of, t) are removed. Subsequently, if $v = 0$, the edge e is added, and the obtained SMG is returned. Otherwise, all remaining has-value edges leading from o to 0 that define fields overlapping with (of, t) are split and/or shortened such that they do not overlap with (of, t), the edge e is added, and the resulting SMG is returned. Again, it is easy to see that this operator is the most precise write reinterpretation from the point of view of preserving information about nullified memory that is possible with the current support of types and values in SMGs.

3.2 Join of SMGs

Join of SMGs is a binary operation that takes two SMGs G_1, G_2 and returns an SMG G that is their common generalisation, i.e., $MI(G_1) \subseteq MI(G) \supseteq MI(G_2)$, and that satisfies the following further requirements intended to minimize the involved information loss: If both input SMGs are semantically equal, i.e., $MI(G_1) = MI(G_2)$, denoted $G_1 \simeq G_2$, we require the resulting SMG to be semantically equal to both the input ones, i.e., $MI(G_1) = MI(G) = MI(G_2)$. If $MI(G_1) \supset MI(G_2)$, denoted $G_1 \sqsupset G_2$, we require that $MI(G) = MI(G_1)$. Symmetrically, if $MI(G_1) \subset MI(G_2)$, denoted $G_1 \sqsubset G_2$, we require that $MI(G) = MI(G_2)$. Finally, if the input SMGs are semantically incomparable, i.e., $MI(G_1) \not\supseteq MI(G_2) \land MI(G_1) \not\subseteq MI(G_2)$, denoted $G_1 \bowtie G_2$, no further requirements are put on the result of the join (besides the inclusion stated above, which is required for the soundness of our analysis). In order to distinguish which of these cases happens when joining two SMGs, we tag the result of our join operator by the so-called *join status* with the domain $\mathbb{J} = \{\simeq, \sqsupset, \sqsubset, \bowtie\}$ referring to the corresponding relations above.

Moreover, we allow the join operation to fail if the incurred information loss becomes too big. Below, we give an informal description of our join operator, for a full description see [8].

The basic idea of our join algorithm is the following. The algorithm simultaneously traverses a given pair of source SMGs and tries to join each pair of nodes (i.e., objects or values) encountered at the same time into a single node in the destination SMG. A single node of one SMG is not allowed to be joined with multiple nodes of the other SMG. This preserves the distinction between different objects as well as between at least possibly different values.

The rules according to which it is decided whether a pair of objects simultaneously encountered in the input SMGs can be joined are the following. First, they must have the same size, validity, and in case of DLSs, the same head, prev, and next offsets. It is possible to join DLSs of different lengths as well as DLSs with regions (approximated as 1+ DLSs). The result is a DLS whose length is the minimum of the lengths of the joined DLSs (hence, e.g., joining a region with a 2+ DLS gives a 1+ DLS). The levels of the joined objects must also be the same up to the following case. When joining a sub-SMG nested below a DLS with a corresponding sub-SMG rooted at a region (restricted by ignoring the next and prev links), objects corresponding to each other appear on different levels: E.g., objects nested right below a DLS of level 0 are on level 1, whereas the corresponding objects directly referenced by a region of level 0 are on level 0 (since for regions, nested and shared sub-SMGs are not distinguished). This difference can, of course, increase when descending deeper in a hierarchically nested data structure as it is essentially given by the different numbers of DLSs passed on the different sides of the join. This difference is tracked by the join algorithm, and only the objects whose levels differ in the appropriate way are allowed to be joined.

When two objects are being joined, a *join reinterpretation* operator is used to ensure that they share the same set of fields and hence have the same number and labels of outgoing edges (which is always possible albeit sometimes for the price of introducing has-value edges leading to unknown values). A formalization of join reinterpretation is available in [8], including a concrete join reinterpretation operator designed to preserve maximum information on nullified blocks in both of the objects being joined. The join reinterpretation allows the fields of the joined objects to be processed in pairs of the same size and type. As for joining values, we do not allow joining addresses with unknown values.[7] Moreover, the zero value cannot be joined with a non-zero value. Further, addresses can be joined only if the points-to edges leading from them are labelled by the same offset, and when they lead to DLSs, they must have the same target specifier. On the other hand, apart from the already above expressed requirement of not joining a single value in one SMG with several values in the other SMG, no further requirements are put on joining non-address values, which is possible since we currently track their equalities only.

To increase chances for successfully joining two SMGs, the basic algorithm from above is extended as follows. When a pair of objects cannot be joined and at least one

---

[7] Allowing a join of an address and an unknown value could lead to a need to drop a part of the allocated heap in one of the SMGs (in case it was not accessible through some other address too), which we consider to be a too big loss of information.

of them is a DLS (call it d and the other object o), the algorithm proceeds as though o was preceded by a 0+ DLS d' that is up to its length isomorphic with d (including the not yet visited part of the appropriate sub-SMG nested below d). Said differently, the algorithm virtually inserts d' before o, joins d and d' into a single 0+ DLS, and then continues by trying to join o and the successor of d. This extension is possible since the semantics of a 0+ DLS includes the empty list, which can be safely assumed to appear anywhere, compensating a missing object in one of the SMGs.

Note, however, that the virtual insertion of a 0+ DLS implies a need to relax some of the requirements from above. For instance, one needs to allow a join of two different addresses from one SMG with one address in the other (the prev and next addresses of d get both joined with the address preceding o). Moreover, the possibility to insert 0+ DLSs introduces some non-determinism into the algorithm since when attempting to join a pair of incompatible DLSs, a 0+ DLS can be inserted into either of the two input DLSs, and we choose one of them. The choice may be wrong, but for performance reasons, we never backtrack. Moreover, we use the 0+ DLS insertion only when a join of two objects fails locally (i.e., without looking at their successors). When a pair of objects can be locally joined, but then the join fails on their successors, one could consider backtracking and trying to insert a 0+ DLS, which we again do not do for performance reasons (and we did not see a need for that in our cases studies so far).

The described join algorithm is used in two scenarios: (1) When joining garbage-free SPCs to reduce the number of SPCs obtained from different paths through the program, in which case the traversal starts from pairs of identical program variables. (2) As a part of the abstraction algorithm for merging a pair of neighbouring objects (together with the non-shared parts of the sub-SMGs rooted at them) of a doubly-linked list into a single DLS, in which case the algorithm is started from the neighbouring objects to be merged. In the join algorithm, the join status is computed on-the-fly. Initially, the status is set to $\simeq$. Next, whenever performing a step that implies a particular relation between G_1 and G_2 (e.g., joining a 0+ DLS from G_1 with a 1+ DLS from G_2 implies that $G_1 \sqsupset G_2$, assuming that the remaining parts of G_1 and G_2 are semantically equal), we appropriately update the join status.

3.3 Abstraction

Our abstraction is based on *merging uninterrupted sequences* of neighbouring objects, together with the $\{nfo, pfo\}$-restricted sub-SMGs rooted at them, into a single DLS. This is done by repeatedly applying a slight extension of the join algorithm on the $\{nfo, pfo\}$-restricted sub-SMGs rooted at the neighbouring objects. The sequences to be merged are identified by the so-called *candidate DLS entries* that consist of an object o_c and next, prev, and head offsets such that o_c has a neighbouring object with which it can be merged into a DLS linked through the given offsets. The abstraction is driven by the *cost* to be paid in terms of the loss of precision caused by merging certain objects and the sub-SMGs rooted at them (in particular, we distinguish joining of equal, entailed, or incomparable sub-SMGs). The higher the loss of precision is, the longer sequence of mergeable objects is required to enable a merge of the sequence.

In the extended join algorithm used in the abstraction (cf. [8]), the two simultaneous searches are started from two neighbouring objects o_1 and o_2 of the same SMG G that are the roots of the $\{nfo_c, pfo_c\}$-restricted sub-SMGs G_1, G_2 to be merged. The extended join algorithm constructs the sub-SMG $G_{1,2}$ that is to be nested below the DLS resulting from the join of o_1 and o_2. The extended join algorithm also returns the sets O_1, V_1 and O_2, V_2 of the objects and values of G_1 and G_2, respectively, whose join gives rise to $G_{1,2}$. Unlike when joining two distinct SMGs, the two simultaneous searches can get to a single node at the same time. Clearly, such a node is shared by G_1 and G_2, and it is therefore *not* included into the sub-SMG $G_{1,2}$ to be nested below the join of o_1 and o_2.

Below, we explain in more detail the particular steps of the abstraction. For the explanation, we fix an SPC $C = (G, \nu)$ where $G = (O, V, \Lambda, H, P)$ is an SMG with the sets of regions R, DLSs D, and addresses A.

Candidate DLS Entries. A quadruple $(o_c, hfo_c, nfo_c, pfo_c)$ where $o_c \in O$ and hfo_c, $nfo_c, pfo_c \in \mathbb{N}$ such that $nfo_c < pfo_c$ is considered a *candidate DLS entry* iff the following holds: (1) o_c is a valid heap object. (2) o_c has a neighbouring object $o \in O$ with which it is doubly-linked through the chosen offsets, i.e., there are $a_1, a_2 \in A$ such that $H(o_c, nfo_c, \mathtt{ptr}) = a_1$, $P(a_1) = (hfo_c, tg_1, o)$ for $tg_1 \in \{\mathtt{fst}, \mathtt{reg}\}$, $H(o, pfo_c, \mathtt{ptr}) = a_2$, and $P(a_2) = (hfo_c, tg_2, o_c)$ for $tg_2 \in \{\mathtt{lst}, \mathtt{reg}\}$.

Longest Mergeable Sequences. The *longest mergeable sequence* of objects given by a candidate DLS entry $(o_c, hfo_c, nfo_c, pfo_c)$ is the longest sequence of distinct valid heap objects whose first object is o_c, all objects in the sequence are of level 0, all DLSs that appear in the sequence have hfo_c, nfo_c, pfo_c as their head, next, prev offsets, and the following holds for any two neighbouring objects o_1 and o_2 in the sequence (for a formal description, cf. [8]): (1) The objects o_1 and o_2 are doubly linked through their nfo_c and pfo_c fields. (2) The objects o_1 and o_2 are a part of a sequence of objects that is not pointed from outside of the detected list structure. (3) The $\{nfo_c, pfo_c\}$-restricted sub-SMGs G_1 and G_2 of G rooted at o_1 and o_2 can be joined using the extended join algorithm into the sub-SMG $G_{1,2}$ to be nested below the join of o_1 and o_2. Let O_1, V_1 and O_2, V_2 be the sets of non-shared objects and values of G_1 and G_2, respectively, whose join gives rise to $G_{1,2}$. (4) The non-shared objects and values of G_1 and G_2 (other than o_1 and o_2 themselves) are reachable via o_1 or o_2, respectively, only. Moreover, the sets O_1 and O_2 contain heap objects only.

Merging Sequences of Objects into DLSs. Sequences of objects are merged into a single DLS *incrementally*, i.e., starting with the first two objects of the sequence, then merging the resulting new DLS with the third object in the sequence, and so on. Each of the *elementary merge operations* is performed as follows (see Fig. 4 for an illustration).

Assume that G is the SMG of the current SPC (i.e., the initial SPC or the SPC obtained from the last merge) with the set of points-to edges P and the set of addresses A, o_1 is either the first object in the sequence or the DLS obtained from the previous elementary merge, o_2 is the next object of the sequence to be processed, and hfo_c, nfo_c, pfo_c are the offsets from the candidate DLS entry defining the sequence to be merged. First, we merge o_1 and o_2 into a DLS d using hfo_c, nfo_c, and pfo_c as its defining offsets (cf. [8]). The sub-SMG nested below d is created using the above mentioned extended join algorithm. Next, the DLS-linking pointers arriving to o_1 and o_2 are redirected to d. In particular, if there is $a_f \in A$ such that $P(a_f) =$

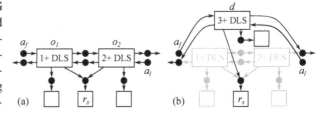

Fig. 4. The elementary merge operation: (a) input (b) output

(o_1, hfo_c, tg) for some $tg \in \{\texttt{fst}, \texttt{reg}\}$, then P is changed such that $P(a_f) = (d, hfo_c, \texttt{fst})$. Similarly, if there is $a_l \in A$ such that $P(a_l) = (o_2, hfo_c, tg)$ for some $tg \in \{\texttt{lst}, \texttt{reg}\}$, then P is changed such that $P(a_l) = (d, hfo_c, \texttt{lst})$. Finally, each heap object and each value (apart from the null address and null object) that are not reachable from any static or stack object of the obtained SPC are removed from its SMG together with all the edges adjacent to them.

The Top-level Abstraction Algorithm. Assume we are given an SMG G, and a candidate DLS entry $(o_c, hfo_c, nfo_c, pfo_c)$ defining the longest mergeable sequence of objects $\sigma = o_1 o_2 \ldots o_n$ in G of length $|\sigma| = n \geq 2$. We define the *cost* of merging a pair of objects o_1, o_2, denoted $cost(o_1, o_2)$, as follows. First, $cost(o_1, o_2) = 0$ iff the $\{nfo_c, pfo_c\}$-restricted sub-SMGs G_1 and G_2 rooted at o_1, o_2 are equal (when ignoring the kinds of o_1 and o_2). This is indicated by the $\simeq$ status returned by the modified join algorithm applied on G_1, G_2. Further, $cost(o_1, o_2) = 1$ iff G_1 entails G_2, or vice versa, which is indicated by the status $\sqsupset$ or $\sqsubset$. Finally, $cost(o_1, o_2) = 2$ iff G_1 and G_2 are incomparable, which is indicated by status $\bowtie$. The cost of merging a sequence of objects $\sigma = o_1 o_2 \ldots o_n$, denoted $cost(\sigma)$, is defined as the maximum of $cost(o_1, o_2)$, $cost(o_2, o_3)$, ..., $cost(o_{n-1}, o_n)$.

Our abstraction is parameterized by associating each cost $c \in \{0, 1, 2\}$ with the *length threshold*, denoted $lenThr(c)$, defining the minimum length of a sequence of mergeable objects allowed to be merged for the given cost. Intuitively, the higher is the cost, the bigger loss of precision is incurred by the merge, and hence a bigger number of objects to be merged is required to compensate the cost. In our experiments discussed in Section 5, we, in particular, found as optimal the setting $lenThr(0) = lenThr(1) = 2$ and $lenThr(2) = 3$. Our tool, however, allows the user to tweak these values.

Based on the above introduced notions, the process of *abstracting an SPC* can now be described as follows. First, all candidate DLS entries are identified, and for each of them, the corresponding longest mergeable sequence is computed. Then each longest mergeable sequence σ for which $|\sigma| < lenThr(cost(\sigma))$ is discarded. Out of the remaining ones, we select those that have the lowest cost. From them, we then select those that have the longest length. Finally, out of them, one is selected arbitrarily. The selected sequence is merged, and then the entire abstraction process is repeated till there is a sequence that can be merged taking its length and cost into account.

3.4   Checking Equality and Inequality of Values

Checking equality of values in SMGs amounts to simply checking their identity. For checking inequality, we use an algorithm which is sound and efficient but incomplete. It is designed to succeed in most common cases, but in order not to harm its efficiency, we allow it to fail in some exceptional cases (e.g., when comparing addresses out of bounds of two distinct objects). The basic idea of the algorithm is as follows (cf. [8]): Let v_1 and v_2 be two distinct values of level 0 to be checked for inequality (other levels cannot be directly accessed by program statements). First, if the same value or object can be reached from v_1 and v_2 through 0+ DLSs only (using the next/prev fields when coming through the fst/lst target specifiers, respectively), then the inequality between v_1 and v_2 is not established. This is due to v_1 and v_2 may become the same value when the possibly empty 0+ DLSs are removed (or they may become addresses of the first and last node of the same 0+ DLS, and hence be equal in case the list contains a single node). Otherwise, v_1 and v_2 are claimed different if the final pair of values reached from them through 0+ DLSs represents different addresses due to pointing (1) to different valid objects (each with its own unique address) with offsets inside their bounds, (2) to the null object and a non-null object (with an in-bound offset), (3) to the same object with different offsets, or (4) to the same DLS with length at least 2 using different target specifiers. Otherwise, the inequality is not established.

3.5   A Brief Note on Symbolic Execution

The symbolic execution algorithm based on SMGs is similar to [1]. It uses the read reinterpretation operator for memory lookup (as well as type-casting) and the write reinterpretation operator for memory mutation. Whenever a DLS is about to be accessed (or its address with a non-head offset is about to be taken), a materialisation (as described in Section 2.3) is performed so that the actual program statements are always executed over concrete objects. If the minimum length of the DLS being materialised is zero, the computation is split into two branches—one for the empty segment and one for the non-empty segment. In the former case, the DLS is removed (as described in Section 2.3) while in the latter case, the minimum length of the DLS is incremented. When executing a conditional statement, the algorithm for checking (in)equality of values from Section 3.4 is used. If neither equality nor inequality are established, the execution is split into two branches, one of them assuming the compared values to be equal, the other assuming them not to be equal. This may again involve removing 0+ DLSs in one of the branches and incrementing their length in the other (cf. [8]).

A Note on Soundness of the Analysis. In the described analysis, program statements are always executed on concrete objects only, closely following the C semantics. The read reinterpretation is defined such that it cannot change the semantics of the input SMG, and the write reinterpretation can only over-approximate the semantics in the worst case. Likewise, our abstraction and join algorithms are allowed to only over-approximate the semantics—indeed, when joining a pair of nodes, the semantics of the resulting node is always generic enough to cover the semantics of both of the joined nodes (e.g., the join of a 2+ DLS with a compatible region results in a 1+ DLS, etc.). Moreover, the entailment check used to terminate the analysis is based on the join operator and consequently conservative. Hence, it is not difficult to see that the proposed analysis is sound (although a full proof of this fact would be rather technical).

4   Extensions of SMGs

In this section, we point out that the notion of SMGs can be easily extended in various directions, and we briefly discuss several such extensions (including further kinds of abstract objects), most of which are already implemented in our tool Predator.

Explicit Non-equivalence Relations.   When several objects have the same concrete value stored in their fields, this is expressed by that the appropriate has-value edges lead from these objects to the same value node in the SMG. On the other hand, two different value nodes in an SMG do not necessarily represent different concrete values. To express that two abstract values represent distinct concrete values, SMGs can be extended with a symmetric, irreflexive relation over values, which we call an *explicit non-equivalence relation*. Clearly, SMGs can be quite naturally extended by allowing more predicates on data, which is, however, beyond the scope of this paper (up to a small extension by tracking more concrete values than 0 that is mentioned below).

Singly-linked List Segments (SLSs).   Above, we have presented all algorithms on SMGs describing doubly-linked lists only. Nevertheless, the algorithms work equally well with singly-linked lists represented by an additional kind of abstract objects, SLSs, that have no *pfo* offset, and their addresses are allowed to use the `fst` and `all` target specifiers only. The algorithm looking for DLS entry candidates then simply starts looking for SLS entry candidates whenever it does not discover the back-link.

0/1 Abstract Objects.   In order to enable summarization of lists whose nodes can *optionally* point to some region or that point to nested lists whose length never reaches 2 or more, we introduce the so-called *0/1 abstract objects*. We distinguish three kinds of them with different numbers of neighbour pointers. The first of them represents 0/1 SLSs with one neighbour pointer, another represents 0/1 DLSs with two neighbour pointers. These objects can be later joined with compatible SLSs or DLSs. The third kind has no neighbour pointer, and its address is assumed to be NULL when the region is not allocated. This kind is needed for optionally allocated regions referred from list nodes but never handled as lists themselves. The 0/1 abstract objects are created by the join algorithm when a region in one SMG cannot be matched with an object from the other SMG and none of the above described join mechanisms applies.

Offset Intervals and Address Alignment.   The basic SMG notion labels points-to edges with scalar offsets within the target object. This labelling can be generalized to *intervals of offsets*. The intervals can be allowed to arise by joining objects with incoming pointers compatible up to their offset. This feature is useful, e.g., to handle lists arising in higher-level memory allocators discussed in the next section where each node points to itself with an offset depending on how much of the node has been used by sub-allocation. Offset intervals also naturally arise when the analysis is allowed to support *address alignment*, which is typically implemented by masking several lowest bits of pointers to zero, resulting in a pointer whose offset is in a certain interval wrt. the base address. Similarly, one can allow the *object size* to be given by an interval, which in turn allows one to abstract lists whose nodes are of a variable size.

Integral Constants and Intervals. The basic SMG notion allows one to express that two fields have the same value (by the corresponding has-value edges leading to the same value node) or that their values differ (using the above mentioned explicit non-equivalence relation). In order to improve the support of dealing with integers, SMGs can be extended by associating value nodes with concrete integral numbers. These can be respected by the join algorithm (at least up to some bound), or they can be abstracted to intervals or some other abstract numerical domains.

5   Implementation

We have implemented the above described algorithms (including the extensions) in a new version of our tool called Predator.[8] Predator is a GCC plug-in, which allows one to experiment with industrial source code without manually preprocessing it first. The verified program must, however, be closed in that it must allocate and initialize all the data structures used. Modular verification of code fragments is planned for the future. By default, Predator disallows calls to external functions in order to exclude any side effect that could potentially break memory safety. The only allowed external functions are those that Predator recognizes as built-in functions and properly models them wrt. proving memory safety. Besides `malloc` and `free`, the set of supported built-in functions includes certain memory manipulating functions defined in the C standard, such as `memset`, `memcpy`, or `memmove`. Predator uses the same style of error and warning messages as GCC itself, and hence it can be used with any IDE that can use GCC. It also supports error recovery to report multiple program errors during one run. For example, if a memory leak is detected, Predator only reports a warning, the unreachable part of SMG is removed, and the symbolic execution then continues.

Predator implements an inter-procedural analysis based on [13]. It does not support recursive programs yet, but it supports indirect calls, which is necessary for verification of programs with callbacks (e.g., Linux drivers). Regions for stack variables are created automatically as needed and destroyed as soon as they become dead according to a static live variables analysis, performed before running the symbolic execution. When working with initialized variables, we take advantage of our efficient representation of nullified blocks—we first create a has-value edge $o \xrightarrow{0, \text{char}[size(o)]} 0$ for each initialized variable represented by a region o, then we execute all explicit initializers, which themselves automatically trigger the write reinterpretation. The same approach is used

---

[8] http://www.fit.vutbr.cz/research/groups/verifit/tools/predator/

for `calloc`-based heap allocation. Thanks to this, we do not need to initialize each structure member explicitly, which would not scale for complex structures.

The algorithms for abstraction and join implemented in Predator use some further optimizations of the basic algorithms described in Section 3. While objects in SMGs are type-free, Predator tracks their *estimated type* given by the type of the pointers through which objects are manipulated. The estimated type is used during abstraction to postpone merging a pair of objects with incompatible types. Note, however, that this is really a heuristic only—we have a case study that constructs list nodes using solely `void` pointers, and it can still be successfully verified by Predator. Another heuristic is that certain features of the join algorithm (e.g., insertion of a non-empty DLS or introduction of an 0/1 abstract object) are disabled when joining SMGs while enabled when merging nodes during abstraction. Predator tracks integral values precisely up to a certain bound (± 10 by default) and once the bound is reached, the values are abstracted out. Predator also supports intervals aligned to a power of two as well as tracking of simple dependences between intervals, such as a shift by a constant and a multiplication by -1. All these features are optional and can be easily disabled.

Predator iteratively computes sets of SMGs for each basic block entry of the control-flow graph of the given program, covering all program configurations reachable at these program locations. Termination of the analysis is aided by the abstraction and join algorithms described above. Since the join algorithm is expensive, it is used at loop boundaries only. When updating states of other basic block entries, we compare the SMGs for equality only, which makes the comparison way faster, especially in case a pair of SMGs cannot be joined. Similarly, the abstraction is by default used only at loop boundaries in order not to introduce abstract objects where not necessary (reducing the space for false positives that can arise due to breaking assumptions sometimes used by programmers for code inside loops as witnessed by some of our case studies).

Predator is able to discover or prove absence of various kinds of *memory safety errors*, including various forms of illegal dereferences (null dereferences, dereferences of freed or unallocated memory, out-of-bound dereferences), illegal free operations (double free operations, freeing non-heap objects), as well as memory leakage. Moreover, Predator also uses the fact that SMGs allow for easy checking whether a given pair of memory areas overlap. Indeed, if both of them are inside of two distinct valid regions, they have no overlaps, and if both of them are inside the same region, one can simply check their offset ranges for intersection. Such checks are used for reporting invalid uses of `memcpy` or the C-language assignment, which expose undefined behavior if the destination and source memory areas (partially) overlap with each other.

6   Experiments

The new version of Predator based on the above proposed method was successfully tested on a number of case studies. Among them there are more than 256 case studies (freely available with Predator) illustrating various programming constructs typically used when dealing with linked lists. These case studies include various advanced kinds of lists used in the Linux kernel and their typical manipulation, typical error patterns that appear in code operating with Linux lists, various sorting algorithms (insert sort, bubble

Table 1. Selected experimental results showing either the verification time or one of the following outcomes: FP = false positive, FN = false negative, T = time out (900 s), x = parsing problems

Test Origin	Test	Invader	SLAyer	Predator 2011-10	Predator 2013-02
SLAyer	`append.c`	<0.01 s	10.47 s	<0.01 s	<0.01 s
	`cromdata_add_remove_fs.c`	<0.01 s	FN	<0.01 s	<0.01 s
	`create_kernel.c`	T	FN	<0.01 s	<0.01 s
	`cromdata_add_remove.c`	T	FN	<0.01 s	<0.01 s
	`reverse_seg_cyclic.c`	FP	0.68 s	<0.01 s	<0.01 s
	`is_on_list_via_devext.c`	T	34.43 s	0.20 s	0.02 s
	`callback_remove_entry_list.c`	T	71.46 s	0.14 s	0.10 s
Invader	`cdrom.c`	FN	x	2.44 s	0.66 s
Predator	`five-level-sll-destroyed-top-down.c`	FP	x	FP	0.05 s
	`linux-dll-of-linux-dll.c`	T	x	0.41 s	0.05 s
	`merge-sort.c`	FP	x	1.08 s	0.21 s
	`list-of-arena-pools-with-alignment.c`	FP	x	FP	0.50 s
	`lvmcache_add_orphan_vginfo.c`	x	x	FP	1.07 s
	`five-level-sll-destroyed-bottom-up.c`	FP	x	FP	1.14 s

sort, merge sort), etc. These case studies have up to 300 lines of code, but they consist almost entirely of complex memory manipulation (unlike larger programs whose big portions are often ignored by tools verifying memory safety). Next, we successfully tested Predator on the driver code snippets distributed with SLAyer [2] as well as on the cdrom driver originally checked by Space Invader [17]. As discussed below, in some of these examples, we identified errors not found by the other tools due to their more abstract (not byte-precise) treatment of memory.

Further, we also considered two real-life low-level programs (which, to the best of our knowledge, have not yet been targeted by fully automated formal verification tools): a memory allocator from the Netscape portable runtime (NSPR) and a module taken from the lvm2 logical volume manager. The NSPR allocator allocates memory from the operating system in blocks called *arenas*, grouped into singly-linked lists called *arena pools*, which can in turn be grouped into lists of arena pools (giving lists of lists of arenas). User requests are then satisfied by sub-allocation within a suitable arena of a given arena pool. We have considered a fixed size of the arenas and checked safety of repeated allocation and deallocation of blocks of aligned size randomly chosen up to the arena size from arena pools as well as lists of arena pools. For this purpose, a support for offset intervals as described above was needed. The intervals arise from abstracting lists whose nodes (arenas) point with different offsets to themselves (one byte behind the last sub-allocated block within the arena) and from address alignment, which the NSPR-based allocator is also responsible for. Our approach allowed us to verify that pointers leading from each arena to its so-far free part never point beyond the arena and that arena headers never overlap with their data areas, which are the original assertions checked by NSPR arena pools at run-time. Our lvm2-based case studies then exercise various functions of the module implementing the volume metadata cache. As in the case of NSPR arenas, we use the original (unsimplified) code of the module, but (for now) we use a simplified test harness where the lvm2 implementation of hash tables is replaced by the lvm2 implementation of doubly-linked lists.

We have compared the capabilities and performance of Invader, SLAyer, and Predator on the above case studies on an Intel® Core™ i7-3770K machine. The memory consumption was below 128 MB in all cases. As we can see in Table 1, Predator successfully verified even the test-cases that were causing problems to Invader or SLAyer. We have also revealed issues of memory safety violation in the examples distributed with Invader and SLAyer because Invader did not check memory manipulation via array subscripts and SLAyer did not check size of the blocks allocated on the heap.[9] All the tools were run in their default configurations. Better results can sometimes be obtained for particular case studies by tweaking certain configuration options (abstraction threshold, call cache size, etc.). However, while such changes may improve the performance in some case studies, they may harm it in others, trigger false positives, or even prevent the analysis from termination.

We have also compared the new version of Predator with its older version that participated in the 1st International Competition on Software Verification (SV-COMP'12). The old Predator produced false positives on many of the more advanced case studies, including NSPR arenas and lvm2, and it was also slower. For example, the merge-sort case study, presented as the most expensive in [7] (Predator 2011-02), now runs approximately $25\times$ faster on the same machine ($5\times$ due to the algorithms presented above and $5\times$ due to an improved live variable analysis). The new Predator participated in the 2nd International Competition on Software Verification (SV-COMP'13) [4], where it won three categories. Moreover, the fact that Predator did not have any false negative over the whole SV-COMP'13 benchmark confirms the soundness of our analysis algorithm.

7   Conclusion and Future Work

We have presented a new approach to fully automated formal verification of list manipulating programs capable of handling various features of low-level memory manipulation. We have experimentally validated the approach on a number of case studies showing its efficiency and capability of handling program behaviour that is beyond what current fully automated shape analysis tools can handle. In the future, a number of extensions of our approach are possible. We are planning a support of (low-level) tree structures, a better support of integer data, a support of arrays and hash tables, as well as a support for modular verification in order to remove the burden of having to write environments for the code to be verified.

References

1. Berdine, J., Calcagno, C., Cook, B., Distefano, D., O'Hearn, P.W., Wies, T., Yang, H.: Shape Analysis for Composite Data Structures. In: Damm, W., Hermanns, H. (eds.) CAV 2007. LNCS, vol. 4590, pp. 178–192. Springer, Heidelberg (2007)
2. Berdine, J., Cook, B., Ishtiaq, S.: SLAYER: Memory Safety for Systems-Level Code. In: Gopalakrishnan, G., Qadeer, S. (eds.) CAV 2011. LNCS, vol. 6806, pp. 178–183. Springer, Heidelberg (2011)

---

[9] We used the latest publicly available version of SLAyer from [2]. The version from [3] was not available, but [3] targets mainly checking of spuriousness of counterexamples.

3. Berdine, J., Cox, A., Ishtiaq, S., Wintersteiger, C.M.: Diagnosing Abstraction Failure for Separation Logic-Based Analyses. In: Madhusudan, P., Seshia, S.A. (eds.) CAV 2012. LNCS, vol. 7358, pp. 155–173. Springer, Heidelberg (2012)
4. Beyer, D.: Second competition on software verification. In: Piterman, N., Smolka, S.A. (eds.) TACAS 2013 (ETAPS 2013). LNCS, vol. 7795, pp. 594–609. Springer, Heidelberg (2013)
5. Calcagno, C., Distefano, D., O'Hearn, P.W., Yang, H.: Beyond Reachability: Shape Abstraction in the Presence of Pointer Arithmetic. In: Yi, K. (ed.) SAS 2006. LNCS, vol. 4134, pp. 182–203. Springer, Heidelberg (2006)
6. Chang, B.-Y.E., Rival, X., Necula, G.C.: Shape Analysis with Structural Invariant Checkers. In: Riis Nielson, H., Filé, G. (eds.) SAS 2007. LNCS, vol. 4634, pp. 384–401. Springer, Heidelberg (2007)
7. Dudka, K., Peringer, P., Vojnar, T.: Predator: A Practical Tool for Checking Manipulation of Dynamic Data Structures Using Separation Logic. In: Gopalakrishnan, G., Qadeer, S. (eds.) CAV 2011. LNCS, vol. 6806, pp. 372–378. Springer, Heidelberg (2011)
8. Dudka, K., Peringer, P., Vojnar, T.: Byte-Precise Verification of Low-Level List Manipulation. Technical report FIT-TR-2012-04, FIT BUT (2012),
   http://www.fit.vutbr.cz/~idudka/pub/FIT-TR-2012-04.pdf
9. Habermehl, P., Holík, L., Rogalewicz, A., Šimáček, J., Vojnar, T.: Forest Automata for Verification of Heap Manipulation. In: Gopalakrishnan, G., Qadeer, S. (eds.) CAV 2011. LNCS, vol. 6806, pp. 424–440. Springer, Heidelberg (2011)
10. Kreiker, J., Seidl, H., Vojdani, V.: Shape Analysis of Low-Level C with Overlapping Structures. In: Barthe, G., Hermenegildo, M. (eds.) VMCAI 2010. LNCS, vol. 5944, pp. 214–230. Springer, Heidelberg (2010)
11. Laviron, V., Chang, B.-Y.E., Rival, X.: Separating Shape Graphs. In: Gordon, A.D. (ed.) ESOP 2010. LNCS, vol. 6012, pp. 387–406. Springer, Heidelberg (2010)
12. Marron, M., Hermenegildo, M.V., Kapur, D., Stefanovic, D.: Efficient Context-Sensitive Shape Analysis with Graph Based Heap Models. In: Hendren, L. (ed.) CC 2008. LNCS, vol. 4959, pp. 245–259. Springer, Heidelberg (2008)
13. Reps, T., Horwitz, S., Sagiv, M.: Precise Interprocedural Dataflow Analysis via Graph Reachability. In: Proc. of POPL 1995. ACM Press (1995)
14. Sagiv, M., Reps, T., Wilhelm, R.: Parametric shape analysis via 3-valued logic. In: ACM Transactions on Programming Languages and Systems (TOPLAS), 24(3) (2002)
15. Tuch, H.: Formal Verification of C Systems Code. Journal of Automated Reasoning 42(2-4) (2009)
16. Yang, H., Lee, O., Calcagno, C., Distefano, D., O'Hearn, P.W.: On Scalable Shape Analysis. Technical report RR-07-10, Queen Mary, University of London (2007)
17. Yang, H., Lee, O., Berdine, J., Calcagno, C., Cook, B., Distefano, D., O'Hearn, P.W.: Scalable Shape Analysis for Systems Code. In: Gupta, A., Malik, S. (eds.) CAV 2008. LNCS, vol. 5123, pp. 385–398. Springer, Heidelberg (2008)

Abstract Semantic Differencing for Numerical Programs

Nimrod Partush and Eran Yahav

Technion, Israel

Abstract. We address the problem of computing semantic differences between a program and a patched version of the program. Our goal is to obtain a precise characterization of the difference between program versions, or establish their equivalence when no difference exists.

We focus on computing semantic differences in numerical programs where the values of variables have no a-priori bounds, and use abstract interpretation to compute an over-approximation of program differences. Computing differences and establishing equivalence under abstraction requires abstracting relationships between variables in the two programs. Towards that end, we first construct a *correlating program* in which these relationships can be tracked, and then use a *correlating abstract domain* to compute a sound approximation of these relationships. To better establish equivalence between correlated variables and precisely capture differences, our domain has to represent non-convex information using a partially-disjunctive abstract domain. To balance precision and cost of this representation, our domain over-approximates numerical information while preserving equivalence between correlated variables by dynamically partitioning the disjunctive state according to equivalence criteria.

We have implemented our approach in a tool called DIZY, and applied it to a number of real-world examples, including programs from the GNU core utilities, Mozilla Firefox and the Linux Kernel. Our evaluation shows that DIZY often manages to establish equivalence, describes precise approximation of semantic differences when difference exists, and reports only a few false differences.

1 Introduction

Understanding the semantic difference between two versions of a program is invaluable in the process of software development. A developer applying a patch is often interested in answering questions like: (i) did the patch add/remove the desired functionality? (ii) does the patch introduce other, *unexpected*, behaviors? (iii) which regression tests should be run? Answering these questions manually is difficult and time consuming.

Semantic differencing has received much attention in classical work (e.g., [11,12,10]) and has recently seen growing interest for various applications ranging from testing concurrent programs [5], understanding software upgrades [15], to automatic generation of security exploits [3].

Problem Definition. We define the problem of *semantic differencing* as follows: Given a pair of programs (P, P') that agree on the number and type of input and output variables, for every execution π of P that originates from an input i and a corresponding execution π' of P' that originates from the *same input* i our goal is: (i) Check whether π and π' have the same output i.e. are output-equivalent, and (ii) In case of difference in output variables, provide a description of the difference.

F. Logozzo and M. Fähndrich (Eds.): SAS 2013, LNCS 7935, pp. 238–258, 2013.
© Springer-Verlag Berlin Heidelberg 2013

Existing Techniques. Existing techniques mostly offer solutions based on under approximation, the most prominent of which is regression testing which provides limited assurance of behavior equivalence while consuming significant time and compute resources. Other approaches for computing semantics differences [22,24] rely on symbolic execution techniques, may miss differences, and are generally unable to prove equivalence. Previous work for equivalence checking [9] rely on unsound bounded model checking techniques to prove (input-output) equivalence of two closely related numerical programs, under certain conditions (see Section 8 for more details).

Our Approach. We present an approach based on abstract interpretation [7] for producing a *sound* representation of changed program behaviors and proving equivalence between a program and a patched version of the program. Our method focuses on abstracting relationships between variables in both versions allowing us to achieve a precise description of the difference and prove equivalence. Our solution is sound in the sense that it computes an over approximation of the difference between the two versions, therefore guaranteeing equivalence when no difference is found.

We focus on output equivalence in the final state. This is sufficient as mid-execution output can be modeled as added variables in the final state. This limitation also means that we assume all program executions to be finite (i.e. equivalence/difference holds if indeed both executions terminate). Note that the definition limits program difference to the final state which alleviates the need for matching the different stages of (P, P'). Finding equivalence/difference in earlier stages of the program requires program matching (we first need to find a suitable location in both programs for checking for equivalence, otherwise it has no meaning). The problem of program matching is orthogonal and can be addressed via various techniques ranging in complexity and precision - from syntactic diff [13] to execution indexing [29] and others. In this work we employ a simple matching strategy to achieve better precision as described in Section 6. We found this technique to be sufficient for our experiments.

To answer the question of semantic differencing for infinite-state programs, we employ abstract interpretation. Though the notion of difference is well defined in the concrete case, defining and soundly computing it under abstraction is challenging:

- Differencing requires correlation of *different program executions.* The abstraction must be able to capture and compare only the input-equivalent executions, and avoid comparing ones that are not input-equivalent.
- Equivalence of abstract output values does not entail concrete value equivalence.

To address these challenges, we introduce two new concepts: (i) *correlating program* - a single program $P \bowtie P'$ that captures the behaviors of both P and P' in a way that facilitates abstract interpretation; (ii) *correlating abstract domain* - a domain for tracking relationships between variables in P and variables in P' using $P \bowtie P'$.

Correlating Program. We create a single program which captures the behavior of both the original program and its patched version. A *correlating program* $P \bowtie P'$ contains both programs flow and data, however program flow is arranged so to reflect a (simple) matching between the stages of the two programs. This matching is key for precision as otherwise we will not be able to maintain equivalence throughout the entire run of the program, particularly in the face of loops.

Correlating Abstraction. Abstracting relationships allows us to maintain focus on differences while over-approximating (whenever necessary for scalability) equivalent behaviors. We abstract variables of both programs together, starting off by assuming equality over all matched variables (variable matching is discussed in Section 4). Thus we can reflect relationships without necessarily knowing the actual value of variables. We focus on numerical programs and use numerical domains such as Octagon [18] and Polyhedra [8] to capture the relationship between variables. Our current implementation does not track pointer equivalences, but such equivalences can be tracked by a using a correlating shape analysis domain [1]. To maintain equivalence as much as possible, our domain was designed to represent non-convex information (e.g. so we will not immediately lose equivalence taking a condition of the form $x \neq 0$ into account). We use a powerset domain of convex sub-states. Our domain uses a partitioning strategy that abstracts together states that have the same set of equivalent variables, thus avoiding exponential blowup (as explained in Section 5). This strategy helps us preserve equivalence even across widening. Therefore our domain may over-approximate numerical information as long as equivalence between correlated variables is preserved.

1.1 Main Contributions

The main contributions of this paper are as follows:

- We present a novel approach for computing abstract semantic difference between a program P and a patched version of the program P'. We focus on numerical programs where the values of variables have no a-priori bounds.
- We reduce the problem of analyzing the two programs P, P' to the problem of analyzing a single *correlating program* $P \bowtie P'$ that captures the behavior of P and P'.
- We present a *correlating abstract domain* that captures an over-approximation of the difference between P and P' by tracking relationships between variables in $P \bowtie P'$. The domain applies a partitioning strategy for scaling the analysis while maintaining precision in equivalence.
- We have implemented our approach in a tool based on the LLVM compiler infrastructure and the APRON numerical abstract domain library, and applied it to several real-world programs. Our evaluation shows that the tool often manages to establish equivalence, reports useful approximation of semantic differences when differences exists, and reports only a few false differences.

2 Overview

In this section, we provide an informal overview of our approach using a simple illustrating example. In Section 7 we show how our approach is applied to real-world programs. Consider the two versions of a program for computing sign in Fig. 1, inspired by an example from [25]. For these programs, we would like to establish that the output of $sign$ and $sign'$ differs *only* in the case where $x = 0$ and that the difference is $sgn = 1 \neq sgn' = 0$.

```
int sign(int x) {        int sign'(int x') {       int sign(int x) {
  int sgn;                  int sgn';                  int x' = x;
  if (x < 0)               if (x' < 0)                 guard g1 = (x < 0);
    sgn = -1                 sgn' = -1                 guard g1' = (x' < 0);
  else                    else                         int sgn;
    sgn = 1                 sgn' = 1                    int sgn' = sgn;
  return sgn               if (x'==0)                  if (g1) sgn = -1;
}                           sgn' = 0                    if (g1') sgn' = -1;
                          return sgn'                   if (!g1) sgn = 1;
                        }                               if (!g1') sgn' = 1;
                                                        guard g2' = (x' == 0);
                                                        if (g2') sgn' = 0;
                                                      }
```

$$sign \qquad\qquad sign' \qquad\qquad sign \bowtie sign'$$

Fig. 1. Two simple implementations of the *sign* operation and their correlating program

Separate Analysis is Unsound. As a first naïve attempt to achieve this, one could try to analyze each version of the program separately and compare the (abstract) results. However, this is clearly unsound, as equivalence under abstraction does not entail concrete equivalence. For example, using an interval domain [8] would yield that in both programs the result ranges in the same interval $[-1, 1]$, missing the fact that *sign* never returns the value 0 where *sign'* does.

Establishing Equivalence under Abstraction. To establish equivalence under abstraction, we need to abstract *relationships between the values of variables* in *sign* and *sign'*. Specifically, we need to track the relationship between the values of sgn and sgn'. This requires a joint representation in which these relationships can be tracked.

As our approach dictates the joint analysis of two programs for maintaining variable relationships, we need to determine an order in which the different stages of the programs are analyzed. One solution would be to analyze the programs sequentially. However, such an analysis will be forced to retain full path sensitivity, withholding over-approximation, since abstracting together paths will result in a non-restorable loss of equivalence. For example, analyzing *sign* first will result in an abstract state where $\sigma = sgn \mapsto [-1, 1]$. As we continue on towards *sign'*, we could never restore in σ the fact that sgn' is equal to sgn for all paths except where x is zero.

Intuitively, establishing equivalence using the sequential composition $P; P'$ requires full path sensitivity, leading to an inherently non-scalable solution. Further, in the presence of loops and widening, applying widening separately to the loops of P and to those of P' does not allow maintaining variable relationships under abstraction.

Correlating Program. To address these challenges, we construct a *correlating program* $P \bowtie P'$ where operations of P and P' are interleaved to achieve correlation throughout the analysis. Fig. 1 shows the correlating program $sign \bowtie sign'$. The programs were transformed to a guarded command language form to allow for interleaving. A key feature of the correlating program for closely related program versions is the ability to keep matched instructions, that appear in both versions, closely interleaved. This allows the analysis to better maintain relationships as the program executions are better aligned. Using the correlating program, we can directly track the relationship between sgn in *sign* and its corresponding variable sgn' in *sign'*.

We note that the set of tracked relationships is determined by a matching of P and P' variables denoted VC and defined in Section 4. We match variables in the two versions using variable names as we found that these do not vary greatly over patches. However, this matching can also be provided by the user.

We describe the specifics of creating $P \bowtie P'$ in Section 6 and only briefly note that the interleaving is chosen according to a syntactic diff process over a guarded command language version of the programs.

Correlating Abstract Domain. We introduce a *correlating abstract domain* that tracks relationships between corresponding variables in P and P' using the correlating program $P \bowtie P'$. Unfortunately, any domain with convex constraints will fail to capture the precise relationship between variables in many cases. For example, using the polyhedra abstract domain [8] to analyze the sign example from Fig. 1, the relationship between the sgn and sgn$'$ variables in the correlating program would be lost, leaving only the trivial $\langle 1 \geq sgn \geq -1, 1 \geq sgn' \geq -1 \rangle$ constraint. Although the result soundly reports a difference (as we do not explicitly know that $\equiv_{sgn}$), we still know nothing about the difference between the programs.

An obvious, but prohibitively expensive, solution to the problem is to use disjunctive completion, moving to a powerset domain where the abstract state is a set of convex objects (e.g., set of polyhedra). A state in such domain is a set of convex abstract representations (e.g., polyhedra [8] or octagon [18]). For example, analyzing $sign \bowtie sign'$ using a powerset domain would yield:

$$\sigma_1 = \{x = x' < 0, sgn = sgn' \mapsto -1\}, \sigma_2 = \{x = x' \mapsto 0, sgn \mapsto 1, sgn' \mapsto 0\}$$
$$\sigma_3 = \{x = x' > 0, sgn = sgn' \mapsto 1\}$$

However, using such domain would significantly limit the applicability of the approach. The desirable solution is a partially disjunctive domain, where only certain disjunctions are kept separate during analysis. The challenge in our setting is in keeping the partition fine enough such that equivalence could be preserved, without reaching exponential blowup. This is accomplished by applying partitioning.

Partitioning. As the goal of this work is to distinguish equivalent from dissimilar behaviors, using equivalence as criteria for merging paths is apt. The partitioning will abstract together paths that hold equivalence for the same set of variables, allowing for a maximum of $2^{|VC|}$ disjunctions in the abstract state.

For example partitioning the above-mentioned result of analyzing $sign \bowtie sign'$ according to our criteria would abstract behaviors σ_1 and σ_3 together, as they hold equivalence for sgn. The merge would abstract away data regarding x and represent sgn as the $[-1, 1]$ interval, losing precision but gaining reduction in state size. This loss of precision is acceptable as it is complemented by the offending state σ_2.

$$\sigma_1 = \{x = x', sgn = sgn' \mapsto [-1, 1]\}, \sigma_2 = \{x' = 0, sgn \mapsto 1, sgn' \mapsto -1\}$$

To reduce state size, we must perform partitioning dynamically during analysis. This cannot be achieved using a sequential composition $P; P'$. Intuitively, this is because an operation in P has to "wait" for its equivalent operation to occur in P'. To overcome this, our correlating program $P \bowtie P'$ interleaves P and P' commands, and informs the analysis when programs have reached a point where correlation may be established by annotating $P \bowtie P'$ with special markers called *correlation points* denoted CP and defined also in Section 6.

```
int sum(int arr[], unsigned len) {          int sum'(int arr[], unsigned len) {
  int result = 0;                             int result = 0;
  for (unsigned i = 1; i < len; i+=2)         unsigned i = 0;
    result += arr[i];                         while (i + 1 < len) {
  return result;                                i++;
}                                               result += arr[i];
                                                i++;
                                              }
                                              return result;
                                            }
```

Fig. 2. Two equivalent versions of a looping program for partial array summation

Widening. Although we achieved a reduction in state size using partitioning, we have yet to account for programs with loops. Handling loops is where most previous approaches fall short [9,16,22,24]. To overcome this, we define a widening operator for our domain, based on the convex sub-domain widening operator (e.g., interval, octagon, polyhedra). The main challenge here, as our state is a set of convex objects belonging to the sub-domain, is finding an optimal pairwise matching between objects for a precise widened result. Ideally, we would like to pair objects that adhere to the same "looping path" meaning we would like to match a path π_i's abstraction with a path π_{i+1} that results from taking another step in the loop. This requires encoding path information along with the sub-state abstraction. This information is acquired by keeping *guard values* explicitly, as they appear in our correlating program, inside the state. As guard values (*true* or *false*) reflect branch outcomes, they can be used to match sub-states that advanced on the loop by matching their guard values.

We note that the correlating program is crucial to maintaining equivalence over loops. To demonstrate this we perform the simple exercise of checking equivalence of a small looping program with itself. Consider the array summation program in Fig. 2. Equivalence for these two small programs cannot be established soundly by approaches based on under approximation. To emphasize the importance of the correlating program, we will first show the result of an analysis of $sum; sum'$ which will be:

$$\sigma_1 = \{len = len' \leq 1, result = result' \mapsto 0\}, \sigma_2 = \{len = len' > 1\}$$

This loss of equivalence occurred due to the inability to precisely track the relationship of result and result' over $sum; sum'$. As we widened the first loop to converge, all paths passing through that loop were merged together, losing the ability to be "matched" with the second loop waiting further down the road. Performing the same analysis on $sum \bowtie sum'$ instead as seen in Fig. 3, allows maintaining equivalence, as the loops are interleaved to allow establishing $\equiv_{result}$ as a loop invariant. This invariant survives the widening process to prove equivalence at the end as the result would be: $\sigma_1 = \{\equiv_{result}\}$. We note that we implicitly assume equivalence in array content for sum and sum'.

3   Preliminaries

We use the following standard concrete semantics definitions for a program:

- *Var*, *Val*, *Loc* denote the set of program variable identifiers, variable values and program locations respectively. Program locations are also denoted *lab* for label. The labels *begin* and *end* mark the start and exit locations of the program.

```
int sum(int arr[], unsigned len) {
   unsigned len' = len;
   int arr'[] = arr;
   int result = 0;
   int result' = 0;
   {
      unsigned i = 1;
      unsigned i' = 0;
1:    guard g = (i < len);
1':   guard g' = (i' + 1 < len');
      if (g') i'++;
      if (g)  result += arr[i];
      if (g') result' += arr'[i'];
      if (g') i'++;
      if (g)  i+=2;
      if (g)  goto 1;
      if (g') goto 1';
   }
}
```

Fig. 3. $sum \bowtie sum'$

- A concrete program state σ is a tuple $(loc, values) \in \Sigma$ mapping the set of program variables to their concrete value at a certain program location loc. The set of all possible states of a program P is denoted Σ_P.
- We describe an imperative program P, as a tuple $(Val, Var, \rightarrow, \Sigma_0)$ where $\rightarrow$: $\Sigma_P \times \Sigma_P$ is a transition relation and Σ_0 is a set of initial states of the program.
- A program trace $\pi \in \Sigma_P^*$, is a sequence of states $\langle \sigma_0, \sigma_1, ... \rangle$ describing a single execution of the program. The set of all possible traces for a program is denoted $[\![P]\!]$. We also define $last : \Sigma_P^* \rightarrow \Sigma_P$ which returns the last state in a trace.

We note that our formal semantics need not deal with errors states therefore we ignore crash states of the programs, as well as inter-procedural programs since our work deals with function calls by either assuming output-equivalence (for functions that were proven to be equivalent) or by inlining them (this work excludes recursion).

4   Concrete Semantics

In this section, we define the notion of concrete difference between programs, based on a standard concrete semantics.

4.1   Concrete State Differencing

Comparing two programs P and P' under concrete semantics means comparing their *traces*, but only those that originates from the same input. Towards that end, we first define the difference between two concrete states.

Intuitively, given two concrete states, the difference between them is the set of variables (and their values) where the two states map corresponding variables to different values. As variable names may differ between programs, we parameterize the definition with a mapping that establishes a correspondence between variables in P and P'. Thus concrete state differencing is restricted to comparing values of corresponding variables.

Definition 1 (Variable Correspondence). *A variable correspondence $VC \subseteq Var \times Var'$, is a partial mapping between two sets of program variables. The VC mapping can be taken as input from the user however, our evaluation indicates that is sufficient to use a name-based mapping for a program and a patched version:*

$$VC_{EQ} \triangleq \{(v, v')|v \in Var \wedge v' \in Var' \wedge name(v) = name(v')\}$$

Definition 2 (Concrete State Delta). *Given two concrete states $\sigma \in \Sigma_P$, $\sigma' \in \Sigma_{P'}$, and a correspondence VC, the concrete state delta is defined as:*

$$\triangle_S(\sigma, \sigma') \triangleq \{(v, val)|(v, v') \in VC \wedge \sigma(v) = val \neq \sigma'(v')\}$$

Informally, $\triangle_S$ means the "part of the state σ where corresponding variables do not agree on values (with respect to σ')". Note that $\triangle_S$ is not symmetric. In fact, the direction in which $\triangle_S$ is used has meaning in the context of a program P and a patched version of it P'. We define $\triangle_S^- = \triangle_S(\sigma, \sigma')$ which means the values of the state that was "removed" in P' and $\triangle_S^+ = \triangle_S(\sigma', \sigma)$ which stands for the values "added" in P'. When there is no observable difference between the states we get that $\triangle_S^+(\sigma, \sigma') = \triangle_S^-(\sigma, \sigma') = \emptyset$, and say that the states are *equivalent* denoted $\sigma \equiv \sigma'$.

Example 1. *Consider two concrete states $\sigma = (x \mapsto 1, y \mapsto 2, z \mapsto 3)$ and $\sigma' = (x' \mapsto 0, y' \mapsto 2, w' \mapsto 4)$ and using VC_{EQ} then $\triangle_S^- = \{(x \mapsto 1)\}$ since x and x' match and do not agree on value, y and y' agree (thus are not in delta) and z' is not in VC_{EQ}. Similarly, $\triangle_S^+ = \{(x' \mapsto 0)\}$.*

We now use our notion of concrete state difference to define the difference between concrete program traces.

Definition 3 (Trace Delta). *Given two traces $\pi \in [\![P]\!]$ and $\pi' \in [\![P']\!]$ that originate from equivalent input states, we define the trace delta as simply the difference between the traces final states. Formally: $\triangle_T(\pi, \pi') = \{\triangle_S(last(\sigma), last(\sigma'))\}$*

The definition adheres to our problem definition in Section 1, where we defined program difference as difference between matched variables in the terminating state. Since $\triangle_T(\pi, \pi')$ is based on state difference, we define $\triangle_T^+$ and $\triangle_T^-$ similarly to their underlying states difference operations.

Now, we will move past the concrete semantics towards *abstract semantics*. This is required as it is unfeasible to describe difference based on traces. Before doing so, we must adjust our concrete semantics since a concrete semantics based on individual traces *will not allow us to correlate traces that originate from the same input*. This is the first formal indication of how a separate abstraction, that considers each of the programs by itself, cannot succeed.

4.2 Concrete Correlating Semantics

We define the correlating state and trace which bind the executions of both programs, P and P', together and define the notion of delta in this setting. This allows us to define the *correlating abstract semantics* which is key for successful differencing.

Definition 4 (Correlating Concrete State). *A correlating concrete state* $\sigma_{\bowtie} : Var \cup Var' \to Val$ *is a unified concrete state, mapping variables from both programs* (P, P') *to their values.*

Definition 5 (Correlating Concrete Trace). *A correlating trace* $\pi_{\bowtie}$, *is a sequence of correlating states* ..., $\sigma_{\bowtie_i}$, ... *describing an execution of* $P \bowtie P'$.

Note that an attribute of the correlating programs (as defined in Section 6) is that it restricts to traces that originate from equivalent input states i.e., $\sigma_{\bowtie_0} \equiv \sigma'_{\bowtie_0}$.

We must remember however, that the number of traces to be compared is potentially unbounded which means that the delta we compute may be unbounded too. Therefore we must use an abstraction over the concrete semantics that will allow us to represent executions in a bounded way.

5   Abstract Correlating Semantics

In this section, we introduce our correlating abstract domain which allows bounded representation of correlating program state while maintaining equivalence between correlated variables.

5.1   Abstract Correlating State

We represent variable information using standard relational abstract domains. As our analysis is path sensitive, we allow for a set of abstract sub-states, each adhering to a certain path in the product program. This abstraction is similar to the trace partitioning domain as described in [25].

Our power-set domain records precise state information but does not scale due to exponential blowup. As a first means of reducing state size, we define a special join operation that *dynamically partitions* the abstract state according to the set of equivalences maintained in each sub-state and joins all sub-states in the same partition together (using the sub-domain join operation). This join criteria allows separation of equivalence preserving paths thus achieving better precision. Second, to allow a feasible bound abstraction for programs with infinite number of paths, we define a widening operator which utilizes the sub-domain's widening operator but cleverly chooses which sub-states are to be widened, according to path information encoded in state. We start off by abstracting the correlating trace semantics in Sec. 4.2.

In the following, we assume an abstract relational domain $(D^{\sharp}, \sqsubseteq_D)$ equipped with operations $\sqcap_D$, $\sqcup_D$ and ∇_D, for representing sets of concrete states in $\Sigma_{P \bowtie P'}$. We separate the set of program variables into original program variables denoted Var (which also include a special added variable for return value, if such exists) and the added guard variables denoted $Guard$ that are used for storing conditional values alone ($Guard$ also include a special added guard for return flag). We assume the abstract values in $D^{\sharp}$ are constraints over the variables and guards (we denote $D^{\sharp}_{Guard}$ for sub-domain abstraction of guards and $D^{\sharp}_{Var}$ for original variables), and do not go into further details regarding the particular abstract domain as it is a parameter of the analysis. We also assume that the sub-domain $D^{\sharp}$ allows for a sound over-approximation of the concrete semantics (given a sound interpretation of program operations). In our experiments, we use the polyhedra abstract domain [8] and the octagon abstract domain [18].

Definition 6 (Correlating Abstract State). *A correlating abstract program state* $\sigma^\sharp \in Lab \to 2^{D^\sharp_{Guard} \times D^\sharp_{Var}}$, *is a mapping from a correlating program label* $l_{\bowtie}$ *to a set of pairs* $(ctx, data)$, *where* $ctx \in D^\sharp_{Guard}$ *is the execution context i.e. an abstraction of guards values via the relational numerical domain and data* $\in D^\sharp_{Var}$ *is an abstraction of the variables.*

We separate abstractions over guard variables added by the transformation to Guarded command language (GCL) format (see Section 6) from original program variables as there need not be any relationships between guard and regular variables.

5.2 Abstract Correlating Semantics

Tab. 1 describes the abstract transformers. The table shows the effect of each statement on a given abstract state $\sigma^\sharp = l_{\bowtie} \mapsto S$. The abstract transformers are defined using the abstract transformers of the underlying abstract domain $D^\sharp$. We assume that any program P can be transformed such that it only contains the operations described in Tab. 1 (this is achieved by the GCL format). We also assume that for $[\![g := e]\!]^\sharp$ operations, e is a logical operation with boolean value.

Table 1. Abstract transformers

$[\![v := e]\!]^\sharp$	$l_{\bowtie} \mapsto \{\langle ctx, [\![v := e]\!]^\sharp_{D^\sharp}(data)\rangle | \langle ctx, data\rangle \in S\}$
$[\![g := e]\!]^\sharp$	$l_{\bowtie} \mapsto \{\langle [\![g := true]\!]^\sharp_{D^\sharp}(ctx), [\![e]\!]^\sharp_{D^\sharp}(data)\rangle | \langle ctx, data\rangle \in S\}$
	$\cup \{\langle [\![g := false]\!]^\sharp_{D^\sharp}(ctx), [\![\neg e]\!]^\sharp_{D^\sharp}(data)\rangle | \langle ctx, data\rangle \in S\}$
$[\![\text{ if }(g)\{s_0\}\text{ else }\{s_1\}]\!]^\sharp$	$l_{\bowtie} \mapsto \{\langle [\![g = true]\!]^\sharp_{D^\sharp}(ctx), [\![s_0]\!]^\sharp_{D^\sharp}(data)\rangle | \langle ctx, data\rangle \in S\}$
	$\cup \{\langle [\![g = false]\!]^\sharp_{D^\sharp}(ctx), [\![s_1]\!]^\sharp_{D^\sharp}(data)\rangle | \langle ctx, data\rangle \in S\}$
$[\![\text{ goto lab }]\!]^\sharp$	$\sigma^\sharp$

Next, we define the abstraction function $\alpha : 2^{\Sigma^*_{P \bowtie P'}} \to 2^{D^\sharp \times D^\sharp}$ that abstracts together a set of concrete correlating traces T. As in our domain traces are abstracted together if they share the exact same path, we first define an operation $path : \Sigma^*_{P \bowtie P'} \to Lab^*$ which returns a sequence of labels for a trace's states i.e. what is the path taken by that trace. We also allow applying $path$ on a set of traces to denote the set of paths resulting by applying the function of each of the traces. Finally we define the trace abstraction as follows:

$$\alpha(T) \triangleq \{\sqcup_{path(\pi)=p}\beta(last(\pi))|p \in path(T)\}$$

where $\beta(\sigma) = \langle \beta_{D^\sharp}(\sigma|_{Guard}), \beta_{D^\sharp}(\sigma|_{Var})\rangle$ i.e. applying the abstraction function of the abstract sub-domain $\beta_{D^\sharp}$ on parts of the concrete state applying to $Guards$ (denoted

$\sigma|_{Guard})$ and $Vars$ (denoted $\sigma|_{Var}$) separately. Our abstraction partitions trace prefixes π by path and abstracts together the concrete states reached by the prefix - $last(\pi)$, using the sub-domain.

Every path in the correlating program will be represented by a single sub-state of the sub-domain. As a result, all *trace prefixes* that follow the same path to $l_{\bowtie}$ will be abstracted into a single sub-state of the underlying domain. This abstraction fits semantics differencing well, as inputs that follow the same path display the same behavior and will usually either keep or break equivalence together, allowing us to separate them from other behaviors (it is possible for a path to display both behaviors as in Fig. 4 and we will discuss how we are able to manipulate the abstract state and separate equivalent behaviors from ones that offend equivalence). Another issue to be addressed is the fact that our state is still potentially unbounded as the number of paths in the program may be exponential and even infinite (due to loops).

```
int f(int x) {          int f'(int x) {
    return x;               return 2*x;
}                       }
```

Fig. 4. Single path differentiation candidates

5.3   Dynamic Partitioning

Performing analysis with the powerset domain does not scale as the number of paths in the correlated program may be exponential (we defer the case of unbound paths to widening of loops). We must allow for reduction of state $\sigma^{\sharp} = l_{\bowtie} \mapsto S$ with acceptable loss of precision. This reduction via partitioning can be achieved by joining the abstract sub-states in S (using the standard join of the sub-domain). However this can only be accomplished after first deciding which of the sub-states should be joined and then choosing the program locations for the partitioning to occur. To choose a strategy, we start by taking a closer look at the final state of the fully disjunctive analysis of Fig. 1:

$$\sigma^{\sharp}(end) = [\langle(g1, \neg g2', \equiv_{g1}), (x > 0, sgn = 1, \equiv_{x,sgn})\rangle,$$
$$\langle(\neg g1, \neg g2', \equiv_{g1}), (x < 0, sgn = -1, \equiv_{x,sgn})\rangle,$$
$$\langle(\neg g1, g2', \equiv_{g1}), (x = 0, sgn = 0, sgn' = 1, \equiv_{x})\rangle]$$

One may observe that were we to join the two sub-states that maintain equivalence on $\{x, sgn, g1\}$, it would result in an acceptable loss of precision (losing the x related constraints). This is achieved by partitioning sub-states according to *the set of variables which they preserve equivalence for*. This bounds the state size at $2^{|VC|}$, where VC is the set of correlating variables we wish to track. As mentioned, another key factor in preserving equivalence and maintaining precision is the program location at which the partitioning occurs. The first possibility, which is somewhat symmetric to the first proposed partitioning strategy, is to partition at every join point i.e. after every branch converges. Let use examine $sign \bowtie sign'$ state after processing the first guarded instruction if (g1) sgn = -1; (we ignored $g2'$ effect at this point for brevity):

$$\sigma^{\sharp} = [\langle(g1, \equiv_{g1}), (x \geq 0, \equiv_{x,sgn})\rangle, \langle(g1, \equiv_{g1}), (x < 0, sgn' = -1, \equiv_{x})\rangle]$$

This suggests that partitioning at join points will perform badly in many scenarios, specifically here as we will lose all data regarding sgn. However if we could delay the partitioning to a point where the two programs "converge" (after the following `if (g1')` `sgn'` = -1; line), we will get a more precise temporary result which preserves equivalence. To accomplish this, we define special program locations we name *correlating points* which present places where programs have likely converged. These are a sub-product of the correlating program construction process described in Section 6.

```
                                        unsigned max' = ...;
                                        int sum(int arr[], unsigned len) {
                                          unsigned len' = len;
                                          int arr'[] = arr;
                                          int result = 0;
                                          int result' = 0;
                                          guard r' = (len' > max');
                                          if (r') retval' = -1;
unsigned max = ...;                       if (r') r' = 0;
int sum''(int arr[], unsigned len) {      {
  int result = 0;                           unsigned i = 1;
  if (len > max)                            unsigned i' = 1;
    return -1;                        1:    guard g = (i < len);
  for (unsigned i = 1; i < len; i+=2) 1':   guard g' = 0;
    result += arr[i];                       if (r') g' = (i' < len');
  return result;                            if (g) result += arr[i];
}                                           if (r') if (g') result' += arr'[i'];
                                            if (g) i+=2;
                                            if (r') if (g') i'+=2;
                                            if (g) goto 1;
                                            if (r') if (g') goto 1';
                                          }
                                        }
```

Fig. 5. Patched `sum"` and correlating `sum` ⋈ `sum"`

5.4   Widening

In order for our analysis to handle loops we require a means for reaching a fixed point. As our analysis iterates over a loop, sub-states may be added or transformed continuously, never converging. We therefore need to define a widening operator for our new domain. We have the widening operator of our sub-domain at our disposal, but we are faced with the question of how to lift this operator, i.e., which pairs of sub-states $\langle ctx, data \rangle$ from $\sigma^\sharp$ should be widened with which. This problem has been addressed in the path in other settings [2], and our approach can be viewed as a specialized form of lifting that is tailored for tracking equivalences. A first viable strategy is to perform an overall join operation on all pairs which will result in a single pair of sub-states and then simply apply the widening to this sub-state using the sub-domain's ∇ operator. If we examine applying this strategy to $sum \bowtie sum'$ from Fig. 3, we get that it will successfully arrive at a fixed point that also maintains equivalence as all sub-states maintain equivalence at loop back-edges. Now let us try to apply the strategy to the more complex $sum \bowtie sum''$ of Fig. 5. First we mention that as sum' introduces a return statement under the $len > max$ condition, the example shows an extra r' guard and $retval'$ variable for representing a return (this exists in all GCL programs but we omitted it so far for brevity). While analyzing, once we pass that first conditional, our state is split to reflect the return effect:

$$\sigma^{\sharp} = [d_1 = \langle(\neg r'), (len \leq max, result = 0, \equiv_{len,result})\rangle,$$
$$d_2 = \langle(r'), (len > max, retval' = -1, result = 0, \equiv_{len,result})\rangle]$$

As we further advance into the loop, d_1 will maintain equivalence but d_2 will continue to update the part of the state regarding untagged variables (since r' is $false$), specifically it will change $result$ continuously, preventing the analysis from reaching fixed point. We would require widening here but using the naive strategy of a complete join will result in aggressive loss of precision, specifically losing all information regarding $result$. The problem originates from the fact that prior to widening, we joined substates which adhere to two different loop behaviors: one where both sum and sum' loop together (that originated from $len < max$) and the other where sum' has exited but sum continues to loop ($len \geq max$). Ideally, we would like to match these two behaviors and widen them accordingly. We devised a widening strategy that allows us to do this as it basically matches sub-states that adhere to the same behavior, or loop-paths. This strategy dictates using *guards* for the matching. If two sub-states agree on their set of guards, it means they represent the same loop path and can be widened as the latter originated from the former (widening operates on subsequent iterations). In our example, using this strategy will allow the correct matching of states after consequent $k, k + 1$ loop iterations:

$$\sigma^{\sharp}_k = [d_1 = \langle(\neg r', g, \equiv_g), (len \leq max, i = 2k + 1, \equiv_{i,len,result})\rangle,$$
$$d_2 = \langle(r', \neg g, g'), (len > max, retval' = -1, result' = 0, i' = 2k + 1, i = 1, \equiv_{len})\rangle]$$

And:

$$\sigma^{\sharp}_{k+1} = [d_1 = \langle(\neg r', g, \equiv_g), (len \leq max, i = 2k + 3, \equiv_{i,len,result})\rangle,$$
$$d_2 = \langle(r', \neg g, g'), (len > max, retval' = -1, result' = 0, i' = 2k + 3, i = 1, \equiv_{len})\rangle]$$

As we can identify the states predecessors by simply matching the guards. d_1 will be widened for a precise description of the difference shown as $\langle len = len' > max',$ $retval' = -1, retval = \top \rangle$.

5.5   Differencing for Abstract Correlating States

Given an abstract state in our correlating domain, we want to determine whether equivalence is kept and if so under which conditions it is kept (for partial equivalence) or determine there is difference and characterize it. As our state may hold several pairs of sub-states, each holding different equivalence data, we can provide a verbose answer regarding whether equivalence holds. We partition our sub-states according to the set of variables they hold equivalence for and report the state for each equivalence partition class. Since we instrument our correlating program to preserve initial input values, for some of these states we will also be able to report input constraints thus informing the user of the input ranges that maintain equivalence. When equivalence could not be proved, we report the offending states and apply a differencing algorithm for extracting of the delta. Fig. 4 shows an example of where our analysis is unable to prove equivalence, although part of the state does maintain equivalence (specifically for $x = 0$). This is due to the abstraction being too coarse. We describe an algorithm that given a sub-state $d \in D^\sharp$, computes the differentiating part of the sub-state (where correlated variables disagree on values) by splitting it into parts according to equivalence. This is done by treating the relational constraints in our domain as geometrical objects and formulating delta based on that.

Definition 7 (Correlating Abstract State Delta). *Given a sub-state d and a correspondence VC, the correlating state delta $\triangle_A(d)$, computes abstract state differentiation over d. The result is an abstract state $\sqsubseteq d$ approximating all concrete values for variables correlated by VC, that differ between P and P'. Formally, the delta is simply the abstraction of the concrete trace deltas:*

$$\triangle_A(d)^+ \triangleq \alpha(\cup_{path}\triangle_T^+), \triangle_A(d)^- \triangleq \alpha(\cup_{path}\triangle_T^-)$$

where deltas are grouped together by path and then abstracted.

The algorithm for the extraction of delta from a correlating state, is as follows:

1. $d_\equiv$ is a state abstracting the concrete states *shared* by the original and patched program. Obtained by computing: $d_\equiv \triangleq d|_{V=V'} \equiv d \sqcap \bigwedge\{v = v' | (v, v') \in VC\}$.
2. $\overline{d_\equiv}$ is the negated state i.e. $D^\sharp \setminus d_\equiv$ and it is computed by negating $d_\equiv$ (as mentioned before, all logical operations, including negation, are defined on our representation of an abstract state).
3. Eventually: $\triangle_A(d) \triangleq d \sqcap \overline{d_\equiv}$ abstracts all states in $P \times P'$ where correlated variables values do not match.
4. $\triangle_A(d)^+ = \triangle_A(d)|_{V'}$ is a projection of the differentiation to display values of P' alone i.e. "added values".
5. $\triangle_A(d)^- = \triangle_A(d)|_V$ is a projection of the differentiation to display values of P alone i.e. "removed values".

Example 2. *Applying the algorithm on Fig. 4's P and P' where $d = \{retval' = 2retval\}$ will result in the following:*

1. $d_\equiv = \langle retval' = 0, retval = 0 \rangle$.
2. $\overline{d_\equiv} = [\langle retval' > 0 \rangle, \langle retval' < 0 \rangle, \langle retval > 0 \rangle, \langle retval < 0 \rangle]$
3. $\triangle_A(d) = [\langle retval' = 2retval, retval' > 0 \rangle, \langle retval' = 2retval, retval' < 0 \rangle, \langle retval' = 2retval, retval > 0 \rangle, \langle retval' = 2retval, retval < 0 \rangle]$
4. $\triangle_A(d)^+ = [\langle retval' > 0 \rangle, \langle retval' < 0 \rangle]$
5. $\triangle_A(d)^- = [\langle retval > 0 \rangle, \langle retval < 0 \rangle]$

We note that as a sub-state is basically a conjunction of constraints, negating it by splitting to constraints and negating each individually reflects correctly the effect of negating a conjunction as we are left with a disjunction of negations, as seen in step 2. We also see that displaying the result in the form of projections is ill-advised as in some states differentiation data is represented by relationships on correlated variables alone, thus projecting will lose all data and we will be left with a less informative result. A geometrical representation of $\triangle_A$ calculation can be seen in Fig. 7 in Appendix A.

From this point forward any mention of "delta" (denoted $\triangle$) refers to the correlating abstract state delta ($\triangle_A$). We claim that $\triangle$ is a correct abstraction for the concrete state delta which allows for a scalable representation of difference we aim to capture.

6 Correlating Program

In this section, we describe how to construct a correlating program $P \bowtie P'$. The process attempts to find an interleaving of programs for a more precise differentiation. The construction also instruments $P \bowtie P'$ with the required correlation points CP which define the locations for our partitioning. We also allow a user defined selection of CP.

6.1 Construction of $P \bowtie P'$

The idea of a correlating program is similar to that of self-composition [27], but the way in which statements in the correlating program are combined is designed to keep the steps of the two programs close to each other. Analysis of the correlating program can then recover equivalence between values of correlated variables even when equivalence is *temporarily* violated by an update in one version, as the corresponding update in the other version follows shortly thereafter.

The correlating program is an optimized reduction over $P \times P'$ where not all pairs of $(\sigma^{\sharp}, \sigma'^{\sharp})$ are considered, but only pairs in a controlled execution, where correlating instructions in P and P' execute adjacently. This allows for superior precision.

The input for the correlation process are two C programs (P, P'). The first step involves transforming both programs to a normalized guarded instruction form (P_G, P'_G). Next, a vector of *imperative commands* I (and I' respectively) is extracted from each program for the purposes of performing the syntactic diff. An imperative command in our GCL format is defined to be either one of v := e | goto l | f(...) as they effectively change the program state (variable values, excluding guards) and control. Function calls are either inlined, in case equivalence could not be proven for them, or left as is, in case they are equivalent or are external system calls. Continuing the construction process, a syntactical diff [13] is computed over the vectors (I, I'). One of the inputs to the diff process is VC as it is needed to identify correlated variables and the diff comparison will regard commands differing by variable names which are correlated by VC as equal. The result of the last step will be a vector $I_\triangle$ specifying for each command in I, I' whether it is an added command in P' (for I') marked $+$, a deleted command from P (for I) marked $-$, or a command existing in both versions marked $=$. This diff determines the order in which the commands will be interleaved in the resulting $P \bowtie P'$ as we will iterate over the result vector $I_\triangle$ and use it to construct the correlating program. We remind that since I, I' contain only the imperative commands, we cannot use it directly as $P \bowtie P'$. Instead we will use the imperative commands as markers, specifying which chunk of program from P_G or P'_G should be taken next and put in the result. The construction goes as follows: iterate over $I_\triangle$ and for every command c (c') labeled l_c ($l_{c'}$):

- read P_G (P'_G) up to label l_c ($l_{c'}$) including into block B_c (B'_c)
- for B'_c, tag all variables in the block.
- emit the block to the output.
- delete B_c (B'_c) from P_G (P'_G).

The construction is now complete. We only add that at the start of the process, we strip P'_G of its prototype and add declarations for the tagged input variables, initializing them to the untagged version (thus assuring $P \bowtie P'$ will only co-execute traces that originate from the same input for P and P'). As mentioned, CP is also a product of the construction, and it's defined using = commands: after two = commands are emitted to the output, we add an instrumentation line, telling the analysis of the correlation point. One final observation regarding the correlating program is that it is a legitimate program that can be run to achieve the effect of running both versions. We plan to leverage this ability to use dynamic analysis and testing techniques such as fuzzing [21] and directed automated testing [4] on the correlating program in our future work.

7 Evaluation

We evaluated DIZY on a number of real world programs where the patches affect numerical variables. As benchmarks, we used several programs from the GNU core utilities, as well as a few handpicked patches from the Linux kernel and the Mozilla Firefox web browser. We also include results for illustrative examples used throughout the paper.

7.1 Prototype Implementation

We implemented a correlating compiler named CCC which creates correlating programs from any two C programs. We also implemented a differencing analysis for analyzing correlated programs. Both tools are based on LLVM and CLANG compiler infrastructure. We analyze C code directly since it is more structured, has type information and keeps a low number of variables, as opposed to intermediate representation. We also benefit from our delta being computed over original variables. As mentioned in Section 6, we normalize the input programs before correlating them. This also allows for a simpler analysis. Our analysis is intra-procedural and we handle function calls by either modularly proving their equivalence and assuming it once encountered or, in case equivalence could not be proved, by inlining. Calls to external system functions do not change local state in our examples and thus were ignored. We used the APRON abstract numerical domain library and conducted our experiments using several domains including Interval, Octagon [18] and Polyhedra [8]. All of our experiments were conducted running on a Intel(R) Core-i7(TM) processor with 4GB.

7.2 Results

Tab. 2 summarizes the results of our analysis. The columns indicate the benchmark name, lines of code for the analyzed program, the number of lines added and removed by the patch, whether it required widening, and the result of each benchmark run alongside its run time in minutes. We included three different setting in the results: with and without partitioning and with an Interval, Octagon [18] and Polyhedra [8] abstract domains. Generally, the results are ordered in increasing order of precision from left to right. Results marked with ✓ presented abstract states with acceptable precision i.e., mostly variables that indeed differ between variables were reported, and the description of the difference was useful for producing actual values for the differencing variables.

Table 2. Experimental Results

Name	#LOC	#P	Widen	Interval		Octagon		Polyhedra	
				Part	**No Part**	**Part**	**No Part**	**Part**	**No Part**
remove	16	4	N	✗(0)	✗(0)	✓(0:03)	✓(0:03)	✓(0:01)	✓(0:01)
copy	44	2	N	✗(0:33)	✗(0:33)	✓(0:23)	✓(3:11)	✓(0:07)	✓(0:47)
fmt	42	5	Y	✗(0:16)	✗(13:20)	✗(3:13)	TO	✓(0:22)	✓(1:46)
md5sum	40	3	Y	✓(0:04)	✓(0:15)	✓(5:24)	TO	✓(1:38)	✓(5:52)
pr	100	10	Y	✗(2:35)	TO	TO	TO	✓(18:49)	TO
savewd	86	1	N	TO	TO	✓(2:53)	✓(12:37)	✓(0:46)	✓(2:08)
seq	23	15	Y	✗(0:25)	✗(2:04)	✗(12:21)	TO	✗(3:24)	✗(8:12)
addr	77	1	N	✗(0:14)	✗(0:46)	✓(20:00)	TO	✓(6:46)	TO
nsGDDN	47	11	N	✗(0:02)	✗(0:21)	✗(0:24)	✗(1:56)	✓(0:11)	✓(0:35)
sign	8	2	N	✗(0)	✓(0)	✓(0)	✓(0)	✓(0)	✓(0)
sum	7	5	Y	✗(0:03)	✗(0:10)	✗(0:12)	✗(0:33)	✓(0:04)	✓(0:14)
nested	10	1	Y	✗(1:02)	TO	✗(0:35)	✗(1:37)	✓(0:12)	✓(0:30)

As precision increases, the resulting delta was more precise and contained more numerical information describing the difference. Results marked with ✗ produced false positives, reporting equivalent variables as different or providing too abstract of a description of the difference (i.e., ⊤). Results marked in TO represent runs that were stopped after 20 minutes. In either case, the results maintained soundness (equivalence was never reported falsely).

Runs without partitioning presented the most precise results with the most detailed abstract states describing the differencing paths. However this setting could not be applied towards all benchmarks since it leads to state explosion as shown by larger benchmarks that timed out. Applying partitioning allowed us to scale the analysis while maintaining precision. Results from runs that included partitioning described difference with less detail since some numerical data was abstracted away.

As expected, the Interval domain usually produced the fastest, least accurate results, while maintaining soundness as difference was reported for the appropriate variables but numerical data was almost completely abstracted away. In some case, like in the copy benchmark, Interval performed worse than Octagon and Polyhedra (in run time) for runs with partitioning. This is due to the Interval domain's limited ability to capture variable relationships which led to the partitioning algorithm failing in grouping together the different sub-states (as the equivalences they kept varied greatly). This resulted in a close to $2^{|VC|}$ number of equivalence groups.

Surprisingly, runs using the Octagon domain presented poor performance (run time), even compared to the more expensive Polyhedra domain, with less precision. This is due to the Octagon domain being less successful in capturing equivalences as it is built upon linear inequalities. This meant that more constraints were needed to represent variable equality, resulting in bigger states and a slower analysis.

The addr and nsGDDN benchmarks taken from the net/sunrpc/addr.c module in the Linux kernel SUNRPC implementation v2.6.32-rc6 and Firefox 3.6 security advisory CVE-2010-1196 (adapted to C from C++) respectively. The results produced by DIZY can be directly used towards exploiting known security flaws mentioned in advisories from which these patches originate, as the resulting abstract state describes the difference between versions which is exactly the range of exploitable values.

```
bool bsd_split_3 (char *s, size_t s_len,...) {
    int i = s_len;
    i--;
+   if (s_len == 0) return false;
    while (i && s[i] != ')') {
        i--;
    }
    ...
}
```

Fig. 6. Original and patched version of coreutils md5sum.c's bsd_split_3 procedure

In the md5sum benchmark, all paths in the programs contain loops and only some of them maintain equivalence. Fig. 6 shows part of the benchmark that was patched to disallow 0-length inputs (patch line is marked with '+'). The main challenge in this example, is separating the path where s_len is 0, which results in the loop index i ranging within negative values (producing an array access out of bounds fault), from the rest of the behaviors that maintain equivalence, throughout the widening process which is required for the analysis to reach a fixed point. As the partitioning maintains equivalence, the path where $s\_len = s\_len' \mapsto 0, ret \mapsto false, ret' \mapsto true$ will not be abstracted together with all other paths (that maintain equivalence). The offending path will be widened separately, precisely reporting difference in the final program state for the particular value.

The seq benchmark presented poor results, reporting difference on all variables although the semantic difference is small. This is due to the patch introducing a considerable amount of structural syntactic change to the code. We added the nested benchmark to demonstrate results for a simple nested loop program correlated with itself.

8   Related Work

Our work has been mainly inspired by recent work identifying program differencing as having vast security implications [3,26] as well as advancements made in the field of under-approximations of program equivalence [9,16,22,24].

The problem of program differencing is fundamental [10] and early work mainly focused on computing syntactical difference [13]. These solutions are an important stepping stone and we used syntactical diff as a means to achieve interleaving of programs in our correlating program. Another possibility for creating this program is to rely on the editing sequence that creates the new version from the original program [11].

We rely on classic methods of abstract interpretation [7] for presenting an over approximating solution for semantic differencing and equivalence. To achieve this we devised a static analysis over a correlating program. The idea of a correlating program is similar to that of self-composition [27] except that we compose two different programs in a interleaving designed to maintain a close correlation between them. The use of a correlating construct for differencing is novel as previous methods mainly use sequential composition [9,22,24], disregarding possible program correlation.

We base our analysis on numerical abstractions [8,18] that allow us to reason about variables of different programs. The abstraction is further refined in a way similar to trace partitioning [25] with an equivalence-based partitioning criteria.

Jackson and Ladd [14] proposed a tool for computing data dependencies between input and output variables and comparing these dependencies along versions of a program for discovering difference. This method may falsely report difference as semantic difference may occur even if data dependencies have not changed. Furthermore, data dependencies offer little insight as to the meaning of difference i.e. input and output values. Nevertheless, this was an important first step in employing program analysis as a means for semantic differencing.

Several works on the problem of equivalence of combinatorial circuits [17,19,6] made important contributions in establishing the problem of equivalence as feasible, producing practical solutions for hardware verification.

Symbolic execution methods [22,24] offer practical equivalence verification techniques for loop and recursion free programs with small state space. These works complement each other in regards to reporting difference as one [22] presents an over approximating description of difference and the other [24] presents an under approximating description including concrete inputs for test cases demonstrating difference in behavior. An interesting question is how could these methods be combined iteratively to achieve better precision. Also, this work can be used to complement our work in cases where equivalence could not be proven and the description of difference can be leveraged for the extraction of concrete input that leads to offending states.

Bounded model checking based work [9] presents the notion of partial equivalence which allows checking for equivalence under specific conditions, supplied by the user but are bound by loops. They employ a technique based on theorem provers for proving an equivalence formula which embeds program logic (in SSA form) alongside the requirement for input and output equivalence and user provided constraints.

[1] introduced a correlating heap semantics for verifying linearizability of concurrent programs. In their work, a correlating heap semantics is used to establish correspondence between a concurrent program and a sequential version of the program at specific linearization points.

In previous work regarding translation validation [23,20,30], in order to establish equivalence for a (looping) code fragment being translated or optimized by a compiler, a simulation relation between the basic blocks of the translated code is found. This method is limited in the context of semantic differencing as, for instance, a simulation relation for examples such as Fig. 2 cannot be automatically established (it needs to be crafted manually as this is not one of the classic transformations). However, the correlating program method we propose is generic enough to establish equivalence for many cases, without requiring special tailoring.

9   Conclusions

We presented an abstract interpretation approach for program equivalence and differencing. We defined a correlating program construct, that allows reasoning over both programs and establishing of equivalence. We defined a correlating abstract domain, that allows us to maintain variable relationships. This partially disjunctive domain allows to differentiate equivalent from differencing paths and we introduce a dynamic partitioning strategy to abstract together paths according to equivalence criteria and avoid exponential blowup. We also defined a widening operator for the disjunctive domain, which over approximates looping paths and is able to maintain equivalences for programs with unbound loops. We showed that this approach is feasible and can be applied successfully to challenging real world patches.

References

1. Amit, D., Rinetzky, N., Reps, T., Sagiv, M., Yahav, E.: Comparison under abstraction for verifying linearizability. In: Damm, W., Hermanns, H. (eds.) CAV 2007. LNCS, vol. 4590, pp. 477–490. Springer, Heidelberg (2007)
2. Bagnara, R., Hill, P.M., Zaffanella, E.: Widening operators for powerset domains. Int. J. Softw. Tools Technol. Transf. 8(4), 449–466 (2006)
3. Brumley, D., Poosankam, P., Song, D., Zheng, J.: Automatic patch-based exploit generation is possible: Techniques and implications. In: S&P 2008, pp. 143–157 (2008)
4. Cadar, C., Dunbar, D., Engler, D.R.: Klee: Unassisted and automatic generation of high-coverage tests for complex systems programs. In: OSDI, pp. 209–224 (2008)
5. Chaki, S., Gurfinkel, A., Strichman, O.: Regression verification for multi-threaded programs. In: Kuncak, V., Rybalchenko, A. (eds.) VMCAI 2012. LNCS, vol. 7148, pp. 119–135. Springer, Heidelberg (2012)
6. Clarke, E.M., Kroening, D.: Hardware verification using ansi-c programs as a reference. In: ASP-DAC, pp. 308–311 (2003)
7. Cousot, P., Cousot, R.: Abstract interpretation: A unified lattice model for static analysis of programs by construction of approximation of fixed points. In: POPL (1977)
8. Cousot, P., Halbwachs, N.: Automatic discovery of linear restraints among variables of a program. In: POPL 1978, pp. 84–97 (1978)
9. Godlin, B., Strichman, O.: Regression verification. In: DAC, pp. 466–471 (2009)
10. Hoare, C.A.R.: An axiomatic basis for computer programming. Commun. ACM 12(10), 576–580 (1969)
11. Horwitz, S.: Identifying the semantic and textual differences between two versions of a program. In: PLDI 1990, pp. 234–245 (1990)
12. Horwitz, S., Prins, J., Reps, T.: Integrating noninterfering versions of programs. ACM Trans. Program. Lang. Syst. 11(3)
13. Hunt, J.W., McIlroy, M.D.: An algorithm for differential file comparison. Tech. rep., Bell Laboratories (1975)
14. Jackson, D., Ladd, D.A.: Semantic diff: A tool for summarizing the effects of modifications. In: ICSM, pp. 243–252 (1994)
15. Jin, W., Orso, A., Xie, T.: BERT: a tool for behavioral regression testing. In: FSE 2010, pp. 361–362. ACM (2010)
16. Kawaguchi, M., Lahiri, S. K., and Rebelo, H. Conditional equivalence. Tech. rep., MSR (2010)
17. Kuehlmann, A., Krohm, F.: Equivalence checking using cuts and heaps. In: DAC, pp. 263–268 (1997)
18. Miné, A.: The octagon abstract domain. Higher Order Symbol. Comput. 19, 31–100 (2006)
19. Mishchenko, A., Chatterjee, S., Brayton, R.K., Eén, N.: Improvements to combinational equivalence checking. In: ICCAD, pp. 836–843 (2006)

20. Necula, G.C.: Translation validation for an optimizing compiler, pp. 83–95
21. Nethercote, N., Seward, J.: Valgrind: A framework for heavyweight dynamic binary instrumentation. In: PLDI 2007 (2007)
22. Person, S., Dwyer, M.B., Elbaum, S.G., Pasareanu, C.S.: Differential symbolic execution. In: FSE 2008 (2008)
23. Pnueli, A., Siegel, M., Singerman, E.: Translation validation. In: Steffen, B. (ed.) TACAS 1998. LNCS, vol. 1384, p. 151. Springer, Heidelberg (1998)
24. Ramos, D.A., Engler, D.R.: Practical, low-effort equivalence verification of real code. In: Gopalakrishnan, G., Qadeer, S. (eds.) CAV 2011. LNCS, vol. 6806, pp. 669–685. Springer, Heidelberg (2011)
25. Rival, X., Mauborgne, L.: The trace partitioning abstract domain. ACM Trans. Program. Lang. Syst. 29(5) (August 2007)
26. Song, Y., Zhang, Y., Sun, Y.: Automatic vulnerability locating in binary patches. In: CIS 2009,
27. Terauchi, T., Aiken, A.: Secure information flow as a safety problem. In: Hankin, C., Siveroni, I. (eds.) SAS 2005. LNCS, vol. 3672, pp. 352–367. Springer, Heidelberg (2005)
28. Verdoolaege, S., Janssens, G., Bruynooghe, M.: Equivalence checking of static affine programs using widening to handle recurrences. In: Bouajjani, A., Maler, O. (eds.) CAV 2009. LNCS, vol. 5643, pp. 599–613. Springer, Heidelberg (2009)
29. Xin, B., Sumner, W.N., Zhang, X.: Efficient program execution indexing. In: Proceedings of the 2008 ACM SIGPLAN Conference on Programming Language Design and Implementation, PLDI 2008, pp. 238–248 (2008)
30. Zuck, L., Pnueli, A., Fang, Y., Goldberg, B., Hu, Y.: Translation and run-time validation of optimized code. Electr. Notes Theor. Comput. Sci. 70(4) (2002)

A   Appendix

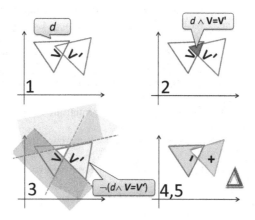

Fig. 7. Delta computation geometrical representation

Precise Slicing in Imperative Programs via Term-Rewriting and Abstract Interpretation

Raghavan Komondoor

Indian Institute of Science, Bangalore
`raghavan@csa.iisc.ernet.in`

Abstract. We propose a new approach for producing precise constrained slices of programs in a language such as C. We build upon a previous approach for this problem, which is based on term-rewriting, which primarily targets loop-free fragments and is fully precise in this setting. We incorporate abstract interpretation into term-rewriting, using a given arbitrary abstract lattice, resulting in a novel technique for slicing loops whose precision is linked to the power of the given abstract lattice. We address pointers in a first-class manner, including when they are used within loops to traverse and update recursive data structures. Finally, we illustrate the comparative precision of our slices over those of previous approaches using representative examples.

1 Introduction

Program slicing was introduced by Weiser [16] as a program transformation technique, in order to extract a smaller program P' from a given program P wrt to a given slicing *criterion*. In his setting the criterion is the value of a variable x at a given program point l. The semantics of slicing, intuitively, is that over all possible executions, P and P' result in identical value(s) for variable x at point l. Subsequently, the notion of the slicing criterion has been generalized in many ways, e.g., by allowing *constraints* [5] or *conditions* [2,8] on the initial and final states of the program's executions. Slicing has found varied applications, including debugging, software testing, software metrics, program comprehension, program parallelization, and state-space reduction for efficient verification; numerous techniques have also been proposed for slicing, e.g., as surveyed by Tip [15] and by Xu et al. [17].

The problem we address is precise, path-sensitive constrained slicing of looping programs in C-like languages, that may potentially access and manipulate heap structures via pointers.

1.1 Motivating Example

Consider the example program in Fig. 1(a). Say our criterion – shown within the box after line 9 – is the value in the variable z at the end of the program. (Let us ignore the two boxes above line 8 for now.) It can be seen that the conditional

F. Logozzo and M. Fähndrich (Eds.): SAS 2013, LNCS 7935, pp. 259–282, 2013.

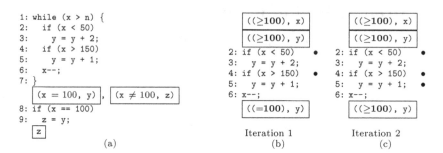

Fig. 1. Illustrative examples

statement "if (x < 50) y = y + 2" inside the loop need not be included in the slice. This is because the value of x decreases monotonically within the loop; therefore, in any execution in which control flows through the *true* branch of the above statement, control will eventually not reach the statement "z = y" in line 9, which means that the value written into y at line 3 will not affect the criterion.

In general, we express each slicing criterion as a pair of the form (g, v), where v is a variable (or address, in general) whose value we are interested in, and g is the condition (at the point where the criterion is expressed) under which we are interested in this value. Upon back-propagating the given criterion at the end of the program in Fig. 1(a), one would get the two criteria shown within boxes above line 8 in Fig. 1(a). Note the importance of the guards on the criteria; if there were no guards, line 3 in the loop would end up being pulled into the slice (unnecessarily) by the first of the two criteria (the one for variable y), because *all* assignments to y would have to be considered relevant.

Let us ignore the second criterion (the one for variable z), for now, and consider only the criterion for variable y (i.e., '(x = 100, y')). A naive (but precise) approach to slicing the loop would be to repeat the following steps iteratively: Propagate the criterion in hand back through the loop body, and identify the statements that impact it. Then, collect the variables that are *used* in these impacting statements before being *defined* in the loop body. For each such variable, create a new criterion for it, with the criterion's guard being the condition under which the variable is used. Then, slice the loop body using these criteria (each time we slice the loop body using a criterion we call it an *iteration*). Keep repeating this process until no new guarded criteria get generated. Finally, the statements that are found to impact any of the criteria in any of the iterations are taken together as the slice of the loop wrt the original criterion. Note that in each iteration we need to analyze the complete loop body, and *not* the parts of the loop body that were found relevant in preceding iterations. That is, the approach "grows" the slice iteratively.

In the example, in the first iteration, for the criterion '(x = 100, y)', none of the assignments in the loop are found to be impacting it. Basically, this is because both the statements that assign to y are controlled by conditions that would have to evaluate to *false* in order for x to have the value 100 at the end of the iteration. The two conditionals themselves, in lines 2 and 4, however impact the criterion, and are included in the slice[1]. Now, the use of x in lines 2 and 4 cause the criterion '(x = 101, x)' to be generated ('(x = 101)' is the weakest pre-condition wrt the loop body of the guard of the criterion that was processed in the current iteration). Also, since y was not unconditionally assigned to by any impacting statement in this iteration (in fact, it was not even conditionally assigned), we re-generate a criterion '(x = 101, y)' for y.

We now process the above two criteria in the subsequent two iterations. The first one of these criteria (the one involving variable x) causes line 6 to be pulled into the slice, while the other criterion does not cause any new statement to be pulled into the slice. The process then continues; we keep generating criteria for x and for y, with guards '(x = 102)', '(x = 103)', etc., until we produce the criterion '(x = 150, y)'. Due to this criterion, finally, line 5 in the program is found to be impacting and is pulled into the slice. Now, continuing the process, we end up generating a never-ending sequence of criteria, with guards '(x = 151)', '(x = 152)', etc. Note that Line 3 itself never gets pulled into the slice. In fact, this naive approach is *fully* precise. The problem with it is the impossibility of ensuring its termination, in general, while guaranteeing soundness as well as full precision.

1.2   Our Approach

The motivation behind our proposal is a need for a principled way to trade off on the precision of slicing, while guaranteeing termination. The key idea underlying our approach is to use *abstract* guards rather than concrete guards in slicing criteria. An abstract guard l is an element of an abstract lattice that is provided as a parameter to the approach. An abstract criterion is of the form (l, v), where v is an address; this criterion basically expresses interest in the value in location v in the *subset* of concrete stores that are abstractly represented by l (i.e., that belong to $\gamma(l)$) and that arise at the point where the criterion is given.

Coming back to the example, say we are provided an abstract lattice that is meant to track the value of variable x only (for simplicity), and contains the abstract elements $\{\bot, = 100, \leq 100, \geq 100, \neq 100, \top\}$. '$= 100$' indicates that the value of x is 100, '≤ 100' indicates that the value of x is at most 100, and so on. The elements ≥ 100 and ≤ 100 dominate the element $= 100$; as usual, $\top$ dominates all elements, and every element dominates $\bot$. Now, considering the criterion '(x = 100, y)' in Fig. 1(a). We first "abstract out" its guard, thus obtaining the abstract criterion '((=100), y)' (we show abstract guards in bold in the figure). We then analyze the loop body for the first time (see Fig. 1(b)). As before, only the conditionals in lines 2 and 4 are found to impact the criterion, and are included in the slice (as indicated by the bullet signs). Now, at the end of this iteration, rather than generate a criterion for x with the concrete guard

---

[1] This is following the definition of a correct slice as proposed by Field et al. [5], on whose approach we are based. As per their definition a condition is considered as impacting a criterion unless replacing it with a non-deterministic condition makes no difference to the criterion.

'$(x = 101)$', we generate a criterion whose guard is an *abstraction* of this concrete condition, namely, '(≥ 100)'. Similarly, because y was not unconditionally defined by an impacting statement, we generate a criterion for y with the same abstract guard. These two abstract criteria are shown at the top of Fig. 1(b). Say, we process the criterion '$((\geq 100), y)$', in the next iteration, as shown in Fig. 1(c); line 5 is found impacting in this iteration, and is pulled into the slice. The same two abstract criteria get generated in this iteration as in the first iteration. (Processing the abstract criterion '$((\geq 100), x)$' that was generated in the first iteration produces back the same criterion; this iteration is omitted from the figure.) Therefore, since a fix-point has been reached wrt the abstract criteria that can be generated, we terminate the analysis. Note in the example that Line 3 got excluded from the slice, as is desired.

Once the loop has been sliced, we use all the criteria that were generated across all the iterations to continue slicing the part of the program that precedes the loop.

Assuming a finite set of addresses that can be used in criteria, and assuming a finite lattice of abstract guards, the total number of possible criteria is finite. Therefore, reaching a fix-point is guaranteed. If the lattice is of finite *height* (as opposed to being finite), we can still ensure that a fix-point is reached by always *broadening* the guard of any newly generated criterion by joining it with the guard(s) of other criteria generated so far for the same address.

1.3   Novelty and Contributions

From the point of view of the previous literature in constrained slicing of programs in C-like languages, our approach is novel and more powerful in several ways. (1) We are the first to allow an arbitrary abstract lattice to be plugged in, and for the elements of this abstract lattice to be used as guards of criteria, in order to perform slicing of looping programs. The precision of our approach is linked to the power of the abstract lattice chosen. (2) To our knowledge ours is the first slicing approach to specifically address heap-manipulating programs, and to produce slices with non-trivial precision on typical programs that access and manipulate heap structures. Two key ingredients that enable this are: (a) A novel notion, in the context of the slicing literature, of a symbolic address, that we call a *compressed* access path; e.g., x.next.*. A compressed access path can be used in the place of an address in a criterion, and in general, represents an infinite family of concrete access paths; e.g., x.next, x.next.next, etc. (b) Plugging in an abstract domain such as shape analysis [13] in our analysis in order to identify statements that impact a criterion with high precision.

The underlying part of our approach that identifies the statements in a fragment that are relevant to a criterion (e.g., during an iteration in our analysis while slicing a loop) is built upon the *term-rewriting* approach of Field et al. [5]. Their approach performs *fully* precise slicing of loop-free fragments, including in the presence of pointers, via term rewriting. A fundamental contribution of our paper is to introduce a new rewrite rule to go along with PIM's rewrite rules, that is effective in situations wherein the term to be rewritten contains a loop inside it (e.g., when a loop body contains a nested loop). The base PIM rules in this scenario can essentially only perform term simplifications whose safety can be established by (limited) unrolling of the loop. The key idea underlying our rule, on the other hand, is to use abstract interpretation [4] to perform *fix-point* reasoning about loops inside terms, and to use this reasoning to perform (semantics-preserving) simplifications that the base rules might not be able to do. Our abstract-interpretation based rewrite rule can be interleaved freely and used along with the base PIM rewrite rules during the term-rewriting sequence. We hypothesize that our generalization of term rewriting will find other applications, too, in precise analysis and transformation of imperative programs.

The rest of this paper is structured as follows. Section 2 introduces the term rewriting approach (PIM) of Field et al., upon which our approach is based. Section 3 spells out our approach in detail; in this section we consider loops and pointers, but assume that there are no heap-allocated objects. Section 4 gives an informal overview of how we address programs that manipulate heap objects; finally, Section 5 discusses related work.

Due to space constraints we include several related discussions in an associated technical report [11]: (1) An outline of an argument regarding the correctness of our approach. (2) The details of how we employ compressed access paths to slice heap-accessing programs. (3) Two new examples, one being a program that manipulates two linked data structures using a loop, and another being a "batch" program that reads a record from a file in each iteration of a loop and processes different kinds of records differently. We provide interesting slicing criteria for both these programs, and illustrate our approach. We believe ours is the first proposed slicing approach to be demonstrated to produce non-trivial slices in these kinds of challenging scenarios. (5) Expanded discussions corresponding to various sections in this paper.

2   Background on Term-Rewriting

In this section we give an informal overview of the term-rewriting system for C programs proposed by Field et al., called *PIM*. We also discuss how Field et al. apply the system to the slicing problem. For full details and a complete discussion on PIM we refer the reader to their paper. This relevance of our overview is in that our approach, which is described subsequently in Section 3, builds upon PIM in a closely-coupled manner, inheriting all of PIM's features and then adding extra features.

2.1   PIM Intermediate Representation

PIM has two components, a graph or term representation for programs, which we introduce first, and an equational logic on these graphs, which we introduce in Section 2.2. PIM graphs are directed acyclic graphs, which can also be interpreted as terms after "flattening". Terms (or subterms) are of two basic types: *store structures* and *merge structures*. A *store cell* is the simplest form of store structure, representing a single assignment statement; it associates an *address expression* (the lhs) with a merge structure (the rhs). For example, if x is a program variable, the store cell $\{a(x) \mapsto [1]\}$ maps $a(x)$, which represents the (constant) address of variable x, to the constant value 1. In general, an address expression is an expression that evaluates to an address. '$\emptyset_s$' represents the empty store (i.e., no addresses are mapped to values). The '$\circ_s$' operator can be used to sequentially compose store structures. Sequential composition has the usual semantics; i.e., if stores s_1 and s_2 both map an address a to something, the mapping provided by s_2 takes precedence in the composed store $s_1 \circ_s s_2$.

A merge structure is a recursive structure, and is basically a sequence of one or more inner merge structures or expressions, each *guarded* by a boolean expression. The simplest kind of merge structure is a *merge cell*, of the form $m \equiv [g \triangleright e]$, where g is the guard (a boolean expression) and e is an (arithmetic or boolean) expression. m evaluates to e if g is *true*, else it evaluates to the null value $\emptyset_m$. The operator '!' is used to "select" a constituent merge structure or expression from a composite merge structure. Basically, the term $((g_1 \triangleright m_1) \circ_m (g_2 \triangleright m_2) \circ_m \ldots \circ_m (g_n \triangleright m_n))!$ evaluates to m_k iff g_k evaluates to *true* and the guards $g_{k+1}, g_{k+2}, \ldots, g_n$ all evaluate to *false*. Thus, merge structures resemble Lisp **cond** expressions. Where there is no ambiguity we omit the subscripts m and s from the symbols '$\emptyset$' and '$\circ$'. Also, where the guard g of a merge cell is *true*, we omit the guard (thus, the expression e is "coerced" into a merge cell).

Expressions in PIM make use of the usual arithmetic and boolean operators. A leaf in an expression may be a constant (including a constant address), or an *address lookup*, which is the lookup of the value in a memory location in a store. Address lookups take the syntactic form '$!(s @ a)$', where s is a store structure and a is an address expression. (As we will see later, just '$s @ a$' evaluates to a composite merge structure, which encodes the possible values that reside in location a under different conditions.)

For illustration, we refer to the example program P in Fig. 2(a), and its graph representation S_P in Fig. 2(b). Ignore, for now, the address-lookup at the root of the term in Fig. 2(b), as well as the term in Fig. 2(c). Children of a node are depicted *above* or to the right of the node, to emphasize the correspondence

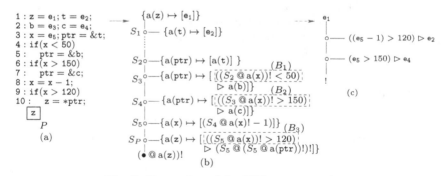

Fig. 2. Illustration of the PIM representation

between source-code constructs and their corresponding PIM subgraphs. Store cells (i.e., statements) are enclosed in curly braces; the composite stores are labeled S_1, S_2, etc., for convenience of notation, so that they can be referred to wherever required. Merge structures within store structures are enclosed within square brackets. We use e_1, e_2, etc., as placeholders in the notation, representing merge structures whose actual contents are not relevant for the purpose of this discussion. Note that (a) "if" conditions are *flattened*, by making each statement inside the conditional become an (unconditional) assignment whose rhs is a merge structure that is guarded by the "if"s condition, and (b) a variable reference in any statement in the program gets translated into a address-lookup on the store-structure that represents the portion of the program that precedes the statement. The Field et al. paper discusses a simple syntax-directed scheme for translating any program into its graph representation.

PIM also includes the notion of *meta variables*, that represent input parameters to the program. We ignore this construct in our discussion for the sake of brevity.

2.2   Rewriting in PIM

In addition to the graph representation of statements and programs, PIM contains an equational logic on these graphs. The logic consists of two subsystems: (a) an "operational" subsystem of directed *rewrite* rules, which completely define the operational semantics of the language and can be used to "execute" graphs, and (b) an additional set of non-oriented equational rules for reasoning about operational equivalences of graphs. We begin by introducing two of the key PIM rewrite rules. Rule S4[2] converts an address lookup on a composite store structure into a composite merge structure:

$$\text{S4: } (s_1 \circ_s s_2) @ a \longrightarrow (s_1 @ a) \circ_m (s_2 @ a)$$

$1:$ $B_3 \rhd (S_5 @ \text{a}(\text{ptr}))!$

$2: B_3 \rhd (((\text{a}(\text{ptr}) = \text{a}(\text{z})) \rhd e_1) \circ ((\text{a}(\text{ptr}) = \text{a}(\text{t})) \rhd e_2) \circ \ldots \circ ((\text{a}(\text{ptr}) = \text{a}(\text{x})) \rhd ((S_4 @ \text{a}(\text{x}))! - 1)))!$

$3:$ $B_3 \rhd (\text{a}(\text{t}) \circ (B_1 \rhd \text{a}(\text{b})) \circ (B_2 \rhd \text{a}(\text{c})))!$

$4:$ $((B_3 \rhd \text{a}(\text{t})) \circ ((B_3 \wedge B_1) \rhd \text{a}(\text{b})) \circ ((B_3 \wedge B_2) \rhd \text{a}(\text{c})))!$

$5:$ $((B_3 \rhd \text{a}(\text{t})) \circ ((B_3 \wedge B_2) \rhd \text{a}(\text{c})))!$

Fig. 3. Illustration of rewriting, based on the example in Fig. 2(b)

Rule S1 says that the value written into a location a_2 by the merge cell '$\{a_1 \mapsto m\}$' is m if $(a_1 = a_2)$ simplifies to *true* (i.e., a_1 and a_2 are the same address), else is the null value:

$$\text{S1: } \{a_1 \mapsto m\} @ a_2 \longrightarrow (a_1 = a_2) \rhd m$$

To illustrate these rewrite rules we consider the subterm '$(S_5 @ \text{a}(\text{ptr}))!$' in Fig. 2(b) (corresponding to line 10 in the source code); this sub-term, along with

---

[2] We use the same rule names as in the Field et al. paper.

its guard B_3, is shown in line 1 in Fig. 3 (B_1, B_2, and B_3 are labels that are used for notational convenience only). The subsequent lines in Fig. 3 illustrate a sequence of rewrite steps that the subterm undergoes, one step per line. Line 2 results from an application of Rules S4 and S1. Intuitively, since the store S_5 is a composition of several store cells, the value in address a(ptr) as per this store structure is the merge structure in the rhs of the last store cell that is a constituent of S_5 and whose lhs is a(ptr). The term in line 3 results from an application of the following four rules:

L1: $(\emptyset \circ l) \longrightarrow l$, L2: $(l \circ \emptyset) \longrightarrow l$

L5: $(true \rhd l) \longrightarrow l$, L6: $(false \rhd l) \longrightarrow \emptyset$

As a result of these rules, the merge structures that take part in the composition in line 2 whose guards are $false$ have gotten eliminated. Intuitively, the term in line 3 indicates that the value in a(ptr) in store S_5 is the address of c, which happens when B_2 is $true$, else is the address of b, when B_1 is $true$, else is the address of t. We now use the following PIM rewrite rules:

L7: $p \rhd (l_1 \circ l_2) \longrightarrow (p \rhd l_1) \circ (p \rhd l_2)$, L8: $(p_1 \rhd (p_2 \rhd l)) \longrightarrow ((p_1 \wedge p_2) \rhd l)$

These rules yield the term in line 4 in Fig. 3. Now, the condition $B_1 \wedge B_3$ reduces to $false$, yielding the term in line 5. This step illustrates the fully precise nature of PIM rewriting. Intuitively, the term in line 5 indicates that the value in a(ptr) in S_5 $under$ the condition B_3 is either the address of c or the address of t, but definitely not the address of b.

For an illustration of how the PIM rewrite rules natively address pointer operations, consider the subterm '$B_3 \rhd (S_5 @ (S_5 @ a(\texttt{ptr}))!)!$' in Fig. 2(b). Given that '$(S_5 @ a(\texttt{ptr}))!$' evaluates to either the address of c or the address of t, upon simplification of the subterm above the store-cell 'a(b) $\mapsto$ e_3' gets eliminated. What this means intuitively is that the value of '*ptr' in line 10 in Fig. 2(a) may be equal to e_2 or e_4, but cannot be equal to e_3.

2.3 Slicing via Term Rewriting

Field et al. encode the slicing criterion $plus$ the program itself as an address lookup on the store-structure that represents the program. For instance, for the program P in Fig. 2(a), and for a slicing criterion ($true$, z), the combined encoding would be the term '$(S_P @ a(\texttt{z}))!$', where S_P is the store-structure corresponding to the program P. This term is the one shown in Fig. 2(b). For the same program, if the slicing criterion were to be (x $<$ n, z), then the combined encoding would be the term '$((S_P @ a(\texttt{x}))! < (S_P @ a(\texttt{n}))!) \rhd (S_P @ a(\texttt{z}))!$.

Note that the combined encoding, e.g., the term shown in Fig. 2(b), is itself a $semantic$ $slice$ of the program P wrt the given criterion. This term can be syntactically simplified (while preserving its semantics) by rewriting it. Going back to the example, Fig. 2(c) shows the fully simplified term, which is a normal form or minimal semantic slice.

A $syntactic$ $slice$ is one that's a projection of the original program (i.e., certain statements and conditionals are removed). In many applications of slicing, where the slice is to be used to perform some analysis or transformation on the $original$ program, what is desired is a syntactic slice. Each term that is produced during rewriting, on the other hand, is essentially a semantic slice. In order to map back semantic slices to the original program to yield syntactic slices, Field et al. introduce the idea of *dependence tracking*. Whenever a term t is rewritten into a term t', the rewrite rule that was used also indicates the *dependences* of the subterms in t' on the subterms in t, in the form of a binary relation. At any point in the rewriting process, the subterms of the initial term (e.g., the one in Fig. 2(b)) on which the current term (e.g., the one in Fig. 2(c)) depends *transitively* constitute the syntactic slice of the program. In the example, the subterm e_1 in Fig. 2(c) transitively depends on the store-cell 'a(z) $\mapsto$ [e_1]', as well on the boolean expression B_3 (this is intuitively the case because the final value of z is e_1 only when B_3 evaluates to *false*). The subterm e_2 depends transitively on the store-cell 'a(t) $\mapsto$ [e_2]', the store-cell 'a(ptr) $\mapsto$ [a(t)]', as well on the boolean expressions B_1, B_2, and B_3. The subterm e_4 depends transitively on the store-cell 'a(c) $\mapsto$ [e_4]', the store-cell 'a(ptr) $\mapsto$ [a(c)]', as well on the boolean expressions B_1, B_2, and B_3. Therefore, the syntactic slice corresponding to the term in Fig. 2(c) consists of all parts of the term in Fig. 2(b) except the store-cells 'a(b) $\mapsto$ [e_3]' and 'a(ptr) $\mapsto$ [a(b)]'.

Note that although dependence-tracking from any of the rewritten terms yields a correct syntactic slice, the degree of precision of the slice depends on the degree to which the term that represents the criterion is rewritten (i.e., simplified). If the term is reduced to a normal form then the resultant syntactic slice is guaranteed to be *minimal* (the Field et al. paper has more details on this.)

2.4   Loops in PIM

We now touch upon how PIM handles loops. A loop is represented in PIM by a term of the form $Loop(\lambda x_S.body(v_E, u_S), s)$. Informally, v_E is the loop's predicate (a boolean expression), u_S is a store structure representing the loop's body, both being functions of the store x_S at the beginning of a loop iteration. The second argument s is the incoming store (i.e., the store that precedes the loop). For e.g., if a program has two statements s_1, s_2, followed by a loop whose predicate is v_E and body is s_3, followed by a statement s_4, its PIM graph would be $s_1 \circ s_2 \circ Loop(\lambda x_S.body(v_E, s_3), (s_1 \circ s_2)) \circ s_4$. The term $Loop(\lambda x_S.body(v_E, u_S), s)$ itself denotes the store resulting from repeated execution of the loop body until the predicate evaluates to *false*. This is captured by a rewrite rule:

$Loop(\lambda x_S.body(v_E, u_S), s) \longrightarrow (\lambda x_S. v_E \triangleright (u_S \circ Loop(\lambda x_S.body(v_E, u_S), x_S \circ u_S)))s$

This rule basically expresses the semantics of a loop using unrolling. For instance, a single application of this rule on the example loop-structure mentioned above, would result in:

$v_E[(s_1 \circ s_2)/x_S] \triangleright (s_3[(s_1 \circ s_2)/x_S] \circ Loop(\lambda x_S.body(v_E, s_3), s_1 \circ s_2 \circ s_3[(s_1 \circ s_2)/x_S]))$

The simplest way in which PIM slices looping programs is using the above rewrite rule (repeatedly). Field et al. call this technique *pure dynamic slicing*; this approach terminates only when the input- and/or output-side constraints imply a bound on the number of iterations of the loop. Note that premature forced termination of the rewriting process will result in the entire loop being included in the slice. Whenever the approach terminates it computes a fully precise slice. PIM also includes other, somewhat more sophisticated techniques to slice loops, which we will touch upon in Section 3.4.

3   Our Extensions to PIM

Our slicing framework is the same as that of PIM. That is, we encode the program plus the slicing criterion as a PIM term, rewrite the term, and finally use the tracked dependences to emit the syntactic slice. We inherit their term representation, as well as all their rewrite rules. The new aspects of our approach over PIM are in the form of (1) A new rewrite rule that simplifies guards (i.e., boolean expressions) to *false* more aggressively (yet safely) than PIM's rules, using abstract interpretation on terms. (2) Letting merge structures (and hence, slicing criteria) use "abstract" guards (as illustrated in Fig. 1, parts (b) and (c)), in conjunction with the "concrete" guards that PIM allows. (3) A technique to slice loops by fix-point analysis of the loop body, using abstract guards, as illustrated intuitively in Section 1.2. Note that we use the same *representation* of loops as PIM, namely, the one discussed in Section 2.4. In the rest of this section we first introduce some notation and terminology, and then discuss in detail the three aspects mentioned above.

3.1   Notation and Terminology

A *scope* is a store structure that represents either the entire program, or the body of a loop in a program. Therefore, the scopes corresponding to a program form a hierarchical tree structure due to nesting. Associated with each scope $\mathcal{F}$ is a *store variable* $x_{\mathcal{F}}$, which represents the *incoming* store into $\mathcal{F}$. When $\mathcal{F}$ is the full program $x_{\mathcal{F}}$ represents the initial memory configuration of the program. When $\mathcal{F}$ is a loop, $x_{\mathcal{F}}$ is nothing but the formal store parameter x_S used in our representation of loops (see Section 2.4). Different scopes never refer to shared store- or merge- structures, even when the scopes are related by nesting. Therefore, rewriting within different scopes can be seen as independent activities. However, rewriting within a scope can trigger rewriting of contained as well as containing scopes, as will become clear in Section 3.4.

Let *Abs* denote the given abstract interpretation lattice; this is a finite or a finite-height lattice, with associated transfer functions for each kind of statement and conditional in the language. The precision of our approach depends on the power of this lattice; however, in the worst case, if a meaningful lattice is not provided, the trivial lattice $\{\bot, \top\}$ can be used. Associated with the incoming store variable $x_{\mathcal{F}}$ of each scope $\mathcal{F}$ is an abstract value $l_{\mathcal{F}} \in Abs$, which over-approximates the set of concrete states that $x_{\mathcal{F}}$ may take on. When $\mathcal{F}$ is the program then $l_{\mathcal{F}}$ is the abstraction of the incoming store into the program (this needs to be provided). When $\mathcal{F}$ is a loop body we compute $l_{\mathcal{F}}$ automatically using the fragment of the program that precedes the loop (more on this in Section 3.4).

(a)

(i)

```
(S₂)
1 : x = e  (S₁)
2 : if (x is odd)
3 :   z = z + 1
4 : while(x < n)
5 :   x = x + 2

6 : if(x is even)
7 :   y = z + 2
          (Sₚ)
      y
```

(ii)

```
x = e;              ⎤ from
x1 = x;             ⎦ (S₁ @ x)!

x = e;
while(x < n)    from
    x = x + 2;   (S₂ @ x)!
x2 = x;         ⎦

v1 = (x1 is odd) &&
        (x2 is even);
if (v1)
    no-op;
```

(b)

Procedure $translExp(e)$

Input: e, a PIM expression
Output: (val, cfg), where val is a *fresh*
     variable name, and cfg is a CFG
     that computes e and stores its
     result in val
1: Let val be a fresh variable name
2: **if** e is a(v)
3:     **return** (val, asgn(val, &v))
4: **else if** $e = (s @ a)!$
5:     c1 = $translStore(s)$
6:     (v,c2) = $translExp(a)$
7:     **return** (val, (c1 ; c2 ; asgn(val, *(v))))
8: **else if** e is (e_1 op e_2)
9:     (v1,c1) = $translExp(e_1)$
10:     (v2,c2) = $translExp(e_2)$
11:     **return** (val, (c1 ; c2 ; asgn(val, op(v1, v2))))
12: **end if**

(c)

Procedure $translStore(s)$

Input: s, a store structure
Output: a CFG representing s
1: **if** s is $x_{\mathcal{F}}$
2:     **return** {empty CFG}
3: **else if** s is a store cell $\{a \mapsto m\}$
4:     (v1,c1) = $translExp(a)$
5:     (v2,c2) = $translMerge(m)$
6:     **return** (c1 ; c2; asgn(*(v1),v2))
7: **else if** s is a loop
8:     Construct a CFG c from s
         using v_E and u_S
9:     **return** c
10: **else if** $s = s_1 \circ s_2$
11:     cfg1 = $translStore(s_1)$
12:     cfg2 = $translStore(s_2)$
13:     **return** (cfg1 ; cfg2)
14: **end if**

(d)

Procedure $translMerge(m)$

Input: m, a merge structure
Output: (val, cfg), where val is a *fresh*
     variable name, and cfg is a CFG
     that computes m and stores its
     result in val
1: Let val be a fresh variable name
2: **if** m is an expression
3:     (v1,c1) = $translExp(m)$
4:     **return** (val, (c1 ; asgn(val,v1)))
5: **else if** $m = (g_1 \triangleright m_1) \circ (g_2 \triangleright m_2)$
6:     (v1,c1) = $translExp(g_1)$
7:     (v2,c2) = $translMerge(m_1)$
8:     cfg1 = asgn(c1; c2 ; if(v1, asgn(val, v2)))

9:     *Similarly, create* cfg2 *from* $(g_2 \triangleright m_2)$
10:     **return** (val, (cfg1 ; cfg2))
11: **end if**

Fig. 4. (a) Example for abstract analysis of conditionals. (b)-(d): Translating PIM structures into CFGs.

We use the term *store* to mean a store structure, and the term *memory* or *state* to refer to a concrete snapshot of memory. We use the term "address lookup" to refer to a PIM subterm of the form '$s @ a$'. We say "*abstract state* at a program point" to mean the abstract value (from the domain *Abs*) at that program point due to abstract interpretation.

3.2 Rewriting Boolean Expressions Using Abstract Interpretation

Our first major extension on top of PIM is a new rule that can rewrite boolean expressions to *false* in more cases than PIM's native rules. Simplifying boolean expressions to *false* is key to precise slicing; e.g., in the example in Fig. 1, determining that the condition in line 2 had to be *false* for x to be equal to or greater than a hundred after line 6 was what helped exclude line 3 from the slice. While PIM's base rules suffice in that example, they don't suffice in the example in

Fig. 4(a)(i). In this example, let S_P be the store structure corresponding to the entire program, and let S_1 and S_2 be the store structures corresponding to the fragments of the program as shown. The term corresponding to the program plus criterion is '$(S_P @ a(y))!$'. During the rewriting of this term, one of the terms obtained will contain the subterm:

$((S_2 @ a(x))!$ `is even`$) \triangleright$
  $((S_1 @ a(z))!$ `o` $(((S_1 @ a(x))!$ `is odd`$) \triangleright ((S_1 @ a(z))! + 1)))!$

This subterm represents the value in z that is used to compute y. The guard in the first line above indicates that the value of z is relevant only when the condition in line 6 in the example program is *true*. The merge structure in the second line above indicates the two possible values that may reside in z in line 7, namely, the value of z in store S_1, or this value plus one. It can be noted that the second of these two values is infeasible; i.e., if '$(S_2 @ a(x))!$' is even then '$(S_1 @ a(x))!$' cannot be odd. Therefore, line 3 in the program need not be in the slice at all. To detect this we would need to determine during rewriting that the condition '$((S_2 @ a(x))!$ `is even`$) \wedge ((S_1 @ a(x))!$ `is odd`$)$' reduces to *false*. The PIM rules per se will not be able to do this, because the value of x in S_2 is computed in a loop.

Our key idea is to extend the power of the PIM rules that simplify guards by making them reason about loops using abstract interpretation. In the example above, we would basically like to abstractly interpret the term S_2, using an "odd / even" abstract lattice, to determine that '$(S_2 @ a(x))!$' is even iff '$(S_1 @ a(x))!$' is even (note that S_1 is a sub-fragment of S_2).

Our New Rewrite Rule. Our approach is to introduce a new rewrite rule for guards (i.e., boolean expressions), which uses results from abstract interpretation. At this point we focus on abstract interpretation of terms from the base PIM term language; we discuss in Section 3.3 how our approach needs to be extended in the presence of the new operator that we introduce, i.e., "abstract" guards.

Abstract interpretation is traditionally defined over control-flow graphs (CFGs), and not over PIM-like term structures. Therefore, given a PIM term p that is a boolean expression **Step 1** of our approach is to *translate* p (and all store- and merge-structures that it refers to within the current scope $\mathcal{F}$) to a (self-contained) CFG, on which abstract interpretation can be performed subsequently. We do this translation in a syntax-directed fashion, with each kind of PIM construct being translated by a corresponding procedure. The pseudo-code for this is shown in Fig. 4(b)-(d). The pseudo-code is mostly self-explanatory; therefore, we only touch upon some of its key elements below. The procedure *translExp*, which can actually translate any PIM expression e (and not just conditions), returns a pair, the first element being 'val', which is a (fresh) temporary variable name, and the second element being 'cfg', which is a CFG which evaluates e and places the result in 'val'. Note that during the translation of each expression or merge structure we introduce a fresh temporary variable name to hold its value; this is our strategy to translate these kinds of PIM terms, which basically transmit data (to enclosing terms) without going through a store. Notice the "return" statement in line 7 in Fig. 4(b): the second component being returned is a CFG. We use ';' as an infix operator to sequentially compose CFGs; also, asgn(x,y) is a data-constructor which basically constructs an assignment statement 'x := y'. We use other data-constructors for other constructs: 'op(x,y)' to generate the syntactic expression "x op y" (see line 11 in Fig. 4(b)), and 'if(p, stmt)', to generate the statement "if (p) stmt" (see line 8 in Fig. 4(d)). For brevity we omit the (straightforward) details involved in translating a PIM loop structure into a CFG loop, in lines 7-9 in Fig. 4(c).

The root procedure call that we make to translate the given boolean expression p is '$translExp(p)$'. Let (val,cfg) be the return value from this call. The last statement in 'cfg' is necessarily of the form 'asgn(v, exp)', where 'v' is a temporary variable and 'exp' is the translation of p. We finish the construction of the CFG by appending to the end of 'cfg' the statement "if (v) $no\text{-}op$".

Example: Fig. 4(a)(ii) shows the CFG (depicted, for convenience, as program text) obtained by translating the condition '$(((S_2 @ a(x))!$ is even$) \wedge ((S_1 @ a(x))!$ is odd$))$' mentioned earlier. Note that x1, x2, and v1 are the temporary variables that hold the values of expressions '$(S_1 @ a(x))!$', '$(S_2 @ a(x))!$', and the entire condition, respectively.   □

Step 2 is to perform abstract interpretation on the CFG constructed above, using $l_{\mathcal{F}}$ (which is the incoming abstract state into the current scope $\mathcal{F}$) as the initial abstract state. **Step 3** is the actual rewrite step: If the computed abstract state at the *true* edge of the "if" statement that was added to the end of the CFG is $\bot$, then we rewrite the boolean expression p to the value *false*; also, we let the newly introduced *false* value be dependent on p (to enable p, but not the statements that it controls, to be included in the syntactic slice).

Example: In the CFG in Fig. 4(a)(ii), say we use an abstract lattice 2^D, where each element of D, which we call an *abstract valuation* (shown within square brackets below), maps each program variable to *odd*, *even*, or *oddEven*. Say the initial abstract state to this scope is $\{[e \mapsto odd], [e \mapsto even]\}$ (all variables other than e are mapped to *oddEven* in both abstract valuations). At the point before the final "if" condition two abstract valuations arise – one in which both x1 and x2 are mapped to *odd*, and another in which both are mapped to *even*. Therefore, the analysis can determine that the abstract state at the *true* edge out of this condition is the empty set (i.e. $\bot$).   □

Note that our abstract-interpretation based rewrite rule proposed above and the (base) rewrite rules of PIM for simplifying conditionals can be freely interleaved. In fact, there exist natural example programs where (a) initially the PIM rules are not able to reduce any of the conditions to *false*, (b) our technique is able to reduce *some* of the conditions to *false*, (c) *after* the simplification done by our technique the PIM rules are able to reduce other remaining conditions to *false*, and so on.

3.3 Abstract Guards

As discussed in the context of the example in Fig. 1 in the introduction, we need the notion of *abstract* guards (i.e., conditions) to ensure termination during slicing of loops. Therefore, we add to the PIM term language a new boolean operator '$\models$'. The concrete semantics of this operator is as follows: $s \models l$, where s is a store structure and $l \in Abs$, is true if the state that s evaluates to is included in the *concretization* of l (denoted $\gamma(l)$), which is the set of states represented by l. Note that this "abstract comparison" operator '$\models$' will not appear in the initial term obtained by translating a program; it only gets introduced in terms during the rewriting of loops (as will be discussed in Section 3.4). For an illustration of a use of this operator, consider Fig. 1(c); the criterion at the end of that code fragment, namely, '$((\geq 100), y)$', is actually encoded as the merge structure '$(s \models (\geq 100)) \triangleright (s @ a(y))!$', where s is the store structure representing the loop's body. We allow composite boolean expressions that make use of the '$\models$' operator in addition to other (base) PIM operators.

Note that the base PIM rewrite rules cannot reason about the abstract operator '$\models$'. Instead, the new rewrite rule that we had proposed earlier for simplifying boolean expressions addresses this operator, as follows. For any store s that is used as an operand of a '$\models$' operator, we add a *pseudo-statement* at the last program point in the CFG fragment generated from s, whose semantics is to save the abstract state at that point (from domain *Abs*) into a pseudo-variable v_s. Then, we translate any condition '$s \models l$' in the PIM term as the condition '$v_s \models l$' in the CFG. During abstract interpretation this condition is interpreted as *false* if the congratulations of l_s and l are non-intersecting, and as a non-deterministic condition otherwise.

3.4 Slicing Loops

We now discuss our final extension over PIM, which is a technique to slice a loop by fix-point analysis of the loop body, using abstract guards, as illustrated intuitively in Section 1.2. We use the same representation of loops as PIM (which was introduced in Section 2.4). We introduce some additional notation, for convenience: If L is a loop structure $Loop(\lambda x_S.body(v_E, u_S), s)$, $s(L)$ denotes the body u_S of the loop, $b(L)$ denotes the predicate v_E of the loop, and $inStore(L)$ denotes s (which is the "incoming" store into L). As discussed in Section 3.1, we use the notation x_L (rather than x_S) to denote the incoming store into each iteration of the loop L. As mentioned in the introduction, for simplicity of presentation we address pointers (to local variables) in this section, but not heap objects. Our technical report [11] discusses the full approach, including handling of heap accesses.

Procedure *RewriteLoop*. Procedure *RewriteLoop*, described in Fig. 5, is the procedure that performs the fix-point analysis. This procedure needs to be triggered whenever, during term rewriting, a subterm of the form $r = $ '$p \triangleright (L @ \text{aexp\_in})!$' is encountered, where p is a boolean expression, L is the store-structure representing an outermost loop, and aexp_in is an address-expression.

Algorithm *RewriteLoop*

Input: L: a loop-structure. $l_{in}, l_{out} \in Abs$. aexp_in: an address expression.

Output: L': a sliced loop. *uses*: set of pairs of the form (l, aexp), with $l \in Abs$ and aexp being an address expression.

```
 1: inSlice = ∅; worklist = {(l_in, aexp_in)}; allCrit = worklist
 2: while worklist is not empty do
 3:     (l, aexp) = worklist.remove()
 4:     t = (((s(L) ⊨ l) ∧ b(L) ∧ (x_L ⊨ l_in)) ▷ (s(L) @ aexp)!)
 5:     t_init = t
 6:     repeat
 7:         Apply rewrite rules (base PIM rules + our rule for conditions) on t. We now call the thus
            rewritten term as t.
 8:         for all subterms r of the form 'p ▷ (L_1 @ aexp1)!' in t such that the '@' operator in r is
            unmarked do {L_1 is an inner loop inside L, and '(L_1 @ aexp1)!' is a store-lookup subterm
            in L.}
 9:             Let l_{1,out} ∈ Abs be an abstract state such that if execution of L_1 terminates in a state
                that is not in γ(l_{1,out}) then p will not hold.
10:             Let l_{1,in} ∈ Abs be an abstract state that over-approximates the set of states possible
                at the entry of s(L_1) given that l_in over-approximates the possible states at the entry
                of s(L).
11:             (L'_1, u) = RewriteLoop(L_1, l_{1,in}, l_{1,out}, aexp1)
12:             Let every subterm in L'_1 depend on the corresponding subterm in L_1
13:             for all (l_1, aexp2) in u do
14:                 Create a store-cell {__ ↦ [(inStore(L_1) ⊨ l_1) ▷ (inStore(L_1) @ aexp2)!]}
15:             end for
16:             Let S be the concatenation of all store cells created above followed by L'_1
17:             Rewrite t such that the first argument (i.e., the store) of the '@' operator in r becomes
                S (instead of L_1). Also, mark this '@' operator. Call the newly obtained term t.
18:         end for
19:     until (each '@' operator in t is either marked or is a lookup on x_L) AND (no more simplifi-
        cation desired)
20:     Using the dependences from the term t to t_init, add all subterms of t_init that are depended
        upon by subterms of t to inSlice.
21:     for all subterms of the form (p ▷ (x_L @ aexp1)! in t do
22:         Let l_1 ∈ Abs be an abstract state such that if x_L takes on a state that is not in γ(l_1) then
            p will not hold.
23:         Let l_2 = ⊔ {l | (l, aexp1) ∈ allCrit}
24:         if (l_1 ⊔ l_2, aexp1) ∉ allCrit then
25:             Add (l_1 ⊔ l_2, aexp1) to worklist and to allCrit
26:         end if
27:     end for
28: end while
29: Let L' be L minus its subterms that are not in inSlice
30: return (L', allCrit)
```

Fig. 5. Procedure for rewriting a loop

(Address-lookup terms inside loops that refer to inner loops are taken care of explicitly within this procedure, via recursive calls, as in line 11 in the pseudo-code.)

This procedure requires four parameters: L, l_{in}, l_{out}, and aexp_in. l_{out} is an over-approximation of the states that L needs to terminate in order for p to hold. The pair $(l_{out}, \text{aexp\_in})$ essentially constitutes the (abstract) slicing criterion given to the procedure. The abstract state l_{in} is nothing but $l_{\mathcal{F}}$ introduced in Section 3.1 if we treat the body of L as $\mathcal{F}$. *RewriteLoop* computes and returns a slice L' of L for the value in address aexp_in, under the constraint that the states that arise at the initial point of the body of L are contained within $\gamma(l_{in})$ and control leaves L in a state that's in $\gamma(l_{out})$. The original term r mentioned above can then be rewritten as '$p \triangleright (L' @ \text{aexp\_in})!$'.

Procedure *RewriteLoop* also returns a set of pairs of the form (l, aexp). The semantics of such a pair is that the address 'aexp' *may* have an *upwards*

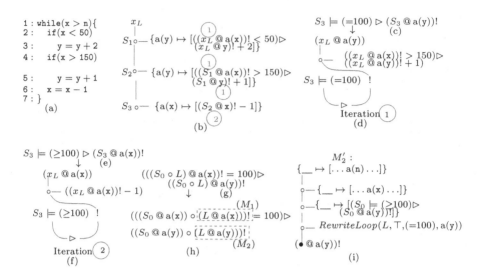

Fig. 6. Illustration of slicing of a loop

exposed use in L' whenever the incoming state into an iteration of L' is in the concretization of $\gamma(l)$. These pairs can be used to slice the part of the program that precedes loop L (this will be discussed in more detail later in this section).

We now provide some intuition on how the parameters l_{in} and l_{out} can be computed; the details have been elided due to lack of space. If $\mathcal{S}$ is the scope that contains the loop L, and $l_{\mathcal{S}}$ is the initial abstract state at the entry to $\mathcal{S}$, l_{in} can be computed from $l_{\mathcal{S}}$ via a standard forward abstract interpretation of $\mathcal{S}$. Regarding l_{out}, the idea is to identify the atomic predicates in p that are implied by p and that refer to values computed in L, and then to lift the conjunction of these predicates to the abstract domain Abs. For instance, if we let L be the loop in Fig. 6(a) (which is the same as the loop in Fig. 1(a)), p be '$((L @ a(x))! = 100)$', and use the lattice $\{\bot, =100, \leq100, \geq100, \neq100, \top\}$ (which was introduced in Section 1.2, and captures the value of variable x alone), then l_{out} could be '$=100$' (or, less desirably, ≥100, or even $\top$).

A very high-level summary of procedure *RewriteLoop* is as follows: The procedure works iteratively. Each iteration of the outermost loop (beginning in line 2 of the pseudo-code) processes a criterion, with the criterion (l_{out}, aexp_in) that was initially passed to the procedure being processed in the first iteration. Processing a criterion consists of rewriting the loop's body using this criterion (line 7 in the pseudo-code). Then, all subterms in the original loop body on which the rewritten term transitively depends are included in the slice (line 20). Then, upwards-exposed uses in the rewritten term are identified, and added to the 'worklist' as criteria to be processed in subsequent iterations (lines 20-27). We use *joins* (line 23-25 in the pseudo-code) to ensure that we generate a finite number of criteria corresponding to each address; since there are a finite number of addresses possible (under our current assumption that there are no heap objects), this ensures termination of the procedure.

Note the loop in lines 8-18 in the pseudo-code. This loop is entered if within the loop's body there exist nested loops. In this case each occurrence of a nested loop is sliced using a recursive invocation of the procedure *RewriteLoop*.

We discuss in the rest of this section some of the detailed aspects of the usage of procedure *RewriteLoop*, as well as its internal functioning, using illustrations.

Invocation of Procedure *RewriteLoop*. Let us consider the example program in Fig. 1(a). The body of the loop L in this example is shown Fig. 6(b) as a PIM store structure. The subterm shown in Fig. 6(g) arises during the slicing of this program using variable z as the criterion; here, let S_0 be the store structure corresponding to the fragment of the program that precedes the loop. This subterm rewrites to the term shown in Fig. 6(h) (using rule S4).

Consider the address-lookup sub-term labeled M_2. Since this is a lookup on a store-structure corresponding to a loop, *RewriteLoop* gets invoked, with the following four arguments: L, $\top$, (=100), a(y). We have assumed here that l_{in} is $\top$. The parameter l_{out} is set to '(=100)', as this is the abstraction of the condition '$(L @ a(x))! = 100$' under which the lookup occurs. Fig. 6(i) shows the rewritten form of the lookup M_2. Note that L has been replaced with the sliced loop, which we denote as '*RewriteLoop*$(L, \top, (=100), a(y))$'.

Note in Fig. 6(i) that three new store-cells have been created and prepended in front of the reference to the sliced loop. Basically, for each address 'aexp2' that is used in the sliced loop before being defined under abstract condition l_1 (recall that these pairs of address expressions and abstract conditions are a return value from the call to *RewriteLoop*), we generate such a store-cell, to look up address 'aexp2' from the incoming store into the loop (S_0, in this case), under the same condition l_1. The store-cell assigns the looked up value to a dummy location (denoted by '__'). For instance, '$\{$__ $\mapsto [(S_0 \models (\geq 100)) \triangleright (S_0 @ a(y))!]\}$', indicates that the loop L looks up the value of y from the incoming store S_0 under the condition '$x \geq 100$' on this store. Our motivation behind creating these store cells is basically to obtain a slice of the program fragment that precedes the loop using the upwards-exposed addresses inside the loop as criteria. In order to ensure that this slicing does happen, we need to ensure during subsequent rewriting steps that the dummy store cells created above are never rewritten away (in spite of the fact that no statements make use of the values that they write to).

(The address-lookup term M_1 in Fig. 6(h) needs to be rewritten, too, just like the term M_2 was; due to lack of space we omit this from the figure.)

We include an optimization in the algorithm, namely marking. Each instance of an '@' operator (i.e., the lookup operator) whose first operand is a loop has 'mark' bit. By default every lookup operator is unmarked when it gets introduced. Whenever we slice the loop referred to by such an operator, we mark the operator so that we will not attempt again to slice the loop referred to by it.

The steps discussed above regarding invoking procedure *RewriteLoop* at each address-lookup subterm that refers to a loop, and rewriting this address lookup subterm using the return value from this procedure, need to be done recursively inside procedure *RewriteLoop*, too, whenever address-lookups on nested loops are encountered. Therefore, our description of these steps in lines 8-18 in the pseudo-code of the procedure is also applicable in the scenario where *RewriteLoop* is invoked at the outermost level.

Iterative Analysis in *RewriteLoop*. We now illustrate the iterative fix-point analysis performed by procedure *RewriteLoop*. Consider the invocation to this procedure mentioned above with arguments L, $\top$, $(=100)$, $a(y)$, where L is the store-structure corresponding to the loop in Fig. 6(a). In the first iteration, following line 3 in the pseudo-code, we pull out the "root" criterion, namely, '$((=100), a(y))$', from the worklist. Let's call this Criterion 0. Following line 4 in the pseudo-code, we construct the term $(S_3 \models (=100)) \rhd (S_3 @ a(y))!$' to represent the desired slice, as shown in Fig. 6(c). Note that S_3 is the store structure representing the body of the loop. (We ought to have also included the predicates '$(x_L @ a(x))! > (x_L @ a(n))!$' and '$x_L \models \top$' in the guard of the above term; however, these predicates turn out to be not useful in this example, and we elide them for brevity.) Following line 7 in the pseudo-code, we simplify this term, yielding the rewritten term shown in Fig. 6(d). Since there are no nested loops in this example, lines 8–18 in the pseudo-code, which are used to simplify inner loops, are not executed.

Note the termination condition for the rewriting, in line 19 of the pseudo-code. The condition says that *all* address lookups in the rewritten term ought to be to the initial store x_L. This property can always be achieved by applying the PIM rule S4 (see Section 2.2) repeatedly in line 7 of the pseudo-code; this property makes it easier for us to generate criteria for subsequent iterations (more on this below). Note that the rewritten term in Fig. 6(d) satisfies this property. The second part of the termination condition (i.e., "no more simplification desired") devolves the decision on whether to keep rewriting until a normal form is reached, or whether to stop the rewriting earlier, to a rewriting strategy. Such rewrite strategies are not a focus of this paper.

We now revert to our illustration using the example. Following line 20 in the pseudo-code, we trace back dependences from the rewritten term in Fig. 6(d) to the original term in Fig. 6(b). The subterms in Fig. 6(b) that are *not* depended upon by the rewritten term are the ones that correspond to lines 3 and 6 in Fig. 6(a). Therefore, we add every other subterm in Fig. 6(b) to the set 'inSlice', which basically represents the subterms of the loop body that are to be included in the slice (we add subterms to this same set in all the iterations). The numbers within circles adjacent to each subterm in Fig. 6(b) indicate the iteration(s) in which that subterm was identified as belonging to the slice. (Recall that the current iteration is Iteration 1.)

The final step in the current iteration (which is the loop in lines 21-27 in the pseudo-code) is to generate criteria for subsequent iterations. We do this by identifying address-lookups in the rewritten term in Fig. 6(d) to the store x_L; these are basically the addresses with upwards-exposed uses in the body of the loop. For instance, the lookup '$(x_L @ a(y))!$' occurs two times. Consider the occurrence in the right child of the '$\circ$' operator, which is under the condition '$(S_3 \models (=100)) \wedge ((x_L @ a(x))! > 150)$'. The abstract state that x_L needs to be described by in order for this condition to hold, as computed in line 22 in the pseudo-code, is '(≥ 100)'. Therefore, we add the criterion '((≥ 100), a(y))', which we call Criterion (1), to 'worklist' and to 'allCrit'. The other occurrence of 'x_L @ a(y)' in the rewritten term, which is under the condition '($S_3 \models (=100)$)', causes the exact same criterion to be generated. Finally, the lookup '(x_L @ a(x))!' under the condition '($S_3 \models (=100)$)' causes Criterion (2) – '((≥ 100), a(x))' – to be generated. With this, Iteration 1 is over.

It turns out that the processing of Criterion 1 mentioned above has the exact same effect as the processing of Criterion 0; therefore, for brevity, we ignore the iteration that's used to process this criterion. We now process Criterion 2 in Iteration 2. This causes the term shown in Fig. 6(e) to be created, which gets eventually rewritten to the term shown Fig. 6(f). This rewritten term depends transitively on the subterm in Fig. 6(b) that corresponds to line 6 in the source; therefore, this subterm gets pulled into the slice. No new criteria get generated from the rewritten term, and so the outer loop of the algorithm terminates. The final slice is nothing but the original program minus the subterm corresponding to line 3 in the source; this subterm is not present in the set 'inSlice' because neither of the two rewritten terms produced in the two iterations depends on it.

Our Contributions over the Base PIM Approach. PIM's naive strategy to slice loops is called *pure dynamic slicing*. As discussed in Section 2.4, the idea here is to unroll loops as part of rewriting. Although this strategy is precise, it does not terminate on many realistic examples, such as the one in Fig. 1(a). PIM also includes three other approaches for slicing loops, which are guaranteed to terminate, but which are not *path sensitive*, and are hence not as precise as our approach. We omit the details of these approaches due to lack of space. When applied on the program in Fig. 1(a) with the value of variable z as the criterion all these approaches return the entire loop as the slice. Furthermore, none of these approaches handle loops that manipulate pointers. Our approach generalizes and subsumes two of these three approaches; the third approach, namely, "invariance sensitive slicing" can, in general, be used in conjunction with our approach (e.g., as a pre-pass).

4   Slicing Loops in Heap Manipulating Programs

Precise slicing of programs that manipulate heap data structures is challenging. Consider the code fragment shown in Fig. 7(a). Assume that the code that precedes the while loop is such that x and y point to *disjoint*, *acyclic*, singly-linked lists. The loop's functionality is to remove elements from a prefix of the list originally pointed to by x and prepend them to the list originally pointed to by y. Say we are interested in the functionality in the loop that removes the elements from the x-list, but *not* in the code that prepends the removed elements to the y-list. The criterion to express this is the value of variable x at the point after the loop; a precise slice, in this case, is one that contains Line 4 only inside the loop. In particular, Line 5 need not be in the slice. This is because, given

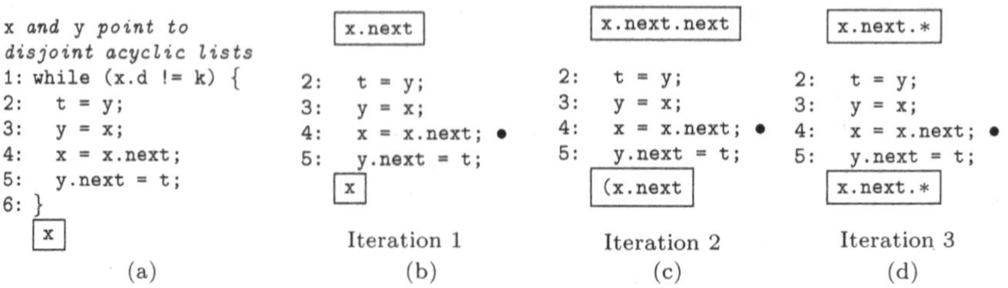

Fig. 7. Slicing a linked-list traversal program

that the lists were originally acyclic, x.next at the point before Line 5 cannot point to the same element as x itself.

Our model of heap is that it is a collection of cells, each cell having one or more fields, fields being scalars or pointers. We allow copying of pointer values, adding the (constant) offset of a declared field to the value of a (base) pointer to yield another pointer, and dereferencing of pointers. However, we do not address arbitrary pointer arithmetic, nor arrays. We handle malloc's in the typical way, by treating each malloc site as returning the (fixed) address of a temporary variable associated with that site.

In the rest of this section we informally introduce the extensions that are required over the base approach described in Section 3 to address heap manipulating programs. A detailed description is available in our associated technical report [11].

Access Paths. Slicing criteria are no longer necessarily just addresses of variables. In general, they might need to be *access paths*. For Iteration 1 in the example in Fig. 7, the given criterion is the simple address a(x). As shown in Fig. 7(b), in this iteration line 4 gets included into the slice. The new criterion (address) that we would get at end of this iteration would be '$(x_L @ a(x))! + next$', with 'next' denoting the constant offset associated with the field of the same name (for simplicity, we show this criterion simply as x.next at the top of Fig. 7(b)). This criterion is not a simple address, but an access path. Similarly, at the end of Iteration 2 the criterion generated would be '$(x_L @ ((x_L @ a(x))! + next))! + next$', and so on.

For convenience of notation, we denote the first of the two access paths shown above as '$([x_L]$ x$) + next$', the second one as '$([x_L]$ x.next$) + next$', and so on. In the figure, we use an even more cryptic notation, e.g., x.next, x.next.next, wherein the store-structure being referred to follows implicitly from the point where the access-path is shown.

Compressed Access Paths. As can be observed with the example above, access path lengths can grow unboundedly. We need a technique to limit their lengths, and hence guarantee termination, while still ensuring soundness (i.e., not missing any required statements from slices), and good precision in typical situations.

Therefore, we introduce the notion of a *compressed access path* in our term language. We denote compressed access paths using the notation '$([x_L]$ v.f.$*)$'. Intuitively, the semantics of this compressed access path is that it *represents* an (infinite) family of (normal) access paths obtained by appending zero or more fields at its end (in place of the '$*$'); e.g., '$([x_L]$ v$) +$ f', and '$([x_L]$ v.f$) +$ g'.

We use compressed access paths to ensure termination of the iterative analysis of loops. We fix a threshold k on the length (i.e.. number of fields in) access paths; this threshold is a parameter to the analysis. Whenever a (normal) access path grows to a length beyond k we compress it, by dropping its last field and adding a '$*$' instead. For e.g., in Fig. 7, Iteration 2 generates the criterion '$([x_L]$ x.next$)$ $+$ next'. Assuming $k = 1$, we would compress this access path, yielding '$([x_L]$ x.next.$*)$', which is used as the criterion in Iteration 3.

Compressed access paths need to be handled specially in Rule S4 (see Section 2.2), where address-expressions need to be compared. The intuition behind our modified rule is that (a) a compressed access path cannot be treated as being definitely equal to any other address expression, and (b) conservative techniques can be used to determine that an access path is not equal to a given other address expression.

One way to simplify address equality comparisons to *false* is to use PIM's concrete reasoning. For e.g., a(v), where v is a program variable, cannot be equal to '$a +$ f' for any address-expression a and field f. That is, intuitively, an address-expression that involves the traversal of one or more fields can never evaluate to the address of a variable. Additionally, by plugging in an abstract-interpretation such as shape analysis [13] into our analysis, one can safely reduce address equality comparisons to *false* in more cases than is possible with only the base PIM rules. For e.g., consider Iteration 2 in Fig. 7, with criterion '$([x_L]$ x$) +$ next'. The PIM rules, even using unrolling, will not be able to prove that the address assigned to in line 5 is never equal to the address '$([x_L]$ x$) +$ next'. However, given that x and y point to disjoint acyclic lists at the point before the loop, using shape analysis we will be able to prove that line 5 is not relevant to the criterion. The same inference can be made in Iteration 3 also; i.e., x.next.$*$ and y.next can be determined to be definitely non-aliased.

5   Related Work

A lot of research has been carried out on the topic of slicing of imperative programs, e.g., as surveyed by Tip [15] and by Xu et al. [17]. Most of these approaches are not about computing constrained slices, are not path-sensitive, are not parameterizable by a user-provided abstract lattice, and do not address heap-manipulating programs specifically. The approach of Snelting et al. [14] is an exception, in being mildly path-sensitive.

Various researchers [2,8,10] have proposed various notions of *conditioned* slicing, whose problem statement is very similar to that of PIM's constrained slicing. These approaches are primarily based on symbolic execution. There are two issues with these approaches. (a) Symbolic execution does not produce as precise slices as term-rewriting even on loop-free fragments[3]. (b) More importantly, these approaches do not treat loops precisely. For e.g., they coalesce all paths that cycle through loops by broadening the path constraints of these paths, due to which examples like the one in Fig. 1(a) and Fig. 4(a) cannot be handled precisely. Our approach does not have this problem, because we keep even cyclic paths distinct using abstract conditions.

Our approach is related to the predicate-abstraction approach of Hong et al. [9]. This approach takes a finite partitioning of the state-space of the program as an input, in the form of a set of predicates. It then performs slicing on the "exploded" control-flow graph of the program, whose nodes basically are the partitions. Note that they support only domains of predicates for this partitioning, and not arbitrary abstract lattices. More importantly, the precision of their approach is tightly linked to the predicate abstraction chosen; whereas, we interleave fully-precise slicing based on concrete term-rewriting in loop-free fragments (even inside loop bodies), and resort to abstraction only when transferring a criterion across a loop boundary or across loop iterations. Consider, for e.g., the program in Fig. 1(a). Their approach is able to compute a precise slice here if given the abstract lattice that we used, namely, $\{\bot, =100, \leq100, \geq100, \neq100, \top\}$, as a partitioning (recall that this lattice tracks only the value of x). However, say the statement "$x--$" in line 6 was replaced with the fragment:

```
y = m + n; x = x - y; if (m < 0) x = x + m; if (n < 0) x = x + n;
```

This fragment does not increase the value of x. Therefore, line 5 in the program still need not be included in the slice. However, their approach will not determine this unless given a much richer set of predicates (e.g., one that track various relationships between the different variables). In general it may be difficult or impractical to devise and use such sets of predicates that give sufficient precision. Term rewriting handles loop-free fragments precisely without the need for any user-input or parameterization.

Amorphous slicing [7] and assertion-based slicing [1] use precise forms of reasoning to compute *semantic* slices. While PIM also performs semantic reasoning (via term-rewriting), it has the additional ability to translate back a semantic slice into a syntactic slice via dependence-tracking. The two approaches mentioned above do not use user-provided abstract lattices to address loops.

To summarize, there are two key contributions of ours over all the approaches mentioned so far in this section: (1) We interleave abstract and concrete reasoning in a seamless way, by building on term rewriting. (2) We address slicing of programs that use pointers, and that manipulate heap structures.

Abstract slicing [18], which is itself based on abstract non-interference [6], is a variant of slicing in which one wishes to obtain a slice of a program that does not necessarily preserve concrete values of variables in the criterion, but certain observable properties of these variables, based on a given abstraction. Statements that modify the concrete value of a criterion variable, but not its observable property, need not be retained in the slice. Our problem is standard

---

[3] We omit the details in the interest of space. The example in Fig. 8 in the PIM paper [5], with the value of x as the criterion, illustrates this.

syntactic slicing, which is quite different from their problem. Note that while abstraction is part of the problem definition itself for them, for us it only a means to an end. This said, there is some high-level similarity between our approach and theirs: they propagate abstract states backward, while we propagate back address-expressions *guarded* by abstract states. They address heap-manipulating programs, like we do. However, our transformation framework is entirely different from theirs, in that we integrate term rewriting and abstract interpretation. Theirs is a pure abstract interpretation approach (on control-flow graphs), and does not address fully-precise analysis on loop-free fragments.

There is an interesting conceptual connection between our approach and the abstract-interpretation-based approaches for *partial evaluation* of functional programs [3] and logic programs [12]. These approaches target languages whose semantics is defined using term rewriting; they specialize programs wrt given abstract criteria using term rewriting, and use abstract interpretation to ensure termination. They do not target slicing, which needs backwards propagation as well as dependence-tracking, nor do they target heap-manipulating programs.

References

1. Barros, J., da Cruz, D., Henriques, P., Pinto, J.: Assertion-based slicing and slice graphs. Formal Aspects of Computing 24(2), 217–248 (2012)
2. Canfora, G., Cimitile, A., De Lucia, A.: Conditioned program slicing. Information and Software Technology 40(11), 595–607 (1998)
3. Consel, C., Khoo, S.: Parameterized partial evaluation. ACM Transactions on Programming Languages and Systems (TOPLAS) 15(3), 463–493 (1993)
4. Cousot, P., Cousot, R.: Abstract interpretation: a unified lattice model for static analysis of programs by construction or approximation of fixpoints. In: Proc. ACM Symp. on Principles of Programming Languages (POPL), pp. 238–252 (1977)
5. Field, J., Ramalingam, G., Tip, F.: Parametric program slicing. In: Proc. Int. Symp. on Principles of Prog. Langs. (POPL), pp. 379–392 (1995)
6. Giacobazzi, R., Mastroeni, I.: Abstract non-interference: Parameterizing non-interference by abstract interpretation. In: Proc. ACM Symp. on Principles of Programming Languages (POPL), pp. 186–197 (2004)
7. Harman, M., Danicic, S.: Amorphous program slicing. In: Proc. Int. Workshop on Program Comprehension, pp. 70–79 (1997)
8. Harman, M., Hierons, R., Fox, C., Danicic, S., Howroyd, J.: Pre/post conditioned slicing. In: Proc. Int. Conf. on Software Maintenance (ICSM), pp. 138–147 (2001)
9. Hong, H., Lee, I., Sokolsky, O.: Abstract slicing: A new approach to program slicing based on abstract interpretation and model checking. In: IEEE Int. Workshop on Source Code Analysis and Manipulation (SCAM), pp. 25–34 (2005)
10. Jaffar, J., Murali, V., Navas, J.A., Santosa, A.E.: Path-sensitive backward slicing. In: Miné, A., Schmidt, D. (eds.) SAS 2012. LNCS, vol. 7460, pp. 231–247. Springer, Heidelberg (2012)
11. Komondoor, R.: Precise slicing in imperative programs via term-rewriting and abstract interpretation (2013),
    http://www.csa.iisc.ernet.in/~raghavan/slicing-loops-TR2013.pdf
12. Puebla, G., Albert, E., Hermenegildo, M.V.: Abstract interpretation with specialized definitions. In: Yi, K. (ed.) SAS 2006. LNCS, vol. 4134, pp. 107–126. Springer, Heidelberg (2006)

13. Sagiv, S., Reps, T.W., Wilhelm, R.: Solving shape-analysis problems in languages with destructive updating. ACM Trans. Program. Lang. Syst. 20(1), 1–50 (1998)
14. Snelting, G., Robschink, T., Krinke, J.: Efficient path conditions in dependence graphs for software safety analysis. ACM Trans. Softw. Eng. Methodol. 15(4), 410–457 (2006)
15. Tip, F.: A survey of program slicing techniques. Journal of programming languages 3(3), 121–189 (1995)
16. Weiser, M.: Program slicing. In: Proc. Int. Conf. on Software Engg (ICSE), pp. 439–449 (1981)
17. Xu, B., Qian, J., Zhang, X., Wu, Z., Chen, L.: A brief survey of program slicing. SIGSOFT Softw. Eng. Notes 30(2), 1–36 (2005)
18. Zanardini, D.: The semantics of abstract program slicing. In: IEEE Int. Working Conf. on Source Code Analysis and Manipulation (SCAM), pp. 89–98 (2008)

Automatic Synthesis of Deterministic Concurrency

Veselin Raychev[1], Martin Vechev[1], and Eran Yahav[2]

[1] ETH Zurich
{veselin.raychev,martin.vechev}@inf.ethz.ch
[2] Technion
yahave@cs.technion.ac.il

Abstract. Many parallel programs are meant to be deterministic: for the same input, the program must produce the same output, regardless of scheduling choices. Unfortunately, due to complex parallel interaction, programmers make subtle mistakes that lead to violations of determinism.

In this paper, we present a framework for static synthesis of deterministic concurrency control: given a non-deterministic parallel program, our synthesis algorithm introduces synchronization that transforms the program into a deterministic one. The main idea is to statically compute inter-thread ordering constraints that guarantee determinism and preserve program termination. Then, given the constraints and a set of synchronization primitives, the synthesizer produces a program that enforces the constraints using the provided synchronization primitives.

To handle realistic programs, our synthesis algorithm uses two abstractions: a thread-modular abstraction, and an abstraction for memory locations that can track array accesses. We have implemented our algorithm and successfully applied it to synthesize deterministic control for a number of programs inspired by those used in the high-performance computing community. For most programs, the synthesizer produced synchronization that is as good or better than the hand-crafted synchronization inserted by the programmer.

1 Introduction

Many parallel programs are meant to be deterministic: for the same input, the program must produce the same output. Unfortunately, concurrent programming mistakes often result in parallel programs that are non-deterministic: for the same input, different executions of the program produce different outputs. Manually enforcing determinism is a time consuming, error-prone and inefficient task: introducing too much synchronization can lead to sequentializing the parallel program, while introducing too little synchronization can produce a non-deterministic program.

In this paper we propose to automatically synthesize deterministic concurrency control: given a non-deterministic (potentially infinite-state) parallel program, our algorithm will statically introduce synchronization that transforms the input program into a deterministic parallel program.

Determinism Verification under Abstraction. Direct verification of determinism requires comparing the output states of different executions starting from the same input state. Equality between states can be easily determined when states are concrete. However, to handle infinite-state programs one must employ abstraction. Under abstraction,

F. Logozzo and M. Fähndrich (Eds.): SAS 2013, LNCS 7935, pp. 283–303, 2013.

the equality relationship between concrete states is lost. Equality between abstract states does not entail equality between the concrete states they represent, and therefore establishing equality between abstract states is insufficient.

Establishing Determinism by Conflict-Freedom. Rather than verifying (and enforcing) determinism directly, we focus on verifying (and enforcing) a stronger property called *conflict-freedom*: if the program is conflict-free then it is deterministic. Informally, a program is conflict-free if in any concrete program state, parallel threads do not access (where at least one access is a write) the same memory location. Conflict-freedom allows us to reason about determinism in a local way – by using a property that can be locally enforced, we ensure that the resulting program is deterministic.

Our approach uses abstract interpretation [9] to compute an over-approximation of the possible concrete program behaviors. Then, the algorithm checks whether the over-approximation is conflict-free and if so, verification of conflict-freedom (and thus determinism) succeeds. Otherwise, the algorithm synthesizes a repair that enforces conflict freedom. It does so by synthesizing an inter-thread ordering constraint on the accesses performed by conflicting threads. That is, the synthesis algorithm *statically determinizes* the order of operations performed by conflicting threads.

Motivation. A comprehensive study [18] shows that nearly a third of all concurrency errors in a variety of open source projects are inter-thread "ordering" violations. As noted in [18], such violations cannot be easily fixed with atomicity and locking constructs. Vasuvedan et al. [28] express desire for a "determinizing compiler", but do not provide any analysis.

Over the years, there has been significant interest in automatically enforcing mutual exclusion properties in parallel programs, usually by inferring locks and atomicity constructs [20,30,8]. Comparatively, there has been little focus on static techniques for enforcing "ordering" relationships or determinism, exceptions being the works of [23,6,14]. Relationship to existing work is discussed in detail in Section 8.

We present a synthesis framework for statically enforcing determinism. The framework consists of a novel thread-modular synthesis algorithm that enables the use of flow-sensitive techniques for analyzing each thread. We instantiate the framework with powerful abstract domains such as Octagon [22] and Polyhedra [10], enabling tracking and avoidance of conflicting memory accesses at a fine granularity.

Main Contributions. Our main contributions are as follows:

- A thread-modular synthesis algorithm which takes as input a potentially non-deterministic parallel program, and "determinizes" the program by synthesizing inter-thread ordering constraints between conflicting statements in a way that preserves program termination.
- An algorithm that takes as input a set of inter-thread ordering constraints produced by the synthesizer and a particular synchronization primitive and realizes the constraints using the synchronization constructs. To illustrate the concept, we show a translation to two kinds of synchronization primitives: the classic *signal/wait* synchronization and the *spawn/sync* constructs used in structured parallel languages such as Cilk [4].

- An implementation of the algorithm in a tool based on Soot [27] and Apron [13], using powerful numerical abstract domains such as Octagon and Polyhedra.
- An evaluation of the tool on a set of Java programs derived from those used in the high performance community. Our results indicate that the tool can be practically useful: for most programs, it produced synchronization that is as good or better than the initial hand-crafted synchronization inserted by the programmer.

The tool's source code, the benchmarks and instructions how to build and run the tool are available open source at: http://www.srl.inf.ethz.ch/dps.php.

Limitations

- We note that for general programs, non-determinism may occur due to other reasons like random number generators, network or user interaction. In this work, we focus on programs for which the non-determinism is only due to conflicts.
- We focus on programs with a constant number of threads. However, this limitation is imposed only by the used synchronization primitives. For example, programs using *signal/wait* synchronization require careful attention to the number of *signal/wait* calls based on the number of threads.

2   Overview

Given a parallel program P, our goal is to synthesize a deterministic parallel program P' by adding synchronization to P. To handle infinite-state programs, our synthesis algorithm is based on abstract interpretation [9], and takes an abstraction α as one of its parameters. In this setting, the problem can be phrased as:

Given a parallel program P, and an abstraction α, our goal is to synthesize a deterministic parallel program P' by adding synchronization to P such that P' can be automatically verified as deterministic under the abstraction α.

Challenges. Any synthesis algorithm targeting the above problem must address at least the following three challenges:

- Scalability: The synthesizer should soundly handle realistic infinite-state concurrent programs.
- Termination: The inferred synchronization should preserve program termination.
- Number of solutions: The synthesizer should provide a mechanism which allows to control the number of solutions.

Next, we illustrate our approach on an example. The formalization and evaluation are provided in later sections.

2.1   Example Program

Consider the simple program shown in Fig. 1(a). Here, a main thread creates two threads using the spawn construct which in turn execute in parallel and access shared variables x and y (both initialized to 0). The conditional at line 7 executes atomically. In this program, different schedules can lead to different final values for x and y. For example, the schedule x = 0;y = 0;x = 1;if (x == 0) y = 1 results in values $x = 1, y = 0$, and the schedule x = 1;x = 0;if (x == 0) y = 1;y = 0 results in values $x = 0, y = 0$. Our goal is to add efficient synchronization to the program such that its result is deterministic, i.e., all executions of the new program yield the same output state when starting from the same initial values for x and y.

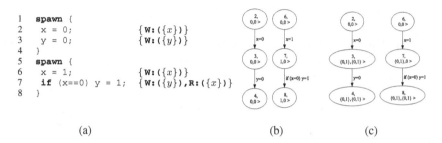

```
1   spawn {
2     x = 0;                {W:({x})}
3     y = 0;                {W:({y})}
4   }
5   spawn {
6     x = 1;                {W:({x})}
7     if (x==0) y = 1;      {W:({y}),R:({x})}
8   }
```

(a)   (b)   (c)

Fig. 1. Example with two spawned threads (a) and its thread-modular transition systems for the threads, (b) before, and (c) after stabilization

2.2   Thread-Modular Synthesis

To add the necessary synchronization, we present a novel synthesis algorithm that generates *inter-thread ordering constraints*, describing an ordering between statements of different threads. A set of inter-thread ordering constraints can then be implemented in various ways, for instance by adding synchronization to the program.

One approach would be to build a global transition system of the program in the style of [16] and use an iterative algorithm to eliminate the "bad" states (states that cause non-determinism) from the transition system. Unfortunately, building a global transitions system does not scale to realistic concurrent programs as one needs to reason about all program interleavings.

Instead, to avoid global reasoning, we introduce a thread-modular synthesis algorithm. To enable thread-modular reasoning the algorithm uses a thread-modular abstraction. The synthesis algorithm consists of the following three phases:

Phase 1: Compute Stable Invariants. First, each thread is analyzed sequentially, initially assuming that all memory locations accessed by the thread are independent from locations accessed by threads that may execute in parallel. Fig. 1 (b) shows the thread-modular transition systems for the two threads in the program of Fig. 1 (a) after each thread is analyzed sequentially. The values in a state are denoted as a tuple $\langle pc, x, y \rangle$. Note that the combination of states (i.e., concretization) in the transition systems of

Fig. 1 (b) does not cover all possible states of the original program: it does not represent a final state $x = 0, y = 1$, clearly possible in the program.

To guarantee soundness, after the initial analysis of each thread, the analyzer checks whether the independence assumption holds. If not, it iteratively weakens the computed invariants until they stop changing as a result of interference with other threads. This stabilization is usually achieved by having each thread include the values of interfering locations produced by other threads (e.g., [21]).

For the program in Fig. 1 (a), the accessed memory locations for each statement are shown in curly braces. The statements x = 0 and x = 1 are *conflicting* as they can execute in parallel and both write to location x. Similarly for x = 0 and if (x==0) y = 1 as well as for y = 0 and if (x==0) y = 1. As conflicts arise, our algorithm needs to weaken the invariants computed in each thread's transition system. In our example, the weakening results in the transition systems of Fig. 1 (c). Note that in these (abstract) transition systems, x and y can have more than one possible value in each state. After the weakening, the result is sound, and indeed, the transition systems do capture the state where $x = 0, y = 1$.

Phase 2: Identify and Resolve Conflicts. After the invariants for each thread are computed, the next step is to synthesize a repair that determinizes each conflict. Determinization of a conflict is achieved via an *inter-thread ordering constraint*. An inter-thread ordering constraint restricts the order in which statements from different threads may be executed. Using the transition systems of Fig. 1 (c), the algorithm produces the following formula: $\psi = (l_2 \prec l_6 \vee l_6 \prec l_2) \wedge (l_2 \prec l_7 \vee l_7 \prec l_2) \wedge (l_3 \prec l_7 \vee l_7 \prec l_3)$.

Each term in the formula is a constraint determinizing two conflicting statements. The meaning of a term $l_2 \prec l_6$ is defined in terms of traces. Informally, the traces which satisfy $l_2 \prec l_6$ are those where if statements at labels l_2 and l_6 are performed in the trace, then l_2 must occur before l_6. The formal semantics of such terms are defined in Section 4.

The models which satisfy the synthesized formula represent *potential solutions* for making the program de-

Table 1. Solutions to ψ

Id	(a) Satisfied terms	(b) Non-redundant terms
1	$l_2 \prec l_6, l_2 \prec l_7, l_3 \prec l_7$	$l_2 \prec l_6, l_3 \prec l_7$
2	$l_6 \prec l_2, l_2 \prec l_7, l_3 \prec l_7$	$l_6 \prec l_2, l_3 \prec l_7$
3	$l_2 \prec l_6, l_7 \prec l_2, l_3 \prec l_7$	—
4	$l_6 \prec l_2, l_7 \prec l_2, l_3 \prec l_7$	—
5	$l_2 \prec l_6, l_2 \prec l_7, l_7 \prec l_3$	$l_2 \prec l_6, l_7 \prec l_3$
6	$l_6 \prec l_2, l_2 \prec l_7, l_7 \prec l_3$	$l_6 \prec l_2, l_2 \prec l_7, l_7 \prec l_3$
7	$l_2 \prec l_6, l_7 \prec l_2, l_7 \prec l_3$	—
8	$l_6 \prec l_2, l_7 \prec l_2, l_7 \prec l_3$	$l_7 \prec l_2$

terministic. For instance, for the formula above, we have eight minimal solutions as shown in Table 1 (column a). Each row in column (a) lists a solution of the formula (we list the terms which are *true*).

Termination and Redundancy. Unfortunately, some of these solutions are undesirable and others can be minimized. In particular, solutions 3, 4 and 7 cause non-termination via deadlock. For instance, solution 3 requires label 3 to execute before label 2, clearly not possible. Further, solutions 1, 2, 5 and 8 contain redundant terms that can lead to unnecessary synchronization when implemented directly. For instance, in solution 1, the term $l_2 \prec l_7$ is redundant because it is subsumed by the term $l_3 \prec l_7$. Intuitively, this is because if the statement at label 3 is executed before the statement at label 7, then the statement at label 2 is also executed before the statement at label 7. Interestingly, solution 6 contains no redundant terms and does not introduce non-termination.

Our algorithm addresses both of these issues: it adds terms to the formula ψ that prevents cycles, and only outputs solutions that do not contain redundant terms. With the new formula (details are in Section 5), our algorithm produces the five solutions shown in Table 1(b). Here, '—' means that the corresponding solution in that row in column (a) does not terminate and hence it is not selected in column (b). Indeed, these solutions do not introduce non-termination and they do not contain redundant terms (up to the thread-modular abstraction as discussed later).

Reducing the number of solutions. Even after the filtering above, it is possible to produce too many solutions. There are three principal approaches to deal with this problem: (i) provide additional specifications that solutions must satisfy. For example, in the case of a read-write conflict, require that the write always takes place before the read as the write initializes the data accessed by the read. This particular specification filters solution 6 from the list. (ii) define criteria that compare solutions. A simple criteria could be to filter solutions that sequentialize the program when there are other solutions which do not. This criteria filters solution 8. (iii) using coarser synchronization constructs to realize the constraints, this arises naturally in phase 3, and is discussed below.

```
1  spawn {                          spawn {                      spawn {
2    o₁.wait(); x = 0;                x = 0;                       x = 1;
3    y = 0; o₂.signal();              y = 0;                       if (x==0) y = 1;
4  }                                }                            }
5  spawn {                          sync; spawn {                sync; spawn {
6    x = 1; o₁.signal();              x = 1;                       x = 0;
7    o₂.wait(); if (x==0) y = 1;      if (x==0) y = 1;             y = 0;
8  }                                }                            }

            (a)                              (b)                          (c)
```

Fig. 2. (a) Enforcing solution $l_6 \prec l_2$, $l_3 \prec l_7$ with signal/wait. (b) Enforcing solution $l_2 \prec l_6$ and $l_3 \prec l_7$ with *sync*. (c) Enforcing solution $l_7 \prec l_2$ with *spawn* and *sync*.

Phase 3: Realization of Solutions. A solution can be enforced with a variety of synchronization mechanisms. To illustrate the issues that arise when realizing solutions into the program, we selected two different synchronization primitives:

- *spawn/signal/wait*: a thread is created with a *spawn*, a thread can notify another thread by invoking *o.signal()* on a signaling object *o* and a thread can wait to be notified with *o.wait()*. Once a thread is notified, it continues execution.
- *spawn/sync*: this synchronization mechanism is used by structured parallel programming languages such as Cilk [4]. A thread is created with a *spawn*. When a thread calls *sync*, the thread blocks and waits until all of its children threads (threads that it has spawned) as well as their descendants complete.

With the first mechanism all five solutions in Table 1(b) can be implemented directly. For instance, the implementation of solution $l_6 \prec l_2$, $l_3 \prec l_7$ is shown in Fig. 2 (a).

Two interesting points need to be noted when using the *spawn/sync* constructs. First, not all of the five solutions are directly implementable with *spawn/sync*. For example, the solution $l_6 \prec l_2$, $l_2 \prec l_7$, $l_7 \prec l_3$ cannot be implemented by placing a *sync* construct anywhere in the program. In fact, from the set of five solutions, only the ordering $l_2 \prec l_6$, $l_3 \prec l_7$ can be implemented by placing a *sync* in the program. The resulting program is shown in Fig. 2 (b). Second, the implemented solution enforces sequentialization of the two threads, that is, the implemented solution is *more coarse* than what the actual constraints require.

Indeed, with certain synchronization primitives, one may obtain fewer and coarser solutions than what the solutions yielded by phase 2 require. Hence, one side-effect of using coarser synchronization constructs is obtaining fewer solutions. Therefore, this is the third mechanism that can lead to fewer solutions produced by the synthesizer. In Section 7 we show an evaluation of the two synchronization mechanisms and their final number of solutions.

***Inferring* spawns.** In addition to *sync* statements, our approach can also infer a placement for *spawn*'s. In our example it is impossible to find a placement of *sync* in the program that realizes the solution $l_7 \prec l_2$. However, if the user had omitted the *spawn* statements, then our algorithm can infer a placement of *spawn*'s (and *sync*) that realizes $l_7 \prec l_2$. The result is shown in Fig. 2 (c).

Precision. Because of abstraction, it is possible to produce unnecessary constraints. This is expected as the abstraction loses information in order to make static analysis tractable. Consider solution $l_2 \prec l_6$, $l_3 \prec l_7$ from Table 1(b). Here, the term $l_3 \prec l_7$ is unnecessary because if $l_2 \prec l_6$ is enforced, y = 1 would not execute and hence there would be no conflict with the statement at label 3. One can attempt to refine the abstraction to avoid unnecessary solutions, but in general it is impossible to completely avoid this effect.

Preserving Termination. The solutions produced in phase 2 should not introduce non-termination. However, when implementing these solutions into a program, deadlock may be introduced.

To illustrate the point, we slightly modify the example of Fig. 1: assume that the statement y = 1 at label 7 is now executed separately from its guard. Suppose that we would like to realize the solution where y = 1 is always performed before y = 0. If we implement this with *signal/wait*, we can introduce non-termination. The reason is that if we place a *signal* right after y = 1 and a *wait* right before y = 0, then it is possible that the execution of statements (in this sequence): x = 0, x = 1, *wait* leads to a deadlock. The reason is that y = 1 will never be reached (and the *signal* will never be invoked). This issue can be addressed at any of the three phases. We address the problem in phase 1 and make sure that the inter-thread constraints in the formula only use labels that are always performed by the program (defined later).

Our approach soundly handles programs with loops and conditionals, the main point here is that care must be taken when conflicting labels participate inside conditionals and loops (the details of our solution can be found in Section 5).

2.3 Abstracting Memory Accesses

So far, we illustrated the steps of our algorithm on a simple example. However, realistic programs introduce additional challenges in the form of unbounded number of dynamically allocated objects, and accesses to arrays of unknown sizes. To address this issue, we use an abstraction of memory locations that combines information from a (simple) heap abstraction with information from a numerical abstraction of array indices. Here, we briefly illustrate the abstractions on the example in Fig. 3.

```
1   void update(double[] B, double[] C) {
2     spawn {
3       for (int i=1;i <= n; i++) {
4         int ci = 2*i;
5         double t1 = C[ci];    {R:({A_C},{2 ≤ ci ≤ 2*n})}
6         B[i] = t1;            {W:({A_B},{1 ≤ i ≤ n})}
7       }
8     }
9     spawn {
10      for (int j=n;j <=2*n; j++) {
11        int cj = 2*j+1;
12        double t2 = C[cj]; {R:({A_C},{2*n+1 ≤ cj ≤ 4*n+1})}
13        B[j] = t2;         {W:({A_B},{n ≤ j ≤ 2*n})}
14      }
15    }
16  }
```

Fig. 3. Simple example for parallel accesses to shared arrays

The threads in the program of Fig. 3 access two arrays B and C passed as parameters. Our abstraction for memory locations over-approximates the memory locations accessed by each statement. We represent the set of (abstract) memory locations accessed by each statement as a pair of heap information and array index range. The heap information records what abstract locations may be pointed to by the array base reference. The array index-range records what indices of the array may be accessed by the statement via constraints on the index variable.

For this program, our pointer analysis is able to establish that B and C correspond to disjoint (abstract) memory locations A_B and A_C, respectively (by analyzing the rest of the program, not shown here). In this example, we used the Polyhedra abstract domain [10] to abstract numerical values, and the array index range is generally represented as a set of linear inequalities on local variables of the thread. For example, in Line 5 of the example, the array base C may point to a single abstract location A_C, and the statement reads from the range $2 \leq ci \leq 2 * n$.

To identify a conflict, our algorithm reasons about potential overlaps between abstract memory locations. In the example of Fig. 3, the ranges of array indices represented by linear inequalities overlap. That is, the writes at Line 6 and Line 13 overlap as the abstract memory locations $(\{A_B\}, 1 \leq i \leq n)$ and $(\{A_B\}, n \leq j \leq 2 * n)$ intersect, leading to potentially conflicting writes by the two threads when i=j=n.

3   Background

Here, we provide basic notations and definitions which we use in the rest of the paper.

Programming Language. Our synthesis algorithms are applicable to standard off-the-shelf concurrent/parallel programming languages. To simplify presentation, we assume a simple sequential imperative language augmented with the *spawn* statement for creating parallel threads. We use *TIds* to denote the set of thread identifiers, *VarIds* to denote the set of local variable identifiers, and *Labs* to denote the set of program labels. We assume the code in each thread is augmented with an initial label (the label of the first statement in the thread) and a final label (the label after the last statement in the thread). We assume that labels are unique to each thread. We denote the thread of a label l by $tid(l)$. For an assignment statement at label l, $lhs(l)$ denotes the left hand side, and $rhs(l)$ the right hand side. To simplify exposition, we assume the language only contains array accesses. The treatment of shared field accesses is similar (and simpler).

Transition System. A transition system is a tuple $\langle \Sigma_0, F, \Sigma, T \rangle$ where Σ is a set of states, $T \subseteq \Sigma \times \Sigma$ is a set of transitions between states, $\Sigma_0 \subseteq \Sigma$ are the initial states and $F \subseteq \Sigma$ are the final states. For a transition $\tau \in T$, we use $src(\tau)$ and $dst(\tau)$ to denote its source and destination states and $tid(\tau)$ to denote the thread which performed τ. A state is final if all threads are at their final label in that state. There are no outgoing transitions from a final state.

Concrete Semantics. We assume standard semantics which define a program state and evaluation of expressions and statements in that program state. The semantic domains are defined in the standard way in Table 2. As we focus our exposition on arrays, each l-value is a pair $(a, n) \in (A^\natural \times \mathbb{N})$.

A *program state* is a tuple: $\sigma = \langle pc^\natural_\sigma, \rho^\natural_\sigma, h^\natural_\sigma, A^\natural_\sigma \rangle \in ST^\natural$, where $ST^\natural = PC \times Env^\natural \times Heap^\natural \times 2^{aobjs^\natural}$. A state σ keeps track of the program counter for each thread ($pc^\natural_\sigma$) (undefined if the thread has not yet been activated), an environment mapping local variables to values ($\rho^\natural_\sigma$), a mapping from allocated array

Table 2. Semantic Domains

$A^\natural \subseteq aobjs^\natural$	allocated arrays
$v^\natural \in Val = aobjs^\natural \cup \{null\} \cup \mathbb{N}$	values
$lv^\natural \in LVal = aobjs^\natural \times \mathbb{N}$	l-values
$pc^\natural \in PC = TIds \rightharpoonup (Labs \cup \bot)$	program counters
$\rho^\natural \in Env^\natural = TIds \times VarIds \rightharpoonup Val$	environment
$h^\natural \in Heap^\natural = LVal \rightharpoonup Val$	heap

objects and indices to values ($h^\natural_\sigma$), and a set of allocated array objects ($A^\natural_\sigma$).

We denote $threads(\sigma)$ the set of thread identifiers in $dom(pc^\natural_\sigma)$ which are not mapped to $\bot$. We use $succ(\sigma)$ to denote the set of states that are direct successors of σ in the transition system. The set of threads which can perform a transition out of state σ is denoted by $succtid(\sigma)$. For a transition τ, we denote by $wr(\tau) \subseteq LVal$ the set of memory locations written by τ, by $rd(\tau) \subseteq LVal$ the set of memory location read by τ, and by $rw(\tau) = wr(\tau) \cup rd(\tau)$ the set of locations accessed by τ.

The transition system of a program P is denoted by $\langle \Sigma_0, F_P, \Sigma_P, T_P \rangle$. Every transition $\tau \in T_P$ is associated with a statement that performed the transition and its label is denoted by $lbl(\tau)$.

A trace $\pi = \tau_0 \cdot \tau_1 \ldots$ of a program P is a sequence of transitions, such that for $i \geq 0$, $\tau_i \in T_P$, $src(\tau_{i+1}) = dst(\tau_i)$ and $src(\tau_0) \in \Sigma_0$. We denote the set of traces of P by $[\![P]\!]$. We denote the first state of a trace π by $first(\pi) = src(\tau_0)$ and the last state of a finite trace π by $last(\pi) = dst(\tau_{n-1})$, $n = |\pi|$.

Determinism. Informally, a program is deterministic if it produces (observationally) equivalent outputs for all (observationally) equivalent inputs. For programming languages where each statement is deterministic, ensuring end-to-end determinism can be achieved if concurrent shared memory accesses are ordered such that the program is *conflict-free*. Conflict-freedom is a strong property which allows us to prove and establish determinism without devising abstractions for automatically reasoning about state equality, a task that can be very challenging when analyzing real programs.

Definition 1 (Conflicting Transitions). *We say that two transitions τ and τ' are conflicting, denoted by $\tau \nparallel \tau'$, when: i) $tid(\tau) \neq tid(\tau')$, ii) $src(\tau) = src(\tau')$ and iii) $wr(\tau) \cap rw(\tau') \neq \emptyset$ or $wr(\tau') \cap rw(\tau) \neq \emptyset$.*

Definition 2 (Conflict State). *A state $\sigma \in \Sigma$ is a conflict state if there are two transitions τ, τ' such that $src(\tau) = \sigma$ and $\tau \nparallel \tau'$.*

A program P is *conflicting* if it has a reachable conflict state $\sigma \in \Sigma_P$. Otherwise, the program is *conflict-free*.

4   Constraints and Termination Guarantees

This section states a theorem which outlines the conditions under which enforcing ordering constraints will preserve termination. To state the theorem, we define necessary concepts such as termination, thread blocking, and (combination of) ordering constraints. Indeed, any synthesis algorithm which operates in the setting outlined in this section can provide the guarantees stated by the theorem. One such synthesis algorithm is provided in Section 5.

4.1   Program Termination

To define that a program P *halts*, it is enough to show that every trace $\pi \in [\![P]\!]$ is finite. This property is sufficient when all states with no outgoing transitions are final states. However programs that deadlock do not reach final state and yet they *halt*. We refine the definition of termination to exclude halting in non-final states.

Definition 3 (Terminating Set of Program Traces). *A set of traces $S \subseteq [\![P]\!]$ is terminating if:*

1. *every trace $\pi \in S$ is finite.*
2. *for any trace $\pi' \in S$, there exists a trace $\pi \in S$ such that π' is a prefix of π and $last(\pi) \in F_P$.*

We say that a program is terminating if the set $[\![P]\!]$ is a terminating set. Note that it is possible for the program to terminate, yet during its execution some threads can be temporarily disabled from making progress. This can happen for instance when a thread is waiting for an external action to occur before it can make a transition. Below we define what it means for a thread to be blocked (or not to be enabled at any point).

Definition 4. *A thread t blocks in a program P if there exists a reachable state $\sigma \in \Sigma_P$, such that $t \notin succtid(\sigma)$ and $pc_\sigma^\natural(t)$ is not a final label of t.*

For example, if a thread calls *wait* then it (temporarily or permanently) blocks.

4.2   Ordering Constraints

In this work we focus on determinization by enforcing ordering between labels that execute *exactly once* — the motivation for this approach is to ensure termination.

Definition 5 (Single-transition label). *A label l in a program P is a single-transition label if for every finite trace $\pi \in [\![P]\!]$ where $last(\pi) \in F_P$, there is exactly one transition $\tau \in \pi$, such that $lbl(\tau) = l$.*

Next, we define the meaning of a constraint $l_m \prec l_n$ in terms of traces that satisfy it.

Definition 6 (Meaning of $l_m \prec l_n$). *Given a program P, we say that a trace $\pi \in [\![P]\!]$ violates an ordering constraint $l_m \prec l_n$ if:*

- *l_m or l_n are not single-transition labels, or*
- *they are single transition labels where $\exists i, j.\ 0 \leq i \leq j < |\pi|$ such that $lbl(\pi_i) = l_n$ and $lbl(\pi_j) = l_m$.*

Any trace which does not violate $l_m \prec l_n$ satisfies the predicate.

The definition above is naturally extended to a set of ordering constraints $C = \{l_1 \prec l_2, \ldots, l_m \prec l_n\}$. That is, a trace satisfies C only if it satisfies each constraint in C. We use $[\![P]\!]_C$ to denote all program traces which satisfy the set of ordering constraints C. Where convenient we treat the set C as a binary relation on labels. We use $labels(C)$ to denote all labels appearing in the constraints of set C and $labels(C)|_t = \{l \mid l \in labels(C), tid(l) = t\}$ to denote the set labels of thread t appearing in $labels(C)$.

4.3   Constraining Traces

Next, we define what it means for a set of constraints to be consistent. Intuitively, this will correspond to what a synthesis algorithm must produce as the output right before this output is implemented with particular synchronization constructs.

Definition 7. *Given a program P, we say that a set of ordering constraints C is consistent w.r.t P, if:*

1. *$labels(C)$ contains only single transition labels.*
2. *C does not contain cycles: $I_{labels(C)} \cap C^* = \emptyset$.*

3. *for every thread t, there exists a unique set* $T \subseteq C$ *such that:*
    (a) T *is a total order on* $labels(C)|_t$.
    (b) $[\![P]\!]_T = [\![P]\!]$.

The first consistency property is self explanatory. The second property requires that the set of constraints does not conflict with itself. Here $I_{labels(C)}$ is the identity function defined over the set $labels(C)$. Property 3a) requires that if two labels of the same thread appear in C (could be in different constraints), then these two labels must be ordered. Property 3b) states that all traces of the program satisfy the total order. The last two conditions prevents a situation where two labels of the same thread always appear in all program traces (i.e., they are single-transition labels), yet in some traces they appear in one order, and in other traces they appear in the opposite order.

Next, we state a key theorem: removing traces induced by a consistent set of ordering constraints will not introduce non-termination.

Theorem 1. *Given a terminating program P where no thread blocks, and a set of constraints C, if C is consistent, then* $[\![P]\!]_C$ *is a terminating set of program traces.*

This theorem means that if we produce a program P_C where C is enforced in P such that $[\![P_C]\!] = [\![P]\!]_C$, the resulting program will still be terminating. Next, we will see a thread-modular synthesis algorithm that takes as input a potentially conflicting program and infers a consistent set of constraints C. Then, we will see how to implement C with particular synchronization primitives so to obtain a final conflict-free program.

5   Thread-Modular Synthesis

In this section, we present our thread-modular synthesis algorithm. The algorithm is based on a thread-modular abstraction which over-approximates the concrete behaviors from Section 3, allowing us to reason in a thread-modular way. The algorithm takes as input a potentially conflicting program and outputs a conflict-free program.

First, we define a thread modular abstraction. This abstracts away the relationship between different threads and leads to semantics that tracks each thread separately, rather than tracking all threads simultaneously. Then, once stabilization is obtained, we check for conflicts by combining pairwise thread states and checking whether the combined state is conflict-free.

5.1   Abstraction

We define the projection $\sigma|_t$ of a state σ on a thread identifier t as $\sigma|_t = \langle pc|_t, \rho|_t, h, A \rangle$, where $pc|_t$ is the restriction of pc to t and $\rho|_t$ is the restriction of ρ to t. Given a concrete state $\sigma \in ST^{\natural}$, the program state for a single thread t is $\sigma|_t \in \widehat{ST}$, where $\widehat{ST} = PC \times Env^{\natural} \times Heap^{\natural} \times 2^{aobjs^{\natural}}$. Given a set of states $S \subseteq ST^{\natural}$, its abstraction is defined as:

$$\alpha_{tm}(S) = \bigcup_{\sigma \in S} \{\sigma|_t \mid t \in threads(\sigma)\}$$

The program counter pc of a state $\hat{\sigma} \in \widehat{ST}$ contains only a single thread in its domain. Similarly, $threads(\hat{\sigma})$ returns a singleton set that contains the single thread represented in $\hat{\sigma}$ (or the empty set if the thread is mapped to $\perp$ in σ).

Abstraction Computation. We have defined what the abstraction does and not how it is computed. There are various techniques which can automatically compute a thread-modular abstraction of a program [21]. Typically, these analysis algorithms begin by computing inductive invariants for each thread. Then, based on the interference between threads, they weaken the proof of a given thread until the interference checking succeeds. In a later section, we will discuss how this stabilization is accomplished in our setting. After the thread-modular abstraction is obtained, one can apply standard abstractions such as heap or numerical in order to abstract unbounded state (we will see an example later).

Algorithm 1. Thread-Modular Synthesis

    Input: Program P with n threads
    Output: Program P' that is conflict-free
1   compute stabilized $\Sigma_P^1, \ldots, \Sigma_P^n$
2   $\psi \leftarrow true$
3   **foreach** i *in* $1, \ldots, n$ **do**
4   **foreach** j *in* $i + 1, \ldots, n$ **do**
5   **foreach** $\hat{\sigma}_i^{tm} \in \Sigma_P^i,$
            $\hat{\sigma}_j^{tm} \in \Sigma_P^j$ **do**
6             $\sigma \leftarrow \hat{\sigma}_i^{tm} \oplus \hat{\sigma}_j^{tm}$
7   **if** $\sigma \neq \perp$ **then**
8                $\psi \leftarrow \psi \wedge resolve(\sigma)$

9   $\varphi \leftarrow \psi \wedge nocycles(\psi)$
10   $S \leftarrow SAT(\varphi)$
11   return implement(P, S)

5.2 Synthesis

Our thread modular synthesizer is shown in Algorithm 1. After computing invariant stabilization, the algorithm checks for conflicts between states and computes ordering constraints to avoid any conflicts. The constraints are accumulated in a global inter-thread constraint formula ψ. Next, we discuss the ingredients of the algorithm.

Step 1: Identifying Conflicts. As defined in Section 3, a conflict is a property of two transitions executed by different threads. Since our abstraction is thread modular, identifying a conflict requires pairwise composition of states of individual threads.

First, we define a pairwise state as a composition of individual thread states. The idea is to define when individual states can be combined into a pairwise state (corresponding to partial concretization, e.g., in [19]). For example, we can define that two individual states can be combined only when they agree on shared data, or when the program locations of the individual threads may indeed occur in parallel.

The combination $pc_1 \oplus pc_2$ of program counter functions pc_1, pc_2 is defined as

$$pc_1 \oplus pc_2 = \begin{cases} \perp, & mhp(dom(pc_1), dom(pc_2)) = false \\ \lambda t.\{pc_1(t) \mid t \in dom(pc_1)\} \cup \{pc_2(t) \mid t \in dom(pc_2)\} & \text{otherwise.} \end{cases}$$

Here, we use the predicate mhp to decide whether two labels may happen in parallel. Our approach is parametric on this predicate's implementation: we can use any existing may-happen analysis to compute the predicate (e.g. [1]). The combination $\rho_1 \oplus \rho_2$ of environments is defined similarly.

Definition 8. *Given two states* $\hat{\sigma}_1 = \langle pc_1, \rho_1, h_1, A_1 \rangle$, $\hat{\sigma}_2 = \langle pc_2, \rho_2, h_2, A_2 \rangle \in \widehat{ST}$, *we say that the states are* matching *when* $pc_1 \oplus pc_2 \neq \bot$, $\rho_1 \oplus \rho_2 \neq \bot$, $h_1 = h_2$ *and* $A_1 = A_2$, *and define the* composed pairwise state $\sigma^{pw} = \hat{\sigma}_1 \oplus \hat{\sigma}_2$ *of matching states as* $\sigma^{pw} = \langle pc_1 \oplus pc_2, \rho_1 \oplus \rho_2, h_1, A_1 \rangle$. *If the states are not matching, we define* $\hat{\sigma}_1 \oplus \hat{\sigma}_2$ *to be* $\bot$.

Definition 9 (Conflicting Program). *Given a program* P *with* n *threads* $(1..n)$, *let the reachable states for each thread be* $\Sigma_P^1, \ldots, \Sigma_P^n$ *respectively, where* $\Sigma_P^i \subseteq \widehat{ST}, 1 \leq i \leq n$. *We say that the program is* conflicting *when there exist matching states* $\hat{\sigma}_i^{tm} \in \Sigma_P^i, \hat{\sigma}_j^{tm} \in \Sigma_P^j$ *such that* $\hat{\sigma}_i^{tm} \oplus \hat{\sigma}_j^{tm}$ *is a conflict state.*

A program that is not conflicting is a conflict-free program.

Step 2: Compute Single-Transition Labels and Total Orders. Next, we show how to build a constraint formula whose satisfying assignments form a consistent set as in Definition 7. First, for each thread t we find a set of single-transition labels $S_t = \{l_i^t\}_{i=1}^n$ such that there exists a total order $TO_t = \{\cup_{i=1}^{n-1}\{l_i^t \prec l_{i+1}^t\}\}$ on the labels in S_t, in a way that each trace in $[\![P]\!]$ satisfies this total order. The set containing the total order of each thread is denoted by $thords = \cup_{t \in TIds} TO_t$.

Next, given a transition τ, we discuss how to compute the functions $l_{pred}(\tau)$ and $l_{succ}(\tau)$ (both of these return a label). Intuitively, the reason we need these functions is to lift labels which participate in a conflict and are not single-transition labels. We assume that l_1^t is the label of the first statement in the thread and l_n^t is the final label in the thread where both are single-transition labels. This guarantees that if a thread t performs a transition τ such that $lbl(\tau) \notin S_t$, then we can always find a transition τ' in a trace π performed by t so that τ' precedes τ in π and $lbl(\tau') \in S_t$. We use the function $l_{pred}(\tau)$ to denote such a label. The function returns the same label regardless in which π the transition τ appears. Similarly, we ensure the existence of a single-transition label of a transition performed after τ in some trace π. We use $l_{succ}(\tau)$ to denote such a label. A trivial solution is to use $l_{pred}(\tau) = l_1^t$ and $l_{succ}(\tau) = l_n^t$, however, we can also choose labels that are "closer" to τ (in all traces where τ appears). In case $lbl(\tau) \in S_t$, we define $l_{pred}(\tau) = l_{succ}(\tau) = lbl(\tau)$.

Step 3: Resolve conflicts. The formula ψ accumulates constraints for each conflict state. Let the conflict transitions of state σ be defined as:

$$conflicts(\sigma) = \{(\tau, \tau') \mid \tau \nparallel \tau', src(\tau) = src(\tau') = \sigma\}$$

Resolving a conflict state with a pair of conflicting transition τ, τ' can be done in two ways: performing τ first or τ' first. Since we would like our formula to contain only single-transition labels, the formula for resolving conflicts in a state becomes:

$$resolve(\sigma) = \bigwedge \{l_{succ}(\tau') \prec l_{pred}(\tau) \vee l_{succ}(\tau) \prec l_{pred}(\tau') \mid (\tau, \tau') \in conflicts(\sigma)\}$$

Up to here, we have ensured that conditions 1 and 3 in Definition 7 are enforced. Next, we make sure that condition 2 (i.e., no solutions with cycles) is also met. Let $terms(\psi)$ be the set of all terms in the boolean formula ψ. Every term has the form $l_a \prec l_b$. Then, the following formula describes all possible ways in which cycles can be eliminated.

$$nocycles(\psi) = \bigwedge \{\vee\{\neg a \mid a \in A, a \in terms(\psi)\} \mid A \subseteq terms(\psi) \cup thords, A \text{ is a cycle}\}$$

After all conflicts are resolved and ψ is computed, the formula $nocycles(\psi)$ is added to ψ obtaining the final formula φ (line 9 of Algorithm 1). Note that all labels of a given thread that appear in $terms(\psi)$ are contained in $thords$, that is, the labels of a given thread are totally ordered. As an optimization, we only need to consider cycles that do not visit the same node multiple times because such cycles can be decomposed into several smaller ones.

Step 4: Compute satisfying assignments to φ. Finally, line 10 of Algorithm 1 computes a satisfying assignment to φ. From this satisfying assignment, we select the constraints with positive truth values, which results in a consistent set of constraints that makes the program conflict-free. Note that this set may contain constraints which are implied by other constraints. This is addressed by performing a transitive reduction on the set. Such a reduction is unique and can be computed with an iterative greedy algorithm that at each step removes a constraint implied by others.

6   From Constraints to a Program

In the previous section, we showed how to obtain a consistent set of constraints S. In this section, we discuss how to enforce S in the program by adding synchronization. This process is realized by the $implement(P, S)$ procedure of Algorithm 1.

Realization with signal/wait synchronization. A synchronization method, which directly corresponds to an ordering constraint between a pair of labels, is a *signal/wait* object. Every *signal/wait* object starts non-signaled and can be signaled by a call to its *signal* method. The *wait* method of a non-signaled object blocks the current thread until the object gets signaled. If l_m and l_n are single-transition labels, then the ordering constraint $l_m \prec l_n$ can be implemented calling $o.signal()$ after the statement at label l_m and calling $o.wait()$ before the statement at label l_n.

Realization with structured synchronization. We also considered a set of constructs used in the structured parallel programming language Cilk [4]. Here, *spawn* creates a new child thread while *sync* blocks until all existing child threads as well as their recursively created children complete.

Consider the program in Fig. 4(a). Here, a main thread spawns two children threads and then updates several variables. Suppose we would like to enforce that $x = 0 \prec x = 1$, $x = 1 \prec x = 3$, $x = 3 \prec x = 2$. Here we abuse notation and use statements instead of labels for readability. Fig. 4(b) shows one possible determinization. To enforce $x = 0 \prec x = 1$, the second thread is spawned only after the $x = 0$ statement, while the thread with $x = 1$ is joined before spawning the next thread in order to enforce its order to take place before $x = 3$. Finally, the last *sync* enforces $x = 3 \prec x = 2$.

In general, as mentioned in Section 2, not every solution can be directly implementable with *spawn/sync*: either some coarsening may take place or the solution may not be directly enforceable. In turn, this leads to fewer overall solutions. In the cases when *spawn/sync* is possible, we would like a solution that allows for maximum parallelism. The same order as Fig. 4(b) may be enforced by using *sync* immediately after the end of the *spawn* statements. However, larger portions of the program will be sequentialized and leading to less parallelism. We can solve this by allowing *sync* statements to be inserted only at single-transition labels right before a conflict or right before *spawn* statements. This leads to Algorithm 2.

In this algorithm, we use a rooted tree of program threads. Each thread is a node and its parent node is the thread who spawned it. The main thread is the root node. We refer to this tree as the thread hierarchy. We define *lca* to return the lowest common ancestor in the thread hierarchy and $spawnlabel(a, b)$ to return the label at which b executes *spawn* of thread a (or a parent thread of a if a is not a direct child of b).

$x = 0;$
 spawn {
 $\quad x = 1;$
 }
 spawn {
 $\quad x = 3;$
 }
 $y = 7;$
 $x = 2;$
 $z = 8;$
	$x = 0;$
	 spawn {
	 $\quad x = 1;$
	 }
	 sync;
	 spawn {
	 $\quad x = 3;$
	 }
	 $y = 7;$
	 sync;
	 $x = 2;$
	 $z = 8;$
		$x = 0;$
		 $y = 7;$
		 $x = 2;$
		 spawn {
		 $\quad x = 1;$
		 }
		 $z = 8;$
		 sync;
		 spawn {
		 $\quad x = 3;$
		 }
			$x = 0;$
			 $y = 7;$
			 $x = 2;$
			 spawn {
			 $\quad x = 1;$
			 }
			 sync;
			 spawn {
			 $\quad x = 3;$
			 }
			 $z = 8;$

(a)	(b)	(c)	(d)

Fig. 4. Example showing different determinizations. (a) the original program, (b) a determinization by adding *sync* statements. (c) a determinization inferring *sync* and *spawn* statements. (d) another determinization inferring *sync* and *spawn* statements.

Inferring **spawn** *statements*. As mentioned earlier, we can realize ordering constraints by inferring not only *sync*, but also *spawn* statements. This is useful in cases where the programmer provides a set of threads without the corresponding *spawn* statement (or they can be only partially specified). Ability to infer both *sync* and *spawn* allows for finer-grained solutions.

Inference of *spawn* statements can produce several solutions for the same set of ordering constraints. For example, programs (c) and (d) in Fig. 4 enforce the same ordering, but they differ in the way they order statement $z = 8$ (z is a non-conflicting variable).

7 Experimental Evaluation

We implemented the thread-modular synthesis algorithm in a tool called DPS and evaluated its effectiveness on a set of parallel programs. The implementation handles programs written in the (sequential) Java language augmented with parallel constructs. The experiments were conducted using Oracle's Java 1.6 VM on a 4-core 3.5GHz Core i7 machine. The input to DPS is a standard Java program optionally augmented with constructs for thread creation (e.g. *spawn*). The output of DPS is a determinization of the program expressed with the desired synchronization primitives: *signal/wait* or *spawn/sync*.

Components of the Synthesizer. Our analysis is based on the Soot analysis engine [27]. First, our analysis computes an abstraction of the heap using a flow-insensitive global pointer analysis [17]. Since the pointer analysis is flow-insensitive, its results are sound even in the presence of concurrency. We use the may-alias information mainly to determine abstract array objects. We perform a thread-modular analysis using numerical abstract domains (based on Apron [13]). For our experiments, we used the Octagon and Polyhedra abstract domains with a simple widening strategy (we identify loops and widen after some constant number of iterations around the loop). The thread modular analysis computes the set of abstract states as required by Algorithm 1. To solve the constraint formulas we used the SAT4J solver [26].

Algorithm 2. Inference of sync

Input: Program P, a set $constraints$
Output: Program P' with added
            $sync$ statements

1 P' = P
2 **foreach** $l_a \prec l_b \in constraints$ **do**
3      $t_a, t_b \leftarrow tid(l_a), tid(l_b)$
4      $t^p \leftarrow lca(t_a, t_b)$
5   **if** $t_a = t^p$ **then** $l_a^p \leftarrow l_a$
6   **else** $l_a^p \leftarrow spawnlabel(t_a, t^p)$
7   **if** $t_b = t^p$ **then** $l_b^p \leftarrow l_b$
8   **else** $l_b^p \leftarrow spawnlabel(t_b, t^p)$
9   **if** $l_a^p \prec l_b^p$ **then**
10   add $sync$ at l_b^p to P'
11   **else**
12   **return** "not realizable"

13 **return** P'

Stabilized Proofs. The particular heap abstract domain we use ensures the sequential analysis of each thread produces a stabilized proof and there is no need for refinement. The reason is that the domain abstracts away the *contents* of an abstract object, meaning all possible interferences on that object are considered. Generally this need not be the case, and refinement may be necessary to compute a stabilized proof.

Experimental Data. To evaluate DPS, we used benchmarks from the Habanero project [25]. We slightly modified the benchmarks to ensure the number of spawned threads is a constant (all modifications preserve the input-output behavior of the program). Also, our numerical analysis and synthesis focus on a program fragment where threads can execute in parallel and interference is possible. All resulting programs listed in Table 3 perform parallel numerical computations and are meant to be deterministic. To evaluate our tool, we first removed all initial synchronization from the program and then ran the synthesizer. The questions we wanted to answer were:

- can the tool discover the initial synchronization and if so, with which abstract domains?
- which methods are useful to reduce the number of solutions?
- can viable determinizations be obtained in reasonable time?

The results for the first question are summarized in the third and fourth columns of Table 3. Except for SPARSE, running with Polyhedra produced at least as good synchronization as the initial one. In fact, for MOLDYN and SERIES, the tool discovered synchronization that allows for more statements to execute in parallel than in the program before removing synchronization.

We found that in some programs, the Octagon domain was too imprecise and led to coarser than necessary synchronization. Still, the tool produced a deterministic program, but forced threads to sequentialize. For SPARSE, we were unable to discover the initial synchronization because the program contains complicated array aliasing manipulations (an array is indexed with the contents of another array) and the Polyhedra numerical domain is too imprecise to establish that parallel array accesses are disjoint. In all cases, the running time of DPS was less than two minutes.

Table 3. Reconstruction of the initial synchronization with different abstract domains and the number of determinizations with Polyhedra

Program	Description	Abstract Domain		Number of Determinizations			
		Octagon	Polyhedra	fine grained	$W \prec R$	sync + spawn	sync
CRYPT	IDEA encryption	✗	✓	6	1	1	1
MOLDYN	Molecular dynamics simulation	✗	✓	992	72	72	1
SOR	Succesive over-relaxation	✗	✓	2	1	1	1
LUFACT	LU Factorization	✓	✓	7	4	2	1
SERIES	Fourier coefficient analysis	✓	✓	3	2	2	1
SPARSE	Sparse matrix multiplication	✗	✗	2	1	1	1

Next, we evaluated different methods for reducing the number of solutions. We experimented with the following:

- Adding a specification that orders writes before reads: in case of a read-write conflict, it is often that the write should be ordered before the read except if this would create a cycle in the constraints. The intuition is that the read should access the most recently updated value.
- Choosing orderings that are implementable only with a coarser set of synchronization primitives (e.g., only *spawn* and *sync*).

The fifth column of Table 3 presents the number of solutions with the most fine grained constraints the algorithm could generate. For some programs, this setting produced a high number of determinizations. The sixth column adds a specification to order the writes before the reads. The last two columns include only solutions, where *both*, *spawn* and *sync* are inferred. The last column contains only one determinization. This can happen if the *spawn* statements are fixed in the program and only *sync* statements are inferred. It is worth noting that even in this setting, the synthesized synchronization for MOLDYN and SERIES allowed for more parallelism than the initial synchronization.

8   Related Work

Next, we survey some of the more closely related work concerning determinism.

The work of Navabi et al. [23] focuses on migrating sequential programs into parallel ones. Our work has a different focus, but shares a similar high level problem: given a potentially non-deterministic parallel program, construct an output program that is deterministic. However, there are a number of key technical differences: (i) we use numerical domains to gain precision while [23] only relies on pointer analysis. Without precise numerical domains such as Octagon or Polyhedra, we will end up sequentializing all threads of our benchmarks. Generally, applications in High Performance Computing require rather precise domains to establish correctness. In contrast, in [23], it is often sufficient to enforce coarse-grained synchronization, as any parallel solution is considered an improvement over the sequential program; (ii) our solutions do not require ta total logical order between threads, resulting in more solutions. This is particularly important when we have a pair of threads but a solution is possible where the thread which is spawned first (but still can run in parallel with the second thread) needs to wait for a transition in the second thread; (iii) in [23], a synchronization point is generated automatically for every shared memory access, even if that access does not conflict with any logically preceding thread. This means that some synchronization may be inserted even if the program is conflict-free. In our approach such synchronization points are unnecessary; (iv) we produce a set of constraints as intermediate form, enabling us to experiment with different synchronization constructs for realizing it.

Next, we examine the technical differences with the work of Botincan et.al. [6]. Here, they start with two sequential programs (e.g. two iterations of a loop) and a proof of some property for each program in separation logic. Then, by examining each assertion in the proof, one can check whether the resources in the proof can be released. Conversely, one can check which resources are needed. Then, a thread can grant these resources to another thread, or block execution until it receives the resources it needs from another thread. Once the releasing and granting of resources is ensured, the programs (i.e., two iterations of a loop) can run in parallel. Our work differs in the following ways: (i) their approach is centered around resources, a concept in separation logic, while our approach is based on abstract interpretation; (ii) the inference algorithms are different: theirs uses logical resources and directly maps (required or unnecessary) resources to specific synchronization primitives, while we use abstract conflict states and produce constraints that can then be mapped to various synchronization primitives (as we show); (iii) their work lacks evaluation, while we present a detailed study of how different specifications and synchronization primitives affect the solution space.

The work of Jin et al. [14] presents a method for enforcing two types of constraints, called *allA-B* and *firstA-B*. While the two works share similar high level goals, the technical details are very different: for instance, their inference algorithm can introduce non-termination via deadlocks. Finally, we present a sound thread-modular synthesizer, while in their work it is assumed that conflicts are provided by an external analysis.

There has been significant interest in various aspects of determinism: automatic verification [29,15], programming models and systems [7,24,11,2,3]. Some of these dynamically ensure that the program is deterministic (e.g., aborts in case of conflicts or performs deterministic merge of conflicts, or uses deterministic schedulers). A concern with some of these approaches is that the program may suffer unnecessary slowdowns. To reduce these overheads, some techniques put stringent requirements on the input program (e.g., [24] requires that the input program is data-race free). Further, there is an issue that a small change to the input may cause a vastly different scheduling strategy, causing unpredictable slowdowns. In contrast, our approach is static and guarantees that the output program is deterministic for *all* input states. We believe that the two approaches are complementary.

Other approaches such as DPJ [5] extend a programming language with deterministic constructs and rely on a type system to verify conflict freedom. However, DPJ's type system handling of numerical computations is not as powerful as classic abstract domains and as such cannot prove conflict-freedom for programs such as SOR. More importantly, it requires explicit annotations of disjointness and suggests no repairs when statements conflict.

Program Synthesis. Program synthesis techniques have been successfully used to help programmers discover tricky details, see [12] for a survey. For instance, inference techniques have been used to automatically synthesize missing synchronization such as atomic sections [30] and locks [20]. All of these approaches effectively synthesize a constraint over the statements of the same thread. In contrast, we consider *inter-thread* constraints where comparatively speaking, there has been significantly less work.

9   Conclusion and Future Work

We introduced a synthesis framework for statically enforcing determinism of infinite-state programs. We presented a thread-modular synthesis algorithm, which given a potentially non-deterministic parallel program, discovers ordering constraints that make the program deterministic, without introducing non-termination.

The algorithm identifies abstract conflict states and then synthesizes an inter-thread constraint formula that describes ways to resolve these conflicts. Then, the synthesizer realizes a satisfying assignment to such a constraint in the program via synchronization constructs. We showed how this is accomplished for *signal/wait* and *spawn/sync* constructs.

We implemented our synthesizer and evaluated it on a set of programs adapted from those used in the high performance community. Our results indicate that the tool is effective: for most programs it managed to quickly synthesize the initial synchronization placement, and in some cases improve it.

There are several interesting directions for future work: (i) defining more expressive inter-thread constraints, (ii) extending the notion of single-transition labels, (iii) refining the thread-modular synthesis algorithm so that stabilization interacts with repairs, and (iv) designing translation algorithms that convert constraints to more expressive synchronization, also enabled by (i).

References

1. Agarwal, S., Barik, R., Sarkar, V., Shyamasundar, R.K.: May-happen-in-parallel analysis of x10 programs. In: PPoPP 2007: Proceedings of the 12th Symposium on Principles and Practice of Parallel Programming, pp. 183–193. ACM (2007)
2. Aviram, A., Weng, S.-C., Hu, S., Ford, B.: Efficient system-enforced deterministic parallelism. In: OSDI (2010)
3. Berger, E.D., Yang, T., Liu, T., Novark, G.: Grace: safe multithreaded programming for c/c++. In: OOPSLA 2009 (2009)
4. Blumofe, R.D., Joerg, C.F., Kuszmaul, B.C., Leiserson, C.E., Randall, K.H., Zhou, Y.: Cilk: an efficient multithreaded runtime system. In: PPoPP 1995 (1995)
5. Bocchino Jr., R.L., Adve, V.S., Dig, D., Adve, S.V., Heumann, S., Komuravelli, R., Overbey, J., Simmons, P., Sung, H., Vakilian, M.: A type and effect system for deterministic parallel java. In: OOPSLA 2009 (2009)
6. Botincan, M., Dodds, M., Jagannathan, S.: Resource-sensitive synchronization inference by abduction. In: POPL 2012 (2012)
7. Burckhardt, S., Baldassin, A., Leijen, D.: Concurrent programming with revisions and isolation types. In: OOPSLA 2010 (2010)

8. Cherem, S., Chilimbi, T., Gulwani, S.: Inferring locks for atomic sections. In: PLDI 2008 (2008)
9. Cousot, P., Cousot, R.: Abstract interpretation: A unified lattice model for static analysis of programs by construction of approximation of fixed points. In: POPL 1997 (1977)
10. Cousot, P., Halbwachs, N.: Automatic discovery of linear restraints among variables of a program. In: POPL 1978 (1978)
11. Devietti, J., Lucia, B., Ceze, L., Oskin, M.: Dmp: deterministic shared memory multiprocessing. In: ASPLOS 2009 (2009)
12. Gulwani, S.: Dimensions in program synthesis. In: PPDP 2010 (2010)
13. Jeannet, B., Miné, A.: APRON: A library of numerical abstract domains for static analysis. In: Bouajjani, A., Maler, O. (eds.) CAV 2009. LNCS, vol. 5643, pp. 661–667. Springer, Heidelberg (2009)
14. Jin, G., Zhang, W., Deng, D., Liblit, B., Lu, S.: Automated concurrency-bug fixing. In: OSDI 2012 (2012)
15. Kawaguchi, M., Rondon, P., Bakst, A., Jhala, R.: Deterministic parallelism via liquid effects. In: PLDI 2012 (2012)
16. Kuperstein, M., Vechev, M., Yahav, E.: Automatic inference of memory fences. In: FMCAD 2010 (2010)
17. Lhoták, O., Hendren, L.: Scaling Java points-to analysis using SPARK. In: Hedin, G. (ed.) CC 2003. LNCS, vol. 2622, pp. 153–169. Springer, Heidelberg (2003)
18. Lu, S., Park, S., Seo, E., Zhou, Y.: Learning from mistakes: a comprehensive study on real world concurrency bug characteristics. In: SIGOPS Oper. Syst. Rev. (2008)
19. Manevich, R., Lev-Ami, T., Sagiv, M., Ramalingam, G., Berdine, J.: Heap decomposition for concurrent shape analysis. In: Alpuente, M., Vidal, G. (eds.) SAS 2008. LNCS, vol. 5079, pp. 363–377. Springer, Heidelberg (2008)
20. McCloskey, B., Zhou, F., Gay, D., Brewer, E.: Autolocker: synchronization inference for atomic sections. In: POPL 2006 (2006)
21. Miné, A.: Static analysis of run-time errors in embedded critical parallel c programs. In: Barthe, G. (ed.) ESOP 2011. LNCS, vol. 6602, pp. 398–418. Springer, Heidelberg (2011)
22. Miné, A.: The octagon abstract domain. Higher Order Symbol. Comput. 19, 31–100 (2006)
23. Navabi, A., Zhang, X., Jagannathan, S.: Quasi-static scheduling for safe futures. In: PPoPP 2008 (2008)
24. Olszewski, M., Ansel, J., Amarasinghe, S.: Kendo: efficient deterministic multithreading in software. ASPLOS 2009 (2009)
25. Habanero Multicore Software Research project, http://habanero.rice.edu/hj
26. The SAT4J SAT solver, http://www.sat4j.org/.
27. Vallée-Rai, R., et al.: Soot - a Java Optimization Framework. In: Proceedings of CASCON 1999, pp. 125–135 (1999)
28. Vasudevan, N., Edwards, S.A.: A determinizing compiler. In: PLDI, FIT Session (2009)
29. Vechev, M., Yahav, E., Raman, R., Sarkar, V.: Automatic verification of determinism for structured parallel programs. In: Cousot, R., Martel, M. (eds.) SAS 2010. LNCS, vol. 6337, pp. 455–471. Springer, Heidelberg (2010)
30. Vechev, M., Yahav, E., Yorsh, G.: Abstraction-guided synthesis of synchronization. In: POPL 2010 (2010)

Witnessing Program Transformations

Kedar S. Namjoshi[1] and Lenore D. Zuck[2]

[1] Bell Laboratories, Alcatel-Lucent
kedar@research.bell-labs.com
[2] University of Illinois at Chicago
lenore@cs.uic.edu

Abstract. We study two closely related problems: (a) showing that a program transformation is correct and (b) propagating an invariant through a program transformation. The second problem is motivated by an application which utilizes program invariants to improve the quality of compiler optimizations. We show that both problems can be addressed by augmenting a transformation with an auxiliary *witness generation* procedure. For every application of the transformation, the witness generator constructs a relation which guarantees the correctness of that instance. We show that *stuttering simulation* is a sound and complete witness format. Completeness means that, under mild conditions, every correct transformation induces a stuttering simulation witness which is strong enough to prove that the transformation is correct. A witness is self-contained, in that its correctness is independent of the optimization procedure which generates it. Any invariant of a source program can be turned into an invariant of the target of a transformation by suitably composing it with its witness. Stuttering simulations readily compose, forming a single witness for a sequence of transformations. Witness generation is simpler than a formal proof of correctness, and it is comprehensive, unlike the heuristics used for translation validation. We define witnesses for a number of standard compiler optimizations; this exercise shows that witness generators can be implemented quite easily.

1 Introduction

An optimizing compiler is commonly structured as a sequence of passes. Each pass has a source program, which is analyzed and transformed to a target program, which then becomes the source for the next pass in the sequence. By augmenting the analysis phase of an optimization pass with information from externally supplied program invariants, it is possible to significantly enhance the quality and the effectiveness of the optimization.

To illustrate this point, consider a program which uses McCarthy's 91 function [12], which we write as $M91(x)$. The original function is doubly recursive, but has the simple property that the result is 91, if $x \leq 100$, and is $(x - 10)$ otherwise. Suppose that a programmer supplies this invariant, perhaps as part of a larger correctness proof. A compiler may then replace an invocation of this function, say M91(a), with the substantially simpler conditional statement: if (a <= 100) then 91 else (a-10).

F. Logozzo and M. Fähndrich (Eds.): SAS 2013, LNCS 7935, pp. 304–323, 2013.

Program invariants that enable new and improved optimization may arise from multiple sources: they may be computed by a static program analysis, be supplied as part of a correctness proof, or be generated by the analysis phase of an earlier optimization pass. The key technical challenge is to accurately propagate an invariant through multiple optimization passes. The difficulty arises because an optimization may alter program structure in arbitrary ways. For instance, a dead-code elimination removes portions of the program, expression simplification may add fresh variables and statements, and loop optimization reorders statement executions. Therefore, an invariant cannot simply be copied over unchanged from the source to the target of an optimization.

Moreover, one would like a generic and systematic propagation procedure which works for all optimizations. The questions of correctness and propagation are closely related: if there is no assurance that an optimization is correct, a target program invariant cannot be derived from an invariant for its source program, but must be computed afresh.

In this work we suggest a methodology which resolves both questions. We propose that every optimization[1] procedure is augmented with an auxiliary *witness generator*. For each instance of optimization, the generator constructs a *witness relation* between the target and source programs which guarantees correctness for that instance. We show that a *stuttering simulation* relation forms a sound and complete witness format. Stuttering simulation has several advantages. First, checking if a relation is a stuttering simulation can be done by considering only single program steps (even if stuttering is unbounded), resulting in a generic, easily implemented, and independent procedure to check for the correctness of a transformation. Second, stuttering simulation is closed under composition; thus, a sequence of witnesses, corresponding to a sequence of transformations, can be collapsed into a single witness for the entire sequence. Third, we show that a source program invariant can be propagated to the target program simply by computing its pre-image with respect to the witness relation. And, finally, we show that this format is complete: under mild conditions, a valid stuttering simulation relation can be defined for every correct transformation.

Unlike witness propagation, witness generation is not expected to be performed automatically. It assumes accesss to the optimization code and familiarity with the procedure. The additional effort required is compensated for with a better optimization that can utilize externally supplied invariants, and whose correctness can be proved independently with theorem provers.

Witness generation differs in crucial respects from the known alternatives to showing correctness of compiler optimizations. Formally proving the correctness of a transformation over all legal inputs is a daunting task[2]. Moreover, a correctness proof does not directly result in a method for propagating invariants.

---

[1] In this paper, we use "transformation" and "optimization" interchangeably.

[2] The remarkable effort described in [10] shows how much work is needed to construct correctness proofs for an optimizing compiler. As another estimate of the difficulty, the implementation of sparse conditional constant propagation requires over 2000 lines of C++ code in LLVM [9].

Translation validation (TV) (cf. [24]) employs heuristics to guess a witness relation for every instance of an *unknown* transformation. The heuristics, however, may fail to produce a witness for some instances.

Witness generation falls in-between these two options. Crucially, we assume full knowledge of the optimization procedure, as for formal correctness proofs, but define a generator to construct a witness for every run of the optimizer, as with TV. Full knowledge of the optimization procedure eliminates the need for heuristics, while generating a witness for each run is significantly simpler than constructing a correctness proof. The possible drawback is in the overhead of witness generation and the need to check a witness for correctness.

```
L1: y := 3;
L2: x := 10;          L1: y := 3;
L3: x := 20;          L3: x := 20;
L4: y := 2*x + y;     L4: y := 2*x + y;

(a) source            (b) target
```

Fig. 1. Dead-code elimination

The use of stuttering simulation is a departure from the common method of showing refinement, which is to establish a simulation relation from the target to the source program. Simulation is, however, incomplete: for instance, the dead-code elimination transformation shown in Figure 1 cannot be shown correct with a standard simulation relation, as the target has fewer instructions than the source. Our proof that stuttering simulation is complete is a specialization of results [1,14] on the completeness of refinement mappings; the details of this connection are laid out in Section 2. The witness relations defined in the completeness proof are necessarily complex. As we show in Section 3, however, many common optimizations may be witnessed with simple relations. This is because the complexity lies in the analysis phase which is used to determine whether a transformation is feasible, rather than in the transformation itself. A witness generator can re-use the information gathered in the analysis to define a witness.

To summarize, our contributions in this work are as follows:

- We propose augmenting each optimization pass with a *witness generator*, which creates a witness relation for every run of the optimizer.
- We show that stuttering simulation is a sound and (under mild conditions) complete witness format. As a consequence, witness checking can be made independent of the optimizations being considered.
- We show how to propagate program invariants using a stuttering simulation witness. The construction preserves inductiveness: an inductive invariant for the source turns into an inductive invariant for the target program;
- We show how to define witnesses generators for several standard compiler optimizations. The generator procedure freely uses analysis information that has been gathered for the optimization.

2   Transformations and Witnesses

We define the notion of correctness for a program transformation, and show that establishing a stuttering simulation relation from target to source is a sound and complete method for establishing correctness. We also show how to propagate invariants across a transformation using witnesses.

2.1   Background and Notation

Following Dijkstra and Scholten[8], the notation $[\varphi]$ for a formula φ represents that φ is a validity. For clarity, we often omit displaying the variables that a predicate depends on; thus, for instance, we may write $[f \Rightarrow g]$ instead of $[f(x,y) \Rightarrow g(y)]$ or the even more verbose $(\forall x, y : f(x,y) \Rightarrow g(y))$.

The *inverse* of a binary relation R is written as R^{-1}. The composition of relations R and S, written $R; S$, is the relation $\{(u,w) \mid (\exists v : (u,v) \in R \wedge (v,w) \in S)\}$. For a relation R on $D \times E$ and a predicate θ on E, the notation $\langle R \rangle \theta$ defines the set $\{d \in D \mid (\exists e : e \in E : (d,e) \in R \wedge e \in \theta)\}$. Its negation dual, denoted $[R]\theta$, defines the set $\{d \in D \mid (\forall e : e \in E \wedge (d,e) \in R : e \in \theta)\}$.

For a program A and predicate φ, $\mathbf{wlp}(A, \varphi)$ is the weakest liberal precondition operator, and $\mathbf{wp}(A, \varphi)$ is the weakest precondition operator, both defined in [7].

2.2   Programs and Transformations

Example programs in this paper are written in a C-like notation. For the formal framework, it is simpler to consider a program as a symbolic transition system.

Definition 1 (Program). *A program is described as a tuple* $(V, \Theta, \mathcal{T})$, *where*

- *V is a finite set of (typed)* state variables, *including a distinguished* program location variable, π,
- *Θ is an* initial condition *characterizing the initial states of the program,*
- *$\mathcal{T}$ is a* transition relation, *relating a state to its possible successors.*

A program *state* is a type-consistent interpretation of its variables. For a state s and a variable $v \in V$, we denote by $s[v]$ the value that s assigns to v. The transition relation is denoted syntactically as a predicate on V and V', which is a primed copy of V. For every variable x in V, its primed version x' refers to the value of x in the successor state.

There is a unique initial program location, S, such that $[\Theta \rightarrow (\pi = \mathsf{S})]$, and a unique terminal program location, F, such that $[\mathcal{T} \wedge (\pi = \mathsf{F}) \rightarrow \mathit{false}]$. An *initial state* is one where the location is S; a *final state* is one where the location is F; all other states are *intermediate* states. We assume that a program has no direct transition from an initial to a final state, and that there are no transitions to an initial state.

We assume that the transition relation of a program is *complete*; that is, for every non-final state s, there is a state s' such that $\mathcal{T}(s, s')$ holds, and that a final state has no successor. We also assume that the transition relation is *location-deterministic*, in that there is a unique transition between any two locations. Formally, $[(\mathcal{T}(s,t) \ \wedge \ \mathcal{T}(s,v) \ \wedge \ t[\pi] = v[\pi]) \ \Rightarrow \ t = v]$. This allows non-determinism in the sense of Dijkstra's **if-fi** and **do-od** constructs where multiple guards may be true at a state, since the successor states have different locations.

A *computation* of a program is a maximal finite or infinite sequence of states $\sigma \colon s_0, s_1, \ldots$, where s_0 is an initial state and every two consecutive states on σ are related by the transition relation. Maximality implies that the last state of σ (if any) is a final state.

The notion of correct implementation ("program B implements program A") is parameterized with respect to a *compatibility* relation from the state space of B to the state space of A. Intuitively, this suggests how the initial and final states of a B-computation correspond to similar states of A.

We give some examples of compatibility relations. A renaming transformation maps every variable of program A, say x_i, to a corresponding variable, say y_i, and replaces all occurrences of the x-variables with their corresponding y-variables. The compatibility relation is simply the conjunction of terms $(x_i = y_i)$, for all i. A different transformation may replace one variable, x_0, of A with a bit-vector $b_0, \ldots, b_{31}$ in B, while renaming all other variables $x_1, x_2, \ldots$ to corresponding variables $y_1, y_2, \ldots$ as in the renaming transformation. The compatibility relation is the conjunction of $(x_0 = \sum_{k=0}^{31} b_k \cdot 2^k)$ with the terms $(x_i = y_i)$ for $i \geq 1$.

Definition 2 (Computation Matching). *Let A and B be programs, and σ^B and σ^A be maximal computations of B and A respectively. Then σ^B is matched by σ^A up to a compatibility relation α if the following all hold:*

- *The initial states of σ^B and σ^A are related by α,*
- *If σ^B is terminating, so is σ^A and their final states are related by α, and*
- *If σ^B is infinite then so is σ^A.*

The definition does not require that intermediate states of σ^B and σ^A are compatible. We make this simplifying choice for this work because, typically, an optimizing transformation preserves sequential semantics, which depends only on initial and final states. It is straightforward to modify this definition to require matching of intermediate states.

Definition 3 (Implementation). *Given programs A and B and a compatibility relation α, we say that B implements A up to α if for every maximal computation of B, there is a maximal computation in A that matches it up to α.*

Requiring non-terminating computations of B to be matched to non-terminating computations of A rules out pathological "implementations" where B does not terminate on any input.

Theorem 1. *The implementation formulation has the following properties.*

1. *(Composition) If B implements A up to α, and C implements B up to β, then C implements A up to $\beta; \alpha$.*

2. *(Preservation)* If B implements A up to α, then for any predicates pre and post, if $[\langle\alpha^{-1}\rangle pre \Rightarrow \mathbf{wlp}(A, [\alpha^{-1}]post)]$ then $[pre \Rightarrow \mathbf{wlp}(B, post)]$, and $[\langle\alpha^{-1}\rangle pre \Rightarrow \mathbf{wp}(A, [\alpha^{-1}]post)]$ then $[pre \Rightarrow \mathbf{wp}(B, post)]$.

Proof. (Sketch)The composition property follows directly from the definitions. We sketch a proof of the preservation property for $\mathbf{wlp}$. Suppose there is an initial state u of B which satisfies *pre* and a terminating computation of B from u which ends in a final state v. As B implements A up to α, there is a terminating computation of A starting from an initial state s and ending in a final state t; these states match u and v, respectively, by α. As $(u, s) \in \alpha$, the state s satisfies $\langle\alpha^{-1}\rangle pre$. Therefore, the state t satisfies $[\alpha^{-1}]post$. As $(v, t) \in \alpha$, it follows that v satisfies *post*.

The proof for $\mathbf{wp}$ uses the identity $[\mathbf{wp}(S, q) \equiv \mathbf{wlp}(S, q) \wedge \mathbf{wp}(S, true)]$ from [7]. It remains to prove that $[pre \Rightarrow \mathbf{wp}(B, true)]$ under the assumption $[\langle\alpha^{-1}\rangle pre \Rightarrow \mathbf{wp}(A, true)]$. Consider state u and s as before. If $\mathbf{wp}(B, true)$ does not hold at u, there is an infinite computation from u in B, which must be matched by an infinite computation from s in A. As s satisfies $\langle\alpha^{-1}\rangle pre$, this leads to a contradiction.   □

A *transformation* is a *partial* function on the set of programs. A transformation τ is *correct* up to a parametric compatibility function α if for every program A in its domain, $B = \tau(A)$ implements A up to $\alpha(A)$. In practical terms, a transformation is partial because it need not apply to all programs. Indeed, much of the effort in compiler optimization is on the analysis required to determine whether a particular transformation can be applied.

2.3 Stuttering Simulation

The definition of implementation requires matching computations of unbounded length, which is difficult to verify. A more directly verifiable formulation is in terms of simulation, which matches single transitions.

It is simpler to define simulation in terms of a *transition system*, given by a tuple (S, I, R), where S is a set of states, I is the subset of initial states and $R \subseteq S \times S$ is a transition relation. A program $(V, \Theta, \mathcal{T})$ induces the transition system where the states are interpretations of V, the initial states are those satisfying Θ, and the relation R is that defined symbolically by $\mathcal{T}$.

Definition 4 (Step Simulation). *Given transition systems B and A, a relation $X \subseteq S_B \times S_A$ is a* step simulation *if (a) every state in I_B is related by X to some state in I_A, and (b) for every u, s and v such that $(u, s) \in X$ and $(u, v) \in R_B$, there is some $t \in S_A$ such that $(s, t) \in R_A$ and $(v, t) \in X$.*

The following theorem is immediate.

Theorem 2 (Step Soundness). *For programs B and A and a compatibility relation α, the program B implements A up to α if there is a step simulation X from B to A, such that (1) for every initial state s^B of B, there is an initial* state s^A of A such that (s^B, s^A) is in both X and α, and (2) for every final state t^B of B, if $(t^B, t^A) \in X$ then t^A is a final state of A and $(t^B, t^A) \in \alpha$.

Thus, checking the single-transition conditions of step simulation, together with the two additional conditions of Theorem 2, suffices to show that B is an implementation of A up to α. These checks can be encoded as validity questions and (possibly) resolved with a decision procedure.

Step simulation implies that matching finite computations have the same length. As pointed out in the introduction, this requirement makes it impossible to show the correctness of certain transformations using step simulation. Stuttering simulation [6] relaxes this condition to allow successive non-empty segments of the two computations to match by X, as is illustrated in Figure 2(a). However, these segments may be of arbitrary length, which makes it difficult to check a candidate relation.

For this reason, we use an equivalent single-step definition of stuttering simulation, formulated in [16] and refined in [14]. This requires, in addition to the state relation, a ranking function whose value decreases strictly at each stuttering step, ensuring that every maximal stuttering segment is finite. We use a simpler form of the definition, which is illustrated in Figure 2(b).

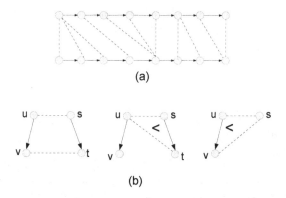

Fig. 2. Stuttering Simulation. Part (a) shows matching computations; states related by X are connected with a dashed line. Part(b) illustrates the single-step formulation.

Definition 5 (Stuttering Simulation with Ranking). *Consider transition systems B and A, a relation $X \subseteq S_B \times S_A$, a well-founded domain $(D, \prec)$, and a partial ranking function, rank : $S_B \times S_A \to D$. The relation X is a stuttering simulation if (a) every state in I_B is related by X to some state in I_A, and (b) for every $u, v \in S_B$ and $s \in S_A$ such that $(u, s) \in X$ and $(u, v) \in R_B$, one of the following holds:*

- *There is t such that $(s, t) \in R_A$ and $(v, t) \in X$, or*

- *There is t such that $(s,t) \in R_A$ and $(u,t) \in X$ and $rank(u,t) \prec rank(u,s)$ (stuttering in A), or*
- *$(v,s) \in X$ and $rank(v,s) \prec rank(u,s)$ (stuttering in B)*

The strict decrease in rank on every stuttering step ensures that any stuttering sequence must be of finite length.

2.4   Soundness and Completeness of Stuttering Simulations

Definition 6 (Witness). *Let A and B be programs with α as a compatibility relation from B to A. An α-witness for (A,B) is a relation X from the state space of B to that of A which is a stuttering simulation and satisfies the additional conditions*

- *For every initial state u of B, there is an initial state s of A such that (u,s) is in X and α, and*
- *For every final B-state v, and any A-state t, if $(v,t) \in X$, then t is final for A and $(v,t) \in \alpha$.*

It is a well known fact that stuttering simulations are closed under composition and union (see [13] for a proof). It is straightforward to show that the union and the composition of witnesses satisfies the two additional conditions. Hence, we obtain the following theorem.

Theorem 3. *[Closure Properties] The union of witness relations is a witness. If X is an α-witness for (A,B) and Y is a β-witness for (B,C), then $Y;X$ is a $\beta;\alpha$-witness for (A,C).*

Theorem 4. *[Soundness] If X is an α-witness for the program pair (A,B), then B implements A up to α.*

Proof. Suppose that σ^B is a maximal computation of B with start state u. By the first condition of Definition 6, there is an initial state s of A that is related to u by both X and α. As X is a stuttering simulation, one can inductively construct a maximal computation σ^A of A from s which matches σ^B. Formally, matching requires that that σ^A and σ^B can be partitioned into corresponding non-empty segments where any pair of states in corresponding segments are related by X. A full proof showing the inductive construction can be found in [16].

Matching implies that the first condition of Definition 2 is met by the choice of initial state for σ^A. We now show the second condition. Suppose σ^B is finite, so its last state, say v, is final for B. This state is X-related to some state, say t, on σ^A. By condition (2) of the witness definition, t is final for A, and therefore the last state of σ^A, and (v,t) is in α. This meets the second condition of Definition 2. On the other hand, if σ^B is infinite, so is σ^A, by construction. This meets the third condition of Definition 2.

Thus, every maximal computation of B has a matching computation in A, so that B implements A up to α by Definition 3.   □

In [1], Abadi and Lamport showed that establishing a simulation is complete for showing language containment after the two transition systems are augmented with history and prophecy variables. Prophecy variables are needed to account for stuttering and branching. In [14], Manolios sketches a proof that stuttering simulation is complete when augmented with history and prophecy variables, where prophecy variables are used only to account for non-determinism. We prove in Theorem 5 that stuttering simulation is complete for programs with deterministic transitions, where unbounded non-determinism is allowed in the choice of initial state. The proof shows that prophecy variables are unnecessary in this situation, while history can be folded into the definition of stuttering simulation. As compiler optimizations are performed on deterministic internal representations, the assumptions made are valid in practice.

Theorem 5. *[Completeness] Consider programs B and A both of which have a deterministic transition relation. If B implements A up to α, there is an α^h-witness for the pair (A^h, B^h). Here, P^h and α^h are augmentations of program P and relation α with respect to a history variable h.*

We first sketch out the idea of the proof. By the definition of implementation, every computation σ of B has a matching computation δ of A. As A and B are deterministic, the computations are non-branching. The stuttering simulation relation connects initial states of the two computations, final states (if any), and every pair of intermediate states. A history variable is used to differentiate occurrences of the same program state on different computations; as there is no branching, it suffices to record the initial state of a computation.

Proof. (of Theorem 5) Given a program $P = (V, \Theta, \mathcal{T})$, construct P^h, an extension of P with a history variable h. The history variable is an array that records a value for every program variable. The new program has variable set $V^h = V \cup \{h\}$, transition relation $\mathcal{T}^h = \mathcal{T} \wedge (h' = h)$, and initial condition $\Theta^h = \Theta \wedge (\wedge x : x \in V : h(x) = x)$. The new initial condition ensures that the initial values of all program variables are recorded in the history variable.

For a state s of an extended program, the initial state corresponding to it is denoted $init(s)$. In this state, the location is S, every program variable x has the value stored for it in the history h, i.e., $init(s)[x] = (s[h])(x)$, and the history variable has the value stored in the history; i.e., $init(s)[h] = s[h]$. The state of the original program which state s corresponds to is called $orig(s)$. In this state, the location is the location of s, and every program variable has the value it has in s, i.e., $orig(s)[x] = s[x]$ for all $x \in V$.

Suppose that programs B and A have been extended in this manner to B^h and A^h respectively. Determinism and completeness of transitions ensures that there is a single computation from every initial state. The relation X between B^h and A^h is defined as follows. For a state u of B^h and a state v of A^h, the pair (u, v) is in X iff the following conditions hold:

- (Reachability) u is on the computation from $init_B(u)$ in B^h and v is on the computation from $init_A(v)$ in A^h,

- (Matching) The computation in B starting at $orig_B(init_B(u))$ is matched (as in Definition 2) by the computation in A starting at $orig_A(init_A(v))$.
- (Position) u and v are either both initial states, both final states, or both intermediate states.

The function $rank(u, v)$ is defined only if $(u, v) \in X$ and u and v are both on a path to a final state. It has the value (m, n) where m is the number of steps to the final state from u and n is the number of steps to the final state from v. (By determinism, at most one final state can be reached from any state.) The comparison function compares rank values point-wise.

We claim that X is a stuttering simulation relation. Consider a pair (u, v) in X. The definition of X implies that for any descendant u' of u (including $u' = u$) and descendant v' of v (including $v' = v$), the pair (u', v') satisfies the reachability and matching conditions. This follows as the definition of the history variable and its update imply that $init_B(u) = init_B(u')$ and $init_A(v) = init_A(v')$. Hence, in the following, we focus on re-establishing the Position condition for successor states.

(1) If u is on a path to a final state, so must v by the Matching constraint. Consider a transition (u, u'). By the definitions, u' must be either an intermediate or a final state.

Suppose u' is a intermediate state. If v is a intermediate state, then $(u', v) \in X$; moreover, $rank(u', v) \prec rank(u, v)$ as u' is closer to its final state than u. If v is an initial state, its unique successor v' must be an intermediate state, so $(u', v') \in X$. It is not possible for v to be final state, as u would also have to be a final state by the definition of X, and would not have a successor.

Suppose u' is a final state. Then u (and therefore v) must be an intermediate state. If v has a final successor v', then $(u', v') \in X$. If not, then v has a successor v' that is an intermediate state. Then $(u, v') \in X$; moreover, $rank(u, v') \prec rank(u, v)$ as v' is closer to its final state than v.

(2) If u has no path to a final state, neither can v by the path matching condition. Consider a transition (u, u'). If u is an initial state, so is v, by the definition of X, so there is an intermediate successor v' of v such that $(u', v') \in X$. If u is an intermediate state, so are v and u'; hence, by completeness of the transition relation, v has an intermediate successor v', and $(u', v') \in X$.

This proof establishes that X is a stuttering simulation. We now establish the two additional conditions that are required for X to be a witness. Define α^h so that $(u, v) \in \alpha^h$ iff $(orig_B(u), orig_A(v)) \in \alpha$.

Consider an initial state u of B^h. Then $s = orig_B(u)$ is an initial state of B which, as B implements A up to α, is related to an initial state t of A such that $(s, t) \in \alpha$. Consider the initial state v of A^h formed by extending t with the initial value of the history variable. Then $orig_A(v) = t$, so that $(u, v) \in \alpha^h$.

Suppose u, v are states such that $(u, v) \in X$ and u is final. From the Position condition, v must also be final. As the history variable is purely auxiliary, the computation from $init_B(u)$ to u has a corresponding computation in B from $orig_B(init_B(u))$ to $orig_B(u)$. Similarly, the computation from $init_A(v)$ to v has a corresponding computation in A from $orig_A(init_A(v))$ to $orig_A(v)$. By the

Matching condition, these computations match, so that $(orig_B(u), orig_A(v))$ is in α, as $orig_B(u)$ is a final state of B. Hence, $(u, v) \in \alpha^h$.   □

2.5   Invariant Propagation

Program invariants may arise from multiple sources: for instance, they may be supplied externally via a correctness proof or a static analysis of the source program, or computed internally as part of the analysis phase of an optimization pass. Having a witness relation helps to propagate both types of invariants for use in later stages of optimization. Note that the propagated invariant does not depend on the ranking function used to show that W is a stuttering simulation.

Theorem 6. *Let W be a stuttering simulation witness for a transformation from program A to program B. If θ is an invariant for A, the set $\langle W \rangle \theta$ is an invariant for B. Moreover, if θ is inductive, so is $\langle W \rangle \theta$.*

Proof. Let σ be a computation of B. From the stuttering simulation definition, there is a computation δ of A such that every state on σ is related to some state on δ. As δ is a computation of A, every state along it satisfies θ. It follows that every state on σ satisfies $\langle W \rangle \theta$. Hence, the assertion $\langle W \rangle \theta$ is an invariant for B.

Now assume that θ is inductive; we show that $\langle W \rangle \theta$ is inductive as well. The base case, that every initial state of B satisfies $\langle W \rangle \theta$, holds as all such states are related to some initial state of A. Consider any state u of B which satisfies $\langle W \rangle \theta$. Therefore, there is a state s of A such that $(u, s) \in W$ and s satisfies θ. Consider a transition in B from u to v. By the stuttering simulation definition, v corresponds by W to a state t that is reachable by a finite (possibly empty) path in A from s. As θ is inductive, every state on this path, including t, satisfies θ; hence, v satisfies $\langle W \rangle \theta$.   □

2.6   Computational Questions

Consider a sequence of transformations, with respective witnesses $W_1, W_2, \ldots,$ W_k. An invariant θ for the source program may be transferred in stages to the invariant $\langle W_K \rangle (\langle W_{K-1} \rangle (\ldots \langle W_2 \rangle (\langle W_1 \rangle \theta) \ldots))$ for the target. As the pre-image operator distributes over composition, this is equivalent to $\langle W_K; \ldots; W_2; W_1 \rangle \theta$. Witnesses are closed under composition by Theorem 3, so letting $X = W_K; \ldots;$ $W_2; W_1$ be the witness for the entire transformation sequence, this expression can be written succinctly as $\langle X \rangle \theta$.

An interesting question is whether to perform invariant propagation in an eager or lazy manner. Eager propagation transfers the invariant for each stage. Since not all stages necessarily use the transferred invariant, an alternative is to transfer an invariant only when needed.

We expect that the primary use of a transferred invariant will be to check the validity of Hoare-triples under the invariant. The checks, therefore, have the shape $[(\langle W \rangle \theta \wedge pre) \Rightarrow \mathbf{wlp}(S, post)]$. This can be written equivalently as $[(W \wedge \theta \wedge pre \wedge S) \Rightarrow post]$, which eliminates the existential quantification in $\langle W \rangle$. The quantifier-removal is important as, for many logics, efficient decision procedures are known only for their quantifier-free fragments.

3   Witnesses for Common Optimizations

In this section we define witnesses for several standard optimizations. The optimizations are chosen for their commonality and in order to illustrate features of the witness generation. We consider conditional constant propagation, dead-code elimination, control-flow graph compression, and a number of loop optimizations. For constant propagation, the witness is a step simulation; however, dead-code elimination and control-flow graph compression requires stuttering simulation, as the target code is shorter than the original. Loop optimizations, such as interchange, tiling, and reversal require more complex witnesses which maintain invariants about the loop. In each case, witness generation makes explicit the implicit invariants gathered during the analysis.

3.1   Conditional Constant Propagation

In conditional constant propagation, the analysis algorithm does not propagate constants through conditional branches which can be derived to be "dead"; i.e., those which have a guard which evaluates to false. This produces more accurate results. For instance, in the example of Figure 3, determining that the "then" branch of the conditional is dead allows y to be a constant after the conditional.

```
L1:  x := 10;
L2:  y := x*x;
L3:  z := 2*x + 30;
L4:  if(3*z < y){
L5:    y := y+1;
L6:  }else{
L7:    y := y+2;
L8:  }
L9:  z := y+10;
L10:
```

```
L1: x := 10;
L2: y := 100;
L3: z := 50;
L4: skip;
L7: y := 102;
L8: skip;
L9: z := 112;
L10:
```

(a) source   (b) target

Fig. 3. Conditional Constant Propagation

Constant propagation determines a set of variables that are known to be constant at each location, along with their values. This set can be represented as an assertion. For instance, at L3, the assertion is $\pi = L3 \wedge x = 10 \wedge y = 100$. The set of such assertions forms an inductive invariant of the source program.

We use a symbolic representation to specify the relation between target and source programs. For a source variable x, we use $\overline{x}$ to represent the same variable in the target program. The general shape of the witness relation for constant propagation is the following. A target state t is related to a source state s iff (a) program locations of s and t correspond, (b) all variables have identical values in s and t, and (c) the inductive invariant representing constant values holds of the source program. In our example, for simplicity, we rename locations in the target so that the correspondence is obvious (e.g., $L3$ in the source corresponds to $L3$ in the target) but such renaming is not required.

The witness relation for the example program includes the following clause. Note that the invariant for the source program has been "folded-in" to the relation through the assertions $x = 10 \land y = 100 \land z = 50$.

$$(\pi = L4) \land (\overline{\pi} = L4) \land (x = \overline{x}) \land (y = \overline{y}) \land (z = \overline{z}) \land x = 10 \land y = 100 \land z = 50$$

Carrying the invariants in the relation is necessary to match transitions as required for a step simulation. For instance, the unconditional transition from the target location $L4$ to $L7$ can be matched by the conditional source transition from $L4$ to $L7$ only because the values of y and z are known to be the constant values. We obtain the following theorem.

Theorem 7. *For any correct constant propagation, the defined relation is a step simulation witness which preserves all variables.*

3.2 Dead Code Elimination (DCE)

Dead code elimination is based on an analysis of "live" variables. A variable is live at a program point if there is program path starting at that point where the variable is used before it is redefined. (All variables are considered live at S and F nodes.) If the transition from location m to location n assigns a value to a variable v that is dead (i.e., not live) at n, the assignment is replaced with a *skip* statement. This is illustrated in Figure 4 which performs dead-code detection for the output of the conditional analysis.

```
L1: x := 10;              L1: x := 10;
L2: y := 100;             L2: skip;
L3: z := 50;              L3: skip;
L4: skip;                 L4: skip;
L7: y := 102;             L7: y := 102;
L8: skip;                 L8: skip;
L9: z := 112;             L9: z := 112;
L10:                      L10:
```

(a) source   (b) target

Fig. 4. Dead code elimination

The result of the liveness analysis is a set, denoted $live(l)$, for each location l of the source program. The witness relation for DCE is the following. A target state t is related to a source state s if (a) the program locations are identical for s and t, and (b) every variable that is live at the source location has the same value in target and source states – i.e., for every variable v such that $v \in live(s[\pi])$): $s[v] = t[\overline{v}]$. For the example programs, the relation includes the clause

$$(\pi = L3) \wedge (\overline{\pi} = L3) \wedge (x = \overline{x})$$

as only the variable x is live at $L3$.

Theorem 8. *For any correct dead code elimination, the defined relation is a step simulation witness which preserves all variables.*

Proof. Every initial state of the target is an initial state of the source. Consider a pair of related states (t, s). Let m be the common location in s and t. Now consider a transition from t to t'. There is a corresponding transition from s to s' where s' and t' have the same location, as the control flow of the program is unchanged. The transition from t to t' is either a *skip* that is a result of eliminating an assignment of a dead variable at l, or corresponds to an identical transition in the source. Note that the transition in the source must be based only on variables live at m. In the latter case, as s and t agree on the values of live variables, the result of the transition is identical in both source and target.

In the first case, the source transition from s must have the form $y := e$ for some variable y that is dead at the successor location m'. Consider a variable x that is live at m'. Hence, $x \neq y$, so that $s'[x] = s[x]$. By the skip transition, $t'[x] = t[x]$. Variable x must also be live at m, thus, $s[x] = t[x]$ by the witness relation, so that $s'[x] = t'[x]$, as desired. Finally, as all variables are considered live at S and F nodes, the two additional conditions in the witness definition hold for the compatibility relation which preserves all program variables. □

3.3   Control-Flow Graph Compression (CFG)

The output of the dead code elimination has several unnecessary skip statements. These may be removed using the rewrite rule which replaces `skip;S` by `S`, for any statement S. This compresses the control flow graph of the program. Other instances of compression may occur in the following situations: (1) a sequence such as `goto L1; L1:S` is replaced with `L1:S`, or (2) the sequence `S1;S2` replaces the sequence `S1;if (C) skip else skip;S2`. In each case, the target program is shorter than the source. There cannot, therefore, be a step simulation witness; it is necessary to introduce stuttering.

The general witness definition relates a target state t to a source state s if for all $v \neq \pi$, $s[v] = t[v]$ and either $s[\pi] = t[\pi]$ or $s[\pi]$ lies on a linear chain of skip statements starting from $s[\pi]$ in the source graph. For our example, the witness relation connects $L1$ in the target to $\{L1, L2, L3, L4\}$ in the source, and $L7$ to $\{L7, L8\}$, while $L9$ and $L10$ are connected to $L9$ and $L10$, respectively.

As for the ranking, note that every *skip*-sequence occurs in the same basic block. Hence, we can assign a rank to each stuttering pair that measures its distance from the end of the source *skip*-sequence, while non-stuttering pairs are given a sufficiently high rank. Thus, one possible ranking is $(L1, L1) \mapsto 3$, $(L1, L2) \mapsto 2$, $(L1, L3) \mapsto 1$, $(L1, L4) \mapsto 0$, $(L7, L7) \mapsto 3$, $(L7, L8) \mapsto 2$, $(L9, L9) \mapsto 3$, and $(L10, L10) \mapsto 3$.

```
L1: x := 10;
L2: skip;
L3: skip;
L4: skip;
L7: y := 102;              L1: x := 10;
L8: skip;                  L7: y := 102;
L9: z := 112;              L9: z := 112;
L10:                       L10:
```

(a) source   (b) target

Fig. 5. Control-Flow-Graph compression

Theorem 9. *For a correct control-flow graph compression, the defined relation is a stuttering simulation witness which preserves all variables.*

Proof. (Sketch)Suppose that target state t is related to source state s. Then location $s[\pi]$ is on a linear chain of skip statements from $t[\pi]$ in the source graph. This chain must be of bounded length; the distance to the end of the chain provides the rank function needed for the stuttering simulation proof. A transition from t is matched either by a transition from s, or by a stuttering skip transition from s to s', where s' and t are matched by the witness while the rank decreases along the step. The two additional conditions of the witness definition hold for the compatibility relation which preserves all program variables.   □

As stuttering simulations are closed under composition, the witnesses for constant propagation, dead-code elimination, and control-flow graph compression can be composed to form a single witness for the transformation from the program in Figure 3(a) to the program in Figure 5(b).

4   Reordering Transformations

A *reordering transformation* is a program transformation that merely changes the order of execution of the code, without adding or deleting any executions of any statement [2]. It preserves a dependence if it preserves the relative execution order of the source and target of that dependence, and thus preserves the meaning of the program. Reordering transformations include many loop optimizations including fusion, distribution, interchange, and tiling.

A generic loop can be described by the statement "**for** $i \in \mathcal{I}$ **by** $\prec_{\mathcal{I}}$ **do** B(i)" where i is the loop induction variable and $\mathcal{I}$ is the set of the values assumed by i through the different iterations of the loop. The set $\mathcal{I}$ can typically be characterized by a set of linear inequalities.

4.1   Loop Invariant Code Motion

This is a simple reordering transformation, also referred to as "hoisting" or "scalar promotion". In it, a statement (or a group of statements) in the loop body B(i) that does not depend on any of the loop iterations is taken out of the loop body. See for example Fig. 6, which is a simplified version of an example from [15]. The assignments to a and c are not dependent on any statement in the loop body. Moreover, the loop body is executed at least once. These facts can be established by a static dependency analysis. Therefore, the two assignments may be moved before the loop without changing the overall semantics.

The stuttering simulation maps the first few statements of the target program ($L1, L12, L13$) and the first iteration of the target loop into the first iteration of the source loop. This requires stuttering, as there are more instructions in the target program segment than in the source program segment. The corresponding symbolic (stuttering simulation) matching may thus include $(\pi = L5) \wedge (\overline{\pi} = L5) \wedge (i = \overline{i}) \wedge (a = \overline{a}) \wedge (b = \overline{b}) \wedge (c = \overline{c}) \wedge (i = 1) \wedge (a = 3) \wedge (b = 2) \wedge (c = 2)$. From the second iteration onwards, the two loops are linked in a step simulation as, by that stage, the values of a, b, and c are established as identical constants in both programs. This pattern, of matching up the first iterations of the loops using a stuttering simulation, while subsequent iterations are in a step simulation, applies to the general instance of loop invariant code motion. For these iterations, the matching may include $(\pi = L5) \wedge (\overline{\pi} = L5) \wedge (i = \overline{i}) \wedge (a = \overline{a}) \wedge (b = \overline{b}) \wedge (c = \overline{c}) \wedge (d = \overline{d}) \wedge (i > 1) \wedge (a = 3) \wedge (b = 2) \wedge (c = 2)$. An alternative treatment of this transformation can be found in [23].

```
L1:   b := 2;                              L1:    b := 2;
L2:   for i=1 to 100 do{                   L12:   a := 3;
L3:       a := b + 1;                      L13:   c := 2;
L4:       c := 2;                          L2:    for i=1 to 100 do{
L5:       d := (i mod 2) * c;}             L5:        d := (i mod 2) * 2;}
L6:                                        L6:
```

(a) source   (b) target

Fig. 6. Loop Invariant Code Motion

4.2   Loop Reordering Transformations

"Loop transformations" usually refer to a group of transformations that reorder the loop bodies themselves, rather than the statements inside the loop body, and have the generic form:

$$\textbf{for } i \in \mathcal{I} \textbf{ by } \prec_{\mathcal{I}} \textbf{ do } \text{B}(i) \quad \Longrightarrow \quad \textbf{for } j \in \mathcal{J} \textbf{ by } \prec_{\mathcal{J}} \textbf{ do } \text{B}(F(j)) \qquad (1)$$

In such a transformation, we may possibly change the domain of the loop indices from $\mathcal{I}$ to $\mathcal{J}$, the names of loop indices from i to j, and possibly introduce an additional linear transformation in the loop's body, changing it from the source B(i) to the target body B($F(j)$). An example of such a transformation is *loop reversal*, that can be described as

$$\textbf{for } i = 1 \textbf{ to } N \textbf{ do } B(i) \quad \Longrightarrow \quad \textbf{for } j = N \textbf{ to } 1 \textbf{ (by } -1) \textbf{ do } B(j)$$

Here $\mathcal{I} = \mathcal{J} = [1..N]$, the transformation F is the identity, and the two orders are given by $i_1 \prec_{\mathcal{I}} i_2 \iff i_1 < i_2$ and $j_1 \prec_{\mathcal{J}} j_2 \iff j_1 > j_2$, respectively. Since we expect the source and target programs to execute the same instances of the loop's body (possibly in a different order), the mapping $F : \mathcal{J} \mapsto \mathcal{I}$ is a bijection from $\mathcal{J}$ to $\mathcal{I}$.

The work in [24] includes a comprehensive table of common loop transformations expressed in this form. There, "structure preserving" and "reordering" transformations are treated differently, here we claim that witnesses allow for uniform treatment of the two types of transformations. There, it is shown that the following *commutation conditions* suffice for a correct loop transformation:

1. The mapping F is a bijection from $\mathcal{J}$ onto $\mathcal{I}$.
2. For every $i_1 \prec_{\mathcal{I}} i_2$ such that $F^{-1}(i_2) \prec_{\mathcal{J}} F^{-1}(i_1)$, $B(i_1); B(i_2) \sim B(i_2); B(i_1)$.

Establishing simulation iteration by iteration may be difficult (perhaps even useless at times); the commutation conditions are sufficient to establish stuttering simulation for states before and after the loop body. Propagation of inner loop invariants, however, may be beneficial to perform further optimizations. While a general scheme for establishing such a transformation may require complex logics and reasoning, in many cases the obvious scheme — of replacing a source invariant $\varphi(i)$ by its counterpart $F^{-1}(\varphi(i))$ — is correct. For example, consider the programs in Fig. 7 and let AssertionA be the assertion $\varphi_A(i)$: $sum = \sum_{k=1}^{i-1} a[i]$. Since for every $i = 1, \ldots, N$, $F^{-1}(i) = N - j + 1$, we replace $k = 1$ with $k = N - 1 + 1 = N$, $i - 1$ with $F^{-1}(i - 1) = N - j$, and $a[i]$ with $a[j]$ to obtain $\varphi_B(j)$: $sum = \sum_{k=N-j}^{N} a[k]$ for AssertionB.

```
BO                                         BO
L1:   sum := 0;                            L1:   sum := 0;
B1    {sum = 0}                            B1    {sum = 0}
L2:       for i=1 to N do{                 L2:       for j=N to 1 by (-1) do{
****AssertionA                             ****AssertionB
L3:         sum := sum + a[i];}            L3:         sum := sum + a[j];}
B2                                         B2
L4:                                        L4:

(a) source                                 (b) target
```

Fig. 7. Vector summation reversal

5   Discussion, Conclusions, and Related Work

Ensuring the correctness of program transformations – in particular, compiler optimizations – is a long-standing research problem. In [11], Leroy gives a nice technical and historical view of approaches to this question. A primary approach is to formally prove each transformation correct, over all legal input programs. This is done, for example, in the CompCert project [10], and in [5], which derives and proves correct optimizations using denotational semantics and a relational version of Hoare's logic. However, formal verification of a full-fledged optimizing compiler, as one would verify any other large program, is often infeasible, due to its size, evolution over time, and, possibly, proprietary considerations. *Translation Validation* offers an alternative to full verification. The idea is to construct a *validating tool* which, after every run of the compiler, formally confirms that the target code produced is a correct translation of the source program. (Proof-carrying code [19] is related but certifies specific properties of programs.) A primary assumption of this approach is that the validator has limited knowledge of the transformation process. Hence, a variety of methods for translation validation arise (cf. [20,18,21,23,24,22]), each making choices between the flexibility of the program syntax and the set of possible optimizations that are handled. As details of the optimization are assumed to be unknown, each method employs heuristics to set up an inductive correctness proof for a run of the optimizer. This approach is, therefore, naturally limited in its reach by the heuristics that are used to compute a correctness proof.

More recently, [4] study *certificate translation*, which transforms a correctness proof of a source program into a correctness proof of the program's transformation, and *certificate analysis*, which transforms a proof of correctness from one formalism into another. In [3], a method for proving semantic equivalence programs based on relational Hoare logic is presented. While there are similarities to our use of stuttering simulation relations as witnesses, the general thrust is closer to translation validation rather than witness generation, and has similar limitations.

Our approach, while close to translation validation, differs crucially in that it supposes that the optimization procedure is known and can be examined and augmented. Hence, we suppose that the optimization procedure can be augmented with a witness generator which produces witnesses which are checked – as in the translation validation – at run-time. As the optimization process is visible to the witness generator, the generator is able to make use of auxiliary invariants derived by the optimizer in order to produce a witness. This implies that witness generation is, in principle, applicable to any optimization. The particular form of witness that is considered here ensures that it is complete; hence, a witness checker may be written once and reused for the witnesses produced by a variety of transformations. The completeness result applies to deterministic programs. This may seem like a limitation; however, program optimizations are, for the most part, applied to deterministic sections of code, although the full program may have non-determinism from inputs and thread-level scheduling.

In practice, limits may arise from the complexity of the witness relation that must be produced. For instance, the logics needed to express the witness may not have decision procedures, so that fully automated witness checking is not possible. However, in several cases – a selection of which is presented in Section 3 – witnesses can be expressed in terms of simple logics which are solvable using current SMT solvers. An interesting question, which we plan to address in future work, is the extent to which specialized forms of witnesses may be generated for efficient checking.

We also state and provide a solution for the problem of invariant propagation. This is prompted by recent (ongoing) work to crowd-sourced formal verification, which will enable an application to use manually generated invariants to enhance and extend compiler optimizations. However, one need not rely solely on crowd-sourcing or expert intervention for invariants; sound static analysis tools often produce deep invariants for program code, especially loops, which are not uncovered by the quick analysis carried out inside a compiler.

Invariant propagation is a special case of the proof propagation that is discussed in [17]; however, that work considers only propagation of inductive invariants through a step simulation. Theorem 6 extends the propagation result to general invariants and stuttering simulation. While invariant propagation of a kind is standard in optimizing compilers (e.g., the results of a points-to analysis on the source program may be used in several subsequent optimizations), to the best of our knowledge, the problem of invariant propagation had not been addressed in the general form discussed here. An interesting practical issue with invariant propagation is whether it should be performed in an eager or lazy manner, as discussed briefly in Section 2.5.

In this paper, we have considered a simple, procedure-free model of programs. A large number of standard optimizations fit this model. Extending witness generation and checking to inter-procedural optimizations is a topic of ongoing work. In current work, we are developing witness generators for several of the commonly applied optimization routines in LLVM [9], using SMT solvers to check the correctness of the generated witnesses.

Acknowledgements. This material is based on research sponsored by DARPA under agreement number FA8750-12-C-0166. The U.S. Government is authorized to reproduce and distribute reprints for Governmental purposes notwithstanding any copyright notation thereon. The views and conclusions contained herein are those of the authors and should not be interpreted as necessarily representing the official policies or endorsements, either expressed or implied, of DARPA or the U.S. Government.

References

1. Abadi, M., Lamport, L.: The existence of refinement mappings. Theor. Comput. Sci. 82(2), 253–284 (1991)
2. Allen, R., Kennedy, K.: Optimizing Compilers for Modern Architectures. Morgan Kaufmann (2002)
3. Barthe, G., Crespo, J.M., Kunz, C.: Beyond 2-safety: Asymmetric product programs for relational program verification. In: Artemov, S., Nerode, A. (eds.) LFCS 2013. LNCS, vol. 7734, pp. 29–43. Springer, Heidelberg (2013)
4. Barthe, G., Kunz, C.: An abstract model of certificate translation. ACM Trans. Program. Lang. Syst. 33(4), 13 (2011)

5. Benton, N.: Simple relational correctness proofs for static analyses and program transformations. In: POPL, pp. 14–25 (2004)

6. Browne, M.C., Clarke, E.M., Grumberg, O.: Reasoning about networks with many identical finite state processes. Inf. Comput. 81(1), 13–31 (1989)

7. Dijkstra, E.: Guarded commands, nondeterminacy, and formal derivation of programs. CACM 18(8) (1975)

8. Dijkstra, E., Scholten, C.: Predicate Calculus and Program Semantics. Springer (1990)

9. Lattner, C., Adve, V.S.: LLVM: A compilation framework for lifelong program analysis & transformation. In: CGO, pp. 75–88 (2004), Webpage at llvm.org

10. Leroy, X.: Formal certification of a compiler back-end or: programming a compiler with a proof assistant. In: POPL, pp. 42–54. ACM (2006)

11. Leroy, X.: Formal verification of a realistic compiler. Commun. ACM 52(7), 107–115 (2009)

12. Manna, Z., McCarthy, J.: Properties of programs and partial function logic. Journal of Machine Intelligence 5 (1970)

13. Manolios, P.: Mechanical Verification of Reactive Systems. PhD thesis, University of Texas at Austin (2001)

14. Manolios, P.: A compositional theory of refinement for branching time. In: Geist, D., Tronci, E. (eds.) CHARME 2003. LNCS, vol. 2860, pp. 304–318. Springer, Heidelberg (2003)

15. Muchnick, S.: Advanced Compiler Design & Implementation. Morgan Kaufmann, San Francisco (1997)

16. Namjoshi, K.S.: A simple characterization of stuttering bisimulation. In: Ramesh, S., Sivakumar, G. (eds.) FST TCS 1997. LNCS, vol. 1346, pp. 284–296. Springer, Heidelberg (1997)

17. Namjoshi, K.S.: Lifting temporal proofs through abstractions. In: Zuck, L.D., Attie, P.C., Cortesi, A., Mukhopadhyay, S. (eds.) VMCAI 2003. LNCS, vol. 2575, pp. 174–188. Springer, Heidelberg (2002)

18. Necula, G.: Translation validation of an optimizing compiler. In: Proceedings of the ACM SIGPLAN Conference on Principles of Programming Languages Design and Implementation, PLDI 2000, pp. 83–95 (2000)

19. Necula, G.C., Lee, P.: Safe kernel extensions without run-time checking. In: OSDI, pp. 229–243. ACM (1996)

20. Pnueli, A., Siegel, M., Shtrichman, O.: The code validation tool (CVT)- automatic verification of a compilation process. Software Tools for Technology Transfer 2(2), 192–201 (1998)

21. Rinard, M., Marinov, D.: Credible compilation with pointers. In: Proceedings of the Run-Time Result Verification Workshop (July 2000)

22. Tristan, J.-B., Govereau, P., Morrisett, G.: Evaluating value-graph translation validation for LLVM. In: PLDI, pp. 295–305 (2011)

23. Zuck, L.D., Pnueli, A., Goldberg, B.: Voc: A methodology for the translation validation of optimizing compilers. J. UCS 9(3), 223–247 (2003)

24. Zuck, L.D., Pnueli, A., Goldberg, B., Barrett, C.W., Fang, Y., Hu, Y.: Translation and run-time validation of loop transformations. Formal Methods in System Design 27(3), 335–360 (2005)

Formal Verification of a C Value Analysis Based on Abstract Interpretation*

Sandrine Blazy[1], Vincent Laporte[1], André Maroneze[1], and David Pichardie[2]

[1] IRISA - Université Rennes 1
[2] Harvard University / INRIA

Abstract. Static analyzers based on abstract interpretation are complex pieces of software implementing delicate algorithms. Even if static analysis techniques are well understood, their implementation on real languages is still error-prone.

This paper presents a formal verification using the Coq proof assistant: a formalization of a value analysis (based on abstract interpretation), and a soundness proof of the value analysis. The formalization relies on generic interfaces. The mechanized proof is facilitated by a translation validation of a Bourdoncle fixpoint iterator.

The work has been integrated into the CompCert verified C-compiler. Our verified analysis directly operates over an intermediate language of the compiler having the same expressiveness as C. The automatic extraction of our value analysis into OCaml yields a program with competitive results, obtained from experiments on a number of benchmarks and comparisons with the Frama-C tool.

1 Introduction

Over the last decade, significant progress has been made in developing tools to support mathematical and program-analytic reasoning. Proof assistants like ACL2, Coq, HOL, Isabelle and PVS are now successfully applied both in mathematics (e.g., a mechanized proof of the 4-colour theorem [15] and of the Feit-Thompson theorem [16]) and in formal verification of critical software systems (e.g., the CompCert C-compiler [20] and the verified operating system kernel seL4 [18]).

Over the same time, automatic verification tools based on model-checking, static analysis and program proof have become widely used by the critical software industry. The main reason for their success is that they strengthen the confidence we can have in critical software by providing evidence of software correctness. The next step is to strengthen the confidence in the results of these verification tools, and proof assistants seem to be mature and adequate for this task. This paper presents a foundational step towards the formal verification of a static analysis based on abstract interpretation [10]: the formal verification using the Coq proof assistant of a value-range analysis operating over a real-world language.

---

* This work was supported by Agence Nationale de la Recherche, grant number ANR-11-INSE-003 Verasco.

F. Logozzo and M. Fähndrich (Eds.): SAS 2013, LNCS 7935, pp. 324–344, 2013.
© Springer-Verlag Berlin Heidelberg 2013

Static analyzers based on abstract interpretation are complex pieces of software that implement delicate symbolic algorithms and numerical computations. Their design requires a deep understanding of the targeted programming language. Misinterpretations of the programming language informal semantics may lead to subtle soundness bugs that may be hard to detect by using only testing techniques. Implementing a value analysis raises specific issues related to low-level numeric computations. First, the analysis must handle the machine arithmetic that is (more or less) defined in the programming language. Second, some computations done by the analyzer rely on this machine arithmetic.

Thus, a prerequisite for implementing a static analyzer operating over a C-like language is to rely on a formal semantics of the programming language defining precisely the expected behaviors of any program execution (and including low-level features such as machine arithmetic). Such formal semantics are defined in the CompCert compiler (and it is unusual for a compiler). More precisely, each language of the compiler is defined by a formal semantics (in Coq) associating observable behaviors to any program. Observable behaviors include normal termination, divergence, abnormal termination and undefined behaviors (such as out-of-bounds array access). We have chosen one language of the compiler (the main intermediate language that has the same expressiveness as C, see Section 2) and we have formalized a static analyzer operating over this language. The advantage of this approach is that our analyzer as well as the formal semantics operate exactly over the same language.

The main peculiarity of the CompCert C-compiler is that it is equipped with a proof of semantic preservation [20]. This proof is made possible thanks to the formal semantics of the languages of the compiler. The proof states that any compiled program behaves exactly as specified by the semantics of its original program. It consists of the composition of correctness proofs for each compiler pass and thus involves reasoning on the different intermediate languages of the compiler.

All results presented in this paper have been mechanically verified using the Coq proof assistant. The complete Coq development is available online at http://www.irisa.fr/celtique/ext/value-analysis.

The paper makes the following contributions.

- It provides the first verified value analysis for a realistic language such as C and hence demonstrates the usability of theorem proving in static analysis of real programs.
- It presents a modular design with strong interfaces aimed at facilitating any further extension.
- It provides a reference description of basic techniques of abstract interpretation and thus gives advice on how to use the abstract interpretation methodology for this kind of exercice while maintaining a sufficiently low cost in terms of formal proof effort.
- It compares the performances of our tool (that has been generated automatically from our formalization and integrated into the CompCert compiler) with those of two interval-based value analyzers for C.

The paper exposes many examples taken from the formal development. It is structured to follow the development of a C value analysis based on abstract interpretation; from generic abstract domains (section 3), to fixpoint resolution (section 4) and numerical and memory abstractions (sections 5 and 6). Section 7 describes the experimental evaluation of our implementation. Related work is discussed in Section 8, followed by concluding remarks.

2   Background

This section starts with a short introduction to the Coq proof assistant. It is followed by a brief presentation of the CompCert architecture and memory model. The language our analyzer operates over is described at the end of this section.

2.1   Short Introduction to Coq

Coq is an interactive theorem prover. It consists in a strongly typed specification language and a language for conducting machine-checked proofs interactively. The Coq specification language is a functional programming language as well as a language for inductively defining mathematical properties, for which it has a dedicated type (Prop). Induction principles are automatically generated by Coq from inductive definitions, thus inductive reasoning is very convenient. Data structures may consist of properties together with dependent types. Coq's type system includes type classes. Coq specifications are usually defined in a modular way (e.g., using record types and functors, that are functions operating over structured data such as records). The user is in charge to interactively build proofs in the system but those proofs are automatically machine-checked by the Coq kernel. OCaml programs can be automatically generated by Coq from Coq specifications. This process is called extraction.

2.2   The CompCert Memory Model

There are 11 languages in the CompCert compiler, including 9 intermediate languages. These languages feature both low-level aspects such as pointers, pointer arithmetic and nested objects, and high-level aspects such as separation and freshness guarantees. A memory model [21] is shared by the semantics of all these languages. Memory states (of type mem) are collections of blocks, each block being an array of abstract bytes. A block represents a C variable or an invocation of malloc. Pointers are represented by pairs (b,i) of a block identifier and a byte offset i within this block. Pointer arithmetic modifies the offset part of a pointer value, keeping its block identifier part unchanged.

Values stored in memory are the disjoint union of 32-bit integers (written as vint(i)), 64-bit floating-point numbers, locations (written as vptr(b,i)), and the special value undef representing the contents of uninitialized memory. Pointer values vptr(b,i) are composed of a block identifier b and an integer byte offset i within this block. Memory chunks appear in memory operations load and store, to describe concisely the size, type and signedness of the value being stored.

Values: $v ::= \mathtt{vint}(i) \mid \mathtt{vfloat}(f) \mid \mathtt{vptr}(b, i)$
                 $\mid \mathtt{undef}$

Mem. chunks: $\kappa ::= \mathtt{Mint8signed} \mid \mathtt{Mint8unsigned}$ 8-bit integers
                 $\mid \mathtt{Mint16signed} \mid \mathtt{Mint16unsigned}$ 16-bit integers
                 $\mid \mathtt{Mint32}$ 32-bit integers or pointers
                 $\mid \mathtt{Mfloat32}$ 32-bit floats
                 $\mid \mathtt{Mfloat64}$ 64-bit floats

In CompCert, a 32-bit integer (type int) is defined as a Coq arbitrary-precision integer (type Z) plus a property called intrange that it is in the range 0 to 2^{32} (excluded). The function signed (resp. unsigned) gives an interpretation of machine integers as a signed (resp. unsigned) integer. The properties signed_range and unsigned_range are examples of useful properties for machine integers.

Definition max_unsigned : Z := 2^{32} - 1.
Definition max_signed : Z := 2^{31} - 1.
Definition min_signed : Z := - 2^{31}.
Record int := { intval: Z;
                    intrange: $0 \leq$ intval $< 2^{32}$ }.
Definition unsigned (n: int) : Z := intval n.
Definition signed (n: int) : Z := **if** unsigned(n) $< 2^{31}$ **then** unsigned(n)
                                        else unsigned(n) - 2^{32}.
Theorem signed_range: $\forall$ i, min_signed $\leq$ signed(i) $\leq$ max_signed.
   Proof.   (* Proof commands omitted here *)   **Qed.**
Theorem unsigned_range: $\forall$ i, $0 \leq$ unsigned(i) $\leq$ max_unsigned.
   Proof.   (* Proof commands omitted here *)   **Qed.**

2.3   The CFG Intermediate Language

The main intermediate language of the CompCert compiler is called Cminor, a low-level imperative language structured like C into expressions, statements and functions. Historically, Cminor was the target language of the compiler front-end. There are four main differences with C [20]. First, arithmetic operators are not overloaded. Second, address computations are explicit, as well as memory access (using load and store operations). Third, control structures are if-statements, infinite loops, nested blocks plus associated exits and early returns. Last, local variables can only hold scalar values and they do not reside in memory, making it impossible to take a pointer to a local variable like the C operator & does. Instead, each Cminor function declares the size of a stack-allocated block, allocated in memory at function entry and automatically freed at function return. The expression addrstack(n) returns a pointer within that block at constant offset n.

Cminor was designed to be the privileged language for integrating within CompCert other tools operating over C and other compiler front-ends. For instance, two front-end compilers from functional languages to Cminor have been connected to CompCert using Cminor, and a separation logic has been defined for Cminor [2]. The Concurrent Cminor language extends Cminor with concurrent features and lies at the heart of the Verified Software Toolchain project [1].

As control-flow is still complex in Cminor (due to the presence of nested blocks and exits), we have first designed a new intermediate language called CFG that is adapted for static analysis: 1) its expressions are Cminor expressions (i.e., side-effect free C expressions), 2) its programs are represented by their control flow graphs, with explicit program points and 3) the control flow is restricted to simple unconditional and conditional jumps. The CFG syntax is defined in Figure 1. Floating-point operators are omitted in the figure, as our analysis does not compute any information about floats. Statements include assignment to local variables, memory stores, if-statements and function calls. Expressions include reading local variables, constants and arithmetic operations, reading store locations, and conditional expressions. As in the memory model, loads and stores are parameterized by a memory chunk κ.

The CFG language is integrated into the CompCert compiler, as shown in Figure 2. There is a translation from Cminor to CFG and a theorem stating that any terminating or diverging execution of a CFG program is also a terminating or diverging execution of the original Cminor program. Thus, instead of analyzing Cminor programs, we can analyze CFG programs and use this theorem to propagate the results of the CFG analysis on Cminor programs. For instance, in order to show that Cminor is memory safe, we only need to show that CFG is memory safe.

For the purpose of the experiments that we conduct in Section 7, we use an inlining pass recently added to the CompCert compiler. It was implemented and proved correct by X.Leroy for another language of the compiler, RTL, that is similar to CFG except that it only handles flat expressions. Since our analysis operates on CFG, we have adapted this inlining pass to CFG. Adapting the soundness proof of this transformation to CFG has been left for future work.

The concrete semantics of CFG is defined in small-step style as a transition relation between execution states. An execution state is a tuple called σ. Among the components of σ are the current program point (i.e., a node in the control-flow graph), the memory state (type mem) and the environment (type env) mapping program variables to values. We use $\sigma.E$ to denote the environment of a state σ, and $\mathrm{dom}(\sigma.E)$ to denote its domain (i.e., the set of its variables). We use $\mathrm{reach}(P)$ to denote the set of states belonging to the execution trace of P.

Our value analysis (called value_analysis) computes for each program point the estimated values of the program variables. When the value of a variable is an integer i or a pointer value of offset i, the estimate provides two numerical ranges signed_range and unsigned_range. The first one over-approximates the signed interpretation of i and the other range over-approximates its unsigned interpretation. We note ints_in_range (signed_range, unsigned_range) i this fact. Thus, given a program P, value_analysis(P) yields a map such that for each node l in its control flow graph and each variable v, value_analysis $(P)[l, v]$ is a pair of sound ranges for v. The following theorem states the soundness of the value analysis: for every program state that may be reached during the execution

Constants:	$c ::= n \mid f$	integer and floating-point constants
	$\mid \mathtt{addrsymbol}(id, n)$	address of a symbol plus an offset
	$\mid \mathtt{addrstack}(n)$	stack pointer plus a given offset
Expressions:	$a ::= id$	variable identifier
	$\mid c$	constant
	$\mid op_1 \ a$	unary arithmetic operation
	$\mid a_1 \ op_2 \ a_2$	binary arithmetic operation
	$\mid a_1?\ a_2 : a_3$	conditional expression
	$\mid \mathtt{load}(\kappa, a)$	memory load
Unary op.:	$op_1 ::= \mathtt{cast8unsigned}$	8-bit zero extension
	$\mid \mathtt{cast8signed}$	8-bit sign extension
	$\mid \mathtt{cast16unsigned}$	16-bit zero extension
	$\mid \mathtt{cast16signed}$	16-bit sign extension
	$\mid \mathtt{boolval}$	0 if null, 1 if non-null
	$\mid \mathtt{negint}$	integer opposite
	$\mid \mathtt{notbool}$	boolean negation
	$\mid \mathtt{notint}$	bitwise complement
Binary op.:	$op_2 ::= \mathtt{+} \mid \mathtt{-} \mid \mathtt{*} \mid \mathtt{/} \mid \mathtt{\%}$	arithmetic integer operators
	$\mid \mathtt{<<} \mid \mathtt{>>} \mid \mathtt{\&} \mid \mathtt{\mid} \mid \mathtt{\char`^}$	bitwise operators
	$\mid \mathtt{/}_u \mid \mathtt{\%}_u \mid \mathtt{>>}_u$	unsigned operators
	$\mid \mathtt{cmp}(b)$	integer signed comparisons
	$\mid \mathtt{cmpu}(b)$	integer unsigned comparisons
Comparisons:	$b ::= \mathtt{<} \mid \mathtt{<=} \mid \mathtt{>} \mid \mathtt{>=} \mid \mathtt{==} \mid \mathtt{!=}$	relational operators
Statements:	$i ::= \mathtt{skip}(l)$	no operation (go to l)
	$\mid \mathtt{assign}(id, a, l)$	assignment
	$\mid \mathtt{store}(\kappa, a, a, l)$	memory store
	$\mid \mathtt{if}(e, l_{true}, l_{false})$	if statement
	$\mid \mathtt{call}(sig, id^?, a, a*, l)$	function call
	$\mid \mathtt{return}(a)^?$	function return

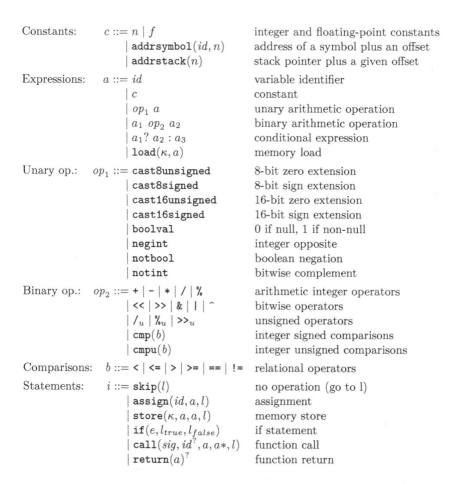

Fig. 1. Abstract syntax of CFG

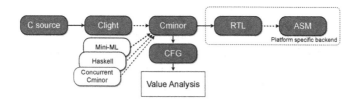

Fig. 2. Integration of the value analysis in the CompCert toolchain

of a program, any program point and variable, every variable valuation computed by the analysis is a correct estimation of the exact value given by the concrete semantics.

Theorem 1 (Soundness of the value analysis). *Let P be a program, $\sigma \in$* reach(P) *and res $=$* value_analysis (P) *be the result of the value analysis. Then, for each program point l, for each local variable $v \in$ dom$(\sigma.E)$ that contains an integer i (i.e., $\sigma.E(v) =$ vint$(i) \lor \exists b, \sigma.E(v) =$ vptr(b,i)), the property* (ints_in_range $res[l,v]$ i) *holds.*

2.4   Overview of a Modular Value Analysis

Our value analysis is designed in a modular way: a generic fixpoint iterator operates over generic abstract domains (see Section 3). The iterator is based on the state-of-the-art Bourdoncle [6] algorithm that provides both efficiency and precision (see Section 4).

The modular design of the abstract domains is inspired from the design of the Astrée analyzer. It consists in three layers that are showed in Figure 3. The simplest domains are numerical abstract domains made of intervals of machine integers. These domains are not aware of the C memory model.

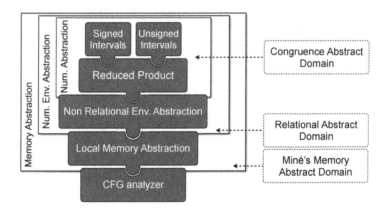

Fig. 3. Design of abstract domains: a three-layer view

In a C program, a same piece of data can be used both in signed and unsigned operations, and the results of these operations differ from one interpretation to the other. Thus, we have two numerical abstract domains, one for each interpretation. Our analysis computes the reduced product of the two domains in order to make a continuous fruitful information exchange between these two domains (see Section 5).

Then, we build abstract domains representing numerical environments. We provide a non-relational abstraction that is parameterized by a numerical abstract domain. The last layer is the abstract domain representing memory. It is parameterized by the previous layer and links the abstract interpreter with the numerical abstract domains (see Section 6).

This modular design is targeted to connect at each layer other abstract domains. They are represented in dotted lines in Figure 3. For example, several abstract memory models can be used instead of the current one while maintaining the same interfaces with the rest of the formal development. The ultimate goal is to enhance our current abstract interpreter in order to connect it to a memory domain à la Miné [23]. The current interfaces are also compatible with any relational numerical abstract domain. At the top, more basic numerical abstractions as congruence could be added and plugged into our reduced product.

3   Abstract Domain Library

This section describes the library we have designed to represent our abstract domains. First, it defines generic abstract domains. Then, it details the interval abstract domain. Last, it explains how to combine abstract domains.

3.1   Abstract Domain Interface

Abstract interpretation provides various frameworks [10] for the design of abstract semantics. The most well-known framework is based on Galois connections but some relaxed frameworks exist. They are generally used when some useful abstraction does not fulfill standard properties (e.g., polyhedral abstract domains [12] do not form a complete lattice). In our context, a relaxed framework is required because of the associated lightweight proof effort.

Since our main goal is to provide a formal proof of soundness for the result of an analysis, some additional properties such as best approximation or completeness do not require a machine checked proof. In some previous work of the last author, a framework has been defined for the purpose of machine checked proofs [14]. In this paper, we push further this initiative and provide a more minimalist framework. The signature of abstract domains is of the following form.[1]

```
Notation P(A) := (A → Prop).          (* identify sets and predicates *)
Notation x ∈ P := (P x).
Notation P1 ⊆ P2 := (incl P1 P2).     (* property inclusion *)

Record adom (A:Type) (B:Type) : Type := {
    le: A → A → bool;                 (* partial order test           *)
    top: A;                           (* greatest element             *)
    join: A → A → A;                  (* least upper bound            *)
    widen: A → A → A;                 (* widening operator            *)
    gamma: A → P(B);                  (* concretization function      *)
    gamma_monotone:                   (* monotonicity of gamma        *)
        ∀ a1 a2, le a1 a2 = true → (gamma a1) ⊆ (gamma a2);
    top_sound:                        (* top over-approximates any    *)
```

---

[1] In this paper, for the sake of simplicity, we only use records to structure our formalization. However, in our development, we also use more advanced Coq features such as type classes.

```
    ∀ x, x ∈ (gamma top);              (*    concrete property      *)
  join_sound : ∀ x y:A,                (* join over-approximates    *)
    (gamma x) ∪ (gamma y) ⊆ gamma (join x y);  (* concrete union  *)
}.
```

Here, A is the type of abstract values, B is the type of concrete values, and the type of the abstract domain is (adom A B). This type is a record with various operators (described on the right part) and properties about them. This record contains only three properties: the monotonicity of the gamma operator, the soundness of the top element and the soundness of the least upper bound operator join. We do not provide formal proof relating the abstract order with top or join. Indeed any *weak-join* will be suitable here. The lack of properties about the widening operator is particularly surprising at first sight. In fact, as we will explain in Section 4, the widening operator is used only during fixpoint iteration and this step is validated *a posteriori*. Thus, only the result of this iteration step is verified and we don't need a widening operator for that purpose.

The gamma operator of *every* abstract domain will be noted γ. The type class mechanism enables Coq to infer which domain it refers to.

3.2   Example of Abstract Domain: Intervals

Our value analysis operates over compositions of abstract domains. The most basic abstract domain is the domain of intervals. Figure 4 defines the abstract domain of intervals made of machine integers, that are interpreted as signed integers. This instance is called signed_itv_adom. The definitions are standard and only some of them are detailed in the figure. An interval represents the range of the signed interpretation of a machine integer. Thus, top is defined as the largest interval with bounds min_signed and max_signed. The concretization is defined as follows. A machine integer n belongs to the concretization of an interval itv iff signed(n) belongs to itv. The proof of the lemma top_sound follows from the signed_range theorem given in Section 2.2.

```
Record itv := {min: Z; max: Z}.

Definition signed_itv_adom : adom itv int := {
    le := (λ itv1 itv2, ...);              (* definition omitted here *)
    top := { min:= min_signed; max:= max_signed};
    join := (λ itv1 itv2, ...);            (* definition omitted here *)
    widen := (λ itv1 itv2, ...);           (* definition omitted here *)
    gamma := (λ itv n, itv.min ≤ signed(n) ≤ itv.max);
    top_sound := (...);                    (* proof term omitted here *)
    gamma_monotone := (...);               (* proof term omitted here *)
    join_sound := (...);                   (* proof term omitted here *)
}.
```

Fig. 4. An instance called signed_itv_adom: the domain of intervals (made of signed machine integers) with a concretization to $\mathcal{P}(\text{int})$

We also define a variant of this domain with a concretization using an unsigned interpretation of machine integers: (λ itv n, itv.min$\leq$unsigned(n)$\leq$itv.max). As explained in Section 5, combining both domains recovers some precision that may be lost when using only one of them.

The itv record type provides only lower and upper bounds of type Z. Using the expressiveness of the Coq type system, we could choose to add an extra field requiring a proof that min $\leq$ max holds. While elegant at first sight, this would be rather heavyweight in practice, since we must provide such a proof each time we build a new interval. For the kind of proofs we perform, if such a property was required, we would generally have an hypothesis of the form i $\in$ (γ itv) in our context and it would trivially imply that itv.min $\leq$ itv.max holds.

3.3   Abstract Domain Functors

Our library provides several functors that build complex abstract domains from simpler ones.

Direct Product. A first example is the product (adom (A*A') B) of two abstract domains (adom A B) and (adom A' B), where the concretization of a pair (a,a'):A*A' is the intersection (γ a) $\cap$ (γ a').

Lifting a Bottom Element A bottom element is not mandatory in our definition of abstract domains because some sub-domains do not necessarily contain one. For instance, the domain of intervals does not contain such a least element. Still in our development, the bottom element plays a specific and important role since we use it for reduction. We hence introduce a polymorphic type A+$\perp$ that lifts a type A with an extra bottom element called Bot. We then define a simple functor lift_bot that lifts any domain (adom A B) on a type A to a domain on A+$\perp$. In this new domain, the concretization function extends the concretization of the input domain and γ Bot = $\emptyset$.

Definition botlift (A:**Type**): **Type** := Bot | NotBot (x:A).
Notation A+$\perp$:= (botlift A).
Definition lift_bot (A B: **Type**): adom A B $\rightarrow$ adom (A+$\perp$) B :=
    (* definition omitted here *)

Finite Reduced Map. Lifted domains are used for instance as input for an important functor of finite maps. CompCert uses intensively the TREE interface. Given an implementation T of the interface TREE and a type A, an element of type (TREE.t A) represents a partial map from keys (of type T.elt) to values of type A. The interface is implemented for several kinds of keys in the CompCert libraries. In our development, we use it to map variables to abstract values, but also program points to abstract environments. The functor implements the following type.

AbTree.make(T:TREE)(A B:**Type**): adom A B $\rightarrow$ adom (T.t A)+$\perp$ (T.elt $\rightarrow$ B)

An element in (T.t A)+$\perp$ is turned into a function of type T.elt $\rightarrow$ A+$\perp$ via the function get that satisfies the following equations.

```
get(Bot)(k)       = Bot
get(NotBot m)(k) = top        (* if m[k] is undefined *)
get(NotBot m)(k) = NotBot m[k] (* otherwise *)
```

As a consequence, the top element is represented in a lazy way: a key is associated to it as soon as it is not bound in the partial map. Furthermore, the map is reduced w.r.t. the bottom element of the input domain: as soon as we try to bind a key to the bottom element, the whole map is shrunk to Bot. This situation is interesting for dead code elimination and more generally for the whole precision of an analysis.

4   Fixpoint Resolution

From a proof point of view, the main lesson learned from the CompCert experiment is the following. When formally verifying a complex piece of software relying on sophisticated data structures and delicate algorithms, it is not realistic to write the whole software using exclusively the specification language of the proof assistant. A more pragmatic approach to formal verification consists in reusing an existing implementation in order to separately verify its results. This approach is not optimal, but it is worthwhile when the algorithm is a sophisticated piece of code and when the formal verification of each of the results is much easier than the formal verification of the algorithm itself.

The CompCert compiler combines both approaches in order to facilitate the proofs. Most of the compiler passes are written and proved in Coq. A few compiler passes (e.g., the register allocation [26]) are not written directly in Coq, but formally verified in Coq by a translation validation approach. Our value analysis also combines both approaches. We have formally verified a checker that validates *a posteriori* the untrusted results of a fixpoint engine written in OCaml, that finds fixpoints using widening and narrowing operators.

As many data flow analyses, our value analysis can be turned into the fixpoint resolution of an equation system on a lattice. CompCert already provides a classical Kildall iteration framework to iteratively find the least fixpoint of an equation system. But using such a framework is impossible here for two reasons. First, the lattice of bounded intervals contains very long ascending chains that make standard Kleene iterations too slow. Second, the non-monotonic nature of widening and narrowing makes fixpoint iteration sensible to the iteration order of each equation.

We have then designed a new fixpoint resolution framework that relies on the general iteration techniques defined by Bourdoncle [6]. First, Bourdoncle provides a strategy computation algorithm based on Tarjan's algorithm to compute strongly connected subcomponents of a directed graph and find loop headers for widening positioning. This algorithm also orders each strongly connected subcomponent in order to obtain an iteration strategy that iterates inner loops until stabilization before iterating outer loops. Bourdoncle then provides an efficient fixpoint iteration algorithm that iterates along the previous strategy and requires a minimum number of abstract order tests to detect convergence.

This algorithm relies on advanced reasoning in graph theory and formally verifying it would be highly challenging. This frontal approach would also certainly be too rigid because widening iteration requires several heuristic adjustments to reach a satisfactory precision in practice (loop unrolling, delayed widenings, decreasing iterations). We have therefore opted for a more flexible verification strategy: as Bourdoncle strategies, fixpoints are computed by an external tool (represented by the function called `get_extern_fixpoint`) and we only formally verify a fixpoint checker (called `check_fxp`).

Our fixpoint analyzer is defined below, given an abstract domain `ab`, a program `P` and its entry point `entry`, the transfer functions `transfer` and initial abstract values `init`.

```
Definition solve_pfp (ab: adom t B) (P: PTree.t instruction)
    (entry: node) (transfer: node→instruction→list(node*(t→t)))
    (init: t) : node → t :=
    let fxp := get_extern_fixpoint entry ab P transfer init in
    if check_fxp entry ab P transfer init fxp then fxp else top.
```

The verification of the fixpoint checker yields the following property: the concretization of the result of the `solve_pfp` function is a post-fixpoint of the concrete transfer function. That is, given the analysis result `fxp`, for each node `pc` of the program, applying the corresponding transfer function `tf` to the analysis result yields an abstract value included in the analysis result.

```
Lemma solve_pfp_postfixpoint: ∀ ab entry P transfer init fxp,
    fxp = solve_pfp ab P entry transfer init →
    ∀ pc i, P[pc] = i →
    ∀ (pc',tf) ∈_list (transfer pc i), γ(tf(fxp pc))⊆γ(fxp pc').
Proof. (* proof commands are omitted here *) Qed.
```

5   Numerical Abstraction

Following the design of the Astrée analyzer [11], our value analysis is parameterized by a numerical abstract domain that is unaware of the C memory model. We first present the interface of abstract numerical environments, then how we abstract numerical values in order to build non relational abstract environments. Finally, we show concrete instances of numerical domains and how they can be combined.

5.1   Abstraction of Numerical Environments

The first interface captures the notion of numerical environment abstraction. Given a type `t` for abstract values and a notion of variable `var` (simple positive integers in our development), we require an abstract domain that concretizes to $\mathcal{P}(\text{var} \to \text{int})$ and provide three sound operators `range`, `assign` and `assume`.

```
sign_flag ::= Signed | Unsigned
Definition ints_in_range (r:sign_flag → itv+⊥) : int :=
                        (γ (r Signed)) ∩ (γ (r Unsigned)).
Record int_dom (t:Type) := {
```

```
int_adom: adom t (var → int);    (* abstract domain structure *)
(* signed/unsigned range of an expression *)
range: nexpr → t → sign_flag → itv+⊥;
range_sound: ∀ e ρ ab,
    ρ ∈ γ ab → eval_nexpr ρ e ⊆ ints_in_range (range e ab);
(* assignment of a variable by a numerical expression *)
assign: var → nexpr → t → t;
assign_sound: ∀ x e ρ n ab,
    ρ ∈ γ ab → n ∈ eval_nexpr ρ e → (upd ρ x n) ∈ γ (assign x e ab);
(* assume a numerical expression evaluates to true *)
assume: nexpr → t → t;
assume_sound: ∀ e ρ ab,
    ρ ∈ γ ab → Ntrue ∈ eval_nexpr ρ e → ρ ∈ γ (assume e ab)
}.
```

This interface matches with any implementation of a relational abstract domain [12] on machine integers. To increase precision, it relies on a notion of expression tree (type nexpr) defined as follows and relying on CFG operators.

$$e_{tr} ::= \text{NEvar } id \mid \text{NEconst } c \mid \text{NEunop } op_1 \, e_{tr} \mid \text{NEbop } op_2 \, e_{tr} \, e_{tr} \mid \text{NEcond } e_{tr} \, e_{tr} \, e_{tr}$$

These expressions are associated with a big-step operational semantics eval_nexpr of type (var→int) → nexpr → $\mathcal{P}$(int) that we define as a partial function represented by a relation. The semantics is not detailed in this paper.

5.2   Building Non-relational Abstraction of Numerical Environments

Implementing a fully verified relational abstract domain is a challenge in itself and it is not in the scope of this paper. We implement instead the previous interface with a standard non relational abstract environment of the form var → V$^\sharp$ where V$^\sharp$ abstracts numerical values. The notion of abstraction of numerical values is captured by the following interface.

```
Record num_dom (t:Type) := {
    num_adom : adom t int;                  (* abstract domain structure *)
    meet: t → t → t+⊥;              (* over-approximation of the concrete *)
    meet_sound: ∀ x y, (γ x) ∩ (γ y) ⊆ γ (meet x y); (* intersection *)
    range: t → sign_flag → itv+⊥;            (* signed/unsigned range *)
    range_sound: ∀ x:t, γ x ⊆ ints_in_range (range x);
    const: constant → t; const_sound:  (*omitted*);
    forward_unop: unary_operation → t → t+⊥;
    forward_unop_sound: ∀ op x,
        Eval_unop op (γ x) ⊆ γ (forward_unop op x);
    forward_binop: (* omitted *); forward_binop_sound: (* omitted *);
    backward_unop: (* omitted *); backward_unop_sound: (* omitted *);
    backward_binop: binary_operation → t → t → t → t+⊥ * t+⊥;
    backward_binop_sound: ∀ op x y z i j k,
        eval_binop op i j k → i ∈ (γ x) → j ∈ (γ y) → k ∈ (γ z) →
    let (x',y') := backward_binop op x y z in
        i ∈ (γ x') ∧ j ∈ (γ y')
}.
```

It is defined as a carrier t, an abstract domain structure num_adom and a bunch of *abstract transformers*. Some operators are forward ones: they provide properties about the output of an operation. For instance, the operator const builds an abstraction of a single value. Some operators are backward ones: given some properties about the input and expected output of an operation, they provide a refined property about its input. Each operator comes with a soundness proof.

We also implement a functor that lifts any abstraction of numerical values into a numerical environment abstraction. It relies on the functor for finite reduced maps that we have presented at the end of Section 3. Here, PTree provides an implementation of the TREE interface for the var type.

$$\text{NonRelDom.make(t): num\_dom t} \rightarrow \text{int\_dom ((PTree.t t)+}\bot)$$

The most advanced operator in this functor is the assume function. It relies on a backward abstract semantics of expressions.

```
Fixpoint backward_expr (e:nexpr) (ab:t) (itv:Val) : t :=
  match e with
  | ...
  | NEcond b l r ⇒
      join
        (backward_expr b (backward_expr r ab itv) (const Nfalse))
        (backward_expr b (backward_expr l ab itv)
            (backward_unop boolval (eval_expr b ab) (const Ntrue)))
  end.
```

We just show and comment the case of conditional expressions. Given such an expression NEcond b l r, an abstract environment ab and the expected value itv of this expression, we explore the two branches of the condition. In one case, the condition b evaluated to Nfalse and the *right* branch r evaluated to itv. In the other case, the condition b evaluated to anything whose boolean value is Ntrue and the *left* branch l evaluated to itv. Then we have to consider that any of the two branches might have been taken, hence the join.

Equipped with such backward operators, the analysis is then able to deal with complex conditions like the following: if (0 <= x && x < y && y < z && z < t && t < u && u < v && v < 10). When analysing the true branch of this if, it is sound to assume that the condition holds. The backward operator will propagate this information and infer one bound for each variable. Since backward evaluation of conditions goes right to left, the following bounds are inferred: $v < 10$, $u < 9$, $t < 8$, $z < 7$, $y < 6$, and $0 \leq x < 5$. Unfortunately, no information is propagated from left to right. However applying again the assume function does propagate information between the various conditions. Iterating this process finally yields the most precise intervals for all variables involved in this condition.

Notice that inferring such precise information is possible thanks to the availability of complex expressions in the analyzed CFG program. Compare for example with Frama-C which, prior to any analysis, destructs boolean operations into nested ifs; it is thus unable to give both bounds for each variable.

5.3 Abstraction of Numerical Values: Instances and Functor

We gave two instances of the numerical value abstraction interface: the intervals of signed integers and the intervals of unsigned integers. Several operations are defined on intervals together with their proofs of correctness. We have to take into account machine arithmetic. We do not try to precisely track integers that wrap-around intentionally. Instead we systematically test if an overflow may occur and fall back to top when we can't prove the absence of overflow.

```
Definition repr  (i: itv): itv := if leb i top then i else top.
Definition add (i j: itv): itv :=
  repr { min := i.min + j.min; max := i.max + j.max}.
```

We also rely on a reduction operator when the result of an operation may lead to an empty interval. Since our representation of intervals contains several elements with the same (empty) concretization, it is important to always use a same representative for them.[2]

```
Definition reduce (min max:Z): itv+⊥ :=
    if min ≤ max then NotBot (ITV min max) else Bot.

Definition backward_lt (i j: itv): itv+⊥ * itv+⊥ :=
      (meet i (reduce min_signed (j.max-1)),
      meet j (reduce (i.min+1) max_signed)).
```

At run-time, there are no *signed* or *unsigned* integers; there are only *machine* integers that are bit arrays whose interpretation may vary depending on the operations they undergo. Therefore choosing one of the two interval domains may hamper the precision of the analysis. Consider the following example C program.

```
1   int main(void) { signed s; unsigned u;
2      if (*) u = 2³¹ - 1; else u = 2³¹;
3      if (*) s = 0; else s = -1;
4      return u + s;  }
```

At the end of line 2, an unsigned interval can exactly represent the two values that the variable u may hold. However, the least signed interval that contains them both is top. Similarly, at the end of line 3, a signed interval can precisely approximate the content of variable s whereas an unsigned interval would be extremely imprecise. Moreover, comparison operations can be precisely translated into operations over intervals (e.g., intersections) only when they share the same signedness. Therefore, so as to get as precise information as possible, we need to combine the two interval domains. This is done through reduction.

To combine abstractions of numerical values in a generic and precise way, we implement a functor that takes two abstractions and a sound reduction operator and returns a new abstraction based on their reduced product.

```
Definition reduced_product (t t':Type) (N:num_dom t) (N':num_dom t')
   (R:reduction N N') : num_dom (t*t') := (* omitted definition *)
```

A reduction is made of an operator ρ and a proof that this operator is a sound reduction.

```
Record reduction (A B:Type) (N1:num_dom A) (N2:num_dom B) := {
   ρ: A+⊥ → B+⊥ → (A * B)+⊥;
   ρ_sound: ∀ a b, (γ a) ∩ (γ b) ⊆ γ (ρ a b)                    }
```

---

[2] Otherwise the analyzer may encounter two equivalent values without noticing it and lose precision.

Each operator of this functor is implemented by first using the operator of both input domains and then reducing the result with ρ. We hence ensure that each encountered value is systematically of the form ρ a b but we do not prove this fact formally, avoiding the heavy manipulation of quotients. Note also that, for soundness purposes, we do not need to prove that reduction actually reduces (i.e., returns a lower element in the abstract lattice)!

6   Memory Abstraction

The last layer of our modular architecture connects the CFG abstract interpreter with numerical abstract domains. It aims at translating every C feature into useful information in the numerical world. On the interpreter side, the interface with this *abstract memory model* is called mem_dom. It consists in trees made of CFG expressions and four basic commands forget, assign, store and assume.

```
Record mem_dom (t:Type) := { (* abstract domain with concretization
    to local environment and global memory *)
  mem_adom: adom t (env * mem);
  (* consult the range of a local variable *)
  range: t → ident → sign_flag → itv+⊥;
  range_sound: ∀ ab e m x i,
    (e,m) ∈ γ ab → (e[x] = vint(i) ∨ ∃ b, e[x] = vptr(b,i)) →
    i ∈ (ints_in_range (range ab x));
  (* project the value of a local variable *)
  forget: ident → t → t;
  forget_sound: ∀ x ab, Forget x (γ ab) ⊆ γ (forget x ab);
  (* assign a local variable *)
  assign: ident → expr → t → t;
  assign_sound: ∀ x e ab, Assign x e (γ ab) ⊆ γ (assign x e ab);
  (* assign a memory cell *)
  store: memory_chunk → expr → expr → t → t;
  store_sound: ∀ κ l r ab,
    Store κ l r (γ ab) ⊆ γ (store κ l r ab);
  (* assume an expression evaluates to non-zero value *)
  assume: expr  → t → t;
  assume_sound: ∀ e ab, Assume e (γ ab) ⊆ γ (assume e ab)
}.
```

Our final analyzer is parameterized by a structure of this type.

```
value_analysis (t:Type) :   mem_dom t →
   program → node → (ident → sign_flag → Interval.itv +⊥)
```

A structure of type mem_dom is built with a functor of the following form.

```
AbMem.make (t:Type) : int_dom t → mem_dom (t*type_info)
```

The numerical abstraction is associated with a flow sensitive type information (of type type_info) that we compute at the same time. This type information tries to recover some information to disambiguate integer and pointer values. The abstract domain is built using the product functor presented in Section 3. The concretization function of the numeric domain is lifted from a concretization of type t → $\mathcal{P}$(var→int) to a concretization of type t → $\mathcal{P}$(env * mem) with the following definition. [3]

---

[3] The types env and mem are introduced in Section 2.

```
Definition gamma_mem (ab:t) := λ (e,m):(env*mem).
   ∃ ρ:var → int, ρ ∈ (γ ab) ∧
      (∀ x i, (e[x] = vint(i) ∨ ∃ b, e[x] = vptr(b,i)) → ρ x = i).
```

For each transfer function that takes as argument a C expression, we convert it
into a numerical expression in order to feed the numerical abstract domain. For
instance, the assign operator takes the following form.

```
Definition assign (id:ident) (e:expr) (ab:t*type_info): t*type_info :=
  let (nm,tp) := ab in
  (* convert expression e into a numeric form using type infos *)
  match convert tp e with
  | None ⇒ forget id ab (* if we fail, we just project *)
  | Some ne ⇒
      (* otherwise we call the numerical assignment operator *)
      (num.assign id ne nm, ... (* type info update omitted *))
end.
```

Removing some ambiguity between pointers and integers is mandatory for soundness. As an example, consider the unsigned equality expression (x ==u y). For
the sake of precision of the analysis, it is important to convert it into a simple
numerical equality x == y before using the assume operator of the numerical
abstract domain. However if x contains a numerical value and y a pointer, the
first formula is always false while assuming the second formula in the numerical
world would lead to a spurious assumption about the offset of the pointer in y.

7 Experimental Evaluation

Our verified value analyzer takes as input a CFG program and outputs ranges
for every variable at every point of the program. Our formal development adds
about 7,500 lines of Coq code (consisting of 4,000 lines of Coq functions and
definitions and 3,500 lines of Coq statements and proof scripts) and 200 lines
of OCaml to the 100,000 lines of Coq and 1,000 lines of OCaml provided in
CompCert 1.11.

We have conducted some experiments to evaluate the precision and the efficiency of our analyzer. Indeed, an analyzer that always returns "top" is easily proved correct, but useless. It is therefore important to distinguish between
bounded and unbounded variables. Moreover, a precise but non-scalable analyzer
has limited applicability. In order to evaluate the precision and efficiency of our
value analysis, we use the OCaml extracted code to compile our benchmark
programs into CFG programs and to run our analyzer on them.

We compare our analyzer to two interval-based analyzers operating over C programs: a state-of-the-art industrial tool, Frama-C [13], and an implementation
of a value-range analyzer [24]. Frama-C is an industrial-strength framework for
static analysis, developed at CEA. It integrates an abstract interpretation-based
interprocedural value analysis on interval domains with congruence, k-sets and
memory analysis. It operates over C programs and has a very deep knowledge
of its semantics, allowing it to slice out undefined behaviors for more precise
results. It currently does not handle recursive functions. The value-range analyzer, which will be referred to as Wrapped is described in [24]. It relies on

LLVM and operates over its intermediate representation to perform an interval analysis in a signedness-agnostic manner, using so-called "wrapped" intervals to deal with machine integer issues such as overflows while retaining precision. It is an intraprocedural tool, but can benefit from LLVM's inlining to perform interprocedurally in the absence of recursion.

The 3 tools have been compared on significant C programs from CompCert's test suite. They range from a few dozen to a few thousand statements. To relate information from different analyses, we annotated the programs to capture information on integer variables at function entries and exits and at loops (for iteration variables). This amounts to 545 annotations in the 20 programs considered. For each program point, we counted the number of bounded variables. We consider as bounded any variable whose inferred interval has no more than 2^{31} elements, and hence rule out useless intervals like $x \in [-2^{31}, 2^{31} - 2]$, inferred after a guard like $x<y$. Finally, to be able to compare the results of an interprocedural analysis with those of two intraprocedural analyses with inlining, we considered for each annotation the union of the intervals of all call contexts. Less than 10% of intervals present a union of different intervals, and among those several preserve the boundedness for all contexts. Overall, its impact on the results is negligible.

The results are shown in Figure 5, which displays the number of bounded variables per program and per analyzer. In total, Frama-C bounded 398 variables, our analyzer got 355, and Wrapped ended up with 305. The main differences between our analyzer and Frama-C, especially on the larger benchmarks (lzw, arcode and lzss) result from global variable tracking and congruence information. Such reasoning is not handled by our analyzer. On the other hand, the precision of our product of signed and unsigned domains allows us to bound more variables (e.g., on fannkuch), where Wrapped also obtains a good score, mainly due to variables bounded as $[0, 2^{31} - 1]$ and similar values. Some issues with the inlining used by Wrapped explain its worse results in fft, knucleotide and spectral.

We also compared the execution times of the analyses. Overall, our analysis runs faster than Frama-C because we track less information, such as pointers

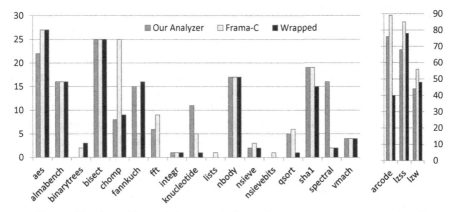

Fig. 5. Number of bounded intervals (bounded per program and analyzer)

and global variables. For programs without these features, both analyses run in roughly the same time, from a few tenths of seconds for the smaller programs up to a few seconds for the larger ones. Wrapped's analysis is faster than the others. On a larger benchmark (over 3,000 lines of C code and about 10,000 CFG instructions after inlining) our analysis took 34 seconds to perform.

It is hard to draw final conclusions about the precision of our tool from these experiments. Frama-C, for instance, is likely to perform better on specific industrial critical software for which it has been specially tuned. Nevertheless we give evidence that our analyzer performs non-trivial reasoning over the C semantics, close to that of state-of-the-art (non-verified) tools.

8   Related Work

While mechanization of research paper proofs attracts an increasing number of practitioners, it should not be confused with the activity of developing a formally verified compiler or static analyzer. Our work is initially inspired by the achievement of the CompCert compiler [20] but we target the area of abstract-interpretation-based static analyzers.

Previous work on mechanized verification of static analyses has been mostly based on classic data flow frameworks: Klein and Nipkow instantiate this framework for inference of Java bytecode types [19]; Coupet-Grimal and Delobel [9] and Bertot et al. [3] for compiler optimizations, and Cachera et al. [7] for control flow analysis. Vafeiadis et al. [28] rely on a simple data flow analysis to verify a fence elimination optimization for concurrent C programs. Compared to these prior works, our value analysis relies on fixpoint iterations that are accelerating with widening operators. Cachera and Pichardie [8] and Nipkow [25] describe a verified static analysis based on widenings but their technique is restricted to structured programs and targets languages without machine arithmetic nor pointers. Leroy and Robert [22] have developed a points-to analysis in the CompCert framework. This static analysis technique is quite orthogonal to what we formalize here. Their verified tool is not compared to any existing analyzer. Hofmann et al. [17] provide a machine-checked correctness proof in Coq for a generic post-fixpoint solver named RLD. The formalized algorithm is not fully executable and cannot be extracted to OCaml code.

Of course the area of non-verified static analysis for C programs is a broader topic. In our context, the most relevant and inspiring works are the static analyses devoted to a precise handling of signed and unsigned integers [27,24] and the Astrée static analyzer [11]. Our current formalization is directly inspired by Astrée's design choices, trying to capture some of its key interfaces. Our current abstract memory model is aligned with the model developed by Miné [23] because we connect a C abstract semantics with a generic notion of numerical abstract domain. Still our treatment of memory is simplified since we only track values of local variables in the current implementation of our analyzer.

9   Conclusion

This work provides the first verified value analysis for a realistic language as C. Implementing a precise value analysis for C is highly error-prone. We hope that our work shows the feasibility of developing such a tool together with a machine-checked proof. The precision of the analysis has been experimentally evaluated and compared on several benchmarks. The paper's technology performs comparably to existing off-the-shelf (unverified!) tools, Frama-C [13] and Wrapped [24]. Our contribution is also methodological. Our formalization, its lightweight interfaces and its proofs can be easily reused to develop different formally verified analyses.

Now that the main interfaces are defined, we expect to improve our analyzer in several challenging directions. First, we want to replace the current memory abstraction with a domain similar to Miné's memory model [23]. Verifying such a domain raises specific challenges not only in terms of semantic proofs but also in terms of efficient implementation of the transfer functions. Without special care, the domain may not be able to scale to large enough programs. We also intend to connect relational abstract domains to the interface for numerical environments. We would like to develop efficient validation techniques following Besson *et al.* [4] approach and test their efficiency on large programs. The last and important challenge concerns floats. Astrée relies on subtle reasoning and manipulation on floats. CompCert has recently been enhanced with a fully verified implementation of floating-point arithmetic [5] and we hope to be able to incorporate them in our own value analysis.

Acknowledgements. We thank Antoine Miné, David Monniaux and Xavier Rival for many fruitful discussions on the Astrée static analyzer. We thank Jacques-Henri Jourdan and Xavier Leroy for integrating the CFG language into the CompCert compiler.

References

1. Appel, A.W.: Verified software toolchain. In: Barthe, G. (ed.) ESOP 2011. LNCS, vol. 6602, pp. 1–17. Springer, Heidelberg (2011)
2. Appel, A.W., Blazy, S.: Separation logic for small-step Cminor. In: Schneider, K., Brandt, J. (eds.) TPHOLs 2007. LNCS, vol. 4732, pp. 5–21. Springer, Heidelberg (2007)
3. Bertot, Y., Grégoire, B., Leroy, X.: A structured approach to proving compiler optimizations based on dataflow analysis. In: Filliâtre, J.-C., Paulin-Mohring, C., Werner, B. (eds.) TYPES 2004. LNCS, vol. 3839, pp. 66–81. Springer, Heidelberg (2006)
4. Besson, F., Jensen, T., Pichardie, D., Turpin, T.: Certified result checking for polyhedral analysis of bytecode programs. In: Wirsing, M., Hofmann, M., Rauschmayer, A. (eds.) TGC 2010, LNCS, vol. 6084, pp. 253–267. Springer, Heidelberg (2010)
5. Boldo, S., Jourdan, J., Leroy, X., Melquiond, G.: A formally-verified C compiler supporting floating-point arithmetic. In: Proc. of ARITH 21. IEEE Computer Society Press (to appear, 2013)
6. Bourdoncle, F.: Efficient chaotic iteration strategies with widenings. In: Pottosin, I.V., Bjorner, D., Broy, M. (eds.) FMP&TA 1993. LNCS, vol. 735, pp. 128–141. Springer, Heidelberg (1993)
7. Cachera, D., Jensen, T.P., Pichardie, D., Rusu, V.: Extracting a data flow analyser in constructive logic. Theoretical Computer Science 342(1), 56–78 (2005)

8. Cachera, D., Pichardie, D.: A certified denotational abstract interpreter. In: Kaufmann, M., Paulson, L.C. (eds.) ITP 2010. LNCS, vol. 6172, pp. 9–24. Springer, Heidelberg (2010)
9. Coupet-Grimal, S., Delobel, W.: A uniform and certified approach for two static analyses. In: Filliâtre, J.-C., Paulin-Mohring, C., Werner, B. (eds.) TYPES 2004. LNCS, vol. 3839, pp. 115–137. Springer, Heidelberg (2006)
10. Cousot, P., Cousot, R.: Abstract interpretation frameworks. Journal of Logic and Computation 2(4), 511–547 (1992)
11. Cousot, P., Cousot, R., Feret, J., Mauborgne, L., Miné, A., Monniaux, D., Rival, X.: The Astrée analyzer. In: Sagiv, M. (ed.) ESOP 2005. LNCS, vol. 3444, pp. 21–30. Springer, Heidelberg (2005)
12. Cousot, P., Halbwachs, N.: Automatic discovery of linear restraints among variables of a program. In: Proc. of POPL 1978, pp. 84–97. ACM Press (1978)
13. Cuoq, P., Kirchner, F., Kosmatov, N., Prevosto, V., Signoles, J., Yakobowski, B.: Frama-C. In: Eleftherakis, G., Hinchey, M., Holcombe, M. (eds.) SEFM 2012. LNCS, vol. 7504, pp. 233–247. Springer, Heidelberg (2012)
14. Pichardie, D.: Interprétation abstraite en logique intuitionniste : extraction d'analyseurs Java certifiés. PhD thesis, Université Rennes 1 (2005) (in French)
15. Gonthier, G.: The Four Colour Theorem: Engineering of a Formal Proof. In: Kapur, D. (ed.) ASCM 2007. LNCS (LNAI), vol. 5081, p. 333. Springer, Heidelberg (2008)
16. Gonthier, G.: Engineering mathematics: the odd order theorem proof. In: Proc. of POPL 2013, pp. 1–2. ACM (2013)
17. Hofmann, M., Karbyshev, A., Seidl, H.: Verifying a local generic solver in Coq. In: Cousot, R., Martel, M. (eds.) SAS 2010. LNCS, vol. 6337, pp. 340–355. Springer, Heidelberg (2010)
18. Klein, G., Andronick, J., Elphinstone, K., Heiser, G., Cock, D., Derrin, P., Elkaduwe, D., Engelhardt, K., Kolanski, R., Norrish, M., Sewell, T., Tuch, H., Winwood, S.: SeL4: formal verification of an operating-system kernel. Comm. of the ACM 53(6), 107–115 (2010)
19. Klein, G., Nipkow, T.: A machine-checked model for a Java-like language, virtual machine and compiler. ACM TOPLAS 28(4), 619–695 (2006)
20. Leroy, X.: A formally verified compiler back-end. Journal of Automated Reasoning 43(4), 363–446 (2009)
21. Leroy, X., Appel, A.W., Blazy, S., Stewart, G.: The CompCert memory model, version 2. Research report RR-7987, INRIA (June 2012)
22. Robert, V., Leroy, X.: A formally-verified alias analysis. In: Hawblitzel, C., Miller, D. (eds.) CPP 2012. LNCS, vol. 7679, pp. 11–26. Springer, Heidelberg (2012)
23. Miné, A.: Field-sensitive value analysis of embedded C programs with union types and pointer arithmetics. In: Proc. of LCTES 2006, pp. 54–63. ACM (June 2006)
24. Navas, J.A., Schachte, P., Søndergaard, H., Stuckey, P.J.: Signedness-agnostic program analysis: Precise integer bounds for low-level code. In: Jhala, R., Igarashi, A. (eds.) APLAS 2012. LNCS, vol. 7705, pp. 115–130. Springer, Heidelberg (2012)
25. Nipkow, T.: Abstract interpretation of annotated commands. In: Beringer, L., Felty, A. (eds.) ITP 2012. LNCS, vol. 7406, pp. 116–132. Springer, Heidelberg (2012)
26. Rideau, S., Leroy, X.: Validating register allocation and spilling. In: Gupta, R. (ed.) CC 2010. LNCS, vol. 6011, pp. 224–243. Springer, Heidelberg (2010)
27. Simon, A., King, A.: Taming the wrapping of integer arithmetic. In: Riis Nielson, H., Filé, G. (eds.) SAS 2007. LNCS, vol. 4634, pp. 121–136. Springer, Heidelberg (2007)
28. Vafeiadis, V., Zappa Nardelli, F.: Verifying fence elimination optimisations. In: Yahav, E. (ed.) SAS 2011. LNCS, vol. 6887, pp. 146–162. Springer, Heidelberg (2011)

Efficient Generation of Correctness Certificates for the Abstract Domain of Polyhedra*

Alexis Fouilhe, David Monniaux, and Michaël Périn

Verimag – Centre Équation – 2, Avenue de Vignate, 38610 Gières, France

Abstract. Polyhedra form an established abstract domain for inferring runtime properties of programs using abstract interpretation. Computations on them need to be certified for the whole static analysis results to be trusted. In this work, we look at how far we can get down the road of a posteriori verification to lower the overhead of certification of the abstract domain of polyhedra. We demonstrate methods for making the cost of inclusion certificate generation negligible. From a performance point of view, our single-representation, constraints-based implementation compares with state-of-the-art implementations.

In static analysis by abstract interpretation [1], sets of reachable states, which are in general infinite or at least very large and not amenable to tractable computation, are over-approximated by elements of an *abstract domain* on which the analyzer applies forward (resp. backward) steps corresponding to program operations (assignments, tests. . .) as well as "joins" corresponding to control points with several incoming (resp. outgoing) edges. When dealing with numerical variables in the analyzed programs, one of the simplest abstract domains consists in keeping one interval per variable, and the forward analysis is known as *interval arithmetic*. Interval arithmetic however does not keep track of relationships between variables. The domain of *convex polyhedra* [2] tracks relationships of the form $\sum_i a_i x_i \bowtie b$ where the a_i and b are integer (or rational) constants, the x_i are rational program variables, and $\bowtie$ is $\leq$, $<$ or $=$.

The implementor of an abstract domain faces two hurdles: the implementation should be reasonably efficient and scalable; it should be reasonably bug-free. As an example, the Parma Polyhedra Library (PPL) [3], version 1.0, which implements several relational numerical abstract domains, comprises 260,000 lines of C++; despite the care put in its development, it is probable that bugs have slipped through. The same applies to the APRON library [4].

Such hurdles are especially severe when the analysis is applied to large-scale critical programs (e.g. in the ASTRÉE system [5], targeting avionics software). For such systems, normal compilers may not be trusted, resulting in expensive post-compilation checking procedures, and prompting the development of the COMPCERT certified compiler [6]: this compiler is programmed, specified and proved correct in COQ [7]. We wish to extend this approach to obtain a trusted static analyzer; this article focuses on obtaining a trusted library for convex

---

* This work was partially supported by ANR project "VERASCO" (INS 2011).

F. Logozzo and M. Fähndrich (Eds.): SAS 2013, LNCS 7935, pp. 345–365, 2013.
© Springer-Verlag Berlin Heidelberg 2013

polyhedra, similar in features to the polyhedra libraries at the core of PPL and APRON.

One method for certifying the results of a static analysis is to store the invariants obtained by an untrusted analyzer at (roughly) all program points, then check that they are inductive using a trusted checker: each statement is then a Hoare triple that must be checked. Unfortunately, storing invariants everywhere proved impractical in the ASTRÉE analyzer due to memory consumption; we then opted to recompute them. Our (future) analyzer will thus store invariants only at loop heads, and thus, for control programs consisting of one huge control loop plus small, unrolled, inner loops, will store only a single invariant. It will then enter a checking phase which will recompute, in a trusted fashion, all intermediate invariants. Efficiency is thus important.

The main contribution of our article is an efficient way of implementing a provably correct abstract domain of polyhedra. Efficiency is two-fold:

1. In proof effort: most of the implementation consists in an untrusted oracle providing *certificates* of the correctness of its computations; only a much smaller certificate checker, consisting in simple algorithms (multiplying and adding vectors, replacing a variable by an expression), needs to be proven correct in the proof assistant.
2. In execution time: the expensive parts of the computations (e.g. linear programming) are inside the untrusted oracle and may use efficient programming techniques unavailable in parts that need formal proofs. We do not compute certificates as an afterthought of polyhedral computations: close examination of the algorithms implementing the polyhedral operators revealed that they directly expose the elements needed to build certificates. Simple bookkeeping alleviates the need to rebuild them after the fact. The overhead of making the operators certifying is thus very limited. This contrasts with earlier approaches [8] based on *a posteriori* generation of witnesses, which had to be recomputed from scratch using linear programming.

A second contribution is a complete implementation of the abstract domain of polyhedra in a purely constraints-based representation. Most libraries used in static analysis, including PPL and APRON, use a double description: a polyhedron is both an intersection of half-spaces (constraints) or the convex hull of vertices, half-lines and lines (generators), with frequent conversions. Unfortunately, the generator representation is exponential in the number of constraints, including for common cases such as hypercubes (e.g. specification of ranges of inputs for the program). We instead chose to represent the polyhedra solely as lists of constraints, with pruning of redundant ones. Our implementation uses sparse matrices of rational numbers and uses efficient techniques for convex hull [9] and emptiness testing by linear programming [10].

We applied our library to examples of polyhedral computations obtained by running the PAGAI static analyzer [11] on benchmark programs. Despite a common claim that implementations based on the double representation are more efficient than those based on constraints only, our library reaches performance comparable to the APRON library together with the high-level of trust brought by our COQ certificate checker.

The remainder of this paper is organized as follows. After having stated the conventions we are using (§1), we define correctness criteria for the operators of the abstract domain (§2), which all reduce to inclusion properties for which certificates are presented as *Farkas coefficients* (also known as Lagrange multipliers) (§3). Such certificates may also be cheaply generated for the convex hull (§4). Both forward step and convex hull operations reduce internally to a form of projection. Some design choices of our implementation are then described (§5), including how to keep the representation size of the polyhedra reasonable. Last before conclusion (§7), an experimental evaluation and accompanying results are presented (§6).

1   Definitions and Notations

In the remainder of this article, we use the following notations and definitions.

1. C: a linear constraint of the form $\boldsymbol{a} \cdot \boldsymbol{x} \leq b$ where $\boldsymbol{a}$ is a vector of rational constants, b is a rational and $\boldsymbol{x} \in \mathbb{Q}^n$ is the vector of the analyzed program variables. Such a linear constraint, or constraint for short, can be viewed as a half-space in an n-dimensional space. We write $\overline{C} \stackrel{\text{def}}{=} \boldsymbol{a} \cdot \boldsymbol{x} > b$ for the complementary half-space.

2. P: a convex polyhedron, not necessarily closed, represented as a set of constraints. We call "size of the representation of P" the number of constraints that P is made of.

3. satisfaction: saying that point $\boldsymbol{y}$ of $\mathbb{Q}^n$ satisfies a constraint $C \stackrel{\text{def}}{=} \boldsymbol{a} \cdot \boldsymbol{x} \leq b$ means that $\boldsymbol{a} \cdot \boldsymbol{y} \leq b$. By extension, a point $\boldsymbol{y}$ satisfies (or is in) polyhedron P if it satisfies all of its constraints. We write this: Sat P $\boldsymbol{y}$. Given that a constraint C can be regarded as polyhedron with only one constraint, we also write: Sat C $\boldsymbol{y}$.

4. Given our focus on the abstract domain of polyhedra we shall adopt the following vocabulary.
   (a) The order relation on polyhedra $\sqsubseteq$ is geometrical inclusion.
   (b) The least upper bound $\sqcup$ is the convex hull.
   (c) The greatest lower bound $\sqcap$ is geometrical intersection.
   We will further distinguish the definition of abstract domain operators from their actual implementation, which can have bugs. The implemented version of the operators will be written with a hat: $\widehat{\sqsubseteq}, \widehat{\sqcup}$ and $\widehat{\sqcap}$ implement the ideal operators $\sqsubseteq, \sqcup$ and $\sqcap$, respectively.

5. inclusion: a polyhedron P_1 is included in a polyhedron P_2 (noted $P_1 \sqsubseteq P_2$) if and only if
$$\forall \boldsymbol{y}, \text{Sat } P_1 \ \boldsymbol{y} \Rightarrow \text{Sat } P_2 \ \boldsymbol{y} \tag{1}$$

Inclusion for constraints $C_1 \stackrel{\text{def}}{=} \boldsymbol{a}_1 \cdot \boldsymbol{x} \leq b_1$ and $C_2 \stackrel{\text{def}}{=} \boldsymbol{a}_2 \cdot \boldsymbol{x} \leq b_2$ is a special case which is easy to decide: $C_1 \sqsubseteq C_2$ holds if and only if there exists $k > 0$ such that $k \cdot \boldsymbol{a}_1 = \boldsymbol{a}_2$ and $k \cdot b_1 \leq b_2$. This latter case is thus proven correct directly inside COQ.

2   Correctness of the Abstract Domain Operators

Let us now see what needs to be proven for the implementation of each operator of an abstract domain so that the correctness of its result can be established.

Inclusion test $P_1 \mathrel{\widehat{\sqsubseteq}} P_2 \Rightarrow P_1 \sqsubseteq P_2$

Convex hull $P_1 \sqsubseteq P_1 \mathbin{\widehat{\sqcup}} P_2$ and $P_2 \sqsubseteq P_1 \mathbin{\widehat{\sqcup}} P_2$

Intersection $\forall \boldsymbol{x}, \mathrm{Sat}\ P_1\ \boldsymbol{x} \wedge \mathrm{Sat}\ P_2\ \boldsymbol{x} \Rightarrow \mathrm{Sat}\ P_1 \mathbin{\widehat{\sqcap}} P_2\ \boldsymbol{x}.$

> For now, we will assume a naive implementation of the intersection: $P_1 \mathbin{\widehat{\sqcap}} P_2$ is the union of the constraints of P_1 with these of P_2, which trivially satisfies the desired property.

Assignment in a forward analysis, $x := e$ amounts to intersection by the equality constraint $x' = e$ (where x' is a fresh variable), projection of x and renaming of x' to x.[1] When analyzing backward, assignment is just substitution.

Projection if P_2 is the returned polyhedron for the projection of P_1 parallel to variables $x_{i_1}, \ldots, x_{i_p}$ we check that $P_1 \sqsubseteq P_2$ and that variables $x_{i_1}, \ldots, x_{i_p}$ do not appear in the constraints defining P_2.

Widening : no correctness check needed. Widening (∇) is used to accelerate the convergence of the analysis to a candidate invariant. For partial correctness of the analyzer, no property is formally needed of the widening operator, since iterations stop when the inclusion test reports that an inductive invariant has been obtained. There exist formalizations of the widening operator suitable for proving the total correctness of the analysis (that is, that it eventually converges to an inductive invariant) [12] but we avoided this question by assuming some large upper bound on the number of iterations after which the analyzer terminates with an error message.

Remark that we only prove that the returned polyhedron *contains* the polyhedron that it should ideally be (which is all that is needed for proving that the results of the analysis are sound), not that it *equals* it: for instance, we prove that the polyhedron returned by the convex hull operator includes the convex hull, not that it is the true convex hull. The *precision* of our algorithms (that is, the property that they do not return polyhedra larger than needed) is not proved formally; it is however ensured by usual software engineering methods (informally correct algorithms, comparing the output of our implementation to that of other polyhedra libraries...).

3   A Posteriori Verification of the Inclusion Test

We shall now describe a way to ensure the correctness of the inclusion test. Recall we represent polyhedra as sets of constraints only. Our certificate for

---

[1] Other polyhedra libraries distinguish invertible assignments (e.g. $x := x + 1$, more generally $\boldsymbol{x'} = A \cdot \boldsymbol{x}$ with A an invertible matrix), which can be handled without projection, from non-invertible ones (e.g. $x := y + z$). Because our library automatically keeps a canonical system of equalities, which it uses if possible when projecting, no explicit detection of invertibility is needed; it is subsumed by the canonicalization.

proving that a polyhedron P, composed of the constraints $C_1, \ldots, C_n$ satisfies a constraint C relies on the following trivial fact:

Lemma 1. *If a point $\boldsymbol{y}$ satisfies a set of constraints $\{C_1, \ldots, C_n\}$, it satisfies any linear positive combination $\sum_{i=1}^n \lambda_i C_i$ with $\lambda_i \geq 0$.*

If we can find a constraint C' that is a linear positive combination of $C_1, \ldots, C_n$ and such that $C' \sqsubseteq C$ then it follows that P is included in C. Farkas' lemma states that such linear combinations necessarily exist when inclusion holds, which justifies our approach.

The motivation for *a posteriori* verification of inclusion results stems from this formulation: while finding an appropriate linear combination requires advanced algorithms, a small program checking that a particular set of λ_i's entails $P \sqsubseteq C$ can easily be proven correct in a proof assistant. We call these λ_i's the *certificate* for $P \sqsubseteq C$.

3.1   A Certificate Checker Certified in Coq

Our certificate checker has COQ type:

`inclusion_checker` $(P_1\ P_2 : \textbf{Polyhedra})\ (cert : \textbf{Cert}) : \textbf{Exception}\ (P_1 \sqsubseteq P_2)$

where the type **Polyhedra** is a simple representation of a polyhedron as a list of linear constraints and the type **Cert** is a representation for inclusion certificates. If a proof of $P_1 \sqsubseteq P_2$ can be built from *cert*, then the `inclusion_checker` returns it wrapped in the constructor VALUE. However *cert* might be incorrect due to a bug in $\widehat{\sqsubseteq}$. In this case, the `inclusion_checker` fails to build a proof of $P_1 \sqsubseteq P_2$ and returns ERROR.

When extracting the OCAML program from the COQ development, proof terms are erased and the type of the checker function becomes that which would have been expected from a hand-written OCAML function:[2]

$$\texttt{inclusion\_checker} : \textbf{Polyhedra} \to \textbf{Polyhedra} \to \textbf{Cert} \to \textbf{bool}$$

In reality, our implementation is slightly more complicated because the untrusted part of our library, for efficiency reasons, operates on fast rational and integer arithmetic, while the checker uses standard COQ types that explicitly represent integers as a list of bits (see §5.6).

3.2   A Certificate-Generating Inclusion Test

Let us now go back to the problem of building a proof of $P \sqsubseteq C$ by exhibiting an appropriate linear combination. From [8], this can be rephrased as a pure satisfiability problem in linear programming:

$$\left(\forall y, \neg \text{Sat}\ \left(P \sqcap \overline{C}\right)\ y\right) \Rightarrow P \sqsubseteq C$$

---

[2] We chose to replace the constructors VALUE and ERROR of the type **Exception** by OCAML booleans instead of letting the extraction define an OCAML type "exception" with two nullary constructors due to proof terms being erased.

This problem can be solved by the simplex algorithm [13]. For this purpose, the simplex variant proposed by [10], designed for SMT-solvers, is particularly well-suited. This algorithm only implements the first of the two phases of the simplex algorithm: finding a feasible point, that is a point satisfying all the constraints of the problem. If there is no such point, a witness of unsatisfiability is extracted as a set of mutually exclusive bounds on linear terms and suitable Farkas coefficients λ, in the same way that blocking clauses for theory lemmas are obtained for use in SMT-solving modulo linear rational arithmetic. Furthermore, this algorithm is designed for cheap backtracking (addition and removal of constraints), which is paramount in SMT-solving and also very useful in our application (§5.2).

Our approach to certificate generation differs from previous suggestions [8] where inclusion is first tested by untrusted means, and, if the answer is positive, a vector of Farkas coefficients is sought as the solution of a dual linear programming problem with optimization, which has a solution, the Farkas coefficients, if and only if the primal problem has no solution. Ours uses a primal formulation without optimization.

3.3   From an Unsatisfiability Witness to an Inclusion Certificate

Inclusion certificates are derived from unsatisfiability witness in a way similar to [14]. To illustrate how they are built as part of the inclusion test, a global idea of the inner workings of the simplex variant from [10] is needed. We insist on the following being a coarse approximation.

We aim at building, given P non-empty and C, an inclusion certificate for $P \sqsubseteq C$, otherwise said $P \wedge \overline{C}$ having no solution. P is composed of n constraints $C_1, \ldots, C_n$ of the form $\sum_{j=1}^{n} a_{ij} \cdot x_j \leq b_i$, where i is the constraint subscript. We refer to $\overline{C} \stackrel{\text{def}}{=} b_0 < \sum_{j=1}^{n} a_{0j} \cdot x_j$ as C_0.

Let us start by describing the organization of data. Each constraint C_i is split into an equation $x'_i = \sum_{j=1}^{n} a_{ij} \cdot x_j$ and a bound $x'_i \leq b_i$ where x'_i is a fresh variable. For the sake of simplicity, in this presentation, a constraint $x_i \leq b_i$ is represented as $x'_i = x_i \wedge x'_i \leq b_i$; the actual implementation avoids introducing such extra variable. Therefore, each x'_i uniquely identifies C_i by construction and the original variables x_i are unbounded. We call *basic* the variables which are defined by an equation (*i.e.* on the left-hand side, with unit coefficient) and *non-basic* the others. Last, the algorithm maintains a candidate feasible point, that is a value for every variable x'_i and x_j, initially set to 0.

From this starting point, the algorithm iterates pivoting steps while ensuring preservation of the invariant: *the candidate feasible point always satisfy the equations and the values of the non-basic variables always satisfy their bounds (‡).* At each iteration and prior to pivoting, a basic variable x'_i is chosen such that its value does not satisfy its bounds. Either there is no such x'_i, and the candidate feasible point is indeed a solution of $P \wedge \overline{C}$, thereby disproving $P \sqsubseteq C$; or there is such a basic variable x'_i. In this case, we shift its value to fit its bounds and we seek a non-basic variable x'_n such that its value can be adjusted to compensate the shift: through a pivoting step, x'_i becomes non-basic, and x'_n becomes basic.

If there is no such x'_n (because all the non-basic variables already have reached their bound), the equation which defines x'_i exhibits incompatible bounds of the problem and is of the form $x'_i = \sum_{j \neq i} \lambda_j \cdot x'_j$ (only x'_j's appear in this equation: recall that the x_j's are unbounded). We now show how to transform this unsatisfiability result into an inclusion certificate.

Since we supposed that P is not empty, the unsatisfiability necessarily involves C_0. Thus, x'_0, which represents C_0, has a non-zero coefficient λ_0 in the equation. Without loss of generality, we suppose that the incompatible bounds involve an upper bound on x'_i and that λ_0 is positive. The above equation can be rewritten so that x'_0 appears on the left-hand side:

$$x'_0 = \sum_{j=1}^{n} \lambda'_j \cdot x'_j$$

where the lower bound $b_0 < x'_0$ and the upper bound $\sum_{j=1}^{n} \lambda'_j \cdot x'_j \leq b'$ are such that $b' \leq b_0$. Recall that the x'_i's were defined as equal to linear terms $l_i \overset{\text{def}}{=} \sum_{j=1}^{n} a_{ij} \cdot x_j$ of the constraints C_i. Let us now substitute the x'_i's by their definition, yielding

$$l_0 = \sum_{j=1}^{n} \lambda'_j \cdot l_j$$

Noting that C is $l_0 \leq b_0$ (since $C_0 = b_0 < l_0$ is $\overline{C}$), that $\sum_{j=1}^{n} \lambda'_j \cdot l_j \leq b$ and that $b' \leq b_0$, the λ'_j's form an inclusion certificate for $P \sqsubseteq C$.

4   A Posteriori Verification of the Convex Hull

We saw in §2 that the result of the convex hull of two polyhedra P_1 and P_2 must verify inclusion properties with respect to both P_1 and P_2. Computing $P \overset{\text{def}}{=} P_1 \sqcup P_2$, then $P_1 \sqsubseteq P$ and $P_2 \sqsubseteq P$ and then checking the certificates would produce a certified convex hull result, at the expense of two extra inclusion tests. From a development point of view, this is the lightest approach. However, careful exploitation of the details of $\sqcup$ can save us the extra cost of certificate generation, at the expense of some development effort.

Before delving into the details, let us introduce some more notations for the sake of brevity. In this section, a polyhedron P is regarded as a column vector of the constraints $C_1, \ldots, C_n$ it is composed of. This allows for a matrix notation: $P \overset{\text{def}}{=} \{x \mid A \cdot x \leq b\}$, where the linear term of C_i is the ith line of A and the constant of C_i is the ith component of b.

Then, an inclusion certificate, $\lambda_1, \ldots, \lambda_n$, for $P \sqsubseteq C'$ is a line vector Λ, such that $\Lambda \cdot P = C$ and $C \sqsubseteq C'$. Now, an inclusion certificate for $P \sqsubseteq P'$ is a set of inclusion certificates $\Lambda_1, \ldots, \Lambda_n$, one for each constraint C'_i of P'. Such a set can be regarded as a matrix F such that

$$F \overset{\text{def}}{=} \begin{pmatrix} \Lambda_1 \\ \vdots \\ \Lambda_n \end{pmatrix} \text{ and } F \times P \sqsubseteq P'$$

where the ith line of $F \times P$ is a constraint C such that $C \sqsubseteq C'_i$. We call Λ a *Farkas vector* and F a *Farkas matrix*.

4.1   A Convex Hull Algorithm on Constraints Representation

The convex hull $P_1 \sqcup P_2$ is the smallest polyhedron containing all line segments joining P_1 to P_2. Thus, a point x of $P_1 \sqcup P_2$ is the barycenter of a point x_1 in P_1 and a point x_2 in P_2. Exploiting this remark, [15] defined $P_1 \sqcup P_2$, with $P_i = \{x \mid A_i \cdot x \leq b_i\}$, as the set of solutions of the constraints $A_1 \cdot x_1 \leq b_1 \wedge A_2 \cdot x_2 \leq b_2 \wedge x = \alpha_1 \cdot x_1 + \alpha_2 \cdot x_2 \wedge \alpha_1 + \alpha_2 = 1 \wedge 0 \leq \alpha_1 \wedge 0 \leq \alpha_2$ using $2n + 2$ auxiliary variables $x_1, x_2, \alpha_1, \alpha_2$ where $n = |x|$ is the number of variables of the polyhedron. Still following [15], the variable changes $x'_1 = \alpha_1 \cdot x_1$ and $x'_2 = \alpha_2 \cdot x_2$ remove the non-linearity of the equation $x = \alpha_1 \cdot x_1 + \alpha_2 \cdot x_2$.

The resulting polyhedron can regarded as the 3-block system S_{bar} below. The auxiliary variables $x'_1, x'_2, \alpha_1, \alpha_2$ are then projected out to stick to the tuple x of program variables. Therefore, the untrusted convex hull operator $\hat{\sqcup}$ mainly consists in a sequence of projections: $P_1 \,\hat{\sqcup}\, P_2 \overset{\text{def}}{=} \widehat{proj}\; S_{bar} \,(x'_1, x'_2, \alpha_1, \alpha_2)$ where

$$S_{bar} = \left(\begin{array}{c} \boxed{A_1 x'_1 \leq \alpha_1 b_1} \\[6pt] \boxed{A_2 x'_2 \leq \alpha_2 b_2} \\[6pt] \boxed{\begin{array}{c} x = x'_1 + x'_2 \\ \alpha_1 + \alpha_2 = 1 \\ 0 \leq \alpha_1 \\ 0 \leq \alpha_2 \end{array}} \end{array} \right)$$

4.2   Instrumenting the Projection Algorithm

Projecting a variable x_k from a polyhedron P represented by constraints can be achieved using Fourier-Motzkin elimination (e.g. [13]). This algorithm partitions the constraints of P into three sets: $E^0_{x_k}$ contains the constraints where the coefficient of x_k is nil, $E^+_{x_k}$ contains those having a strictly positive coefficient for x_k and $E^-_{x_k}$ contains those which coefficient for x_k is strictly negative.

Then, the result P_{proj} of the projection of x_k from P is defined as

$$P_{\text{proj}} = proj\, P\, x_k \overset{\text{def}}{=} E^0_{x_k} \cup \left(map\; elim_{x_k}\, (E^+_{x_k} \times E^-_{x_k})\right)$$

where $E^+_{x_k} \times E^-_{x_k}$ is the set of all possible pairs of inequalities, one element of each pair belonging to $E^+_{x_k}$ and the other belonging to $E^-_{x_k}$. The $elim_{x_k}$ function builds the linear combination with positive coefficients of the members of a pair such that x_k has a zero coefficient in the result.

Illustrating on an example, projecting x from

$$P \overset{\text{def}}{=} \{y \leq 1, 2 \cdot x + y \leq 2, -x - y \leq 1\} \text{ gives}$$

$$E^0_x = \{y \leq 1\} \text{ and } E^+_x \times E^-_x = \{(2 \cdot x + y \leq 2, -x - y \leq 1)\}$$

From $1 \cdot (2 \cdot x + y \leq 2) + 2 \cdot (-x - y \leq 1) = -y \leq 4$, we get $P_{\text{proj}} = \{y \leq 1, -y \leq 4\}$.

Note that every constraint C of P_{proj} is either a constraint of P, or the result of a linear combination with non-negative coefficients λ_1, λ_2 of two constraints C_1 and C_2 of P, such that $\lambda_1 \cdot C_1 + \lambda_2 \cdot C_2 = C$. It is therefore possible, with some bookkeeping, to build a matrix F such that $F \times P = P_{\text{proj}}$. This extends to the projection of several variables: if $proj\ P\ \boldsymbol{x}_k = P_{\text{proj}} = F \times P$ and $proj\ P_{\text{proj}}\ \boldsymbol{x}_l = P'_{\text{proj}} = F' \times P_{\text{proj}}$, then $P'_{\text{proj}} = F'' \times P$ with $F'' = F' \times F$.

Fourier-Motzkin elimination can generate a lot of redundant constraints, which make the representation size of P_{proj} unwieldy. In the worst case, the n constraints split evenly into $E^+_{x_k}$ and $E^-_{x_k}$, and thus, after one elimination, one gets $n^2/4$ constraints; this yields an upper bound of $n^{2^p}/4^p$ where p is the number of elimination steps. Yet, the number of true faces can only grow in single exponential [16, §4.1]; thus most generated constraints are likely to be redundant.

The algorithm inspired from [9], which we use in practice, adds these refinements to Fourier-Motzkin elimination:

1. Using equalities when available to make substitutions. A substitution is no more than a linear combination of two constraints, the coefficients of which can be recorded in F. Note that there is no sign restriction on the coefficient applied to an equality.
2. Discarding trivially redundant constraints. The corresponding line F can be discarded just as well.
3. Discarding constraints proved redundant by linear programming, as in §5.2.

Note that, since discarding a constraint only *adds* points to the polyhedron, there is no need to prove these refinements to be correct or to provide certificates for them. We could thus very easily add new heuristics.

4.3   On-the-Fly Generation of Inclusion Certificates

In order to establish the correctness of static analysis, the convex hull operator should return a superset of the true convex hull; we thus need proofs of $P_1 \sqsubseteq P_1 \mathbin{\widehat{\sqcup}} P_2$ and $P_2 \sqsubseteq P_1 \mathbin{\widehat{\sqcup}} P_2$. The converse inclusion is not needed for correctness, though we expect that it holds; we will not prove it. A certifying operator $\widehat{\sqcup}$ must then produce for each constraint C of $P_1 \mathbin{\widehat{\sqcup}} P_2$ a certificate Λ_1 (resp. Λ_2) proving the inclusion of P_1 (resp. P_2) into the single-constraint polyhedron C. The method we propose for on-the-fly generation of a correctness certificate is based on the following remark.

For each constraint C of $P_1 \mathbin{\widehat{\sqcup}} P_2$, the projection operator $\widehat{proj}$ provides a vector Λ such that $\Lambda \times S_{bar} = C$, where S_{bar} is the system of constraints defined in §4.1. An examination of the certificate reveals that Λ can be split into three parts $(\Lambda_1, \Lambda_2, \Lambda_3)$ such that Λ_1 refers to the constraints $A_1.\boldsymbol{x}'_1 \leq \alpha_1 \boldsymbol{b_1}$ derived from P_1 ; Λ_2 refers to the constraints $A_2.\boldsymbol{x}'_2 \leq \alpha_2 \boldsymbol{b_2}$ derived from P_2 and Λ_3 refers to the barycenter part $\boldsymbol{x} = \boldsymbol{x}'_1 + \boldsymbol{x}'_2 \wedge \alpha_1 + \alpha_2 = 1 \wedge 0 \leq \alpha_1 \wedge 0 \leq \alpha_2$. Let us apply the substitution $\sigma = [\alpha_1/1, \alpha_2/0, \boldsymbol{x}'_1/\boldsymbol{x}, \boldsymbol{x}'_2/0]$, that characterizes the points of P_1 as some extreme barycenters, to each terms of the equality $\Lambda \times S_{bar} = C$. This only changes S_{bar}: Indeed, $\Lambda\sigma = \Lambda$ since Λ is a constant vector and $C\sigma = C$

since none of the substituted variables appears in C (due to projection). We obtain the equality (below) where many constraints of $S_{bar}\sigma$ became trivial.

$$(\Lambda_1, \Lambda_2, \Lambda_3) \times \begin{pmatrix} \boxed{A_1 x \leq b_1} \\ \boxed{0 \leq 0} \\ \boxed{\begin{matrix} x = x \\ 1 = 1 \\ 0 \leq 1 \\ 0 \leq 0 \end{matrix}} \end{pmatrix} = C$$

This equality can be simplified into $\Lambda_1 \times (A_1 x \leq b_1) + \lambda(0 \leq 1) = C$ where λ is the third coefficient of Λ_3. This shows that Λ_1 is a certificate[3] for $P_1 \sqsubseteq C$. The same reasoning with $\sigma = [\alpha_1/0, \alpha_2/1, x'_1/0, x'_2/x]$ shows that Λ_2 is a certificate for $P_2 \sqsubseteq C$.

5   Notes on the Implementation

The practical efficiency of the abstract domain operators is highly sensitive to implementation details. Let us thus describe our main design choices.

5.1   Extending to Equalities and Strict Inequalities

Everything we discussed so far deals with non-strict inequalities only. The inclusion test algorithm however complements such non-strict inequalities, which yields strict ones. Adaptation could have been restricted to the simplex algorithm on which the inclusion test relies, and such an enhancement is described in [10]. We have however elected to add full support for strict inequalities to our implementation. Once the addition of two constraints has been defined, almost no further change to the algorithms we discussed previously was needed.

Proper support and use of equalities was more involving. As [9] points out, equalities can be used for projecting variables. Such substitutions do not increase the number of constraints, contrary to Fourier-Motzkin elimination. We ended up splitting the constraint set into a set of equalities, each serving as the definition of a variable, and a set of inequalities in which these variables have been substituted by their definitions. Minimization (see §5.2) was augmented to look for implicit equalities in the set of inequalities. Last, testing inclusion of P in C was split into two phases: substituting in C the variables defined by the equalities of P and then using the simplex-based method described earlier without putting the equalities of P in, which reduces the problem size.

Inclusion certificates were adapted for equalities. If $P \sqsubseteq C$, with $C \stackrel{def}{=} a \cdot x = b$, cannot be proven using a linear combination of equalities, it is split as $\{a \cdot x \leq b, a \cdot x \geq b\}$ and P is proven to be included in each separately.

---

[3] The shift λ of the bound is lost and will be computed again by our CoQ-certified checker.

5.2   Minimization

The intersection $P_1 \widehat{\cap} P_2$ is a very simple operation. As §2 described, a naive implementation amounts to list concatenation. However, some constraints of P_1 may be redundant with constraints of P_2. Keeping redundant constraints leads to a quick growth of the representation sizes and thus of computation costs. In addition, one condition for the good operations of widening operators on polyhedra is that there should be no implicit equality in the system of inequalities and no redundant constraint [17].

It is therefore necessary to *minimize* the size of the representation of polyhedra, that is, removing all redundant constraints, and to have a system of equality constraints that exactly defines the affine span of the polyhedron. We call $P_{\min}$ the result of the minimization on P. The correctness of the result is preserved as long as $P_{\min}$ is an over-approximation of P, which means $P \sqsubseteq P_{\min}$.

First, we check whether P has points in it using the simplex algorithm from §3.3. If P is empty, $\bot$ is returned as the minimal representation. The certificate is built from the witness of contradictory bounds returned by the simplex algorithm. It is a linear combination which result is a trivially contradictory constraint involving only constants (e.g. $0 \leq -1$) and which, in other words, has no solution.

The next step is implicit equality detection. It builds on $\boldsymbol{a} \cdot \boldsymbol{x} \leq b \wedge \boldsymbol{a} \cdot \boldsymbol{x} \geq b \Rightarrow \boldsymbol{a} \cdot \boldsymbol{x} = b$. For every $C^{\leq} \stackrel{\text{def}}{=} \boldsymbol{a} \cdot \boldsymbol{x} \leq b$ of P (by definition $P \sqsubseteq C^{\leq}$), we test whether $P \sqsubseteq C^{\geq} \stackrel{\text{def}}{=} \boldsymbol{a} \cdot \boldsymbol{x} \geq b$. If the inclusion holds, the certificate of the resulting equality is composed of a linear combination yielding $C^{\geq}$ and a trivial one, $1 \cdot C^{\leq}$, yielding $C^{\leq}$. Once this is done, the representation of P can be split into a system of equalities P_e and a system of inequalities P_i with no implicit equality. P_e is transformed to be in echelon form using Gaussian elimination, which has two benefits. First, redundant equations are detected and removed. Second, each equation can now serve as the definition of one variable. The so-defined variables are then substituted in P_i, yielding P_i'. Although our implementation tracks evidence of the correctness of this process, it should be noted that the uses of equalities decribed above are standard practice.

At this point, if redundancy remains, it is to be found in P_i' only. It is detected using inclusion tests: for every $C \in P_i'$, if $P_i' \setminus \{C\} \sqsubseteq P_i'$, C is removed. Removing a constraint is, at worst, an over-approximation for which no justification needs to be provided.

All that we describe above involve many runs of the simplex algorithm. The key point which makes this viable in practice is the following: they are all strongly related and many pivoting steps are shared among the different queries. We described (§3.3) the data representation used by the simplex variant we use: it splits each constraint of P in linear term and bound by inserting new variables. These variables can have both an upper and a lower bound. Let us now illustrate the three steps of minimization on constraint $C \stackrel{\text{def}}{=} \boldsymbol{a} \cdot \boldsymbol{x} \leq b$, split as $x' = \boldsymbol{a} \cdot \boldsymbol{x}$ and $\boldsymbol{x}' \leq b$. The first step, satisfiability, solves this very problem. Then, implicit equalities detection checks whether $x' = \boldsymbol{a} \cdot \boldsymbol{x}$ and $x' < b$ is unsatisfiable. Last, redundancy elimination operates on $x' = \boldsymbol{a} \cdot \boldsymbol{x}$ and $x' > b$.

For all these problems, we only changed the bound on x', without ever touching either the constraint $x' = \boldsymbol{a} \cdot \boldsymbol{x}$ or the other constraints of P. These changes can be done dynamically, while preserving the simplex invariant (‡ of §3.3), by making sure that the affected x' is a basic variable. This remark, once generalized to a whole polyhedron, enables the factorization of the construction of the simplex problem. Actually, it is only done once for each minimization. It is also hoped that the feasible point of one problem is close enough to that of the next problem, so that convergence is quick.

Minimization also plays an important role in the convex hull algorithm. We mentioned (§4.2) that projection increases the representation size of polyhedra and described some simple counter-measures from [9]. When projecting a lot of variables, as is done for computing the convex hull of two polyhedra, each redundant constraint can trigger a lot of extra computation. Applying a complete minimization after the projection of each variable mitigates this. More precisely, only the third of the steps described above is used: projection cannot make a nonempty polyhedron empty and it cannot reduce the dimension of a polyhedron, no implicit equality can be created.

5.3   A More Detailed Intuition on Bookkeeping

We mentioned in §3.2 and §4 that simple bookkeeping makes it possible to build inclusion certificates. We now give a more precise insight on what is involved, on the example of the projection.

The main change is an extension of the notion of constraint, which is now a pair (f, C) of a certificate fragment and a linear constraint as we presented them so far. A certificate fragment f is a list of pairs (n_i, id_i), n_i being a rational coefficient and id_i a natural number uniquely identifying one constraint of P. The meaning of f is the following

$$\sum_i n_i \cdot C_{id_i} = C, \text{ with } C_{id_i} \in P \text{ and } (n_i, id_i) \in f$$

The $elim_{\boldsymbol{x}_k}$ function introduced in §4.2 is extended to take two extended constraints (f_1, C_1) and (f_2, C_2), and return an extended constraint (f, C). Recall that the original $elim_{\boldsymbol{x}_k}$ chooses λ_1 and λ_2 such that the coefficient of $\boldsymbol{x}_k$ in the resulting C is nil. The extended version returns $(\lambda_1 \cdot f_1 \ @ \ \lambda_2 \cdot f_2, \lambda_1 \cdot C_1 + \lambda_2 \cdot C_2)$, where @ is the list concatenation operator and $\lambda_i \cdot f_i$ is a notation for:

$$map \ (fun \ (n, id) \rightarrow (\lambda_i \cdot n, id)) \ f_i$$

The certificate fragment keeps track of how a constraint was generated from an initial set of constraints. For a single projection $proj \ P \ \boldsymbol{x}_k$, the fragments are initialized as $[(1, id_C)]$ for every constraint C before the actual projection starts. For a series of projection as done for the convex hull, the initialization takes place before the first projection.

5.4   Polyhedron Representation Invariants

The data representation our implementation uses for polyhedra satisfies a number of invariants which relate to minimality.

(1) There is no implicit equality among the inequalities.
(2) There is no redundant constraint, equality or inequality.
(3) In a given constraint, factors common to all the coefficients of variables are removed.
(4) Each equality provides a definition for one variable, which is then substituted in the inequalities.
(5) Empty polyhedra are explicitly labeled as such.

(3) helps keeping numbers small, hopefully fitting machine representation, resulting in cheaper arithmetic. (1) implies in particular that if an implicit equality is created when adding a constraint C to a polyhedron P, then C is necessarily involved in that equality. It follows that the search for implicit equalities can be restricted to those involving newly added constraints. Because of (2), the same holds for redundancy elimination: if C is shown to be redundant, P remains unaffected by the intersection. Furthermore, (4) allows for the reduction of the problem dimension when testing for $P_1 \sqsubseteq P_2$. Once the same variables are substituted in P_1 and P_2, only the inequalities need to be inserted in the simplex problem. Last, (3) and (4) give a canonical form to constraints, which make syntactic criteria for deciding inclusion of constraints more powerful. These criteria, suggested by [9], are used whenever possible in the inclusion test and the projection.

5.5   Data Structures

Radix Trees. Capturing linear relations between program variables with polyhedra generally leads to sparse systems, as noted by [9]. Our implementation uses a tree representation of vectors[4] where the path from the root to a node identifies the variable whose coefficient is stored at that node. This offers a middle ground between dense representation, as used by other widely-used implementation of the abstraction domain of polyhedra, and sparse representation which makes random access costly as sparsity diminishes.

Numbers Representation. Rational vector coefficients can grow so as to overflow native integer representation during an analysis. Working around this shortcoming requires the use of an arithmetic library for arbitrarily large numbers. This has a serious impact on overall performance. Our implementation uses the ZARITH[18] OCAML front-end to GMP[19]. ZARITH tries to lower the cost of using GMP by using native integers as long as they don't overflow.

Our experiments show that, in many practical cases, extended precision arithmetic is not used. This echoes similar findings in SMT-solvers such as Z3 or

---

[4] The idea was borrowed from [8].

OpenSMT [20]: in most cases, extended precision is not used, thus the great importance of an arithmetic library that operates on machine words as much as possible, without allocating extended precision numbers. In the case of polyhedra, however, the situation occasionally degenerates when the convex hull operator generates large coefficients.

The extracted OCAML code of inclusion_checker does not use this efficient representation. Because of the need for correctness of computations, the checker instead uses the COQ representation of numbers (lists of bits), which is inefficient on numerical computations. Alternatively, assuming trust in ZARITH and GMP, it is possible to configure the COQ extractor to base the checker on ZARITH.

5.6   A Posteriori Certification vs. Full COQ-Certified Development

Even though our library is planned to be used in a COQ-certified analyzer, we preferred *a posteriori* certification over a fully COQ-certified development. Keeping COQ only for the development of checkers of external computations reduces the development cost and reconciles efficiency of the tool and confidence in its implementation through certificates.

First, it reduces the proof effort: verifying that a guess is the solution to a problem involves weaker mathematic arguments than proving correctness and termination of the solver. To illustrate the simplicity of our COQ development, Figure 1 shows some excerpts which are self-explanatory. The last function, inclusion_checker, is representative of the difficulty of the proofs. This function is close to its extraction in OCAML except that it returns either an ERROR or a proof of $P_1 \sqsubseteq P_2$ wrapped in the VALUE constructor (Line 38). In the case where P_1 is an empty polyhedron (established by *eproof*) the proof of inclusion in P_2 is built from that proof of emptiness. The missing proof of Line 38 is done in the interactive prover (Lines 43-45) and automatically placed in the function. It consists in an induction on the list of constraints of P_2 that shows that the empty polyhedron P_1 is included in every constraint of P_2.

Our external library acts as an oracle: it efficiently performs the operation and returns a certificate which serves two purposes: it can be used to check the correctness of the computations but it is also a short cut toward the result. For instance, the convex hull $P_1 \sqcup P_2$ is easy to obtain from the complete inclusion certificates (F_1, λ_1) related to P_1 or (F_2, λ_2) related to P_2. Indeed, $P_1 \sqcup P_2 = F_1 \cdot P_1 + \lambda_1 = F_2 \cdot P_2 + \lambda_2$ (see §4.3). This way, the expensive computations that involve numerous calls to our simplex algorithm are done by our OCAML implementation using ZARITH and the result is reflected in COQ at the cost of just a matrix product using the COQ-certified representation of numbers. If we work in such a manner, we never actually have to transfer polyhedra from the untrusted to the trusted side.

From a general point of view, splitting a tool into an untrusted solver and a correctness checker makes it more amenable to extensions and optimizations. *A posteriori* certification has a cost each time the correctness of a result needs to be proved (only during the last phase of the analysis to ascertain the stability of the inferred properties). However, it allows optimizations whose correctness would be difficult to prove and usage of untrusted components (e.g. GMP).

6   Experimental Results

In order to evaluate the viability of our solution, we compared experimentally our library (referred to as LIBPOLY) with mature implementations.

In addition to the efficiency of the polyhedra computation, we wished to measure the cost of the inclusion checker. Our approach guarantees that, if our certificate checker terminates successfully on a given verification, the result of the operation which produced the certificate is correct. However, this assertion currently only applies to the polyhedra as known to the COQ checker: a translation occurs between the OCAML representation of numbers, ZARITH, and their representation in the COQ language as lists of bits. This means that the checker has to compute on this inefficient representation, and thus we wished to ascertain whether the cost was tolerable.[5]

The best approach to evaluating LIBPOLY would have been to rely on it for building a complete static analyzer. Although this is our long-term goal, a less demanding method was needed for a more immediate evaluation. We chose to compare computation results from LIBPOLY to those of widely used existing implementations of the abstract domain of polyhedra: the NEWPOLKA library and the PPL. More precisely, we used them through their APRON front end [4].

6.1   The Method

As [21] points out, randomly-generated polyhedra do not give a faithful evaluation: a more realistic approach was needed. Because of the lack of a static analyzer supporting both APRON and LIBPOLY, we carried out the comparison by logging and then replaying with LIBPOLY the abstract domain operations done by the existing PAGAI analyzer [11] using APRON.

Technically, logging consists in intercepting calls to the APRON shared library (using the wrap functionality of the GNU linker ld), analyzing the data structures passed as operands and generating equivalent OCAML code for LIBPOLY. NEWPOLKA and PPL results are logged too, for comparison purposes. At the end of the analysis, the generated OCAML code forms a complete program which replays all the abstract domain operations executed by the NEWPOLKA library or the PPL on request of the analyzer.

---

[5] An alternative would be to map, at checker extraction time, COQ numbers to ZARITH numbers, at the expense of having both ZARITH and GMP in the trusted computing base. One may consider that we already make assumptions about ZARITH and GMP: we assume they respect memory safety, and thus will not corrupt the data of the OCAML code extracted from COQ, or at least that, if they corrupt memory, they will cause a crash in the analyzer (probably in the garbage collector) instead of a silent execution with incorrect data. This seems a much less bold assumption than considering that they always compute correctly, including in all corner cases.

```
1    From module LinearCsrt:
2    Record LinearCstr: Set := mk {coefs: Vec; cmp_op: Cmp; bound: Num}.
3
4    Definition Sat (c:LinearCstr) (x:Vec) : Prop :=
5      denote  (Vec.eval (coefs c) x) (cmp_op c) (bound c).
6
7    From module List:
8    Inductive Forall (A : Type) (pred : A → Prop) : list A → Prop :=
9     | FORALL_NIL: Forall pred nil
10    | FORALL_CONS: ∀ (x:A) (l:list A),
11                      pred x → Forall pred l → Forall pred (x :: l)
12
13   From module Polyhedra:
14   Definition Polyhedra : Set := list (id * LinearCstr).
15
16   Definition Sat (P:Polyhedra) (x:Vec) : Prop :=
17     List.Forall (fun c => LinearCstr.Sat (snd c) x) P.
18
19   Definition Incl (P:Polyhedra) (C:LinearCstr) : Prop :=
20     ∀ x:Vec, Sat P x → LinearCstr.Sat C x.
21
22   Definition (infix ⊑) (P_1 P_2 : Polyhedra) : Prop :=
23     ∀ x:Vec, Sat P_1 x → Sat P_2 x.
24
25   Definition CertOneConstraint : Set := list (id * Num)
26
27   Inductive Cert : Set :=
28    | INCL: list (id * CertOneConstraint) -> Cert
29    | EMPTY: CertOneConstraint -> Cert.
30
31   Lemma Empty_is_included: ∀ (P:Polyhedra) (C:LinearCstr),
32     (Empty P) → (Incl P C).
33
34   Definition inclusion_checker (P_1 P_2:Polyhedra) (cert:Cert) : Exc(P_1⊑P_2).
35   refine ( match cert with
36              | INCL icert => checkInclusion P_1 P_2 icert
37              | EMPTY ecert => match (checkEmptyness P_1 ecert) with
38                                | VALUE eproof => VALUE _ ← missing proof
39                                | ERROR => ERROR
40                              end
41          end
42   ). The missing proof is provided by the following proof script:
43   induction P_2 with IH;
44    exact (List.FORALL_NIL _ _) ;
45    exact (List.FORALL_CONS _ _ c _ (Empty_is_included P_1 (snd c) eproof) IH).
46   Defined.
```

Fig. 1. Excerpts of our COQ-certified inclusion checker

The comparison was done for the following operations: parallel assignment, convex hull, inclusion test and intersection on the analysis of the following programs:

1. **bf**: the Blowfish cryptographic cipher
2. **bz2**: the bzip2 compression algorithm
3. **dbz2**: the bzip2 decompress algorithm
4. **jpg**: an implementation of the jpeg codec
5. **re**: the regular expression engine of GNU **awk**
6. **foo**: a hand-crafted program leading to polyhedra with many constraints, large coefficients and few equalities

6.2   Precision and Representation Size Comparison

The result of each operator we evaluated is a well-defined geometrical object. For every logged call, the results from NEWPOLKA, PPL and LIBPOLY were checked for equality (double inclusion). The certificates generated by LIBPOLY were then systematically checked. Furthermore, polyhedra have a minimal constraints representation, up to the variable choices in the substitutions of equalities. It was systematically checked whether LIBPOLY, NEWPOLKA and the PPL computed the same number of equalities and inequalities. In all the cases we tried, the tests of correctness and precision passed. It is to be noted that the PPL does not systematically minimize representations: its results often have redundant constraints.[6]

Besides giving confidence in the results computed by LIBPOLY, ensuring that our results are identical to those of NEWPOLKA or the PPL lead us to believe that the analyzer behavior would not have been very different, had it used the results from LIBPOLY. There is no noticeable difference between the analyses carried out using NEWPOLKA and the PPL.

6.3   Timing Measurements

Timing measurements were made difficult because of the importance of the state of polyhedra in the double representation NEWPOLKA and the PPL use. We were concerned that logging and replaying as described above would be unfair towards these libraries, since it would force the systematic recomputation of generator representations that, in a real analyzer, would be kept internally. We thus opted for a different approach.

We measured the timings for NEWPOLKA and the PPL directly inside PAGAI by wrapping the function calls between calls to a high precision timer. We made sure that the overhead of the timer system calls was sufficiently small so as to produce meaningful results. For LIBPOLY, timing measurements were done

---

[6] This is due to the lazy-by-default implementation of the operators of the PPL. Since support for the eager version of the operators has been deprecated in and is being removed from the PPL (see [22], § A Note on the Implementation of the Operators), we could not configure the library to have the same behavior as NEWPOLKA.

Table 1. Timing comparison between NEWPOLKA (N), PPL (P), LIBPOLY (L) and LIBPOLY with certificate checker (C): total time (in milliseconds) spent in each of the operations; trivial problems are excluded

prog.	assignment			convex hull				inclusion				intersection		
	N	P	L	N	P	L	C	N	P	L	C	N	P	L
bf	3.7	11.4	0.5	3.2	1.2	2.7	2.8	0.2	0.4	0.1	0.1	10.7	13.4	1.2
bz2	14.6	54.1	2.9	23.5	11.5	66.8	68.7	1.6	2.8	0.7	1.2	52.3	61.1	7.9
dbz2	1618	4182	83.8	1393	231.9	532.8	535.3	32.3	35.6	2.1	3.6	1687	1815	28.3
jpg	23.7	68.3	3.8	28.2	7.5	24.0	24.9	1.2	1.8	0.5	0.8	39.7	51.0	6.0
re	5.7	17.2	0.7	20.2	8.4	17.9	19.2	1.1	1.3	0.5	0.7	37.3	47.2	3.3
foo	9.2	14.8	8.5	4.2	0.6	941.8	943.7	0.2	0.2	0.9	0.9	6.7	7.1	5.5

during the replay and exclude the time needed to parse and rebuild the operand polyhedra.

We present two views of the same timing measurements, carried out on the programs introduced in §6.1. Table 1 gives, for each benchmark program, the total time spent in each operation of the abstract domain. Such a table does not inform us of the typical distribution of problem sizes and the relationship between problem size and computation time, thus we compiled Table 2 which shows computation times aggregated according to the "problem size", defined as the sum of the number of constraints of all the operands of a given operation.

For the assignment and the convex hull, all the constraints of the two operands are put together after renaming and many projections follow. The inclusion test $P_1 \sqsubseteq P_2$, in the worst case, solves as many linear programming problems as there are constraints in P_2, but each is of size the number of constraints of $P_1 + 1$. Last, the intersection operator minimizes the result of the union of the sets of constraints. Note that the sums in Table 1 exclude operations on trivial problems of size zero or one.

The presented results show that LIBPOLY is efficient on small problems. Yet, the performance gap between LIBPOLY and the other implementations closes on bigger problems. This is especially true for the convex hull, which is a costly operation in the constraint representation. At least part of the difference in efficiency on small problems can be explained by the generality APRON provides: it provides a unified interface to several abstract domains at the expense of an extra abstraction layer which introduces a significant overhead on small problems.

More generally, the use of ZARITH in LIBPOLY is likely to lower the cost of arithmetic when compared to NEWPOLKA and the PPL, which use GMP directly. The foo program illustrates this: the analysis creates constraints with big coefficients, likely to overflow native number representation. However, precise measurement of the effect of using ZARITH would be a hard task.

Last, Table 1 seems to show that problems are most often of rather small size, but this may well be due to our limited experimentation means.

In spite of the shortcomings of our evaluation method, these results seem promising for a constraints-only implementation of the abstract domain of polyhedra. Some progress still needs to be made on the convex hull side (see §7). It is also interesting to notice the performance differences between the

Table 2. Timing comparison between NEWPOLKA (N), PPL (P) and LIBPOLY (L). Computation times (in milliseconds) are aggregated according to operation and problem size. (n) is the total number of problems of the size range in the benckmarks.

problem size		0–1	2–5	6–10	11–15	16–20	21–25	26–30	31+
assignment	N	33.8	601.8	385.4	20.9	78.3	537.4	59.5	13.1
	P	47.5	1176	519.7	87.4	247.6	2111	81.7	77.9
	L	1.1	6.6	14.3	10.7	5.2	39.2	15.2	11.6
	n	*539*	*667*	*981*	*58*	*64*	*480*	*30*	*16*
convex hull	N	687.9	679.7	434.1	119.5	68.8	37.9	6.4	3.5
	P	167.5	141.0	68.4	22.8	16.8	9.2	1.9	0.9
	L	7.0	57.1	133.7	131.2	1050	106.4	50.1	27.8
	n	*3354*	*3373*	*1092*	*354*	*135*	*65*	*14*	*7*
inclusion	N	7.2	9.7	9.7	3.3	5.8	4.0	4.0	0
	P	6.5	12.8	10.6	4.2	7.0	3.9	3.4	0
	L	0.6	1.6	1.3	0.5	1.0	0.3	0.1	0
	n	*1482*	*1881*	*673*	*277*	*111*	*52*	*17*	*4*
intersection	N	1389	1752	52.3	27.4	1.3			
	P	1933	1740	158.6	91.4	4.8			
	L	35.0	30.9	18.4	8.8	0.6			
	n	*11458*	*4094*	*322*	*156*	*6*	*0*	*0*	*0*

NEWPOLKA and the PPL. At least part of them can be explained by the eagerness of NEWPOLKA and the lazyness of the PPL.

6.4 Certificate Checking Overhead

The certificate checking overhead shown in Table 1 includes the translation between OCAML and COQ representations. Inside a certified static analyzer, this overhead could be reduced by only transferring the certificates, as opposed to the full polyhedra, and using them to simulate the polyhedra computations, without bothering to check after every call that the polyhedron inside the OCAML library corresponds to the one inside the certified checker. In addition to translation costs, there is the general inefficiency of computations on COQ integers, which are represented as lists of bits; this is considerably more expensive than using native integers, or even arrays of native integers as GMP would do.

However, it should be noted that the checking of inclusion certificates occurs only during the final step of the certified static analysis which consists in verifying that the inferred invariant candidates are indeed inductive invariants for the program.

Last, the overhead of certificate checking is relatively greater for inclusion than for convex hull. Although the actual checking burden is bigger for the convex hull, due to certificate composition densifying the resulting certificate, the inclusion test algorithm is much cheaper than the convex hull in terms of computations. More precisely, the convex hull algorithm involves inclusion tests as part of representation minimization.

7 Conclusions

The previous sections demonstrated that a realistic implementation of the abstract domain of polyhedra can be certified using a posteriori verification of results. This approach has a key benefit: the time-consuming development inside the COQ proof assistant is reduced to the bare minimum. A tight integration of the certification concern enables on-the-fly certification generation as a by-production of the actual computations, thereby making the associated cost negligible. The same procedures can be used for fixed point iterations (with certificate generation turned off for efficiency) and for fixed point verification (with certificates generated and checked).

The complete implementation which has been developed operates only on a constraints representation of polyhedra; our motivations for this choice were the ease of generation of certificates as well as the absence of combinatorial explosion on common cases such as hypercubes. This is made possible through careful choice of data structures and exploitation of recent algorithmic refinements [9,10]. Possible future developments include designing efficient techniques for generating Farkas certificates for a library based on the double representation (generators and constraints) and providing heuristics for choosing when to operate over constraints only and when to use the double representation.

Prior to this, however, there remains room for both enhancement and extension of our current implementation. A simple enhancement would be to have both an upper and a lower bound for linear terms, which would further condense the representation of polyhedra. The implicit equality detection algorithm could be made less naive by exploiting the fact that a point in a polyhedron P which has implicit equalities E_i necessarily reaches the bounds of the inequalities involved in the proof of $P \sqsubseteq E_i$.

Finally, our library is planned to be part of a certified static analyzer, such as the one being built in the VERASCO project. Beyond a certified implementation of the abstract domain of polyhedra, our library could also serve to verify the numerical invariants discovered by untrusted analysis using a combination of abstract domains (intervals, octagons, ... which are special cases of polyhedra). The discovered invariants could be stored in the form of polyhedra and the verification of their stability could be done with our certified library. Currently, our polyhedron library only deals with linear constraints, but a general-purpose analyzer has to handle nonlinearity. Our library should therefore include linearization techniques [23] at the condition that these be proven correct.

Acknowledgements. We would like to thank Bertrand Jeannet for his advice on proper ways to evaluate LIBPOLY against his NEWPOLKA library.

References

1. Cousot, P., Cousot, R.: Abstract interpretation: a unified lattice model for static analysis of programs by construction or approximation of fixpoints. In: Principles of Programming Languages (POPL), pp. 238–252. ACM (1977)

2. Cousot, P., Halbwachs, N.: Automatic discovery of linear restraints among variables of a program. In: Principles of Programming Languages (POPL), pp. 84–97. ACM (1978)
3. Bagnara, R., Hill, P.M., Zaffanella, E.: The Parma Polyhedra Library: Toward a complete set of numerical abstractions for the analysis and verification of hardware and software systems. Science of Computer Programming 72(1-2), 3–21 (2008)
4. Jeannet, B., Miné, A.: Apron: A library of numerical abstract domains for static analysis. In: Bouajjani, A., Maler, O. (eds.) CAV 2009. LNCS, vol. 5643, pp. 661–667. Springer, Heidelberg (2009)
5. Blanchet, B., Cousot, P., Cousot, R., Feret, J., Mauborgne, L., Miné, A., Monniaux, D., Rival, X.: A static analyzer for large safety-critical software. In: Programming Language Design and Implementation (PLDI), pp. 196–207. ACM (2003)
6. Leroy, X.: Formal verification of a realistic compiler. Communications of the ACM 52(7), 107–115 (2009)
7. The Coq Development Team: The Coq proof assistant reference manual. INRIA. 8.4. edn. (2012)
8. Besson, F., Jensen, T., Pichardie, D., Turpin, T.: Result certification for relational program analysis. Technical Report RR-6333, INRIA (2007)
9. Simon, A., King, A.: Exploiting sparsity in polyhedral analysis. In: Hankin, C., Siveroni, I. (eds.) SAS 2005. LNCS, vol. 3672, pp. 336–351. Springer, Heidelberg (2005)
10. Dutertre, B., De Moura, L.: Integrating simplex with DPLL(T). Technical Report SRI-CSL-06-01, SRI International, computer science laboratory (2006)
11. Henry, J., Monniaux, D., Moy, M.: PAGAI: a path sensitive static analyser. In: Jeannet, B. (ed.) Tools for Automatic Program Analysis (TAPAS) (2012)
12. Monniaux, D.: A minimalistic look at widening operators. Higher Order and Symbolic Computation 22(2), 145–154 (2009)
13. Dantzig, G., Thapa, M.N.D.: Linear Programming. Springer (2003)
14. Necula, G.C., Lee, P.: Proof generation in the Touchstone theorem prover. In: McAllester, D. (ed.) CADE 2000. LNCS (LNAI), vol. 1831, pp. 25–44. Springer, Heidelberg (2000)
15. Benoy, F., King, A., Mesnard, F.: Computing convex hulls with a linear solver. Theory and Practice of Logic Programming 5(1-2), 259–271 (2005)
16. Monniaux, D.: Quantifier elimination by lazy model enumeration. In: Touili, T., Cook, B., Jackson, P. (eds.) CAV 2010. LNCS, vol. 6174, pp. 585–599. Springer, Heidelberg (2010)
17. Bagnara, R., Hill, P.M., Ricci, E., Zaffanella, E.: Precise widening operators for convex polyhedra. Science of Computer Programming 58(1-2), 28–56 (2005)
18. Miné, A., Leroy, X.: ZArith, http://forge.ocamlcore.org/projects/zarith
19. Free Software Foundation: The GNU Multiple Precision Arithmetic Library. 5.0 edn. (2012)
20. Barbosa, C., de Oliveira, D., Monniaux, D.: Experiments on the feasibility of using a floating-point simplex in an SMT solver. In: Workshop on Practical Aspects of Automated Reasoning (PAAR), CEUR Workshop Proceedings (2012)
21. Monniaux, D.: On using floating-point computations to help an exact linear arithmetic decision procedure. In: Bouajjani, A., Maler, O. (eds.) CAV 2009. LNCS, vol. 5643, pp. 570–583. Springer, Heidelberg (2009)
22. Bugseng: The Parma Polyhedra Library. 1.0 edn. (2012)
23. Miné, A.: Symbolic methods to enhance the precision of numerical abstract domains. In: Emerson, E.A., Namjoshi, K.S. (eds.) VMCAI 2006. LNCS, vol. 3855, pp. 348–363. Springer, Heidelberg (2006)

Static Provenance Verification
for Message Passing Programs

Rupak Majumdar[1], Roland Meyer[2], and Zilong Wang[1]

[1] MPI-SWS, Germany
[2] University of Kaiserslautern, Germany

Abstract. Provenance information records the source and ownership history of an object. We study the problem of provenance tracking in concurrent programs, in which several principals execute concurrent processes and exchange messages over unbounded but unordered channels. The provenance of a message, roughly, is a function of the sequence of principals that have transmitted the message in the past. The provenance verification problem is to statically decide, given a message passing program and a set of allowed provenances, whether the provenance of all messages in all possible program executions, belongs to the allowed set.

We formalize the provenance verification problem abstractly in terms of well-structured provenance domains, and show a general decidability result for it. In particular, we show that if the provenance of a message is a sequence of principals who have sent the message, and a provenance query asks if the provenance lies in a regular set, the problem is decidable and EXPSPACE-complete.

While the theoretical complexity is high, we show an implementation of our technique that performs efficiently on a set of Javascript examples tracking provenances in Firefox extensions. Our experiments show that many browser extensions store and transmit user information although the user sets the browser to the private mode.

1 Introduction

Controlled access and dissemination of data is a key ingredient of system security: we do not want secret information to reach untrusted principals and we do not want to receive bad information (indirectly) from untrusted principals. Many organizations receive private information from users and this information is passed around within the organization to carry out business-critical activities. These organizations must ensure that the data is not accidentally disclosed to unauthorized users, as the potential cost of disclosure can be high. Moreover, in many domains, such as healthcare and finance, the control of data is required by regulatory agencies through legislation such as HIPAA and GLBA.

We present an abstract model of information dissemination in message passing systems, and a static analyzer to verify correct dissemination. We model systems as concurrent message passing processes, one process for each principal in the system. Processes communicate by sending and receiving messages via a shared

F. Logozzo and M. Fähndrich (Eds.): SAS 2013, LNCS 7935, pp. 366–387, 2013.

set of channels. Channels are unbounded, but can reorder messages. Sends are non-blocking, but receive actions block until a message is available.

To track information about the origin and access history of a message, we augment messages with *provenance* annotations. Roughly, the provenance of a message is a function of the sequence of principles that have transmitted the message in the past. Depending on the function, we get different provenance annotations. For example, the annotation can simply be the sequence of principals. Whenever a principal sends a message, we append the name of the principal to the current provenance of the message. The *provenance verification problem* asks, given a message passing program, a variable in the program, and a set of allowed provenance annotations, whether the provenance of every message stored in the variable, on every run of the program, belongs to the set of allowed provenances.

Consider a healthcare system in which a patient sends health questions to a secretary or a nurse, who in turn, forwards the question to doctors. An information-dissemination policy may require that every health answer received by the patient has been seen by at least one doctor. That is, the provenance of every message received by the patient must belong to the regular language Patient(Secretary + Nurse) Doctor$^+$.

We consider provenance verification for general provenance domains satisfying an algebraic requirement. Static provenance verification is hard because of two sources of unboundedness in the model. First, the provenance information associated with a single message can be unbounded. For example there is no bound on the number of doctors who see a health question before an answer is sent back. Second, the number of pending messages in the system can be unbounded. We tackle these two sources of unboundedness as follows.

We give a reduction from provenance verification problem to coverability in *labeled* Petri nets, where tokens carry (potentially unbounded) provenance data. As a result, we obtain a general decidability result for provenance verification problem, when the domain of provenance annotations is well-structured [1,8]. Specifically, we show verification is EXPSPACE-complete for the set provenance domain, that tracks the set of principals that have seen a message, as well as for the language provenance domain, in which provenance information is stored as ordered sequences of principals that have seen the message and policies are regular languages. Our proofs combine well-structuredness arguments with symbolic representations; we analyze coverability in a product of a Petri net modeling the system and a symbolic domain encoding the set of allowed provenances.

While our decision procedures reduce the verification problems to problems on Petri nets, our experiences with a direct implementation of provenance verification based on existing Petri net coverability tools have been somewhat disappointing. Mostly, this is because after the reduction to Petri nets, the coverability tools fail to utilize the structure of message passing programs, in particular potential state-space reductions arising from partial order reduction (POR) [11].

We implemented a coverability checker that is tuned for message passing programs on top of the Spin model checker [14]. Our implementation uses the expand-enlarge-check (EEC) pradigm [10]. The EEC algorithm explores a sequence of finite-state approximations of the message passing program. Intuitively, the approximation is obtained by replacing the counters in the Petri net with "abstract" counters that count precisely up to a given parameter k, and then set the count to ∞. Since the induced state space is finite for each approximation, we can use a finite-state reachability engine (such as Spin) to explore its state space. Additionally, we use partial order reduction, already implemented in Spin, to reduce the explored state space, allowing local actions of different processes to commute.

Our choice of a message passing programming model with unbounded but unordered buffers was inspired by the communication model in browser extensions, where several components communicate asynchronously. Specifically, we checked the following property of extensions. Most browsers have a "private mode" that allow users to browse the internet without saving information about pages visited. Browser extensions should respect the private mode and not save user information (or worse, upload user information to remote servers) while the user is browsing in the private mode. We checked this property and found that several widely-used Firefox extensions, including some extensions whose purpose is to improve user privacy, do not properly handle "private mode" settings. Among nine browser extensions using message passing, local storage, and sometimes remote database accesses, we found five extensions store user data even in the private mode. Thus, our experiments demonstrate that a precise static tool can be useful in detecting privacy violations in this domain.

One can view our result as a general compilation procedure from a provenance verification problem for a program P to a safety verification problem for an instrumented program P'. The instrumentation P' adds some counters to P but keeps the other features (e.g., complex control flow and data structures) the same: program P' is safe iff P satisfies the provenance properties. After the reduction, we can harness any verification technique that has been developed for the underlying class of programs (e.g., abstract interpretation or software model checking). Our experiments use a simple dataflow abstraction, but other abstract domains could be used for more precision. We chose message passing programs for our presentation as they capture the essence of provenance tracking: concurrency, unbounded provenance information, and unbounded channels. This focus allows us to settle the complexity of provenance verification without mixing it with the complexity of features in the programming model.

Related Work. Provenance annotation on data has been studied extensively in the database community [6,3,12], both for annotating query results and for tracking information through workflows. Provenance information is usually tracked for a fixed database and a fixed query in a declarative query language. Seen as a program, the query has exactly one "execution path." The connection between provenance tracking and dependency analysis in (sequential) programs was made in [5]. A provenance-tracking semantics for asynchronous π-calculus was given in [27], but the static analysis problem was not considered. Most previous work focused on dynamic tracking and enforcement along one execution path, and the

```
patient {                          secretary {
    var p1, p2, p3;                    var s1, s2;
    while (true) {                     while (true) {
        choose                     S1: recv(ch0, s1);
P1: [] p1 = HQ; send(ch0, p1);     S2: if (s1 == HQ)
P2: [] p1 = AR; send(ch0, p1);     S3:     send(ch2, s1);
P3: [] recv(ch1, p2);              S4: else {
P4:    if (p2 == HA) p3 = p2;      S5:     s2 = AA(s1);
    }                              S6:     send(ch1, s2);
}                                      }
                                   }
                               }
```

```
doctor{
    var d1, d2;
    while(true) {
D1: recv(ch2, d1);
D2: d2 = HA(d1);
D3: choose
D4: [] send(ch1, d2);
D5: [] send(ch2, d2);
    }
}
```

Fig. 1. Medical system example

static meet-over-all-paths solution was not considered. In contrast, we provide algorithms to track provenances in concurrent message passing programs, and give algorithms to check provenance queries over all execution paths of programs. We were inspired by the algebraic framework of provenance semirings [12] to give a similar algebraic description of provenance domains.

Our algorithm for provenance verification generalizes algorithms for explicit information flow studied in the context of sequential programs [25], e.g., through taint analysis. Taint analysis problems [15,19] classify methods as *sources*, *sinks*, and *sanitizers*, and require that any data flow from sources to sinks must go through one or more sanitizers. In our model, this property can be formulated by requiring that the provenance of every message received by a sink must conform to the regular specification $(source^+ \ sanitizer^+)^*$. We are able to verify such properties for message passing programs, where the source, sanitizer, and sink can be concurrently executing processes sharing unbounded channels, and with other intermediary processes as well. Previous work, too numerous to enumerate here, either dealt with dynamic enforcement or provided imprecise static checks for these domains. We show *precise* static analysis remains decidable!

2   Example

We motivate our results by modeling a simple online health system described in [2], which allows patients to interact with their doctors and other healthcare professionals using a web-based message passing system. In the system, users have different roles, such as Patient, Secretary, and Doctor. Patients can ask health questions and receive answers by exchanging messages with their doctors.

For simplicity of exposition, we describe a subset of the functionality of the system as a message passing program. (In Section 5, we modeled the entire system as a case study.) Intuitively, a message passing program is a collection of imperative processes running concurrently, one for each principal in the system. In our example, each role (Patient, Doctor, etc.) is modeled as a different principal. The processes run by the principals have local variables, and in addition, communicate with each other by sending to and receiving from shared channels. We assume shared channels are potentially unbounded, but may reorder messages. Message sends are non-blocking, the execution continues at the control point following the send. Receives are blocking: a process blocks until some message from the channel is received.

Figure 1 shows a simple implementation of the system, written in a simple imperative language. We have three principals: Patient (modeling the set of patients using the system), Secretary (modeling secretaries who receive and forward messages), and Doctor (modeling the set of doctors using the system). The choose construct nondeterministically chooses and executes one of its branches. A send action sends a message to a channel, and a recv receives a message from a channel into a local variable.

There are four kinds of messages in the system. The patient can send a health question (HQ) or an appointment request (AR). The healthcare providers can send back a health answer (HA) or an appointment confirmation (AA). The principals communicate through shared channels ch0, ch1, and ch2.

The patient process runs in a loop. In each step, it nondeterministically decides to either send an HQ or an AR to ch0, or to receive an answer on channel ch1. The secretary process runs a loop. In each step, it receives a message from channel ch0. If it is an HQ, the message is forwarded to doctors on channel ch2. If it is an AR, the secretary answers the patient directly on channel ch1. The doctor process receives health questions on channel ch2. It computes a health answer based on the received message (the assignment on line D2). It can either reply directly to the patient (on channel ch1), or put the answer back to channel ch2 for further processing.

Figure 1 also shows a possible message sequence for a health question, where the patient sends a health question to the secretary, the secretary forwards it to the doctor, and the doctor looks at the message several times before replying with a health answer. We capture the flow of messages through the principals using provenance annotations with each message; the provenance captures the history of all the principals that have forwarded the message. While in Section 3 we give a general algebraic definition of a *provenance domain*, for the moment, think of a provenance as a string over the principals. When a message is initially assigned, e.g., on line P1, the provenance is the empty string ε. After the patient sends the message, the channel ch0 contains an HQ message with provenance Patient. When the message is forwarded to channel ch2, its provenance becomes

Fig. 2. Complemented finite automaton for provenance property. We omit an accepting sink to which all unspecified edges go.

Patient Secretary. Finally, when the message is sent back on ch1, its provenance is a string in the regular language Patient Secretary Doctor$^+$, indicating that it has been sent originally by the patient, seen by the secretary next, and then seen by the doctor one or more times.

The *provenance verification problem* asks, given the message passing program, a variable v, and a regular language R of provenances, whether the content of v has a provenance in R along all program executions. In the example, we can ask if the provenance of variable p3 is in the set

$$\varepsilon + \text{Patient Secretary Doctor}^+, \tag{1}$$

capturing the requirement that any health answer must be initiated by a health question from the patient, and must be seen by a doctor at least once, after it has been seen by a secretary.

Notice that the example is unbounded in two dimensions. First, the channels can contain unboundedly many messages. For example, the patient process can send unboundedly many messages on channel ch0 before the secretary process receives them. Second, the provenance annotations can be unbounded: a message in channel ch2 can have an unbounded number of Doctor annotations.

We show the provenance verification problem is decidable. The first observation is that, if we ignore provenances, we can keep a counter for each channel ch and each message type m, that counts the number of messages with value m that are currently in ch. A send action increases the counter, a receive decrements it. We can then show that the transition system of a message passing program is *well-structured* [1,8]: an action that could be taken in a state can also be taken if there are more messages in the channels. Formally, we give a reduction to Petri nets, an infinite-state well-structured system with good decidability properties.

In the presence of provenances, we have to be more careful. Unlike a normal Petri net, now the "tokens" (the messages in the channels) will carry potentially unbounded provenance annotations. However, given the regular set R, we only need to distinguish two provenance annotations that behave differently with respect to a deterministic finite automaton A for R. So, we keep more counters that are now of the form $\langle \text{ch}, m, q \rangle$: one counter for each combination of channel ch, message type m, and state q of A. The state of the automaton A remembers where the automaton would go to, starting with its initial state, on seeing the provenance annotation. Similarly, for each variable in the program, we distinguish the contents of the variable based on the message type m as well as the state q of the automaton.

```
patient {
  var p1, p2, p3;
  while (true) {
    choose
P1' [] p1 = ⟨HQ,q0⟩; ⟨ch0, HQ,q1⟩++;
P2' [] p1 = ⟨AR,q0⟩; ⟨ch0, AR,q1⟩++;
P31 [] if ⟨ch1,HQ,q⟩ > 0 (for each q ∈ Q)
          p2 = ⟨HQ,q⟩; ⟨ch1,HQ,q⟩--;
P32 [] if ⟨ch1,HA,q⟩ > 0 (for each q ∈ Q)
          p2 = ⟨HA,q⟩; ⟨ch1,HA,q⟩--;
P4'     if (p2 == (HA, ·) ) p3 = p2;
P33 [] if ⟨ch1,AA,q⟩ > 0 (for each q ∈ Q)
          p2 = ⟨AA,q⟩; ⟨ch1,AA,q⟩--;
P34 [] if ⟨ch1,AR,q⟩ > 0 (for each q ∈ Q)
          p2 = ⟨AR,q⟩; ⟨ch1,AR,q⟩--;
  }
}
```

Fig. 3. Translation of `patient`. We have simplified some statements for readability: the actual translation performs a case split over `p1` in lines P1' and P2', and performs the check on line P4' after each statement $P3_i$.

Figure 2 shows a deterministic automaton accepting the complement of the language in (1). Using this automaton, we describe the reduction to a well-structured system as follows. Let $Q = \{q_0, q_1, q_2, q_3, q_4\}$ be the set of states of the automaton (q_4 is the omitted sink state). We have a set of integer-valued counters $\langle \text{ch}i, m, q \rangle$, for $i = 0, 1, 2$, $m \in \{\text{HQ}, \text{HA}, \text{AA}, \text{AR}\}$, and $q \in Q$. For example, the counter $\langle \text{ch0}, \text{HQ}, q_1 \rangle$ stores the number of HQs in `ch0` for which the automaton is in state q_1. Figure 3 shows the translation of the `patient` process. The send actions are replaced by incrementing the appropriate counter. For example, the action `send(ch0,p1)` in line P1 is replaced with incrementing the counter $\langle \text{ch0}, \text{HQ}, q_1 \rangle$, the state of the automaton is q_1 because the principal Patient takes the automaton from its initial state q_0 to the state q_1. The receive action non-deterministically selects a non-zero counter and decrements it, while storing the message and the state into the local variable.

After the translation, we are left with a well-structured system. Verifying the provenance specification reduces to checking if there is a reachable configuration of the system in which v contains a message whose provenance automaton is in a final state. This reachability question can be solved as a *coverability problem* on the well-structured system, which is decidable. In fact, we show a symbolic encoding that gives an optimal algorithm.

3   Message Passing Programs

Preliminaries. A *multiset* m over a set Σ is a function $\Sigma \to \mathbb{N}$ with finite support (i.e., $m(\sigma) \neq 0$ for finitely many $\sigma \in \Sigma$). By $\mathbb{M}[\Sigma]$ we denote the set of all multisets over Σ. As an example, we write $m = [\![\sigma_1^2, \sigma_3]\!]$ for the multiset $m \in \mathbb{M}[\{\sigma_1, \sigma_2, \sigma_3\}]$ with $m(\sigma_1) = 2, m(\sigma_2) = 0$, and $m(\sigma_3) = 1$. We write $\emptyset$ for the empty multiset, mapping each $\sigma \in \Sigma$ to 0. Two multisets are ordered by $m_1 \leq m_2$ if for all $\sigma \in \Sigma$, we have $m_1(\sigma) \leq m_2(\sigma)$. Let $m_1 \oplus m_2$ (resp. $m_1 \ominus m_2$) be the multiset that maps every element $\sigma \in \Sigma$ to $m_1(\sigma) + m_2(\sigma)$ (resp. $\max\{0, m_1(\sigma) - m_2(\sigma)\}$).

For a set X, a relation $\preceq \subseteq X \times X$ is a *well-quasi-order* (wqo) if it is reflexive, transitive, and such that for every infinite sequence $x_0, x_1, \ldots$ of elements from X, there exists $i < j$ such that $x_i \preceq x_j$. Given a wqo $\preceq$, we define its *induced equivalence* $\equiv \subseteq X \times X$ by $x \equiv y$ if $x \preceq y$ and $y \preceq x$.

A subset X' of X is *upward closed* if for each $x \in X$, if there is a $x' \in X'$ with $x' \preceq x$ then $x \in X'$. A subset X' of X is *downward closed* if for each $x \in X$, if there is a $x' \in X'$ with $x \preceq x'$ then $x \in X'$. A function $f : X \to X$ is called $\preceq$-*monotonic* if for each $x, x' \in X$, if $x \preceq x'$ then $f(x) \preceq f(x')$.

A *transition system* $TS = (\mathcal{C}, c_0, \to)$ consists of a set $\mathcal{C}$ of configurations, an initial configuration $c_0 \in \mathcal{C}$, and a transition relation $\to \subseteq \mathcal{C} \times \mathcal{C}$. We write $\to^*$ for the reflexive transitive closure of $\to$. A configuration $c \in \mathcal{C}$ is *reachable* if $c_0 \to^* c$. A *well-structured transition system* is a $TS = (\mathcal{C}, c_0, \to)$ equipped with a well-quasi order $\preceq \subseteq \mathcal{C} \times \mathcal{C}$ such that for all $c_1, c_2, c_3 \in \mathcal{C}$ with $c_1 \preceq c_2$ and $c_1 \to c_3$, there exists $c_4 \in \mathcal{C}$ with $c_3 \preceq c_4$ and $c_2 \to c_4$.

3.1   Programming Model

Syntax. We work in the setting of asynchronous message passing programs. For simplicity, we assume that the programming language has a single finitely-valued datatype $\mathcal{M}$ of messages. A *channel* is a (potentially unbounded) multiset of messages supporting two actions: a *send* action (written $ch!x$) that takes a message stored in variable x and puts it into the channel, and a *receive* action (written $ch?x$) that takes a message m from the channel and copies it to the variable x. Let C be a finite set of channels.

A *control flow graph* (CFG) $G = (X, V, E, v^0)$ consists of a set X of message variables, a set V of control locations including a unique *start location* $v^0 \in V$, and a set E of labeled directed edges between the control locations in V. Every edge in E is labeled with one of the following actions:

- an *assignment* $y := \otimes(x)$, where $x, y \in X$ and $\otimes$ is an uninterpreted unary operation on messages;
- an *assume action* $\mathsf{assume}(x = m)$, where $x \in X$ and $m \in \mathcal{M}$;
- a *send action* $ch!x$, or a *receive action* $ch?x$, where $x \in X$ and $ch \in C$.

A *message passing program* $\mathcal{P} = (Prin, C, \{G_p\}_{p \in Prin})$ consists of a finite set $Prin$ of principals, a set C of channels, and for each $p \in Prin$, a control flow graph G_p.

Intuitively, a message passing program consists of a finite set of processes. Each process is owned by a named entity or a principal. The processes have local variables which can be updated using unary operators, and communicate with other processes by asynchronously sending to and receiving messages from the set of channels C.

We shall use the notation $v \xrightarrow{a,p} v'$ to denote that the CFG G_p of principal p has an edge $(v, v') \in E_p$ labeled with the action a. Given the set $\{G_p\}_{p \in Prin}$ of CFGs, we define $X^\star = \uplus\{X_p \mid p \in Prin\}$, $V^\star = \uplus\{V_p \mid p \in Prin\}$, and $E^\star = \uplus\{E_p \mid p \in Prin\}$ as the disjoint unions of local variables, control locations, and control flow edges, respectively.

Semantics. We now give a *provenance-carrying* semantics to message passing programs. Let U be a (not necessarily finite) set of *provenances*. We shall associate with each message in a message passing program a provenance from U.

Let $\mathcal{P} = (Prin, C, \{G_p\}_{p \in Prin})$ be a message passing program. A *provenance domain* $\mathcal{U} = (U, \preceq, \psi)$ for $\mathcal{P}$ consists of a set U of provenances, a well-quasi ordering $\preceq$ on U, and for each principal $p \in Prin$ and for each operation $op \in \otimes \cup \{!, ?\}$, a $\preceq$-monotonic function $\psi(p, op) : U \to U$. A provenance domain is decidable if $\preceq$ is a decidable relation and ψ is a computable function. We assume all provenance domains below are decidable.

Since channels are unordered, we represent contents of a channel as a multiset of pairs of messages and provenances. A *configuration* $(\ell, \mathbf{c}, \pi)$ consists of a location function $\ell : Prin \to V^\star$ mapping each principal to a control location; a channel function $\mathbf{c} : C \to \mathbb{M}[\mathcal{M} \times U]$ mapping each channel to a multiset of pairs of messages from $\mathcal{M}$ and provenances from U; and a store function $\pi : X^\star \to \mathcal{M} \times U$ mapping each variable to a message and its provenance.

Define $\ell_0 : Prin \to V^\star$ as the function mapping $p \in Prin$ to the start location $v_p^0 \in V_p$ and $\mathbf{c}_0 : C \to \mathbb{M}[\mathcal{M} \times U]$ as the function mapping each $ch \in C$ to the empty multiset $\emptyset$. Let $\pi_0 : X^\star \to \mathcal{M} \times U$ be a mapping from variables in $X^\star$ to a default initial value m_0 from $\mathcal{M}$ and a default initial provenance ε from U.

The provenance-carrying semantics of a message passing program $\mathcal{P}$ with respect to the provenance domain $(U, \preceq, \psi)$ is defined as the transition system $TS(\mathcal{P}) = (\mathcal{C}, c_0, \to)$ where $\mathcal{C}$ is the set of configurations, the initial configuration $c_0 = (\ell_0, \mathbf{c}_0, \pi_0)$, and the transition relation $\to \subseteq \mathcal{C} \times \mathcal{C}$ is defined as follows.

For a function $f : A \to B$, $a \in A$, and $b \in B$, let $f[a \mapsto b]$ denote the function that maps a to b and all $a' \neq a$ to $f(a')$. We define $(\ell, \mathbf{c}, \pi) \to (\ell', \mathbf{c}', \pi')$ if there exists $p \in Prin$ and $(\ell(p), a, \ell'(p)) \in E^\star$ such that for all $p' \neq p$, we have $\ell(p') = \ell'(p')$; and

1. if $a \equiv y := \otimes(x)$ and $(m, u) = \pi(x)$ then $\mathbf{c}' = \mathbf{c}$ and $\pi' = \pi[y \mapsto (\otimes(m), \psi(p, \otimes)(u))]$;
2. if $a \equiv \mathsf{assume}(x = m)$ then $\mathbf{c}' = \mathbf{c}$, $\pi' = \pi$, and $\pi(x) = (m, \cdot)$;
3. if $a \equiv ch!x$ then $\pi' = \pi$ and if $(m, u) = \pi(x)$, then $\mathbf{c}' = \mathbf{c}[ch \mapsto \mathbf{c}(ch) \oplus [\![(m, \psi(p, !)(u))]\!]]$;
4. if $a \equiv ch?x$ and there is (m, u) such that $\mathbf{c}(ch)(m, u) > 0$ then $\mathbf{c}' = \mathbf{c}[ch \mapsto \mathbf{c}(ch) \ominus [\![(m, u)]\!]]$ and $\pi' = \pi[x \mapsto (m, \psi(p, ?)(u))]$.

Intuitively, in each step, one of the principals executes a local action. An assignment action $y := \otimes(x)$ transforms the message contained in x by applying the operation $\otimes$ and transforms the provenance of x by applying ψ, storing the new message and its provenance in y. An assume checks that a variable has a specific message. Sends and receives model asynchronous communication to shared channels. Send actions are non-blocking, receive actions are blocking, and a channel can reorder messages.

Let $\mathcal{P}$ be a message passing program and $\mathcal{U} = (U, \preceq, \psi)$ a provenance domain. We consider provenance specifications given by downward closed sets over U. Downward closed sets capture the "monotonicity" property that holds in many domains. For example, a security policy that holds when a given set of trusted principals looks at a message, is also met when fewer principals look at it. Conversely, bad behaviors are captured by upward closed sets.

The *provenance verification problem* asks, given a variable x of $\mathcal{P}$ and a downward closed set $D \subseteq U$, if the provenance of the content of variable x is always in D along all runs of the program. Dually, the specification is violated if there exists a reachable configuration where the provenance of variable x is in the upward closed set $I = U \backslash D$. Such a configuration indicates a violation of security policies. We shall use the dual formulation in our algorithms.

3.2   Examples

We now give illustrative examples of provenance domains.

Example 1. [**The Language Provenance Domain**] Consider $U = Prin^*$, the set of finite sequences over principals. Let $(Q, Prin, q_0, \delta)$ be a deterministic finite automaton, and let $\preceq$ be defined as $u \preceq v$ iff $\delta(q_0, u) = \delta(q_0, v)$. Let ψ be the function defined as $\psi(p, !)(u) = u \cdot p$, and $\psi(\cdot, \cdot)(u) = u$ for all other operations. Intuitively, the language provenance domain associates a list of principals with each message: the sequence of principals who have sent this message along the current computation.

A downward closed set D in the language provenance domain is a regular language that prescribes a set $F \subseteq Q$ of final states for the finite automaton A. The corresponding upward closed set I is a regular language that prescribes a set $Q \setminus F$ of final states for the complement automaton $\overline{A}$. The provenance verification problem asks, for example, if the provenance of the message in p3 always belongs to the regular language Patient Secretary Doctor$^+$ along all runs of the program.

Example 2. [**The Set Provenance Domain**] Let $U = 2^{Prin}$, the set of sets of principals. Let $\preceq$ be set inclusion. Since the set of principals is finite, this is a wqo. Let ψ be the function defined as $\psi(p, !)(u) = u \cup \{p\}$, and $\psi(\cdot, \cdot)(u) = u$ for all other operations. The set provenance domain associates a set of principals with each message: the set contains all the principals who have sent this message (potentially multiple times). An upward closed set I corresponds to a set of sets of principals, such that if a set of principals is in I, each of its supersets is also in I. As an example, suppose the set of principals $Prin$ is divided into "trusted" and "untrusted" principals. A downward closed set D specifies the sets all of whose elements are "trusted". As a result, the corresponding upward closed set I captures all sets containing at least one "untrusted" principal. The provenance verification problem asks, given a variable x, if there is a message stored in x along a run that has a provenance which is one of the sets in I.

4   Model Checking

We now give a model checking algorithm for provenance verification by reduction to labeled Petri nets.

4.1   Labeled Petri Nets

A *Petri net* (PN) is a tuple $N = \langle S, T, (I, O) \rangle$ where S is a finite set of places, T is a finite set of transitions, and functions $I : T \to S \to \{0, 1\}$ and $O : T \to S \to \{0, 1\}$ encodes pre- and post-conditions of transitions.

A *marking* is a multiset over S. A transition $t \in T$ is *enabled* at a marking μ, denoted by $\mu[t\rangle$, if $\mu \geq I(t)$. An enabled transition t at μ may *fire* to produce a new marking μ', denoted by $\mu[t\rangle\mu'$, where $\mu' = \mu \ominus I(t) \oplus O(t)$. We naturally lift the enabledness and firing notions from one transition to a sequence $\sigma \in T^*$ of transitions. A PN N and a marking μ_0 define a transition system $TS(N) = (\mathbb{M}[S], \mu_0, \to)$, where $\mu \to \mu'$ if there is a transition t such that $\mu[t\rangle\mu'$.

The encoding of a PN N is given by a list of pairs of lists. Each transition $t \in T$ is encoded by two lists corresponding to $I(t)$ and $O(t)$. Each list $I(t)$ or $O(t)$ is encoded as a bitvector of size $|S|$. The size of N, written $\|N\|$, is the sum of the representations of all the lists.

Let N be a Petri net and μ_0 and μ markings. The *coverability problem* asks if there is $\mu' \geq \mu$ that is reachable from μ_0, so $\mu_0 \to^* \mu' \geq \mu$. In this case, we say μ is coverable from μ_0.

Theorem 1. *[18,24] The coverability problem for Petri nets is EXPSPACE-complete.*

In the usual definition of Petri nets, tokens are simply uninterpreted "dots" and markings count the number of dots in each place. We now extend the Petri net model with tokens labeled with elements from a decidable provenance domain $\mathcal{U}$. A $\mathcal{U}$-labeled Petri net $N = \langle S, T, (I, O), \Lambda \rangle$ is a Petri net $\langle S, T, (I, O) \rangle$ that is equipped with a labeling function Λ specifying how provenance markings are updated when a transition is fired. Consider a transition $t \in T$. Let $p_1, \ldots, p_k$ be an ordering of all the places in S for which $I(t)(p) = 1$. For each place $p' \in S$ with $O(t)(p') = 1$, the labeling function $\Lambda(t, p')$ is a $\preceq$-monotonic function $U^k \to U$. We assume the labeling function Λ is computable.

A *labeled marking* μ is a mapping from places S to multisets over U, i.e., it labels each token in a marking with an element of U. A labeled marking μ induces a marking $\mathsf{erase}(\mu)$ that maps each $p \in S$ to $\sum_{u \in U} \mu(p)(u)$ obtained by erasing all provenance information carried by tokens. Fix a transition t, and let

$p_1, \ldots, p_k$ be an ordering of the places such that $I(t)(p) = 1$. The transition t is enabled at a labeled marking μ if for each $p \in S$ with $I(t)(p) = 1$, we have $\mathsf{erase}(\mu)(p) \geq 1$. An enabled transition t at μ can fire to produce a new labeled marking μ', denoted (by abuse of notation) $\mu[t\rangle\mu'$, defined as follows. To compute μ' from μ, first pick and remove arbitrarily tokens from p_1 to p_k with labels u_1 to u_k respectively. Then, for each p' with $O(t)(p') = 1$, add a token whose label is $\Lambda(t, p')(u_1, \ldots, u_k)$ to p'. All other places remain unchanged. We extend the firing notion to sequences of transitions, as well as notions of transition system, size, reachability, and coverability to labeled Petri nets in the obvious way.

To prove the coverability problem is decidable for $\mathcal{U}$-labeled Petri nets, we argue that their transition systems $(\mathbb{M}[U]^S, \mu_0, \hookrightarrow)$ are *well-structured* in that the labeled markings can be equipped with an order that allows larger labeled markings to mimic the behaviour of smaller ones, i.e. there is a wqo $\ll \subseteq \mathbb{M}[U]^S \times \mathbb{M}[U]^S$ that is compatible with the transitions: for all $\mu_1 \hookrightarrow \mu_1'$ and $\mu_1 \ll \mu_2$ there is $\mu_2 \hookrightarrow \mu_2'$ so that $\mu_1' \ll \mu_2'$.

To define a suitable wqo on labeled markings, we first compare the multisets on a place. Intuitively, $\mu(p) \ll \mu'(p)$ with $\mu, \mu' \in \mathbb{M}[U]^S$ and $p \in S$ if for every u in $\mu(p)$ there is an element u' in $\mu'(p)$ such that $u \preceq u'$ in the wqo $\preceq$ of the provenance domain. Hence, $\mu \ll \mu'$ if for each $p \in S$ there is an injective function $f_p : \mu(p) \to \mu'(p)$ so that for each $u \in \mu(p)$, we have $u \preceq f_p(u)$. The result is a wqo by Higman's lemma [13] and the fact that wqos are stable under Cartesian products. The ordering is also compatible with the transitions by the monotonicity requirement on labelings. The following theorem follows using standard results on well-structured transition systems [1,8].

Theorem 2. *The coverability problem for $\mathcal{U}$-labeled Petri nets is decidable and EXPSPACE-hard for decidable provenance domains $\mathcal{U}$.*

The coverability problem for labeled Petri nets need not be in EXPSPACE, even when the operations on $\mathcal{U}$ are provided by an oracle. For example, nested Petri nets [20] can encode reset nets, for which a non-primitive recursive lower bound is known for coverability [26].

4.2 From Message Passing Programs to Labeled Petri Nets

Let $\mathcal{P} = (Prin, C, \{G_p\}_{p \in Prin})$ be a message passing program and $\mathcal{U} = (U, \preceq, \psi)$ a provenance domain. We now give a labeled Petri net semantics to the program.

Define the labeled Petri net $N(\mathcal{P}, \mathcal{U}) = \langle S, T, (I, O), \Lambda \rangle$ as follows. There is a place for each program location, for each local variable and message value, and each channel and message value: $S = V^\star \cup (X^\star \times \mathcal{M}) \cup (C \times \mathcal{M})$.

In the definition of labels, we use variable $\mathsf{prov}(p)$ for the token (which is a provenance) in place $p \in S$ that is used for firing. The set T is the smallest set that satisfies the following conditions.

1. For each $e \equiv v \xrightarrow{y := \otimes(x), p} v'$ in $E^\star$, and for each $m, m' \in \mathcal{M}$, there is a transition t with $I(t) = [\![v, (x, m), (y, m')]\!]$ and $O(t) = [\![v', (x, m), (y, \otimes m)]\!]$. Also, $\Lambda(t, (x, m)) = \mathsf{prov}(x, m)$, $\Lambda(t, (y, \otimes m)) = \psi(p, \otimes)(\mathsf{prov}(x, m))$, and $\Lambda(t, v') = \varepsilon$.

2. For each $e \equiv v \xrightarrow{\mathsf{assume}(x=m),p} v'$ in $E^{\star}$, there is a transition t with $I(t){=}[\![v,(x,m)]\!]$ and $O(t){=}[\![v',(x,m)]\!]$. Also, $\Lambda(t,v') = \varepsilon$, and $\Lambda(t,(x,m)) = \mathsf{prov}(x,m)$.

3. For each $e \equiv v \xrightarrow{ch!x,p} v'$ in $E^{\star}$, and for each $m{\in}\mathcal{M}$, there is a transition t with $I(t){=}[\![v,(x,m)]\!]$, $O(t){=}[\![v',(x,m),(ch,m)]\!]$. Also, $\Lambda(t,v'){=}\varepsilon$, $\Lambda(t,(x,m)){=}\mathsf{prov}(x,m)$, and $\Lambda(t,(ch,m)){=}\psi(p,!)(\mathsf{prov}(x,m))$.

4. For each $e \equiv v \xrightarrow{ch?x,p} v'$ in $E^{\star}$, for each $m,m'{\in}\mathcal{M}$, there is a transition t with $I(t) = [\![v,(x,m),(ch,m')]\!]$ and $O(t) = [\![v',(x,m')]\!]$. Also, $\Lambda(t,v') = \varepsilon$ and $\Lambda(t,(x,m')) = \psi(p,?)(\mathsf{prov}(ch,m'))$.

To relate $\mathcal{P}$ with its Petri nets semantics $N(\mathcal{P},\mathcal{U})$, we define a bijection ι between configurations and labeled markings: $\iota(\ell,\mathbf{c},\pi) = \mu$ iff all of the three conditions hold: (1) $\mu(v) = [\![\varepsilon]\!]$ iff there is $p \in Prin$ with $\ell(p) = v$; (2) for all $x \in X^{\star}$, for all $m \in \mathcal{M}$, and for all $u \in U$, $\mu(x,m) = [\![u]\!]$ iff $\pi(x) = (m,u)$; (3) for all $ch \in C$, for all $m \in \mathcal{M}$, and for all $u \in U$, $\mu(ch,m)(u) = k$ iff $\mathbf{c}(ch)(m,u) = k$. Define the initial labeled marking $\mu_0 = \iota(\ell_0,\mathbf{c}_0,\pi_0)$. The following observation follows from the definition of ι.

Lemma 1. $TS(\mathcal{P})$ and $TS(N(\mathcal{P},\mathcal{U}))$ are isomorphic.

Complexity-wise, the problem inherits the hardness of coverability in (unlabeled) Petri nets for any non-trivial provenance domain.

Theorem 3. Given a message passing program $\mathcal{P}$ and a decidable provenance domain $\mathcal{U} = (U,\preceq,\psi)$, the provenance verification problem is decidable. It is EXPSPACE-hard for any provenance domain with at least two elements.

Proof. From the construction of the labeled Petri net, Lemma 1, the provenance verification problem is reducible in polynomial time to coverability for labeled Petri nets. Thus, by Theorem 2, provenance verification problem is decidable.

For EXPSPACE-hardness, we reduce Petri net coverability to provenance verification. To simulate a Petri net with a message passing program, we introduce a channel for every place and then serialize the reading of tokens. Consider $N = \langle S,T,(I,O)\rangle$. We construct a message passing program with one principal, one message, and a channel for each place in S. The control flow graph of the only principal has a central node from which loops simulate the Petri net transitions. At each step, the central node picks a transition $t \in T$ non-deterministically and simulates first the consumption and then the production of tokens — one by one. To consume a token from place p with $I(t)(p) = 1$, the principal receives a message from channel p. For the production, it sends a message to the channel p' with $O(t)(p') = 1$. Additionally, the principal non-deterministically checks if the current configuration of channels covers the target marking. If so, it writes a message into a special variable x. The provenance verification problem asks whether x ever contains a message with non-trivial provenance. EXPSPACE-hardness follows from Theorem 1. ∎

4.3 EXPSPACE Upper Bounds

For set and language provenance domains, we can in fact show a matching upper bound on the complexity. It relies on a fairly general product construction and reduction to Petri nets. We say that a provenance domain $\mathcal{U}$ is of *finite index* if the equivalence induced by $\preceq$ has finitely many classes. We denote this equivalence by $\equiv$. Clearly, any finite provenance domain (thus, the set domain) is of finite index. The language domain is also of finite index: take the equivalence relation induced by the Myhill-Nerode classes of the language. The following lemma characterizes the structural properties of provenance domains of finite index.

Lemma 2. *Consider a Petri net $N = \langle S, T, (I, O), \Lambda \rangle$ that is labelled by $\mathcal{U}$ of finite index. (1) The equivalence classes are closed under Λ: for any tuple $e_1, \ldots, e_k$ of $\equiv$-equivalence classes, the image $\Lambda(e_1, \ldots, e_k)$ is fully contained in another equivalence class e. (2) The upward-closure of any $u \in U$ is a finite union of $\equiv$-classes.*

Let $N = \langle S, T, (I, O), \Lambda \rangle$ be a $\mathcal{U}$-labeled Petri net, and suppose $\mathcal{U}$ is of finite index. We now define a product construction that reduces N to an ordinary Petri net $N' = \langle S', T', (I', O') \rangle$. Intuitively, for each place $p \in S$ and each equivalence class e, there is a place (p, e) in S' that keeps track of all tokens in N at place p and having their label in the equivalence class e. We define $S' = S \times \{[u]_\equiv \mid u \in U\}$. Each transition in N is simulated by a family of transitions in T', one for each combination of equivalence classes for the source tokens. More precisely, T' is the smallest set that contains the following family of transitions for each $t \in T$. Let $p_1, \ldots, p_k$ be the places in S with $I(t)(p_i) = 1$. For each sequence $\bar{p} = \langle e_1, \ldots, e_k \rangle$ of k-tuples of $\equiv$-equivalence classes, we have a transition $t_{\bar{p}} \in T'$ such that $I'(t_{\bar{p}})((p_i, e_i)) = 1$ for $i = 1, \ldots, k$ and $I'(t_{\bar{p}})(p) = 0$ for all other places. Moreover, for each $p \in S$ with $O(t)(p) = 1$ labeled with Λ, we have that $O'(t_{\bar{p}})((p, e)) = 1$ with $\Lambda(e_1, \ldots, e_k) \subseteq e$. Note that this inclusion is well-defined by Lemma 2(1). This product construction reduces a labelled coverability query in N to several unlabelled queries in N'. What are the unlabelled queries we need? Consider a token u in a labelled marking $\mu \in \mathbb{M}[U]^S$. We use the equivalence classes that, with Lemma 2(2), characterize the upward closure of u. In the following proposition, we assume that these classes are effectively computable. This is the case for set and language domains.

Proposition 1. *If $\mathcal{U}$ is of finite index, coverability for $\mathcal{U}$-labeled Petri nets is reducible to coverability for Petri nets.*

Proposition 1 provides a 2EXPSPACE upper bound for the set and language domains, which is not optimal. Consider the set domain. Each subset of principals yields an equivalence class of provenances. Hence, there is an exponential number of classes and the above product net is exponential. A similar problem occurs for the language domain if the provenance specification is given by a non-deterministic finite automaton. There are regular languages where this non-deterministic representation is exponentially more succinct than any deterministic one. The deterministic one, however, is needed in the product. To derive an optimal upper bound, we give compact representations of these exponentially many classes.

Theorem 4. *Provenance verification problem is in EXPSPACE for set and language domains.*

Proof. To establish membership in EXPSPACE, we implement the above reduction from labeled to unlabeled coverability in a compact way, so that the size of the resulting Petri net is polynomial in the size of the input. The challenge is to avoid the multiplication between places and equivalence classes, which may be exponential. Instead, we first encode the classes into polynomially many additional places, and maintain the relationship between a place and a class in the marking of the new net. Second, we only keep the provenance information for tokens in the goal marking, and omit the provenance of the remaining tokens.

Let E be the set of equivalence classes of a provenance domain of finite index. Let $\kappa = \lceil \log |E| \rceil$. The symbolic representation of E uses 2κ places. Let the places be $b_0, d_0, \ldots, b_{\kappa-1}, d_{\kappa-1}$. We maintain the invariant that in any reachable marking, exactly one of b_i, d_i contains a single token, for $i = 0, \ldots, (\kappa - 1)$. Intuitively, a token in b_i specifies the bit i is one, and a token in d_i specifies the bit i is zero. Using constructions on (1-safe) Petri nets, one can "copy" a bitvector, remove all tokens from a bitvector, or update a bitvector to a value.

For example, to empty out a bitvector, we introduce $\kappa + 1$ places $p_0, \ldots, p_\kappa$, with an initial token in p_0. Each p_i, $i \in \{0, \ldots, \kappa - 1\}$, has two transitions: they take a token from p_i and from b_i (resp. d_i), and put a token in p_{i+1}. When p_κ is marked, all the bits have been cleared. Similarly, to copy the configuration from places $b_0, d_0, \ldots, b_{\kappa-1}, d_{\kappa-1}$ to empty places $b'_0, d'_0, \ldots, b'_{\kappa-1}, d'_{\kappa-1}$, we use the following gadget. We add additional $\kappa + 1$ places $p_0, \ldots, p_\kappa$, with an initial token on p_0. For each p_i, $i \in \{0, \ldots, \kappa - 1\}$ there are two transitions: one takes a token from p_i and one token from b_i and puts a token in p_{i+1}, one in b_i, and one in b'_i; the other takes a token from p_i and one from d_i and puts a token in p_{i+1}, one in d_i, and one in d'_i. When the place p_κ is marked, the bits in $b_0, d_0, \ldots, b_{\kappa-1}, d_{\kappa-1}$ have been copied to $b'_0, d'_0, \ldots, b'_{\kappa-1}, d'_{\kappa-1}$.

Now, in the translation of the Petri net, instead of a place (x, m, e) for each variable x, message m, and equivalence class $e \in E$, we keep 2κ places for each place (x, m), encoding the equivalence class e for x and m. If all 2κ places for (x, m) are empty in a marking, it implies that the current content of x is not m; otherwise, the provenance equivalence class $e \in E$ of (x, m) is encoded by the 2κ bits. The transitions of the net are updated with the gadgets to copy the provenance bitvectors in case of assignments.

Moreover, for each channel ch, we maintain the provenance information of one message, and drop the provenance of every other message in the channel. That is, each channel ch is modeled using places (ch, m) for each $m \in \mathcal{M}$, and in addition, $2\kappa \cdot |\mathcal{M}|$ places that encode the provenance equivalence class of one message for each value in $\mathcal{M}$ stored in the channel. Intuitively, tokens in (ch, m) denote messages with value m in the channel ch whose provenance has been "forgotten" and tokens in the bitvectors encode one message (per message type) in the channel whose provenance is encoded using 2κ places. We use non-determinism to guess which messages contribute to the message with provenance in the target. When a message is sent to a channel, we non-deterministically decide to keep its provenance (thus using the bitvectors, moving any tokens already there) or to drop its provenance.

Similarly, when we receive from a channel, we non-deterministically decide to either read from the "special" places for the encoding of an equivalence class, or from the "normal" place.

Now, for the set domain, we use $2|Prin|$ places to encode sets of principals. For the language domain, where the specification is given by a non-deterministic automaton with states Q, we use $2|Q|$ places to encode the subsets of states. The encoding allows us to perform the subset construction on the fly. Each action of the program requires at most a polynomial number of additional places to encode the gadgets. Thus, we get a Petri net that is polynomial in the size of the message passing program and the specification. Thus, using Theorem 1, we get the EXPSPACE upper bound. ∎

5   Implementation and Experiments

We have implemented a tool for the provenance verification problem for language provenance domains. Our tool takes as input a message passing program encoded in an extended Promela syntax in which channels are marked asynchronous and have the semantics described in Section 3. It reduces the provenance verification problem to Petri net coverability using the algorithm from Section 4. We first used state-of-the-art tools for Petri net coverability [9,21]. Unfortunately, the times taken to verify the provenance properties were high. This is because Petri net coverability tools are optimized for nets with many places that can be unbounded and for high concurrency. Instead, message passing programs only have few places that are unbounded (the channels). Our second observation is that message passing programs have a lot of scope for partial-order reduction, by allowing a process to continue executing until it hits a blocking receive action. To take advantage of these features, we implemented a coverability checker that combines expand-enlarge-check (EEC) [10] with partial order reduction [11].

5.1   Expand-Enlarge-Check and Partial Order Reduction

The EEC procedure [10] performs *counter abstraction* over a Petri net. We observe that only the places representing shared channels can have more than one token in our Petri nets. Instead of counting the exact number of messages in a channel, we fix a parameter $k \geq 0$ and count precisely up to k. If at any point, the number of messages in a channel exceeds k, we replace the number by ∞. Once the count goes to ∞, we do not decrease the count even when messages are removed from the channel. For example, if $k = 0$, the abstraction of a channel distinguishes two cases: either the channel has no messages or it has an arbitrary number of messages.

The abstraction is sound, in that if a marking is coverable in the original net, it is also covered in the abstraction. However, the abstraction can add spurious counterexamples, in that a marking can be considered coverable in the abstraction, even though it is not coverable in the original net. By concretely simulating a specific counterexample path, we can decide if the counterexample is genuine or spurious. In case the counterexample is spurious, we increase the parameter k and continue. This abstraction-refinement process is guaranteed to terminate, by either finding a genuine path that covers a given marking, or by proving that the target marking is not coverable for some parameter k in the abstraction [10]. We have found that $k = 1$ is usually sufficient to soundly abstract the state space and to prove a provenance property; this is consistent with other uses of counter abstractions in verification [23,17].

Additionally, we note that once the parameter k is fixed, the state space of the system is finite, since each channel can have at most $k + 2$ messages ($\{0, \ldots, k\} \cup \{\infty\}$). Thus, for each k, we can perform reachability analysis using a finite-state reachability engine. In our implementation, we choose the Spin model checker [14] to perform reachability analysis in every iteration where k is fixed. In Spin models, for each channel, each message type, and each state of the provenance automaton, we have a variable that takes $k + 2$ values, implementing the k-abstraction.

Additionally, message passing programs have the potential for partial order reduction. For example, each process in the program can be executed until it reaches a blocking receive action, and the local actions of different processes commute. Since Spin already implements partial order reduction, we get the benefits of partial order reduction for free.

5.2   Case Studies: Message Passing Benchmarks

We first describe our evaluation on a set of three message passing systems (see Table 1). The example MyHealth Portal is described in [2]. We checked if the provenance of a variable is always in the regular language Patient (Secretary + ε) Nurse Doctor$^+$ + ε. The bug tracking system [16] manages software bug reports. It has five principals and eight types of messages (bug report, closed, fix-again, fix, must-fix, more-information, pending, and verified). The provenance specification, given as an automaton with nine states, encodes the flow of events leading from a bug report to a bug fix. We found that the original system violated the specification because a message was sent to an incorrect channel. After fixing the bug, we were able to prove the property for the new system. The Service Incident Exchange Standard (SIS) specifies a system to share service incident data and facilitate resolutions. The standard envisages interactions between service requesters and providers. We took the system model from [4], which consists of 16 principals, 18 channels, and 9 message types. The property to check is once a service request is terminated, it is never reopened.

Results. Table 2 lists the analysis results. All experiments were performed on a 2 core Intel Xeon X5650 CPU machine with 64GB memory and 64bit Linux (Debian/Lenny). We compare state-of-the-art Petri net coverability tools (Mist2 [9] and Petruchio [21]) with our Spin-based coverability checker. We run Petruchio and three different options of Mist2 and report the best times. A timeout indicates that all the tools timed out. The "Markings" row indicates the number of coverability checks required to prove correctness. The time denotes the sum of the times for all the coverability checks to finish, where for each check, we take the best time by any tool.

For our Spin-based checker, we report the parameter k for which either a genuine counterexample was found, or the system was proved correct. We compare the results with and without partial order reduction. For each run, we give three numbers: the number of states and transitions explored by our checker and the time taken. There is a significant reduction when partial order reduction is turned on. Moreover, our Spin-based implementation is orders of magnitude faster than the Petri net coverability tools.

5.3 Private Mode and Firefox Extensions

We performed a larger case study on provenance in browser extensions. Modern browsers provide a "private mode" that deletes cookies, forms, and browsing history at the end of each browsing session. Browsers also provide an extension mechanism, through which third-party developers can add functionality to browsers. Extensions can communicate between their front- and back-ends by asynchronous messages passing, and between each other via temporary files. Moreover, Firefox lets extension developers manage SQLite databases in user machines by invoking a service called *mozIStorageService*. It provides a set of asynchronous APIs for extensions to communicate with databases through SQL queries. If extension developers do not properly handle the private mode, user data may be stored in the database while the user is browsing in private mode.

It is expected that browser extensions should respect the private mode. Unfortunately, browsers do not restrict an extension's capability in private mode, and it is the responsibility of developers not to record user data in private mode. In the second set of case studies, we check if extension developers for Firefox obey the privacy concerns when the user is browsing in private mode.

Our goal is to check if extensions using *mozIStorageService* can store user data while in private mode. We formulate the problem of tracking information flow in private mode as a provenance verification problem. Consider a set of browser extensions cooperating with each other, and a principal Db modelling a database. For each extension A, we introduce two principals NormA and PrivA that represent two instances of A running in the normal and in

Table 1. Message passing benchmarks. "Principals" is the number of principals, "Messages" the possible values of messages, "Channels" is the number of shared channels, and "Automaton" is the number of states in the provenance automaton.

Example	Principals	Messages	Channels	Automaton
Health Care	4	4	5	6
Bug Tracking	5	8	5	9
SIS	16	9	18	2

Table 2. Results of the message passing benchmarks. Bug Tracking (1) is the buggy version.

PN tools	Health Care	Bug Tracking (1)	Bug Tracking (2)	SIS
Markings	12	1	40	127
Time	125.6s	2308.940s	timeout	1152.07s
Our Checker	Health Care	Bug Tracking (1)	Bug Tracking (2)	SIS
k	0	1	0	1
States (No POR)	6351	39	4905516	3738754
States (POR)	2490	39	995468	893786
Trans (No POR)	23357	39	24850365	17274836
Trans (POR)	4249	39	1707682	1736062
Time (No POR)	0.04s	0.01s	38.6s	58.7s
Time (POR)	0.01s	0.01s	3.37s	6.10s

the private mode, respectively. For each extension A that saves data to the database, there are two channels ch_{Db}, ch'_{Db} for NormA and PrivA to interact with Db. Moreover, for each pair of extensions (A, B) where A sends data to B, for instance, by writing and reading files, there are four combinations: (NormA, NormB), (PrivA, NormB), (NormA, PrivB), and (PrivA, PrivB). For each case, we introduce a channel ch to model the message flow from A to B. The property we check is whether some PrivA directly or indirectly updates the database. Note that it is not sufficient to ensure every write to the database is guarded by a check that the browser is not in private mode. There can be indirect flows where data is stored in a temporary file in private mode, or communicated to a different extension, and later stored in the database.

We use Firefox 13.0.1 in our experiments. We selected nine popular extensions from Firefox's extension repository, by filtering them based on the keywords *form*, *history*, and *shopping*, and then filtering based on their use of *mozIStorageService*. The extensions we chose have about 50000 users on average.

Our tool works as follows. We first use JSure [7], a Javascript parser and static analyzer, to obtain the control flow from the extension source code, and to produce a message passing program in Promela syntax. As the access to a database is either via calling the *mozIStorageService* APIs directly or via helper extensions, we capture along the control flow the information about when an extension calls these APIs to update the database, and the information about when extensions communicate with each other by writing and reading temporary files. Our front end abstracts away complex data structures in the program. In particular, we do not track the contents inserted into the database. This may lead to false positives in the analysis. We then run our Spin-based back-end to verify the message passing program.

Table 3 lists the results. Five out of the nine examples are found to store user information even in private mode. All examples can be verified efficiently (in a few milliseconds) because usually a small portion of code is related to database accesses and extension communications, and complex data structures are abstracted out. For all unsafe cases, we have successfully replayed executions that violate the private mode in Firefox.

6 Extensions

We have described a general algebraic model of provenance in concurrent message passing systems and an algorithm for statically verifying provenance properties. For these expressive programs, only dynamic checks or imprecise static checks had been studied so far. While the complexity may seem high, reachability analysis in message passing programs is already EXPSPACE-complete, so provenance verification does not incur an extra cost.

Table 3. Experimental results for Firefox extensions

Name	LOC	Leak	Usage	Leak Details	Time
Amazon Price History and More 4.1.4	8124	Yes	Provide comparative pricing for searched products. Inform pricing drops for searched products.	Records shopping history while in private mode.	57ms
Facebook Chat History Manager 1.5	2798	Yes	Help users organize conversations by time and names of persons.	Records the person to whom users talk, the conversation content, and the time in private mode.	60ms
FVD Speed Dial with Online Sync 4.0.3	21278	Yes	Provide a dashboard holding favorite websites of users. Cross-platform bookmark synchronization.	Keeps counting how often users look at the websites on their Speed Dial in private mode and lists them.	57ms
Privad 1.0	17593	Yes	Uses differential privacy to prevent ad targeting.	Records user browsing history while in private mode.	60ms
Shopping Assist 3.2.4.6	15263	Yes	Provide comparative pricing for searched products.	Records shopping history while in private mode.	57ms
Form History Control 1.2.10.3	16560	No	Autosave text on forms, search bar history, for crash recovery.		63ms
History Deleter 2.4	3027	No	Utilities to delete history automatically by user defined rules.		90ms
Lazarus: Form Recovery 2.3	10839	No	Autosave text on forms, search bar history, for crash recovery.		64ms
Session Manager 0.7.9	14010	No	Autosave sessions by time for crash recovery.		104ms

Our decidability results continue to hold under some extensions to the programming model. For example, our decidability results also hold when programs can test the provenance of a message against an upward closed set in a conditional, or in the presence of a spawn instruction that dynamically generates a new thread of execution. Informally, to decide provenance verification in the presence of provenance-tests, we extend the product construction to track the membership in each upward closed set appearing syntactically in some conditional. To handle spawn, we modify the reduction to Petri nets to keep a place for each spawned instance (that is, each tuple of control location and valuation to local variables).

On the other hand, many other extensions are easily seen to be undecidable. For example, if each principal executes a recursive program, or if messages come from an unbounded domain such as the natural numbers, or if channels preserve the order of messages, the provenance verification problem becomes undecidable by simple reductions from known undecidable problems [22].

References

1. Abdulla, P.A., Cerans, K., Jonsson, B., Tsay, Y.-K.: General decidability theorems for infinite-state systems. In: LICS 1996, pp. 313–321. IEEE (1996)
2. Barth, A., Mitchell, J., Datta, A., Sundaram, S.: Privacy and utility in business processes. In: CSF, pp. 279–294. IEEE (2007)
3. Buneman, P., Khanna, S., Tan, W.-C.: Why and where: A characterization of data provenance. In: Van den Bussche, J., Vianu, V. (eds.) ICDT 2001. LNCS, vol. 1973, pp. 316–330. Springer, Heidelberg (2000)
4. Chaki, S., Rajamani, S., Rehof, J.: Types as models: model checking message-passing programs. In: POPL, pp. 45–57. ACM (2002)
5. Cheney, J., Ahmed, A., Acar, U.: Provenance as dependency analysis. Math. Struct. in Computer Science 21, 1301–1337 (2011)
6. Cui, Y., Widom, J., Wiener, J.: Tracing the lineage of view data in a warehousing environment. ACM TODS 25, 179–227 (2000)
7. Durak, B.: JSure, https://github.com/berke/jsure
8. Finkel, A., Schnoebelen, P.: Well-structured transition systems everywhere! Theoretical Computer Science 256(1-2), 63–92 (2001)
9. Ganty, P., Raskin, J.-F., Begin, L.V.: From many places to few: Automatic abstraction refinement for Petri nets. Fund. Informaticae 88(3), 275–305 (2008)
10. Geeraerts, G., Raskin, J.-F., Van Begin, L.: Expand, enlarge and check: new algorithms for the coverability problem of WSTS. In: Lodaya, K., Mahajan, M. (eds.) FSTTCS 2004. LNCS, vol. 3328, pp. 287–298. Springer, Heidelberg (2004)
11. Godefroid, P. (ed.): Partial-Order Methods for the Verification of Concurrent Systems. LNCS, vol. 1032. Springer, Heidelberg (1996)
12. Green, T., Karvounarakis, G., Tannen, V.: Provenance semirings. In: PODS, pp. 31–40. ACM (2007)
13. Higman, G.: Ordering by divisibility in abstract algebras. Proc. London Math. Soc (3) 2, 326–336 (1952)
14. Holzmann, G.: The Spin model checker. IEEE Transactions on Software Engineering 23(5), 279–295 (1997)

15. Huang, Y.-W., Yu, F., Hang, C., Tsai, C.-H., Lee, D.-T., Kuo, S.-Y.: Securing web application code by static analysis and runtime protection. In: WWW, pp. 40–52 (2004)
16. Janák, J.: Issue tracking systems. Diplomová práce, Masarykova univerzita, Fakulta informatiky (2009)
17. Jhala, R., Majumdar, R.: Interprocedural analysis of asynchronous programs. In: POPL 2007, pp. 339–350. ACM (2007)
18. Lipton, R.: The reachability problem is exponential-space hard. Technical Report 62, Department of Computer Science, Yale University (1976)
19. Livshits, B., Lam, M.: Finding security errors in Java programs with static analysis. In: Usenix Security Symposium, pp. 271–286 (2005)
20. Lomazova, I.A., Schnoebelen, P.: Some decidability results for nested Petri nets. In: Bjorner, D., Broy, M., Zamulin, A.V. (eds.) PSI 1999. LNCS, vol. 1755, pp. 208–220. Springer, Heidelberg (2000)
21. Meyer, R., Strazny, T.: Petruchio: From dynamic networks to nets. In: Touili, T., Cook, B., Jackson, P. (eds.) CAV 2010. LNCS, vol. 6174, pp. 175–179. Springer, Heidelberg (2010)
22. Minsky, M.: Finite and Infinite Machines. Prentice-Hall (1967)
23. Pnueli, A., Xu, J., Zuck, L.D.: Liveness with $(0, 1, \infty)$-counter abstraction. In: Brinksma, E., Larsen, K.G. (eds.) CAV 2002. LNCS, vol. 2404, pp. 107–122. Springer, Heidelberg (2002)
24. Rackoff, C.: The covering and boundedness problems for vector addition systems. Theoretical Computer Science 6(2), 223–231 (1978)
25. Sabelfeld, A., Myers, A.: Language-based information-flow security. IEEE J. Selected Areas in Communications 21, 5–19 (2003)
26. Schnoebelen, P.: Revisiting Ackermann-hardness for lossy counter machines and reset Petri nets. In: Hliněný, P., Kučera, A. (eds.) MFCS 2010. LNCS, vol. 6281, pp. 616–628. Springer, Heidelberg (2010)
27. Souilah, I., Francalanza, A., Sassone, V.: A formal model of provenance in distributed systems. In: Workshop on the Theory and Practice of Provenance (2009)

Verification as Learning Geometric Concepts

Rahul Sharma[1], Saurabh Gupta[2], Bharath Hariharan[2],
Alex Aiken[1], and Aditya V. Nori[3]

[1] Stanford University
{sharmar,aiken}@cs.stanford.edu
[2] University of California at Berkeley
{sgupta,bharath2}@eecs.berkeley.edu
[3] Microsoft Research India
adityan@microsoft.com

Abstract. We formalize the problem of program verification as a learning problem, showing that invariants in program verification can be regarded as geometric concepts in machine learning. Safety properties define *bad states*: states a program should not reach. Program verification explains why a program's set of reachable states is disjoint from the set of bad states. In Hoare Logic, these explanations are predicates that form inductive assertions. Using samples for reachable and bad states and by applying well known machine learning algorithms for classification, we are able to generate inductive assertions. By relaxing the search for an exact proof to classifiers, we obtain complexity theoretic improvements. Further, we extend the learning algorithm to obtain a sound procedure that can generate proofs containing invariants that are arbitrary boolean combinations of polynomial inequalities. We have evaluated our approach on a number of challenging benchmarks and the results are promising.

Keywords: loop invariants, verification, machine learning.

1 Introduction

We formalize the problem of verification as a learning problem, showing that loop invariants can be regarded as geometric concepts in machine learning. Informally, an invariant is a predicate that separates good and bad program states and once we have obtained strong invariants for all the loops, standard techniques can be used to generate program proofs. The motivation for using machine learning for invariant inference is twofold: guarantees and expressiveness.

Standard verification algorithms observe some small number of behaviors of the program under consideration and extrapolate this information to (hopefully) get a proof for all possible behaviors of the program. The extrapolation is a heuristic and systematic ways of performing extrapolation are unknown, except for the cases where they have been carefully designed for a particular class of programs. SLAM [6] generates new predicates from infeasible counterexample traces. Interpolant based techniques [37] extrapolate the information obtained from proving the correctness of finite unwindings of loops. In abstract interpretation [21], fixpoint iterations are performed for a few iterations of the

F. Logozzo and M. Fähndrich (Eds.): SAS 2013, LNCS 7935, pp. 388–411, 2013.
© Springer-Verlag Berlin Heidelberg 2013

loop and this information is extrapolated using a widening operator. In any of these heuristics, and others, there is no formal characterization of how well the output of the extrapolation strategy approximates the true invariants.

Extrapolation is the fundamental problem attacked by machine learning: A learning algorithm has some finite training data and the goal is to learn a function that generalizes for the infinite set of possible inputs. For classification, the learner is given some examples of good and bad states and the goal is to learn a predicate that separates all the good states from all the bad states. Unlike standard verification approaches that have no guarantees on extrapolation, learning theory provides formal generalization guarantees for learning algorithms. These guarantees are provided in learning models that assume certain oracles. However, it is well known in the machine learning community that extrapolation engines that have learning guarantees in the theoretical models tend to have good performance empirically. The algorithms have been applied in diverse areas such as finance, biology, and vision: we apply learning algorithms to the task of invariant inference.

Standard invariant generation techniques find invariants of a restricted form: there are restrictions on expressiveness that are not due to efficiency considerations but instead due to fundamental limitations. These techniques especially have trouble with disjunctions and non-linearities. Predicate abstraction restricts invariants to a boolean combination of a given set of predicates. Existing interpolation engines cannot generate non-linear predicates [1]. Template based approaches for linear invariants like [35] require a template that fixes the boolean form of the invariant and approaches for non-linear invariants [53] can only find conjunctions of polynomial equalities. Abstract interpretation over convex hulls [23] handles neither disjunctions nor non-linearities. Disjunctions can be obtained by performing disjunctive completion [22,26], but widening [3] places an ad hoc restriction on the number of disjuncts. Our learning algorithm is strictly more expressive than these previous approaches: It can generate arbitrary boolean combinations of polynomial inequalities (of a given degree). Hence there are no restrictions on the number of disjuncts and we go beyond linear inequalities and polynomial equalities.

Unsurprisingly, our learning algorithm, with such expressive power, has high computational complexity. Next, we show how to trade expressiveness for computational speedups. We construct efficient machine learning algorithms, with formal generalization guarantees, for generating arbitrary boolean combinations of constituent predicates when these predicates come from a given set of predicates (predicate abstraction), when the size of integer constants in the predicates are bounded, or from a given abstract domain (such as boxes or octagons). Note that these efficient algorithms with reduced expressiveness still generate arbitrary boolean combinations of predicates.

Our main insight is to view invariants as geometric concepts separating good and bad states. This view allows us to make the following contributions:

- We show how to use a well known learning algorithm [13] for the purpose of computing candidate invariants. This algorithm is a PAC learner: it has generalization guarantees in the PAC (probably approximately correct) learning model. The learning algorithm makes no assumption about the syntax of the program and outputs a candidate invariant that is as expressive as arbitrary boolean combinations of linear inequalities.

– The algorithm of [13] is impractical. We parametrize the algorithm of [13] by the abstract domain in which the linear inequalities constituting the invariants lie, allowing us to obtain candidates that are arbitrary boolean combinations of linear inequalities belonging to the given abstract domain. We obtain efficient PAC learning algorithms for generating such candidates for abstract domains requiring few variables, such as boxes or octagons and finite domains such as predicate abstraction.

– We augment our learning algorithms with a theorem prover to obtain a sound procedure for computing invariants. This idea of combining procedures for generating likely invariants with verification engines has been previously explored in [49,55,54] (see Section 6). We evaluate the performance of this procedure on challenging benchmarks for invariant generation from the literature. We are able to generate invariants, using a small amount of data, in a few seconds per loop on these benchmarks.

The rest of the paper is organized as follows: We informally introduce our technique using an example in Section 2. We then describe necessary background material, including the learning algorithm of [13] (Section 3). Section 4 describes the main results of our work. We first give an efficient algorithm for obtaining likely invariants from candidate predicates (Section 4.1). Next, in Section 4.1, we obtain efficient algorithms for the case when the linear inequalities constituting the invariant lie in a given abstract domain. In Section 4.2, we extend [13] to generate candidates that are arbitrary boolean combinations of polynomial inequalities. Finally, Section 4.3 describes our sound procedure for generating invariants. Section 5 describes our implementation and experiments. We discuss related work in Section 6 and conclude in Section 7.

2   Overview of the Technique

```
1: x := i; y := j;
2: while (x != 0) { x--; y--; }
3: if (i == j) assert (y == 0);
```

Fig. 1. Motivating example

Consider the program in Figure 1 [37]. To prove that the assertion in line 3 is never violated, we need to prove the following Hoare triple:

$$\{x = i \land y = j\}\texttt{while (x != 0) do x--; y--}\{i = j \Rightarrow y = 0\}$$

In general, to prove $\{P\}$ `while` E `do` S $\{Q\}$, where E is the loop condition and S is the loop body, we need to find a *loop invariant* I satisfying $P \Rightarrow I$,

$\{I \wedge E\}S\{I\}$, and $I \wedge \neg E \Rightarrow Q$. Thus, to verify that the program in Figure 1 does not violate the assertion, we need a loop invariant I such that $(x = i \wedge y = j) \Rightarrow I$, $\{I \wedge x \neq 0\}S\{I\}$, and $I \wedge x = 0 \Rightarrow (i = j \Rightarrow y = 0)$. The predicate $I \equiv i = j \Rightarrow x = y$ is one such invariant [37].

There is another way to view loop invariants. For simplicity of exposition, we restrict our attention to *correct* programs that never violate assertions (e.g., Figure 1). A *state* is a valuation of the program variables, for example $(i, j, x, y) = (1, 0, 1, 0)$. Consider the set of states at the loop head (the `while` statement of Figure 1) when the program is executed. All such states are *good* states, that is, states that a correct program can reach. A *bad* state is one that would cause an assertion violation. For example, if we are in the state $(i, j, x, y) = (1, 1, 0, 1)$ at the loop head, then execution does not enter the loop and violates the assertion.

An invariant strong enough to prove the program correct is true for all good states and false for all bad states. Therefore, if one can compute the good states and the bad states, an invariant will be a predicate that *separates* the good states from the bad states. Of course, in general we cannot compute the set of all good states and the set of all bad states. But we can always compute some good and bad states by sampling the program.

To generate samples of good states, we simply run the program on some inputs. If we run the program in Figure 1 with the initial state $(1, 0, 1, 0)$, we obtain the good samples $(1, 0, 1, 0)$ and $(1, 0, 0, -1)$. To compute bad states, we can sample from predicates under-approximating the set of all bad states. For Figure 1, $(x = 0 \wedge i = j \wedge y \neq 0)$ is the set of bad states that do not enter the loop body and violate the assertion, and $(x = 1 \wedge i = j \wedge y \neq 1)$ is the set of bad states that execute the loop body once and then violate the assertion. Note that such predicates can be obtained from the program using a standard weakest precondition computation. Finally, we find a predicate separating the good and bad samples.

But how can we guarantee that a predicate separating the good samples from the bad samples also separates *all* good states from *all* bad states? In machine learning, formal guarantees are obtained by showing that the algorithm generating these predicates *learns* in some learning model. There are several learning models and in this paper we use Valiant's PAC (probably approximately correct) model [56]. An algorithm that learns in the PAC model has the guarantee that if it is given enough independent samples then with a high probability it will come up with a predicate that will separate almost all the good states from the bad states. Hence, under the assumptions of the PAC model, we are guaranteed to find good candidate invariants with high probability. However, just like any other theoretical learning model, the assumptions of PAC model are generally impossible or at least very difficult to realize in practice. We emphasize that in the variety of applications in which PAC learning algorithms are applied, the assumptions of the PAC model are seldom met. Hence, the question whether generalization guarantees in a learning model are relevant in practice is an empirical one. PAC has intimate connections with complexity theory and cryptography and is one of the most widely used models. We demonstrate empirically in Section 5 that PAC learning algorithms successfully infer invariants.

Bshouty et al. [13] presented a PAC learning algorithm for geometric concepts (see Section 3.2). This algorithm can produce predicates as expressive as arbitrary boolean combinations of linear inequalities. In particular, the invariant required for Figure 1 is expressible using this approach. However, this expressiveness has a cost: the algorithm of [13] is exponential in the number of program variables. To obtain polynomial time algorithms in the number of samples and program variables we must restrict the expressiveness. Assume, for example, that we knew the invariant for the program in Figure 1 is a boolean combination of octagons (which it is). For octagons, the linear inequalities are of the form $\pm x \pm y \leq c$, where x and y are program variables and c is a constant (Section 4.1). We extend [13] to obtain a PAC learning algorithm for obtaining a predicate, separating good and bad samples, that is an arbitrary boolean combination of linear inequalities belonging to a given abstract domain. The time complexity of our algorithm increases gracefully with the expressiveness of the chosen abstract domain (Section 4.1). For example, the complexity for octagons is higher than that for boxes.

We augment our learning algorithm with a theorem prover (Section 4.3), obtaining a sound algorithm for program verification. Empirically, we show that the predicates discovered by our approach are provably invariants using standard verification engines (Section 5).

2.1   Finding Invariants for the Example

We now explain how our sound algorithm (Section 4.3) for program verification (parametrized by octagons) proves the correctness of the program in Figure 1. To sample the good states, assume we run the program on inputs where $i, j \in \{0, 1, 2\}$. As suggested above, we obtain bad states by sampling the predicate representing violations of the assertion after going through at most one loop iteration: $x = 0 \wedge i = j \wedge y \neq 0 \vee x = 1 \wedge i = j \wedge y \neq 1$. In total, for this example, we generated 18 good samples and 24 bad samples. The algorithm of [13] first generates a large set of candidate hyperplanes representing all linear inequalities possibly occurring in the output predicate. We build this set by constructing all possible hyperplanes (of the form $\pm x \pm y = c$) passing through every state. For instance, the state $(2, 2, 0, 0)$ generates twenty four hyperplanes: $x = 0$, $x = y$, $i \pm x = 2, \ldots$. Section 4.1 justifies this choice of the set of candidates.

From this large set of hyperplanes, we pick a subset that successfully separates the good and bad samples. Note that every good sample must be separated from every bad sample. Several algorithms can be used to solve this problem. We describe how a standard greedy approach would work. We keep track of the pairs of samples, one good and the other bad, that have not yet been separated by any hyperplane, and repeatedly select from the set of candidate hyperplanes the one that separates the maximum number of remaining unseparated pairs, repeating until no unseparated pairs remain.

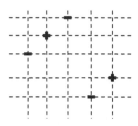

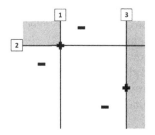

Fig. 2. Candidate inequalities passing through all states

Fig. 3. Separating good states and bad states using boxes

We illustrate this process in Figures 2 and 3. The +'s are the good states, and the −'s are the bad states. Assume that our abstract domain is the box or interval domain, that is, the predicates are inequalities of the form $\pm x \leq c$. We first generate our candidates, that is, hyperplanes of the form $x = c$ passing through all the good and bad states. These corresponds to all possible horizontal and vertical lines passing through all the + and − states as shown in Figure 2. Next, from this set of candidate lines, we initially select line 3, separating one good state from three bad states, which is the maximum number of pairs separated by any of the lines. Next, we select line 1 because it separates one good state from two bad states. Finally, we select line 2, separating the final pair of one good state and one bad state. The lines tessellate the space into cells, where each cell is a conjunction of boxes bounding the cell and no cell contains both a good and a bad state. Each shaded cell in Figure 3 represents a conjunction of boxes that includes only the good states. The returned predicate is the set of all shaded cells in Figure 3, which is a disjunction of boxes.

By a similar process, for the 42 states generated from Figure 1 and using the octagon domain, our tool infers the predicate $I \equiv i \leq j + 1 \lor j \leq i + 1 \lor x = y$ in 0.06 seconds. We annotated the loop of Figure 1 with this predicate as a candidate loop invariant and gave it to the BOOGIE [7] program checker. BOOGIE was successfully able to prove that I was indeed a loop invariant and was able to show that the assertion holds. As another example, on parametrizing with the Octahedron [16] abstract domain, our technique discovers the simpler conjunctive loop invariant: $i + y = x + j$ in 0.09s.

3   Preliminaries

This section presents necessary background material, including the learning algorithm of [13]. Our goal is to verify a *Hoare triple* $\{P\}S\{Q\}$ for the simple language of *while programs* defined as follows:

$$S ::= x{:=}M \mid S; S \mid \text{if } E \text{ then } S \text{ else } S \text{ fi} \mid \text{while } E \text{ do } S$$

The while program S is defined over integer variables, and we want to check whether, for all states s in the precondition P, executing S with initial state

s results in a state satisfying the postcondition Q. In particular, if $L \equiv \mathtt{while}\ E\ \mathtt{do}\ S$ is a while program, then to check $\{P\}L\{Q\}$, Hoare logic tells us that we need a predicate I such that $P \Rightarrow I$, $\{I \wedge E\}S\{I\}$, and $I \wedge \neg E \Rightarrow Q$. Such a predicate I is called an *inductive invariant* or simply an *invariant* of the loop L. Once we have obtained invariants for all the loops, then standard techniques can generate program proofs [7]. We first focus our attention on invariants in the theory of *linear arithmetic*:

$$\phi ::= w^T x + d \geq 0 \mid true \mid false \mid \phi \wedge \phi \mid \phi \vee \phi \mid \neg\phi$$

where $w = (w_1, \ldots, w_n)^T \in \mathbb{Q}^n$ is a *point*, an n-dimensional vector of rational number constants. The vector $x = (x_1, \ldots, x_n)^T$ is an n-dimensional vector of variables. The *inner product* $\langle w, x \rangle$ of w and x is $w^T x = w_1 x_1 + \ldots + w_n x_n$. The equation $w^T x + d = 0$ is a *hyperplane* in n dimensions with *slope* w and *bias* d. Each hyperplane *corresponds* to an intersection of two *half-spaces*: $w^T x + d \geq 0$ and $w^T x + d \leq 0$. For instance, $x - y = 0$ is a 2-dimensional hyperplane, $x - y + 2z = 0$ is a 3-dimensional hyperplane, and $x \geq y$ and $x \leq y$ are half-spaces corresponding to the hyperplane $x = y$.

3.1   Invariants and Binary Classification

Assume that the Hoare triple $\{P\}\mathtt{while}\ E\ \mathtt{do}\ S\{Q\}$ is valid. Let the loop L have n variables $x = \{x_1, \ldots, x_n\}$. Therefore, the precondition $P(x)$ and postcondition $Q(x)$ are predicates over x. If the loop execution is started in a state satisfying P and control flow reaches the loop head after zero or more iterations, then the resulting state is said be *reachable* at the loop head. Denote the set of all reachable states at the loop head by $\mathcal{R}$. Since the Hoare triple is valid, all the reachable states are *good* states. On the other hand, if we execute the loop from a state y satisfying $\neg E \wedge \neg Q$, then we will reach a state at the end of the loop that violates the postcondition, that is, y satisfies $\neg Q$. We call such a state a *bad state*. Denote the set of all bad states by $\mathcal{B}$. Observe that for a correct program, $\mathcal{R} \Rightarrow \neg\mathcal{B}$. Otherwise, any state satisfying $\mathcal{R} \wedge \mathcal{B}$ is a reachable bad state. $\mathcal{R}$ is the strongest invariant, while $\neg\mathcal{B}$ is the weakest invariant sufficient to prove the Hoare triple. Any inductive predicate $\mathcal{I}$ satisfying $\mathcal{R} \Rightarrow \mathcal{I}$ and $\mathcal{I} \Rightarrow \neg\mathcal{B}$ suffices for the proof: $\mathcal{I}$ contains all the good states and does not contain any bad state. Therefore, $\mathcal{I}$ *separates* the good states from the bad states, and thus the problem of computing an invariant can be formulated as finding a separator between $\mathcal{R}$ and $\mathcal{B}$. In general, we do not know $\mathcal{R}$ and $\mathcal{B}$ – our objective is to compute a separator $\mathcal{I}$ from under-approximations of $\mathcal{R}$ and $\mathcal{B}$. For the Hoare triple $\{P\}\mathtt{while}\ E\ \mathtt{do}\ S\{Q\}$, any subset of states reachable from P is an under-approximation of $\mathcal{R}$, while any subset of states satisfying, but not limited to, the predicate $\neg E \wedge \neg Q$ is an under-approximation of $\mathcal{B}$.

Computing separators between sets of points is a well-studied problem in machine learning and goes under the name *binary classification*. The input to the binary classification problem is a set of points with labels from $\{1, 0\}$. Given points and their labels, the goal of the binary classification is to find a *classifier*

C : *points* $\rightarrow$ {*true, false*}, such that $C(a) = true$, for every point a with label 1, and $C(b) = false$ for every point b with label 0. This process is called *training* a classifier, and the set of labeled points is called the *training data*.

The goal of classification is not to just classify the training points correctly but also to be able to predict the labels of previously unseen points. In particular, even if we are given a new labeled point w, with label l, not contained in the training data, then it should be very likely that $C(w)$ is *true* if and only if $l = 1$. This property is called *generalization*, and an algorithm that computes classifiers that are likely to perform well on unseen points is said to *generalize* well.

If C lies in linear arithmetic, that is, it is an arbitrary boolean combination of half-spaces, then we call such a C a *geometric concept*. Our goal is to apply machine learning algorithms for learning geometric concepts to obtain invariants. The good states, obtained by sampling from $\mathcal{R}$, will be labeled 1 and the bad states, obtained by sampling from $\mathcal{B}$, will be labeled 0. We want to use these labeled points to train a classifier that is likely to be an invariant, separating all the good states $\mathcal{R}$ from all the bad states $\mathcal{B}$. In other words, we would like to compute a classifier that generalizes well enough to be an invariant.

3.2   Learning Geometric Concepts

Let R and B be under-approximations of the good states $\mathcal{R}$ and the bad states $\mathcal{B}$, respectively, at a loop head. The classifier $\vee_{r \in R} x = r$ trivially separates R from B. However, this classifier has a large generalization error. In particular, it will *misclassify* every state in $\mathcal{R} \setminus R$; a candidate invariant misclassifies a good state r when $I(r) = false$ and a bad state b when $I(b) = true$. It can be shown if a predicate or classifier grows linearly with the size of training data ($\vee_{r \in R} x = r$ being such a predicate), then such a classifier cannot generalize well. On the other hand, a predicate that is independent of the size of training data can be proven to generalize well [11].

To reduce the size of the predicates, Bshouty et al. [13] frame the problem of learning a general geometric concept as a *set cover* problem. Let X be a set of n points. We are given a set $F \subseteq 2^X$ with k elements such that each element $F_i \in F$ is a subset of X. We say that an element $x \in X$ is *covered* by the set F_i if $x \in F_i$. The goal is to select the minimum number of sets F_i such that each element of X is covered by at least one set. For example, if $X = \{1, 2, 3\}$ and $F = \{\{1, 2\}, \{2, 3\}, \{1, 3\}\}$, then $\{\{1, 2\}, \{2, 3\}\}$ is a solution, and this minimum set cover has a size of two. The set cover problem is NP-complete and we have to be satisfied with approximation algorithms [12,15]. Bshouty et al. [13] formalize learning of geometric concepts as a set cover problem, solve it using [12], and show that the resulting algorithm PAC learns. Note that experiments of [12] show that the performance of the naive greedy algorithm [15] is similar to the algorithm of [12] in practice. Hence, we use the simple to implement greedy set cover for our implementation (Section 5).

We are given a set of samples $V = \{x_i\}_{i=1,\dots m}$, some of which are good and some bad. We create a bipartite graph $\mathcal{U}$ where each sample is a node and there is an edge between nodes x_+ and x_- for every good sample x_+ and every bad

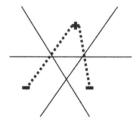

Fig. 4. Separating three points in two dimensions. The solid lines tessellate $\mathbb{R}^2$ into seven cells. The $-$'s are the bad states and the $+$'s are the good states. The dotted lines are the edges to be cut.

sample x_-. In Figure 4, there is one good state, two bad states, and dotted lines represent edges of $\mathcal{U}$. Next, we look for hyperplanes that cut the edges of the graph $\mathcal{U}$. A hyperplane cuts an edge if the two endpoints of the edge lie on different sides of the hyperplane. Note that for every solution, each good sample needs to be separated from every bad sample. This implies that we will need to "cut" every edge in graph $\mathcal{U}$. Intuitively, once we have collected a set S of hyperplanes such that every edge in graph $\mathcal{U}$ is cut by at least one hyperplane in S we can perfectly separate the good and bad samples. The hyperplanes in S tessellate $\mathbb{R}^d$ into a number of cells. (In Figure 4, the three solid lines tessellate $\mathbb{R}^2$ into seven cells.) No cell contains both a good sample and a bad sample – if it does, then the edge between a good sample and a bad sample in the cell is not cut by any hyperplane in S. Thus, each cell contains only good samples, or only bad samples, or no samples at all. We can therefore label each cell, as "good" in the first case, "bad" in the second case, and with an arbitrary "don't care" label in the last case.

Each cell is bounded by a set of hyperplanes, and therefore corresponds to an intersection of half-spaces. The "good" region of $\mathbb{R}^d$ (where d is the number of variables in the program) is then a union of cells labeled "good", and hence a union of intersections of half-spaces, that we output. Thus, the union of intersections of half-spaces we output contains all the good samples, no bad samples, and separates all the good from all the bad samples.

This discussion shows that all we need to do is to come up with the set S of hyperplanes that together cut every edge of graph $\mathcal{U}$. To achieve this goal, we consider a universal set of hyperplanes $\mathcal{F}$ corresponding to all possible partitions of states. Every hyperplane defines a partition of states: some states lie above the plane and some lie below it. $\mathcal{F}$ contains one hyperplane for every possible partition. By Sauer's lemma, such a set $\mathcal{F}$ has cardinality $\mathcal{O}(m^d)$ [13]. We say that an edge is covered by a hyperplane from $\mathcal{F}$ if the hyperplane cuts it. We want to cover all edges of graph $\mathcal{U}$ by these hyperplanes. This set cover problem can be solved in several ways that have comparable performance in practice [15,12]. The simplest solution is to greedily select the hyperplane from $\mathcal{F}$ that covers the maximum number of uncovered edges of graph $\mathcal{U}$, and repeating the greedy selection until all edges in $\mathcal{U}$ are cut. For Figure 4, $\mathcal{F}$ contains three hyperplanes, and graph $\mathcal{U}$ has two edges (edges between $-$'s and $+$'s.). The horizontal plane cuts both the edges and divides the space into two cells: one above and one below. Since the cell above the horizontal plane contains a '$+$', we will label it "good". Similarly, the cell below is labeled "bad". The output predicate is the half-space above the horizontal hyperplane. If the good and bad samples, total m in number, require a minimum number of s hyperplanes to separate them, then the greedy approach has the guarantee that will compute a predicate that uses $\mathcal{O}(s \log m)$ hyperplanes. Using [12], we can obtain a predicate using $\mathcal{O}(sd \log sd)$ hyperplanes. This implies that the number of inequalities of the classifier approximates the number of the inequalities of the simplest true invariant by a logarithmic factor. Such a relationship between candidate and true invariants appears to be new in the context of invariant inference.

3.3   PAC Learning

By enumerating a plane for each partition and performing a set cover, the algorithm of [13] finds a geometric concept that separates the good samples from the bad samples. But how well does it generalize? Bshouty et al. [13] showed that under the assumptions of the PAC model [56] this process is likely to produce a geometric concept that will separate all the good states from all the bad states with high probability. The major assumption of the PAC model is that there is an oracle that knows the true classifier and it generates training data by drawing independent and identically distributed samples from a distribution and assigning them labels, either good or bad, using the true classifier.

Independent samples are theoretically justified as otherwise one can construct data with an arbitrary number of samples by duplicating one sample an arbitrary number of times and then the term "amount of training data" is not well defined. Practically, if one draws a sample randomly from some distribution, then deciding whether it is good or bad is undecidable. Hence such an oracle cannot be implemented and in our experiments we make do with a simple technique for obtaining samples, where the samples are not necessarily independent.

The proof of PAC learning in [13] uses the following result from the seminal paper of Blumer et al. [11].

Theorem 1. *If an algorithm outputs f consistent with a sample of size max $\left(\frac{4}{\epsilon} \log \frac{2}{\delta}, \frac{8VC}{\epsilon} \log \frac{13}{\epsilon}\right)$ then f has error at most ϵ with probability at least $1 - \delta$.*

Intuitively, this theorem states that if an algorithm can separate a large number of good and bad samples then the classifier has a low probability of misclassifying a new sample. Here VC is the Vapnik-Chervonenkis dimension, a quantity determined by the number of hyperplanes in the geometric concepts we are learning and the number of variables. In [13], by using algorithms for set cover that have a good approximation factor [12], Bshouty et al. are able to bound the number of planes in the output predicate f, and hence the quantity VC. Since the output of [13] is consistent with all good and bad samples, given enough samples the algorithm outputs a predicate that is very likely to separate all the good states from all the bad states. For the full proof the reader is referred to [13].

Hence, [13] can produce predicates that are likely to separate all good states and bad states, under PAC assumptions. This is a formal guarantee on the extrapolation we have performed using some good and bad samples, that is, using some finite behaviors of the program. Although this guarantee is in a model, we are unaware of any previous program verification engine with any guarantee, in a model or otherwise, on the heuristic extrapolation they perform. Even though this guarantee is not the best possible guarantee that one would desire, the undecidability of program verification prevents strong results for the problem we consider. It is well known that the PAC learners tend to have good performance in practice for a variety of learning tasks. Our experiments show that the PAC learners we construct have good performance for the task of invariant inference. We believe that by finding candidate invariants separating all good samples from all bad samples and misclassifying unseen points with low probability leads our technique to produce true invariants.

3.4   Complexity

If we have m states in d dimensions, then we need to cover $\mathcal{O}(m^2)$ edges of graph $\mathcal{U}$ using $\mathcal{O}(m^d)$ hyperplanes of $\mathcal{F}$. Greedy set cover has a time complexity of $\mathcal{O}(m^2|\mathcal{F}|)$. Considering $\mathcal{O}(m^d)$ hyperplanes is, however, impractical. With a thousand samples for a four variable program, we will need to enumerate 10^{12} planes. Hence this algorithm has a very high space complexity and will run out of memory on most benchmarks of Section 5.

Suppose the invariant has s hyperplanes. Hence the good states and bad states can be separated by s hyperplanes. To achieve learning, we require that $\mathcal{F}$ should contain s hyperplanes that separate the good samples and the bad samples – since the planes constituting the invariant could be any arbitrary set, in general we need to select a lot of candidates to ensure this. By adding assumptions about the invariant, the size of $\mathcal{F}$ can be reduced. Say for octagons, for thousand samples and four variables, the algorithm of Section 4.1 considers 24000 candidates.

3.5   Logic Minimization

The output of the algorithm of Section 3.2 is a set S of hyperplanes separating every good sample from every bad sample. As described previously, these hyperplanes tessellate $\mathbb{R}^d$ into cells. Recall that S has the property that no cell contains both a good state and a bad state.

Now we must construct a predicate containing all good samples and excluding all bad samples. One obvious option is the union of cells labeled "good". But this might result in a huge predicate since each cell is an intersection of half-spaces. Our goal is to compute a predicate with the smallest number of boolean operators such that it contains all the "good" cells and no "bad" cells. Let $\mathcal{H}$ be the set of half-spaces constituting the "good" cells. Define a boolean matrix M with m rows and $|\mathcal{H}|$ columns, and an m-dimensional vector y as follows.

$$M(i,j) = true \Leftrightarrow \{i^{th}state \in j^{th} \text{ half-space of } \mathcal{H}\}$$
$$y(i) = true \Leftrightarrow \{i^{th}state \text{ is a good state}\}$$

This matrix M together with the vector y resembles a partial truth table – the ith row of M identifies the cell in which the ith state lies and $y(i)$ (the label of the ith state) gives the label for the cell (whether it is a cell containing only good states or only bad states). Now, we want to learn the simplest boolean function (in terms of the number of boolean operators) $f : \{true, false\}^{|\mathcal{H}|} \rightarrow \{true, false\}$, such that $f(M_i) = y(i)$ (M_i is the ith row of M). This problem is called logic minimization and is NP-complete. Empirically, however, S has a small number of hyperplanes, at most eight in our experiments, and we are able to use standard exponential time algorithms like the Quine-McCluskey algorithm [44] to get a small classifier.

In summary, we use set covering for learning geometric concepts (Section 3.2) to compute predicates with a small number of hyperplanes. Combining this with logic minimization, we compute a predicate with a small number of boolean connectives. Empirically, we find that these predicates are actual invariants for *all* the benchmarks that have an arbitrary boolean combination of linear inequalities as an invariant.

4 Practical Algorithms

The algorithm discussed in Section 3.2, although of considerable interest, has limited practical applicability because its space and time complexity is exponential in the dimension, which in our case, is the number of program variables (Section 3.4). This complexity is not too surprising since, for example, abstract interpretation over the abstract domain of convex hulls [23] is also exponential in the number of variables. In this paper, we make the common assumption that the invariants come from a restricted class, which amounts to reducing the number of candidate sets for covering in our set cover algorithm. Therefore, we are able to obtain polynomial time algorithms in the number of samples and the dimension to generate classifiers under mild restrictions (Section 4.1).

4.1 Restricting Generality

Let s denote the number of hyperplanes in the invariant. Then for PAC learning, we say the set $\mathcal{F}$ of candidate hyperplanes is *adequate* if it contains s hyperplanes that completely separate the good samples from the bad samples. Recall that the complexity of the procedure of Section 3.2 is $\mathcal{O}(m^2|\mathcal{F}|)$, and therefore a polynomial size set $\mathcal{F}$ makes the algorithm polynomial time. In addition, the set covering step can be parallelized for efficiency [8].

In the following two sections we will give two PAC learning algorithms. The formal proofs that these algorithms learn in the PAC model are beyond the scope of this paper and are similar to the proofs in [13]. However, we do show the construction of adequate sets $\mathcal{F}$ that coupled with a good approximation factor of set cover [12] give us PAC learning guarantees.

Predicate Abstraction. Suppose we are given a set of predicates $\mathcal{P}$ where each predicate is a half-space. Assume that the invariant is a boolean combination of predicates in $\mathcal{P}$, and checking whether a given candidate I is an invariant is co-NP-complete. If the invariant is an intersection or disjunction of predicates in $\mathcal{P}$, then Houdini [27] can find the invariant in time P^{NP} (that is, it makes a polynomial number of calls to an oracle that can solve NP problems). When the predicates are arbitrary boolean combinations of half-spaces from $\mathcal{P}$, then the problem of finding the invariant is much harder, NP^{NP}-complete [39]. We are not aware of any previous approach that solves this problem.

Now suppose that instead of an exact invariant, we want to find a PAC classifier to separate the good states from the bad states. If the set of candidates $\mathcal{F}$ is $\mathcal{P}$, then this trivially guarantees that there are s hyperplanes in $\mathcal{F}$ that do separate all the good states from the bad states – all we need to do now to obtain a PAC algorithm is to solve a set cover problem [12]. This observation allows us to obtain a practical algorithm. By using the greedy algorithm on m samples, we can find a classifier in time $\mathcal{O}(m^2|\mathcal{P}|)$. Therefore, by relaxing our problem to finding a classifier that separates good samples from bad samples, rather than finding an exact invariant, we are able to solve a NP^{NP} complete problem in time $\mathcal{O}(m^2|\mathcal{P}|)$ time, a very significant improvement in time complexity.

Abstract Interpretation. Simple predicate abstraction can be restrictive because the set of predicates is fixed and finite. Abstract interpretation is another approach to finding invariants that can deal with infinite sets of predicates. For scalable analyses, abstract interpretation assumes that invariants come from restricted abstract domains. Two of the most common abstract domains are boxes and octagons. In boxes, the predicates are of the form $\pm x + c \geq 0$, where x is a program variable and c is a constant. In octagons, the predicates are of the form $\pm x \pm y + c \geq 0$. Note that, by varying c, these form an infinite family of predicates. These restricted abstract domains amount to fixing the set of possible slopes w of the constituent half-spaces $w^T x + b \geq 0$ (the bias b that corresponds to c, is however free).

Suppose now that we are given a finite set of slopes, that is, we are given a finite set of weight vectors $\Sigma = \{w_i \mid i = 1, \ldots, |\Sigma|\}$, such that the invariant only involves hyperplanes with these slopes. In this case, we observe that we can restrict our attention to hyperplanes that pass through one of the samples, because any hyperplane in the invariant that does not pass through any sample can be translated until it passes through one of the samples and the resulting predicate will still separate all the good samples from the bad samples. In this case, the set $\mathcal{F}$ is defined as follows:

$$\mathcal{F} = \{(w, b) \mid w \in \Sigma \text{ and } w^T x_i + b = 0 \text{ for some sample } x_i \in V\} \qquad (1)$$

The size of $\mathcal{F}$ is $|\Sigma|m$. Again, this set contains s hyperplanes that separate all the good samples from all the bad samples (the s hyperplanes of the invariant, translated to where they pass through one of the samples), and therefore this set is adequate and coupled with set covering [12] gives us a PAC learning algorithm.

The time complexity for greedy set cover in this case also includes the time taken to compute the bias for each hyperplane in $\mathcal{F}$. There are $|\mathcal{F}| = |\Sigma|m$ such hyperplanes, and finding the bias for each hyperplane takes $\mathcal{O}(d)$ time. The time complexity is therefore $\mathcal{O}(m^2|\mathcal{F}| + d|\mathcal{F}|) = \mathcal{O}(m^3|\Sigma|)$.

If we want to find classifiers over abstract domains such as boxes and octagons, then we can work with the appropriate slopes. For boxes $|\Sigma|$ is $\mathcal{O}(d)$ and for octagons $|\Sigma|$ is $\mathcal{O}(d^2)$. Interestingly, the increase in complexity when learning classifiers as we go from boxes to octagons mirrors the increase in complexity of the abstract interpretation. By adding more slopes we can move to more expressive abstract domains. Also note that the abstract domain over which we compute classifiers is much richer than the corresponding abstract interpretation. Conventional efficient abstract interpretation can only find invariants that are conjunctions of predicates, but we learn arbitrary boolean combinations of half-spaces, that allows us to learn arbitrary boolean combinations of predicates in abstract domains.

Again, we observe that by relaxing the requirement from an invariant to a classifier that separates good and bad samples, we are able to obtain predicates in polynomial time that are richer than any existing symbolic program verification tool we are familiar with.

4.2   Non-linear Invariants

Our geometric method of extracting likely invariants carries over to polynomial inequalities. Assume we are given a fixed bound k on the degree of the polynomials. Consider a d-dimensional point $\vec{x} = (x_1, \ldots, x_d)$. We can map $\vec{x}$ to a $\binom{d+k-1}{k}$-dimensional space by considering every possible monomial involving the components of $\vec{x}$ of maximum degree k as a separate dimension. Thus,

$$\phi(\vec{x}) = (x_1^{\alpha_1} x_2^{\alpha_2} \ldots x_d^{\alpha_d} \mid \sum_i \alpha_i \leq k, \alpha_i \in \mathbb{N}) \tag{2}$$

Using the mapping ϕ, we can transform every point $\vec{x}$ into a higher dimensional space. In this space, polynomial inequalities of degree k are linear half-spaces, and so the entire machinery above carries through without any changes. In the general case, when we have no information about the invariant then we will take time exponential in d. When we know the slopes or the predicates constituting the invariants then we can get efficient algorithms by following the approach of Section 4.1. Therefore, we can infer likely invariants that are arbitrary boolean combinations of polynomial inequalities of a given degree.

4.3   Recovering Soundness

Once we obtain a classifier, we want to use it to construct proofs for programs. But the classifier is not guaranteed to be an invariant. To obtain soundness, we augment our learning algorithm with a theorem prover using a standard *guess-and-check* loop [55,54]. We sample, perform learning, and propose a candidate invariant using the set cover approach for learning geometric concepts as described in Section 3.2 (the guess step). We then ask a theorem prover to check whether the candidate invariant is indeed an invariant (the check step). If the check succeeds we are done. Otherwise, the candidate invariant is not an invariant and we sample more states and guess again. When we terminate successfully, we have computed a sound invariant. For a candidate invariant I, we make the following queries:

1. The candidate invariant is weaker than the pre-condition $P \Rightarrow I$.
2. The candidate invariant implies the post-condition $I \wedge \neg E \Rightarrow Q$.
3. The candidate invariant is inductive $\{I \wedge E\} S \{I\}$.

If all three queries succeed, then we have found an invariant. Note that since we are working with samples, I is neither an under-approximation nor an over-approximation of the actual invariant. If the first constraint fails, then a counter-example is a good state that I classifies as bad. If the second constraint fails, then a counter-example is a bad state that I classifies as good. If the third constraint, representing inductiveness, fails then we get a pair of states (x, y) such that I classifies x as good, y as bad, and if the loop body starts its execution from state x then it can terminate in state y. Hence if x is good then so is y and (x, y) refutes the candidate I. However, x is unlabelled, i.e., we do not know whether it is a good state or not and we cannot add x and y to samples directly.

Now, we want our learning algorithm to generate a classifier that respects the pair (x, y) of counter-example states: if the classifier includes x then it also includes y. If the invariant has s hyperplanes then the greedy set cover can be extended to generate a separator between good and bad samples that respects such pairs. The basic idea is to greedily select the hyperplanes which make the most number of pairs consistent. Moreover the number of hyperplanes in the output is guaranteed to be $\mathcal{O}(s(\log m)^2)$: the size of the predicate can increase linearly with the number of pairs. This algorithm can be used to guide our learning algorithm in the case it finds an invariant that is not inductive. Note that the need for this extension did not arise in our experiments. Using a small amount of data, greedy set cover was sufficient to find an invariant. For buggy programs, a good state g, a bad state b, and a sequence of pairs $(x_1, x_2), (x_2, x_3), \ldots, (x_{k-1}, x_k)$ such that $g = x_1$ and $b = x_k$ is an error trace, i.e., certificate for a bug.

When we applied guess-and-check in our previous work [55,54] to infer relevant predicates for verification, we checked for only two out of the three constraints listed above (Section 6). Hence, these predicates did not prove any program property and moreover they were of limited expressiveness (no disjunctions among other restrictions). Checking fewer constraints coupled with reduced expressiveness made it straightforward to incorporate counter-examples. In contrast, we now must deal with the kinds of counter-examples (good, bad, and unlabeled) for an expressive class of predicates. Handling all three kinds is necessary to guarantee progress, ensuring that an incorrect candidate invariant is never proposed again. However, if the candidates are inadequate then the guess-and-check procedure will loop forever: Inadequacy results in candidate invariants that grow linearly with the number of samples.

If we want to analyze a single procedure program with multiple loops, then we process the loops beginning with the last, innermost loop and working outwards and upward to the first, outermost loop. The invariants of the processed loops become assertions or postconditions for the to-be-processed loops. While checking the candidate invariants, the condition that the candidate invariant should be weaker than the pre-condition is only checked for the topmost outermost loop L and not for others. If this check generates a counter-example then the program is executed from the head of L with the variables initialized using the counter-example. This execution generates new good states for the loops it reaches and invariant computation is repeated for these loops.

5   Experimental Evaluation

We have implemented and evaluated our approach on a number of challenging C benchmarks. Greedy set cover is implemented in one hundred lines of MATLAB

Table 1. Program is the name, LOC is lines, #Loops is the number of loops, and #Vars is the number of variables in the benchmark. #Good is the maximum number of good states, #Bad is the maximum number of bad states, and Learn is the maximum time of the learning routine over all loops of the program. Check is time by BOOGIE for proving the correctness of the whole program and Result is the verdict: OK is verified, FAIL is failure of our learning technique, and PRE is verified but under certain pre-conditions.

Program	LOC	#Loops	#Vars	#Good	#Bad	Learn(s)	Check(s)	Result
fig6 [31]	16	1	2	3	0	0.030	1.04	OK
fig9 [31]	10	1	2	1	0	0.030	0.99	OK
prog2 [31]	19	1	2	10	0	0.034	1.00	OK
prog3 [31]	29	1	4	8	126	0.106	1.05	OK
test [31]	30	1	4	20	0	0.162	1.00	OK
ex23 [36]	20	1	2	111	0	0.045	1.05	OK
sas07 [29]	20	1	2	103	6112	2.64	1.02	OK
popl07 [32]	20	1	2	101	10000	2.85	0.99	OK
get-tag [35]	120	2	2	6	28	0.092	1.04	OK
hsort [35]	47	2	5	15	435	0.19	1.05	OK
maill-qp [35]	92	1	3	9	253	0.11	1.05	OK
msort [35]	73	6	10	9	77	0.093	1.12	OK
nested [35]	21	3	4	49	392	0.24	0.99	OK
seq-len1 [35]	44	6	5	36	1029	0.32	1.04	PRE
seq-len [35]	44	6	5	224	3822	4.39	1.04	OK
spam [35]	57	2	5	11	147	1.01	1.05	OK
svd [35]	50	5	5	150	1708	4.92	0.99	OK
split	20	1	5	36	4851	FAIL	NA	FAIL
div [53]	28	2	6	343	248	2.03	1.04	OK

code. We use HAVOC [5] to generate BOOGIEPL programs from C programs annotated with candidate invariants. Next, BOOGIE [7] verification condition generator operates on the BOOGIEPL programs to check the candidate invariants by passing the verification conditions to Z3 theorem prover [45]. All experiments were performed on a 2.67GHz Intel Xeon processor system with 8 GB RAM running Windows 7 and MATLAB R2010b.

Implementation Notes. Our implementation analyzes single procedure C programs with integer variables and assertions. Since all these programs contain loops, we need to compute invariants that are strong enough to prove the assertions. For every loop, our technique works as follows: first, we instrument the loop head to log the values of the variables in scope. Next, we run the program till termination on some test inputs to generate data. All internal non-deterministic choices, such as non-deterministic tests on branches, are randomly selected. All states reaching the loop head are stored in a matrix good. We then compute the null space of good to get the sub-space J in which the good states lie: J represents the equality relationships that the good states satisfy. Working in the lower dimensional sub-space J improves the performance of our algorithms by effectively reducing d, the number of independent variables.

Next, from the loop body, we statically identify the predicate B representing the states that will violate some assertion after at most one iteration of the loop. We then sample the bad states from the predicate $B \wedge J$. The good and bad samples are then used to generate the set of candidate hyperplanes $\mathcal{F}$ using the specified slopes – octagons are sufficient for all programs except seq-len.

We perform another optimization: we restrict the candidates to just the octagons passing through the good states, thus reducing the number of candidates. Note that this optimization still leads to an adequate set of candidates and we retain our learning guarantees. Next, using the greedy algorithm, we select the hyperplanes that separate the good from the bad states, and return a set of half-spaces $\mathcal{H}$ and a partial boolean function $f\colon f(b_1, \ldots, b_{|\mathcal{H}|})$ that represents the label of the cell that lies inside the half-spaces for which b_i's are *true* and outside the half-space for which b_i is *false*. This algorithm is linear in the number of bad states and its complexity is governed almost entirely by the number of good states. For our benchmarks, $|\mathcal{H}|$ was at most 8. We use the Quine-McCluskey algorithm for logic minimization (Section 3.5) that returns the smallest total boolean function g that agrees with f. Conjoining the predicate obtained using g and $\mathcal{H}$ with J yields a candidate invariant. This invariant is added as an annotation to the original program that is checked with BOOGIE for assertion violations.

Evaluation. An important empirical question is how much data is sufficient to obtain a sound invariant. To answer this question, we adopt the following method for generating data: we run the programs on all possible inputs s.t. all input variables have their values between $[-1, N]$ where N is initially zero. This process generates good states at the loop head. Next we generate bad states and check whether our first guess is an invariant. If not then we continue generating more bad states and checking if the guess is an invariant. If we have generated 10,000 bad states and still have not found an invariant then we increment N by one and repeat the process. We are able to obtain a sound invariant within four iterations of this process for our linear benchmarks; div needs ten iterations: it needs more data as the (non-linear) invariant is found in a higher dimensional space.

Now we explain our approach of sampling bad states given a set of good states. Each variable x at the loop head takes values in some range $[L_x, M_x]$ for the good states. To sample the bad states, we exhaustively enumerate states (in the subspace in which the good states lie) where the value of each variable x varies over the range $[L_x, M_x]$. For deterministic programs with finite number of reachable states, any enumerated state that is unreachable is labeled bad. For others, bad states are generated by identifying the enumerated states satisfying the predicate B representing bad states. Because this process can enumerate a very large number of states unless the range or number of variables is small, we incrementally enumerate the states until we generate 10,000 bad states. The results in Table 1 show the number of good states (column 5) and bad states (column 6) that yield a sound invariant.

We observe that only a few good states are required for these benchmarks, which leads us to believe that existing test suites of programs should be sufficient for generating sound invariants. We observe that our sampling strategy based on enumeration generates many bad states that are not useful for the algorithm. The candidate invariant is mainly determined by the bad states that are close to the good states and not those that are further away and play no role in determining the good state/bad state boundary. The complexity of our algorithm is governed mainly by the good states, due to our optimizations, and hence generating superfluous bad states is not an issue for these benchmarks. Since the candidate inequalities are determined by the good and bad states, the good and bad samples should be generated with the goal of including the inequalities of the invariants in the set of candidates. Note that we use a naive strategy for sampling. Better strategies directed towards the above goal are certainly possible and may work better.

The benchmarks that we used for evaluating our technique are shown in the first column (labeled Program) of Table 1. LEE-YANNAKAKIS partition refinement algorithm [42] does not work well on fig6; SYNERGY [31] fails to terminate on fig9; prog2 has a loop with a large constant number of iterations and predicate abstraction based tools like SLAM take time proportional to the number of loop iterations. The program prog3 requires a disjunctive invariant. For test we find the invariant $y = x + lock$: SLAM finds the disjunctive invariant $(x = y \Rightarrow lock = 0 \land x \neq y \Rightarrow lock = 1)$. For ex23, we discovered the invariant $z = counter + 36y$. This is possible because the size of constants are bounded only for computing inequalities: the equalities in J have no restriction on the size of constants. Such relationships are beyond the scope of tools performing abstract interpretation over octagons [40]. The equalities in J are sufficient to verify the correctness of the benchmarks containing a zero in column #Bad of

Table 1. The programs sas07 and pop107 are deterministic programs requiring disjunctive invariants. We handle these without using any templates [35]. The programs get-tag through svd are the benchmarks used to evaluate the template based invariant generation tool INVGEN [35]. As seen from Table 1, we are faster than INVGEN on half of these programs, and slower on the other half.

We modify seq-len to obtain the benchmark seq-len1; the program seq-len1 assumes that all inputs are positive. We are able to find strong invariants for the loops, using octagons for slopes, that are sufficient to prove the correctness of this program. These invariants include sophisticated equalities like $i+k = n0+n1+n2$. Since we proved the correctness by assuming a pre-condition on inputs, the Result column says PRE. Next, we analyze seq-len, that has no pre-conditions on inputs, using octagons as slopes. We obtain a separator that has as many linear inequalities as the number of input states; such a predicate will not generalize. For this example, there is no separator small in size if we restrict the domain of our slopes to octagons. Therefore, we add slopes of hyperplanes that constitute invariants of seq-len1 and similar slopes to our bag of slopes. We are then able to prove seq-len correct by discovering invariants like $i + k \geq n0 + n1 + n2$. This demonstrates how we can find logically stronger invariants in specialized contexts.

The split program requires an invariant that uses an interpreted function *iseven*. Our approach fails on this program as the desired invariant cannot be expressed as an arbitrary boolean combinations of half-spaces. For the div program, the objective is to verify that the computed remainder is less than the divisor and the quotient times divisor plus remainder is equal to dividend. Using the technique described in Section 4.2 with a degree bound of 2, we are able to infer a invariant that proves the specification. We are unaware of any previous technique that can prove the specification of this benchmark.

6   Related Work

In this section, we compare our approach with existing techniques for linear and non-linear invariant generation. Since the literature on invariant inference is rich, we only discuss the techniques closest to our work.

6.1   Comparison with Linear Invariant Generation

Invariant generation tools that are based on either abstract interpretation [23,21], or constraint solving [19,35], or their combination [18], cannot handle arbitrary boolean combinations of half-spaces. Similar to us, CLOUSOT [41] improves its performance by conjoining equalities and inequalities over boxes. Some approaches like [25,26,52,32,34,29,43] can handle disjunctions, but they restrict the number of disjunctions by widening, manual input, or trace based heuristics. In contrast, [28] handles disjunctions of a specific form.

Predicate abstraction based tools are geared towards computing arbitrary boolean combinations of predicates [6,9,31,1,10,30]. Among these, YOGI [31] uses test cases to determine where to refine its abstraction. However, just like [47], it uses the trace and not the concrete states generated by a test. INVGEN [35] uses test cases for constraint simplification, but does not generalize from them with provable generalization guarantees. Amato et al. [2] analyze data from program executions to tune their abstract interpretation. Recently, we ran support vector machines [20], a widely used machine learning algorithm, in a guess-and-check loop to obtain a sound interpolation procedure [55]. However, [55] cannot handle disjunctions and computed interpolants need not be inductive.

Daikon [24] is a tool for generating likely invariants using tests. Candidate invariants are generated using templates, and candidates that violate some test case are removed. Since the invariants are based on templates, Daikon is less expressive than our approach. It is interesting to note that our empirical results are consistent with those reported in [49]: a small number of states can cover most program behaviors. Random interpretation [33] trade-offs complexity of program analysis for a small probability of unsoundness. In contrast, our guarantees are sound and we trade expressiveness for efficiency.

6.2   Comparison with Tools for Non-linear Invariants

Existing sound tools for non-linear invariant generation can produce invariants that are conjunctions of polynomial equalities [51,38,50,14,46,53,17]. However, by imposing strict restrictions on syntax (such as no nested loops) [51,38] do not need to assume the degree of polynomials as the input. Bagnara et al. [4] introduce new variables for monomials and generate linear invariants over them by abstract interpretation over convex polyhedra. Our domain is more expressive: arbitrary boolean combinations of polynomial inequalities.

Nguyen et al. [48] give an unsound algorithm for generation of likely invariants that are conjunctions of polynomial equalities or inequalities. For equalities, they compute the null space of good samples (obtained from tests) in the higher dimensional space described in Section 4.2, that is also one of the steps of our technique. For generation of candidate polynomial inequalities they find the convex hull of the good samples in the higher dimensional space. In addition to limiting the expressiveness to just conjunction of polynomial inequalities, this step is computationally very expensive. In a related work, we ran [48] in a guess-and-check loop to obtain an algorithm [54], with soundness and termination guarantees, for generating polynomial equalities as invariants. A termination proof was possible as [54] can return the trivial invariant *true*: it is not required to find invariants strong enough to prove some property of interest. This technique can handle only the benchmarks that require zero bad states in Table 1, whereas our current technique can handle all the benchmarks of [54].

7   Conclusion

We have presented a machine learning perspective to verifying safety properties of programs and demonstrated how it helps us achieve guarantees and expressiveness. The learning algorithm performs a set cover and given an adequate set of candidate inequalities, it has the guarantee that the output candidate invariant uses at most a logarithmic number of inequalities more than the simplest true invariant. Hence the algorithm is biased towards simple invariants and hence parsimonious proofs. The PAC learning guarantees for this algorithm formally capture the generalization properties of the candidate invariants. Disjunctions and non-linearities are handled naturally with no a priori bound on the number of disjunctions. We trade expressiveness for efficiency by changing the abstract domains and demonstrate our approach on challenging benchmarks. The literature on classification algorithms is rich and it will be interesting to see how different classification algorithms perform on the task of invariant inference. Learning algorithms for data structures manipulating programs are left as future work.

Acknowledgements. We thank Hongseok Yang and the anonymous reviewers for their constructive comments. Praneeth Netrapalli, Divya Gupta, and Prateek Jain helped in extending the classification algorithm to handle pairs. Sharma performed part of the work reported here during a summer internship at Microsoft Research India. This material is based on research sponsored by NSF grant CCF-0915766 and the Air Force Research Laboratory, under agreement number FA8750-12-2-0020. The U.S. Government is authorized to reproduce and distribute reprints for Governmental purposes notwithstanding any copyright notation thereon.

References

1. Albarghouthi, A., Gurfinkel, A., Chechik, M.: Craig interpretation. In: Miné, A., Schmidt, D. (eds.) SAS 2012. LNCS, vol. 7460, pp. 300–316. Springer, Heidelberg (2012)
2. Amato, G., Parton, M., Scozzari, F.: Discovering invariants via simple component analysis. J. Symb. Comput. 47(12), 1533–1560 (2012)
3. Bagnara, R., Hill, P.M., Zaffanella, E.: Widening operators for powerset domains. STTT 9(3-4) (2007)
4. Bagnara, R., Rodríguez-Carbonell, E., Zaffanella, E.: Generation of basic semi-algebraic invariants using convex polyhedra. In: Hankin, C., Siveroni, I. (eds.) SAS 2005. LNCS, vol. 3672, pp. 19–34. Springer, Heidelberg (2005)
5. Ball, T., Hackett, B., Lahiri, S.K., Qadeer, S., Vanegue, J.: Towards scalable modular checking of user-defined properties. In: Leavens, G.T., O'Hearn, P., Rajamani, S.K. (eds.) VSTTE 2010. LNCS, vol. 6217, pp. 1–24. Springer, Heidelberg (2010)
6. Ball, T., Rajamani, S.K.: The SLAM toolkit. In: Berry, G., Comon, H., Finkel, A. (eds.) CAV 2001. LNCS, vol. 2102, pp. 260–264. Springer, Heidelberg (2001)
7. Barnett, M., Chang, B.-Y.E., DeLine, R., Jacobs, B., M. Leino, K.R.: Boogie: A modular reusable verifier for object-oriented programs. In: de Boer, F.S., Bonsangue, M.M., Graf, S., de Roever, W.-P. (eds.) FMCO 2005. LNCS, vol. 4111, pp. 364–387. Springer, Heidelberg (2006)
8. Berger, B., Rompel, J., Shor, P.W.: Efficient NC algorithms for set cover with applications to learning and geometry. J. Comput. Syst. Sci. 49(3), 454–477 (1994)

9. Beyer, D., Henzinger, T.A., Jhala, R., Majumdar, R.: The software model checker BLAST. STTT 9(5-6), 505–525 (2007)
10. Beyer, D., Henzinger, T.A., Majumdar, R., Rybalchenko, A.: Path invariants. In: PLDI, pp. 300–309 (2007)
11. Blumer, A., Ehrenfeucht, A., Haussler, D., Warmuth, M.K.: Learnability and the Vapnik-Chervonenkis dimension. JACM 36(4), 929–965 (1989)
12. Brönnimann, H., Goodrich, M.T.: Almost optimal set covers in finite VC-dimension. In: SoCG, pp. 293–302 (1994)
13. Bshouty, N.H., Goldman, S.A., Mathias, H.D., Suri, S., Tamaki, H.: Noise-tolerant distribution-free learning of general geometric concepts. In: STOC, pp. 151–160 (1996)
14. Cachera, D., Jensen, T., Jobin, A., Kirchner, F.: Inference of polynomial invariants for imperative programs: A farewell to gröbner bases. In: Miné, A., Schmidt, D. (eds.) SAS 2012. LNCS, vol. 7460, pp. 58–74. Springer, Heidelberg (2012)
15. Chvatal, V.: A greedy heuristic for the set-covering problem. Mathematics of Operations Research 4(3), 233–235 (1979)
16. Clarisó, R., Cortadella, J.: The octahedron abstract domain. In: Giacobazzi, R. (ed.) SAS 2004. LNCS, vol. 3148, pp. 312–327. Springer, Heidelberg (2004)
17. Colón, M.A.: Approximating the algebraic relational semantics of imperative programs. In: Giacobazzi, R. (ed.) SAS 2004. LNCS, vol. 3148, pp. 296–311. Springer, Heidelberg (2004)
18. Colón, M.A., Sankaranarayanan, S.: Generalizing the template polyhedral domain. In: Barthe, G. (ed.) ESOP 2011. LNCS, vol. 6602, pp. 176–195. Springer, Heidelberg (2011)
19. Colón, M.A., Sankaranarayanan, S., Sipma, H.B.: Linear invariant generation using non-linear constraint solving. In: Hunt Jr., W.A., Somenzi, F. (eds.) CAV 2003. LNCS, vol. 2725, pp. 420–432. Springer, Heidelberg (2003)
20. Cortes, C., Vapnik, V.: Support-vector networks. Machine Learning 20(3), 273–297 (1995)
21. Cousot, P., Cousot, R.: Abstract interpretation: A unified lattice model for static analysis of programs by construction or approximation of fixpoints. In: POPL, pp. 238–252 (1977)
22. Cousot, P., Cousot, R.: Systematic design of program analysis frameworks. In: POPL, pp. 269–282 (1979)
23. Cousot, P., Halbwachs, N.: Automatic discovery of linear restraints among variables of a program. In: POPL, pp. 84–96 (1978)
24. Ernst, M.D., Perkins, J.H., Guo, P.J., McCamant, S., Pacheco, C., Tschantz, M.S., Xiao, C.: The Daikon system for dynamic detection of likely invariants. Sci. Comput. Program. 69(1-3), 35–45 (2007)
25. Fähndrich, M., Logozzo, F.: Static contract checking with abstract interpretation. In: Beckert, B., Marché, C. (eds.) FoVeOOS 2010. LNCS, vol. 6528, pp. 10–30. Springer, Heidelberg (2011)
26. Filé, G., Ranzato, F.: Improving abstract interpretations by systematic lifting to the powerset. In: GULP-PRODE, vol. (1), pp. 357–371 (1994)
27. Flanagan, C., Leino, K.R.M.: Houdini, an annotation assistant for ESC/Java. In: Oliveira, J.N., Zave, P. (eds.) FME 2001. LNCS, vol. 2021, pp. 500–517. Springer, Heidelberg (2001)
28. Ghorbal, K., Ivančić, F., Balakrishnan, G., Maeda, N., Gupta, A.: Donut domains: Efficient non-convex domains for abstract interpretation. In: Kuncak, V., Rybalchenko, A. (eds.) VMCAI 2012. LNCS, vol. 7148, pp. 235–250. Springer, Heidelberg (2012)

29. Gopan, D., Reps, T.: Guided static analysis. In: Riis Nielson, H., Filé, G. (eds.) SAS 2007. LNCS, vol. 4634, pp. 349–365. Springer, Heidelberg (2007)
30. Gulavani, B.S., Chakraborty, S., Nori, A.V., Rajamani, S.K.: Automatically refining abstract interpretations. In: Ramakrishnan, C.R., Rehof, J. (eds.) TACAS 2008. LNCS, vol. 4963, pp. 443–458. Springer, Heidelberg (2008)
31. Gulavani, B.S., Henzinger, T.A., Kannan, Y., Nori, A.V., Rajamani, S.K.: Synergy: a new algorithm for property checking. In: FSE 2006, pp. 117–127 (2006)
32. Gulwani, S., Jojic, N.: Program verification as probabilistic inference. In: POPL, pp. 277–289 (2007)
33. Gulwani, S., Necula, G.C.: Discovering affine equalities using random interpretation. In: POPL, pp. 74–84 (2003)
34. Gulwani, S., Srivastava, S., Venkatesan, R.: Program analysis as constraint solving. In: PLDI, pp. 281–292 (2008)
35. Gupta, A., Majumdar, R., Rybalchenko, A.: From tests to proofs. In: Kowalewski, S., Philippou, A. (eds.) TACAS 2009. LNCS, vol. 5505, pp. 262–276. Springer, Heidelberg (2009)
36. Ivancic, F., Sankaranarayanan, S.: NECLA Static Analysis Benchmarks, http://www.nec-labs.com/research/system/ systems_SAV-website/small_static_bench-v1.1.tar.gz
37. Jhala, R., McMillan, K.L.: A practical and complete approach to predicate refinement. In: Hermanns, H., Palsberg, J. (eds.) TACAS 2006. LNCS, vol. 3920, pp. 459–473. Springer, Heidelberg (2006)
38. Kovács, L.: A complete invariant generation approach for p-solvable loops. In: Pnueli, A., Virbitskaite, I., Voronkov, A. (eds.) PSI 2009. LNCS, vol. 5947, pp. 242–256. Springer, Heidelberg (2010)
39. Lahiri, S.K., Qadeer, S.: Complexity and algorithms for monomial and clausal predicate abstraction. In: Schmidt, R.A. (ed.) CADE-22. LNCS, vol. 5663, pp. 214–229. Springer, Heidelberg (2009)
40. Lalire, G., Argoud, M., Jeannet, B.: The Interproc Analyzer, http://pop-art.inrialpes.fr/people/bjeannet/ bjeannet-forge/interproc/index.html
41. Laviron, V., Logozzo, F.: Subpolyhedra: a family of numerical abstract domains for the (more) scalable inference of linear inequalities. STTT 13(6), 585–601 (2011)
42. Lee, D., Yannakakis, M.: Online minimization of transition systems (extended abstract). In: STOC, pp. 264–274 (1992)
43. Mauborgne, L., Rival, X.: Trace partitioning in abstract interpretation based static analyzers. In: Sagiv, M. (ed.) ESOP 2005. LNCS, vol. 3444, pp. 5–20. Springer, Heidelberg (2005)
44. McCluskey, E.J.: Minimization of boolean functions. Bell Systems Technical Journal 35(6), 1417–1444 (1956)
45. de Moura, L., Bjørner, N.: Z3: An efficient SMT solver. In: Ramakrishnan, C.R., Rehof, J. (eds.) TACAS 2008. LNCS, vol. 4963, pp. 337–340. Springer, Heidelberg (2008)
46. Müller-Olm, M., Seidl, H.: Computing polynomial program invariants. Information Processing Letters 91(5), 233–244 (2004)
47. Naik, M., Yang, H., Castelnuovo, G., Sagiv, M.: Abstractions from tests. In: POPL, pp. 373–386 (2012)
48. Nguyen, T., Kapur, D., Weimer, W., Forrest, S.: Using dynamic analysis to discover polynomial and array invariants. In: ICSE (2012)
49. Nimmer, J.W., Ernst, M.D.: Automatic generation of program specifications. In: ISSTA, pp. 229–239 (2002)

50. Rodríguez-Carbonell, E., Kapur, D.: Automatic generation of polynomial invariants of bounded degree using abstract interpretation. Sci. Comput. Program. 64(1), 54–75 (2007)

51. Rodríguez-Carbonell, E., Kapur, D.: Generating all polynomial invariants in simple loops. J. Symb. Comput. 42(4), 443–476 (2007)

52. Sankaranarayanan, S., Ivančić, F., Shlyakhter, I., Gupta, A.: Static analysis in disjunctive numerical domains. In: Yi, K. (ed.) SAS 2006. LNCS, vol. 4134, pp. 3–17. Springer, Heidelberg (2006)

53. Sankaranarayanan, S., Sipma, H., Manna, Z.: Non-linear loop invariant generation using Gröbner bases. In: POPL, pp. 318–329 (2004)

54. Sharma, R., Gupta, S., Hariharan, B., Aiken, A., Liang, P., Nori, A.V.: A data driven approach for algebraic loop invariants. In: Felleisen, M., Gardner, P. (eds.) ESOP. LNCS, vol. 7792, pp. 574–592. Springer, Heidelberg (2013)

55. Sharma, R., Nori, A.V., Aiken, A.: Interpolants as classifiers. In: Madhusudan, P., Seshia, S.A. (eds.) CAV 2012. LNCS, vol. 7358, pp. 71–87. Springer, Heidelberg (2012)

56. Valiant, L.G.: A theory of the learnable. Commun. ACM 27(11), 1134–1142 (1984)

Interpolation-Based Verification
of Floating-Point Programs
with Abstract CDCL[*]

Martin Brain[1], Vijay D'Silva[3], Alberto Griggio[2,**],
Leopold Haller[1], and Daniel Kroening[1]

[1] University of Oxford
first.last@cs.ox.ac.uk
[2] Fondazione Bruno Kessler, Trento, Italy
griggio@fbk.eu
[3] University of California, Berkeley
vijayd@eecs.berkeley.edu

Abstract. One approach for SMT solvers to improve efficiency is to delegate reasoning to abstract domains. Solvers using abstract domains do not support interpolation and cannot be used for interpolation-based verification. We extend Abstract Conflict Driven Clause Learning (ACDCL) solvers with proof generation and interpolation. Our results lead to the first interpolation procedure for floating-point logic and subsequently, the first interpolation-based verifiers for programs with floating-point variables. We demonstrate the potential of this approach by verifying a number of programs which are challenging for current verification tools.

1 Introduction

Numeric software that manipulates floating-point variables is ubiquitous in automotive, avionic, medical, public transportation and other safety critical systems. The IEEE 754 standard defines the format of, operations on, and exceptions concerning floating-point computations. To alleviate the complexity of floating-point reasoning, some solvers use abstract domains to manipulate and approximate the semantics of formulae [2,14,22,24].

In this paper, we study solvers that implement the *Abstract Conflict Driven Clause Learning* (ACDCL) algorithm [9]. ACDCL solvers lift the Conflict Driven Clause Learning (CDCL) algorithm in SAT solvers to operate on abstract domain elements instead of propositional formulae. To enable the use of ACDCL solvers in interpolation-based verification, we extend ACDCL with proof generation and

[*] Supported by the Toyota Motor Corporation, ERC project 280053, EPSRC project EP/J012564/1, and the FP7 STREP PINCETTE.

[**] Supported by Provincia Autonoma di Trento and the European Community's FP7/2007-2013 under grant agreement Marie Curie FP7 – PCOFUND-GA-2008-226070 "progetto Trentino", project ADAPTATION.

F. Logozzo and M. Fähndrich (Eds.): SAS 2013, LNCS 7935, pp. 412–432, 2013.

interpolant construction. We apply our theoretical results to derive verifiers for programs with floating-point variables.

The intuition behind our work stems from the construction of propositional interpolants. Clause learning SAT solvers can generate resolution proofs [25] and interpolants can be constructed in time linear in the size of a proof [18]. We introduce ACDCL proofs, which extend propositional resolution with reasoning about abstract domain elements. Under certain conditions, discussed later, ACDCL proofs can be rewritten to obtain proofs with the structure generated by DPLL(T) solvers. Existing techniques can be used to construct interpolants from such proof [19]. The major difference between our work and existing work is not in the interpolation procedure we use but in the solver algorithm used to generate proofs. Extending ACDCL to generate proofs with the same structure as DPLL(T) solvers is useful because there are cases where DPLL(T) solvers time out out but an ACDCL solver does not [1].

Contributions and Contents. In this paper, we present and evaluate the first interpolation-based verification procedures for programs with floating-point variables. Our work makes the following contributions.

1. Generation of proofs for ACDCL based on the notion of abstract resolution. Abstract resolution generalises resolution to accommodate formula manipulation in an abstract domain.
2. Sufficient conditions for computing interpolants from ACDCL proofs, and for linear-time interpolation in a theory.
3. The first interpolation-based verifiers for floating-point logic. We implement both the Bounded Model Checking-based interpolation algorithm of [18], and two variants of lazy abstraction with interpolants [20,3].
4. Our implementations perform better than existing state-of-the-art verification tools on a set of small but challenging floating-point programs.

The paper is organised as follows: Section 2 contains a recap of ACDCL, and Section 3 presents our extension of resolution and of ACDCL to generate proofs. Our results on interpolation appear in Section 4, which includes a treatment of the issues arising in the floating point context. We present our empirical results in Section 5, followed by related work in Section 6.

2   Abstract Conflict Driven Clause Learning

We recall the abstract satisfaction framework, which allows us to study satisfiability problems in terms of lattices and transformers and is the basis for ACDCL. We refer the reader to [9] for a deeper treatment of ACDCL, and to [14] for an instantiation of ACDCL for floating-point reasoning.

2.1   The Abstract Satisfaction Framework

Logic. We work with standard first-order notions of predicates, functions and terms. An *atomic predicate* is a predicate symbol composed with terms. A *literal* is an atomic predicate or its negation. A *clause* is a disjunction of literals, and a *cube* is a conjunction of literals. A CNF formula is a conjunction of clauses, and one in DNF is a disjunction of cubes.

We assume a *satisfaction relation* $\models$ between structures in a set *Structs* and formulae. A structure σ is a *model* of φ if $\sigma \models \varphi$, otherwise, σ is a *countermodel*. A formula is *satisfiable* if it has a model and is *unsatisfiable* otherwise. The *satisfiability problem* is to determine whether a given formula is satisfiable. We write SAT for the satisfiability problem for propositional logic.

Lattices. A *lattice* $(L, \sqsubseteq, \sqcup, \sqcap)$ is a partially ordered set with a meet and a join. The *powerset lattice* over a set X, written $(\wp(S), \subseteq, \cup, \cap)$, contains subsets of S order by inclusion. Two functions $f, g : Q \to L$ from a set Q to L can be *ordered pointwise*, denoted $f \sqsubseteq g$, if $f(x) \sqsubseteq g(x)$ holds for all x in Q. Functions on L also lift pointwise to $Q \to L$. The least and greatest fixed points of a monotone function f on a complete lattice will be denoted $\mathsf{lfp}(f)$ and $\mathsf{gfp}(f)$, respectively.

Let id_S be the identity function on a set S. A *Galois connection* between posets $(C, \sqsubseteq)$ and $(A, \preccurlyeq)$, written $(C, \sqsubseteq) \xleftrightarrow[\alpha]{\gamma} (A, \preccurlyeq)$, is a pair of monotone functions $\alpha : C \to A$ and $\gamma : A \to C$ satisfying the pointwise constraints $\alpha \circ \gamma \preccurlyeq id_A$ and $id_C \sqsubseteq \gamma \circ \alpha$.

Concrete Semantics of Formulae. We recall a fixed point characterisation of satisfiability [9]. The *concrete domain of structures* is $(\wp(Structs), \subseteq, \cup, \cap)$. A formula φ defines two *structure transformers*. The name structure transformers is used by analogy to state transformers and predicate transformers. Let X be a set of structures. The *model transformer* $mods_\varphi$ removes all countermodels of φ from X, and the *conflict transformer* $confs_\varphi$ adds all countermodels of φ to X.

$$mods_\varphi(X) \,\hat{=}\, \{\sigma \in X \mid \sigma \models \varphi\} \quad confs_\varphi(X) \,\hat{=}\, \{\sigma \in Structs \mid \sigma \not\models \varphi \text{ or } \sigma \in X\}$$

Properties of a formula can be expressed with transformers. The set of models of φ is $mods_\varphi(Structs)$ and the set of countermodels of φ is $confs_\varphi(\emptyset)$.

Theorem 1. *The following statements are equivalent.*

1. *A formula φ is unsatisfiable.*
2. *The greatest fixed point $\mathsf{gfp}(mods_\varphi)$ contains no structures.*
3. *The least fixed point $\mathsf{lfp}(confs_\varphi)$ contains all structures.*

Applying the transformers above amounts to solving the ALL-SAT problem and is at least as hard as satisfiability. For efficiency, we use abstraction.

Abstract Satisfaction. We overapproximate models and underapproximate countermodels. Let $(O, \sqsubseteq, \sqcup, \sqcap)$ be an overapproximation of the domain of structures and $(U, \preccurlyeq, \curlyvee, \curlywedge)$ be an underapproximation. The approximation is formalised by the Galois connections below. The orders $\sqsubseteq$ and $\preccurlyeq$ both refine set inclusion on structures. That is, $a \sqsubseteq b$ implies $\gamma(a) \subseteq \gamma(b)$, and $x \preccurlyeq y$ implies $\gamma(x) \subseteq \gamma(y)$.

$$(\wp(Structs), \subseteq) \xleftrightarrow[\alpha_O]{\gamma_O} (O, \sqsubseteq) \qquad (\wp(Structs), \supseteq) \xleftrightarrow[\alpha_U]{\gamma_U} (U, \succcurlyeq)$$

An *abstract model transformer* $amods_\varphi : O \to O$, and an *abstract conflict transformer* $aconfs_\varphi : U \to U$ satisfy the pointwise constraints below.

$$mods_\varphi \circ \gamma_O \subseteq \gamma_O \circ amods_\varphi \qquad\qquad confs_\varphi \circ \gamma_U \supseteq \gamma_U \circ aconfs_\varphi$$

The basic soundness result of abstract interpretation can be used to derive sound but incomplete satisfiability solvers.

Theorem 2. *A formula φ is unsatisfiable over a set of structures Structs if at least one of the conditions below hold.*

1. *The set $\gamma_O(\mathsf{gfp}(amods_\varphi))$ is empty.*
2. *The set $\gamma_U(\mathsf{lfp}(aconfs_\varphi))$ contains all structures.*

If $\mathsf{gfp}(amods_\varphi)$ concretises to the empty set, φ must be unsatisfiable. Due to imprecision in the abstraction, $\gamma_O(\mathsf{gfp}(amods_\varphi))$ may not be empty even if φ is unsatisfiable. Similar intuition applies to reasoning with $aconfs_\varphi$.

2.2 A Recap of ACDCL

Recent work has given an abstract interpretation characterisation of the clause learning algorithm in SAT solvers [9]. This characterisation builds upon the observation that the data structures and operations in propositional SAT solvers are defined entirely by the notion of a literal. Propositional literals are the generators of CNF formulae, partial assignments (the data structure for deduction) and clauses (used in learning). The unit rule, decisions, and conflict analysis, can all be formulated in terms of literals. If we can generalise the notion of a literal, all else follows. The work in [9] shows that *complementable meet irreducibles* are a mathematical generalisation of literals to abstract domains. We review this characterisation next.

Irreducible Elements. Irreducible elements in a lattice cannot be derived from other elements using meets and joins. A lattice element x is *completely meet irreducible* if for all $X \subseteq L$, the equality $x = \bigsqcap X$ implies x is in X. The set of meet irreducibles of L is denoted $Irr_\sqcap(L)$. A *meet decomposition* is a function $mdc : L \to \wp(Irr_\sqcap(L))$ satisfying $x = \bigsqcap mdc(x)$ for all x. We shorten 'completely meet irreducible' to 'meet irreducible' in this paper. A meet irreducible m of an abstract domain is *complementable* if there is an element $\overline{m}$ satisfying that $\neg\gamma(m) = \gamma(\overline{m})$. A domain *has complementable meet irreducibles* if every element is the meet of meet irreducibles, and every meet irreducible is complementable.

Domains to Logic. ACDCL uses both abstract domain elements and formulae. We use lower case letters such as p, q, r for logical literals, φ, ψ for formulae, and m, n for domain elements. Our work applies to abstract domains that satisfy the requirements below. The first two conditions enforce that the semantics of logical formulae and abstract domain elements are both given in terms of a set of structures. The fourth condition ensure that meet irreducibles of the abstract domain can be represented by logical formulae. The formula representation is required to generate proofs. In Section 4.3 we show that choosing a representation is non-trivial.

Assumption 1. *Let $\mathcal{L}$ be set of formulae in the logic we consider and O be an abstract domain. We make the following assumptions.*

1. *Formulae in $\mathcal{L}$ are interpreted over structures in a set Structs.*
2. *The concretisation function γ is in $O \rightarrow \wp(Structs)$.*
3. *The abstract domain O has complementable meet irreducibles.*
4. *There exists a function $\langle \cdot \rangle : Irr_\sqcap(O) \rightarrow \mathcal{L}$ which maps every meet irreducible m to a formula $\langle m \rangle$ such that $\gamma(m)$ is the set of models of $\langle m \rangle$.*

We write P, Q, M, N for objects that are formulae or logical representations of meet irreducibles, and $\overline{P}$ denotes $\neg P$ if P is a formula, or $\langle \overline{m} \rangle$, if P is the representation of the meet irreducible m. Assumption 1 allows us to represent logical negations of abstract domain elements as clauses. We adopt the standard convention of writing clauses as sets of literals. Even if an abstract domain is not complemented, we can exploit meet irreducibles to represent the negation of a lattice element as a clause. The *clausal negation* of an abstract element a is the set $neg(a) \hat{=} \{\langle \overline{m} \rangle \mid m \in mdc(a)\}$.

Learning as Transformer Refinement. ACDCL discovers regions of the search space that do not contain models of a formula and uses learning to navigate subsequent search away from such regions. An abstract element a is a *conflict* if $mods_\varphi(\gamma(a))$ is the empty set. The *best learning transformer* for a conflict a, defined below, prunes abstract elements using conflicts.

$$Learn_a : O \rightarrow O \qquad\qquad Learn_a \hat{=} x \mapsto \alpha(\gamma(x) \cap \neg\gamma(a))$$

A *learning transformer* is one that overapproximates the best learning transformer. A learning transformer removes countermodels from an abstract element, but may not remove all. ACDCL discovers conflicts, synthesises learning transformers, and uses these transformers to refine the analysis. We now elaborate on the details of conflict discovery and learning transformer synthesis.

The propositional unit rule asserts that if a region of the search space contains no model for all but one literal in a clause, every model of the clause must be a model of the remaining literal. The *abstract unit rule* lifts this intuition to abstract domains. Let θ be the clausal negation $neg(c)$ of some conflict c.

$$Unit_\theta(a) \hat{=} \begin{cases} \bot & \text{if } \gamma(p \sqcap a) = \emptyset \text{ for all } p \text{ in } \theta \\ a \sqcap q & \text{otherwise, if there exists } q \text{ in } \theta \\ & \quad \text{and for all } p \neq q \text{ in } \theta, \gamma(a \sqcap p) = \emptyset \\ a & \text{otherwise} \end{cases} \tag{1}$$

Learning corresponds to synthesising abstract unit rules from conflicts. ACDCL can be understood as generating a sequence of transformers, as below.

$$amods_\varphi^0 \mathrel{\hat{=}} \prod_{\theta \in \varphi} Unit_\theta \quad amods_\varphi^{i+1} \mathrel{\hat{=}} amods_\varphi^i \sqcap Unit_{neg(c)}, \text{ for some conflict } c$$

ACDCL begins with unit rules for clauses in the formula, and alternates between two phases, *model search*, where conflicts are discovered, and *conflict analysis*, where the conflicts are generalised. Eventually, a satisfying assignment is found, or the formula is shown to be unsatisfiable, or the precision limit of the abstract domain is reached with an inconclusive result, or, in certain cases, the procedure may not terminate. Algorithmic details of ACDCL relevant for proof generation are discussed in the next section.

3   Proofs from ACDCL

The contribution of this section is to generalise resolution to encode abstract domain reasoning, and extend ACDCL with proof generation.

3.1   Abstract Resolution

The resolution rule asserts that if the conjunction of $\theta \vee p$ with $\neg p \vee \psi$ is satisfiable, the clause $\theta \vee \psi$ must also be satisfiable. The rule is formulated entirely in terms of literals, and can be lifted to complementable meet irreducibles. We generalise resolution in two directions illustrated below.

Example 1. We consider a variable x interpreted as an interval, and write a constraint $x \in [0, \infty]$ as $x \geq 0$ for convenience. Of the three inferences below, standard resolution permits the first one.

$$\frac{\theta \vee \langle x \leq 0 \rangle \quad \neg \langle x \leq 0 \rangle \vee \psi}{\theta \vee \psi} \qquad \frac{\theta \vee \langle x \leq 0 \rangle \quad \langle \overline{x \leq 0} \rangle \vee \psi}{\theta \vee \psi} \qquad \frac{\theta \vee \langle x \leq 0 \rangle \quad \langle x \geq 1 \rangle \vee \psi}{\theta \vee \psi}$$

The second inference uses complementable meet irreducibles for Boolean reasoning about certain abstract domain elements. The third inference requires theory reasoning, namely that $(x \leq 0) \sqcap (x \geq 1)$ is $\bot$.

We formalise the inferences above with an extension of the resolution rule that eliminates pairs of meet irreducibles. We encode theory reasoning by a *semantic resolution* rule that applies if a pair of elements reduce to bottom in an abstract domain

Definition 1 (Abstract Resolution). *Let θ and ψ be clauses. Abstract resolution consists of three rules. The literal resolution rule lRES is standard resolution, and mRES extends the standard rule to complementable meet irreducibles.*

$$\frac{\theta \vee p \quad \neg p \vee \psi}{\theta \vee \psi} \; l\text{RES} \qquad\qquad \frac{\theta \vee \langle m \rangle \quad \langle \overline{m} \rangle \vee \psi}{\theta \vee \psi} \; m\text{RES}$$

The semantic resolution rule sRES below uses the meet in the abstract domain to eliminate elements.

$$\frac{\theta \vee \langle m \rangle \quad \langle n \rangle \vee \psi}{\theta \vee \psi} \;\; s\text{RES}, \;\; if \; m \sqcap n = \bot,$$

After applying resolution, a literal may occur multiple times in a resolvent if it occurs in both antecedents. When dealing with a theory, a resolvent may be of the form $\langle m \rangle \vee \langle n \rangle$, where m and n are meet irreducibles satisfying $m \sqsubseteq n$. Such a clause can be *semantically folded* to the equivalent clause $\langle n \rangle$. More generally, the semantic folding of a clause

Definition 2 (Folding). *The semantic folding of a clause θ is the clause*

$$s\text{FOLD}(\theta) \;\hat{=}\; \{\langle m \rangle \in \varphi \mid \not\exists \langle n \rangle \in \varphi \; such \; that \; m \sqsubseteq n\}$$

containing syntactic representations of the maximal elements of θ.

In addition to the abstract resolution rules, ACDCL solvers reason using conflicts. A conflict is a region of the space with no models, so its negation, when viewed as a formula is a tautology. The standard proof-theoretic treatment of conflicts in the SMT literature is to treat them as theory lemmas. We adopt the same convention.

Definition 3. *A theory lemma is a clause $\theta \vee \psi$ satisfying that θ is the clausal negation $neg(c)$ of an element satisfying $c \sqsubseteq aconfs_{\neg\psi}(\bot)$.*

Intuitively, c contains only countermodels of $\neg\psi$, so c "implies" ψ, and the contrapositive of this statement is a tautology that we encode as a clause.

Definition 4 (ACDCL proof). *Consider a CNF formula φ. The hypothesis rule HYP and lemma rule LEMMA are given below.*

$$\frac{}{\theta} \;\text{HYP}, \; if \; \theta \in \varphi \qquad\qquad \frac{}{\theta \vee P} \;\text{LEMMA}, \; if \; \left\{ \begin{array}{l} \theta \vee P \text{ is a theory lemma,} \\ and \; P \text{ is a literal of } \varphi \\ or \; P \text{ is a meet irreducible} \end{array} \right\}$$

A clause θ is derived from a CNF formula φ by ACDCL if θ is introduced by HYP or LEMMA, or if θ is derived by applying either the abstract resolution rules or semantic folding to clauses derived from φ by ACDCL. An ACDCL refutation is an ACDCL derivation of $\bot$.

Theorem 3 extends the soundness of resolution to ACDCL proofs.

Theorem 3. *If there exists an ACDCL derivation of a clause θ from a formula φ then $\varphi \models \theta$.*

Proof. The proof is by induction on the structure of an ACDCL derivation. For the base case, consider the hypothesis and lemma rules.

1. Clauses introduced by HYP belong to φ.
2. A clause $\theta \vee P$ with $\theta = neg(c)$ is derived from an element $c \sqsubseteq aconfs_{\neg P}(\bot)$, so by the soundness of abstract transformers, $\gamma(c) \subseteq confs_{\neg P}(\emptyset)$, and by negation $\neg\gamma(c) \supseteq \neg confs_{\neg P}(\emptyset)$, and by negation of the formula, $\neg\gamma(c) \cup mods_P(Structs) = Structs$, so $neg(c) \vee P$ is valid.

For the induction step, we assume that the theorem holds for clauses derived by ACDCL. The case for lRES is standard, and the reasoning for mRES and sRES are similar, so we only consider mRES. Let σ be a model of $c_1 \vee \langle l_1 \rangle$ and of $c_2 \vee \langle l_2 \rangle$. There are three cases. If σ does not satisfy $\langle l_1 \rangle$ or $\langle l_2 \rangle$, it satisfies $c_1 \vee c_2$. If σ does not satisfy l_1, it must satisfy c_1, hence satisfies $c_1 \vee c_2$. The case for not satisfying l_2 is identical. Note σ cannot satisfy both l_1 and l_2 because they are logical representations of a complemented pair. □

Corollary 1 (Soundness). *If there exists an ACDCL refutation for φ, then φ is unsatisfiable.*

3.2   Proofs from Runs of ACDCL

We now discuss the algorithmic details of ACDCL and show how the algorithm can be extended with proof generation. The algorithm operates on a sequence of meet-irreducibles called an *abstract trail*.

Model Search. Model search can be viewed as a way to guide conflict analysis. The meet of elements in the trail, say a, represents the region considered for model search. If the set $\gamma(a)$ contains a model, the fixed point $\mathsf{gfp}(amods^i_\varphi \sqcap \lambda x.a)$ will be non-empty. If this fixed point is strictly smaller than a, new meet irreducibles are added to the trail. Elements added to the trail are deduced facts and are associated with a *reason*. The reason is either a subformula of φ, or a formula representing the learned transformer $Unit_{neg(c)}$.

Example 2. Consider the following CNF formula φ in linear integer arithmetic:

$$\varphi \hateq (x \geq 3) \wedge (x + y \leq 5) \wedge ((x \leq 0) \vee (y \geq 6))$$

ACDCL over the interval abstract domain produces the following trail during model search:

i	$trail_i$	$reason[i]$
1 :	$\langle x \geq 3 \rangle$	$\leftarrow (x \geq 3)$
2 :	$\langle y \leq 2 \rangle$	$\leftarrow (x + y \leq 5)$
3 :	$\bot$	$\leftarrow (x \leq 0) \vee (y \geq 6)$

The meet irreducible $\langle y \leq 2 \rangle$ is deduced in step 2 from the trail $\langle x \geq 3 \rangle$ and the reason $(x + y \leq 5)$. A conflict is discovered in step 3.

If a conflict is not found, ACDCL makes decisions. A decision is a meet irreducible that when conjoined with the current trail, yields a strictly smaller element. If a does represent the empty set, ACDCL enters the conflict analysis phase.

Conflict Analysis. The goal of conflict analysis is to generalise a conflict a to a larger, still conflicting region. Proof generation only takes place during conflict analysis phase, so we discuss it in greater detail. Conflict analysis is detailed by the uncoloured lines in Algorithm 1 (see [14] for details). Given a reason r for a conflict a the analysis uses an transformer $aconfs_{r,a}$ satisfying two properties:

1. $aconfs_{r,a}$ is sound in the sense that it underapproximates the transformer $\lambda x.\ confs_r(x) \cup \gamma(a)$, and
2. $aconfs_{r,a}$ generalises, meaning that $aconfs_{r,a}(b) \sqsupseteq a$ for all elements b.

Conflict analysis steps backwards through the trail and generalises each meet irreducible by applying the conflict transformer with respect to the associated reason. The generalised result is stored in the *marking* array. An invariant of the algorithm is that after each main loop iteration, the meet of elements in *marking* is a conflict. This conflict is used to synthesise a learning transformer. If $\top$ is not conflicting after the analysis, a backjump undoes part of the trail to return to an earlier, non-conflicting state from which model search continues.

Proof Generation. Proof construction mirrors the construction of resolution proofs from runs of a propositional SAT solver [25]. We walk backwards along the trail and identify proofs steps encoding the reasoning that was performed. The main difference to the propositional case is that an ACDCL proof has to account for the reasoning performed by *aconfs* in the abstract domain.

The proof-producing extension of ACDCL conflict analysis is given by the coloured lines of Algorithm 1. The algorithm uses an array called *proof* to map clauses to proof fragments. We reuse the names of proof rules as functions that construct proof steps. In the case of resolution rules, the second argument is the resolved literal, and the other arguments are antecedents. We write RES for lRES and mRES, because both encode Boolean reasoning, so the distinction is not important for correctness of the algorithm.

The *proof* array is initialized by associating each clause in the input formula with an HYP application. Lines 11-17 constructs a proof to justify that *marking*$[i]$ can be deduced from q by applying the abstract unit rule to *reason*$[i]$. Line 18 constructs a proof for the propagation of *marking*$[i]$ in the trail. The piecewise proofs in the *pl* array are consolidated in lines 23-25 to derive a proof for the learnt clause.

Example 3. We revisit the formula φ and trail in Example 2 and illustrate both conflict analysis and proof construction. In this example, we do distinguish between lRES and mRES. Abstract conflict analysis starts from index 3 in the trail. Suppose that applying $aconfs_{reason[3]}$ to $\bot$ yields the set of meet irreducibles $q \mathrel{\hat{=}} \{\langle y \le 5\rangle, \langle x \ge 1\rangle\}$. Then *marking* is updated as below.

$$marking[1] \leftarrow \langle x \ge 1\rangle \qquad\qquad marking[2] \leftarrow \langle y \le 5\rangle$$

The element *reason*$[3]$ is unit under q, with $amods_{(y\ge 6)}(q) = \bot$. We obtain the proof below

$$r \mathrel{\hat{=}} \frac{\overline{(x \le 0) \vee (y \ge 6)}^{\text{ HYP}} \quad \overline{\langle x \ge 1\rangle \vee \langle y \le 5\rangle \vee \neg(y \ge 6)}^{\text{ LEMMA}}}{(x < 0) \vee \langle x \ge 1\rangle \vee \langle y \le 5\rangle}\ l\text{RES}$$

which we extend to $\mathcal{P}_3$:

$$\mathcal{P}_3 \doteq \cfrac{\overline{\neg(x \leq 0) \vee \langle x \geq 1 \rangle \vee \langle y \leq 5 \rangle} \ \text{LEMMA} \qquad r}{\langle x \geq 1 \rangle \vee \langle y \leq 5 \rangle} \ l\text{RES}$$

At the next iteration, we have $marking[2] = \langle y \leq 5 \rangle$. Applying $aconfs_{reason[2]}$ to $marking[2]$ returns $q \doteq \{\langle x \geq 0 \rangle\}$. Then $marking[1]$ is set to $\langle x \geq 1 \rangle \sqcap \langle x \geq 0 \rangle = \langle x \geq 1 \rangle$, and the following proof $\mathcal{P}_2$ is generated:

$$\mathcal{P}_2 \doteq \cfrac{\overline{\neg(x+y \leq 5) \vee \langle x \geq 0 \rangle \vee \langle y \leq 5 \rangle} \ \text{LEMMA} \qquad \overline{(x+y \leq 5)} \ \text{HYP}}{\langle x \geq 0 \rangle \vee \langle y \leq 5 \rangle} \ l\text{RES}$$

Finally, at the last iteration, we have $marking[1] = \langle x \geq 1 \rangle$, and applying $aconfs_{reason[1]}$ to $marking[1]$ returns $\top$. The following proof $\mathcal{P}_1$ is generated:

$$\mathcal{P}_1 \doteq \cfrac{\overline{\neg(x \geq 3) \vee \langle x \geq 1 \rangle} \ \text{LEMMA} \qquad \overline{(x \geq 3)} \ \text{HYP}}{\langle x \geq 1 \rangle} \ l\text{RES}$$

The final refutation $\mathcal{P}_a$ is obtained by combining $\mathcal{P}_3, \mathcal{P}_2$ and $\mathcal{P}_1$ as follows:

$$\mathcal{P}_a \doteq \cfrac{\cfrac{\mathcal{P}_3 \quad \mathcal{P}_2}{\langle x \geq 1 \rangle} \ s\text{RES} \qquad \mathcal{P}_1}{\bot} \ s\text{RES},$$

where in the first sRES application we applied sFOLD to eliminate $\langle x \geq 0 \rangle$.

We conclude the section with a correctness proof.

Theorem 4. *Let learnt be the clause returned by the proof-producing abstract conflict analysis algorithm of* ACDCL *(Algorithm 1). Then proof[learnt] is an abstract resolution proof for learnt.*

Proof. Assume by induction that $proof[reason[i]]$ is an abstract resolution proof for $reason[i]$, for each non-decision position i in the trail.

First, we show that the LEMMA and RES applications at lines 14, 17 and 18 are correct. For the LEMMAs, the side conditions hold by the correctness of $amods$ and $aconfs$ and by the definition of the abstract unit rule (1). For the RES at line 17, $\bar{l} \in p$ by construction, and $l \in p_i$ by the inductive hypothesis. Similarly, for the RES at line 18, $u \in p_i$ because $u \in proof[reason[i]]$ by the inductive hypothesis and $u \notin unitreason$ by construction. As a consequence of the correctness of such LEMMA and RES applications, the proof p_i generated at line 18 is a correct abstract resolution proof for the clause $marking[i] \vee \bar{q}$ (since all literals $L \in reason[i] \setminus q$ are eliminated by the sequence of resolutions at line 17). Moreover, $q \subseteq \{c \mid \exists 1 \leq j < i \text{ such that } marking[j] \sqsubseteq c\}$. Because of this, in the applications of sRES at line 24, $l \in p$ and P contains a literal l_2 such that $\bar{l_2} \sqsubseteq \bar{l}$. Therefore, the side conditions of sRES are satisfied. In order

---

Algorithm 1. ACDCL proof generation during abstract conflict analysis.

---

1 **abstract-conflict-analysis**($trail$, $reason$, $proof$)
2 | $i \leftarrow |trail|$; $marking \leftarrow \{1 \mapsto \top, \ldots, (i-1) \mapsto \top, i \mapsto \bot\}$;
3 | $pl \leftarrow nil$;
4 | **loop**
5 | | **if** $marking[i] \neq \top$ **then**
6 | | | $a \leftarrow \bigsqcap_{1 \leq j < i} trail[j]$;
7 | | | $q \leftarrow aconfs_{reason[i],a}(marking[i])$;
8 | | | **foreach** c **in** $mdc(q)$ **do**
9 | | | | $r \leftarrow$ smallest index r' s.t. $trail_{r'} \sqsubseteq c$;
10 | | | | $marking[r] \leftarrow marking[r] \sqcap c$;
11 | | | $unitreason \leftarrow nil$; $u \leftarrow \top$;
12 | | | **foreach** l **in** $reason[i]$ **do**
13 | | | | **if** $amods_l(q) = \emptyset$ **then**
14 | | | | | **if** $\bar{l} \not\subseteq q$ **then** $unitreason \leftarrow unitreason : (l, \text{LEMMA}(\bar{l} \vee \bar{q}))$;
15 | | | | **else** $u \leftarrow l$;
16 | | | $p_i \leftarrow proof[reason[i]]$;
17 | | | **foreach** (l, p) **in** $unitreason$ **do** $p_i \leftarrow \text{RES}(p_i, l, p)$;
18 | | | **if** $u \neq \top$ **then** $p_i \leftarrow \text{RES}(p_i, u, \text{LEMMA}(\overline{u} \vee \bar{q} \vee marking[i]))$;
19 | | | $pl \leftarrow pl : (marking[i], p_i)$;
20 | | $marking[i] \leftarrow \top$; $i \leftarrow i - 1$;
21 | | **if** **stopping-criterion**($trail$, $marking$) **then**
22 | | | $confl \leftarrow \bigsqcap_{1 \leq i \leq |trail|} marking[i]$; $learnt \leftarrow \overline{confl}$;
23 | | | $(\_, P) \leftarrow pl[1]$;
24 | | | **foreach** (l, p) **in** $pl[2 \ldots |pl|]$ **do** $P \leftarrow s\text{RES}(P, l, p)$;
25 | | | $proof[learnt] \leftarrow P$;
26 | | | **return** $learnt$;

---

to prove the theorem, it remains to show that the literals of P not involved in the sequence of sRES applications of line 24 are exactly those in the set $\{marking[i] \mid 1 \leq i \leq |trail| \text{ and } marking[i] \neq \top\}$. Since the elements of $marking$ are meet irreducibles, after the update $marking[r] \leftarrow marking[r] \sqcap c$ at line 10, either $marking[r]$ is set to $c \in q$, or $marking[r]$ was already set to an element c' of the result q' of $amods$ of a previous iteration of the loop of Algorithm 1. In both cases, the new value of $marking[r]$ will occur in some proof in the list pl, and hence in the root of P. Also the old value of $marking[r]$ before the update at line 10 will occur in some proof in the list pl, if it was not $\top$. However, such values will not occur in the root of P thanks to the use of sFOLD in the applications of sRES. □

Corollary 2. *Let φ be a* CNF *formula. If* ACDCL *can prove the unsatisfiability of φ, then there exists an abstract resolution refutation for it.*

4   Interpolation for ACDCL

The contribution of this section is sufficient conditions for deriving interpolants from ACDCL proofs. We show how to reuse interpolant constructions for resolution proofs as well as proofs from DPLL(T) solvers to compute interpolants. This allows us to take advantage of the large body of results about interpolation in SAT and SMT, while still retaining the performance benefits that ACDCL might have over DPLL(T) (see e.g. [1]).

4.1   ACDCL and DPLL(T) Proofs

DPLL(T) solvers generate Boolean resolution proof with leaves that are input clauses or theory lemmas [19]. We define such proofs in our setting below.

Definition 5. *Given a* CNF *formula* φ *and a clause* θ, *a* DPLL(T) *proof of* θ *from* φ *is an abstract resolution proof containing no* sRES *applications.*

It should not come as a surprise that an abstract resolution proof can be transformed into a DPLL(T) proof satisfying the definition above. The transformation can be achieved by replacing sRES steps by a combination of mRES and LEMMA steps, as indicated below.

1. An sRES step involving $\langle l_1 \rangle$ and $\langle \overline{l_1} \rangle$ can be replaced by an mRES step.
2. An sRES step involving $\langle l_1 \rangle$ and $\langle l_2 \rangle$ can be replaced by a combination of two mRES and one LEMMA steps as below.

$$\frac{c_1 \vee \langle l_1 \rangle \quad c_2 \vee \langle l_2 \rangle}{c_1 \vee c_2} \text{ sRES} \quad \longrightarrow \quad \frac{c_1 \vee \langle l_1 \rangle \quad \dfrac{c_2 \vee \langle l_2 \rangle \quad \overline{\dfrac{}{\langle \overline{l_1} \rangle \vee \langle \overline{l_2} \rangle}} \text{ LEMMA}}{c_2 \vee \langle \overline{l_1} \rangle} \text{ mRES}}{c_1 \vee c_2} \text{ mRES}$$

3. An sFOLD step which removes an element $\langle l_2 \rangle$ because of an element $\langle l_1 \rangle$ satisfying $l_2 \sqsubseteq l_1$ can be rewritten as follows:

$$\frac{c \vee \langle l_2 \rangle \vee \langle l_1 \rangle \quad \overline{\dfrac{}{\langle \overline{l_2} \rangle \vee \langle l_1 \rangle}} \text{ LEMMA}}{c \vee \langle l_1 \rangle} \text{ mRES}$$

Example 4. Consider again the formula φ and the refutation of Example 3. We convert it into a DPLL(T) proof with the transformation below.

$$\frac{\dfrac{\mathcal{P}_3 \quad \mathcal{P}_2}{\langle x \geq 1 \rangle} \text{ sRES} \quad \mathcal{P}_1}{\bot} \text{ sRES}$$

$$\frac{\dfrac{\dfrac{\mathcal{P}_3 \quad \mathcal{P}_2}{\langle x \geq 0 \rangle \vee \langle x \geq 1 \rangle} \text{ mRES} \quad \overline{\dfrac{}{\langle x \geq 0 \rangle \vee \langle x \geq 1 \rangle}} \text{ LEMMA}}{\langle x \geq 1 \rangle} \text{ mRES} \quad \mathcal{P}_1}{\bot} \text{ mRES}$$

4.2   Generation of Interpolants

Constructing a DPLL(T) refutation from an abstract resolution refutation is the first step towards using existing interpolation algorithms like e.g. [19] with ACDCL. Such algorithms do not typically apply to arbitrary DPLL(T) proofs but require proofs to satisfy a syntactic condition commonly called *colourability*.[1].

Definition 6 (Colourability). *Let Σ be a set of symbols, let t be a term in a theory T, and let* syms(t) *be the set of symbols which occur in t and are uninterpreted in T. Then t is Σ-colourable iff* syms(t) $\subseteq \Sigma$. *Given two formulas A and B in T, t is A-colourable if it is* syms(A)*-colourable, and B-colourable if it is* syms(B)*-colourable. If t is* syms(A)$\cup$syms(B)*-colourable but neither A-colourable nor B-colourable, t is AB-mixed.*

Instantiating ACDCL to work on abstract domains that do not allow AB-mixed terms enables interpolant generation for theories in which interpolation exists for conjunctions of literals. A more interesting case is to wonder whether it is possible to use ACDCL to compute interpolants for theories for which there is no known efficient interpolation procedure. The lemma below provides sufficient conditions on proof structure.

Lemma 1. *Let $\mathcal{P}_{\mathrm{DPLL(T)}}$ be a DPLL(T) proof generated from an abstract resolution refutation for a formula $\varphi_A \wedge \varphi_B$ in a given theory T. If all the lemmas occurring in $\mathcal{P}_{\mathrm{DPLL(T)}}$ are either A-colourable or B-colourable, then it is possible to compute an interpolant I for (φ_A, φ_B) from $\mathcal{P}_{\mathrm{DPLL(T)}}$.*

Proof. Let

$$\psi_A \,\hat{=}\, \varphi_A \wedge \bigwedge \{c \text{ is an } A\text{-colorable lemma of } \mathcal{P}_{\mathrm{DPLL(T)}}\}$$

$$\psi_B \,\hat{=}\, \varphi_B \wedge \bigwedge \{c \text{ is a } B\text{-colorable lemma of } \mathcal{P}_{\mathrm{DPLL(T)}}\}$$

By the hypothesis, each lemma in $\mathcal{P}_{\mathrm{DPLL(T)}}$ occurs in either ψ_A or ψ_B. Therefore, $\psi_A \wedge \psi_B$ is propositionally unsatisfiable, and $\mathcal{P}_{\mathrm{DPLL(T)}}$ is a Boolean resolution refutation for $\psi_A \wedge \psi_B$. Thus, we can compute an interpolant I for (ψ_A, ψ_B) by applying an off-the-shelf Boolean interpolation algorithm to $\mathcal{P}_{\mathrm{DPLL(T)}}$. Since the lemmas of $\mathcal{P}_{\mathrm{DPLL(T)}}$ are by definition valid clauses in the theory T, ψ_A and ψ_B are logically equivalent to φ_A and φ_B in T. Therefore, I is an interpolant also for (φ_A, φ_B). $\qquad\square$

One candidate for satisfying the conditions of Lemma 1 is to use a Cartesian abstract domain because every meet irreducible represents a predicate with one variable and can be coloured. Domain structure alone is insufficient because the conflict transformer must also respect the colorability requirement. We say a conflict transformer *aconfs* is *locality preserving* with respect to a formula $\varphi_A \wedge \varphi_B$ if for all colorable θ and elements a, all elements in the meet decomposition of $aconfs_\theta(a)$ are A-colorable or all are B-colorable.

---

[1] Preprocessing to enforce colourability in restricted cases is known [5].

Corollary 3. *If* ACDCL *is instantiated over a Cartesian domain and it produces an abstract resolution refutation* $\mathcal{P}_a$ *for an unsatisfiable formula* $\varphi_A \wedge \varphi_B$, *then an interpolant* I *for* (φ_A, φ_B) *can be computed from* $\mathcal{P}_a$.

Proof. In a Cartesian domain, complementable elements contain only one variable, and so they are always colorable. Therefore, $\mathcal{P}_a$ does not contain AB-mixed terms. Let $\mathcal{P}_{\text{DPLL(T)}}$ be a DPLL(T) refutation corresponding to $\mathcal{P}_a$. By the side conditions of LEMMA rule, lemmas in $\mathcal{P}_{\text{DPLL(T)}}$ consist of some complementable elements and at most one literal occurring in either φ_A or φ_B (or both). Therefore, assuming the conflict transformer is locality preserving, all the lemmas in $\mathcal{P}_{\text{DPLL(T)}}$ are colorable. By Lemma 1, then, we can compute an interpolant for (φ_A, φ_B) from $\mathcal{P}_{\text{DPLL(T)}}$. □

Example 5. We give an example showing that not all abstract resolution proofs are amenable to interpolation with existing DPLL(T)-based algorithms. Consider the following pair of formulas in linear arithmetic:

$$\varphi_A \,\hat{=}\, (x_3 + y_1 \leq x_1 + x_2) \wedge (x_1 \leq x_3) \wedge (x_2 \leq 0)$$
$$\varphi_B \,\hat{=}\, (z_1 \leq y_1) \wedge (1 \leq z_1)$$

An interpolant for (φ_A, φ_B) is the formula $(y_1 \leq 0)$.

Suppose that ACDCL is instantiated over the non-Cartesian abstract domain of octagons. A run of ACDCL might produce the following trail:

$$
\begin{array}{rll}
i & trail_i & reason[i] \\
1: & \langle -x_1 + x_3 \geq 0 \rangle & \leftarrow (x_1 \leq x_3) \\
2: & \langle y_1 - z_1 \geq 0 \rangle & \leftarrow (z_1 \leq y_1) \\
3: & \langle x_2 - z_1 \geq 0 \rangle & \leftarrow (x_3 + y_1 \leq x_1 + x_2) \\
4: & \langle x_2 \geq 1 \rangle & \leftarrow (1 \leq z_1) \\
5: & \bot & \leftarrow (x_2 \leq 0)
\end{array}
$$

A DPLL(T) proof for this trail is the following:

$$P \,\hat{=}\, \cfrac{\cfrac{\cfrac{P_5 \quad P_4}{\langle x_2 - z_1 \geq 0 \rangle} \quad P_3}{\cfrac{\langle -x_1 + x_3 \geq 0 \rangle \vee \langle y_1 - z_1 \geq 0 \rangle \quad P_2}{\cfrac{\langle -x_1 + x_3 \geq 0 \rangle \quad P_1}{\bot}}}}{}$$

where:

$$P_5 \,\hat{=}\, \frac{\langle x_2 \geq 1 \rangle \vee \neg(x_2 \leq 0) \quad (x_2 \leq 0)}{\langle x_2 \geq 1 \rangle}$$

$$P_4 \,\hat{=}\, \frac{\langle x_2 \geq 1 \rangle \vee \langle x_2 - z_1 \geq 0 \rangle \vee \neg(1 \leq z_1) \quad (1 \leq z_1)}{\langle x_2 \geq 1 \rangle \vee \langle x_2 - z_1 \geq 0 \rangle}$$

$$P_3 \,\hat{=}\, \frac{\langle -x_1 + x_3 \geq 0 \rangle \vee \langle y_1 - z_1 \geq 0 \rangle \vee \neg(x_3 + y_1 \leq x_1 + x_2) \vee \langle x_2 - z_1 \geq 0 \rangle \quad (x_3 + y_1 \leq x_1 + x_2)}{\langle -x_1 + x_3 \geq 0 \rangle \vee \langle y_1 - z_1 \geq 0 \rangle \vee \langle x_2 - z_1 \geq 0 \rangle}$$

$$P_2 \,\hat{=}\, \frac{\langle y_1 - z_1 \geq 0 \rangle \vee \neg(z_1 \leq y_1) \quad (z_1 \leq y_1)}{\langle y_1 - z_1 \geq 0 \rangle}$$

$$P_1 \,\hat{=}\, \frac{\langle -x_1 + x_3 \geq 0 \rangle \vee \neg(x_1 \leq x_3) \quad (x_1 \leq x_3)}{\langle -x_1 + x_3 \geq 0 \rangle}$$

Since some of the leaves of P contain both A-colorable and B-colorable atoms, Boolean interpolation algorithms are not applicable to it. Moreover, P contains also the AB-mixed atom $\langle x_2 - z_1 \geq 0 \rangle$, which prevents also the use of off-the-shelf DPLL(T)-based interpolation algorithms for linear arithmetic (e.g. [19]).

4.3 An Interpolation Procedure for Floating Point Arithmetic

Using Corollary 3, we build a complete interpolation procedure for floating-point arithmetic (FPA), by instantiating ACDCL over the interval abstract domain for floating-point variables [14].

Floating Point Arithmetic. Floating-point numbers are approximate representations of the reals that allow for fixed size bit-vector encoding. A floating-point number represents a real number as a triple of positive integers (s, m, e), consisting of a *sign bit* s taken from the set of Booleans $\{0, 1\}$, a *significand* m and an *exponent* e. Its real interpretation is given by $(-1)^s \cdot m \cdot 2^e$. A floating-point format determines the number of bits used for encoding significand and exponent. For a given format, we define $\mathbb{F}$ to be the set of all floating-point numbers plus the *special values* positive infinity $+\infty$, negative infinity $-\infty$, and *NaN*, which represents an invalid arithmetic result. *Terms* in FPA are constructed from floating-point variables, constants, standard arithmetic operators and special operators such as square roots and combined multiply-accumulate operations. Most operations are parameterized by one of five rounding modes. The result of floating-point operations is defined to be the real result (computed with 'infinite precision') rounded to a floating-point number using the chosen rounding mode. *Formulas* in FPA are Boolean combinations of predicates over floating-point terms. In addition to the standard equality predicate $=$, FPA offers a number of floating-point specific predicates including a special floating-point equality $=_\mathbb{F}$, and floating-point specific arithmetic inequalities $<$ and $\leq$. Since these operators approximate real comparisons they have unusual properties. For example, every comparison with the value *NaN* returns false, therefore $=_\mathbb{F}$ is not reflexive since $NaN =_\mathbb{F} NaN$ does not hold.

ACDCL-Based Interpolation for FPA. We build our interpolation procedure upon FP-ACDCL, a sound and complete ACDCL-based satisfiability algorithm for FPA presented in [14]. More specifically, we instantiate ACDCL over the Cartesian abstract domain of intervals of floating-point values. In order to to this, we define a total order $\preceq$ over all floating-point values, including special values such as *NaN*. In particular, $\preceq$ is such that *NaN* is the minimum element, $-0 \preceq 0$, and $f_1 \preceq f_2 \iff f_1 \leq f_2$ in all other cases. Meet irreducibles in this domain are half-open intervals, which we denote with $\langle x \preceq f \rangle$ or $\langle x \succeq f \rangle$ for a variable x and a floating-point value f.

We extend FP-ACDCL with proof-generation capabilities, and compute the interpolants using existing off-the-shelf proof-based interpolation algorithm for propositional logic (such as e.g. [19]), as described in the previous sections. The only thing to observe here is that, in general, the computed interpolants will contain predicates corresponding to some meet irreducibles $\langle x \preceq f \rangle$, which are not part of the signature of FPA as defined above. However, we can eliminate such predicates with a post-processing step on the generated interpolant, simply by replacing them with equivalent formulas in FPA. Notice that, because of the unusual properties of operations in FPA, in general a single meet irreducible cannot be represented by a single atom in FPA, but non-atomic formulas are needed. For example, the equivalent of $\langle x \preceq -0 \rangle$ in the syntax of FPA is the formula $(x = NaN) \vee ((x \leq 0) \wedge \neg(x = +0))$.

Example 6. Consider the following two formulas φ_A and φ_B in FPA (where "$\cdot_e$" denotes an operation with a "round to nearest even" rounding mode):

$$\varphi_A \hat{=} (x \geq 1.0) \wedge (x +_e y \leq 1.1)$$
$$\varphi_B \hat{=} (z \geq 0.2) \wedge (z < 0.22) \wedge (z *_e y > 0.05).$$

Suppose that FP-ACDCL generates the following DPLL(T) proof P for $\varphi_A \wedge \varphi_B$:

$$P \hat{=} \cfrac{\cfrac{\cfrac{P_5 \quad P_4}{\langle \overline{x \succeq 1.0} \rangle \vee \langle z \succeq 0.2 \rangle \vee \langle z \succeq 0.22 \rangle} \quad P_3}{\langle x \succeq 1.0 \rangle \vee \langle z \succeq 0.22 \rangle} \quad P_2}{\cfrac{\langle x \succeq 1.0 \rangle \qquad P_1}{\perp}}$$

where:

$$P_5 \hat{=} \frac{\neg(x +_e y \leq 1.1) \vee \langle x \succeq 1.0 \rangle \vee \langle y \succeq 0.1001\sim \rangle \quad (x +_e y \leq 1.1)}{\langle x \succeq 1.0 \rangle \vee \langle y \succeq 0.1001\sim \rangle}$$

$$P_4 \hat{=} \frac{\neg(z *_e y > 0.05) \vee \langle \overline{z \succeq 0.2} \rangle \vee \langle y \succeq 0.1001\sim \rangle \vee \langle z \succeq 0.22 \rangle \quad (z *_e y > 0.05)}{\langle \overline{z \succeq 0.2} \rangle \vee \langle y \succeq 0.1001\sim \rangle \vee \langle z \succeq 0.22 \rangle}$$

$$P_3 \hat{=} \frac{\neg(z \geq 0.2) \vee \langle z \succeq 0.2 \rangle \quad (z \geq 0.2)}{\langle z \succeq 0.2 \rangle}$$

$$P_2 \hat{=} \frac{\neg(z < 0.22) \vee \langle \overline{z \succeq 0.22} \rangle \quad (z < 0.22)}{\langle \overline{z \succeq 0.22} \rangle} \qquad P_1 \hat{=} \frac{\neg(x \geq 1.0) \vee \langle x \succeq 1.0 \rangle \quad (x \geq 1.0)}{\langle x \succeq 1.0 \rangle}$$

By applying the Boolean interpolation algorithm of [19] to $\mathcal{P}_{\text{DPLL(T)}}$, we obtain the interpolant $I \hat{=} \langle y \succeq 1.001\sim \rangle$, which is equivalent to the FPA formula $\neg(y \geq 1.001\sim)$.

5   Evaluation

In order to evaluate the utility of our interpolation procedure for FPA, we have implemented several interpolation-based program verifiers, and performed experiments on a number of small but challenging floating-point programs. In this section, we present the results of our experimental evaluation.

5.1   Implementation

Interpolating Decision Procedure. We have implemented our interpolating decision procedure within the MATHSAT5 SMT solver [4]. Details of the ACDCL solver for floating-point intervals are given in [14]. We have extended this solver with proof generation and interpolation. The implementation allows to choose among three different propositional interpolation algorithms for constructing interpolants from ACDCL proofs, and it also provides the option to combine ACDCL-based interpolation with the simple procedure based on inlining "definitional equalities" described in [12], which was shown to be particularly effective for formulas arising in software verification.

Program Verifiers. We have implemented three different program verifiers based on interpolants. The first one, called "Monolithic" here, is the procedure proposed by McMillan in [18], which uses interpolants for computing overapproximations of postimages in symbolic transition systems for verifying circuits. The two others are variants of the "lazy abstraction with interpolants" algorithm of [20] for the verification of imperative sequential programs. We have implemented the original algorithm as described in [20] (called "Impact"), as well as the variant proposed in [3], which combines Impact with techniques inspired by the IC3 algorithm (called "TreeIC3+ITP" in [3], and simply "Impact with IC3-like strenghtening" here).[2]

5.2   Experimental Results and Discussion

Benchmarks. We use three sets of benchmarks to demonstrate the range of application of floating-point interpolation. The first set of benchmarks, dcblock-simple, is derived from a simple filter in the CSound audio processing system. The programs contain infinite loops with a per-cycle input and non-linear arithmetic. Assertions check the variable ranges for each iteration. Proving correctness requires the verification system to be able to reason about the 'eventual' behaviour of the code.

The second set of benchmarks, rangevMain, is based on a widely-used iterative algorithm for computing square roots [21]. The main loop always terminates, but the number of steps is determined by the input and the initial guess, which are both non-deterministic. Proving properties of the result after the loop requires finding consequences of the loop invariant and reasoning about non-linear behaviour including division.

The final set of benchmarks, test, are synthetic tests, which require accurate reasoning about floating-point semantics. These demonstrate the limitation of using the 'standard model' of floating point [21] to convert the analysis into a non-linear real decision problem. Termination of loops and the reachability and

---

[2] Notice that in the TreeIC3+ITP algorithm of [3], interpolants are combined with underapproximated preimage computations based on quantifier elimination. Here, we only use interpolants, since we do not have an effective quantifier elimination procedure for FPA.

truth of assertions in these benchmarks require precise reasoning about floating-point arithmetic, including rounding and loss of precision.

Experimental Setup. We present a comparison of interpolation-based verification using our technique with model checking and conventional abstract interpreters. We compare with SatAbs [6] (release 3.2 with Boom revision 201), a model checker that implements predicate abstraction, and Wolverine [17] (revision 69), an interpolant-based model checker. To the authors' knowledge, these are the only model checking tools that support bit-precise reasoning about floating point. In both cases, this is realized via 'bit-blasting', i.e., a translation to bit-vectors. We also compare with the commercial abstract interpretation systems Fluctuat [8] (version 3.1228) and Astrée [7] (version 12.10). In all cases, tools were run with their default options. We suspect that with expert assistance in their configuration, particularly the abstract interpretation tools, results could likely be improved.

The experiments were run on a 2.83 GHz Intel Core2 Q9550 using Fedora Core 17. Each experiment was limited to 1200 seconds and 3 GB RAM and was run sequentially to avoid inaccuracies due to cache and memory contention.

Table 1. IMPACT with IC3-like strengthening vs. ACDCL and other tools

	TreeIC3+ITP	Model Checking		Abstract Interpretation	
		SatAbs	Wolverine	Fluctuat	Astrée
dcblock-simple-1	117.25	TO	MO	UN	**0.18**
dcblock-simple-2	117.47	TO	MO	UN	**0.19**
dcblock-simple-3	2.31	TO	MO	UN	**0.20**
dcblock-simple-4	727.26	TO	MO	UN	**0.15**
rangevMain1	**0.23**	TO	MO	UN	UN
rangevMain2	**0.23**	TO	MO	UN	UN
rangevMain2b	**0.17**	TO	MO	UN	UN
rangevMain5	**0.28**	TO	MO	UN	UN
rangevMain10	**0.34**	TO	MO	UN	UN
test1	**0.01**	2.16	TO	UN	UN
test2	0.90	**0.13**	MO	UN	UN
test3	6.89	**0.14**	9.94	UN	UN
test4	23.67	**0.13**	TO	UN	UN

Results and Discussion. Table 1 compares Impact with IC3-like strengthening and equality inlining based on ACDCL with state-of-the-art research model checkers and commercial abstract interpretation tools. Times are recorded in seconds, where "TO" and "MO" denote experiments that reached the time and memory limits, respectively. Here, "UN" denotes experiments where safety could not be proven due to limitations of the abstraction. Further comparisons between different interpolation-based verification algorithms and between different interpolation schemes may be found in the appendix.

From the results it is clear that interpolation-based verification using ACDCL is a powerful technique that can verify a range of programs that are beyond the reach of current tools. Further discussion may be found in the appendix.

The performance of SatAbs and Wolverine shows the limitations of 'bit blasting' as an approach to deciding FPA theories. As they are bit precise, the test benchmarks can be handled, but they are unable to generate sufficiently concise invariants to allow other benchmarks to be verified. Conversely, the abstract interpretation tools are very fast (there were no runs that took more than 1 second) but in almost all cases they could not verify the assertions. The benchmarks that Astrée verified were likely due to having explicit domains for digital filters. Experimenting with the number of loop unrollings and the widening operators used may yield positive results as in some cases the computed ranges were close or were clearly converging before widening to the full interval.

6   Related Work

Our work resides in the context of interpolating SMT solvers. There is a performance gap between solvers and their interpolating counterparts, as well as a theoretical gap because proof generation is not well understood within all solver architectures. Interpolating solvers for first-order theories with use-cases in verification were introduced by McMillan [19], who follows the DPLL(T) paradigm, and supports linear rational arithmetic and integer difference arithmetic.

Interpolation frameworks have been developed for first-order theories by controlling the structure of proofs in a superposition-based theorem prover [15]. Another framework for computing interpolants in extensions of a base theory with additional symbols and axioms, by exploiting interpolation algorithms for the base theory appeared in [23]. This paper presents a framework for ACDCL procedures, with an instantiation for the floating-point solver in [14].

The challenge addressed by our work is to study interpolation for a solver in which the notion of a proof is not obvious. The same challenge was addressed in [16] "lifting" propositional interpolants to equality logic in solvers that used Boolean encoding of equality formulae, and in [12] to derive bit-vector interpolants from interpolants for propositional logic and linear integer arithmetic. Our work differs from these by its focus on abstract interpretation-based solvers. We believe that our work is the first to attempt interpolation and proof generation in an abstract interpretation-based solver.

We now summarize applications of interpolating solvers in program analysis. The first application of an interpolating solver in software verification was for predicate discovery in Blast [19]. Wolverine [17] and the analyser in Sec. 5 implement the Impact algorithm [20]. We use abstract interpretation as building-block inside an interpolating solver. Conversely, interpolation is used in an abstract interpreter in [13] for automatically refining abstract interpretations. ACDCL can be applied directly to programs by extending the logic supported by the solver with fixed-point operators [10].

Finally, the combination of abstract interpretation and decidable logics for invariant generation has been recently explored by Garoche et al. [11]. In [22] constraint programming techniques are used for refining abstract interpretations of floating-point programs.

7   Conclusion

One approach to improving performance of decision procedures is to delegate some reasoning to an abstract domain. However, solvers that use abstract domains do not support interpolation and proof generation. We have presented proof generation and interpolation techniques for the family of ACDCL solvers, in which all reasoning is performed within an abstract domain. We have built upon these techniques to implement the first interpolation-based verifiers for programs with floating-point variables, and demonstrated that our verifiers extend the range of what can be automatically verified.

We observe a curious reversal of traditional roles in ours and related work. Abstract interpretation has historically been applied to reason about programs, while proofs and interpolation have been developed in a decision procedure context. We have however used abstract interpretation to design our decision procedure and interpolation to design our program verifier. The broad question for extending this line of work is to identify further techniques from abstract interpretation that can improve decision procedures, and to import techniques from decision procedures to develop program verifiers.

References

1. Brain, M., D'Silva, V., Haller, L., Griggio, A., Kroening, D.: An abstract interpretation of DPLL(T). In: Giacobazzi, R., Berdine, J., Mastroeni, I. (eds.) VMCAI 2013. LNCS, vol. 7737, pp. 455–475. Springer, Heidelberg (2013)

2. Brillout, A., Kroening, D., Wahl, T.: Mixed abstractions for floating-point arithmetic. In: Proc. of Formal Methods in Computer-Aided Design, pp. 69–76. IEEE Computer Society Press (2009)

3. Cimatti, A., Griggio, A.: Software model checking via IC3. In: Madhusudan, P., Seshia, S.A. (eds.) CAV 2012. LNCS, vol. 7358, pp. 277–293. Springer, Heidelberg (2012)

4. Cimatti, A., Griggio, A., Schaafsma, B.J., Sebastiani, R.: The mathSAT5 SMT solver. In: Piterman, N., Smolka, S.A. (eds.) TACAS 2013. LNCS, vol. 7795, pp. 93–107. Springer, Heidelberg (2013)

5. Cimatti, A., Griggio, A., Sebastiani, R.: Efficient generation of Craig interpolants in satisfiability modulo theories. ACM Transactions on Computational Logic 12(1), 7 (2010)

6. Clarke, E.M., Kroening, D., Sharygina, N., Yorav, K.: Predicate abstraction of ANSI-C programs using SAT. Formal Methods in Systems Design 25(2-3), 105–127 (2004)

7. Cousot, P., Cousot, R., Feret, J., Mauborgne, L., Miné, A., Monniaux, D., Rival, X.: The ASTREÉ analyzer. In: Sagiv, M. (ed.) ESOP 2005. LNCS, vol. 3444, pp. 21–30. Springer, Heidelberg (2005)

8. Delmas, D., Goubault, E., Putot, S., Souyris, J., Tekkal, K., Védrine, F.: Towards an industrial use of FLUCTUAT on safety-critical avionics software. In: Alpuente, M., Cook, B., Joubert, C. (eds.) FMICS 2009. LNCS, vol. 5825, pp. 53–69. Springer, Heidelberg (2009)
9. D'Silva, V., Haller, L., Kroening, D.: Abstract conflict driven learning. In: Proc. of Principles of Programming Languages, pp. 143–154 (2013)
10. D'Silva, V., Haller, L., Kroening, D., Tautschnig, M.: Numeric bounds analysis with conflict-driven learning. In: Proc. of Tools and Algorithms for the Construction and Analysis of Systems, pp. 48–63 (2012)
11. Garoche, P.-L., Kahsai, T., Tinelli, C.: Invariant stream generators using automatic abstract transformers based on a decidable logic. CoRR, abs/1205.3758 (2012)
12. Griggio, A.: Effective word-level interpolation for software verification. In: Proc. of Formal Methods in Computer-Aided Design (2011)
13. Gulavani, B.S., Chakraborty, S., Nori, A.V., Rajamani, S.K.: Automatically refining abstract interpretations. In: Ramakrishnan, C.R., Rehof, J. (eds.) TACAS 2008. LNCS, vol. 4963, pp. 443–458. Springer, Heidelberg (2008)
14. Haller, L., Griggio, A., Brain, M., Kroening, D.: Deciding floating-point logic with systematic abstraction. In: Proc. of Formal Methods in Computer-Aided Design, pp. 131–140 (2012)
15. Kovács, L., Voronkov, A.: Interpolation and symbol elimination. In: Schmidt, R.A. (ed.) CADE 2009. LNCS, vol. 5663, pp. 199–213. Springer, Heidelberg (2009)
16. Kroening, D., Weissenbacher, G.: Lifting propositional interpolants to the word-level. In: FMCAD, pp. 85–89. IEEE (2007)
17. Kroening, D., Weissenbacher, G.: Interpolation-based software verification with Wolverine. In: Gopalakrishnan, G., Qadeer, S. (eds.) CAV 2011. LNCS, vol. 6806, pp. 573–578. Springer, Heidelberg (2011)
18. McMillan, K.L.: Interpolation and SAT-based model checking. In: Hunt Jr., W.A., Somenzi, F. (eds.) CAV 2003. LNCS, vol. 2725, pp. 1–13. Springer, Heidelberg (2003)
19. McMillan, K.L.: An interpolating theorem prover. Theoretical Computer Science 345(1), 101–121 (2005)
20. McMillan, K.L.: Lazy abstraction with interpolants. In: LPAR-18 2012, pp. 123–136. Springer (2006)
21. Muller, J.-M., Brisebarre, N., de Dinechin, F., Jeannerod, C.-P., Lefèvre, V., Melquiond, G., Revol, N., Stehlé, D., Torres, S.: Handbook of Floating-Point Arithmetic. Birkhäuser, Boston (2010)
22. Ponsini, O., Michel, C., Rueher, M.: Refining abstract interpretation based value analysis with constraint programming techniques. In: Milano, M. (ed.) CP 2012. LNCS, vol. 7514, pp. 593–607. Springer, Heidelberg (2012)
23. Totla, N., Wies, T.: Complete instantiation-based interpolation. In: Proc. of Principles of Programming Languages, pp. 537–548. ACM Press (2013)
24. Truchet, C., Pelleau, M., Benhamou, F.: Abstract domains for constraint programming, with the example of octagons. In: Symbolic and Numeric Algorithms for Scientific Computing, pp. 72–79 (2010)
25. Zhang, L., Malik, S.: The quest for efficient Boolean satisfiability solvers. In: Voronkov, A. (ed.) CADE 2002. LNCS (LNAI), vol. 2392, pp. 295–313. Springer, Heidelberg (2002)

Concise Analysis Using Implication Algebras for Task-Local Memory Optimisation

Leo White and Alan Mycroft

Computer Laboratory, University of Cambridge
William Gates Building, 15 JJ Thomson Avenue,
Cambridge CB3 0FD, UK
Firstname.Lastname@cl.cam.ac.uk

Abstract. OpenMP is a pragma-based extension to C to support parallelism. The OpenMP standard recently added support for task-based parallelism but in a richer way than languages such as Cilk. Naïve implementations give each task its own stack for task-local memory, which is very inefficient.

We detail a program analysis for OpenMP to enable tasks to share stacks without synchronisation—either unconditionally or dependent on some cheap run-time condition which is very likely to hold in busy systems.

The analysis is based on a novel implication-algebra generalisation of logic programming which allows concise but easily readable encodings of the various constraints. The formalism enables us to show that the analysis has a unique solution and polynomial-time complexity.

We conclude with performance figures.

1 Introduction

Task-based parallelism is a high level parallel programming model made popular by languages such as Cilk [1]. It uses lightweight cooperative threads called *tasks*, which may *spawn* new tasks and *synchronise* with the completion of the tasks that they have spawned.

OpenMP is a shared-memory parallel programming language that has recently introduced support for task-based parallelism—in a less restricted form than Cilk. OpenMP task implementations have struggled to compete with other task-based systems [2,3] as they have been too heavyweight, allocating a whole stack for each task and then restricting parallelism at some cut-off to limit memory consumption.

However, in many cases two or more OpenMP tasks could share stacks without any synchronisation. This paper describes the analysis required to implement such an optimisation. It revolves around analysing the stack usage of a program's tasks.

1.1 OpenMP

OpenMP was originally designed for scientific applications on shared-memory multi-processors. Parallelism is expressed by annotating a program with compiler directives. The language originally only supported data parallelism and

F. Logozzo and M. Fähndrich (Eds.): SAS 2013, LNCS 7935, pp. 433–453, 2013.

static task parallelism. However the emergence of multi-core architectures has brought mainstream applications into the parallel world. These applications are more irregular and dynamic than their scientific counterparts, and require more expressive forms of parallelism. With this in mind, the OpenMP Architecture Review Board released OpenMP 3.0 [4], which includes support for task-based parallelism.

The execution model of OpenMP within the parallel sections of a program consists of *teams* of *threads* executing *tasks* and *workshares*. These threads are heavyweight and preemptively scheduled—typically implemented using system threads. Workshares support data parallelism: they divide work amongst the threads in a team; e.g. the `for` workshare allows iterations of a `for` loop to be divided amongst the threads.

Tasks express more dynamic forms of parallelism. Tasks are sequences of instructions to be executed by a thread. They need not be executed immediately, but can be deferred until later or executed by a different thread in the team. When a team of threads is created each thread begins executing an initial task. These tasks can in turn *spawn* more tasks using the `task` directive. A task can also perform a *sync* operation using the `taskwait` directive, which prevents that task from being executed until all of the tasks that it has spawned have finished.

One point to note, in contrast to languages like Cilk, is that OpenMP tasks can outlive the task which spawned them. This breaks a theorem (Blumofe et al. [5]) for Cilk-like languages about existence of time- and space-optimal execution schedules, and complicates our stack size analysis.

1.2   Optimising Task-Local Memory Allocation

We develop an optimisation that allows multiple tasks to share a single stack. In general, two concurrent tasks sharing a stack would require time-consuming synchronisation between the tasks and would require garbage collection to avoid wasting a potentially unbounded amount of space. However, in some cases a parent task may safely share its stack with some of its child tasks. Consider the OpenMP function shown in Fig. 1. Both tasks only require a bounded amount of space, and they both must finish before the parent task (the one which executed the `work` function) finishes. This means that their stack frames could safely be allocated from the parent task's stack (by using different offsets within it). We say that the child tasks' stacks can be *merged* with their parent task's stack.

The stacks of the child tasks created by the spawn instructions in Fig. 1 can always safely be merged. Other spawn instructions create child tasks whose stacks can safely be merged in most, but not all, instances. Consider the post-order tree traversal OpenMP function shown in Fig. 2. There is no guarantee that the first child task will finish before the second child task begins and they both use unbounded stack space, so they cannot generally be merged. However, our OpenMP implementation executes tasks in post-order: when a thread encounters a spawn instruction it will suspend its current task and begin executing the newly created task. After that new task has finished it will resume its original task (assuming it has not been stolen for execution on another thread).

```
void add_tree(struct tree_node *root) {
    #pragma omp task untied       // OpenMP spawn
    {   tree_node *p = root;
        while (p) { left_sum += p->value;
                    p = p->left;
        }
    }
    #pragma omp task untied       // OpenMP spawn
    {   tree_node *q = root;
        while (q) { right_sum += q->value;
                    q = q->right;
        }
    }
    #pragma omp taskwait          // OpenMP sync
}
```

Fig. 1. OpenMP example—where spawned stacks can be merged

```
void postorder_traverse( struct tree_node *p ) {
    if (p->left)
        #pragma omp task untied      // OpenMP spawn
            postorder_traverse(p->left);
    if (p->right)
        #pragma omp task untied      // OpenMP spawn
            postorder_traverse(p->right);
    #pragma omp taskwait          // OpenMP sync
    process(p);
}
```

Fig. 2. OpenMP example—stack merge is often possible subject to a cheap test

This means that, if the parent task has not been stolen, the first child task in Fig. 1 will definitely finish before the second child task begins.

We can merge spawn instructions like the second one in Fig. 1 as long as their parent task has not been stolen. This can be checked at run-time cheaply and without synchronisation. We say that such spawn instructions are *merged guarded*, while spawn instructions that can always be merged are *merged unguarded*.

To support this optimisation the compiler must determine sets M of spawn instructions whose stacks can safely be merged (the *merged set*), and $U \subseteq M$ of spawn instructions whose stacks can safely be merged unguarded (the *unguarded set*).

1.3   Concise Analysis

In order to express our analysis concisely, we develop a generalisation of logic programming. We use a multi-valued logic, with the values representing possible stack sizes.

First we use a *program* in this logic to represent finding the sizes of stacks for a particular pair of merged set and unguarded set. Then, using the notion of a *stable model* which was developed as a semantics for negation in logic programming, we are able to extend this program to express the whole analysis.

By showing a stratification result about the program representing the analysis, we show that the analysis has a single solution and can be solved in polynomial time.

2   Logic Programming: Negation and Multi-valued Logic

Logic programming is a paradigm where computation arises from proof search in a logic according to a fixed, predictable strategy. It arose with the creation of Prolog [6]. This work uses a variant of logic programming where we restrict terms to be variables or constants (the Datalog restriction) but also allow negation and multi-valued logic.

Syntax. A (traditional) *logic program* P is a set of rules of the form

$$A \longleftarrow B_1, \ldots, B_k$$

where $A, B_1, \ldots, B_k$ are *atoms*. An *atom* is a formula of the form $F(t_1, \ldots, t_k)$ where F is a *predicate symbol* and $t_1, \ldots, t_k$ are *terms*. A is called the *head* and $B_1, \ldots, B_k$ the *body* of the rule. Logic programming languages differ according to the forms of terms allowed. We give a general explanation below, but our applications will only consider Datalog-style terms consisting of variables and constants. A logic program defines a model in which *queries* (syntactically bodies of rules) may be evaluated. We write $ground(P)$ for the ground instances of rules in P.

Note that we do not require P to be finite. Indeed the program analyses we propose naturally give infinite such P, but Section 8 shows these to have an equivalent finite form.

Interpretations, Models and Immediate Consequence Operator. To *evaluate* a query with respect to a logic program we use some form of reduction process (SLD-resolution for Prolog, bottom-up model calculation for Datalog), but the *semantics* is simplest expressed model-theoretically. We present the theory for a general complete lattice $(\mathfrak{L}, \sqsubseteq)$ of truth values (the traditional theory uses $\{false \sqsubseteq true\}$). We use $\sqcup$ to represent the join operator of this lattice and $\sqcap$ to represent the meet operator of this lattice. Members of $\mathfrak{L}$ may appear as nullary atoms in a program.

Given a logic program P, its *Herbrand base* $\mathcal{HB}_P$ is the set of ground atoms that can be constructed from the predicate symbols and function symbols that appear in P. A *Herbrand interpretation* I for a logic program P is a mapping of $\mathcal{HB}_P$ to $\mathfrak{L}$; interpretations are ordered pointwise by $\sqsubseteq$.

Given a ground rule $r = (A \longleftarrow B_1, \ldots, B_k)$, we say a Herbrand interpretation I *respects* rule r, written $I \models r$, if $I(B_1) \sqcap \cdots \sqcap I(B_k) \sqsubseteq I(A)$. A Herbrand interpretation I of P is a *Herbrand model* iff $I \models r$ $(\forall r \in ground(P))$. The least such model (which always exists for the rule-form above) is the canonical representation of a logic program's semantics.

Given logic program P we define the *immediate consequence operator* T_P from Herbrand interpretations to Herbrand interpretations as:

$$(T_P(I))(A) = \bigsqcup_{(A \leftarrow B_1, \ldots, B_k) \in ground(P)} I(B_1) \sqcap \cdots \sqcap I(B_k)$$

Note that I is a model of P iff it is a pre-fixed point of T_P (i.e. $T_P(I) \sqsubseteq I$). Further, since the T_P function is monotonic (i.e. $I_1 \sqsubseteq I_2 \Rightarrow T_P(I_1) \sqsubseteq T_P(I_2)$), it has a least fixed point, which is the least model of P.

2.1   Negation and Its Semantics

It is natural to consider extending logic programs with some notion of negation. This leads to the idea of a *general logic program* which has rules of the form $A \longleftarrow L_1, \ldots, L_k$ where L is a *literal*. A literal is either an atom (*positive literal*) or the negation of an atom (*negative literal*).

The immediate consequence operator of a general logic program is not guaranteed to be monotonic. This means that it may not have a least fixed point, so that the canonical model of logic programs cannot be used as the canonical model of general logic programs. It is also one of the strengths of adding negative literals: support for non-monotonic reasoning. A classic example of non-monotonic reasoning is the following:

$$\texttt{fly}(X) \longleftarrow \texttt{bird}(X), \neg \texttt{penguin}(X)$$
$$\texttt{bird}(X) \longleftarrow \texttt{penguin}(X)$$
$$\texttt{bird(tweety)} \longleftarrow$$
$$\texttt{penguin(skippy)} \longleftarrow$$

It seems obvious that the "intended" model of the above logic program is:

$$\{\texttt{bird(tweety)}, \texttt{fly(tweety)}, \texttt{penguin(skippy)}, \texttt{bird(skippy)}\}$$

Two approaches to defining such a model are to *stratify programs* and to use *stable models*.

Stratified Programs.   One approach to defining a standard model for general logic programs is to restrict our attention to those programs that can be *stratified*.

A predicate symbol F is *used* by a rule if it appears within a literal in the body of a rule. If all the literals that it appears within are positive then the use is positive, otherwise the use is negative. A predicate symbol F is *defined* by a rule if it appears within the head of that rule.

A general logic program P is *stratified* if it can be partitioned $P_1 \cup \cdots \cup P_k = P$ so that, for every predicate symbol F, if F is defined in P_i and used in P_j then $i \leq j$, and additionally $i < j$ if the use is negative.

Any such stratification gives the *standard model*[1] of P as M_k below:

$$M_1 = \text{The least fixed point of } T_{P_1}$$
$$M_i = \text{The least fixed point of } \lambda I. \left(T_{P_i}(I) \sqcup M_{i-1} \right)$$

Stable Models. *Stable models* (Gelfond et al. [8]) give a more general definition of standard model using *reducts*. For any general logic program P and Herbrand interpretation I, the *reduct* of P with respect to I is a logic program defined as:

$$\mathcal{R}_P(I) = \{ A \longleftarrow red_I(L_1), \ldots, red_I(L_k) \mid (A \longleftarrow L_1, \ldots, L_k) \in ground(P) \}$$

$$\text{where } red_I(L) = \begin{cases} L & \text{if } L \text{ is positive} \\ \hat{I}(L) & \text{if } L \text{ is negative} \end{cases}$$

where $\hat{I}$ is the natural extension of I to ground literals.

A *stable model* of a program P is any interpretation I that is the least model of its own reduct $\mathcal{R}_P(I)$.

Unlike the standard models of the previous sections, a general logic program may have multiple stable models or none. For example, both $\{p\}$ and $\{q\}$ are stable models of the general logic program having two rules: $(p \longleftarrow \neg q)$ and $(q \longleftarrow \neg p)$. A stratified program has a unique stable model. The stable model semantics for negation does not fit into the standard paradigm of logic programming. Traditional logic programming hopes to assign to each program a single "intended" model, whereas stable model semantics assigns to each program a (possibly empty) set of models. However, the stable model semantics can be used for a different logic programming paradigm: *answer set programming*. Answer set programming treats logic programs as a system of constraints and computes the stable models as the solutions to those constraints. Note that finding all stable models needs a backtracking search rather than the traditional bottom-up model calculation in Datalog.

2.2   Implication Algebra Programming

We use logic programs to represent stack-size constraints using a multi-valued logic. To represent operations like addition on these sizes it is convenient to allow operators other than negation in literals—a form of *implication algebra* (due to Damasio et al. [9])—to give *implication programs*.

Literals are now terms of an algebra $\mathfrak{A}$. A *positive* literal is one where the formula corresponds to a function that is monotonic (order preserving) in the atoms that it contains. Similarly, *negative* literals correspond to functions that are anti-monotonic (order reversing) in the atoms they contain. We do not consider operators which are neither negative nor positive (such as subtraction).

---

[1] Apt et al. [7] show that this standard model does not depend on which stratification of P is used.

Implication Programs and Their Models. An *implication program* P is a set of *rules* of the form $A \longleftarrow L_1, \ldots, L_k$ where A is an atom, and $L_1, \ldots, L_k$ are positive literals.

Given an implication program P, we extend the notion of *Herbrand base* $\mathcal{HB}_P$ from the set of atoms to the set, $\mathcal{HL}_P$, of all ground literals that can be formed from the atoms in $\mathcal{HB}_P$. A *Herbrand interpretation* for an implication program P is a mapping $I : \mathcal{HB}_P \to \mathcal{L}$ which extends to a valuation function $\hat{I} : \mathcal{HL}_P \to \mathcal{L}$.

Given rule $r = (A \longleftarrow L_1, \ldots, L_k)$, now a Herbrand interpretation I *respects* rule r, written $I \models r$, if $\hat{I}(L_1) \sqcap \cdots \sqcap \hat{I}(L_k) \sqsubseteq I(A)$. Definitions of Herbrand model, canonical semantics, immediate consequence operator etc. are unchanged.

General Implication Programs and Their Models. *General implication programs* extend implication programs by also allowing negative literals. The concepts of stratified programs and stable models defined in Section 2.1 apply to general implication programs exactly as they do to general logic programs.

3   Stack Sizes

The safety of merging stacks depends on the potential size of those stacks at different points in a program's execution. We represent the potential size of a stack by $\mathbb{N}^\infty = \mathbb{N} \cup \{\infty\}$, writing $\sqsubseteq$ for its usual order $\leq_\mathbb{N}$ extended with $(\forall z \in \mathbb{N}^\infty) \; z \sqsubseteq \infty$. Note that $(\mathbb{N}^\infty, \sqsubseteq)$ is a complete lattice. To emphasise this, we will often represent 0 by the symbol $\bot$ and ∞ by the symbol $\top$. The join of this lattice ($\sqcup$) is max and the meet ($\sqcap$) is min.

We use this lattice as the basis for implication programs, using literals of the form:
$$L ::= \neg L \mid \sim L \mid L + L \mid A$$

We use the usual addition operator extended such that $(\forall z \in \mathbb{N}^\infty) \; z + \infty = \infty + z = \infty$.

There are natural definitions for both implication and difference operators on this lattice[2]:

$$\forall z_1, z_2 \in \mathbb{N}^\infty. \quad z_1 \to z_2 \;\overset{\text{def}}{=}\; \begin{cases} z_2 & \text{if } z_2 \sqsubseteq z_1 \\ \top & \text{otherwise} \end{cases}$$

$$\forall z_1, z_2 \in \mathbb{N}^\infty. \quad z_1 \smallsetminus z_2 \;\overset{\text{def}}{=}\; \begin{cases} z_1 & \text{if } z_2 \sqsubseteq z_1 \\ \bot & \text{otherwise} \end{cases}$$

Both operators can be used to define pseudo-complement operations:

$$\forall z \in \mathbb{N}^\infty. \quad \neg z \;\overset{\text{def}}{=}\; z \to \bot$$
$$\forall z \in \mathbb{N}^\infty. \quad \sim z \;\overset{\text{def}}{=}\; \top \smallsetminus z$$

To distinguish them we will call $\neg$ the *complement* and $\sim$ the *supplement*.

---

[2] This follows from $\mathbb{N}^\infty$ being a bi-Heyting algebra—both it and its dual are Heyting algebras

The complement gives $\top$ when applied to 0, and $\bot$ otherwise. We use it conveniently to mean "equals zero". The supplement gives $\bot$ when applied to ∞, and $\top$ otherwise. We use it conveniently to mean "is not ∞". Note that both are anti-monotonic, so they form negative literals.

4   OpenMP Program Representation

We represent OpenMP programs as a triple $(\mathcal{F}, body, \mathcal{S})$ where $\mathcal{F}$ is the set of function names, $body$ is a function that maps function names to their flowgraph (CFG), and $\mathcal{S} \subseteq \mathcal{F}$ gives the entry points to the program. We make various assumptions: function names are unique, program flowgraphs are disjoint and the bodies of tasks have been *outlined* into their own separate functions. (For example, Fig. 1 would be treated as three function definitions, one for the work function and one each for the two task bodies.) We assume that every function is call-graph reachable from $\mathcal{S}$ and that every node in a flowgraph is reachable within its associated function.

Each flowgraph is a tuple (N, E, s, e) with nodes N, edges E, entry node s and exit node e. For a given function $f \in \mathcal{F}$ we write $start(f) = s$, $end(f) = e$, $Nodes(f) = N$ and $Edges(f) = E$. Our analysis is not concerned with detailed intraprocedural execution, so control flow is considered non-deterministic along edges in E, and local variables are summarised by their total size, $frame(f)$.

Flowgraph nodes n are labelled with instructions $instr(n)$. These form four classes: calls, spawns, syncs and local computation. Given $f \in \mathcal{F}$ we write $Calls(f)$ (resp. $Spawns(f)$, $Syncs(f)$) for the subset of $Nodes(f)$ labelled with function calls (resp. task spawns, task syncs). Additionally, provided $instr(n)$ calls or spawns function g, we write $func(n) = g$.

4.1   Paths, Synchronising Instructions and the Call Graph

Paths. A *path* through a function f is an edge-respecting sequence of nodes $(n_0, \ldots, n_k)$ in $body(f)$. The set of all paths between nodes n and m is

$$Paths(n, m) = \{(l_0, \ldots, l_k) \mid l_0 = n \wedge l_k = m \wedge \forall 0 \le i < k. \, (l_i, l_{i+1}) \in Edges(f)\}$$

Notation: $Paths(n, \_) = \bigcup_m Paths(n, m)$ $Paths(\_, n) = \bigcup_m Paths(m, n)$

Synchronising Instructions. A *synchronising instruction* is one whose execution necessarily involves the execution of a sync instruction. These are either sync instructions themselves or calls to functions with a synchronising instruction on every possible path. We define the sets of synchronising instructions, one for each function, as the smallest sets closed under the rules:

$$Synchronising(f) \supseteq Syncs(f)$$

$$Synchronising(f) \supseteq \Big\{ n \in Calls(f) \mid g = func(n) \wedge$$
$$\forall (m_0, \ldots, m_k) \in Paths(start(g), end(g))$$
$$\exists 0 \le i \le k. \, m_i \in Synchronising(g) \Big\}$$

Unsynchronised Paths. An unsynchronised path is a path that may pass through no synchronising instructions. We define the set of unsynchronised paths between two instructions of a function f as follows:

$$Upaths(n, m) = \{(l_0, \ldots, l_k) \in Paths(n, m) \mid \forall 0 < i < k.\ l_i \notin Synchronising(f)\}$$

Notation: $Upaths(n, \_) = \bigcup_m Upaths(n, m)$ $Upaths(\_, n) = \bigcup_m Upaths(m, n)$

Call Graph. The call graph is a relation *CallGraph* on instructions:

$$CallGraph(n, m) \stackrel{\text{def}}{\Leftrightarrow} m \in Calls(f) \cup Spawns(f) \qquad \text{where } f = func(n)$$

We use this relation on spawn and call instructions to order merged sets M and unguarded sets U by dominance (rooted in $\mathcal{S}$, the set of program entry points).

5   Stack Size Analysis Using Implication Programs

This section formulates the stack size analysis as an implication program in a logic using $\mathbb{N}^\infty$ as logic values. Although predicates in the implication program are written as having parameters, these parameters are all constants rather than run-time variables as could be found in Prolog. We emphasise this by writing parameters within $\langle\rangle$ instead of $(\ )$. The framework is monotonic in that only conjunction (min), disjunction (max) and sum are used (we address the benefits in expressiveness and efficiency of using *general* implication programs in Section 6).

We do not analyse OpenMP programs in isolation, but rather in a context of a choice of merged set M and unguarded set U . Hence the result of analysing an OpenMP program is an implication program $P_{(M,U)}$.

Only some choices of M and U are safe and of these we wish to choose a 'best' solution (Section 5.3). Finally, we show how a context-sensitive variant of the analysis naturally follows (Section 5.5).

This section focuses on ease of expression and does not address efficiency, or even computability (note that the analyses here can produce infinite logic programs—Section 8 shows that these are equivalent to finite logic programs).

We represent the amount of stack space that may be required by a function at different points in its execution by four separate values:

Total Size. An upper bound on the total amount of stack space that may be used during a function's execution. This includes the space used by any child functions that it calls, and the space used by any child tasks that it spawns whose stacks have been merged.

Post Size. An upper bound on the amount of stack space that the function may use after it returns[3]. This size represents how the function may interfere with functions or tasks executed after it has finished. It includes the space used by any merged child tasks that it spawns whose execution may not have completed when the function returns.

---

[3] In task-based systems like Cilk this value is always zero because all tasks wait for their children to complete, but this is not the case in OpenMP.

```
void foo (...)
{
#pragma omp task
    bar (...);

#pragma omp taskwait

#pragma omp task
    baz (...);
}
```

Size	Value
Total	$frame(\texttt{foo})+$ $(frame(\texttt{bar}) \sqcup frame(\texttt{baz}))$
Post	$frame(\texttt{baz})$
Pre	$frame(\texttt{foo}) + frame(\texttt{bar})$
Through	0

Fig. 3. Example of different stack sizes

Pre Size. An upper bound on the amount of stack space that the function may use while an existing child task is still executing. This size represents how the function may interfere with tasks spawned before it started executing. It is similar to the total size, but includes neither tasks whose stacks are merged guarded nor any space used after the execution of a sync instruction.

Through Size. An upper bound on the amount of stack space that the function may use after it returns, while an existing child task is still executing. This size represents how the function may simultaneously interfere with tasks spawned before it started executing, and functions or tasks executed after it has finished. It is similar to the post size, but includes neither tasks whose stacks are merged guarded nor space used after the execution of a sync instruction.

For example, consider the program in Fig. 3. If we assume that the spawns of `bar()` and `baz()` are merged unguarded then the sizes are as shown on the right-hand side. We also extend these size definitions to apply to individual instructions, for instance the *total size* of a call instruction is an upper bound on the total amount of stack space that may be used during that call's execution.

We represent these sizes with the predicate symbols `TotalSize`, `PostSize`, `PreSize` and `ThroughSize` parameterised with function names or instruction nodes. The next two subsections describe the rules that make up $P_{(M,U)}$.

5.1   Rules for Functions

Total Size. Each function's total size must be greater than its stack frame plus the total size of any of its individual instructions. We can represent this by the following rule family:

$$[f \in \mathcal{F},\ n \in Nodes(f)] \quad \texttt{TotalSize}\langle f \rangle \longleftarrow frame(f) + \texttt{TotalSize}\langle n \rangle$$

The notation here $[f \in \mathcal{F}]$ represents a meta-level 'for all', in that one rule is generated for every function f (and in this case for each node n).

The above rules ensure that a function's total size is greater than the total size of any of its instructions executing on their own. A function's total size must also be greater than any combination of its instructions that may use stack space simultaneously. This can be represented by the following rule family:

$$[f \in \mathcal{F}, \; n \in \mathit{Nodes}(f), \; (m_0, \ldots, m_k) \in \mathit{Upaths}(\_, n)]$$

$$\texttt{TotalSize}\langle f \rangle \longleftarrow \mathit{frame}(f) + \texttt{PostSize}\langle m_0 \rangle$$

$$+ \sum_{0 < i < k} \texttt{ThroughSize}\langle m_i \rangle$$

$$+ \texttt{PreSize}\langle m_k \rangle$$

Post Size, Pre Size and Through Size. A function's post size must be greater than the post size of any combination of its instructions that may use stack space simultaneously, and which lie on an unsynchronised path to the function's exit. A function's pre size must be greater than its stack frame plus the pre size of any combination of its instructions that may use stack space simultaneously, and which lie on an unsynchronised path from the function's entry. A function's through size must be greater than the through size of any combination of its instructions that may use stack space simultaneously, and which lie on an unsynchronised path from the function's entry to its exit. These observations encode directly as rule families:

$$[f \in \mathcal{F}, \; (n_0, \ldots, n_k) \in \mathit{Upaths}(\_, \mathit{end}(f))]$$

$$\texttt{PostSize}\langle f \rangle \longleftarrow \texttt{PostSize}\langle n_0 \rangle$$

$$+ \sum_{0 < i \leq k} \texttt{ThroughSize}\langle n_i \rangle$$

$$[f \in \mathcal{F}, \; (n_0, \ldots, n_k) \in \mathit{Upaths}(\mathit{start}(f), \_)]$$

$$\texttt{PreSize}\langle f \rangle \longleftarrow \mathit{frame}(f) + \sum_{0 \leq i < k} \texttt{ThroughSize}\langle n_i \rangle$$

$$+ \texttt{PreSize}\langle n_k \rangle$$

$$[f \in \mathcal{F}, \; (n_0, \ldots, n_k) \in \mathit{Upaths}(\mathit{start}(f), \mathit{end}(f))]$$

$$\texttt{ThroughSize}\langle f \rangle \longleftarrow \sum_{0 \leq i \leq k} \texttt{ThroughSize}\langle n_i \rangle$$

5.2 Rules for Instructions

Call Instructions. Since all call instructions use the stack of the caller, their sizes must be greater than the corresponding size of the functions they call. This is represented by the following rule family:

$$[f \in \mathcal{F}, \; n \in \mathit{Calls}(f)]$$

$$\texttt{TotalSize}\langle n \rangle \longleftarrow \texttt{TotalSize}\langle \mathit{func}(n) \rangle$$

$$\texttt{PreSize}\langle n \rangle \longleftarrow \texttt{PreSize}\langle \mathit{func}(n) \rangle$$

$$\texttt{PostSize}\langle n \rangle \longleftarrow \texttt{PostSize}\langle \mathit{func}(n) \rangle$$

$$\texttt{ThroughSize}\langle n \rangle \longleftarrow \texttt{ThroughSize}\langle \mathit{func}(n) \rangle$$

Spawn Instructions. For any *merged* spawn instruction, the spawned task may use the stack of the caller and may be deferred until some point after the spawn instruction has completed. This means that both the total size and post size of the instruction must be greater than the total size of the spawned task. If the spawn instruction is merged *unguarded* then the pre size and through size of the instruction must also be greater than the size of the spawned task. This leads to the following rule families:

$$[n \in M] \quad \texttt{TotalSize}\langle n \rangle \longleftarrow \texttt{TotalSize}\langle \mathit{func}(n) \rangle$$
$$\texttt{PostSize}\langle n \rangle \longleftarrow \texttt{TotalSize}\langle \mathit{func}(n) \rangle$$

$$[n \in U] \quad \texttt{PreSize}\langle n \rangle \longleftarrow \texttt{TotalSize}\langle \mathit{func}(n) \rangle$$
$$\texttt{ThroughSize}\langle n \rangle \longleftarrow \texttt{TotalSize}\langle \mathit{func}(n) \rangle$$

5.3   Optimising Merged and Unguarded Sets

A solution to our analysis is a pair (M, U) of merged set M and unguarded set U. Our analysis must choose the "best" safe solution. We now explore: (i) which solutions are safe, and (ii) which safe solution is the "best".

Which Solutions Are Safe? Using the implication program $P_{(M,U)}$, we can now decide whether a particular solution (M, U) is a safe choice of merged and unguarded sets. There are two situations that we consider unsafe:

1. A child task using its parent task's stack after that parent task has finished.
2. Two tasks simultaneously using unbounded amounts of the same stack.

In situation 1 the parent task may delete the stack after it has finished while the child task is still using it. In situation 2 both tasks may try to push and pop data onto the top of the stack concurrently, which our optimisation does not support (it would require synchronisation). Note that it would be safe if one of the tasks only required a bounded amount of space because then that much space could be reserved on the stack in advance.

Situation 1 is equivalent to spawning a function with a non-zero post size. To avoid this situation, under the least model of $P_{(M,U)}$ for a safe solution (M, U), the following family of formulae must all evaluate to $\top$:

$$[f \in \mathcal{F}, \; n \in \mathit{Spawns}(f)] \quad \neg \, \texttt{PostSize}\langle \mathit{func}(n) \rangle$$

Situation 2 is equivalent to some of a task's child tasks using unbounded stack space whilst at the same time the parent task (and possibly some of its other child tasks) also uses unbounded stack space. To avoid this situation, under the least model of $P_{(M,U)}$ for a safe solution (M, U), the following family of formulae must all evaluate to $\top$:

$$[f \in \mathcal{F}, \quad n_0 \in \mathit{Nodes}(f), \quad (n_0, \ldots, n_k, m_0, \ldots, m_l) \in \mathit{Upaths}(n_0, \_)]$$

$$\sim \left(\sum_{\substack{0 < i \leq k \\ + \, \texttt{PostSize}\langle n_0 \rangle}} \texttt{ThroughSize}\langle n_i \rangle \;\; \bigsqcap \;\; \sum_{\substack{0 \leq i < l \\ + \, \texttt{PreSize}\langle m_l \rangle}} \texttt{ThroughSize}\langle m_i \rangle \right)$$

These formulae mean that the tasks spawned by instructions $n_0, \ldots, n_k$, and the instructions $m_0, \ldots, m_l$ which may execute simultaneously with them, cannot both use unbounded stack space.

If both of these conditions are met then we say that a solution (M, U) is a safe choice for merged and unguarded sets.

Which Safe Solution Is the "Best"? Our aim is to merge as many stacks at run time as we can, and for as many as possible of those merges to be unguarded. It is also more important to increase the total number of stacks merged than to increase the number of stacks merged unguarded. Hence we order solutions lexicographically:

$$(M, U) \sqsubseteq (M', U') \quad \Leftrightarrow \quad M \subset M' \vee (M = M' \wedge U \subseteq U')$$

We would like to choose as the result of our analysis the greatest safe solution according to this ordering. However, not every program has a unique greatest safe solution. Every program does have a unique set of maximal safe solutions, whose members are each either greater than or incomparable with all other safe solutions. In order to chose the best solution from the set of maximal safe solutions, we must use heuristics.

One simple heuristic is preferring to merge spawns that are further from the root of the run-time call graph, because they are likely to be executed more often. We can approximate this using the static call graph by preferring maximal solution (M, U) over maximal solution (M', U') if, letting $Lost = M' \setminus M$ and $Gained = M \setminus M'$, we have that every node $n \in Lost$ dominates (in $CallGraph$ with respect to paths starting at $\mathcal{S}$) every node $m \in Gained$. Note that this is a heuristic for choosing between maximal solutions, rather than an ordering on all solutions, because the reasoning behind it assumes that there are no safe solutions greater than (M, U) or (M', U').[4]

Even with this heuristic programs may still have several equally preferred safe solutions. We call such solutions *optimal*. In Section 5.5 we discuss context sensitivity; the context-sensitive version of our analysis has only a single optimal solution.

5.4   Finding an Optimal Solution

Finding the greatest safe solution according to both the ordering on solutions and our call-graph heuristic is a kind of *constraint optimisation problem (COP)*.

A traditional COP consists of a constraint problem (often represented by a set of variables with domains and a set of constraints on those variables) and an objective function. The aim is to optimise the objective function while obeying the constraints. In our case, the safety conditions are our constraint problem, and instead of an objective function we have the ordering on solutions and our call-graph heuristic.

---

[4] Including this heuristic as part of the ordering on all solutions can lead to cycles in the ordering.

Many COPs are inherently non-monotonic: as the variables are increased the value of the objective function increases, until a constraint is broken—which is equivalent to the objective function being zero. This is true of finding an optimal solution for our analysis: we prefer solutions which merge more spawn instructions, but as more spawn instructions are merged the sizes increase, and as the sizes increase the solution becomes more likely to be unsafe.

COPs are usually solved using some form of backtracking search. This tries to incrementally build solutions, abandoning each partial candidate as soon as it determines that it cannot possibly be part of a valid solution. Such an approach can easily be adopted for finding the optimal solution to our analysis: keep merging more spawn instructions until it is unsafe, then backtrack and try merging some different spawn instructions.

The search space of a COP is exponential in the number of variables, and our problem requires us to recompute the stack sizes for each solution that we try. A naïve search could be very expensive, however there are two simple methods for improving our search:

1. We can use the stack sizes to prune the search tree. For instance, if the current solution causes two tasks to have unbounded size and their spawn instructions have an unsynchronised path between them, then there is no point in trying a solution that merges both of them unguarded.
2. Instead of recomputing the stack sizes for each possible solution, we can start from the stack sizes of a similar solution and just compute the changes.

We shall see in Section 6 that this approach can be encoded as a general implication program; this enables a more efficient solver.

5.5 Adding Context Sensitivity

It is clear from our safety conditions that whether a spawn can be safely merged is *context-sensitive*. By context-sensitive we mean that it does not just depend on the details of the function that contains it, but also on the details of the function that called that function, and the details of the function that called that second function, and so on.

While the safety conditions are context-sensitive, the optimisation and analysis described so far are context-insensitive. This means that some stacks will not be merged even though it would be safe to do so, because it would not have been safe if the function had been called from a different context.

In order to allow more spawn points to be merged at run time, we can make the optimisation and analysis context-sensitive. This involves making the behaviour of functions depend on the context that called them.

In our model we achieve this by creating multiple versions of the same function for different contexts, but in practice we simply add extra arguments containing information about the calling context.

A recursive program may have an infinite number of contexts, however we are only interested in the restrictions placed on a function by its context. These restrictions can be represented by four boolean values (see Section 6.1), so we can also represent our context by four boolean values.

Making our optimisation context-sensitive is very cheap; other than the extra context arguments it only requires a few additional logic operations before some calls and stack frame allocations. A simple analysis can detect and remove unused or unnecessary context arguments.

The aim of making the optimisation context-sensitive is to separate run-time function calls when they are called from contexts which require them to merge fewer spawns. This means that the context that a call is in depends on the stack sizes of related instructions, but the stack sizes of instructions depend on the contexts that they are given. This recursive relationship is also non-monotonic: as stack sizes increase more calls are assigned more restrictive contexts, but as more calls are placed in more restrictive contexts stack sizes decrease.

This situation is very similar to the one that exists between stack sizes and the merged and unguarded sets. Similarly it can be resolved using a backtracking search and it can be encoded as a general implication program.

6   The Analysis as a General Implication Program

This section describes how to represent the context-sensitive version of our analysis as a single general implication program—the idea is that meta-level constraints on U and M are now expressed within the logic using negation.

6.1   Stack Size Restrictions

We represent the safety conditions, within this general implication program, as various restrictions on individual stack sizes. There are four kinds of restriction:

1. Restricting the post size to 0. This is equivalent to making the *complement* of the post size $\top$.
2. Restricting the post size to be not unbounded. This is equivalent to making the *supplement* of the post size $\top$.
3. Restricting the pre size to be not unbounded. This is equivalent to making the *supplement* of the pre size $\top$.
4. Restricting the through size to be 0. This is equivalent to making the *complement* of the through size $\top$.

We place these restrictions on instructions using the predicates CompPostSize, SuppPostSize, SuppPreSize and CompThroughSize. We do not need to have explicit predicates to place these restrictions on functions, because we use these restrictions as the contexts for functions. Each function f is replaced by 16 versions of the function $f_{(cr,sr,sg,cgr)}$, one for each possible combination of restrictions.

Note that these restrictions can only affect stack sizes by preventing or guarding merges. So a function whose pre size is restricted may still have unbounded pre size if that unboundedness is caused by ordinary recursive calls, rather than by recursive spawns.

The `CompPostSize` restriction is placed on functions that are spawned, to prevent our first safety condition from being broken. It is propagated by the rule family:

$$[f \in \mathcal{F}, \quad \gamma \in (\{\mathtt{T}\} \times \mathbb{B} \times \mathbb{B} \times \mathbb{B}), \quad (n_0, \ldots, n_k) \in \mathit{Upaths}(\_, \mathit{end}(f_\gamma))]$$
$$\mathtt{CompPostSize}\langle n_0 \rangle \longleftarrow \top$$

The other restrictions are used to prevent our second safety condition from being broken. They are propagated by the rule families:

$$[f \in \mathcal{F}, \quad \gamma \in (\mathbb{B} \times \{\mathtt{T}\} \times \mathbb{B} \times \mathbb{B}), \quad (n_0, \ldots, n_k) \in \mathit{Upaths}(\_, \mathit{end}(f_\gamma))]$$
$$\mathtt{SuppPostSize}\langle n_0 \rangle \longleftarrow \top$$

$$[f \in \mathcal{F}, \quad \gamma \in (\mathbb{B} \times \mathbb{B} \times \{\mathtt{T}\} \times \mathbb{B}), \quad (n_0, \ldots, n_k) \in \mathit{Upaths}(\mathit{start}(f_\gamma), \_)]$$
$$\mathtt{SuppPreSize}\langle n_k \rangle \longleftarrow \top$$

$$[f \in \mathcal{F}, \gamma \in (\mathbb{B} \times \mathbb{B} \times \mathbb{B} \times \{\mathtt{T}\}),$$
$$(n_0, \ldots, n_k) \in \mathit{Upaths}(\mathit{start}(f_\gamma), \mathit{end}(f_\gamma)), \ 0 \le i \le k]$$
$$\mathtt{CompThroughSize}\langle n_i \rangle \longleftarrow \top$$

The `CompThroughSize` restriction is used to prevent loops of instructions from using unbounded stack space. It is enforced by the rule:

$$[f \in \mathcal{F}, \gamma \in (\mathbb{B} \times \mathbb{B} \times \mathbb{B} \times \mathbb{B}), \ n \in \mathit{Nodes}(f_\gamma), \ (m_0, \ldots, m_k) \in \mathit{Upaths}(n, n)]$$
$$\mathtt{CompThroughSize}\langle m_0 \rangle \longleftarrow \top$$

The `SuppPreSize` restriction is used to prevent spawn instructions from being merged unguarded if they are unbounded and preceded by a merged spawn instruction which is also unbounded. It is enforced by the rule family:

$$[f \in \mathcal{F}, \gamma \in (\mathbb{B} \times \mathbb{B} \times \mathbb{B} \times \mathbb{B}), \ n \in \mathit{Nodes}(f_\gamma), \ (m_0, \ldots, m_k) \in \mathit{Upaths}(\_, n)]$$
$$\mathtt{SuppPreSize}\langle m_k \rangle \longleftarrow \sim\sim \mathtt{PostSize}\langle m_0 \rangle$$

The `SuppPostSize` restriction is used to prevent spawn instructions from being merged if they are unbounded and followed by a call to a function that may use unbounded stack space (even if all its spawns are merged guarded). Note that we do not prevent a spawn from being merged due to a later unguarded spawn, because we prefer to make the later spawn guarded. This restriction is enforced by the rule family:

$$[f \in \mathcal{F}, \ \gamma \in (\mathbb{B} \times \mathbb{B} \times \mathbb{B} \times \mathbb{B}), \ n \in Nodes(f_\gamma), \ (m_0, \ldots, m_k) \in Upaths(n, \_),$$
$$g = func(m_k), \ cr \in \mathbb{B}, \ sr \in \mathbb{B}, \ crg \in \mathbb{B}]$$

$$\texttt{SuppPostSize}\langle m_0 \rangle \longleftarrow \sim\sim \texttt{PreSize}\langle g_{(cr,sr,\text{T},crg)} \rangle \, ,$$
$$lit(cr, \texttt{CompPostSize}\langle m_k \rangle) \, ,$$
$$lit(sr, \texttt{SuppPostSize}\langle m_k \rangle) \, ,$$
$$lit(crg, \texttt{CompThroughSize}\langle m_k \rangle)$$

where $lit(b, A)$ is a macro for $\begin{cases} \neg\neg A & \text{if } b = \text{T} \\ \neg A & \text{if } b = \text{F} \end{cases}$

Note that the lit macro used in generating the above rules converts the restriction predicates into booleans that can be used as the contexts for functions.

We apply the supplement restrictions to spawns via complement restrictions using the following rules. This is equivalent to preventing unbounded sizes by forcing those sizes to be zero (i.e. preventing the stacks from merging).

$$[f \in \mathcal{F}, \ \gamma \in (\mathbb{B} \times \mathbb{B} \times \mathbb{B} \times \mathbb{B}), \ n \in Spawns(f_\gamma), \ g = func(n)]$$

$$\texttt{CompPostSize}\langle n \rangle \longleftarrow \texttt{SuppPostSize}\langle n \rangle \, ,$$
$$\sim\sim \texttt{TotalSize}\langle g_{(\text{T},\text{T},\text{F},\text{F})} \rangle$$

$$\texttt{CompPreSize}\langle n \rangle \longleftarrow \texttt{SuppPreSize}\langle n \rangle \, ,$$
$$\sim\sim \texttt{TotalSize}\langle g_{(\text{T},\text{T},\text{F},\text{F})} \rangle$$

We refer to these rules as the *bounding rules*.

6.2   Other Rules

The rules for the stack sizes of spawn instructions are as follows:

$$[f \in \mathcal{F}, \ \gamma \in (\mathbb{B} \times \mathbb{B} \times \mathbb{B} \times \mathbb{B}), \ n \in Spawns(f_\gamma), \ g = func(n)]$$

$$\texttt{TotalSize}\langle n \rangle \longleftarrow \texttt{TotalSize}\langle g_{(\text{T},\text{T},\text{F},\text{F})} \rangle \, , \ \neg\, \texttt{CompPostSize}\langle n \rangle$$

$$\texttt{PostSize}\langle n \rangle \longleftarrow \texttt{TotalSize}\langle g_{(\text{T},\text{T},\text{F},\text{F})} \rangle \, , \ \neg\, \texttt{CompPostSize}\langle n \rangle$$

$$\texttt{PreSize}\langle n \rangle \longleftarrow \texttt{TotalSize}\langle g_{(\text{T},\text{T},\text{F},\text{F})} \rangle \, , \ \neg\, \texttt{CompPostSize}\langle n \rangle \, ,$$
$$\neg\, \texttt{CompPreSize}\langle n \rangle \, , \ \neg\, \texttt{CompThroughSize}\langle n \rangle$$

$$\texttt{ThroughSize}\langle n \rangle \longleftarrow \texttt{TotalSize}\langle g_{(\text{T},\text{T},\text{F},\text{F})} \rangle \, , \ \neg\, \texttt{CompPostSize}\langle n \rangle \, ,$$
$$\neg\, \texttt{CompPreSize}\langle n \rangle \, , \ \neg\, \texttt{CompThroughSize}\langle n \rangle$$

The remaining stack size rules are based on those in Section 5 and are omitted for brevity.

6.3   Extracting Solutions

Given a stable model of the rules described in this section, we can extract a solution that is equivalent to the solution that we would have obtained using the methods suggested in Section 5.3. The merged set M and unguarded merge set U are given by:

$$M = \{n \mid \texttt{TotalSize}\langle g_{(\mathrm{T},\mathrm{T},\mathrm{F},\mathrm{F})}\rangle \sqsubseteq \texttt{PostSize}\langle n \rangle,\ g = \mathit{func}(n)\}$$
$$U = \{n \mid \texttt{TotalSize}\langle g_{(\mathrm{T},\mathrm{T},\mathrm{F},\mathrm{F})}\rangle \sqsubseteq \texttt{ThroughSize}\langle n \rangle,\ g = \mathit{func}(n)\}$$

7   Stratification

We could find stable models for the general implication program using back-tracking algorithms similar to those used in answer set programming, based on the DPLL algorithm. However, using stratified models finds them more directly.

It is easy to see that the implication program derived in the previous section cannot be stratified. However looking at the rules we can make the following observations:

1. `CompPostSize` and `CompThroughSize` only depend negatively on other predicates via the *bounding rules*.
2. The bounding rules only apply within a function with context $(\mathrm{T}, \mathrm{T}, \mathrm{F}, \mathrm{F})$ if that function contains an instruction with unbounded `TotalSize`, and such functions have unbounded `TotalSize` with or without the bounding rules. This means that the `TotalSize` of all functions $f_{(\mathrm{T},\mathrm{T},\mathrm{F},\mathrm{F})}$ can be calculated without the bounding rules, and in such a calculation `TotalSize` will only depend negatively on the `CompPostSize` and `CompThroughSize` predicates.
3. For any instruction n, if `SuppPreSize`$\langle n \rangle$ equals $\top$ then the value of `SuppPostSize`$\langle n \rangle$ will not affect the values of `PreSize`$\langle n \rangle$ or `ThroughSize`$\langle n \rangle$. This means that the `PreSize` of any function with a context of the form $(cr, sr, \mathrm{T}, crg)$ only depends negatively on the `TotalSize` of functions with context $(\mathrm{T}, \mathrm{T}, \mathrm{F}, \mathrm{F})$ and on the values of `CompPostSize` and `CompThroughSize` calculated without the bounding rules.
4. If `ThroughSize`$\langle f_{(cr,\mathrm{T},sg,crg)}\rangle \neq$ `ThroughSize`$\langle f_{(cr,\mathrm{F},sg,crg)}\rangle$ then `PostSize`$\langle f_{(cr,\mathrm{T},sg,crg)}\rangle =$ `PostSize`$\langle f_{(cr,\mathrm{F},sg,crg)}\rangle = \top$. Therefore, for any instruction n, the value of `SuppPreSize`$\langle n \rangle$ will not affect the values of `PostSize`$\langle n \rangle$. This means that the `PostSize` of any node only depends negatively on the `TotalSize` of functions with context $(\mathrm{T}, \mathrm{T}, \mathrm{F}, \mathrm{F})$ and on the values of `CompPostSize`, `CompThroughSize` and `SuppPostSize`.

This means that we can create a stratifiable general implication program by using five *layers* of the general implication program from the previous section. Each layer is a more accurate approximation of the full set of rules. All negative literals are made to refer to the literals of the previous layer, so that the program can easily be stratified.

These layers work as follows:

1. The first layer calculates the values of `CompPostSize` and `CompThroughSize` ignoring the bounding rules.
2. The second layer calculates the values of `TotalSize` for all functions with context (T, T, F, F).
3. The third layer calculates the values of `SuppPostSize`.
4. The fourth layer calculates the values of `SuppPreSize`.
5. The fifth layer calculates the values of all the remaining predicates.

It can be shown that the stable models of the previous general implication program are equivalent to the stable models of this stratified general implication program. Since stratifiable general implication programs have a unique stable model, this shows that our analysis has a unique solution.

8   Complexity of the Analysis

The unique stable model of a stratified general implication program $P_1 \cup \cdots \cup P_k$ is the same as its standard model. This standard model can be computed in polynomial time if the least fixed points of each T_{P_i} can be computed in polynomial time.

While some of the rule families of our analysis contain an infinite number of rules this was only for presentation. They can also be expressed by a finite number of rules, using an additional predicate to represent the maximum sum of `ThroughSize` between two instructions:

$$[f \in \mathcal{F}, \quad n, m \in Nodes(f), \quad (l_0, \ldots, l_k) \in Upaths(n, m), \quad \forall 0 < i < k]$$
$$\texttt{PathMax}\langle n, m \rangle \longleftarrow \texttt{PathMax}\langle n, l_i \rangle + \texttt{PathMax}\langle l_i, m \rangle + \texttt{ThroughSize}\langle l_i \rangle$$

Since the number of rules is finite, and the operations within the rules are all polynomial time, each iteration of T_{P_i} can be computed in polynomial time.

Each possible bounded size that can be assigned to a predicate in P is uniquely determined by a set of (context-sensitive) function names and instruction nodes. Otherwise that size would include a recursive call or an unbounded iteration of spawns, and so would be $\top$. This means that the number of times a predicate can increase its size is proportional to the size of the original OpenMP program, so the least fixed points of each T_{P_i} can be computed in polynomial time.

9   Evaluation

We implemented the optimisation within our EMCC prototype compiler. We compared it to our compiler without the optimisation, as well as to three other OpenMP implementations: GCC [10], OpenUH [11] and Nanos [12].

Each of these other implementations uses a stack per-task. To prevent excessive memory consumption they restrict parallelism after a certain number of stacks have been created. By decreasing the required number of stacks, our optimisation allows us to restrict parallelism less often.

Our EMCC implementation and OpenUH are more lightweight than GCC and Nanos: OpenUH uses coroutines to implement its tasks, and our implementation divides tasks into continuations.

We compared the implementations using programs from the Barcelona Tasks Suite [13]: *Alignment*, *NQueens* and *Sort*. Alignment uses an iterative pattern with a parallel loop that spawns multiple tasks. The other two use recursive divide-and-conquer patterns, with each task spawning multiple tasks and then waiting for them to finish. The benchmarks were run on a server with 32 AMD Opteron processors.

The results are shown in Fig. 4. Alignment shows no real difference between implementations. Sort shows performance gains for the lightweight implementations, and further gains due to the optimisation. NQueens shows significant gains due to the optimisation.

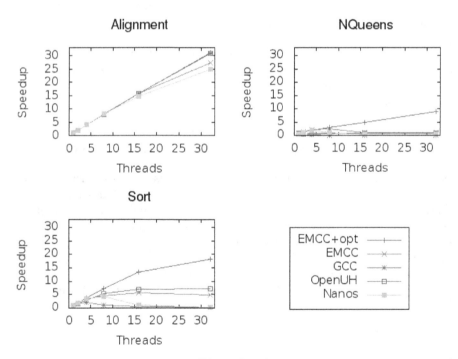

Fig. 4. Results

10   Conclusion

In this paper we have described a program analysis for OpenMP to enable tasks to share stacks for task-local memory. We have shown how a novel implication-algebra generalisation of logic programming allows a concise but easily readable encoding of the various constraints.

Using this formalism we were able to show that the analysis has a unique solution and polynomial-time complexity.

This optimisation has enabled us to implement a very lightweight implementation of OpenMP, and we have shown that this outperforms existing OpenMP implementations that give each task their own stack for task-local memory.

References

1. Supertech Research: Cilk 5.4.6 Reference Manual (1998)
2. Podobas, A., Brorsson, M., Faxén, K.F.: A comparison of some recent task-based parallel programming models (2010)
3. Olivier, S.L., Prins, J.F.: Evaluating OpenMP 3.0 Run Time Systems on Unbalanced Task Graphs. In: Müller, M.S., de Supinski, B.R., Chapman, B.M. (eds.) IWOMP 2009. LNCS, vol. 5568, pp. 63–78. Springer, Heidelberg (2009)
4. OpenMP Architecture Review Board: OpenMP Application Program Interface. Technical report (2008)
5. Blumofe, R.D., Leiserson, C.E.: Space-efficient scheduling of multithreaded computations. In: Proceedings of the Twenty-Fifth Annual ACM Symposium on Theory of Computing, pp. 362–371 (1993)
6. Kowalski, R.: Predicate logic as programming language. Edinburgh University (1973)
7. Apt, K.R., Blair, H.A., Walker, A.: Towards a theory of declarative knowledge. IBM TJ Watson Research Center (1986)
8. Gelfond, M., Lifschitz, V.: The stable model semantics for logic programming. In: Proceedings of the 5th International Conference on Logic Programming, vol. 161 (1988)
9. Damásio, C., Pereira, L.: Antitonic logic programs. Logic Programming and Non-motonic Reasoning, 379–393 (2001)
10. Stallman, R.M.: GNU compiler collection internals. Free Software Foundation (2002)
11. Addison, C., LaGrone, J., Huang, L., Chapman, B.: OpenMP 3.0 tasking implementation in OpenUH. In: Open64 Workshop at CGO 2009 (2009)
12. Teruel, X., Martorell, X., Duran, A., Ferrer, R., Ayguadé, E.: Support for OpenMP tasks in Nanos v4. In: Proceedings of the 2007 Conference of the Center for Advanced Studies on Collaborative Research, pp. 256–259 (2007)
13. Duran, A., Teruel, X., Ferrer, R., Martorell, X., Ayguade, E.: Barcelona OpenMP Tasks Suite: A Set of Benchmarks Targeting the Exploitation of Task Parallelism in OpenMP. In: Proceedings of the 2009 International Conference on Parallel Processing, ICPP 2009, pp. 124–131. IEEE Computer Society, Washington, DC (2009)

Automatic Verification of Erlang-Style Concurrency

Emanuele D'Osualdo, Jonathan Kochems, and C.-H. Luke Ong

University of Oxford

Abstract. This paper presents an approach to verify safety properties of Erlang-style, higher-order concurrent programs *automatically*. Inspired by Core Erlang, we introduce λActor, a prototypical functional language with pattern-matching algebraic data types, augmented with process creation and asynchronous message-passing primitives. We formalise an abstract model of λActor programs called *Actor Communicating System* (ACS) which has a natural interpretation as a vector addition system, for which some verification problems are decidable. We give a parametric abstract interpretation framework for λActor and use it to build a polytime computable, flow-based, abstract semantics of λActor programs, which we then use to bootstrap the ACS construction, thus deriving a more accurate abstract model of the input program.

We evaluate the method which we implemented in the prototype Soter. We find that in practice our abstraction technique is accurate enough to verify an interesting range of safety properties. Though the ACS coverability problem is EXPSPACE-complete, Soter can analyse non-trivial programs in a matter of seconds.

Keywords: Erlang, Infinite-state Systems Verification, Petri Nets.

1 Introduction

This paper concerns the verification of concurrent programs written in Erlang. Originally designed to program fault-tolerant distributed systems at Ericsson in the late 80s, Erlang is now a widely used, open-sourced language with support for higher-order functions, concurrency, communication, distribution, on-the-fly code reloading, and multiple platforms [3,2]. Largely because of a runtime system that offers highly efficient process creation and message-passing communication, Erlang is a natural fit for programming multicore CPUs, networked servers, parallel databases, GUIs, and monitoring, control and testing tools.

The sequential part of Erlang is a higher order, dynamically typed, call-by-value functional language with pattern-matching algebraic data types. Following the *actor model* [1], a concurrent Erlang computation consists of a dynamic network of processes that communicate by message passing. Every process has a unique process identifier (pid), and is equipped with an unbounded mailbox. Messages are sent asynchronously in the sense that send is non-blocking. Messages are retrieved from the mailbox, not FIFO, but First-In-First-Firable-Out

F. Logozzo and M. Fähndrich (Eds.): SAS 2013, LNCS 7935, pp. 454–476, 2013.
© Springer-Verlag Berlin Heidelberg 2013

(FIFFO) via pattern-matching. A process may block while waiting for a message that matches a certain pattern to arrive in its mailbox. For a quick and highly readable introduction to Erlang, see Armstrong's *CACM* article [2].

Challenges. Concurrent programs are hard to write. They are just as hard to verify. In the case of Erlang programs, the inherent complexity of the verification task can be seen from several diverse sources of infinity in the state space.

($\infty\,1$) General recursion requires a (process local) call-stack.
($\infty\,2$) Higher-order functions are first-class values; closures can be passed as parameters or returned.
($\infty\,3$) Data domains, and hence the message space, are unbounded: functions may return, and variables may be bound to, terms of an arbitrary size.
($\infty\,4$) An unbounded number of processes can be spawned dynamically.
($\infty\,5$) Mailboxes have unbounded capacity.

The challenge of verifying Erlang programs is that one must reason about the asynchronous communication of an unbounded set of messages, across an unbounded set of Turing-powerful processes.

Our goal is to verify safety properties of Erlang-like programs *automatically*, using a combination of static analysis and infinite-state model checking. To a large extent, the key decision of which causes of infinity to model as accurately as possible and which to abstract is forced upon us: the class consisting of a fixed set of context-free (equivalently, first-order) processes, each equipped with a mailbox of size one and communicating messages from a finite set, is already Turing powerful [10]. Our strategy is thus to abstract ($\infty\,1$), ($\infty\,2$) and ($\infty\,3$), while seeking to analyse message-passing concurrency, assuming ($\infty\,4$) and ($\infty\,5$).

We consider programs of λActor, a prototypical functional language with actor-style concurrency. λActor is essentially *Core Erlang* [5]—the official intermediate representation of Erlang code, which exhibits in full the higher-order features of Erlang, with asynchronous message-passing concurrency and dynamic process creation. With decidable infinite-state model checking in mind, we introduce *Actor Communicating System* (ACS), which models the interaction of an unbounded set of communicating processes. An ACS has a finite set of control states Q, a finite set of *pid classes* P, a finite set of messages M, and a finite set of transition rules. An ACS transition rule has the shape $\iota: q \xrightarrow{\ell} q'$, which means that a process of pid class ι can transition from state q to state q' with (possible) *communication side effect* ℓ, of which there are four kinds, namely, (i) the process makes an internal transition (ii) it extracts and reads a message m from its mailbox (iii) it sends a message m to a process of pid class ι' (iv) it spawns a process of pid class ι'. ACS models are infinite state: the mailbox of a process has unbounded capacity, and the number of processes in an ACS may grow arbitrarily large. However the set of pid classes is fixed, and processes of the same pid class are not distinguishable.

An ACS can be interpreted naturally as a *vector addition system* (VAS), or equivalently Petri net, using counter abstraction. We consider a particular counter abstraction of ACS, called *VAS semantics*, which models an ACS as a VAS distinguishing two kinds of counters. A counter named by a pair (ι, q) counts the number of processes of pid class ι that are currently in state q; a counter named by (ι, m) counts the sum total of occurrences of a message m currently in the mailbox of p, where p ranges over processes of pid class ι. Using this abstraction, we can conservatively decide properties of the ACS using well-known decision procedures for VAS.

Parametric, Flow-Based Abstract Interpretation. The starting point of our verification pathway is the abstraction of the sources of infinity $(\infty 1)$, $(\infty 2)$ and $(\infty 3)$. Methods such as k-CFA [35] can be used to abstract higher-order recursive functions to a finite-state system. Rather than 'baking in' each type of abstraction separately, we develop a general abstract interpretation framework which is *parametric* on a number of basic domains. In the style of Van Horn and Might [36], we devise a machine-based operational semantics of λActor which is 'generated' from the basic domains of *Time*, *Mailbox* and *Data*. We show that there is a simple notion of *sound abstraction of the basic domains* whereby every such abstraction gives rise to a sound abstract semantics of λActor programs (Theorem 1). Further if a given sound abstraction of the basic domains is finite and the associated auxiliary operations are computable, then the derived abstract semantics is finite and computable.

Generating an ACS. We show that a sound ACS (Theorem 3) can be constructed in polynomial time by *bootstrapping* from the 0-CFA-like abstract semantics. Further, the dimension of the resulting ACS is polynomial in the length of the input λActor program. The idea is that the 0-CFA-like abstract (transition) semantics constitutes a sound but rough analysis of the control-flow of the program, which takes higher-order computation into account but communicating behaviour only minimally. The bootstrap construction consists in constraining these rough transitions with guards of the form 'receive a message of this type' or 'send a message of this type' or 'spawn a process', thus resulting in a more accurate abstract model of the input λActor program in the form of an ACS.

Evaluation. To demonstrate the feasibility of our verification method, we have constructed a prototype implementation called Soter. Our empirical results show that the abstraction framework is accurate enough to verify an interesting range of safety properties of non-trivial Erlang programs.

Outline. In Section 2 we define the syntax of λActor and informally explain its semantics with the help of an example program. In Section 3, we introduce Actor Communicating System and its VAS semantics. In Section 4 we present a machine-based operational semantics of λActor and then, in Section 5, we develop a parametric abstract interpretation from it. In Section 6, we use the analysis to bootstrap the ACS construction. In Section 7 we present the experimental results based on our tool implementation Soter, and discuss the limitations of our approach. We omit proofs for lack of space; they can be found in the extended version of the paper [12]. Please rename the filename of the long version—there should be no reference to POPL13.

Notation. We write A^* for the set of finite sequences of elements of the set A, and ϵ for the null sequence. Let $a \in A$ and $l, l' \in A^*$, we overload '$\cdot$' so that it means insertion at the top $a \cdot l$, at the bottom $l \cdot a$ or concatenation $l \cdot l'$. We write l_i for the i-th element of l. The set of finite partial functions from A to B is denoted $A \rightharpoonup B$. we define $f[a \mapsto b] := (\lambda x.\, \text{if } (x=a) \text{ then } b \text{ else } f(x)); []$ is the everywhere undefined function.

2   A Prototypical Fragment of Erlang

In this section we introduce λActor, a prototypical untyped functional language with actor concurrency. λActor is inspired by single-node *Core Erlang* [5] without built-in functions and fault-tolerant features. It exhibits in full the higher-order features of Erlang, with message-passing concurrency and dynamic process creation. The syntax of λActor is defined as follows:

$$
\begin{aligned}
e \in \text{\textit{Exp}} ::= {}& x \mid c(e_1, \ldots, e_n) \mid e_0(e_1, \ldots, e_n) \mid \text{\textit{fun}} \\
& \mid \textbf{letrec } f_1(x_1, \ldots, x_{k_1}) {=} e_1. \cdots f_n(x_1, \ldots, x_{k_n}) {=} e_n.\ \textbf{in } e \\
& \mid \textbf{case } e \textbf{ of } \text{\textit{pat}}_1 \rightarrow e_1; \ldots; \text{\textit{pat}}_n \rightarrow e_n \textbf{ end} \\
& \mid \textbf{receive } \text{\textit{pat}}_1 \rightarrow e_1; \ldots; \text{\textit{pat}}_n \rightarrow e_n \textbf{ end} \\
& \mid \textbf{send}(e_1, e_2) \mid \textbf{spawn}(e) \mid \textbf{self}\,() \\
\text{\textit{fun}} ::= {}& \textbf{fun}(x_1, \ldots, x_n) \rightarrow e \\
\text{\textit{pat}} ::= {}& x \mid c(\text{\textit{pat}}_1, \ldots, \text{\textit{pat}}_n)
\end{aligned}
$$

where c ranges over a fixed finite set Σ of constructors.

For ease of comparison we keep the syntax close to Core Erlang and use uncurried functions, delimiters, **fun** and **end**. We write '_' for an unnamed unbound variable; using symbols from Σ, we write n-tuples as $\{e_1, \ldots, e_n\}$, the list constructor cons as $[\_|\_]$ and the empty list as $[]$. Sequencing (e_1, e_2) is a shorthand for $(\textbf{fun}(\_) {\rightarrow} e_2)(e_1)$ and we we omit brackets for nullary constructors. The character '%' marks the start of a line of comment. Variable names begin with an uppercase letter. We write fv(e) for the free variables of an expression and we define a λActor program $\mathcal{P}$ to be a closed λActor expression. We associate a unique label l to each sub-expression e of a program and indicate that e is labelled by l by writing $\ell{:}\, e$. Take a term $\ell{:}\, (\ell_0{:}\, e_0(\ell_1{:}\, e_1, \ldots, \ell_n{:}\, e_n))$, we define $\ell.\text{arg}_i := \ell_i$ and arity$(\ell) := n$.

To illustrate λActor's concurrency model we sketch a small-step reduction semantics here. The rewrite rules for function application and λ-abstraction are identical to call-by-value λ-calculus; we write evaluation contexts as $E[\,]$. A state of the computation of a λActor program is a set Π of processes running in parallel. A process $\langle e \rangle_{\mathfrak{m}}^{\iota}$, identified by the pid ι, evaluates an expression e with mailbox $\mathfrak{m}$ holding unconsumed messages. Purely functional reductions performed by each

```
 1  letrec
 2  %
 3  res_start (Res) =
 4      spawn(fun() → res_free (Res)).
 5  res_free (Res) =
 6      receive {lock, P} →
 7          send(P, {acquired, self ()}),
 8          res_locked (Res, P)
 9      end.
10  res_locked (Res, P) =
11      receive
12      {req, P, Cmd} →
13          case Res(P, Cmd) of
14          {NewRes, ok} →
15              res_locked (NewRes, P);
16          {NewRes, {reply, A}} →
17              send(P, {ans, self (), A}),
18              res_locked (NewRes, P)
19          end;
20      {unlock, P} → res_free (Res)
21      end.
22  %
23  res_lock (Q)=
24      send(Q, {lock, self ()}),
25      receive {acquired, Q} → ok end.
26  res_unlock (Q)=
27      send(Q, {unlock, self ()}).
28  res_request (Q, Cmd) =
29      send(Q, {req, self (), Cmd}),
30      receive {ans, Q, X} → X end.
```

```
31  res_do (Q, Cmd) =
32      send(Q, {req, self (), Cmd}).
33  %
34  cell_start () =
35      res_start (cell (zero)).
36  cell (X) = fun(_P, Cmd) →
37      case Cmd of
38      {write, Y} → {cell (Y), ok};
39      read       → {cell (X), {reply, X}}
40      end.
41  %
42  cell_lock    (C) = res_lock (C).
43  cell_unlock  (C) = res_unlock(C).
44  cell_read    (C) = res_request (C, read).
45  cell_write   (C,X)=res_do(C, {write, X}).
46  %
47  inc (C) =
48      cell_lock  (C),
49      cell_write (C, {succ, cell_read (C)}),
50      cell_unlock (C).
51  add_to_cell (M, C) =
52      case M of
53      zero      →    ok;
54      {succ, M'} →
55          spawn(fun() → inc (C)),
56          add_to_cell (M', C)
57      end.
58  %
59  in  C = cell_start (),
60      add_to_cell (N, C).
```

Fig. 1. Locked Resource (running example)

process are independently interleaved. A **spawn** construct, **spawn(fun()→e)**, evaluates to a fresh pid ι' and creates a new process $\langle e \rangle_\epsilon^{\iota'}$, with pid ι':

$$\langle E[\mathbf{spawn}(\mathbf{fun}()\!\to\!e)] \rangle_{\mathsf{m}}^{\iota} \parallel \Pi \quad \longrightarrow \quad \langle E[\iota'] \rangle_{\mathsf{m}}^{\iota} \parallel \langle e \rangle_\epsilon^{\iota'} \parallel \Pi$$

A **send** construct, **send**(ι, v), evaluates to the message v with the side-effect of appending it to the mailbox of the receiver process ι; thus send is non-blocking:

$$\langle E[\mathbf{send}(\iota, v)] \rangle_{\mathsf{m}'}^{\iota'} \parallel \langle e \rangle_{\mathsf{m}}^{\iota} \parallel \Pi \quad \longrightarrow \quad \langle E[v] \rangle_{\mathsf{m}'}^{\iota'} \parallel \langle e \rangle_{\mathsf{m} \cdot v}^{\iota} \parallel \Pi$$

The evaluation of a **receive** construct, **receive** $p_1 \to e_1 \dots p_n \to e_n$ **end**, will block if the mailbox of the process in question contains no message that matches any of the patterns p_i. Otherwise, the first message m that matches a pattern, say p_i, is consumed by the process, and the computation continues with the evaluation of e_i. The pattern-matching variables in e_i are bound by θ to the corresponding matching subterms of the message m; if more than one pattern matches the message, then the first in textual order is fired

$$\langle E[\mathbf{receive}\ p_1 \to e_1 \dots p_n \to e_n\ \mathbf{end}] \rangle_{\mathsf{m} \cdot m \cdot \mathsf{m}'}^{\iota} \parallel \Pi \quad \longrightarrow \quad \langle E[\theta e_i] \rangle_{\mathsf{m} \cdot \mathsf{m}'}^{\iota'} \parallel \Pi;$$

Note that message passing is *not* First-In-First-Out but rather First-In-First-Fireable Out (FIFFO): incoming messages are queued at the end of the mailbox, and the message that a receive construct extracts is not necessarily the first.

Example 1 (Locked Resource). Figure 1 shows an example λActor program. The code has three logical parts, which would constitute three modules in Erlang. The first part defines an Erlang *behaviour*[1] that governs the lock-controlled, concurrent access of a shared resource by a number of clients. A resource is viewed as a generic server implementing the locking protocol, parametrised on a function that specifies how to react to requests. Note the use of higher-order arguments and return values. The function res_start creates a new process that runs an unlocked (res_free) instance of the resource. When unlocked, a resource waits for a {lock, P} message to arrive from a client P. Upon receipt of such a message, an acknowledgement message is sent back to the client and the control is yielded to res_locked. When locked (by a client P), a resource can accept requests {req,P,Cmd} from P—and from P only—for an unspecified command Cmd to be executed. After running the requested command, the resource is expected to return the updated resource handler and an answer, which may be the atom ok, which requires no additional action, or a couple {reply, Ans} which signals that the answer Ans should be sent back to the client. When an unlock message is received from P the control is given back to res_free . Note that the mailbox matching mechanism allows multiple locks and requests to be sent asynchronously to the mailbox of the locked resource without causing conflicts: the pattern matching in the locked state ensures that all the pending lock requests get delayed for later consumption once the resource gets unlocked. The functions res_lock, res_unlock, res_request , res_do hide the protocol from the user who can then use this API as if it was purely functional.

The second part implements a simple shared resource that holds a natural number, which is encoded using the constructors {succ, _} and zero, and allows a client to read its value or overwrite it with a new one. Without lock messages, a shared resource with such a protocol easily leads to inconsistencies.

The last part defines the function inc which accesses a locked cell to increment its value. The function add_to_cell adds M to the contents of the cell by spawning M processes incrementing it concurrently. Finally the entry-point of the program sets up a process with a shared locked cell and then calls add_to_cell . Note that N is a free variable; to make the example a program we can either close it by setting N to a constant or make it range over all natural numbers with the extension described in Section 4.

An interesting correctness property of this code is the mutual exclusion of the lock-protected region (i.e. line 49) of the concurrent instances of inc.

---

[1] I.e. a module implementing a general purpose protocol, parametrised over another module containing the code specific to a particular instance. Note that we simulate modules with higher-order parameters, which is general enough to express in full the dynamic module system of Erlang.

3   Actor Communicating Systems

In this section we explore the design space of abstract models of Erlang-style concurrency. We seek a model of computation that should capture the core concurrency and asynchronous communication features of λActor and yet enjoys the decidability of interesting verification problems. In the presence of pattern-matching algebraic data types, the (sequential) functional fragment of λActor is already Turing powerful [30]. Restricting it to a pushdown (equivalently, first-order) fragment but allowing concurrent execution would enable, using very primitive synchronization, the simulation of a Turing-powerful finite automaton with two stacks. A single finite-control process equipped with a mailbox (required for asynchronous communication) can encode a Turing-powerful queue automaton in the sense of Minsky. Thus constrained, we opt for a model of concurrent computation that has finite control, a finite number of messages, and a finite number of *process classes*.

Definition 1. *An* Actor Communicating System *(ACS)* $\mathcal{A}$ *is a tuple* $\langle P, Q, M, R, \iota_0, q_0 \rangle$ *where P is a finite set of* pid-classes, *Q is a finite set of control-states, M is a finite set of messages, $\iota_0 \in P$ is the pid-class of the initial process, $q_0 \in Q$ is the initial state of the initial process, and R is a finite set of rules of the form* $\iota: q \xrightarrow{\ell} q'$ *where $\iota \in P$, $q, q' \in Q$ and ℓ is a label that can take one of four forms: τ (local transition), $?m$ with $m \in M$ (receive a message), $\iota'!m$ with $\iota' \in P$, $m \in M$ (send a message), $\nu\iota'. q''$ with $\iota' \in P$ and $q'' \in Q$ (spawn a new process in pid-class ι' starting from q'').*

Now we have to give ACS a semantics, but interpreting the ACS mailboxes as FIFFO queues would yield a Turing-powerful model. Our solution is to apply a *counter abstraction* on mailboxes: disregard the ordering of messages, but track the number of occurrences of every message in a mailbox. Since we bound the number of pid-classes, but wish to model dynamic (and hence unbounded) spawning of processes, we apply a second counter abstraction on the control states of each pid-class: we count, for each control-state of each pid-class, the number of processes in that pid-class that are currently in that state.

For soundness, we need to make sure that such an abstraction contains all the behaviours of the semantics with FIFFO mailboxes: if there is a matching term in the mailbox, then the corresponding branch is non-deterministically fired. To see the difference, take the ACS that has one process (named ι), three control states q, q_1 and q_2, and two rules $\iota: q \xrightarrow{?a} q_1$, $\iota: q \xrightarrow{?b} q_2$. When equipped with a FIFFO mailbox containing the sequence $c\,a\,b$, the process can only evolve from q to q_1 by consuming a from the mailbox, since it can skip c but will find a matching message (and thus not look further) before reaching the message b. In contrast, the counter semantics would let q evolve non-deterministically to both q_1 and q_2, consuming a or b respectively: the mailbox is abstracted to $[a \mapsto 1, b \mapsto 1, c \mapsto 1]$ with no information on whether a or b arrived first. However, the abstracted semantics does contain the traces of the FIFFO semantics.

The VAS semantics of an ACS is a state transition system equipped with counters that support increment and decrement (when non-zero) operations. Such infinite-state systems are known as *vector addition systems* (VAS).

Definition 2 (Vector Addition System). *A* vector addition system *(VAS)* $\mathcal{V}$ *is a pair* (I, R) *where* I *is a finite set of indices (called the* places *of the VAS) and* $R \subseteq \mathbb{Z}^I$ *is a finite set of* rules. *Thus a rule is just a vector of integers of dimension* $|I|$, *whose components are indexed (i.e. named) by the elements of* I.
    The state transition system $[\![\mathcal{V}]\!]$ *induced by a VAS* $\mathcal{V} = (I, R)$ *has state-set* $\mathbb{N}^I$ *and transition relation* $\{(\mathbf{v}, \mathbf{v} + \mathbf{r}) \mid \mathbf{v} \in \mathbb{N}^I, \mathbf{r} \in R, \mathbf{v} + \mathbf{r} \in \mathbb{N}^I\}$. *We write* $\mathbf{v} \leq \mathbf{v}'$ *just if for all* i *in* I, $\mathbf{v}(i) \leq \mathbf{v}'(i)$.

The semantics of an ACS can now be given easily in terms of the underlying vector addition system.

Definition 3 (VAS semantics). *The semantics of an ACS* $\mathcal{A} = (P, Q, M, R, \iota_0, q_0)$ *is the transition system induced by the VAS* $\mathcal{V} = (I, \mathbf{R})$ *where* $I = P \times (Q \uplus M)$. *Each ACS rule in* R *is translated into a VAS rule in* $\mathbf{R}$ *as follows:* $\iota: q \xrightarrow{\tau} q'$ *is the vector that decrements* (ι, q) *and increments* (ι, q'), $\iota: q \xrightarrow{?m} q'$ *decrements* (ι, q) *and* (ι, m) *while incrementing* (ι, q'), $\iota: q \xrightarrow{\iota'!m} q'$ *decrements* (ι, q) *and increments both* (ι, q') *and* (ι', m), $\iota: q \xrightarrow{\nu\iota'.\, q''} q'$ *decrements* (ι, q) *while incrementing both* (ι, q') *and* (ι', q''). *Given a* $[\![\mathcal{V}]\!]$*-state* $\mathbf{v} \in \mathbb{N}^I$, *the component* $\mathbf{v}(\iota, q)$ *counts the number of processes in the pid-class* ι *currently in state* q, *while the component* $\mathbf{v}(\iota, m)$ *is the sum of the number of occurrences of the message* m *in the mailboxes of the processes of the pid-class* ι.

While infinite-state, many non-trivial properties are decidable on VAS including reachability, coverability and place boundedness; for more details see [14]. In this paper we focus on coverability, which is EXPSPACE-complete [33]: given two states s and t, is it possible to reach from s a state t' that covers t (i.e. $t' \leq t$)?
    Which kinds of correctness properties of λACTOR programs can one specify by coverability of an ACS? We will be using ACS to *over-approximate* the semantics of a λACTOR program, so if a state of the ACS is not coverable, then it is not reachable in any execution of the program. It follows that we can use coverability to express safety properties such as: (i) unreachability of error program locations (ii) mutual exclusion (iii) boundedness of mailboxes: is it possible to reach a state where the mailbox of pid-class ι has more than k messages? If not we can allocate just k memory cells for that mailbox.

4   An Operational Semantics for λActor

In this section, we define an operational semantics for λACTOR using a *time-stamped CESK* machine*, following an approach by Van Horn and Might [36]. An unusual feature of such machines are *store-allocated continuations* which allow the recursion in a programs's control flow and data structure to be separated from the recursive structure in its state space.

Functional reductions

FunEval

if $\pi(\iota) = \langle \ell \colon (e_0(e_1, \ldots, e_n)), \rho, a, t \rangle$
$\quad b := \mathrm{new}_{\mathrm{kpush}}(\iota, \pi(\iota))$
then $\pi' = \pi[\iota \mapsto \langle e_0, \rho, b, t \rangle]$
$\quad\quad \sigma' = \sigma[b \mapsto \mathsf{Arg}_0\langle \ell, \epsilon, \rho, a \rangle]$

Vars

if $\pi(\iota) = \langle x, \rho, a, t \rangle$
$\quad \sigma(\rho(x)) = (v, \rho')$
then $\pi' = \pi[\iota \mapsto \langle v, \rho', a, t \rangle]$

ArgEval

if $\pi(\iota) = \langle v, \rho, a, t \rangle$
$\quad \sigma(a) = \kappa = \mathsf{Arg}_i\langle \ell, d_0 \ldots d_{i-1}, \rho', c \rangle$
$\quad d_i := (v, \rho)$
$\quad b := \mathrm{new}_{\mathrm{kpop}}(\iota, \kappa, \pi(\iota))$
then $\pi' = \pi[\iota \mapsto \langle \ell.\mathrm{arg}_{i+1}, \rho', b, t \rangle]$
$\quad\quad \sigma' = \sigma[b \mapsto \mathsf{Arg}_{i+1}\langle \ell, d_0 \ldots d_i, \rho', c \rangle]$

Apply

if $\pi(\iota) = \langle v, \rho, a, t \rangle$, $\mathrm{arity}(\ell) = n$
$\quad \sigma(a) = \kappa = \mathsf{Arg}_n\langle \ell, d_0 \ldots d_{n-1}, \rho', c \rangle$
$\quad d_0 = (\mathbf{fun}(x_1 \ldots x_n) \to e, \rho_0) \quad d_n := (v, \rho)$
$\quad b_i := \mathrm{new}_{\mathrm{va}}(\iota, x_i, \mathrm{res}(\sigma, d_i), \pi(\iota))$
$\quad t' := \mathrm{tick}(\ell, \pi(\iota))$
then $\pi' = \pi[\iota \mapsto \langle e, \rho'[x_1 \to b_1 \ldots x_n \to b_n], c, t' \rangle]$
$\quad\quad \sigma' = \sigma[b_1 \mapsto d_1 \ldots b_n \mapsto d_n]$

Fig. 2. Concrete Semantics rules for the functional primitives. The tables define the transition relation $s = \langle \pi, \mu, \sigma, \vartheta \rangle \to \langle \pi', \mu', \sigma', \vartheta' \rangle = s'$ by cases; the primed components of the state are identical to the non-primed components, unless indicated otherwise in the "then" part of the rule. The meta-variable v stands for terms that cannot be further rewritten such as λ-abstractions, constructor applications and un-applied primitives.

A Concrete Machine Semantics. Without loss of generality, we assume that in a λActor program, variables are distinct, and constructors and cases are only applied to variables. The λActor machine defines a transition system on *(global) states* $s \in State := Procs \times Mailboxes \times Store$. An element π of $Procs := Pid \rightharpoonup ProcState$ associates a process with its *(local) state*, and an element μ of $Mailboxes := Pid \rightharpoonup Mailbox$ associates a process with its mailbox. We split a store σ into two partitions $Store := (VAddr \rightharpoonup Value) \times (KAddr \rightharpoonup Kont)$ each with its address space, to separate *values* and *continuations*. By abuse of notation $\sigma(x)$ shall mean the application of the first component when $x \in VAddr$ and of the second when $x \in KAddr$.

The *local state* q of a process is a tuple in $ProcState := (ProgLoc \uplus Pid) \times Env \times KAddr \times Time$ consisting of (i) a pid, or a *program location* which is a subterm of the program, labelled with its occurrence; whenever it is clear from the context, we shall omit the label; (ii) an environment, which is a map from variables to pointers to values $\rho \in Env := Var \rightharpoonup VAddr$; (iii) a pointer to a continuation, which indicates what to evaluate next when the current evaluation returns a value; (iv) a time-stamp, which will be described later.

Values are either closures $d \in Value := Closure \uplus Pid$ or pids $Closure := ProgLoc \times Env$. Note that closures include both functions and constructor terms. All the above domains are naturally partially ordered: $ProgLoc$ and Var are discrete partial orders, all others are defined by pointwise extension.

A *mailbox* is a finite sequence of values: $\mathfrak{m} \in Mailbox := Value^*$. We denote the empty mailbox by ϵ. A mailbox is supported by two operations:

Concurrency

Receive	**Send**

Receive

if $\pi(\iota) = \langle e, \rho, a, t \rangle$

$\quad e = \textsf{receive } p_1 \to e_1 \ldots p_n \to e_n \textsf{ end}$

$\quad \mathrm{mmatch}(p_1 \ldots p_n, \mu(\iota), \rho, \sigma) = (i, \theta, \mathsf{m})$

$\quad \theta = [x_1 \mapsto d_1 \ldots x_k \mapsto d_k]$

$\quad b_j := \mathrm{new}_{\mathrm{va}}(\iota, x_j, \mathrm{res}(\sigma, d_j), \pi(\iota))$

$\quad \rho' := \rho[x_1 \mapsto b_1 \ldots x_k \mapsto b_k]$

then $\pi' = \pi[\iota \mapsto \langle e_i, \rho', a, t \rangle]$

$\quad \mu' = \mu[\iota \mapsto \mathsf{m}]$

$\quad \sigma' = \sigma[b_1 \mapsto d_1 \ldots b_k \mapsto d_k]$

Self

if $\pi(\iota) = \langle \, \textsf{self}\,(), \rho, a, t \rangle$

then $\pi' = \pi[\iota \mapsto \langle \iota, \rho, a, t \rangle]$

Send

if $\pi(\iota) = \langle v, \rho, a, t \rangle$ $\sigma(a) = \mathsf{Arg}_2\langle \ell, d, \iota', \_, c \rangle$

$\quad d = (\textsf{send}, \_)$

then $\pi' = \pi[\iota \mapsto \langle v, \rho, c, t \rangle]$

$\quad \mu' = \mu[\iota' \mapsto \mathrm{enq}((v, \rho), \mu(\iota'))]$

Spawn

if $\pi(\iota) = \langle \textsf{fun}() \to e, \rho, a, t \rangle$ $d = (\textsf{spawn}, \_)$

$\quad \sigma(a) = \mathsf{Arg}_1\langle \ell, d, \rho', c \rangle$ $\iota := \mathrm{new}_{\mathrm{pid}}(\iota, \ell, t)$

then

$$\pi' = \pi \begin{bmatrix} \iota \mapsto \langle \iota', \rho', c, t \rangle, \\ \iota' \mapsto \langle e, \rho, *, t_0 \rangle \end{bmatrix}$$

$$\mu' = \mu[\iota' \mapsto \epsilon]$$

Fig. 3. Concrete Semantic Rules for Concurrency primitives

$$\mathrm{mmatch} \colon pat^* \times Mailbox \times Env \times Store \to (\mathbb{N} \times (Var \rightharpoonup Value) \times Mailbox)_\perp$$
$$\mathrm{enq} \colon Value \times Mailbox \to Mailbox$$

The function mmatch takes a list of patterns, a mailbox, the current environment and a store (for resolving pointers in the values stored in the mailbox) and returns the index of the matching pattern, a substitution witnessing the match, and the mailbox resulting from the extraction of the matched message. To model *Erlang-style* FIFFO mailboxes we set $\mathrm{enq}(d, \mathsf{m}) := \mathsf{m} \cdot d$ and define $\mathrm{mmatch}(p_1 \ldots p_n, \mathsf{m}, \rho, \sigma) := (i, \theta, \mathsf{m}_1 \cdot \mathsf{m}_2)$ such that $\mathsf{m} = \mathsf{m}_1 \cdot d \cdot \mathsf{m}_2$ with $\forall d' \in \mathsf{m}_1$ and $\forall j . \, \mathrm{match}_{\rho,\sigma}(p_j, d') = \perp$, and $\theta = \mathrm{match}_{\rho,\sigma}(p_i, d)$ with $\forall j < i . \, \mathrm{match}_{\rho,\sigma}(p_j, d) = \perp$ where $\mathrm{match}_{\rho,\sigma}(p, d)$ pattern-matches term d against pattern p, using the environment ρ and store σ where necessary, and returns a substitution if successful and $\perp$ otherwise.

Evaluation Contexts as Continuations. Next we represent (in an inside-out manner) evaluation contexts as continuations. A continuation consists of a *tag* indicating the shape of the evaluation context, a pointer to a continuation representing the enclosing evaluation context, and, in some cases, a program location and an environment. Thus $\kappa \in Kont$ consists of the following constructs:

- Stop represents the empty context.
- $\mathsf{Arg}_i\langle \ell, v_0 \ldots v_{i-1}, \rho, a \rangle$ represents the context $E[v_0(v_1, \ldots, v_{i-1}, [\,], e'_{i+1}, \ldots, e'_n)]$ where $e_0(e_1, \ldots, e_n)$ is the subterm located at ℓ; ρ closes the terms e_{i+1}, $\ldots, e_n$ to $e'_{i+1}, \ldots, e'_n$ respectively; the address a points to the continuation representing the enclosing evaluation context E.

Addresses, Pids and Time-Stamps. While the machine supports arbitrary concrete representations of time-stamps, addresses and pids, we present here an instance based on *contours* [35] which shall serve as the reference semantics of λ_{ACTOR}, and the basis for the abstraction.

A way to represent a *dynamic* occurrence of a symbol is the history of the computation at the point of its creation. We record history as *contours* which are strings of program locations $t \in \textit{Time} := \textit{ProgLoc}^*$. The initial contour is just the empty sequence $t_0 := \epsilon$, while the function tick: $\textit{ProgLoc} \times \textit{Time} \rightarrow \textit{Time}$ updates the contour of the process in question by prepending the current program location tick$(\ell, t) := \ell \cdot t$. Addresses for values $b \in \textit{VAddr} := \textit{Pid} \times \textit{Var} \times \textit{Data} \times \textit{Time}$ are represented by tuples comprising the current pid, the variable in question, the bound value and the current time stamp. Addresses for continuations $a, c \in \textit{KAddr} := (\textit{Pid} \times \textit{ProgLoc} \times \textit{Env} \times \textit{Time}) \uplus \{*\}$ are represented by tuples comprising the current pid, program location, environment and time; or $*$ which is the address of the initial continuation (Stop).

The *data domain* ($\delta \in \textit{Data}$) is the set of closed λ_{ACTOR} terms; the function res: $\textit{Store} \times \textit{Value} \rightarrow \textit{Data}$ resolves all the pointers of a value through the store σ, returning the corresponding closed term res$(\sigma, (e, \rho)) := e[x \mapsto \text{res}(\sigma, \sigma(\rho(x))) \mid x \in \text{fv}(e)]$ or, when the value is a pid it just returns it res$(\sigma, \iota) := \iota$.

We extract the relevant components from the context to generate new addresses:

$$\text{new}_{\text{kpush}} \colon \textit{Pid} \times \textit{ProcState} \rightarrow \textit{KAddr}$$
$$\text{new}_{\text{kpush}}(\iota, \langle \ell, \rho, {}_-, t \rangle) := (\iota, \ell.\text{arg}_0, \rho, t)$$
$$\text{new}_{\text{kpop}} \colon \textit{Pid} \times \textit{Kont} \times \textit{ProcState} \rightarrow \textit{KAddr}$$
$$\text{new}_{\text{kpop}}(\iota, \kappa, \langle {}_-, {}_-, {}_-, t \rangle) := (\iota, \ell.\text{arg}_{i+1}, \rho, t) \text{ where } \kappa = \text{Arg}_i \langle \ell, \ldots, \rho, {}_- \rangle$$
$$\text{new}_{\text{va}} \colon \textit{Pid} \times \textit{Var} \times \textit{Data} \times \textit{ProcState} \rightarrow \textit{VAddr}$$
$$\text{new}_{\text{va}}(\iota, x, \delta, \langle {}_-, {}_-, {}_-, t \rangle) := (\iota, x, \delta, t)$$

To enable data abstraction in our framework, the address of a value contains the data to which the variable is bound: by making appropriate use of the embedded information in the abstract semantics, we can fine-tune the data sensitivity of our analysis.

Following the same scheme, pids ($\iota \in \textit{Pid}$) can be identified with the contour of the **spawn** that generated them: $\textit{Pid} := (\textit{ProgLoc} \times \textit{Time})$. Thus the generation of a new pid is defined as

$$\text{new}_{\text{pid}} \colon \textit{Pid} \times \textit{ProgLoc} \times \textit{Time} \rightarrow \textit{Pid}$$
$$\text{new}_{\text{pid}}((\ell', t'), \ell, t) := (\ell, \text{tick}^*(t, \text{tick}(\ell', t')))$$

where tick* is just the simple extension of tick that prepends a whole sequence to another. Note that the new pid contains the pid that created it as a sub-sequence: it is indeed part of its history. The pid $\iota_0 := (\ell_0, \epsilon)$ is the pid associated with the starting process, where ℓ_0 is just the root of the program.

Remark 1. Note that the only sources of infinity for the state space are time, mailboxes and the data component of value addresses. If these domains are finite then the state space is finite.

Definition 4 (Concrete Semantics). *We define a (non-deterministic) transition relation on states* $(\rightarrow) \subseteq State \times State$. *In Figures 2 and 3 we present the rules for application, message passing and process creation; we omit rules for letrec, case and returning pids since they follow the same shape. The transition* $s \rightarrow s'$ *is defined by a case analysis of the shape of s. The initial state associated with a program* $\mathcal{P}$ *is* $s_{\mathcal{P}} := \langle \pi_0, \mu_0, \sigma_0 \rangle$ *where* $\pi_0 = [\iota_0 \mapsto \langle \mathcal{P}, [], *, t_0 \rangle]$, $\mu_0 = [\iota_0 \mapsto \epsilon]$ *and* $\sigma_0 = [* \mapsto Stop]$.

The rules for the purely functional reductions are a simple lifting of the corresponding rules for the sequential CESK* machine: when the currently selected process is evaluating a variable **Vars** its address is looked up in the environment and the corresponding value is fetched from the store and returned. **Apply:** When evaluating an application, control is given to each argument in turn—including the function to be applied; **FunEval** and **ArgEval** are then applied, collecting the values in the continuation. When the machine has evaluated all arguments, it records the new values in the environment and store, and passes control to the function-body. The rule **Receive** fires if mmatch returns a valid match from the process' mailbox and passes control to the expression in the matching clause with the pattern-variables populated by the matching substitution θ. When the machine applies rule **Send** it extracts the recipient's pid from the continuation, and calls enq to dispatch the message. Rule **Spawn** is enabled if the argument evaluates to a nullary function; the machine then creates a new process with a fresh pid running the body of the function.

Concurrent abstract reductions

AbsReceive

if $\widehat{\pi}(\widehat{\iota}) \ni \widehat{q} = \langle e, \widehat{\rho}, \widehat{a}, \widehat{t} \rangle$
  $e = \mathbf{receive}\ p_1 \rightarrow e_1 \ldots p_n \rightarrow e_n\ \mathbf{end}$
  $\widehat{\mathrm{mmatch}}(p_1 \ldots p_n, \widehat{\mu}(\widehat{\iota}), \widehat{\rho}, \widehat{\sigma}) \ni (i, \widehat{\theta}, \widehat{m})$
  $\widehat{\theta} = [x_1 \mapsto \widehat{d}_1 \ldots x_k \mapsto \widehat{d}_k]$
  $\widehat{\delta}_j \in \widehat{\mathrm{res}}(\widehat{\sigma}, \widehat{d}_j)$
  $\widehat{b}_j := \widehat{\mathrm{new}_{\mathrm{va}}}(\widehat{\iota}, x_j, \widehat{\delta}_j, \widehat{q})$
  $\widehat{\rho}' := \widehat{\rho}[x_1 \mapsto \widehat{b}_1 \ldots x_k \mapsto \widehat{b}_k]$
then $\widehat{\pi}' = \widehat{\pi} \sqcup [\widehat{\iota} \mapsto \{\langle e_i, \widehat{\rho}', \widehat{a}, \widehat{t} \rangle\}]$
  $\widehat{\mu}' = \widehat{\mu}[\widehat{\iota} \mapsto \widehat{m}]$
  $\widehat{\sigma}' = \widehat{\sigma} \sqcup [\widehat{b}_1 \mapsto \{\widehat{d}_1\} \ldots \widehat{b}_k \mapsto \{\widehat{d}_k\}]$

AbsSelf

if $\widehat{\pi}(\widehat{\iota}) \ni \langle \mathbf{self}\,(), \widehat{\rho}, \widehat{a}, \widehat{t} \rangle$
then $\widehat{\pi}' = \widehat{\pi} \sqcup [\widehat{\iota} \mapsto \{\langle \widehat{\iota}, \widehat{\rho}, \widehat{a}, \widehat{t} \rangle\}]$

AbsSend

if $\widehat{\pi}(\widehat{\iota}) \ni \langle v, \widehat{\rho}, \widehat{a}, \widehat{t} \rangle$ $\widehat{\sigma}(\widehat{a}) \ni \mathsf{Arg}_2 \langle \ell, \widehat{d}, \widehat{\iota}', \_, \widehat{c} \rangle$
  $\widehat{d} = (\mathrm{send}, \_)$
then $\widehat{\pi}' = \widehat{\pi} \sqcup [\widehat{\iota} \mapsto \{\langle v, \widehat{\rho}, \widehat{c}, \widehat{t} \rangle\}]$
  $\widehat{\mu}' = \widehat{\mu}[\widehat{\iota}' \mapsto \widehat{\mathrm{enq}}((v, \widehat{\rho}), \widehat{\mu}(\widehat{\iota}'))]$

AbsSpawn

if $\widehat{\pi}(\widehat{\iota}) \ni \langle \mathbf{fun}() \rightarrow e, \widehat{\rho}, \widehat{a}, \widehat{t} \rangle$
  $\widehat{\sigma}(\widehat{a}) \ni \mathsf{Arg}_1 \langle \ell, \widehat{d}, \widehat{\rho}', \widehat{c} \rangle$
  $\widehat{d} = (\mathrm{spawn}, \_)$
  $\widehat{\iota}' := \widehat{\mathrm{new}_{\mathrm{pid}}}(\widehat{\iota}, \ell, \widehat{t})$
then
  $\widehat{\pi}' = \widehat{\pi} \sqcup \begin{bmatrix} \widehat{\iota} \mapsto \{\langle \widehat{\iota}', \widehat{\rho}', \widehat{c}, \widehat{t} \rangle\}, \\ \widehat{\iota}' \mapsto \{\langle e, \widehat{\rho}, *, \widehat{t}_0 \rangle\} \end{bmatrix}$
  $\widehat{\mu}' = \widehat{\mu} \sqcup [\widehat{\iota}' \mapsto \widehat{\epsilon}]$

Fig. 4. Abstract Semantic Rules for Concurrency primitives. We write $\sqcup$ for the join operation of the appropriate domain.

One can easily add rules for run-time errors such as wrong arity in function application, non-exhaustive patterns in cases, sending to a non-pid and spawning a non-function.

5   Parametric Abstract Interpretation

We aim to abstract the concrete operational semantics of Section 4 isolating the least set of domains that need to be made finite in order for the abstraction to be decidable. In Remark 1 we identify *Time*, *Mailbox* and *Data* as responsible for the unboundedness of the state space. Our abstract semantics is thus parametric on the abstraction of these basic domains.

Definition 5 (Basic domains abstraction). *A data abstraction is a triple* $\mathcal{D} = \langle \widehat{Data}, \alpha_d, \widehat{res} \rangle$ *where* $\widehat{Data}$ *is a flat (i.e. discretely ordered) domain of abstract data values,* $\alpha_d \colon Data \to \widehat{Data}$ *and* $\widehat{res} \colon \widehat{Store} \times \widehat{Value} \to \mathscr{P}(\widehat{Data})$. *A time abstraction is a tuple* $\mathcal{T} = \langle \widehat{Time}, \alpha_t, \widehat{tick}, \widehat{t_0} \rangle$ *where* $\widehat{Time}$ *is a flat domain of abstract contours,* $\alpha_t \colon Time \to \widehat{Time}$, $\widehat{t_0} \in \widehat{Time}$, *and* $\widehat{tick} \colon ProgLoc \times \widehat{Time} \to \widehat{Time}$. *A mailbox abstraction is a tuple* $\mathcal{M} = \langle \widehat{Mailbox}, \leq_m, \sqcup_m, \alpha_m, \widehat{enq}, \widehat{\epsilon}, \text{mmatch} \rangle$ *where* $(\widehat{Mailbox}, \leq_m, \sqcup_m)$ *is a join-semilattice with least element* $\widehat{\epsilon} \in \widehat{Mailbox}$, $\alpha_m \colon Mailbox \to \widehat{Mailbox}$, $\widehat{enq} \colon \widehat{Value} \times \widehat{Mailbox} \to \widehat{Mailbox}$ *are monotone in mailboxes and* $\text{mmatch} \colon pat^* \times \widehat{Mailbox} \times \widehat{Env} \times \widehat{Store} \to \mathscr{P}(\mathbb{N} \times (Var \rightharpoonup \widehat{Value}) \times \widehat{Mailbox})$. *A basic domains abstraction is a triple* $\mathcal{I} = \langle \mathcal{D}, \mathcal{T}, \mathcal{M} \rangle$ *consisting of a data, a time and a mailbox abstraction.*

An abstract interpretation of the basic domains determines an interpretation of the other abstract domains as follows.

$$\widehat{State} := \widehat{Procs} \times \widehat{Mailboxes} \times \widehat{Store} \qquad \widehat{Procs} := \widehat{Pid} \to \mathscr{P}(\widehat{ProcState})$$

$$\widehat{ProcState} := (ProgLoc \uplus \widehat{Pid}) \times \widehat{Env} \times \widehat{KAddr} \times \widehat{Time}$$

$$\widehat{Store} := (\widehat{VAddr} \to \mathscr{P}(\widehat{Value})) \times (\widehat{KAddr} \to \mathscr{P}(\widehat{Kont}))$$

$$\widehat{Mailboxes} := \widehat{Pid} \to \widehat{Mailbox} \qquad \widehat{Pid} := (ProgLoc \times \widehat{Time}) \uplus \{\widehat{\iota_0}\} \qquad \widehat{\iota_0} := \widehat{t_0}$$

$$\widehat{Env} := Var \rightharpoonup \widehat{VAddr} \qquad \widehat{Value} := \widehat{Closure} \uplus \widehat{Pid} \qquad \widehat{Closure} := ProgLoc \times \widehat{Env}$$

each equipped with an abstraction function defined by an appropriate pointwise extension. We will call all of them α since it will not introduce ambiguities. The abstract domain $\widehat{Kont}$ is the pointwise abstraction of *Kont*, and we will use the same tags as those in the concrete domain. The abstract functions $\widehat{new}_{\text{kpush}}$, $\widehat{new}_{\text{kpop}}$, $\widehat{new}_{\text{va}}$ and $\widehat{new}_{\text{pid}}$, are defined exactly as their concrete versions, but on the abstract domains. When B is a flat domain, the abstraction of a partial map $C = A \rightharpoonup B$ to $\widehat{C} = \widehat{A} \to \mathscr{P}(\widehat{B})$, where $\widehat{f} \leq_{\widehat{C}} \widehat{g} \Leftrightarrow \forall \widehat{a}.\ \widehat{f}(\widehat{a}) \subseteq \widehat{g}(\widehat{a})$, is defined as $\alpha_C(f) := \lambda \widehat{a} \in \widehat{A}.\ \{\alpha_B(b) \mid (a, b) \in f \text{ and } \alpha_A(a) = \widehat{a}\}$.

The operations on the parameter domains need to 'behave' with respect to the abstraction functions: the standard correctness conditions listed below must be satisfied by their instances. These conditions amount to requiring that what we get from an application of a concrete auxiliary function is adequately represented by the abstract result of the application of the abstract counterpart of that auxiliary function. The partial orders on the domains are standard pointwise extensions of partial orders of the parameter domains.

Definition 6 (Sound basic domains abstraction). *A basic domains abstraction $\mathcal{I}$ is sound just if the conditions below are met by the auxiliary operations:*

$$\alpha_t(\text{tick}(\ell, t)) \leq \widehat{\text{tick}}(\ell, \alpha_t(t)) \tag{1}$$

$$\widehat{\sigma} \leq \widehat{\sigma}' \wedge \widehat{d} \leq \widehat{d}' \implies \widehat{\text{res}}(\widehat{\sigma}, \widehat{d}) \leq \widehat{\text{res}}(\widehat{\sigma}', \widehat{d}') \tag{2}$$

$$\forall \widehat{\sigma} \geq \alpha(\sigma). \ \alpha_d(\text{res}(\sigma, d)) \in \widehat{\text{res}}(\widehat{\sigma}, \alpha(d)) \tag{3}$$

$$\alpha_m(\text{enq}(d, \mathfrak{m})) \leq \widehat{\text{enq}}(\alpha(d), \alpha_m(\mathfrak{m})) \quad \alpha_m(\epsilon) = \widehat{\epsilon} \tag{4}$$

if $\text{mmatch}(\boldsymbol{p}, \mathfrak{m}, \rho, \sigma) = (i, \theta, \mathfrak{m}')$ *then* $\forall \widehat{\mathfrak{m}} \geq \alpha(\mathfrak{m}), \ \forall \widehat{\sigma} \geq \alpha(\sigma)$

$$\exists \widehat{\mathfrak{m}}' \geq \alpha(\mathfrak{m}') \ such \ that \ (i, \alpha(\theta), \widehat{\mathfrak{m}}') \in \widehat{\text{mmatch}}(\boldsymbol{p}, \widehat{\mathfrak{m}}, \alpha(\rho), \widehat{\sigma}) \tag{5}$$

Following the Abstract Interpretation framework, one can exploit the soundness constraints to derive, by algebraic manipulation, the definitions of the abstract auxiliary functions which would then be correct by construction [26].

Definition 7 (Abstract Semantics). *Once the abstract domains are fixed, the rules that define the abstract transition relation are straightforward abstractions of the original ones. In Figure 4, we present the abstract counterparts of the concurrency rules for the operational semantics of Figure 3; the full list of the abstract rules can be found in the extended paper [12]. defining the non-deterministic abstract transition relation on abstract states $(\leadsto) \subseteq \widehat{State} \times \widehat{State}$. When referring to a particular program $\mathcal{P}$, the abstract semantics is the portion of the graph reachable from $s_\mathcal{P}$.*

Theorem 1 (Soundness of Analysis). *Given a sound abstraction of the basic domains, if $s \to s'$ and $\alpha_{cfa}(s) \leq u$, then there exists $u' \in \widehat{State}$ such that $\alpha_{cfa}(s') \leq u'$ and $u \leadsto u'$.*

Now that we have defined a sound abstract semantics we give sufficient conditions for its computability.

Theorem 2 (Decidability of Analysis). *If a given (sound) abstraction of the basic domains is finite, then the derived abstract semantics is finite; it is also decidable if the associated auxiliary operations (in Definition 6) are computable.*

Abstracting Mailboxes. For the analysis to be computable abstract mailboxes need to be finite too. Abstracting addresses (and data) to a finite set, values, and thus messages, become finite. We abstract a mailbox by an un-ordered set of messages in the static analysis overcoming the potential unbounded length of mailboxes but loosing information about the sequence and removal of messages. This

abstraction is formalised in the domain $\mathcal{M}_{\mathsf{set}} := \langle \mathscr{P}(\widetilde{Value}), \subseteq, \cup, \alpha_{\mathsf{set}}, \widehat{\mathsf{enq}}_{\mathsf{set}}, \emptyset,$
$\widehat{\mathsf{mmatch}}_{\mathsf{set}} \rangle$ where the abstract versions of enq and the matching function can
be derived from the correctness condition: $\alpha_{\mathsf{set}}(\mathsf{m}) := \{\alpha(d) \mid \exists i. \, \mathsf{m}_i = d\}$,
$\widehat{\mathsf{enq}}_{\mathsf{set}}(\widehat{d}, \widehat{\mathsf{m}}) := \{\widehat{d}\} \cup \widehat{\mathsf{m}}$ and

$$\widehat{\mathsf{mmatch}}_{\mathsf{set}}(p_1 \ldots p_n, \widehat{\mathsf{m}}, \widehat{\rho}, \widehat{\sigma}) := \left\{ (i, \widehat{\theta}, \widehat{\mathsf{m}}) \, \middle| \, \widehat{d} \in \widehat{\mathsf{m}}, \widehat{\theta} \in \widehat{\mathsf{match}}_{\widehat{\rho}, \widehat{\sigma}}(p_i, \widehat{d}) \right\}$$

Abstracting Data. We included data in the value addresses in the definition of
VAddr in order to allow for sensitivity towards data in the analysis. However,
cutting contours is no longer sufficient to make *VAddr* finite. A simple solution
is to use the trivial data abstraction $Data_0 := \{\_\}$, discarding the value, or if
more precision is required, any finite data-abstraction would do: the analysis will
then distinguish states that differ because of different bindings in their frame.

A data abstraction particularly well-suited to languages with algebraic data-
types is the abstraction that discards every sub-term of a constructor term that is
nested at a deeper level than a parameter D. We call $Data_D$ such an abstraction,
the formal definition of which can be found in [12].

Abstracting Time. k-CFA is a specific time abstraction which yields an analysis
that distinguishes dynamic contexts up to a given bound k; this is achieved by
truncating contours at length k to obtain their abstract counterparts obtain-
ing the abstract domain $Time_k := \bigcup_{0 \le i \le k} ProgLoc^i$, $\alpha_t^k(\ell_0 \ldots \ell_k \cdot t) := \ell_0 \ldots \ell_k$.
The simplest analysis we can then define is a 0-CFA with the basic domains
abstraction $\langle Data_0, Time_0, \widehat{Mailbox}_{\mathsf{set}} \rangle$. With this instantiation many of the domains collapse into singletons. However, the analysis keeps a separate store and
mailboxes for each abstract state and leads to an exponential algorithm. To
improve the complexity we apply a widening along the lines of [36, Section 7]:
we replace the separate store and separate mailboxes for each state by a global
copy of each. This reduces significantly the state-space we need to explore: the
algorithm becomes polynomial in the size of the program.

Considering other abstractions for the basic domains easily leads to exponential algorithms; in particular, the state-space grows linearly wrt the size of
abstract data so the complexity of the analysis using $Data_D$ is exponential in D.

Open Programs. Often it is useful to verify an open expression where its input is
taken from a regular set of terms [30]. For this purpose we introduce a new primitive **choice** that non-deterministically calls one of its arguments. For instance,
an interesting way of closing N in Example 1 is to bind it to any_num():

    any_num() = choice(fun() → zero, fun() → {succ, any_num()}).

If the state running two or more instances of inc's critical section is uncoverable,
then mutual exclusion is ensured for arbitrarily many instances of inc.

6   Generating the Actor Communicating System

The CFA algorithm allows us to derive a sound representation of the control-
flow of the program taking into account higher-order computation and some

information about synchronization. The abstract transition relation gives us a rough scheme of the possible transitions that we can 'guard' with communication and process creation actions. These guarded rules will form the definition of an ACS that simulates the semantics of the input λACTOR program.

Terminology. We identify a common pattern of the rules of the abstract semantics. In each rule **R**, the premise distinguishes an abstract pid $\hat{\iota}$ and an abstract process state $\hat{q} = \langle e, \hat{\rho}, \hat{a}, \hat{t}\rangle$ associated with $\hat{\iota}$ i.e. $\hat{q} \in \hat{\pi}(\hat{\iota})$ and the conclusion of the rule associates a new abstract process state—call it $\hat{q}'$—with $\hat{\iota}$ i.e. $\hat{q}' \in \hat{\pi}'(\hat{\iota})$. Henceforth we shall refer to $(\hat{\iota}, \hat{q}, \hat{q}')$ as the *active components* of the rule **R**.

Definition 8 (Generated ACS). *Given a λACTOR program $\mathcal{P}$, a sound basic domains abstraction $\mathcal{I} = \langle \mathcal{T}, \mathcal{M}, \mathcal{D}\rangle$ and a sound data abstraction for messages $\mathcal{D}_{msg} = \langle \widehat{Msg}, \alpha_{msg}, \widehat{res}_{msg}\rangle$ the Actor communicating system generated by $\mathcal{P}, \mathcal{I}$ and $\mathcal{D}_{msg}$ is $\mathcal{A}_{\mathcal{P}} := \langle \widehat{Pid}, \widehat{ProcState}, \widehat{Msg}, R, \alpha(\iota_0), \alpha(\pi_0(\iota_0))\rangle$ where $s_{\mathcal{P}} = \langle \pi_0, \mu_0, \sigma_0, t_0\rangle$ is the initial state with $\pi_0 = [\iota_0 \mapsto \langle \mathcal{P}, [], *, t_0\rangle]$ and the rules in R are defined by induction over the following rules.*

(AcsRec) *If $\hat{s} \rightsquigarrow \hat{s}'$ is proved by **AbsReceive** with active components $(\hat{\iota}, \hat{q}, \hat{q}')$ where $\hat{d} = (p_i, \hat{\rho}')$ is the abstract message matched by $\widehat{mmatch}$ and $\hat{m} \in \widehat{res}_{msg}(\hat{\sigma}, \hat{d})$, then $\hat{\iota}\colon \hat{q} \xrightarrow{?\hat{m}} \hat{q}'$ is in R.*

(AcsSend) *If $\hat{s} \rightsquigarrow \hat{s}'$ is proved by **AbsSend** with active components $(\hat{\iota}, \hat{q}, \hat{q}')$ where $\hat{d}$ is the sent abstract value and $\hat{m} \in \widehat{res}_{msg}(\hat{\sigma}, \hat{d})$, then $\hat{\iota}\colon \hat{q} \xrightarrow{\hat{\iota}'!\hat{m}} \hat{q}'$ is in R.*

(AcsSp) *If $\hat{s} \rightsquigarrow \hat{s}'$ is proved by **AbsSpawn** with active component $(\hat{\iota}, \hat{q}, \hat{q}')$ where $\hat{\iota}'$ is the new abstract pid that is generated in the premise of the rule, which gets associated with the process state $\hat{q}'' = \langle e, \hat{\rho}, *\rangle$ then $\hat{\iota}\colon \hat{q} \xrightarrow{\nu\hat{\iota}'.\hat{q}''} \hat{q}'$ is in R.*

(AcsTau) *If $\hat{s} \rightsquigarrow \hat{s}'$ is proved by any other rule with active components $(\hat{\iota}, \hat{q}, \hat{q}')$, then $\hat{\iota}\colon \hat{q} \xrightarrow{\tau} \hat{q}'$ is in R.*

As we will make precise later, keeping $\widehat{Pid}$ and $\widehat{ProcState}$ small is of paramount importance for the model checking of the generated ACS to be feasible. This is the main reason why we keep the message abstraction independent from the data abstraction: this allows us to increase precision with respect to types of messages, which is computationally cheap, and keep the expensive precision on data as low as possible. It is important to note that these two 'dimensions' are in fact independent and a more precise message space enhances the precision of the ACS even when using $Data_0$ as the data abstraction.

In our examples (and in our implementation) we use a $Data_D$ abstraction for messages where D is the maximum depth of the receive patterns of the program.

Definition 9. *The function $\alpha_{acs}\colon State \to (\widehat{Pid} \times (\widehat{ProcState} \uplus \widehat{Msg}) \to \mathbb{N})$ relating concrete states and states of the ACS is defined as*

$$\alpha_{acs}(\langle \pi, \mu, \sigma\rangle) := \begin{cases} (\hat{\iota}, \hat{q}) & \mapsto \left|\{\iota \mid \alpha(\iota) = \hat{\iota}, \alpha(\pi(\iota)) = \hat{q}\}\right| \\ (\hat{\iota}, \hat{m}) & \mapsto \left|\left\{(\iota, i) \middle| \begin{array}{l} \alpha(\iota) = \hat{\iota}, \\ \alpha_{msg}(res(\sigma, \mu(\iota)_i)) = \hat{m}\end{array}\right\}\right| \end{cases}$$

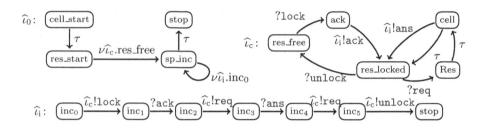

Fig. 5. ACS generated by the algorithm from Example 1

It is important to note that most of the decidable properties of the generated ACS are not even expressible on the CFA graph alone: being able to predicate on the contents of the counters means we can decide boundedness, mutual exclusion and many other expressive properties.

Theorem 3 (Soundness of generated ACS). *For all choices of $\mathcal{I}$ and $\mathcal{D}_{msg}$, for all concrete states s and s', if $s \to s'$ and $\alpha_{acs}(s) \leq \mathbf{v}$ then there exists $\mathbf{v}'$ such that $\alpha_{acs}(s') \leq \mathbf{v}'$, and $\mathbf{v} \to_{\mathrm{acs}} \mathbf{v}'$.*

Let $\mathcal{A}_{\mathcal{P}}$ be the ACS derived from a given λACTOR program $\mathcal{P}$. From Theorem 3 we have that $[\![\mathcal{A}_{\mathcal{P}}]\!]$ simulates the semantics of $\mathcal{P}$: for each run $s \to s_1 \to s_2 \to \ldots$ of $\mathcal{P}$, there exists a $[\![\mathcal{A}_{\mathcal{P}}]\!]$-run $\mathbf{v} \to_{\mathrm{acs}} \mathbf{v}_1 \to_{\mathrm{acs}} \mathbf{v}_2 \to_{\mathrm{acs}} \ldots$ such that $\alpha_{\mathrm{acs}}(s) = \mathbf{v}$ and for all i, $\alpha_{\mathrm{acs}}(s_i) \leq \mathbf{v}_i$. Simulation preserves all paths so reachability (and coverability) is preserved.

Example 2. Figure 5 shows a pictorial representation of the ACS generated by our procedure from the program in Example 1 (with the parametric entry point of Section 4) using a 0-CFA analysis. The three pid-classes correspond to the starting process $\hat{\iota}_0$ and the two static calls of spawn in the program, the one for the shared cell process $\hat{\iota}_c$ and the other, $\hat{\iota}_i$, for all the processes running inc.

The entry point is $(\hat{\iota}_0, \text{cell\_start})$. The second component represents the locking protocol quite faithfully. The VAS semantics is accurate enough to prove mutual exclusion of state 'inc$_2$', which is protected by locks. This property can be stated as a coverability problem for VAS: can inc$_2$ = 2 be covered? We can answer this question algorithmically: in this case the answer is negative and soundness allows us to conclude that our input program satisfies the property.

Complexity of the Generation. Generating an ACS from a program amounts to calculating the analysis of Section 5 and aggregating the relevant ACS rules for each transition of the analysis. Since we are adding $O(1)$ rules to R for each transition, the complexity of the generation is the same as the complexity of the analysis itself. The only reason for adding more than one rule to R for a single transition is the cardinality of $\widetilde{Msg}$ but since this costs only a constant overhead, increasing the precision with respect to message types is not as expensive as adopting more precise data abstractions.

Dimension of the Abstract Model. The complexity of coverability on VAS is EXPSPACE in the dimension of the VAS; hence for the approach to be practical, it is critical to keep the number of components of the VAS underlying the generated ACS small; in what follows we call *dimension* of an ACS the dimension of the VAS underlying its VAS semantics.

Our algorithm produces an ACS with dimension $(|\widehat{ProcState}| + |\widehat{Msg}|) \times |\widehat{Pid}|$. With the 0-CFA abstraction described at the end of Section 4, $\widehat{ProcState}$ is polynomial in the size of the program and $\widehat{Pid}$ is linear in the size of the program so, assuming $|\widehat{Msg}|$ to be a constant, the dimension of the generated ACS is polynomial in the size of the program, in the worst case. Due to the parametricity of the abstract interpretation we can adjust for the right levels of precision and speed. For example, if the property at hand is not sensitive to pids, one can choose a coarser pid abstraction. It is also possible to greatly reduce $\widehat{ProcState}$: we observe that many of the control states result from intermediate functional reductions; such reductions performed by different processes are independent, thanks to the actor model paradigm. This allows for the use of preorder reductions. In our prototype, as described in Section 7, we implemented a simple reduction that collapses internal functional transitions, if irrelevant to the property at hand. This has proven to be a simple yet effective transformation yielding a significant speedup. We conjecture that, after the reduction, the cardinality of $\widehat{ProcState}$ is quadratic only in the number of **send**, **spawn** and **receive** of the program.

7   Evaluation, Limitations and Extensions

To evaluate the feasibility of the approach, we have constructed Soter, a prototype implementation of our method. Written in Haskell, Soter takes as input a single Erlang module annotated with safety properties in the form of simple assertions. Soter supports the full higher-order fragment and the (single-node) concurrency and communication primitives of Erlang; for more details about the tool see [11]. The annotated Erlang module is first compiled to Core Erlang by the Erlang compiler. A 0-CFA-like analysis, with support for the $Data_D$ data and message abstraction, is then performed on the compile; subsequently an ACS is generated. The ACS is simplified and then fed to the backend model-checker along with coverability queries translated from the annotations in the input Erlang program. Soter's backend is the tool BFC [20] which features a fast coverability engine for a variant of VAS. At the end of the verification pathway, if the answer is YES then the program is safe with respect to the input property, otherwise the analysis is inconclusive.

In Table 1 we summarise our experimental results. Many of the examples are higher-order, use dynamic (and unbounded) process creation and non-trivial synchronization. Example 1 appears as reslock and Soter proves mutual exclusion of the clients' critical section. concdb is the example program of [18] for which we prove mutual exclusion. pipe is inspired by the 'pipe' example of [21]; the property proved here is boundedness of mailboxes. sieve is a dynamically spawning higher-order concurrent implementation of Erathostene's sieve inspired by a program by

Table 1. Soter Benchmarks. LOC is the number of lines of compiled Core Erlang. PRP is the number of properties to be proven. ORD is the order of the program. D and M are the data and message abstraction depth. In the "Safe?" column, "no*" means that the verification was inconclusive but the program is safe; "no" means that the program is not safe and Soter finds a genuine counterexample. "Places" is the number of places of the underlying Petri net after simplification; "Ratio" is the ratio between the number of places before and after simplification. All times are in seconds.

Name	LOC	PRP	ORD	SAFE?	ABS D	ABS M	ACS SIZE Places	ACS SIZE Ratio	TIME Analysis	TIME Simpl	TIME BFC	TIME Total
reslock	356	1	2	yes	0	2	40	10%	0.56	0.08	0.82	1.48
sieve	230	3	2	yes	0	2	47	19%	0.26	0.03	2.46	2.76
concdb	321	1	1	yes	0	2	67	12%	1.10	0.16	5.19	6.46
state_factory	295	2	2	yes	0	1	22	4%	0.59	0.13	0.02	0.75
pipe	173	1	2	yes	0	0	18	8%	0.15	0.03	0.00	0.18
ring	211	1	2	yes	0	2	36	9%	0.55	0.07	0.25	0.88
parikh	101	1	1	yes	0	2	42	41%	0.05	0.01	0.07	0.13
unsafe_send	49	1	1	no	0	1	10	38%	0.02	0.00	0.00	0.02
safe_send	82	1	1	no*	0	1	33	36%	0.05	0.01	0.00	0.06
safe_send	82	4	1	yes	1	2	82	34%	0.23	0.03	0.06	0.32
firewall	236	1	2	no*	0	2	35	10%	0.36	0.05	0.02	0.44
firewall	236	1	2	yes	1	3	74	10%	2.38	0.30	0.00	2.69
finite_leader	555	1	2	no*	0	2	56	20%	0.35	0.03	0.01	0.40
finite_leader	555	1	2	yes	1	3	97	23%	0.75	0.07	0.86	1.70
stutter	115	1	1	no*	0	0	15	19%	0.04	0.00	0.00	0.05
howait	187	1	2	no*	0	2	29	14%	0.19	0.02	0.00	0.22

Rob Pike [32]; Soter can prove all the mailboxes are bounded. safe_send, firewall and finite_leader could be successfully verified after refining the data abstraction. All example programs, annotated with coverability queries, can be viewed and verified using Soter at http://mjolnir.cs.ox.ac.uk/soter/.

There are programs and correctness properties that cannot be proved using any of the presented abstractions. Programs whose correctness depends on the order in which messages are delivered are abstracted too coarsely by the counter abstraction on mailboxes; however this is an uncommon pattern. Properties that assume the precise identification of processes are also not amenable to our approach because of the abstraction on pids. Finally, stack-based reasoning is out of reach of the current abstractions. The examples stutter and howait were designed specifically to illustrate Soter's limitations, see [12] for details.

Refinement and Extensions. The parametric definition of our abstract semantics allows us to tune the precision of the analysis. For safety properties, the counter-example witnessing a no-instance is a finite run of the abstract model. We conjecture that, given a spurious counter-example, a suitable refinement of the basic domains abstraction is computable which eliminates the spurious run of the corresponding abstract semantics. The development of a fully-fledged CEGAR loop is a topic of ongoing research.

The general architecture of our approach, combining static analysis and abstract model generation, can be adapted to accommodate different language features and different abstract models. By appropriate decoration of the analysis, it is possible to derive even more complex models for which semi-decision verification procedures have been developed [4,23].

8   Related Work and Conclusions

Verification or bug-finding tools for Erlang [24,29,22,7,8,6] typically rely on static analysis. The information obtained, usually in the form of a call graph, is then used to extract type constraints or infer runtime properties. Examples of static analyses of Erlang programs in the literature include data-flow [6], control-flow [29,22] and escape [7] analyses. Reppy and Xiao [34] and Colby [9] analyse the communication patterns of CML, which is based on typed channels and synchronous message passing, unlike Erlang's Actor-based model. To our knowledge, none of these analyses derives an *infinite-state* system.

Van Horn and Might [27] derive a CFA for a multithreaded extension of Scheme, using the same methodology [36] that we follow. The concurrency model therein is thread-based, and uses a compare-and-swap primitive. Our contribution, in addition to extending the methodology to Actor concurrency, is to use the derived parametric abstract interpretation to bootstrap the construction of an infinite-state abstract model for automated verification.

Venet [37] proposed an abstract interpretation framework for the sanalysis of π-calculus, later extended to other process algebras by Feret [13] and applied to CAP, a process calculus based on the Actor model, by Garoche [17]. In particular, Feret's non-standard semantics can be seen as an alternative to Van Horn and Might's methodology, but tailored for process calculi.

Huch [18] uses abstract interpretation and model checking to verify LTL-definable properties of a restricted fragment of Erlang programs: (i) order-one (ii) tail-recursive, (iii) mailboxes are bounded (iv) programs spawn a fixed, statically computable, number of processes. Given a data abstraction function, his method transforms a program to an abstract, finite-state model. In contrast, our method can verify Erlang programs of every finite order, with no restriction on the size of mailboxes, or the number of processes that may be spawned. Since our method of verification is by transformation to a *decidable infinite-state system* that simulates the input program, it is capable of greater accuracy.

McErlang is a model checker for Erlang programs developed by Fredlund and Svensson [15]. Given a program, a Büchi automaton, and an abstraction function, McErlang explores on-the-fly a product of an abstract model of the program and the Büchi automaton. When the abstracted model has infinitely many reachable states, McErlang's exploration will not terminate. McErlang implements a fully-fledged Erlang runtime system, and it supports a substantial part of the language, including distributed and fault-tolerant features.

Asynchronous Programs, i.e. first-order recursive procedures with finite data which can make an unbounded number of asynchronous calls, can be encoded

474 E. D'Osualdo, J. Kochems, and C.-H. Luke Ong

precisely into VAS and thus verified using reachability [19,16]. This infinite-state model supports call-stacks, through Parikh images, but not message-passing.

ACS can be expressed as processes in a suitable variant of CCS [28]. Decidable fragments of process calculi have been used in the literature to verify concurrent systems. Meyer [25] isolated a rich fragment of the π-calculus called *depth-bounded*. For certain patterns of communication, this fragment can be the basis of an abstract model that avoids the "merging" of mailboxes of the processes belonging to the same pid-class. Erlang programs however can express processes which are not depth bounded. We plan to address the automatic abstraction of arbitrary Erlang programs as depth-bounded process elsewhere.

Dialyzer [22,7,8] is a popular bug finding tool, included in the standard Erlang / OTP distribution. Given an Erlang program, the tool uses flow and escape [31] analyses to detect specific error patterns. Building on top of Dialyzer's static analysis, *success types* are derived. Lindahl and Sagonas' success types [22] 'never disallow the use of a function that will not result in a type clash during runtime' and thus never generate false positives. Dialyzer puts to good use the type annotations that programmers do use in practice; it scales well and is effective in detecting 'discrepancies' in Erlang code. However, success typing cannot be used to *verify* program correctness.

Conclusion. We have defined a generic analysis for λActor, and a way of extracting from the analysis a simulating infinite-state abstract model in the form of an ACS, which can be automatically verified for coverability: if a state of the abstract model is not coverable then the corresponding concrete states of the input λActor program are not reachable. Our constructions are parametric thus enabling different analyses to be easily instantiated. In particular, with a 0-CFA-like specialisation of the framework, the analysis and generation of the ACS are computable in polynomial time. Further, the dimension of the resulting ACS is polynomial in the length of the input program, small enough for the verification problem to be tractable in many useful cases. The empirical results using our prototype implementation Soter are encouraging. They demonstrate that the abstraction framework can be used to prove interesting safety properties of non-trivial programs automatically.

References

1. Agha, G.: Actors: a model of concurrent computation in distributed systems. MIT Press, Cambridge (1986)
2. Armstrong, J.: Erlang. CACM 53(9), 68 (2010)
3. Armstrong, J., Virding, R., Williams, M.: Concurrent programming in Erlang. Prentice Hall (1993)
4. Bouajjani, A., Esparza, J., Touili, T.: A generic approach to the static analysis of concurrent programs with procedures. ACM SIGPLAN Notices 38, 62–73 (2003)
5. Carlsson, R.: An introduction to Core Erlang. In: Proceedings of the PLI 2001 Erlang Workshop (2001)
6. Carlsson, R., Sagonas, K., Wilhelmsson, J.: Message analysis for concurrent programs using message passing. ACM TOPLAS (2006)

7. Christakis, M., Sagonas, K.: Static detection of race conditions in erlang. In: Carro, M., Peña, R. (eds.) PADL 2010. LNCS, vol. 5937, pp. 119–133. Springer, Heidelberg (2010)

8. Christakis, M., Sagonas, K.: Detection of asynchronous message passing errors using static analysis. In: Rocha, R., Launchbury, J. (eds.) PADL 2011. LNCS, vol. 6539, pp. 5–18. Springer, Heidelberg (2011)

9. Colby, C.: Analyzing the communication topology of concurrent programs. In: PEPM, pp. 202–213 (1995)

10. D'Osualdo, E., Kochems, J., Ong, C.-H.L.: Verifying Erlang-style concurrency automatically. Technical report, University of Oxford DCS Technical Report (2011), http://mjolnir.cs.ox.ac.uk/soter/cpmrs.pdf

11. D'Osualdo, E., Kochems, J., Ong, C.-H.L.: Soter: an automatic safety verifier for Erlang. In: AGERE! 2012, pp. 137–140. ACM (2012)

12. D'Osualdo, E., Kochems, J., Ong, C.-H.L.: Automatic verification of Erlang-style concurrency. CoRR, abs/1303.2201 (2013), http://arxiv.org/abs/1303.2201

13. Feret, J.: Abstract interpretation of mobile systems. Journal of Logic and Algebraic Programming 63(1), 59–130 (2005)

14. Finkel, A., Schnoebelen, P.: Well-structured transition systems everywhere! Theoretical Computer Science 256(1-2), 63–92 (2001)

15. Fredlund, L., Svensson, H.: McErlang: a model checker for a distributed functional programming language. In: ICFP, pp. 125–136 (2007)

16. Ganty, P., Majumdar, R.: Algorithmic verification of asynchronous programs. TOPLAS 34(1) (2012)

17. Garoche, P.-L., Pantel, M., Thirioux, X.: Static safety for an actor dedicated process calculus by abstract interpretation. In: Gorrieri, R., Wehrheim, H. (eds.) FMOODS 2006. LNCS, vol. 4037, pp. 78–92. Springer, Heidelberg (2006)

18. Huch, F.: Verification of Erlang programs using abstract interpretation and model checking. In: ICFP, pp. 261–272 (1999)

19. Jhala, R., Majumdar, R.: Interprocedural analysis of asynchronous programs. In: POPL 2007, pp. 339–350. ACM, New York (2007)

20. Kaiser, A., Kroening, D., Wahl, T.: Efficient coverability analysis by proof minimization. In: Koutny, M., Ulidowski, I. (eds.) CONCUR 2012. LNCS, vol. 7454, pp. 500–515. Springer, Heidelberg (2012), www.cprover.org/bfc/

21. Kobayashi, N., Nakade, M., Yonezawa, A.: Static analysis of communication for asynchronous concurrent programming languages. In: Mycroft, A. (ed.) SAS 1995. LNCS, vol. 983, pp. 225–242. Springer, Heidelberg (1995)

22. Lindahl, T., Sagonas, K.: Practical type inference based on success typings. In: PPDP, pp. 167–178 (2006)

23. Long, Z., Calin, G., Majumdar, R., Meyer, R.: Language-Theoretic abstraction refinement. In: de Lara, J., Zisman, A. (eds.) FASE. LNCS, vol. 7212, pp. 362–376. Springer, Heidelberg (2012)

24. Marlow, S., Wadler, P.: A practical subtyping system for Erlang. In: ICFP, pp. 136–149 (1997)

25. Meyer, R.: On boundedness in depth in the π-calculus. In: Fifth Ifip International Conference On Theoretical Computer Science, pp. 477–489 (2008)

26. Midtgaard, J., Jensen, T.: A calculational approach to control-flow analysis by abstract interpretation. In: Alpuente, M., Vidal, G. (eds.) SAS 2008. LNCS, vol. 5079, pp. 347–362. Springer, Heidelberg (2008)

27. Might, M., Van Horn, D.: A family of abstract interpretations for static analysis of concurrent higher-order programs. In: Yahav, E. (ed.) SAS. LNCS, vol. 6887, pp. 180–197. Springer, Heidelberg (2011)

28. Milner, R.: A calculus of communicating systems, vol. 92. Springer, Heidelberg (1980)
29. Nyström, S.: A soft-typing system for Erlang. In: ACM Sigplan Erlang Workshop, pp. 56–71 (2003)
30. Ong, C.-H.L., Ramsay, S.J.: Verifying higher-order functional programs with pattern-matching algebraic data types. In: POPL, pp. 587–598 (2011)
31. Park, Y.G., Goldberg, B.: Escape analysis on lists. ACM SIGPLAN Notices 27, 116–127 (1992)
32. Pike, R.: Concurrency and message passing in Newsqueak. Google Talks Archive, http://youtu.be/hB05UFqOtFA
33. Rackoff, C.: The covering and boundedness problems for vector addition systems. Theoretical Computer Science 6, 223–231 (1978)
34. Reppy, J.H., Xiao, Y.: Specialization of CML message-passing primitives. In: POPL, pp. 315–326 (2007)
35. Shivers, O.: Control-Flow Analysis of Higher-Order Languages. PhD thesis, Carnegie Mellon University (1991)
36. Van Horn, D., Might, M.: Abstracting abstract machines. In: ICFP, pp. 51–62 (2010)
37. Venet, A.: Abstract interpretation of the pi-calculus. In: LOMAPS, pp. 51–75 (1996)

Contextual Locking for Dynamic Pushdown Networks*

Peter Lammich[1], Markus Müller-Olm[2], Helmut Seidl[1], and Alexander Wenner[2]

[1] Technische Universität München, Germany
{lammich,seidl}@in.tum.de
[2] Institut für Informatik, Westfälische Wilhelms-Universität Münster, Germany
{markus.mueller-olm,alexander.wenner}@wwu.de

Abstract. Contextual locking is a scheme for synchronizing between possibly recursive processes that has been proposed by Chadha et al. recently. Contextual locking allows for arbitrary usage of locks within the same procedure call and Chadha et al. show that control-point reachability for two processes adhering to contextual locking is decidable in polynomial time. Here, we complement these results. We show that in presence of contextual locking, control-point reachability becomes PSPACE-hard, already if the number of processes is increased to three. On the other hand, we show that PSPACE is both necessary and sufficient for deciding control-point reachability of k processes for $k > 2$, and that this upper bound remains valid even if dynamic spawning of new processes is allowed. Furthermore, we consider the problem of regular reachability, i.e., whether a configuration within a given regular set can be reached. Here, we show that this problem is decidable for recursive processes with dynamic thread creation and contextual locking. Finally, we generalize this result to processes that additionally use a form of join operations.

1 Introduction

Analysing parallel programs is notoriously hard, especially in the presence of procedures and synchronisation. Ramalingam showed that even simple safety properties like reachability for programs with synchronous communication and procedures are undecidable [17]. The same holds for mutual exclusion via locks [10]. Undecidability can be avoided by using abstraction to over-approximate reachability [2] or by considering restricted classes of executions only to under-approximate reachability [5,16]. Identifying synchronization patterns where exact reachability is decidable remains a challenging problem.

Chadha et al. propose contextual locking, where arbitrary locking may occur as long as it does not cross procedure boundaries [4]. On the one hand, this constraint on lock usage is shown to lead to a decidable simultaneous reachability problem for two processes. On the other hand Chadha et al. demonstrate that

---

* This work was partially funded by the DFG project OpIAT (Optimal Interprocedural Analysis of Programs with Thread Creation, MU 1508/1 and SE 551/13).

F. Logozzo and M. Fähndrich (Eds.): SAS 2013, LNCS 7935, pp. 477–498, 2013.

it is suitable to model common locking patterns and we refer the reader to their paper for a detailed justification of contextual locking and comparison with other locking schemes. The contribution of this paper is to extend their result to more general settings.

The main observation of Chadha et al. is, that it suffices to regard executions where the procedure calls of both processes occur well-nested. This reduces the problem of checking reachability for two processes to reachability of a single pushdown process. However, already for three processes, this reduction is no longer possible. Consider the following three processes T_1, T_2, T_3 with procedures P, Q using contextual locking:

$$T_1 : \text{rel}(B)_5; \ \text{acq}(B)_8; \ \text{rel}(C)_9; \ \text{acq}(C)_{12};$$
$$T_2 : P; \ \text{rel}(D)_{13}; \ \text{acq}(D)_{16};$$
$$T_3 : \text{rel}(A)_1; \ \text{acq}(A)_4; \ Q;$$

$$P : \text{acq}(A)_2; \ \text{rel}(A)_3; \ \text{acq}(C)_{10}; \ \text{rel}(C)_{11};$$
$$Q : \text{acq}(B)_6; \ \text{rel}(B)_7; \ \text{acq}(D)_{14}; \ \text{rel}(D)_{15};$$

Assume that the processes hold locks $\{B, C\}$, $\{D\}$ and $\{A\}$, respectively, at the beginning of the execution. Using further locks, this can be ensured even when starting with the empty set of locks for each process. All three processes can reach the end simultaneously, for example by following the annotated schedule. However, in any execution where all processes reach the end, the calls to procedures P and Q are necessarily non-nested. Lock A forces P to start before Q, locks B and C require Q to start before P ends and lock D ensures that Q only ends after P has ended. Therefore, in general, reachability of multi-pushdown processes cannot be easily reduced to reachability of a single pushdown process.

We show that simultaneous reachability for systems with at least three processes is PSPACE-complete (§2). Furthermore, the problem remains PSPACE-complete for systems with dynamic thread creation (§3), which better fit the concepts of real languages like Java and C with pthreads. While simultaneous reachability focuses on the states of constantly many processes in the configuration, regular reachability concerns the whole configuration, and thus is more natural for systems with an unbounded number of processes. By exploiting well-quasi orderings, similar to [6], for suitably abstracted configurations, we show that regular reachability is decidable for systems with dynamic thread creation (§4) and joins (§5) as additional synchronisation primitive.

In related work Bonnet et al. have recently combined contextual locking with reentrant locking [1]. In this setting simultaneous reachability is shown to be decidable under bounded context switches. Kahlon et al. have shown, that simultaneous reachability for two processes becomes decidable when locks are only used in a well-nested fashion, i.e., when the last lock acquired always is the first lock to be released [10]. This result was later generalized to systems with dynamic process creation [13], regular reachability [14,12], and joins [7]. Furthermore, Kahlon et al. generalized their result to bounded lock-chains, where nesting of locking may be violated, as long as chains of overlapping lock regions are bounded. In this setting, simultaneous reachability for two processes is still decidable [8,9].

2   The Static Case

In [4] an algorithm is presented that decides whether two given control-states are simultaneously reachable by a system of two possibly recursive processes which use contextual locking. Their algorithm is exponential in the number of locks, but polynomial in the size of the program. It remained open whether and how this approach can be generalized to more than two threads. In the following, we provide an algorithm for deciding a slightly more general problem, namely, reachability of a control-sequence, for systems of k recursive processes with $k \geq 1$ which runs in PSPACE. Moreover we show that the original algorithm cannot be easily generalized to more than two threads by showing that reachability already for three processes is PSPACE hard—even for a constant number of locks.

We consider a multi-pushdown system P with a fixed number $k \in \mathbb{N}$ of processes with a shared finite set of locks $\mathcal{L}$. Each process $i \in \{1, \ldots k\}$ maintains a thread-local state which is of the form (q, X) where q is from a finite set Q of process-local information and $X \subseteq \mathcal{L}$ is the set of currently held locks. Furthermore, we are given a finite set Γ of local information of possibly called procedures. Thus, each $\gamma \in \Gamma$ encodes the name of the current procedure together with a finite amount of information about the local state of the current call to the procedure. Accordingly, the current call-stack (or pushdown) of the process is represented by a sequence $w = \gamma_1 \ldots \gamma_k \in \Gamma^*$. For convenience, we assume that the top of the pushdown is on the left side, i.e., equals γ_1. A configuration of a single process thus is given by a pair $((q, X), w)$ where $q \in Q, X \subseteq \mathcal{L}, w \in \Gamma^*$. Each process is defined by a finite set of rules of the form:

$$
\begin{aligned}
&r : (q, \gamma) \xrightarrow{\tau} (q', \gamma') && \text{(computation step)} \\
&r : (q, \gamma) \xrightarrow{\tau} (q', \gamma_1 \gamma_2) && \text{(procedure call)} \\
&r : (q, \gamma) \xrightarrow{\tau} (q', \epsilon) && \text{(procedure exit)} \\
&r : (q, \gamma) \xrightarrow{\mathsf{acq}(l)} (q', \gamma') && \text{(acquire lock } l \in \mathcal{L}) \\
&r : (q, \gamma) \xrightarrow{\mathsf{rel}(l)} (q', \gamma') && \text{(release lock } l \in \mathcal{L})
\end{aligned}
$$

where r is a unique identifier for the corresponding rule, and τ is the empty label. The rules define the effects of actions onto the thread configuration, i.e., the process-local state, the (left end of the) call-stack and the effect onto the set of currently held locks. Let $\mathsf{eff}(r)$ be the effect on the set of locks of a rule r. A step $((q, X), \gamma w) \xRightarrow{r} ((q', X'), w'w)$ on local configurations is defined if there is a rule $r : (q, \gamma) \xrightarrow{e} (q', w')$ and $X' = X \cup \{l\}$ with $l \notin X$ if $\mathsf{eff}(r) = \mathsf{acq}(l)$ or $X' = X \setminus \{l\}$ with $l \in X$ if $\mathsf{eff}(r) = \mathsf{rel}(l)$ or $X = X'$ if $\mathsf{eff}(r) = \tau$. For a sequence $\pi = r_1 \ldots r_m$ of rules, we write $[\![\pi]\!]((q, X), w) = ((q', X'), w')$ if the sequence $r_1, \ldots, r_m$ of rules is successively executable starting from the thread configuration $((q, X), w)$ and results in the configuration $((q', X'), w')$.

A process adheres to *contextual locking* if lock operations do not cross procedure boundaries, i.e. a lock acquired during a procedure call must be released in the same procedure call and no procedure called in the meantime may release it temporarily. Formally for all $X \subseteq \mathcal{L}$ and every call rule $(q, \gamma) \xrightarrow{\tau} (q', \gamma_1 \gamma_2)$ and all sequences π with $[\![\pi]\!] ((q', X), \gamma_1) = ((q'', X'), w)$, the following holds:

1. $X \subseteq X'$;
2. if $w = \epsilon$, then $X = X'$.

A configuration of a multi-pushdown system with k processes is a sequence

$$t = ((q_1, X_1), w_1) \ldots ((q_k, X_k), w_k)$$

where we assume that the sets X_i of locks are pairwise disjoint. W.l.o.g. we may assume that all processes share the same set of rules, but may differ in their respective start configurations. For an initial configuration we assume $X_i = \emptyset$ and $w_i \in \Gamma$ for all $i \in \{1, \ldots, k\}$. An execution of the system can be considered as an interleaving of executions of the participating threads $i \in \{1, \ldots, k\}$. In order to distinguish the action of one process from the same action of another process, we identify actions by means of pairs (i, r) where i identifies the process and r the performed action. A sequence Π of pairs (i, r) starting from configuration t is *executable* resulting in configuration t', if either $\Pi = \epsilon$ and $t' = t$, or $\Pi = \Pi'(i, r)$ and the following holds:

1. Π' is executable for t resulting in $t'' = ((q_1'', X_1''), w_1) \ldots ((q_k'', X_k''), w_k)$;
2. rule r is applicable *thread-locally* to the configuration $((q_i'', X_i''), w_i'')$ of the ith process resulting in some process configuration $((q_i', X_i'), w_i')$;
3. if $\mathsf{eff}(r) = \mathsf{acq}(l)$, then lock l is also *globally* available, i.e., $l \notin X_1'' \cup \ldots \cup X_k''$;
4. $t' = ((q_1', X_1'), w_1') \ldots ((q_k', X_k'), w_k')$, where $((q_j', X_j'), w_j') = ((q_j'', X_j''), w_j'')$ for $j \neq i$.

In this case, we write $t' = [\![\Pi]\!] t$. A configuration t' is *reachable* from a configuration t if $t' = [\![\Pi]\!] t$ for some global execution sequence Π. Likewise, a *set* T of configurations is reachable from t iff there is a configuration $t' \in T$ such that t' is reachable from t. We now extend simultaneous control-state reachability of two processes to *control-state sequence* reachability of k processes and formulate our first result:

Theorem 1. *Assume that $t = ((q_1, \emptyset), \gamma_1) \ldots ((q_k, \emptyset), \gamma_k)$ is the initial configuration and $\sigma = (q_1', X_1') \ldots (q_k', X_k')$ is a sequence of process-local states of length k. Then it is decidable in PSPACE for processes which adhere to contextual locking, whether the set*

$$T = \{((q_1', X_1'), w_1') \ldots ((q_k', X_k'), w_k') \mid w_i' \in \Gamma^*\}$$

is reachable from t or not.

The main observation that leads to a PSPACE algorithm is that reachability is preserved, if only executions are considered where the sizes of occurring pushdowns are polynomially bounded. Intuitively, the pushdown of a process grows whenever a procedure is called. For every such call, two cases can be distinguished. In the first case, the called procedure never returns. In this case, the pushed return location is dead, it will never make it to the top of the pushdown again and thus can be discarded. In the second case, the called procedure eventually returns. Thus, the pushdown grows only temporarily. In presence of recursion, the pushdown still may grow arbitrarily. In the following we therefore show, that in the case of deeply nested recursive calls that eventually return, the execution can be transformed into a shorter execution that still preserves reachability, but uses strictly smaller pushdowns.

For $i = 1, \ldots, k$, let proj_i denote the homomorphism which extracts from a global execution sequence Π, with $t' = [\![\Pi]\!] t$, the execution sub-sequence of the ith process, i.e. the homomorphism proj_i is defined by $\mathsf{proj}_i(i, r) = r$ and $\mathsf{proj}_i(i', r) = \epsilon$ for $i \neq i'$. In particular, $((q'_i, X'_i), w'_i) = [\![\mathsf{proj}_i(\Pi)]\!]((q_i, X_i), w_i)$ if $((q_i, X_i), w_i)$ and $((q'_i, X'_i), w'_i)$ are the configurations of the ith process in t and t', respectively. The proof of Theorem 1 then is based on the following sequence of lemmas. Lemma 2 allows to discard return information of non-returning procedure calls by introducing new rules in the pushdown, that allow to effectively inline such a procedure call.

Lemma 2. *Given a multipushdown-system P, a system P' can be constructed such that any control sequence $\sigma = (q'_1, X'_1) \ldots (q'_k, X'_k)$ is reachable from an initial configuration t in P iff the sequence $\sigma' = (\langle q'_1, \top \rangle, X'_1) \ldots (\langle q'_k, \top \rangle, X'_k)$ is reachable from the initial configuration t in P' and all pushdowns are empty in the final configuration.*

Proof. The set of states of the new system consists of all old states and additional states $\langle q, \bot \rangle, \langle q, \top \rangle$. The set of pushdown symbols contains all old symbols in addition to new symbols $\langle \gamma, \# \rangle$. The system non-deterministically decides whether the execution will return to a level in the pushdown. The lowest level which will be visited again is marked by $\#$ in the pushdown. Since symbols below this level will never be at the top of the pushdown again, we construct the system to remove them directly, thus $\#$ marks the bottom of the pushdown in the new system. $\bot, \top$ in the state mark whether the pushdown is empty or not. The new set of rules consists of transitions $r : (q, \gamma) \xrightarrow{\tau} (\langle q, \bot \rangle, \langle \gamma, \# \rangle)$ which add the markers to the initial configuration. Furthermore, we have a rule $r' : (\langle q, \bot \rangle, \gamma) \xrightarrow{e} (\langle q', \bot \rangle, w')$ working above the marker in the pushdown for each rule $r : (q, \gamma) \xrightarrow{e} (q', w')$ of the old system. Additionally, we add rules that apply to the marked pushdown symbol. Computation- and lock-steps preserve the position of the marker, thus we add $r' : (\langle q, \bot \rangle, \langle \gamma, \# \rangle) \xrightarrow{e} (\langle q', \bot \rangle, \langle \gamma', \# \rangle)$ for every rule $r : (q, \gamma) \xrightarrow{e} (q', \gamma')$. Return below the marked level empties the pushdown and ends the execution, thus we add new rules $r' : (\langle q, \bot \rangle, \langle \gamma, \# \rangle) \xrightarrow{\tau} (\langle q', \top \rangle, \varepsilon)$ that reach a corresponding final state for each rule $r' : (q, \gamma) \xrightarrow{\tau} (q', \varepsilon)$. In case of a call-transition, the system non-deterministically decides whether it will return from the newly pushed symbol or not. For each call-transition $r : (q, \gamma) \xrightarrow{\tau} (q', \gamma_1 \gamma_2)$ we add one rule $r'_1 : (\langle q, \bot \rangle, \langle \gamma, \# \rangle) \xrightarrow{\tau} (\langle q', \bot \rangle, \gamma_1 \langle \gamma_2, \# \rangle)$ that decides that the call is returning and thus preserves the position of the marker. A second rule

$r_2' : (\langle q, \bot \rangle, \langle \gamma, \# \rangle) \xrightarrow{\tau} (\langle q', \bot \rangle, \langle \gamma_1, \# \rangle)$ decides that the call is non-returning, moves the marker and discards the lower pushdown symbol by only pushing the upper symbol. To be able to reach a configuration inside a procedure with an empty pushdown, we finally add rules $r' : (\langle q, \bot \rangle, \langle \gamma, \# \rangle) \xrightarrow{\tau} (\langle q, \top \rangle, \varepsilon)$, that may terminate an execution by emptying a pushdown of size one, preserving the control state. The claim follows by induction on the length of an execution. The size of the resulting system only increases by a constant factor from the size of the original system.

Remark 3. Instead of using $\bot$ and $\#$ in the construction of Lemma 2, one can also use this annotation to store information about the discarded pushdown. For example one can impose a regular constraint on each pushdown in the final configuration. To this end we use states s, s' of a given automaton $\mathcal{A}$ over pushdown symbols and propagate the state when discarding a pushdown symbol, i.e., only add call rules $r_2' : (\langle q, s \rangle, \langle \gamma, s' \rangle) \xrightarrow{\tau} (\langle q', s \rangle, \langle \gamma_1, s'' \rangle)$ of the second kind, where (s'', γ_2, s') is a transition of $\mathcal{A}$, return rules $r' : (\langle q, s \rangle, \langle \gamma, s' \rangle) \xrightarrow{\tau} (\langle q', \top \rangle, \varepsilon)$ where $s = s'$ and rules $r' : (\langle q, s \rangle, \langle \gamma, s' \rangle) \xrightarrow{\tau} (\langle q, \top \rangle, \varepsilon)$ ending the computation where (s, γ, s') is a transition of $\mathcal{A}$. By additionally requiring that s is an initial and s' a final state of $\mathcal{A}$ in rules $r : (q, \gamma) \xrightarrow{\tau} (\langle q, s \rangle, \langle \gamma, s' \rangle)$ for the initial marking, we ensure that reaching a final state implies that the discarded pushdown has an accepting run in the automaton.

Lemma 4 shows that we may disregard nested returning procedure calls, that are executed in a similar context. Recently, a similar statement was developed independently by Bonnet et al. for the main proof of [1].

Lemma 4. *Assume that $t' = [\![\Pi]\!] \, t$ for global configurations t, t' where the configuration of the ith process in t is given by $((q_i, X_i), w_i)$. Assume further that there is a call rule $r : (q, \gamma) \xrightarrow{\tau} (q', \gamma_1 \gamma_2)$ together with a state p such that the following holds:*

- $\mathsf{proj}_i(\Pi)$ *can be written as $c_1 r \pi c_2$ with $((q, X), \gamma w) = [\![c_1]\!] \, ((q_i, X_i), w_i)$ for some w where $[\![\pi]\!] \, ((q', X), \gamma_1) = (p, \epsilon)$; and furthermore,*
- $\pi = u_1 r \pi' u_2$ *such that $((q, X'), \gamma w') = [\![u_1]\!] \, ((q', X), \gamma_1)$ for some w' where $[\![\pi']\!] \, ((q', X'), \gamma_1) = (p, \epsilon)$.*

Consider a factorization of the global execution $\Pi = C_1(i, r) U_1(i, r) \Pi' U_2 C_2$ with $\mathsf{proj}_i(C_j) = c_j$, $\mathsf{proj}_i(U_j) = u_j$ for $j \in \{1, 2\}$ and $\mathsf{proj}_i(\Pi') = \pi'$. Assume that for $j \in \{1, 2\}$, U_j' is obtained from U_j by removing all steps of the ith process. Then the sequence $C_1 U_1'(i, r) \Pi' U_2' C_2$ is an execution for t which also results in t'.

Proof. Let t_1 denote the configuration which is reached by the global execution C_1. In particular, X is the set of locks held by the ith process in t_1. We proceed by considering longer and longer prefixes of the executions. Let V and V' denote a prefix of U_1 and the corresponding prefix of U_1', respectively. By induction on the length of V, we prove that

- The set X is included in the set of locks held by the ith process in the configuration $[\![(i,r)V]\!]\,t_1$.
- V' is executable and the set X equals the set of locks held by the ith process in the configuration $[\![V']\!]\,t_1$.

Now consider the second occurrence of the call transition r of the ith process. We have proven so far, that in particular, $X \subseteq X'$. For all other processes, the sets of acquired locks after the executions $(i,r)U_1(i,r)$ and $U'_1(i,r)$ agree, since these processes have executed the same sequences of actions. Let $t_2 = [\![(i,r)U_1(i,r)]\!]\,t_1$ and $t'_2 = [\![U'_1(i,r)]\!]\,t_1$. Due to contextual locking, the local execution π' of the ith process does not depend on any lock being in X' and only acquires locks that are not in X', thus it may also execute with the smaller initial set of locks X. Therefore, Π' is executable both in configurations t_2 and t'_2 resulting in configurations t_3 and t'_3, respectively. Since the processes adhere to contextual locking, the sets of locks held by the ith process in configurations t_3 and t'_3, respectively, equal again X' and X, respectively. Now let V and V' denote a prefix of U_2 and the corresponding prefix of U'_2, respectively. By induction on the length of V, we prove that

- The set X is included in the set of locks held by the ith process in the configuration $[\![V]\!]\,t_3$.
- V' is executable and the set X equals the set of locks held by the ith process in the configuration $[\![V']\!]\,t'_3$.

Due to contextual locking, the set of locks held by the ith process in configuration $[\![U_2]\!]\,t_3$ precisely equals X. It follows that the two configurations $[\![U_2]\!]\,t_3$ and $[\![U'_2]\!]\,t'_3$ coincide. Accordingly, $C_1U'_1(i,r)U'_2C_2$ is a global execution sequence for t, and the configurations $[\![\Pi]\!]\,t$ and $[\![C_1U'_1(i,r)\Pi'U'_2C_2]\!]\,t$ agree.

Proof (Theorem 1). We can now essentially reduce the problem to checking reachability of a finite state system, whose configurations have polynomial size. Instead of checking reachability in the original system we check for reachability with an empty pushdown in the modified system of Lemma 2. According to Lemma 4, we can eliminate nested returning procedure calls, which have the same initial state q, pushdown symbol γ and final state p. It follows by a simple counting argument, that reachability can be checked using bounded pushdowns of size $O(|Q|^2 \cdot |\Gamma|)$, since each execution using a larger pushdown can be transformed into one using a smaller pushdown.

We now show that the PSPACE algorithm to establish the decidability of reachability in Theorem 1 cannot be improved in general. In fact, we show that control sequence reachability is PSPACE-hard already for three processes using contextual locking with a constant number of locks only. Note that this is in sharp contrast with the result of [4] for two processes with contextual locking where an upper bound is obtained which is polynomial in the size of the processes and exponential only in the number of locks.

Theorem 5. *For three processes using contextual locking with a constant number of locks, control sequence reachability is PSPACE-hard.*

Proof. The construction of the three processes builds on the observation that the set of successful runs of a linear space-bounded Turing Machine can be represented as an intersection $L_1 \cap L_2$ of two languages L_i over an alphabet of fixed size, each of which can be accepted by a pushdown automaton of polynomial size, that uses its pushdown in a disciplined fashion.

Configurations of a linear space-bounded Turing Machine, i.e. the contents of the tape together with the current control state, can be represented by words of fixed length $m = k \cdot (n + 1)$ over a binary alphabet, where n is the space-bound and k depends logarithmically on the size of the alphabet and the number of control states of the Turing Machine. The control state is inserted to the left of the current position of the head on the tape and each tape symbol and the state of the Turing Machine is encoded using k bits.

A word of the language L_1 is a sequence of subwords of length m, where the first subword encodes an initial and the last subword is the reverse of a final configuration of the Turing Machine and the $(2l+1)$-th subword is the reverse of the $(2l + 2)$-th subword. The language L_2 consists of words, where each word is again a sequence of subwords of length m and the $(2l+1)$-th subword is now the reverse encoding of a configuration reachable from the configuration encoded by the $2l$-th subword in one step of the Turing Machine.

We can construct two pushdown processes which accept the languages L_1 and L_2, respectively, together with an additional finite state process that checks the intersection. Instead of formally realizing these three processes as a multi-pushdown system, we prefer to use a more intuitive notation by means of programs with procedures. In our construction, reading a bit $i \in \{0, 1\}$ is simulated by temporarily acquiring the lock A_i associated with that bit using $\mathsf{use}(A_i)$. We write $\mathsf{use}(Z) = \mathsf{acq}(Z); \mathsf{rel}(Z)$ for short for a lock Z. The third process tries to enforce that both pushdown processes read the same bit by only allowing access to one bit at a time. This is achieved by blocking all locks and only temporarily releasing the one associated with the intended bit using $\mathsf{free}(A_i)$, where we write $\mathsf{free}(Z) = \mathsf{rel}(Z); \mathsf{acq}(Z)$ for a lock Z.

This mechanism, though, is not yet sufficient to synchronize the two pushdown processes. The third process may allow a series of bits, but it is not ensured that each of these bits is read by both pushdown processes or that a pushdown does not use one release to read the same bit twice. The second problem can be solved by introducing an additional lock B. Reading a bit $i \in \{0, 1\}$ is then represented by $\mathsf{use}(A_i); \mathsf{use}(B)$ and allowing a bit i to be processed by $\mathsf{free}(A_i); \mathsf{free}(B)$. Since one occurrence of $\mathsf{use}(A_i)$ is no longer directly followed by another one, two separate uses can no longer be associated with the same operation $\mathsf{free}(A_i)$.

Solving the first problem is more intricate. A first idea would be to use the same mechanism in reverse and introduce locks that are blocked by the pushdown processes and are meant to be acquired by the synchronizing process. These could be used after each bit to prevent the synchronizing process from going ahead before both pushdown processes have read the proposed bit. This, however, would violate contextual locking, since the pushdown processes would have to block these locks from the start and only release them temporarily after each bit, which in general, occurs in a context different from the initial context. The second idea therefore is to exploit the disciplined pushdown usage of the two pushdown processes. Both processes read words consisting of pairs of subwords of a fixed length m. Each pair of subwords is independent from the next. Thus, the pushdown processes can be constructed in a way that they return to the initial context after reading $2m$ bits. In order to implement this idea, we introduce locks S_1, S_2, R_1, R_2 that synchronize the third process with the two pushdown processes exactly every $2m$ steps. In the following, we present the programs for each of the three processes.

The synchronizing process does not use push- or pop-operations and thus can be represented by a finite-state program:

$$\mathsf{acq}(A_0); \mathsf{acq}(A_1); \mathsf{acq}(B);$$
$$\mathsf{use}(Z_1); \mathsf{use}(Z_2); \mathsf{acq}(Y);$$
$$s_3 : \mathbf{while}\,(*)\,\{$$
$$((\mathsf{free}(A_0) \vee \mathsf{free}(A_1)); \mathsf{free}(B))^m; \mathsf{use}(R_1); \mathsf{use}(R_2);$$
$$((\mathsf{free}(A_0) \vee \mathsf{free}(A_1)); \mathsf{free}(B))^m; \mathsf{use}(S_1); \mathsf{use}(S_2)$$
$$\}$$
$$l_3 : //\quad \text{program point to be reached}$$

The processes reading L_1 and L_2 are given by:

$$\mathsf{acq}(R_1); \mathsf{acq}(R_2);\qquad\qquad \mathsf{acq}(S_1); \mathsf{acq}(S_2);$$
$$\mathsf{acq}(Z_1); \mathsf{use}(Y);\qquad\qquad \mathsf{acq}(Z_2); \mathsf{use}(Y);$$
$$s_1 : \mathsf{checkInput}; \mathsf{free}(R_1); \mathsf{free}(R_2);\quad s_2 : \mathbf{while}\,(*)\,\{$$
$$\mathbf{while}\,(*)\,\{\qquad\qquad\qquad\qquad \mathsf{checkStep}; \mathsf{free}(S_1); \mathsf{free}(S_2)$$
$$\mathsf{checkRev}; \mathsf{free}(R_1); \mathsf{free}(R_2)\qquad \}$$
$$\}\qquad\qquad\qquad\qquad\qquad\quad l_2 : //\;\text{point to be reached}$$
$$\mathsf{checkFinal};$$
$$l_1 : //\;\text{point to be reached}$$

The locks Y, Z_1, Z_2 and their usage pattern enforce, that all processes first have to reach their starting label s_i, and thus acquire the initial set of locks required to block the other processes. The sub-routines checkInput and checkFinal for verifying the first and last configurations, respectively, can be implemented by a finite-state program in a straight-forward way. The sub routines checkRev and checkStep can be implemented as follows, using procedures C_i with $0 \le i \le m$ and P_i with $3 \le i \le n+1$:

$$\mathsf{checkRev} : C_m$$
$$C_i : (\mathsf{use}(A_0); \mathsf{use}(B); C_{i-1}; \mathsf{use}(A_0); \mathsf{use}(B))$$
$$\vee\,(\mathsf{use}(A_1); \mathsf{use}(B); C_{i-1}; \mathsf{use}(A_1); \mathsf{use}(B))$$
$$C_0 : \mathsf{skip}$$
$$\mathsf{checkStep} : P_{n+1}$$
$$P_i : \bigvee\{\mathsf{read}(a); P_{i-1}; \overline{\mathsf{read}}(a) \mid a \text{ is tape symbol}\}$$
$$\vee\,\bigvee\{\mathsf{read}(a_1 a_2 a_3); C_{(i-3)\cdot k}; \overline{\mathsf{read}}(b_1 b_2 b_3) \mid (a_1 a_2 a_3, b_1 b_2 b_3) \text{ is a step}\}$$

We write $\mathsf{read}(w) = \mathsf{use}(A_{i_0}); \mathsf{use}(B); \ldots \mathsf{use}(A_{i_j}); \mathsf{use}(B);$ for reading the binary encoding $i_0 \ldots i_j$ of a word w over tape symbols and states of the Turing Machine and $\overline{\mathsf{read}}(w)$ for the same operation using the reverse of the encoding of w. A pair $(a_1 a_2 a_3, b_1 b_2 b_3)$ is a step of the Turing Machine if a_2 is the control state, a_1, a_3 are tape symbols and $b_1 b_2 b_3$ describes the rewritten portion of the configuration after a step, including the movement of the head.

The description should have made it clear that, starting from their initial configurations with empty sets of held locks, the control-sequence

$$(l_1, \{R_1, R_2, Z_1\})(l_2, \{S_1, S_2, Z_2\})(l_3, \{A_0, A_1, B, Y\})$$

will be reachable if and only if the simulated Turing Machine has an accepting computation for the given initial configuration.

3   Spawning of New Processes

In this section, we show how the algorithm for control sequence reachability from the last section can be enhanced to multi-pushdown systems where new processes can be dynamically spawned. Programs now additionally may have transitions of the form:

$$r : (q, \gamma) \xrightarrow{(q_1, \gamma_1)} (q_2, \gamma_2) \qquad \text{(spawn step)}$$

where the effect of the transition is the spawning of a new thread with the initial configuration $((q_1, \emptyset), \gamma_1)$. The function $\mathsf{eff}(r)$ is extended accordingly. The pair (q_2, γ_2) on the right-hand side describes the continuation of the process executing this step. The local step relation $\Rightarrow$ affects the current process similar to a compute-rule. The global step relation additionally extends the sequence of processes which are concurrently running, by one more process. As in [3,7], we find it convenient to keep track of the ancestry between processes. For that, each local configuration of a process is equipped with an extra component which is meant to hold all successively spawned processes. Thus, a global configuration is now a rooted tree $(h, (q, X), w)$ where, as before, q is a process state, X is a finite set of locks, $w \in \Gamma^*$ is the pushdown and h is a (possibly empty) sequence of sub-trees representing the child processes. Again, we additionally demand that the different occurrences of sets of locks in a global configuration are mutually disjoint. Initial configurations consist only of a single process and are of the form $(\epsilon, (q, \emptyset), \gamma)$. In order to identify sub-configurations within a global configuration t we use sequences of positive integers called positions. In particular, ϵ is a position in t and the sub-configuration of t at position ϵ, denoted by t/ϵ, equals t itself. Furthermore, if $t = (t_1 \ldots t_k, (q, X), w)$ and η is a position of t_i for $i = 1, \ldots, k$, then $i\eta$ is a position in t with $t/i\eta = t_i/\eta$. Likewise, if $t = (t_1 \ldots t_k, (q, X), w)$, then the root process of t, i.e. the process in t at position ϵ, denoted by $t[\epsilon]$, has the process-local configuration $((q, X), w)$ and has successively spawned the root processes of $t_1, \ldots, t_k$. We write $t[\eta]$ for the root process of t/η, i.e. $t[\eta] = t/\eta[\epsilon]$.

Now, global steps are rules applied to sub-configurations. A global step (η, r) transforms a global configuration t into t', if the following holds:

- $t/\eta = (h, (q, X), w)$, $((q, X), w) \xrightarrow{r} ((q', X'), w')$ and $t'/\eta = (h', (q', X'), w')$
- $l \notin X''$ for all local configurations $t[\eta'] = ((q'', X''), w'')$, if $\mathsf{eff}(r) = \mathsf{acq}(l)$
- if $\mathsf{eff}(r) = (q_1, \gamma_1)$ then $h' = h(\varepsilon, (q_1, \emptyset), \gamma_1)$ else $h' = h$
- all other sub-configurations t/η' are preserved

In this case, we denote the resulting configuration also as $t' = [\![(\eta, r)]\!] t$ and extend the notation to sequences Π of global steps. Note that each newly created process initially holds the empty set of locks. A multipushdown system with dynamic process generation by means of spawn-rules has been called *dynamic pushdown network* or DPN [3]. The DPN adheres to contextual locking if each process of the DPN does so. We first consider reachability of a control sequence of a fixed length for DPNs. This means that we require only a subset of the processes to reach certain control states simultaneously. A control sequence

$$\sigma = (q_1', X_1') \ldots (q_k', X_k')$$

is reachable from a global configuration t if a global configuration t' is reachable such that $t'[\eta_i] = ((q_i', X_i'), w_i')$ for a suitable sequence $\eta_1 < \ldots < \eta_k$ of positions in t' where the ordering $<$ on positions is given by the *left-right* ordering within the textual representation of t', i.e. $\eta < \eta'$ if η' is a proper prefix of η or $\eta = \eta_0 j \eta_1$ and $\eta' = \eta_0 j' \eta_2$ where $j < j'$. In this case, we also say that t' is *compatible* with the control sequence σ at positions $\eta_1, \ldots, \eta_k$. The main theorem of this section is:

Theorem 6. *For every DPN P with contextual locking and control-sequence σ it is decidable in PSPACE whether or not σ is reachable from an initial configuration $(\epsilon, (q, \emptyset), \gamma)$ of the DPN.*

Since the lower-bound result from the last section also applies to DPNs, we conclude that control sequence reachability for DPNs is in fact, PSPACE-complete.

The key observation for the PSPACE upper bound is, that for reachability of a control sequence σ only steps of processes at one of the positions in the control sequence, or ancestors of such a process, must be considered.

Assume that $t_0 = (\epsilon, (p, \emptyset), \gamma)$ is an initial configuration of a DPN and $t = [\![\Pi]\!] t_0$. Then we call a position η *inactive* w.r.t. a global execution sequence Π, if Π does not contain any step (η, r) and thus also no step $(\eta\eta', r)$ for any η'. The following lemma can be proven by induction on the length of prefixes of Π.

Lemma 7. *Assume that t is compatible with the $\sigma = (q_1, X_1) \ldots (q_k, X_k)$ at positions $\eta_1, \ldots, \eta_k$. Let Π' denote the subsequence of Π which is obtained from Π by removing all steps (η, r) where η is not a prefix of any of the η_i. Then the following holds:*

1. *$t' = [\![\Pi']\!] t_0$ is still a global configuration which is compatible with the given control-sequence σ at positions $\eta_1, \ldots, \eta_k$.*
2. *Every position η of t' is either inactive or a prefix of one of the η_i.*   □

Let us call the configuration t' together with the global execution sequence Π' which is constructed according to Lemma 7, *purified* w.r.t. the control-sequence

σ. A purified global execution sequence may still be further reduced while pre-serving compatibility with the given control-sequence. For that, we first add transitions that skip spawning of inactive processes altogether.

For a given DPN P, consider the DPN P' which is obtained from P by adding a transition $r' : (q, \gamma) \xrightarrow{\tau} (p_2, \gamma_2)$ for every transition $r : (q, \gamma) \xrightarrow{(p_1, \gamma_1)} (p_2, \gamma_2)$. The resulting DPN has the same number of states and pushdown symbols as P and at most twice as many transitions. We have:

Lemma 8. *Consider a non-empty control sequence $\sigma = (q_1, X_1) \ldots (q_k, X_k)$. Let $t_0 = (\epsilon, (q_0, \emptyset), \gamma_0)$ be an initial configuration. Then the following statements are equivalent:*

1. *a configuration t is reachable from t_0 w.r.t. P which is compatible with σ;*
2. *a configuration t' is reachable from t_0 w.r.t. P' which is compatible with σ;*
3. *a configuration t'' is reachable from t_0 w.r.t. P' which is compatible with σ at positions $\eta_1, \ldots, \eta_k$ where t' has no inactive processes w.r.t. these positions.*

Proof. Assertion (2) follows from assertion (1) since every execution of DPN P is also an execution of DPN P'. Assertion (3) follows from assertion (2) in two stages. First, we may assume by Lemma 7 w.l.o.g. that the global execution sequence is purified. Then this global execution sequence is modified in such a way that spawning of inactive processes is replaced with the corresponding basic computation step which avoids the new process but preserves the process local successor state and pushdown. Note that not spawning inactive processes may cause a decrease in the number of spawned processes and thus may change the addresses of corresponding processes. Finally, given a global execution reaching t'' from t_0 w.r.t. DPN P' which is compatible with σ and does not spawn inactive processes, a global execution of DPN P can be recovered which is still compatible with σ essentially by introducing spawn-operations r again for the corresponding compute-operations r'. The additionally created processes will be treated as inactive processes.

Henceforth, we call an execution sequence according to statement (3) of Lemma 8 *strongly* purified. In a strongly purified execution, a process may still have an arbitrary number of ancestors. Thus still an arbitrary number of processes would have to be tracked in order to check reachability. However, here our second main observation comes in handy, namely, that similar to deeply nested recursive procedure calls, also deeply nested recursive spawns can be cut out of a given execution. Consider a situation where a process spawns a second process. The second process in turn spawns a third process with the same initial configuration as the second process and no other processes are spawned by the second process. In this case, the execution of the second process can be replaced by the execution of the third process. This eliminates one ancestor from the execution. This observation can be used to derive a bound on the number of processes that must be tracked in order to decide control-sequence reachability.

Lemma 9. *Assume that $t' = [\![\Pi']\!] t_0$ where t' is compatible with the control sequence σ at positions $\eta_1, \ldots, \eta_k$ and t' together with Π' is strongly purified* *w.r.t. the control sequence* σ. *Then there is a subsequence* Π'' *of* Π' *such that the following holds:*

1. $t'' = [\![\Pi'']\!] \, t_0$ *is still a global configuration which is compatible with the given control sequence* σ – *but now at positions* $\eta'_1, \ldots, \eta'_k$ *where the number of distinct non-empty prefixes of* $\eta'_1, \ldots, \eta'_k$ *is at most* $(2k-1) \cdot |Q| \cdot |\Gamma|$.
2. *The number of active positions in* Π'' *is bounded by* $(2k-1) \cdot |Q| \cdot |\Gamma| + 1$.

Proof. For the first statement, we purge positions as follows. Assume that $\eta_i = \eta\eta'\eta''$ and the processes at positions η and $\eta\eta'$ are spawned with the same initial configuration $(\epsilon, (q, \emptyset), \gamma)$ and additionally, there is no proper prefix η''' of η' such that $\eta\eta'''$ is the longest common prefix of η_i and some η_j, $i \neq j$. Then $\eta\eta'$ is replaced in all positions η_j where it occurs as a prefix, with η, and the global execution sequence Π is reduced accordingly. This means that all steps $(\eta\chi, r)$ are removed from Π' where χ is a prefix of η', and then all steps $(\eta\eta'\chi, r)$ are replaced with $(\eta\chi, r)$.

This reduction is performed until it is no longer applicable. Let $\eta'_1, \ldots, \eta'_k$ denote the resulting sequence of positions, and Π'' the resulting global execution sequence. Assume for a contradiction that the number of distinct non-empty prefixes of $\eta'_1, \ldots, \eta'_k$ exceeds $(2k-1) \cdot |Q| \cdot |\Gamma|$. As there are only $|Q| \cdot |\Gamma|$ distinct initial configurations of spawned processes, Π'' must create at least $2k$ of the sub-processes represented by these non-empty prefixes with the same initial configuration, say $(\epsilon, (q, \emptyset), \gamma)$. Let $\rho_1, \ldots, \rho_l$, $l \geq 2k$, be (all) the non-empty prefixes of $\eta'_1, \ldots, \eta'_k$ created with this initial configuration $(\epsilon, (q, \emptyset), \gamma)$. Consider the (potentially multi-rooted) tree induced on $\rho_1, \ldots, \rho_l$ by the prefix relation, i.e. ρ_j is a successor of ρ_i in the tree, if ρ_i is a proper prefix of ρ_j but there is no ρ_h that is a proper prefix of ρ_j and a proper suffix of ρ_i. This tree has at most k leafs as any leaf must be a maximal prefix among the $\rho_1, \ldots, \rho_l$ of one of the positions $\eta'_1, \ldots, \eta'_k$. This implies that at most $k-1$ inner nodes can be branching. On the other hand, there are at least k non-maximal prefixes. Hence, at least one of the non-maximal prefixes, say $\eta = \rho_i$, is non-branching, i.e. has just one successor $\rho_j = \eta\eta'$. This implies that the above reduction can be applied with η and η' resulting in a sequence of shorter positions–contradiction. Due to strong purification only ε and non-empty prefixes of the purged positions $\eta'_1, \ldots, \eta'_k$ can be active in Π''. Hence, the second statement follows from the first one.

Proof (Theorem 6). For deciding whether a control sequence σ of length k is reachable from the initial configuration, it suffices by Lemma 8 to consider strongly purified global executions only. By Lemma 9, only global configurations must be considered where the number of active positions is bounded by $(2k-1) \cdot |Q| \cdot |\Gamma|$. Additionally, the construction of Lemma 2 can be extended to DPNs so that only the case must be considered where all processes in the final configuration have an empty pushdown. Then we proceed analogous to the proof of Lemma 4 and derive a bound on the pushdown of each process. The bound now must take the length k of the control sequence into account, since recursive calls may not be removed in which a process needed for reachability of σ is spawned.

Assume that $t = [\![\Pi]\!] t_0$ for an initial configuration t_0 and a global configuration t. Assume that $\sigma = (q_1', X_1') \ldots (q_k', X_k')$ is a control sequence in t at positions $\eta_1 < \ldots < \eta_k$. Assume further that the execution sequence is strongly purified w.r.t. σ. If during Π a call rule $r : (q, \gamma) \xrightarrow{\tau} (q', \gamma_1\gamma_2)$ is called more often than $k \cdot |Q|$ times for the same position η, then there is a state p such that Π can be factored into $\Pi = C_1(r, \eta)U_1(r, \eta)\Pi_1 U_2 C_2$ and the following holds:

- U_1, U_2 do not spawn any processes;
- $\text{proj}_\eta((r, \eta)\Pi_1)$ as well as $\text{proj}_\eta((r, \eta)U_1(r, \eta)\Pi_1 U_2)$ are same-level computations for the subconfiguration $t[\eta]$ resulting in the same control state p.

For $i = 1, 2$, let U_i' be the sequence obtained from U_i by removing all steps of process η. Then the sequence $\Pi' = C_1 U_1'(r, \eta)\Pi_1 U_2' C_2$ is again a computation sequence for t which is compatible with the control sequence σ at the same positions $\eta_1 < \ldots < \eta_k$.

We conclude that a configuration compatible with σ can be reached by an execution where the depth of each intermediately occurring call-stack is bounded by a polynomial, now in the number of positions in the control sequence and the size of the DPN. Overall, we find that space polynomial in the length of the control-sequence σ and the size of the DPN P is sufficient to verify for P whether σ is reachable by P from the initial configuration $(\epsilon, (p, \emptyset), \gamma)$.

4   Regular Reachability

In this section we introduce *regular control reachability* as a reachability property, that allows to specify properties of configurations of an arbitrary and varying number of processes. Here the word of control states obtained by postorder traversal of a configuration must be contained in a regular language. For that, we define the yield of a configuration $t = (t_1 \ldots t_k, ((q, X), w))$ of a DPN as

$$\text{yield}(t) = \text{yield}(t_1) \ldots \text{yield}(t_k)(q, X)$$

In the following, we show that regular control reachability is decidable for DPNs with contextual locking.

Theorem 10. *For a DPN P with contextual locking and a regular language L over the alphabet $Q \times 2^{\mathcal{L}}$, it is decidable whether or not a configuration t with $\text{yield}(t) \in L$ is reachable from an initial configuration in P.*

In order to prove Theorem 10, we first show that regular control reachability for a DPN can be reduced to *control-set reachability* of a DPN. In a second step we explicitly reduce each pushdown system to a finite state system, using the same argument for recursive calls as before. A DPN without a pushdown is also called dynamic finite-state network (DFN). W.r.t. control-set reachability, configurations of DFNs can be further abstracted by just abstracting configurations to vectors which only keep the multiplicities of occurring process-local states. In the following, we are going to make these ideas precise.

First, we reduce regular control reachability to control-set reachability. For that, we define the state set of a configuration $t = (t_1 \ldots t_k, ((q, X), w))$ by:

$$\mathsf{states}(t) = \mathsf{states}(t_1) \cup \ldots \cup \mathsf{states}(t_k) \cup \{(q, X)\}$$

Lemma 11. *For a DPN P with contextual locking and a regular language L over the alphabet $Q \times 2^{\mathcal{L}}$, there exists a DPN P' with states Q' and contextual locking, and a set $Q'_0 \subseteq Q' \times 2^{\mathcal{L}}$, such that a configuration t with $\mathsf{yield}(t) \in L$ is reachable from an initial configuration in P iff a configuration t' with $\mathsf{states}(t') \subseteq Q'_0$ is reachable from a corresponding initial configuration in P'.*

Proof. Assume that L is given by the finite automaton $\mathcal{A} = (S, Q \times 2^{\mathcal{L}}, \delta, s_0, F)$ where S is the finite set of states of $\mathcal{A}$. We construct a new DPN that encodes the regular reachability into its control states. The yield of a configuration is accepted by the automaton iff there is a run of the automaton that accepts it. The idea is to guess and verify this accepting run during an execution of the DPN. Since the yield of a configuration is constructed from the local process configurations it suffices to guess a partial run for each local configuration and make sure that the partial runs form a run of the automaton. To this end we introduce new control states $\langle s, q, s' \rangle$ where $s, s' \in S$. A control state $\langle s, q, s' \rangle$ signals that s and s' have been guessed as initial and final states for the partial run that recognizes the yield of the subconfiguration generated by this process, and all process it has yet to spawn. As a first step, an initial guess is made. For that, we add transitions $r : (q, \gamma) \xrightarrow{\tau} (\langle s_0, q, s \rangle, \gamma)$ where $s \in F$. We proceed by replacing each non-spawn-transition $r : (q, \gamma) \xrightarrow{e} (q', w')$ with a transition preserving the guess $r' : (\langle s, q, s' \rangle, \gamma) \xrightarrow{e} (\langle s, q', s' \rangle, w')$. In case of a spawn-transition $r : (q, \gamma) \xrightarrow{(q_1, \gamma_1)} (q_2, \gamma_2)$, the guess for the spawned process is initialized by splitting the guess for the parent and distributing it. Therefore, we add transitions $r' : (\langle s, q, s' \rangle, \gamma) \xrightarrow{(\langle s, q_1, s'' \rangle, \gamma_1)} (\langle s'', q_2, s' \rangle, \gamma_2)$. If all processes in an execution of P' reach local configurations $((\langle s_1, q, s_2 \rangle, X), w)$ where $(s_1, (q, X), s_2)$ is a transition of $\mathcal{A}$, then all guesses have been correct, implying that there is an accepting path for the yield of this configuration. If on the other hand an execution of P reaches a configuration whose yield is accepted by $\mathcal{A}$ we can annotate the guesses to obtain an execution of P'. Checking regular reachability thus reduces to checking control set reachability of the set $Q'_0 = \{(\langle s_1, q, s_2 \rangle, X) \mid (s_1, (q, X), s_2) \in \delta\}$.

Remark 12. One can modify the construction from Remark 3 such that it allows to reduce general regular reachability, which also includes the stack content of each process, to regular control reachability. To see this, consider a finite automaton $\mathcal{A}$, now over the input alphabet $(Q \times 2^{\mathcal{L}}) \cup \Gamma$. Then the initial marking of a process can be used to further split the guess from Lemma 11 into parts for the state and the pushdown, i.e. we only add marking rules $r : (\langle s_1, q, s_2 \rangle, \gamma) \xrightarrow{\tau} (\langle \langle s_1, q, s'_2 \rangle, s'_2 \rangle, \langle \gamma, s_2 \rangle)$. The remaining construction proceeds as in Remark 3 using the transitions of $\mathcal{A}$.

In the next step, we reduce control set reachability of a DPN to control set reachability of a DPN without push or pop operations, i.e., a DFN:

Lemma 13. *For a DPN P with contextual locking and a set $Q_0 \subseteq Q \times 2^{\mathcal{L}}$ of control states, there exists a DPN P' with contextual locking, no push or pop operations and a set $Q_0' \subseteq Q' \times 2^{\mathcal{L}}$, such that a configuration t with* states$(t) \subseteq Q_0$ *is reachable from an initial configuration in P iff a configuration t' with* states$(t') \subseteq Q_0'$ *is reachable from a corresponding initial configuration in P'.*

Proof. First we apply the construction of Lemma 2 to only consider reachability where all pushdowns are empty. Using the same arguments as Lemma 4 and the proof of Theorem 6 we can derive a polynomial bound on the size of pushdown needed to check reachability. Assume that a pushdown is reached during an execution whose size exceeds $|Q|^2 \cdot |\Gamma|$ symbols. This translates to a process with more than $|Q|^2 \cdot |\Gamma|$ nested returning procedure calls. Each nested procedure call can be tagged with the initial control state and topmost pushdown symbol together with the final control state. Since the number of procedure calls exceeds the number of possible tags, there are at least two procedure calls, whose starting and ending situation are the same. Then the outer procedure call can be replaced with the inner call, by removing all steps of the outer procedure call as well as of all processes spawned by it. As before, because of contextual locking and processes starting with an empty set of locks, removing these steps does not impose additional constraints on an execution. Since all remaining processes still reach a state in Q_0, whenever that was the case before the replacement, control-set reachability is preserved if the sizes of all occurring pushdowns are restricted to size at most $|Q|^2 \cdot |\Gamma|$.

Using this result a DFN can be defined with states $Q' = \{(q, w) \mid q \in Q, w \in \Gamma^*, |w| \le |Q|^2 \cdot |\Gamma|\}$ where the bounded pushdown is encoded into the control state. We introduce an artificial pushdown symbol $\#$ and define transitions:

$$((q, w), \#) \xrightarrow{\text{eff}(r)} ((q', w'), \#) \text{ if } (q, w) \overset{r}{\Rightarrow} (q', w') \text{ and } \text{eff}(r) \ne (q_1, \gamma_1)$$
$$((q, w), \#) \xrightarrow{((q_1, \gamma_1), \#)} ((q', w'), \#) \text{ if } (q, w) \overset{r}{\Rightarrow} (q', w') \text{ and } \text{eff}(r) = (q_1, \gamma_1)$$

An initial configuration $(\varepsilon, (q, \emptyset), \gamma)$ is translated into an initial configuration $(\varepsilon, ((q, \gamma), \emptyset), \#)$. Finally, the control set for reachability in the new DFN is set to $Q_0' = \{((q, \varepsilon), X) \in Q' \mid (q, X) \in Q_0\}$. The executions of the new DFN are in one-to-one correspondence to the executions of the original DPN that do not violate the pushdown bound. Thus, we have reduced control-set reachability for a DPN to control-set reachability for a (possibly exponentially larger) DFN.

For control-set reachability of a DFN, the precise ordering of processes within a configuration is irrelevant. Therefore, we now abstract configurations of a DFN to multisets of local process configurations. The proof of Theorem 10 then is based on a monotonicity property of control-set reachability. This monotonicity property states that whenever a control set Q_0 is reachable from a (multi set) configuration v, then this is also the case for any multi sub-set of v.

Proof (Theorem 10). We apply Lemma 11 and Lemma 13 to only consider control set reachability of a set Q_0 for a DFN. For the proof, the ordering of processes within a configuration is irrelevant. Therefore, configurations are abstracted as a vector v mapping pairs (q, X) of states and sets of held locks to the number $v(q, X)$ of processes that are currently in state q and hold the set X of locks. Thus, $v(q, X) > 1$ only if $X = \emptyset$, and for $X \neq \emptyset$, $v(q, X) = 1$ implies $v(q', Y) = 0$ for all $q' \neq q$ and $X \cap Y \neq \emptyset$. Let us call such vectors v *abstract* configurations. Every transition of the DFN P induces a corresponding abstract transition on abstract configurations. Let P' denote the transition system on abstract configurations corresponding to the DFN P. Note that, due to unbounded application of spawn-transitions, the transition system P' is still infinite. The initial configuration t_0 of P corresponds to the abstract configuration $v_0 = \{(q_0, \emptyset) \mapsto 1\}$ where q_0 is the initial state of P. Let V_0 be the set of all abstract configurations such that $v(q, X) = 0$ for all $q \notin Q_0$. Then the DFN P may reach a configuration from t_0 where all occurring states are in Q_0 iff a configuration v is abstractly reachable from v_0 where $v \in V_0$. On configurations of P', we consider the elementwise partial ordering defined by $v \preceq v'$ iff $v(q, X) \leq v'(q, X)$ for all (q, X).

By case distinction, we verify that, if $v \preceq v'$ and w' is reachable in P' from v' in one abstract step, then either $v \preceq w'$ or there is an abstract configuration w which is reachable from v in one step such that $w \preceq w'$.

From this fact, we conclude that whenever a configuration in V_0 is reachable from v' and $v \preceq v'$, then a configuration in V_0 is also reachable from v.

Let W denote the set of abstract configurations reachable from v_0 (w.r.t. P') and $\min(W)$ the set of minimal elements in W w.r.t. the ordering $\preceq$. Then $V_0 \cap W \neq \emptyset$ iff $V_0 \cap \min(W) \neq \emptyset$. Thus, it suffices to determine the set of *minimal* configurations which are reachable from v_0. The set $\min(W)$ can be determined by iteratively accumulating the set of reachable configurations where during every step, only those configurations are maintained which are currently minimal. Since in a set of minimal configurations, vectors are pairwise incomparable, Dickson's Lemma can be applied—implying that the algorithm terminates.

5   Joining of Processes

In [7], DPNs have been considered that are additionally equipped with a join operation. A join can only be executed if all immediate children of a process which have been spawned up to this point, have terminated. We show for DPNs extended with such joins that regular control reachability as considered in the last section, is still decidable.

Theorem 14. *Assume that P is a DPN with joins and contextual locking, and L is a regular language over the alphabet $Q \times 2^{\mathcal{L}}$. Then it is decidable if a configuration t with $\mathsf{yield}(t) \in L$ is reachable from an initial configuration in P.*

Formally, a DPN with joins is a DPN where the set of rules additionally may include dedicated transitions of the form

$$r : (q, \gamma) \xrightarrow{\text{join}} (q', \gamma') \qquad \text{(join step)}$$

The intended semantics is that a process may execute the join-transition only after all processes spawned by the process executing the join-transition, have already been terminated. For that, we assume that termination is signaled by reaching a control state in a set $Q_t \subseteq Q$ from which no further transitions can occur. Thus, the following condition must additionally hold for a step as defined in Section 3:

- if $\mathsf{eff}(r) = \mathsf{join}$ and $h = t_1 \ldots t_k$ then $q_i \in Q_t$ for all $i \in \{1, \ldots, k\}$, where $t_i = (h_i, (q_i, X_i), w_i)$.

The same arguments as in Section 4 can be applied to show that regular control reachability of a language L for a DPN P with contextual locking and joins can be reduced to control set reachability of a set Q_0 for a DFN P'. This is due to the fact that removing join operations only lessens the constraints on an execution and otherwise removing steps from an execution does not change a thread from terminating to not terminating. As in Lemma 13, we represent the trivial pushdown of a DFN by means of $\#$.

Remark 15. Using the same method as in in Remark 12 Theorem 14 can be extended to regular reachability which includes all pushdowns.

Control-set reachability for DFNs with joins, however, can no longer be naturally reduced to the computation of minimal elements of suitable sets of vectors of natural numbers. Whether or not a join can be executed, does not depend on the multiplicities by which individual process-local states (q, X) are reached but on whether the right subset of processes have terminated. Accordingly, the abstraction of configurations through vectors of numbers is no longer sufficient. Instead, the nesting of processes as given by configurations must be maintained in order to identify the processes to be waited for. In order to apply an analogous argument as in Section 4, a well-quasi-ordering on (suitably abstracted) configurations is required, that preserves reachability. Since configurations are ordered trees, a candidate ordering is the *embedded subtree ordering*. From $t \preceq t'$, however, it not necessarily follows that every sequence of transitions for t' gives rise to a sequence of transitions for t resulting again in a smaller configuration. Here, a configuration is smaller if it can be obtained from the larger configuration by removing a subtree or by removing a node and replacing it with one of its descendants. But removing and replacing a process may cause its parent to wait for termination of a process which does not terminate. A corresponding monotonicity property, though, is crucial in Section 4 for restricting reachability analysis to maintaining sets of minimal elements only.

We observe that a process may be replaced by a descendant, if all processes in the hierarchy inbetween participate in a join. Since a join requires termination of all children and can only be executed by a process before its termination, this ensures that termination of the original process is preceded by termination of the process it is replaced with. Consequently in the shortened execution no join is blocked, since all required processes are still able to terminate.

We now construct an abstraction of a DFN, where configurations are multisets of unordered trees and indicate how the monotonicity property can be enforced.

The idea is to include processes into the tree only when they participate in a join. All others are added as additional roots to the top-level. We show that abstracting a DFN with joins in this way, preserves control-set reachability. A similar argument as in Section 4, then allows us to show decidability. In the following, we present the outlined proof sketch in detail.

For each spawn-transition $r : (q, \#) \xrightarrow{(q_1, \#)} (q_2, \#)$ we introduce a spawn'-transition with the same semantics:

$$r' : (q, \#) \xrightarrow{\langle q_1, \# \rangle} (q_2, \#) \qquad \text{(spawn' step)}$$

Clearly, each configuration t which was reachable w.r.t. the original DFN is also reachable w.r.t. to the DFN with the extra spawn'-transitions by an execution where the following property holds:

$\mathbf{S_1}$. Every spawn'-transition is eventually followed by a join-transition in the same process;

$\mathbf{S_2}$. After every spawn'-transition, no join-transition occurs in the same process.

Therefore, we may concentrate on control-set reachability of a set Q_0 by means of executions satisfying properties $\mathbf{S_1}$ and $\mathbf{S_2}$. Let us call such executions $\mathbf{S}$-executions. By guessing whether a process eventually executes a join-operation or not and maintaining a corresponding bit in the process-local state, we may enforce that the DFN only performs prefixes of S-executions and reaches the set Q_0 of dedicated control states *only* by means of an $\mathbf{S}$-execution. Let us call such a DFN an $\mathbf{S}$-DFN for control-state reachability of Q_0.

For an $\mathbf{S}$-DFN, we now abandon irrelevant nesting of processes and only keep nesting of processes which is required for simulating join-operations. This means that spawn'-transitions add new processes as leaves to the configuration, while spawn'-transitions add new processes on toplevel as new roots. For that, we consider finite multi-sets m of unordered finite trees t. Each such tree t is of the form $t = (m', (q, X), \#)$ where q is a state of the $\mathbf{S}$-DFN, X is a set of currently held locks and m' is a multiset of trees — each corresponding to a process spawned by a spawn'-transition. We write $\oplus$ for the union of multisets.

For such multisets abstracting configurations of a $\mathbf{S}$-DFN, we define the following abstract transitions. A join-transition $r : (q, \#) \xrightarrow{\text{join}} (q', \#)$ is applicable at $t = (m', (q, X), \#)$ within an abstract configuration m if all subtrees $t' \in m'$ are terminated. In this case, it replaces the subtree t within m by the subtree $t' = (m', (q', X), \#)$. Applying the spawn'-transition $r' : (q, \#) \xrightarrow{\langle q_1, \# \rangle} (q_2, \#)$, at $t = (m', (q, X), \#)$ within an abstract configuration m, replaces t with $t' = (m' \oplus \{(\emptyset, (q_1, \emptyset), \#)\}, (q_2, X), \#)$. A spawn-transition $r : (q, \#) \xrightarrow{(q_1, \#)} (q_2, \#)$ applied to a subtree $t = (m', (q, X), \#)$ within an abstract configuration m, replaces t with $t' = (m', (q_2, X), \#)$ and adds the tree $(\emptyset, (q_1, \emptyset), \#)$ to the multi-set on the toplevel. The abstract execution steps corresponding to the remaining transitions are defined in a straight forward way. We remark that the notion of an S-execution is also applicable to the abstracted DFNs with joins. Let $P^\sharp$ denote the abstract DFN constructed from a $\mathbf{S}$-DFN P in this way. Since every execution of P is a prefix of an S-execution, the same also holds for abstract executions of $P^{\sharp}$. Moreover, we obtain that a configuration t where all states are contained in the control set Q_0, can be reached by P from the initial configuration $t_0 = (\varepsilon, (q_0, \emptyset), \#)$ by means of an S-execution iff a configuration m, where all states are from Q_0, can be reached in $P^{\sharp}$ by means of an abstract S-execution from $m_0 = (\emptyset, (q_0, \emptyset), \#)$. Let V_0 be the set of all multiset configurations m such that all states in m are from Q_0.

On unordered trees t and multisets m, the embedded subtree ordering is the least reflexive and transitive ordering $\preceq$ with the following properties:

- Assume that $t = (m, (q, X), \#)$. Then $t' \in m'$ implies $t' \preceq t$; and also $m' \preceq m$ implies $(m', (q, X), \#) \preceq t$.
- Assume that $m = m_1 \oplus \{t\}$ for some t. Then $m_1 \preceq m$; and $t' \preceq t$ implies $m_1 \oplus \{t'\} \preceq m$.

By Kruskal's Theorem [11], the ordering $\preceq$ on multisets of unordered finite trees is a well-quasi-ordering.

As in the case without join-transitions, we find that if $m \preceq m'$ and w' is reachable in $P^{\sharp}$ from m' in one step, then either $m \preceq w'$ or there is a multiset configuration w which is reachable from m in a corresponding abstract step such that $w \preceq w'$. From this monotonicity, we conclude that whenever a configuration in V_0 is reachable from m' and $m \preceq m'$, then a configuration in V_0 is also reachable from m.

Proof (Theorem 14). Let W denote the set of abstract multiset configurations reachable from $m_0 = \{(\emptyset, (q_0, \emptyset), \#)$ (w.r.t. $P^{\sharp}$) and $\min(W)$ the set of minimal elements in W w.r.t. the ordering $\preceq$ on multisets. Then $V_0 \cap W \neq \emptyset$ iff $V_0 \cap \min(W) \neq \emptyset$. Thus, it suffices to determine the set of *minimal* configurations which are abstractly reachable from m_0. The set $\min(W)$ can be determined by iteratively accumulating the set of abstractly reachable configurations where during every step, only those configurations are maintained which are currently minimal. Since in a set of minimal configurations, multisets are pairwise incomparable, we conclude, now no longer by Dickson's lemma, but by Kruskal's Theorem that the algorithm terminates.

6   Conclusion

We have analyzed the complexity of simultaneous reachability for multiple recursive processes running in parallel which may use contextual locking. While this problem has been shown to be PTIME solvable for two processes in [4], we have shown that this problem becomes PSPACE-complete already for $k > 2$ processes where PSPACE is still sufficient if dynamic thread creation is allowed.

The situation seems to be more complicated if reachability of a regular set of configurations is considered. Such regular sets allow to formalize more intricate properties of configurations. We succeeded to prove decidability by means of Dickson's lemma. The precise complexity of this problem, though, remains open. Interestingly, decidability is preserved even if a join operation is added. Note that fork/join parallelism through parallel procedure calls as considered, e.g., in [15,18], can be expressed by means of DPNs with join. Accordingly, reachability for this model of concurrency remains decidable if contextual locking is allowed. Also there, however, the precise complexity remains open.

References

1. Bonnet, R., Chadha, R.: Bounded context-switching and reentrant locking. In: Pfenning, F. (ed.) FOSSACS 2013. LNCS, vol. 7794, pp. 65–80. Springer, Heidelberg (2013)

2. Bouajjani, A., Esparza, J., Touili, T.: A generic approach to the static analysis of concurrent programs with procedures. Int. J. Found. Comput. Sci. 14(4), 551 (2003)

3. Bouajjani, A., Müller-Olm, M., Touili, T.: Regular symbolic analysis of dynamic networks of pushdown systems. In: Abadi, M., de Alfaro, L. (eds.) CONCUR 2005. LNCS, vol. 3653, pp. 473–487. Springer, Heidelberg (2005)

4. Chadha, R., Madhusudan, P., Viswanathan, M.: Reachability under contextual locking. In: Flanagan, C., König, B. (eds.) TACAS 2012. LNCS, vol. 7214, pp. 437–450. Springer, Heidelberg (2012)

5. Esparza, J., Ganty, P.: Complexity of pattern-based verification for multithreaded programs. In: POPL, pp. 499–510. ACM (2011)

6. Finkel, A., Schnoebelen, P.: Well-structured transition systems everywhere! Theor. Comput. Sci. 256(1-2), 63–92 (2001)

7. Gawlitza, T.M., Lammich, P., Müller-Olm, M., Seidl, H., Wenner, A.: Join-lock-sensitive forward reachability analysis for concurrent programs with dynamic process creation. In: Jhala, R., Schmidt, D. (eds.) VMCAI 2011. LNCS, vol. 6538, pp. 199–213. Springer, Heidelberg (2011)

8. Kahlon, V.: Boundedness vs. unboundedness of lock chains: Characterizing decidability of pairwise cfl-reachability for threads communicating via locks. In: LICS, pp. 27–36. IEEE Computer Society (2009)

9. Kahlon, V.: Reasoning about threads with bounded lock chains. In: Katoen, J.-P., König, B. (eds.) CONCUR 2011. LNCS, vol. 6901, pp. 450–465. Springer, Heidelberg (2011)

10. Kahlon, V., Ivančić, F., Gupta, A.: Reasoning about threads communicating via locks. In: Etessami, K., Rajamani, S.K. (eds.) CAV 2005. LNCS, vol. 3576, pp. 505–518. Springer, Heidelberg (2005)

11. Kruskal, J.B.: Well-quasi-ordering, the tree theorem, and vazsonyi's conjecture. Trans. of the American Math. Society 95(2), 210–225 (1960)

12. Lammich, P.: Lock-Sensitive Analysis of Parallel Programs. Ph.D. thesis, WWU Münster (June 2011)

13. Lammich, P., Müller-Olm, M.: Conflict analysis of programs with procedures, dynamic thread creation, and monitors. In: Alpuente, M., Vidal, G. (eds.) SAS 2008. LNCS, vol. 5079, pp. 205–220. Springer, Heidelberg (2008)

14. Lammich, P., Müller-Olm, M., Wenner, A.: Predecessor sets of dynamic pushdown networks with tree-regular constraints. In: Bouajjani, A., Maler, O. (eds.) CAV 2009. LNCS, vol. 5643, pp. 525–539. Springer, Heidelberg (2009)

15. Mayr, R.: Decidability and Complexity of Model Checking Problems for Infinite-State Systems. Ph.D. thesis, TU München (April 1998)
16. Qadeer, S., Rehof, J.: Context-bounded model checking of concurrent software. In: Halbwachs, N., Zuck, L.D. (eds.) TACAS 2005. LNCS, vol. 3440, pp. 93–107. Springer, Heidelberg (2005)
17. Ramalingam, G.: Context-sensitive synchronization-sensitive analysis is undecidable. ACM Trans. Program. Lang. Syst. 22(2), 416–430 (2000)
18. Seidl, H., Steffen, B.: Constraint-based inter-procedural analysis of parallel programs. Nord. J. Comput. 7(4), 375–400 (2000)

Author Index